No Official Umbrella

By the same author

Fiction:

Angel
Dead On Time
Just In Case
Dead On Target
The Cinelli Vases
The Journeys We Make
The Museum Mysteries & other short stories
Doctor Who & The Space Museum
The Double Deckers
Hildegarde H and Her Friends - Illustrated by Arnold Taraborrelli

Plays:

Beautiful For Ever
Thriller of the Year
Red in the Morning
Peter Pan - A musical fantasy
Champagne Charlie - A music hall entertainment
Oh Brother!
The 88
Generations
Rosemary
Third Drawer from the Top
Women Around

Films:

A King's Story (Columbia Pictures)
River Rivals (Children's Film Foundation)
The Magnificent Six And A Half (Children's Film Foundation)
Bindle (Tannsfeld Films/Rank)

Television:

Doctor Who & The Space Museum (BBC TV)
The Double Deckers (20Th Century Fox (Writer and Script Editor.))
The Gold Robbers (ATV)

No Official Umbrella

Glyn Idris Jones

An Autobiography

First Published in Greece 2008
© Glyn Jones 2005
This Edition 2012

The author's moral rights have been asserted.
All rights reserved.

No part of this book may be reproduced stored in a retrieval system or transmitted in any form by any means with out the prior written permission of the publisher, except by a reviewer who may quote brief passages in a review to be printed in a newspaper, magazine or journal.

Douglas Foote

ISBN 978-960-99470-8-4

www.glynjones.net

It is scarcely to be expected that one who has spent his life beneath an official umbrella, should have at his command the finer analogies between light and shade.

From *Kai Lung's Golden Hours*, by Ernest Bramah.

Acknowledgements

The author is indebted to the following for permission to reproduce illustrations:

James Madison University
Red in the Morning
A View from the Bridge
The Country Wife
Buried Child
The Imaginary Invalid

Dan Savident
Christopher Beeching as Champagne Charlie

BBC Archive
Dr Who & The Space Museum

The majority of the photographs which appear in this autobiography are from the author's own private collection. Certain of the photographs used as illustrations are of unknown provenance and are believed not to be the subject of claimed copyright. If copyright is claimed in any of them the publishers will be pleased to correspond with the claimant and make any arrangements which may prove to be appropriate.

Chapter One

Athens January 2005: Othos Derigny is not a quiet street. It's one-way and, when the lights change at Archeron down the bottom of the block, for two or three minutes the ever speeding Greek traffic tries to outdo New York at its loudest. The flat is our pied à terre and I sit here, facing the laptop, with strict instructions from Chris and Douglas that this is where I stay until I have written at least thirty pages. With luck, and if the muse is with me, there will be more than thirty before I return to our home in Crete.

In three months, on the 27th of April, I celebrate my seventy-fourth birthday. The day after that it will be fifty-two years since I landed in England from that Union Castle ship in which, for three weeks, I had been a lowly bathroom steward. Now, in the twilight of my life I find time, not to finally keep a diary, but to look back on my seventy-four years. Twilight, what a strange word: *The Twilight Zone*, tales of the supernatural, *In the Twi-Twi-Twilight*, Victorian song for young lovers, Their Twilight World, how British tabloids used to describe the homosexual milieu as though like vampires, the living dead, gays only came to life after sunset. Maybe I should have said the autumn of my life.

Whatever, twilight or autumn, here I am with very little hair, more of which leaves me every day and that which is left is steel grey. There are enough lines and wrinkles now to play my age if I had to unlike, as a youngster when called upon to play twice my age or more, in Robert Bolt's *The Tiger and the Horse* or as Baron Hardup in *Cinderella* at Northampton, the lake liner came into its own; on the forehead, around the eyes, either side the nose and the mouth. I can honestly say it wasn't ever really successful. I still looked like a young man made up to look like an old one and have photographs to prove it, but that was one of the problems of being a member of a permanent rep company–play as cast. It's just as well though that I am no longer called upon to play any part at all as I seem to be losing more and more brain cells every day. Names escape me, words escape me and now, living on Crete, I sometimes remember the Greek word for something and have forgotten the English or I learn some Greek one day and by the next it has gone. Sometimes I even have to think hard remembering what I had for dinner the previous evening. I wear glasses to read, I walk distances with the aid of a stick, going uphill takes my breath away and I have to stop every now and again to get it back. I use a state of the art, extremely expensive hearing aid and have no teeth of my own so at least I don't have to worry about the dentist anymore. I am at least two stone overweight, my heart every now and again tends to thud loudly or flutters like a butterfly and the veins in my legs are breaking. I have to take medicine every day for a hiatus hernia and I'm getting a boozer's nose despite being a moderate drinker who hardly ever touches spirits. If ever I was an attractive specimen, I am that no more. Who said growing old is fun? Who knows how much time is left? You only know that time, always the great enemy, is running out. If I were to compare my life with the tragic existence of millions of human beings I have to admit I've had things on the whole pretty good and I am grateful for that.

If you don't believe in karma and reincarnation then, presumably, your being conceived in the first place is a shot in the dark, to coin a phrase. If I did believe in reincarnation I would believe I was a British Tommy killed in the first World War because I have a vision of a long gently rising road, with a park on one side and a terrace of fairly substantial early Edwardian houses on the other, and I am walking up it while wearing a soldier's uniform, a uniform with puttees. I have never been up this road, so vivid in my mind's eye unless, as a four

Chapter One

year old, with my parents on a visit to Great Britain, as it was then called, they walked me up it to visit someone, perhaps a relation or old friends of my father's. But I also have this memory of a battlefield and I have never been on a battlefield. Was it something I saw in a book when I was very young and the memory of it has lingered, exaggerated by imagination? Obviously I was never meant to be a mover and shaker in this world, the darling of the cognoscenti, a celebrity on any list, or to be awarded the glittering prizes even though I have reached out for them, but I could have been born a Jew in Hitler's Europe, I could have been one of Idi Amin's victims in Uganda, or Pol Pot's in Cambodia or even today be trying to stay alive in the Horn of Africa, in Zimbabwe under Robert Mugabe, or in any other country suffering under a malevolent and crazy dictatorship, born in any of the times and places where the four horsemen have had and are having a field day. It would have been ironic had I been born black in apartheid South Africa, instead of to fairly comfortably off, middle-class white parents, so who am I to complain that I've never been flavour of the month?

At various times in my life I thought of keeping a diary; but thinking and doing are two different things and obviously I was never meant to be a latter day Samuel Pepys. Once or twice I made a desultory attempt but I never saw much point in sitting down at the end of the day and recording that day's more of the same mundane events. Let's face it, most days in one's life simply aren't all that red letter or worth recording. Now, having just gone painstakingly through over forty years of "Appointment" diaries in which I did make entries, I realise how useless some of those entries are as archival material. What does one make of an entry that reads "rehearsal" or "performance" or "studio" or "filming"? Which year did I do this? Which year did I do that? Where was I when...? Detective work is called for here. One of the problems is that most theatre programmes and fliers of which we have many don't include the year. For example, I played the part of Herring the bos'n in a number one tour of *Grab me a Gondola*, a musical that had a fairly decent run in London at the Lyric, a spoof on the Venice Film Festival. Part of the show takes place on one of Her Maj's warships and my big number towards the end of the show was *Rocking at the Cannon Ball!* Can you believe that? These days, whenever I tell people, it sounds so dated and such a bad pun, they burst into hysterical laughter. The tour starred Roberta Huby as the platinum blonde Diana Dors take-off, and the tour opened at the King's Theatre, Southsea on Monday, 15th September, according to the flier in front of me. But what year? What year? It doesn't say.

So, had I kept a proper diary, how would it have read? I had a first night, what do I write about it? It would usually be the same… Stood in the wings a bundle of nerves, waiting to go on and thinking, 'We've been rehearsing this play for so many weeks and I don't know a word of it. What do I say? What do I say?' It's no wonder actor's nightmare, when not only do you not know your lines, but you don't even know what play you're supposed to be in, is such a common phenomenon, even late in life when you're no longer performing.

I see the lights on stage, the actors going about their business before my entrance, the setting I'm now more or less familiar with. I sense the audience out there in the semi-dark. That's my cue. I'm on. I'm on. I open my mouth, words come out. After some moments the nerves settle down. Even Laurence Olivier admitted at one point in his life to stage fright. Sheer panic is disaster of course, though it is maintained by some that a certain level of nervousness gives an edge to your performance, and there are performers of course who don't seem to suffer from nerves at all. In a play called *Are You Now or Have You Ever Been?* at Birmingham Rep I was waiting to go on, my usual bundle of fidgety nerves, when Tom Wilkinson who was standing beside me said, 'What's the matter with you?'

'First night nerves,' I whispered.

'If you can't stand the heat get out of the kitchen,' he said.

Strange to say the nerves disappeared immediately. Everyone who has seen Tom's film appearances now appreciates what a splendid actor he is and he deserves his success. At Birmingham he had just returned to England from making a film in Poland, (still Communist

Chapter One

at that time of course) for next to nothing, if anything at all, and was desperately short of money. He had one of those Chinese style padded jackets he had brought back with him and for once I had a few bob to spare so I took it off him for a fiver. It served me well through many a freezing English winter.

Tom Wilkinson & G.I.J.
Are You Now or Have You Ever Been ? - Birmingham Rep

How many first nights have there been? I've really lost count. But, if one imagined beforehand, the thousand and one things that could go wrong at any performance, let alone on a first night, the nerves would not disappear at all. Sometimes, it is worse being in the auditorium, either as writer or director, when you seem to be constantly waiting for that disaster you just know is inevitable. On stage you might be in a position to remedy a potential mishap. Seated in the audience or even roaming around the back of the stalls you are helpless. Sometimes the tension is too much and it's easier to get out of that kitchen and take a walk until it's all over. In the fifties there was still weekly rep and that was the worst. In those days plays were usually written in three acts. Managements liked two intervals so as to increase bar profits so: Tuesday block,[1] act one, Tuesday evening perform in the play currently running; Tuesday night after the show and a late supper learn lines for act one. Wednesday block act two, perform and study. Thursday block act three, play and study. Friday work bits and pieces where needed. Saturday run-thru's, Monday technical and dress (*if time*), and opening night, usually with stage management still putting finishing touches to the set right until curtain up. Strange how sets never seem to get finished in time. Tuesday start the next play and so on through the season.

I was even involved in a musical in a week, *Irma la Douce* at Westcliffe under the direction of chain-smoking Alexander Bridge. After striking the first match of the day he never seemed to need another as each new cigarette was lit from the stub of the old. Bless his heart. He and his mother, Eileen Farrow, were real old time theatricals: "troopers" in old time theatrical parlance. Modern journalists like to refer to them as "luvvies". Despite her advanced age mother was always his leading lady in revivals of early musical comedy and I'm really surprised he didn't take to wearing a fur-collar coat and carry a silver knob cane.

Another old trooper from a 'rep' family was Bessie Watty who was cast to play the 'daily help' in a week's run of *Shop at Sly Corner* at the old Tivoli Theatre, New Brighton; a great barn of a place long since gone. It was meant to hold over a thousand but I don't think audiences the summer of 1956 even reached a hundred. The director's wife was the leading lady, her sister was the ingénue in the company, and Bessie was their mother so it was a real family affair. Bessie claimed that Emlyn Williams named the character in *The Corn is Green* after her.

'You youngsters,' she addressed the junior members of the company one day, 'you youngsters don't know how to get an exit round. You watch me. I'll show you how it's done.' At the performance that evening, instead of the usual nice, clean (if a little laboured–after all she was elderly) exit, she remained on stage intoning, "Oh, my arthriticus,

---
1 Work out movement and stage business.

my arthriticus... Oho! My arthriticus... Ohohoh..." and went on in this fashion clutching at her hip until the audience got so fed up with her arthriticus there was a smattering of applause just to get her off. 'There you are you see?' She crowed triumphantly, 'That's how you do it.'

She wasn't the only disaster at the Tivoli. The company of course was run on a shoestring and the ancient flattage, inherited with the theatre lease I presume, was naturally very tall for what was in fact a large stage with a high proscenium. It was also extremely heavy and somewhat unwieldy and ran to a set and a half so that, while the one set was on stage, the half was being painted for the following week. Saturday night the set was struck and on Sunday and Monday the other half was painted which meant some of it wasn't even dry at curtain up. It was little wonder that one night as the curtain came down on act one of *Reluctant Heroes* the entire set collapsed as well. Fortunately no one on stage was hurt and the tabs[2] took the full brunt of a heavy flat's edge that sliced through the material like a knife, but the curtains certainly saved anyone in the front row from possible decapitation. That was also the play when, cast as the Sergeant Major, I lost my voice and discovered 'Sanderson's Specific.' This was an old actor's standby, a quinine based concoction sold by most chemists. You gargled with it, it tightened your flaccid vocal cords, and it brought the voice back long enough for you to finish a performance if you kept on using it in the intervals. 'Negroids' were another voice-aid: small black pastilles with a very un-PC name. No make-up box was complete without them.

Furniture and props, as was the custom, were borrowed with an acknowledgement in the programme and stage management were sent out to beg, borrow, cajole and turn on the charm in order to secure the necessary. Sometimes it took a bus ride into Birkenhead, an area of long straight roads with small, grimy, soot-blackened, grey stone terraced houses on either side, a couple of which, a little more substantial, were faced with a sign that read THE MAUDE

2 Curtain

AND MARY PICKUP COTTAGES. Poor Maude and Mary, little did they realise the future unintentional message their charitable actions would give out. Cigarettes were donated by a tobacco company, also acknowledged, the packs jealously guarded by stage management, and eagerly rifled by smokers in the company when they could get away with it, usually leaving a shortfall towards the end of the season. Moët & Chandon supplied the ginger ale mock champagne. The lighting and sound equipment was ancient and unreliable so, though there were actor traps a plenty at New Brighton, there were stage management traps as well for the unwary. *The Seventh Veil*, for those who do not know the play, has a young heroine who is destined to be a great concert pianist but, due to the jealousy of her guardian–I think it's her wicked guardian, I am after all dredging up the memory of a play I was in fifty years ago. In the film he was played by James Mason and it was a case of, 'If you don't play for me you don't play for anyone!' with which, as she's seated at her grand piano, he bashes her across the knuckles with his heavy walking stick. It's the same story as *The Red Shoes* really except the heroine is a pianist rather than a ballerina and it has a happy ending. A psychiatrist then has to persuade her to play the piano again and the climax of the play is when she is heard, up in her bedroom, playing Chopin as brilliantly as before. All turn upstage in wonder to listen to the glorious piano music emanating from the bedroom only to hear, one particular night, a full symphony orchestra blasting out at top volume and the ASM[3] sitting at her turntable in the prompt corner paralysed and in floods of tears, while it was just as well the actors in view of the audience were facing upstage. And at one performance, the scene in an anteroom supposedly at a foreign concert hall, instead of hearing the sound of applause, we heard the final movement of a concerto our heroine was about to step out and play!

The play was written by Muriel and Sydney Box, prolific writers of one act plays for amateur companies and Sydney won an Oscar for his screen adaptation. I remember as a schoolboy in South Africa

---
3 Assistant Stage Manager.

Chapter One

seeing the film and playing at being James Mason for quite a while afterwards. I couldn't know then, or during *The Seventh Veil* at New Brighton, that Sydney would later play a part in my life.

The play *Lovely to Look At* is set in the exquisite home of a connoisseur, a collector of beautiful things, of which the most beautiful of course is his lady-love, played by an actress sadly ill-equipped to lay claim to the title of the most beautiful woman in New Brighton, let alone the most beautiful in the world. The designer's idea of the "exquisite" home was realised in yet another landlady-brown set, liberally covered in stencilled cream-coloured leaping gazelles. That is, the first couple of flats stage right were liberally covered but, by the time we got to stage left, the leaping gazelles had dwindled to a couple of pairs. Never mind, the props would give the required feeling of sumptuousness, especially the significant-to-the-plot exquisite Venetian glass bowl. Unfortunately, despite being weakened with a glass cutter, the carefully dipped in cochineal Woolworth's faux cut-glass dessert bowl failed to smash into smithereens as required when dropped, merely bouncing across the stage instead and, worse, stubbornly refused to break even when stamped upon.

When I was very young, *Lovely to Look At* was one of my all time favourite songs on record.

The high point of the season came when the company produced a new play, *Crisis at the Crow's Nest* written by the producer, John Gordon, the first night attended by the Mayor and various dignitaries. I don't remember anything about the play except that a skeleton was involved and I know about the skeleton because I have a photograph of the company complete with said prop, and I know about the play being much much too short because John Gordon, starring in his own play, and another member of the company ad-libbed ad-infinitum as the most absurd, amateurish, unfunny and embarrassing double act that ever was. Who was it? It could have been Michael Vardy who later became a television director and who, at notes on stage one day when the footlights suddenly went out, said to a whooping send-up in unison from the rest of the cast, 'Who turned off the lights? They were so warm.'

New Brighton was my first professional job in England and I joined the company, sent by the agent John Penrose, another South African and a failed actor. I remember seeing him once in an early English movie playing a ticket inspector on a train, appearing at the door of a compartment and saying 'Tickets please.' I wonder what movie that was. The season at New Brighton had already opened with the first play, *The Reluctant Debutante* when I joined the company. Good on John Penrose to take the risk on a total unknown, though I suppose New Brighton was far enough from London for me to make a hash of things that wouldn't rebound on him. *The Stage* was hardly likely to review productions there. (Actor's joke for many years: What are the three most useless things in the world? Answer: a man's tits, the Pope's balls, and a review in *The Stage*.)

I landed in England with my seaman's pay and tips, the biggest of which was £5.00, a grubby rucksack with toiletries and a change of clothes: no contacts, no photographs, no wardrobe. In those days of repertory theatres an actor, according to the Equity contract, had to provide his own wardrobe of sports outfit, two lounge suits and one evening suit. I had no British drama school, Oxford or Cambridge University background and, most important, there was no one who had ever seen me act, so I think it can honestly be said I started with high hopes and a distinct disadvantage. I realised there was every chance of things not working out and I might very well want to leave the way I had come so, before walking away from the docks, I dropped in at the office of the National Union of Seamen, signed on, paid my dues and got my card, just in case. I still have it as a memento though it was never used.

I also have my pay slip, discharge date the 30th April, 1953, in which I see I earned £22.4.8 but with deductions for cash, tobacco, income tax of sixteen shillings and South African insurance eight shillings and nine pence, I was left with the lordly sum of £13.12.5. There

Chapter One

were no deductions for fines, forfeitures, channel money or slops[4] so presumably I handed back my steward's outfits on leaving. What 'channel money' means I have absolutely no idea and no one as yet has been able to enlighten me.

But, in looking for work as an actor, writing to reps, haunting the offices of agents, the inevitable reply was, 'Let me know where I can see you working.' That, of course, was no promise and no guarantee but I just happened to walk into John Penrose's office at the right time, before he could pick up the phone and call anybody else, and I was on my way to New Brighton; play as cast and assistant stage manager. In this business a certain amount of luck is of paramount importance: to be in the right place at the right time, to meet the right people, to have the right face for the part. I remember one of the students at RADA, when I was directing there, who I didn't rate at the time as being particularly talented, leaving and walking straight into a television serial about World War I pilots because, with that blonde hair, blue eyes and peaches and cream complexion he couldn't have suited the role better. More talented actors had to struggle to make themselves known, if they ever did.

At the Tivoli I was paid the princely salary of six pounds a week. Someone once described acting as basically, learning your lines, avoiding the furniture and picking up your pay at the end of the week. Could it have been Coward? The first question a jobbing actor asks is, 'When is treasury?' Possibly adding, 'Do you think I could get a sub?' Half my six pounds went on digs that included breakfast and tea, or was it late supper? Tea, or late supper, whichever it was, invariably consisted of a slice of spam, a slice of tomato, a leaf of lettuce, thinly sliced bread and marge, and tea, but what more could one expect for three pounds a week? My six pounds really didn't stretch far and, by the end of each week, I invariably had to borrow from friends and colleagues, a state of affairs that lasted on and off, mainly on, for a great deal of my life. Later on, when I was more

[4] Seaman's issue of clothing

established and a homeowner with a mortgage, it was bank managers I kowtowed to for overdrafts and credit cards for loans. If I felt a bit down in New Brighton and had a moment to myself during the day I visited Woolworths and just wandered around, almost as if I were in a museum. Woolworths always cheered me up, with its wooden floors, old-fashioned counters, and cheap and cheerful tat. I shouldn't think there's a Woolworth's left that hasn't been modernised and had its wooden floors ripped out more's the pity. I did come across a five and dime in Virginia that hadn't changed in years, which had the same therapeutic effect on me, and a country store near Charlottesville, Walton country. It was a shack complete with pot belly stove, and a wooden stoop where one could spend a lazy summer afternoon sitting in the sun sipping soda, a store the likes of which is usually seen only in the paintings of Norman Rockwell or nostalgic American movies, usually set sometime pre World War II. I only discovered it because my student friend, Gray Lee III, great nephew of that great general of the South, drove us passed it when I was spending a weekend at the Lee farm in Covesville outside Charlottesville and I cried out for him to stop, and we sat in the sun a long while, saying nothing, sipping soda, just content to be with each other. I looked at him through half-closed eyelids and wondered why this beautiful young man should be so taken up with someone thirty years his senior, especially as this beautiful young man was totally girl-crazy and sex was never going to enter the equation. I wonder if that wonderful old store is still there or whether it's been bulldozed to make room for progress.

The other soothe-my-ruffled-soul therapy was to listen to Brahms.

The curtain came down on the penultimate performance of the last play at New Brighton and I went to John Gordon's dressing room to collect my pay at the final treasury, only to discover there was no train fare included for my return to London. Equity contracts stipulated that return fares should be paid but, when I asked where it was, I was informed that, as I hadn't signed a contract, it wasn't up to the company to provide my fare. It had never occurred to me to

Chapter One

ask for a contract. No contract had been placed in front of me for me to sign. I had worked hard and conscientiously the whole season on stage management, and played major roles and that, as far as I was concerned, was as good as any contract and I said as much. My protest was ignored.

'Fine,' I said. 'In that case I don't go on tonight.'

'What!'

'I haven't signed a contract. No contract means I don't have to play. I'm going up to my dressing room, I'm packing my things and I'm leaving the theatre…now.'

'You can't do that!'

'Watch me.'

I stormed up those cold grey uninviting backstage stairs (why are backstage stairs always like that?) and threw open the dressing room door with a crash that nearly sent Philip through the ceiling. Philip Clive is the youngest son of Joe Coral, the bookmaker, and we shared the dressing room. I say, 'is' because, at time of writing, we still keep in touch after all these years. Philip was always of a nervous disposition which later caused him to abandon any idea of a stage career but, at this moment, as I picked up my chair in a truly Taurian rage and hurled it against the wall, he practically had a seizure. A moment later there was a knock at the door, the door opened and there, without a word being spoken, I was handed my train fare, all three pounds odd shillings and pence of it.

My first night back in London, flat broke of course; I stayed with Philip in his parent's apartment near Regents Park. The flat was splendidly furnished as behoves an exceedingly rich bookmaker. I seem to remember velvet was the predominant material and pink the predominant colour, but what I remember most about it, after weeks in the grotty spartan digs in New Brighton, was my wallowing for what seemed like hours in a luxurious, deep, hot hot hot foaming bath. Strange how seemingly small events, like that bath, live on in the memory.

When I first arrived in England my immediate impression of London was chimney pots, rows of small terraced houses back to back and hundreds and hundreds of chimney pots. That's what you saw from the deck of the ship that ended its journey at what were then the George V docks, now either high rise apartments I suppose or expensive lofts in converted warehouses, but I can still see in my mind's eye those rows of chimney pots. I went to Wales and stayed somewhere with friends of the Joneses–Where? I don't remember, and I don't remember who these people were. They could even have been distant relations for all I know. This is the disadvantage of not having kept a diary, not remembering. Anyway, from one of the kids in the family, I borrowed a bike and went cycling around North Wales. I do recall scenes of outstanding beauty but what I remember most was a simple meal. Stopping for an overnight stay at a pub–where was that? Betts-y-Coed? Beddgelert? All the landlady could give me for dinner was ham and eggs. Of all the meals I've consumed over the years I remember that dinner of ham and eggs like I remember that bath in London. Another memory of that trip was listening in a shop to Welsh being spoken like "blah blah blah blah bacon blah blah." Obviously there is no word for bacon in the Welsh language. Either that or the lady ordering had forgotten it.

Another instance of minutiae: walking across Westminster Bridge on a heavily overcast and cold day, a bit down in the dumps, no convenient Woolworths to go to, no Brahms to listen to, probably broke as usual, I stopped to watch as a little old lady opened her handbag, an ancient and wrinkled brown handbag as I recall, and offered a lump of sugar to a policeman's horse and, as the horse took his sugar, suddenly God was in His heaven and all was well with the world. That scene is as vivid now as if it happened yesterday.

I borrowed five quid from Philip, five quid that took quite a long time to repay as my borrowings usually did, and set out to explore possibilities.

Chapter One

Theatrically there were none. Penrose had nothing for me and he was still my only contact. He invited me to dinner in his opulent flat in South Ken which meant he expected me to go to bed with him, but that was a no-no from the start as any attempt to make it with someone I found so physically unattractive could only result in complete failure so there was no point in even trying.

I ended up as a barman in *The Rose and Crown*, Ilford; third stop after Stratford East on the Southend line from Liverpool Street. How I got to be barman in *The Rose and Crown* is lost in the mists of time but there I was, a barman, live-in, all found, salary five pounds a week. Not much of a salary but at least I had a roof over my head, literally, as my eight foot by eight bedroom was in the attic, the window a grimy skylight, very Dickensian and, to quote an old comedian's joke, even the mice were hunchbacked. Is one still allowed to say hunchback? The 'guv'nor' of *The Rose and Crown* was also a Jones, believe it or not. My first day there I called him by his Christian name and was hauled over the coals. 'You address me as Guv,' he ordered, so I have forgotten his Christian name altogether. Short and a little on the tubby side with florid slightly pockmarked features from teenage acne, he dressed quite nattily, always a collar and tie, and I suppose he was in his late thirties or thereabouts. He did have one terrible handicap though: he had the most horrendously, disgustingly, smelly feet. It wasn't noticeable in the pub because his shoes acted as a barrier, but once upstairs where the shoes came off, the odour was almost vomit making and spread through most of the upper floors. I was glad of my attic bedroom where the stench didn't reach, and stench is not too strong a word for it. He also duffed up his missus on occasion but according to the cleaning ladies, Bet and Lil, she enjoyed it, or so they informed me, and I wasn't to interfere. It was nothing to do with me, no matter what my personal feelings. It was little wonder the wife was a dipso. She would run a glass beneath the row of optics: whisky, brandy, vodka, gin, rum, and that, as anyone must admit, is a pretty poisonous concoction to knock back. Also, one afternoon a week, she was off to the local cinema with a bottle opener and an old sort of oilcloth type brown shopping bag filled with bottles of Guinness, and there she would sit through the programme getting happily plastered. There was also a barmaid named Ivy who really did look like the archetypal East End barmaid with her low cut bodice, cheap chunky jewellery and bouffant platinum blonde hair. She very kindly invited me to her home the only Christmas day I was there. I even received a letter from her after I left saying how they missed me and Lil and Bet were telling her to write the most awful things! 'The things they are telling me to say, well you can imagine can't you?'

I got on well with Lil and Bet. They were a pair of real down to earth charmers who came in every Saturday night with their spruced up husbands, always sitting at their regular table enjoying their favourite milk stout. Port and lemon was for a special occasion. Joining in the sing-song to the accompaniment of the old out of tune jangling Joanna: all the old East End favourites; *Knees Up Mother Brown, On Mother Kelly's Doorstep, My Old Man said Follow the Van, If You Were the Only Boy in the World* and many more, plus popular favourites of the day, were played and sung over and over. *You Made Me Love You* was a great favourite and *I Wonder Who's Kissing Her Now*.

It always amazed me, this Saturday night ritual. I would have thought that cleaning the pub every morning would have put them off using it for a social evening. It was Lil I think who told me the story of Old Mother Cat. There was this old woman lived nearby who was known by that appellation and one day Lil was out on her doorstep gossiping with a neighbour who was with her three year old daughter when the old woman passed by. 'Ere,' the neighbour said, nudging her grubby infant, 'who's that then?'

'It's fucking ole muvver cat,' the child squeaked.

'Don't she say it luvly?' Said the proud mother.

Today, with most people, and kids, I suppose that word no longer has the power to shock and is used ad nauseam both in film, theatre, and writing. It's like everyone having discovered they can use it, (in the name of so-called reality I suppose) until total boredom sets in,

Chapter One

but in the fifties it wasn't in public usage. Kenneth Tynan hadn't yet shocked the British public by actually saying it on television.

The Rose and Crown was a large pub right across the road from the rail yards, and it had the longest U-shaped pewter bar in the country which I had to clean every morning, firstly with lashings of metal cleaner which was left to dry, then rubbed off with crinkled up newspaper. It was a job I loathed as metal polish drying on the fingers, like chalk squeaking across a blackboard, invariably set my teeth on edge. By the time I got to the end of that bar with my fingers caked in polish my skin would have crawled across the floor if it could have got away. The pewter was finally polished with a soft cloth. Lil and Bet meanwhile were bent on their own mopping up, invariably chatting away whenever they got close enough to each other without having to raise their voices. Like I said, it was a very large pub. I don't know if it still exists. I haven't been back to that small part of the world since I thankfully left it. Lil and Bet's conversation often ran along the lines of what they had seen on television the night before and normally I didn't take much notice, being lost in my own little dream world. But one morning I was so intrigued by their extravagant praise of a play they'd seen on the telly the night before: something so brilliant it had them totally gob smacked and they just couldn't stop talking about it.

'So what was this play?' I asked.

They had to stop work and think. Obviously the title hadn't registered as deeply as the play itself.

'What was it called, Lil? Can you remember?'

'Hmn' ... Lil rested on her mop handle; 'It'll come to me in a minute. Let me see… What was it now? "The Wild Duck." That's what it was.'

'That's right, "The Wild Duck."'

'Yes, that was it, "The Wild Duck", that's what it was.'

I couldn't believe it. This is not meant to be derogatory in any way but two not very well educated East End ladies who the advertising agencies would definitely place in Category D had been totally enraptured with a nineteenth century Scandinavian playwright, Henrik Ibsen. Who would have credited it? I later wrote this incident into a play, *Are You Sitting Comfortably?* I always maintain if Ibsen were writing today he would be writing for a soap so maybe it's not that surprising.

One incident I have never written into a play was my one and only brush with an East End gangster. One Saturday evening he walked into the pub with his 'associates,' none of whom looked particularly thuggish or menacing, together with their, to use a quaint old American expression, "molls." The pub was packed and we were kept hard at it keeping customers satisfied. The guv'nor's missus had already gone through the optics and was more or less legless, smiling sweetly if somewhat unfocused at the punters, so he and I and the Saturday night barmaid were pretty much rushed off our feet. The gangster was middle aged, tall, slender, quite handsome and immaculate in a natty very expensive looking suit and tie, and sporting a trim moustache. In the course of the evening his companions consumed a fair amount of liquor and the women appeared to be keeping well up with the men; if not forging ahead. I was serving a customer when one of the girls got up and weaved an unsteady path to the bar where she proceeded to bang on it with the flat of her hand. She was quite young, peroxided, dolled up and made up to the nines, definitely a case of overkill and, whether she'd had too much or just couldn't hold her liquor I don't know, but she was obviously nine sheets to the wind. I looked at her and nodded, meaning be with you in a sec. Maybe I should have said something but was too busy finishing what I was doing which evidently, as I didn't jump to her bidding, didn't please her.

'Hey, you! You I'm talking to.'

Now I should have said something. It would have been easy to say, 'be with you in a second' or something equally banal, instead of which I turned my back on her to work the till.

'Hey! You! Are you fucking deaf? You stupid bugger, didn't you hear me?'

Now it was my turn to lose it: that Taurian temper again. I moved over to where she was propped up against the bar and leaned right across it so that our faces were as close as they were ever going to be, which enabled me to say very quietly, 'Of course I heard you, you drunken bitch. The whole fucking pub heard you. And I'm not serving you. If you want a drink, get it elsewhere.'

For a second she seemed taken aback and then she shrieked with laughter. 'Look at his face!' She screamed at the top of her voice. 'Look at his face!'

And a number of people did turn to look in our direction, wondering what was going on. This was getting very hairy. I just had time to clock one of the men from her table getting to his feet, obviously to make his way in our direction, when there was a tug at my sleeve and the guv'nor hauled me around to the other side of the bar where I couldn't be seen from what was euphemistically called the lounge.

'What the hell do you think you're doing?' He hissed and he wasn't angry. He was just scared rigid. 'Don't you know who that is?'

'She's pissed out of her mind,' I said, 'She should be chucked out.'

'Not her! Not her!' His toes must have been really sweating. Those socks were going to stand up on their own come closing time. 'Don't you know that's Lefty Smith?'

I seem to recall that was his name.

'Who's he?' I whispered though I had a suspicion the "Lefty" bit gave me the right clue.

'Jesus!' The guv'nor practically wrung his hands. 'That is his girl friend. For God's sake get back there, apologise and be nice.'

But, when I got back there, she was no longer at the bar. Instead, Lefty himself was standing there. Oh, shit! Every really cowardly barman's nightmare. Visions of sharp cutthroat razors and narrow alleys. Visions of dark rubbish-strewn canals, maybe even railway lines, as they were so handy. He saw I had been stopped in my tracks and flicked back his head to beckon me over. He was smiling. Bad sign.

'What did the guv'nor say to you?' He asked. As befits a neat moustache, freshly laundered shirt and tie, and immaculate suit, his voice was soft and low.

'He told me who you are.'

'And?'

'He said I had to apologise and be nice to your...' I looked across to the table where she was now sitting, rather subdued, 'your girlfriend.'

'Crap,' he said. 'Why should you? If anything she ought to apologise to you. Do you want her to do that?'

I shrugged. 'No. I'd just like to forget it.'

He laid a pound note on the bar. 'Then I apologise on her behalf. Have a drink on me,' he said. 'Keep the change and tell your guv'nor I really can't afford to make trouble over something so stupid.' He gave another smile and a nod and turned away. A true gent was Lefty Smith, though I should imagine he wouldn't have been too gentle with those who really upset him. As for his girl friend, who knows what she was in for after they left? And that, as far as I know, was my only brush with gangsterdom.

One night an extremely attractive young man approached the bar to order drinks and, as he did so, he was humming *La Donna è Mobile* from Verdi's *Rigoletto*.

'Opera?' I said.

'Best music ever written.'

It turned out however that, despite his love of the music, he had never actually been to an opera so on one of my evenings off it was decided we would go to Covent Garden. The opera playing that particular evening was *Carmen*, a good one to start off with and he thoroughly enjoyed it. I also took him to Sheekey's for dinner. I could afford to take him to one of the most famous fish restaurants in London? Somehow or other I could and did. I remember we both had turbot steak in lobster sauce and it was delicious. What was even more delicious was we spent the night in the spare bed in a friend's flat in Chelsea and he was worth twenty servings of turbot in lobster sauce. Unfortunately in the morning I was still extremely horny and had my wicked way with him which was a big mistake. It might have been wonderful by night but not welcome in the cold light of morning. Next time he came into the pub he ignored me and

Chapter One

we never spoke again.

La Donna è Mobile. As mucky-minded little schoolboys who sniggered at "the brown ring test" in chemistry class, the tune of that aria lent itself to dirty words;
Arseholes are cheap today, cheaper than yesterday.
Small boys are half a crown, standing up or lying down.
Bigger boys are seven and six, as they all take bigger pricks,
Tra la la

...and so forth. I don't remember the rest, if there was any rest. Rugby songs were another source of youthful hilarity.
Hasie, Hasie bloubal,
Padda het gepoep.
Sprinkaan sit in die doringboom,
En skilpad se maar fok jou, fok jou, fok jou.

Which, roughly translated goes,
Hare, hare blue balls,
Froggie had a shit.
Locust sat in the thorny tree
And tortoise just said fuck you, fuck you, fuck you.

Not exactly the wittiest of lyrics.

I didn't last much longer at *The Rose and Crown*. Shortly after this I handed in my notice. The guv was really upset. This was something he never expected and, on the spot, he upped my meagre salary. Unfortunately for him I had used a couple of my half days off to travel up to town, looking for another position, and had already been accepted for another barman spot in a pub near Gloucester Road, at just that same improved salary. I'd had enough of smelly feet, stale beer, lingering cigarette smoke (although I was a smoker myself), charmless girls who drank Babycham and squealed loudly, lousy food, Danish Blue cheese was the height of sophistication, and miles and miles of the longest pewter bar in England. So it was goodbye to hard benches, cast iron tables, my hutch beneath the roof, bare wooden floors and the railway yard, and hello to mock leather banquettes, flock wallpaper, carpets, even if stained, curtains, engraved mirrors, clean loos (for the most part), a fairly decent bedroom and a clientele that included faded debs with memories of Hurlingham, Badminton, Wimbledon, Henley, Cowes, the Chelsea Arts and hunt balls, royal garden parties, and their own coming out. Still trying desperately to cling to a long since departed youth, their rouge and lipstick and powder only served to accentuate the passing of the years. All it needed was ghostly background music and it was cinema verité. There were ex-Majors, ex-Squadron Leaders, or so they said, complete with handlebar moustaches, dressed in hard wearing tweed or corduroy reinforced with leather elbow patches, and chattering in wizard prang slang as obsolete as the Spitfire. They existed in pathetically straightened circumstances in the genteel hotels of South Kensington and stretched out their half pints to last most of the evening or, on some memorable occasion, taking a nip of the hard stuff. It says something that, unlike the East End where it was constantly happening, here I was never once offered a drink and, if I had been, I think, out of charity, I would have refused it.

I can't remember how long I stayed at this particular pub. It couldn't have been that long because John Penrose came up with my second summer season, this time at Ventnor on the Isle of Wight.

The quotation used for the title of this biography might not be wholly accurate. I read the book from which it is taken a great many years ago and remember nothing of it but this fragment, which stuck in my youthful mind because I decided, then and there, I would use it one day when fame and fortune were mine. Fame and fortune having eluded me it's still worth using anyway. I still feel it is applicable to my life. For fame, or rather the lack of it, I have no regrets. And that is not sour grapes; it is the voice of experience. Someone once said

Chapter One

that experience is what you get when you don't get what you want. I don't know who said it but I guess it is a truism. For we are like film producers who never seem to know what they really want even when they get it, like Jack Le Vien when we were making the film *A King's Story*. Jack had been gallivanting around the world selling his movie while Harry Booth, the director, and I were sitting day after day in front of a moviola going through what seemed like a million miles of old newsreel footage putting together our version of the Duke of Windsor's life story. Eventually Jack returned from his carpet bagging and the result of our work was screened in a Wardour Street basement cinema. Jack invited a number of people to the screening including, I think, various tea ladies, gophers, and passers-by dragged off the street. This, as far as Harry and I were concerned, with the still to come addition of title, credits, opticals, music, and some voice-overs not yet recorded, was the movie. At the end of the screening Jack stood up in front of us all and said something to the effect that we had done a lot of good work but there was still one hellava long way to go. Later, when we asked him for the changes he wanted, in between trans-Atlantic phone calls and playing at being a big-shot movie mogul, he was pretty vague. So Harry and I went back to our moviola and spent a couple of months dutifully pulling apart and putting together again virtually as was. I don't know how many dollars this exercise in futility added to the budget but Jack, returning from yet another round the world jaunt, loved the result.

For the premiere at The Festival Hall, May 3rd, 1965, I bought myself a dinner suit at Alkits in Cambridge Circus and wore it that once and never wore it again. Should have hired it from Moss Bros in Covent Garden. I was told, probably by Harry, that the film was nominated for an Oscar, something about a specially invented drama-documentary category or some such. In to-day's newspeak would it be called a dramentary? I never did check it out and to this day I don't know if it was true, most likely not, but Sal Mineo later told me he seemed to have some recollection of it. True or not, special category or not, it didn't actually get anything. When the record was released I trotted down to HMV in Oxford Street and took a look at it. There was no screenplay credit on the sleeve. Typical. So I put it back in the rack. Jack also wanted to deny me my credit on the actual film but was dissuaded from this by a letter from Sydney Box that read:-

"I don't care whether Le Vien gives me a credit or not, but he must give one to Glyn Jones, my young contract writer, who actually wrote 90% of the narrative. He was promised a credit and this was confirmed by Mr. Le Vien as recently as the day before yesterday when Glyn sat with him and the Windsor's making all the changes they'd asked for."

Changes to the script were worrying for some people originally involved with the Duke of Windsor. I had to make several journeys into the wilds of Kent to visit the Dowager Lady Hardinge of Penshurst to put her mind at rest, assuring her I would write nothing derogatory about her husband who was equerry to His Royal Highness. A card I received from her read, "With grateful thanks for all your kind co-operation. One thing I forgot to say – There was never any objection to Rip van Winkle's wife because she was American. Something you mentioned about the script made me reminded of this." Rip van Winkle? I had never heard the Duke called that before. Who invented that name for him I wonder, and why?

Duchess of Windsor

Chapter One

Did the Duke really want Mrs. Simpson that much? Or, having made his stand, to coin a phrase, did he feel he had to continue come what may? Did she really want him or was she only, despite her protestations, interested in becoming queen of England? So much has been said and written about this couple you can speculate to your heart's content. The story doing the rounds at the time was that he had masochistic tendencies and liked to be beaten. As the English roses couldn't bring themselves to give the Prince of Wales a good thrashing, it was up to Mrs. Simpson who evidently at parties rode him like a horse, using a crop to obvious good effect on his backside. Why shouldn't royalty, like ordinary mortals, have their own little peccadilloes? My own impression of the couple during filming in Paris and at the mill, their country house, was that they were two unhappy, lonely, separate people and had been so for a long time. So the Duchess of Windsor who, he insisted, everyone refer to as Her Royal Highness, even though this title had been officially denied her, got her fame and her place in the history books but at what price? As for him, he didn't need fame, he was born famous, but the price he paid too was pretty steep for getting what he thought he wanted. My recollection of her is of a silent skeletal ghost wandering around the mill, ashtray in hand and at the ready, just in case some member of the crew thoughtlessly flicked his cigarette ash on the carpet. And the Duke? He had servants at his beck and call, but the moment the telephone rang he would dash to it before anyone else could get there. I had learned from my research that David, as he was known, invariably got his own way and had done so all his life, and I remember one day, called into the Paris studio to do a voice-over re-enacting his abdication speech as I recall, he started to admire the angle-poise lamp illuminating his script. He went on and on about it until it started to become embarrassing. It was the kind of lamp he could have sent out a servant to buy at any department or electrical store for a few francs but it was obvious HRH wanted this one and no other would do. 'Oh, it would be ideal for my bridge table!' He enthused. 'Wouldn't it be ideal?' His tone defied anyone to gainsay him though no one present had actually seen his bridge table.

As we left the studio, the manager presented the Duke with the lamp that he knew from the start he was going to get but which he accepted with great surprise. 'For me? Oh, how kind!' He sat in the back of his car, tartan travelling rug over his knees and the cherished lamp clutched in both hands except for a brief moment to give a royal wave of farewell.

My first meeting with the Duke started inauspiciously. Jack Le Vien, Harry, myself, and some other members of the crew were waiting on His Royal Highness in the study of the Paris house and His Royal Highness was taking a very long time to appear, probably having an interesting telephone conversation elsewhere. So, as is my wont in other people's houses, I started to go through his bookcase. My father used to inspect other people's medicine chests. It was a low bookcase and the chair in front of it on which I was sitting was a low chair without arms, more like a stool with a tall narrow back. The Duke was a small man and some of the furniture was in proportion to his size. He finally entered the room and, as everyone respectfully stood up, I attempted to do the same. Unfortunately, a couple of days previously I had put my back out and, not taking into account the proximity of the chair seat to the floor, I felt the agony of muscles going into spasm and my butt remained glued to the chair. I knew it was going to be a while before I could get to my feet without wanting to yell and possibly keeling over and perhaps I should have explained my predicament only it was also difficult to breathe. So, instead, I stuck my nose six inches from the book spines and studied them intently. There was dead silence. The Duke waited. Everybody waited. There was a discreet cough though fortunately nobody thought of calling me by name. I knew though they were all looking at me and finally, when I felt there was no chance of the spasm being repeated if I were careful, I turned around and rose gingerly to my feet.

'Oh, I'm so sorry, sir,' I said, hoping I sounded truly humble, 'I didn't realise you were here.'

The Duke glared at me. Was I taking the mick or was I hard of

Chapter One

hearing? How come I hadn't been telepathically aware of the august royal presence? As the old cliché has it, you could now cut the atmosphere with a knife, so I thought I had better say something else fast.

'I was amazed to see this in your bookcase, sir,' I said, and held out a large brown covered volume, *A Pictorial History of South Africa.* Uriah Heep had nothing on me at this moment.

'Oh, yes,' he replied, still icy. 'That was presented to me on my tour of the Union of South Africa.' Note, it was still "The Union."

'The only other place I've ever seen this book,' I went on, 'was in my home in Durban. It's a memory of my childhood.'

'You come from Durban?'

'Yes, sir.'

The ice melted.

The Duke of Windsor - His Study in Paris

'Oh, I remember Durban very well. I enjoyed Durban immensely, had the most wonderful time in Durban. Visited the snake park; saw the magnificent rickshaw boys, Zulu dancing at Eshowe. Great hospitality... wonderful people...' and he launched into a long monologue all about his South African tour and the rapturous reception he received from those wonderful people.

Of course they were wonderful, the ones he met, as good as anybody at adoration and he was genuinely popular, especially with the girls, "*I danced with a man who danced with a girl who danced with the Prince of Wales*" was one of the popular songs of the period.

But now the others in the room were all glaring at me, especially Jack who was not being the focus of royal attention, and we were supposed to be having a production meeting, not listening to the Duke's reminiscences on South Africa. Fortunately the ringing of the telephone cut him short as he dashed to his desk to answer it. He must have forgiven me my gross neglect of protocol because, when he saw the finished film, he shook my hand, congratulated me on the writing and thanked me warmly. Which was more than Jack Le Vien ever did. But then Jack never wanted me on the film in the first place. Sydney Box who had been contracted to write *A King's Story* and didn't want to go through with it foisted me onto him. As I was at the time under a year's writing contract to Sydney for the then princely sum of a hundred pounds a week, my first rich period we called it, and as he really didn't have anything for me to do to warrant my weekly salary, he passed me on to Jack who reluctantly accepted he had a new unknown writer for his film, as long as he could still use Sydney's name some way or other, presumably as a selling point. He brought in another writer to add a name to the credits who I don't actually remember doing very much but who, on leaving, presented me with an Edward VIII memorial mug and I still have that and a copy of *A Pictorial History of South Africa* in the library of our house in Crete.

Sometime after the film's release I received a letter from my mother in South Africa saying what a thrill I had given her seeing my name on the screen and photographs outside the cinema of me with the Duke. "We went to the first show yesterday afternoon and the house was full. We loved every moment of it and thought the Duchess looked much younger and prettier in her old age, to her picture on her wedding day. A pathetically lonely lost soul was our final summing

Chapter One

up of the Duke and felt glad he gave up all the pomp and ceremony for love and companionship." Such is the romantic belief in happy ever after fairy tales.

The Duke of Windsor - Rehearsing in his Paris study

When they were issued, my parents bought a set of Edward VIII definitive stamps as an investment and I found and destroyed them by trimming the perforations, which I thought made them look untidy. This resulted in a smacked backside and a severe ticking off as I was informed I had just ruined ten pounds worth of stamps, South African currency then was still pounds, shillings, and pence. It must have been this episode that produced my first known effort at acting. I was discovered curled up on the window seat of my parents' bedroom when, between sobs and apparently talking in my sleep, they heard the words repeated over and over, 'Ten quid... ten jolly old quid... gone! Ten jolly quid!'

My contract with Sydney Box came about because Charles Vance produced my play *Early One Morning* at Chelmsford and Sydney not only bought an option on the play but put me under that year's contract. Charles Vance had once been a member of the J. Arthur Rank charm school of budding film stars, at the same time he informed us as Dirk Bogarde. Charles was someone who did wear a fur collared coat and carry a silver headed cane, the last of the old time actor manager laddies who produced tours and seasons in the sixties, and everyone you knew and bumped into at Chadwick Street Labour Exchange worked for Charlie at some time or other. Chadwick Street in Westminster was the Labour Exchange for actors. You met friends there, exchanged news and gossip, went for coffee after you'd signed on, or collected your three pounds which was the going dole rate at the time. And then some jobs-worthy civil servant put the mockers on it and it became mandatory that everyone had to sign on at their local Labour Exchange instead, which put an end to the socialising at Chadwick Street. The other meeting place at that time was the basement cafe at the Arts Theatre that was always crowded with out of work actors.

Apart from *A King's Story*, no other film was produced in that contract year to give me another screen credit. Together with Sydney's wife, Muriel, we flew to the south of France, to Beaulieu-Sur-Mer, ostensibly to talk to producers about a screenplay for Conan Doyle's *Brigadier Gerrard*. I did write it but my script was rejected and the film was later made with Peter McEnery playing Gerrard and, of course, with someone else's screenplay, and it flopped. Maybe they should have used mine after all. It still lies neglected in my script cupboard together with all the other rejections, with both good work and work

Chapter One

I look back on and shudder over but am forbidden to destroy and all of which is being retyped to put onto CD Rom, even the crap. But at least the stay at Beaulieu was memorable: my first (and only) visit to the South of France: my first experience of how the rich live, Sydney being one of the millionaire socialists; a five star hotel, lunches at La Colombe D'or in St Paul du Vence, renowned as a watering hole of continental film stars and which, some time later, was in the news because of the theft of its collection of fine paintings. In Vence I bought myself a modest painting, a landscape by an artist named Michel Vu about whom I know nothing but whose picture still hangs in our saloni in Crete.

A visit to a casino resulted in my losing all the money Sydney had given me to play with, which wasn't all that much but losing it annoyed me considerably, even though it wasn't mine in the first place. Maybe because money has usually been so tight all my life I am not a good loser. On leaving the casino, we bumped into two furtive figures lingering in the dark outside with a couple of French females in tow. It was hail fellow well met with Sydney and on saying good night, 'Don't tell our wives you saw us.' As I remember it, the truants were Jack Hawkins and Nigel Patrick.

Early One Morning, with Trevor Bannister, and Yolande Turner, South African born actress and wife of Peter Finch, received good notices at Chelmsford, it's first production: not exactly raves but pretty respectable nevertheless and Charles took the play on to Bath and Brighton but, when his option was up, Sydney failed to renew it. This wasn't the end of the story though. The first act of the play takes place in the young man's attic bed-sit and it is predominately the boy's part and Trevor gave a wonderful performance. In the second act which takes place in her lush Belgravia apartment it is the girl who predominates and this was where we had what one might kindly call a hiccup because, instead of taking off and flying with it, Yolande, I hate to say it, was as a piece of wood. She looked great; svelte and so beautiful, every inch the part but that's where it ended. Trevor, opposite her, did his damndest to give it the kiss of life but to no avail.

An option on the play was now taken up by Peter Saunders of *Mousetrap* fame who arranged for an out of town try-out at a theatre close to London. The theatre shall remain nameless as will the director. Actually I asked for a young assistant director at that theatre, Tony Wiles, whose work I had seen and enjoyed, and who I believed had a real flair for directing comedy, but Peter said that wasn't on because, if the play went into the West End, whoever directed it would be on a percentage and so-and-so was not going to give up on that lucrative possibility. Okay, skirmish lost, but what about casting? Well, as Trevor was so good first time round why not use him again if he's willing? He was. So now to find an actress to play opposite him. Suggestions were bandied about. Presumably the play was offered to actresses who for one reason or another wouldn't or couldn't do it and time was pressing when one day the phone rang. It was Peter Saunders.

'Glyn, we've got your leading lady?'

I was highly suspicious. My contract stated I had approval of casting and here was Peter more or less telling me he had signed someone up.

'Oh, yes?' I queried. 'Who?'

And he named a young actress famous for playing a piece of wood in a then long running soap.

'Well, Peter,' was my response, 'with so-and-so directing and so-and-so playing, the result is certain fucking theatrical death.' Believe me, that's exactly how I put it and never was there a truer forecast.

There was the longest silence in theatre history before he replied.

'Don't be unkind,' was all he managed to say and disaster was already on its way. It was just a matter of waiting to see what shape it would take.

First bad sign – On her entrance at the dress rehearsal I couldn't believe what the lady was wearing. The play is called *Early One Morning*, that is when the action takes place, and what was our lady dressed in? A vibrant green sheathe suitable only for a cocktail lounge, certainly not for King's Cross Station at sparrowfart. I made my protest and

Chapter One

got nowhere. Evidently the frock was her own and the only one she thought suitable. She thought it SUITABLE? When it came to the opening night she got her first laugh on her first entrance. She wasn't exactly a flat-chested girl but it also looked as if she had padded up because this pair of shimmering emerald green torpedoes entered followed by an actress. Take a deep breath, I thought, it's going to get worse. However, Trevor had the audience with him all the way and the first interval arrived. I was prowling the back of the stalls when the actress's husband, also a well known actor, came up to congratulate me most enthusiastically, as did a number of others including the playwright Ted Willis which was really heartening.

'Cracking play, Glyn,' he said, 'cracking play!' And off he went to the bar. I started to relax.

Charles Vance, GIJ, Yolande Turner, Peter Finch & Trevor Bannister Back Stage - Early One Morning

Act two, curtain up... end of act two, curtain down... Nobody came up to congratulate me. Somehow everyone seemed to have been spirited away. Somehow the stalls seemed strangely empty... and very lonely. I went backstage and thanked Trevor who shrugged and raised a cynical eyebrow and I knew exactly what he meant. And I did my duty by her but not, I have to admit, with much enthusiasm. That, I presumed, would be the history of the play and, yes, Peter Saunders did drop his option and, no, it wasn't the end because an American gentleman bought it. I think he only did so because he developed the hots for our leading lady. Those boobs must have aroused the beast in him and he bought it, arranging a transfer to a small West End theatre. I was really surprised and grateful that Trevor agreed to go with it.

But disaster was creeping ever closer. For one thing the play was scheduled to open on the same night as two other major openings so I got third string critics who no doubt would have a field day and, in the case of *The Guardian*, Fiona MacCarthy of the women's page who was particularly vitriolic.

At the get-in I stood in the auditorium looking at the set for act one. In front of the bed was a pillar. I went over to where the director was sitting.

'What is that pillar doing in front of the bed?'

'It's to hold down the rostrum. It's a cantilevered set; without that the whole thing will tip up.'

'An awful lot of comedy is played on that bed,' I said to him, 'you cannot, simply CANNOT play comedy behind a pillar! You'll kill it stone dead. Change it.'

'Can't.'

'Tie it to the flies[5]'

He shook his head.

'Use stage weights in the rostrum.'

'Tried it. Doesn't work.'

'So the pillar stays?'

'The pillar stays. What's the problem? It's only six inches wide.'

'Six inches too much,' I said, 'you'll lose all your laughs.' But it was another battle lost. I tottered backstage and knocked on Trevor's

---

5 Overhead Bars

Chapter One

dressing room door. He was a trembling bundle of nerves.

'What's the matter?' I asked him. Need I have asked?

'Do you know what the ASM just said to me?'

'No, but you're going to tell me.'

'Mr. Bannister, how do I give you your cue, do I do this?' And he clicked his fingers. 'They picked her up off the street! One of them fancied her and offered her a job. She's never worked in a theatre in her life.' I wondered what Equity would say about that if only they knew.

Oh, boy! What next? On to the leading lady. Oh, my God! She's still in that awful dress.

'Why are you still wearing that? I thought the management were going to fit you out with another frock.'

'They say they can't afford it.'

That was the proverbial last straw. I went home and phoned my agent, Laurence Fitch of blessed memory.

'Laurence, this play cannot go on. Please, you've got to stop it! I want it stopped. I want my name off it. I don't wish to be associated with it in any way. The critics are going to slaughter it and they'll put all the blame on the play!'

He talked me down. Let it go on. It can't be as bad as I made out, but his first night telegram said it all, "Best of luck always AND IN SPITE OF IT ALL", and I was right. The critics did indeed slaughter it. You would never have credited it was the same play reviewed in Chelmsford and on its second out of town production, despite my reservations even there.

Chelmsford: "*Early One Morning* is a wry, off-beat and amusing examination of motive in one of the basic human relationships."

"The Civic Theatre, Chelmsford has found for itself a merry little comedy called *Early One Morning* by Glyn Jones. This duologue between a poor young schoolmaster and the rich girl he bumps into at King's Cross is marked on the programme as 'prior to London presentation' and for once the legend seems credible. Mr. Jones has a sure theatrical sense. His characters take life on the stage. And though their words and actions are ordinary enough (and must have seemed more so on the page) they catch and hold our surprised attention almost right through the evening. Surprised? Well it is always an achievement for an author to keep us caring when he introduces only two people. *Rattle of a Simple Man* was the most recent example but Mr. Jones scorns such gimmickry. The couple he presents are not stock vaudeville jokes. They are just two strangers out of love… until the end when its undisclosable twist reminds us of the problems of invention, the plotlessness of this chance encounter remains a continuous pleasure."

Second Production: "Plays written for only two characters can be a trifle irksome at times–but not so *Early One Morning*. I have not come across the author, Glyn Jones, in the theatre before and understand he writes mainly for cinema and television. Let us hope that a success for this play will encourage him to do more work in this medium for he has an enviable gift for penning lively, quick-fire and genuinely funny dialogue as well as showing much more than a superficial knowledge of human nature."

Now for London: *Evening Standard's* Tom Pocock: "Who seduces who and who cares?" Say no more.

Daily Mail's Barry Norman: "Somewhere in this overblown mass of words there is a fairly decent little TV play struggling to get out… At the moment it's all chat and no action and for the most part not very good chat either" etc., etc. Oh, so in Mr. Norman's opinion it is not lively, quick-fire and genuinely funny dialogue, just not very good chat.

Malcolm Stuart, *The Sun*: "It was not a dull play – it was sometimes very witty. But it was not memorable either. Just like something you see on the television before making the cocoa."

Chapter One

Basil Boothroyd in *Punch* was quite sweet. I could imagine him drawling it out the side of his mouth with a superior air, maybe drawing on a big fat cigar, "Here was Mr. Jones with this big, fat script, not as funny as *Private Lives*, as moving as *Brief Encounter* or as fierce as *Virginia Woolf*, but looking like a play all the same, yet not being one." Oh, yes, very clever stuff but at least there was a witty cartoon to go with it and, in this case, I don't find the comparisons all that odious.

But now for the real humdinger, Fiona MacCarthy:
"Could this be the most puerile of all the plays in London? *Early One Morning* has quite a claim to the title of the silliest production of the year. For the clumsiness, tediousness, and utter inanity it takes the biscuit. Why is it so awful? First, because it has no plot. Ian and Sheila, after King's Cross brief encounter, spend an act and three quarters [!] sniping at each other. From nonevent to nonevent, the action stumbles on until two hours and 200 flabby wisecracks later a tiny revelation brings the curtain down for good. This, I think, was irony. It was not worth the wait.

The cast desperately grimace and wildly smile and posture their way through the sex war, class war, culture barrier clichés. Loyal to the director and the author of this creaking charade, they almost burst."

This is a slightly condensed version of Malicious McCarthy's bile. I can just imagine her saying to a friend with a newborn babe, 'What an ugly little bugger. Why don't you squeeze its head back into shape while you've got the chance?'

Previously to Charles Vance producing *Early One Morning*, I had been in a play, *Circus Boy* by Michael Redgrave at The Belgrade Theatre, Coventry, directed by James Roose-Evans and when he was Artistic Director at The Hampstead Theatre Club, as it then was, he read *Early One Morning* and offered to do it if I changed the girl to a boy. I didn't fancy this idea. I didn't honestly see the point, and turned it down, but I wonder what the reviews would have been like had I agreed. I gave James another play to read and he came back with: "I just don't understand your writing. You need to give it to Lindsay Anderson or John Dexter." It was the flip of a coin really but Anderson, being more visible at the time with his films, *This Sporting Life*, *If*, I plumped for Anderson. Wrong choice. Not that the alternative would have been a certainty.

The reply from Anderson read, "I have read them with interest and disagree with both James Roose-Evans and David Kossof. In fact I think that the difficulty is not so much that the plays are too offbeat or "way out"–but perhaps they are not offbeat enough. That is to say, they are not quite conventional enough for people who are thinking in conventional terms, yet not completely liberated from certain dramatic conventions, so that they don't achieve a completely new style either.

For instance, *Oh Brother!* which I like the better of the two is essentially (or seems to me) a study of character and mood, in which the intrusion of "drama" at the end is out of place and, in fact, tends to conventionalise the whole thing. I must admit to finding *One Touch of Pity* rather on the sentimental side though, with that proviso, well written. I think you have to beware of too much sentiment. Yours sincerely, Lindsay Anderson."

His reference to David Kossof is interesting because I met Kossof one night on location filming a play, *No Friendly Star* for Chloe Gibson of the BBC and during a break we got to talking about writing. I remember him saying to me, 'Keep at it, dear boy, just keep at it. One day you'll write a huge hit and then, you can write "shit" on a lavatory wall and they'll come running to buy it.' The writer Stanley Miller who was flavour of the month at the time and garnering TV credits by the fistful put it this way, 'The time to carry on writing is when everyone else is giving up.'

I wrote *One Touch of Pity* specifically with Kossof in mind and sent it to him. I was living in a flat above a garage in Well Road, Hampstead at the time and I remember opening the envelope with the returned play and going ice-cold reading Kossof's accompanying letter which went:-

"I have now read the play twice and return it to you. In a letter dated last Feb you speak of lengthening it. Are you serious? It seems to me teased out to a fantastic length. And nothing happens! Only the unbelievable. And this interminable duologue of the girls and Martha containing every cliché in the book! Please Mr. Jones, to tell me this play was written for me presupposes that I have no judgment that cannot be suspended by being told the fact. This is untrue. Nearly every play sent me has been "written for me". It serves only to sharpen the suspicion, not to dull it. Your play seems to me to have no shape and no point. It irritated me.

David Kossof."

This is the same play that Lindsay Anderson thought well written. Andre van Gyseghem was director of productions at Nottingham Playhouse at the time and I sent the play to him. It came back of course but this was his reaction:

"I have at last finished reading your play One Touch of Pity and it grieves me to have to send it back to you. It is only that we have no place for it this season, our list being complete, because I enjoyed reading it and found the end most moving. I hope you have luck in placing it elsewhere."

What had I done to Mr. Kossof to warrant his reaction and the acerbity of his reply? I thought about it long and hard and came up with the following, which may or may not be true. Firstly the central character is Polish. Was Kossof of Russian extraction? Secondly all the characters in the play have names that can be construed as Jewish. Did Kossof think that I, a goy, had had the temerity to write a Jewish play? Who knows? He could have been right in that it is not a very good play, a bit contrived and now certainly well passed its shelf life, but did I tread on a couple of very sensitive toes here? What hurt most was that all the time I was writing I did have David Kossof in mind so, in that way, it was written for him.

As a side note, in the production of *Circus Boy* a young South African actor was playing the part of a chimp. His name was Nicholas Wright, recently making his name with The National Theatre and his much praised play *Vincent in Brixton*. Much earlier I understudied in what was probably his first play, *The Gorky Brigade* at The Royal Court. I have no memory of the play except that it was full-blooded communist propaganda like those posters of hefty women on tractors or marching gangs of Chinese waving red flags or little red books and each scene ended with "*Tableau!*". Why did communist propaganda of that period always make me want to laugh? Bill Gaskill with whom I started to take acting classes at the newly formed 'Actors' Studio' directed the play. I see I am not listed in the programme so I have absolutely no memory of who I might have understudied. Our friend Richard Mayes was also in it and tells me his memory is also a blank.

The Royal Court at one time threatened to ban all critics from the theatre and there was an outcry from Milton Schulman and his coterie: doing critics out of their jobs was one of the whinging complaints. What do critics think they're doing by writing reviews like the above? At this time of writing I read in the papers that this controversy has started up again.

End of story? Not quite. Many years later, the composer Paul Knight talked about wanting to write a two-hander musical so I took *Early One Morning* out of cold storage and rewrote it with songs. It was now called *Fugue in Two Flats*. I don't know if it can really be called a musical. It's difficult to write enough numbers for just two performers so maybe it should be called a play with music unless I plan a rewrite. Anyway, a condensed version was performed as an audition at the Playhouse Theatre in London directed by Donald Sinden's son, Jeremy, who sadly died from cancer in 1996. I put a couple of hundred quid towards it. I could afford it at the time, as I was then teaching in America, so I never saw the audition and it didn't result in anything positive. I notice however in the programme it mentions "the plot" so is there a plot lurking in there after all that the critics just didn't notice? Back into the script cupboard went *Fugue in Two Flats*. Paul had been a concert pianist but gave it up as he hated the living in a suitcase loneliness of the business. Instead he took to accompanying at which he was quite brilliant, and to composing.

With no disrespect to Trevor, I have often wondered what the reviews for *Early One Morning* would have been like had the play been produced on Shaftesbury Avenue by a first class management with money spent on it, directed by a first class director and with, say, Albert Finney and Maggie Smith as the cast.

Some years later I was to face the venom of the London critics a second time but for a completely different reason.

Chapter Two

I wasn't born in a trunk as the song puts it. I was born in a perfectly respectable nursing home in Durban, South Africa on the 27th of April 1931. I believe there was a brother before me but he died either at birth or shortly after. My father was a Jones on both sides. He was born in 1900 in Denbigh, North Wales. His father, Thomas, was a builder who was evidently responsible for building most of the old houses in Prestatyn and, judging by the size of his own house, he was certainly worth a bob or two. My dad had two sisters; Ceridwen, who

Grandparents Thomas & Mary Elizabeth Jones with daughters Ceridwen & Blodwen

was the eldest and who my sister is named after, and Blodwen. Was this ever a Welsh family? My father's name was Llewelyn Idris and Idris is my second name. There is a theory that Arab seafarers settled in Wales many a long year ago as Idris is also an Arabic name and I believe there is a certain similarity in Welsh and Arabic grammar. Welsh scholars can correct me if I'm wrong, and if they know Arabic of course.

My father was a handsome man with, I always thought, a strong resemblance to Somerset Maugham. His nose was definitely hooked, which my mother always insisted was because it pointed continually to his pocket, the Welsh being a race meaner than the proverbial Scot, or so she maintained. It wasn't wholly true. On occasion he could spend lavishly for no ostensible reason but if he put sixpence in a slot machine and it didn't deliver his chocolate you never heard the end of it. I suppose my hating to lose money or waste food amounts to the same thing. He had an uncle who was a ship's captain and, whenever he came home from a voyage, he would take his wife window shopping, but always on a Sunday when the shops were closed, and he took the added precaution of walking on the opposite side of the road in case she grew too enthusiastic over something she saw. This was my dad's story anyway.

He had a bachelor cousin, my uncle Dick who never said much and who lived on his own in a tiny terraced house in Prestatyn and from whom in 1962 I inherited a small sum of money that enabled me to open my first bank account at the Midland Bank, Notting Hill Gate. I believe there was also a well-known composer of light music somewhere on the family tree, a second cousin of my dad's, a cousin once removed or some such. His name was Edward German. Not among the musical giants but his work is pleasant enough and at one time was extremely popular. He dropped his surname, which of course was Jones. Strange thing about names: how come Jones is such a common Welsh name when there is no J in the Welsh alphabet? Or so I'm told. How come Glyn Jones is such a common name? It's the Welsh equivalent of John Smith. There are so many of us I once wondered whether it might be fun to start a Glyn Jones society. At one time I thought of changing my name but then I thought, what the hell, it's what I grew up with and I'm rather fond of it so leave it be; without it I wouldn't be me. I wonder how many actors over the years have been told they can't be called Glyn Jones because I got in first, the Equity ruling being that no two actors can have the same name. Sensible of course; no mix up with credits or royalty cheques. Mind you, you would think with a name as simple as mine people would remember it but I have been called Glen Jones, Glynn Jones, Glyn Llewelyn, Glynn Johns. I've even had it spelt Glynne, Glin and Glinn and, on one occasion, Glun, but that must have been a typo. On *The Double Deckers* album where I should be credited with the lyrics for four songs, I am credited as Glyn Johns. But all that is as nothing compared to a provincial critic who, when I was playing Henry VIII in *A Man for All Seasons* on a tour for Charles Vance wrote, "Terry Collins's Henry is a powerful study, commanding and petulant, but always underlining his respect for More–a respect which heightens the poignancy of the tragedy." Guess there must have been a Terry Collins somewhere in the programme but I don't recall anyone of that name.

I had always believed I was half Welsh, half Italian, my maternal grandfather having come from Reggio Calabria, down there on the toe, right opposite Sicily. His name was Bartolo Paino, pronounced Pi-eeno, though in Australia where a number of Painos have settled, including my first cousins, they pronounce it Pay-no. According to his death certificate, issued in Port Elizabeth in 1911, Bartolo Paino was born in 1853 in Rizzo a short distance up the coast from Reggio. I had always presumed my grandmother too would have been Italian but, a couple of years ago, on a visit to my cousins in Australia and going through old documents and family photos, I got the first glimpse of what our grandmother had looked like and discovered she was in fact, not Italian as I had always imagined, but English. Her name was Maria Charlotte Brockman, daughter of James and Rosie Brockman of Deal in Kent. So they were my great grandparents and I am only one quarter Italian, though I probably have Arab blood in me as well if the

Chapter Two

Welsh theory is true, and possibly Greek as Sicily and southern Italy were colonised by Greeks BC–witness Napoli–Nea Polis–New City. So I must be a regular hybrid. The museum in the town of Caltanissetta in central Sicily has one of the most comprehensive collections of ancient Greek vases and artefacts, mostly in pristine condition as though straight from the manufacturer's shop.

Nobody has been able to tell me how, where, or why Bartolo and Charlotte met or how Bartolo came to end up in South Africa. One

Great grandparents Francesco & Grazia Paino with sons Antonio & Vincenzo - 1887

theory is that he was a seaman who as a young man jumped ship in Port Elizabeth and stayed there because he never obtained a passport until well on in life, making a return visit to Italy with his ten year old daughter, Marie, and acquiring a passport in 1907, when Italy still had a king, Victorio Emanuel III. But what about Charlotte? Well according to her death certificate she was born in South Africa of British descent so presumably her parents had emigrated to settle in Port Elizabeth.

I don't know what my grandfather did for a living when not at sea but his sons were carpenters so maybe he was also a chippy. Ships have their carpenters or, anyway, did have at that time. His death certificate says "Boatman" which could mean anything. The Painos owned three houses in Port Elizabeth, in Bullen Street, Southend. There were seven children: the boys being Francesco (uncle Frank), Antonino (uncle Nin), and Vincenzo (uncle Vincent), and the girls were Grazzia Conzella (auntie Grace), Maria (always called aunt Marie or even just Mary), and my mother, Rosa Angela. Vincent was the youngest and, between Marie and my mother, there was another boy, James, obviously named after Charlotte's father and who died as a child. I go into detail with this family background because, unlike my father's relations thousands of miles away in Wales, Bullen Street still evokes fond and happy memories of schoolboy holidays. I only knew two of the three houses because by the time of our visits one was lived in by uncle Frank and his family and the second by the widow Grace, her two daughters, and my spinster aunt Marie. I presume the third was let.

As I remember it, Bullen Street was a quiet, pleasantly wide, tree-lined street and the two houses, semi-detached, were built on a corner, their frontage on Bullen and with a steep hill running down the side of the first house. The houses were quite small. Each had a narrow veranda with wooden railings and a front door facing Bullen Street. At the side there was a solid wooden gate in a high whitewashed wall. This opened into a narrow courtyard at the back in which, in one corner, there was a bathroom with an ancient temperamental gas boiler that needed a special technique to ignite or you ended up with singed eyebrows. Baths never seemed to be more than an inch deep and usually tepid. Opposite the bathroom was an outside corrugated iron bedroom for boy children and uncle Nin. The beds were of the narrow iron and open springs variety with thin horsehair mattresses and I remember there was a triangular shelf in one corner from the front of which hung a plain blue curtain which served as a wardrobe. There was also a grapevine in the yard whose grapes never seemed to me to grow beyond pea size and which where hard and horribly sour. Not surprising as they were still green; though I could never resist trying one. Maybe we always visited the wrong time of year. There was also some kind of press bolted to a concrete base which I played with one day, got my hand caught in the mechanism and gave myself a nasty and very painful blood blister, screaming blue murder before uncle Nin came running to release me. Behind the timber columns on which the backs of the houses rested, being built on a hill the fronts were at road level, but the backs were a good six or seven feet off the ground, there was a chicken coop. Uncles Frank or Nin would kill a chicken by holding its head and swinging the body around like a great feathered rattle, so wringing the bird's neck. It was then stuffed into the ash can and the lid slammed down to hold it as it flapped about. If it escaped before they could stuff it in the can, though dead, it apparently went berserk, running around the yard flapping wildly until, as we joked, it ran out of petrol. This bizarre display was always a source of fascination to us kids and, when very young, the signal for a leaping about screaming match.

In all the years I knew him, uncle Nin was balding with just a ring of white hair around his ears and the back of his head. He wore a moustache, grey and nicotine stained brown in the centre due to the cigars he smoked, and I remember one day his puffing slowly at a stub while nodding off until it singed his moustache and he woke with a yell. Of course we didn't think to wake him, we were too interested in seeing what would happen. We also ran for our lives when he realised though I'm sure his anger would have been all an act. He spent some time at sea and his favourite cities were "Loose" Angeles and St. Petersburg. In the arctic he contracted frostbite and, thinking the third mate was having a joke at the expense of his pain, he nearly killed the man when he was told to rub his hands with snow, which was evidently the thing to do. He kept his seaman's chest of tools to the end of his days, the tools all beautifully clean, oiled, and properly stowed as though he might, even in old age, be called on at any time to use them again. When he died I was understudying in Brighton and couldn't attend his funeral, an omission that caused his landlady in Bournemouth, having no knowledge of theatre, to write a bitter letter of complaint to my mother, which occasioned a very angry response from me. I would most certainly have been at uncle Nin's funeral if I could have been. Come to think of it, of all the funerals I've attended, not one has been for a member of my family. I wonder what happened to that sea chest of tools.

Uncle Frank, unlike his father, had married an Italian girl, my aunt Rosina who, it is no exaggeration to say; I loved dearly, in a different way to my feeling for aunt Marie, which was more like adoration. Rosina was not a beautiful woman, her nose was far too big and, with her clothes always plain, her hair tied back in a bun, and that sort of harassed look that comes from keeping watch and doing for a large family, I remember her as being a trifle dowdy but warm, lovable, motherly and cuddly. You couldn't enter her house, invariably from around the back and through the kitchen, at any time of day without having food thrust upon you; a curry, a spaghetti, a macaroni as though you hadn't eaten for days.

'You'ra hungry? You'ra hungry. Sitta down. Eat. Why you no eat? Issa good.'

Despite all her years in South Africa she never lost her Italian accent. For example "midnight" was rendered as "milnight" and "goodbye" as "goom-bye." In our house on Crete we still sometimes say it–'Goom-bye.'

Frank and Rosina had five children, at time of writing all still alive.

Chapter Two

Bartolo, the eldest, was a most attractive boy and a real charmer who on a rugby trip to Ireland was unfortunately the recipient of a kick to the head which has left him back in Perth a vegetable in a care home, regularly visited by his brothers and sisters, although there is never any sign of recognition from him. The other two sons are Umberto (Bert or Bertie) who has an encyclopaedic knowledge of poetry and will deliver a line or two or more at the drop of a hat. He also has an unlimited fund of jokes, some of which are so corny you laugh despite yourself. For example, 'innuendo-an Italian suppository.' 'Trisexual-try anything!' The youngster is Vincenzo (Vincent), the black sheep of the family. The only one to stay in South Africa, he moved to Cape Town, married, begat sons and was another who got religion, cousin Bert's joke being 'he's joined the vacuum cleaner set-Jehoover's Witnesses.' He goes from door to door selling *The Watch Tower* and saving people to Jesus. Quite a transformation from a kid brought up in a Catholic family who was always in trouble, always on the scrounge.

The girls were Josepina and Jillorma, now in their eighties, neither of whom married though I am told Jill had the chance and turned it down. As a kid I didn't really get to know the girls. They were that much older and we really only met in passing as it were. They share a house in Australia and, on my visit there, a family reunion was held in their garden during which I tasted kangaroo and met most of the up till then unknown new relations down to the second generation.

Uncle Vincent married a Portuguese girl, Sarah da Costa, Aunt Sally. She was a diabetic who had to inject herself every day with insulin and I thought her terribly brave. They had one son, Tony, who was my age and, I suppose, my favourite cousin and I always loved my visits to their house some distance outside Port Elizabeth. It was a strange square house built of corrugated iron with no windows at the front. The area was very sandy with drought resisting scrub and fir trees. Large round galvanised iron water tanks stood at the corners of the house to catch rain water from the roof and we never took a bath but had all-over washes standing in an enamel basin, aunt Sally rinsing us off with a ewer full of clean water. The house had no electricity so illumination was by candle, paraffin and carbide lamps. The family had a massive brindle Great Dane called Simba who liked his mealie-meal porridge, making great slurping noises as he polished it off and scaring to death local Africans merely by being so huge though, really, he was as soft as a puppy. I would always spend a few days of the holiday there, sometimes travelling in the rumble seat of the Chevvy or in a grossly overloaded and highly decorated Indian bus with treadless tyres swaying alarmingly all over the road. This was before apartheid forbade white boys from travelling in an Indian bus. One holiday Tony and I dug an underground den close to the house, roofed with branches and greenery and entered by a short tunnel. Complete with fireplace to cook things in tin cans, should there actually be something to cook. It did nothing but emit choking smoke. We were ignorant of the fact that fire needs a draught, a fireplace needs a flue. However the smoky fireplace did save our bacon one day when aunt Sally's voice from above called out, 'Are you boys smoking down there?'

Which we were, with cigarettes bought at the Chinese shop, but we quickly stubbed them out and blamed it on the fire which she seemed to accept. We remained stock-still until we heard her moving away then we relit our cigarettes and, together with the smoke from the fire, nearly choked to death.

Tony sometimes stayed overnight in Bullen Street and, when he did, we had to share one of those narrow beds which meant there was nothing for it but to snuggle up spoon fashion. Apart from previously inspecting what equipment each of us possessed, Bert was particularly scornful of my not being circumcised whereas all the cousins were ring barked as the Australians call it, none of us ever indulged in any form of sex but one night Tony must have been particularly horny because I was given the urgent whispered command, 'Feel him.'

Through his pyjamas I dutifully put my hand over a large very hard erection.

Chapter Two

'No, man, feel him raw.'

I felt him raw and that was it. We fell asleep and it was never mentioned.

Tony married in Australia, fathered two sons, and died some years back. Strangely, while in Australia, I learnt his younger son is a commercial pilot who was based in Manchester at what could be called our local airport, so close to where we lived in Yorkshire but nobody thought to tell us.

My chief memory of aunt Grace and aunt Marie's house were the white Staffordshire poodles on a chenille-covered mantel shelf and a large framed portrait of Garibaldi. Grace's two daughters were Joan and Mari Rose. Joan moved to England when she married a no-hoper by the name of Jimmy Toop who left her but, being a devout Catholic, she would never consider a divorce. She died quite young. Mari Rose, the elder of the two who did marry well, became Mrs Gerald Cudmore and their descendents now live in Australia. Aunt Grace, looking at the photographs and making comparison, was the spitting image of her mother who really looked as though she could have been Italian or even have had a touch of the Mulatto about her. That would add an interesting strain to my blood would it not? She certainly didn't seem to have what one thinks of as an English temperament. There is a family story about a young man who tried to court one of the daughters, I don't know whether it was Grace or Marie but, whichever, Charlotte had taken a distinct dislike to this particular suitor which made him definitely persona non grata. However, one day he managed to inveigle himself into the house to do a spot of courting and, hopefully, try and talk his wished-for mother-in-law around. They sat at the kitchen table on which he had placed a shoebox and, when he realised that all the talking in the world was not going to win Charlotte over, he opened the box, took out a revolver and threatened to shoot the two women and then himself. He never had a chance. A well-aimed frying pan to the head put an end to that threat and he was frogmarched from the house, shoebox and all, never to be heard of again.

Aunt Marie was one of the handsomest women I've ever known and it's a great mystery as to why she remained a spinster all her life. Maybe it was the shoebox incident. She had a dressmaking business and her work was always in demand so perhaps she was happy just to stay the way she was. I found her workshop fascinating and, when very young, I loved to play with the empty cotton reels, inspect all the cards with buttons and watch the seamstresses working. Remembering this I used it in a scene in a screenplay I wrote *When the Devil Rides*, on the life of the nineteenth century serial poisoner, William Palmer, another script lingering in the cupboard. It was my agent at Film Rights who suggested I write it and then, when he heard Yorkshire TV had a version in the can, didn't bother with it further. Why? Was the other version so good no one else could write his story? How many films have there been on Oscar Wilde? I believe my script on Palmer went much deeper than the one I watched from Yorkshire TV that, on the whole, I found rather boring considering its subject. The tack I took was to make it the blackest of black comedies, which, in a macabre way, is what it was.

Having been to Italy as a child with her father and then again in Holy Year, Marie was very proud of the fact there was a cardinal in the family, Cardinal Paino, or so she said. She would dearly have loved for me to speak Italian. She taught me a few words and the address of the Paino family in Reggio which I still remember but, alas, have never visited: "Casa Mutilati, Via Torreone, Reggio Calabria, Italia." I've often wanted to go there just to see it if nothing else, and if it still exists, but I was always put off by lack of money and even now by my lack of the language. Once, some years ago, returning from Sicily to Naples by train, we stopped at Reggio and I could have disembarked and paid that longed for visit but, coward that I am, I stayed on the train with regrets as we pulled out of the station. Maybe there is still time. The name of the house is intriguing enough. Why was it called The House of the Mutilated? Do any members of the Paino family still live there? They don't live in Bullen Street anymore. They all emigrated to Western Australia, except for young Vincent and uncle Nin, who never liked a hot climate and moved to England to spend the rest of his days in Bournemouth and, of course, Joan who married the English Mr. Toop.

Bullen Street, I am told, no longer exists, the whole area having been bulldozed and rebuilt. Was this because of the separate areas policy? Because as a child going there on holiday I remember it was a mixed area. Uncle Nin had a very good Indian friend who lived with his family in the neighbourhood and there was the Chinese general store close by I loved to visit. It smelt of paraffin and candle wax, incense and exotic spices. There were sacks on the wooden floor filled with beans and lentils, rice, mealie meal and sugars. The shelves were packed with such a variety of products: tinned foods, packaged foods, dry goods, fly papers, string, clothes-pegs, tobaccos, snuffs, cigarettes and matches, hurricane lamps, utensils, candles, teas, coffees, cakes, biscuits, sweets, spices; bottles of lemonade, orangeade, ginger beer, cream soda (how I loved American cream soda) and strings of red firecrackers from tiny little ones an inch long to great big bangers. Salami and other processed meats hung from racks of which polony was our favourite. A glass display case on the counter held pins and needles, cottons, buttons on cardboard, thimbles, combs, and the cheapest of colourful cheap trinkets. It was indeed a magic emporium, now only a nostalgic memory.

I suppose my grandmother must have seen me as a baby but my first conscious visit to Port Elizabeth was not the happiest. That was in January 1939 when I was seven, almost eight years old. There was no direct railway line from Durban to Port Elizabeth following the coast. To get there the train travelled up country to Bloemfontein and Kimberley in the Orange Free State from where the lines travelled south to the Cape: to East London, Port Elizabeth or Cape Town. It was a long journey involving sleepers and with many a stop, at some

No Official Umbrella

G.I.J. growing up in Durban

of which, during the day and time permitting, my father would get down from our coach, walk up to the engine and have a parley with the driver and his fireman, possibly to inform him how many minutes they was running late. I know this because I sometimes accompanied him. I was always nervous though that the train would start off and leave us stranded at some little dorp[6] in the middle of nowhere, especially in the Great Karoo where the flat landscape stretched away to the horizon in all directions broken only occasionally by koppies[7] and, if the whistle blew and the conductor looked about ready to wave his green flag, my mother, still in our compartment but hanging out the window, and I on the platform, would both panic. But dad assured us he and the engineer were mates. Didn't they both work for South African Railways and Harbours? And he would never go without us.

At Port Elizabeth uncle Vincent picked us up at the station and drove us to Bullen Street. My mother was crying, and when we reached uncle Frank's house we were hugged and kissed and ushered in by sobbing aunts. My mother was led into the darkened front room used only on special occasions and I was almost forcibly guided beyond, into the kitchen, out the back, down the stairs and into the house next door. So I never knew my grandmother. She had died while we were on our way to visit. I wasn't allowed to see her in her coffin and I remember nothing more of that particular holiday. Could I have

---

6 Village.
7 Flat topped hills.

gone to her funeral? I don't know. I have no recollection of it. A great connoisseur of funerals was my auntie Grace. She donned her best blacks and attended a funeral, even a perfect stranger's whenever she felt like a really good weep, which happened quite often. Aunt Marie was disgusted with her for taking my sister to the cemetery to tend family graves. 'Tch, Tch, no place to take a child.'

Strange to say her marriage ceremony was conducted by the Reverend Alfred Ebden Padday, an Anglican friend of the family. Presumably her husband, Charles Willis, was Church of England and, after his death, Grace reverted to Catholicism. When making plans to do anything her sentences always ended with 'God willing.' St Anthony was her best friend and always found anything she had lost, and she was reputed to be psychic through dreams, contrary to her religion.

The train journey was always one of the highlights of our visits to the Cape. I love trains. I loved standing in the corridor and risking painful clinkers in the eyes by sticking my head out the window. You can't do that with modern carriages. I liked it when the train went round a wide bend and I could see the engine, sometimes two of them, big black monsters, hissing steam, billowing smoke up a heavy incline and, looking the other way, seeing all the carriages following behind. I enjoyed drinking from the glass water container strapped in on a metal shelf at the end of the coach even if the water was tepid, and hearing the steward as he walked by playing a little tune on his marimba and calling the sitting for breakfast, lunch, or dinner. In the dining car there was linen on the tables, the plates were china, there was proper cutlery and everything served out of metal dishes engraved with S.A.R.&.H, South African Railways & Harbours or S.A.S.&.H, Suid Afrikanse Spoorwee & Hawens. The 2nd class compartment was comfortable in simulated green leather with two lower and two upper bunks and a pull up table under the window. In the evening the steward came around to lower the bunks and make the beds. Even going to the loo was a little adventure. You were admonished not to flush while the train was standing in the station but who would want to when you could flush and, keeping the pan open with your foot, you could watch the track beneath you disappearing at fifty miles an hour and listen to the roar it made? Outside the window of your compartment or standing in the corridor the countryside was forever changing. What can you see from an aeroplane?

Other highlights of the holidays were picnics, with masses of watermelon that everyone slurped with relish, all except me who hated it and still do, I find the flesh so insipid. We picked prickly pears which I love and which we never got in Natal. They were definitely a Cape thing and, no matter how careful I was in picking and peeling them, I invariably got itchy hairs imbedded in my fingers. I remember my aunts would then smother them with butter to ease out the hairs. There was swimming at Happy Valley and, with cousins, drinking shakes in a milk bar near the campanile, a landmark feature of Port Elizabeth. A giant milkshake cost pennies, gave you two full glasses and a bit more to linger over, and strawberry was my favourite.

Cousin Joan was not the only one to marry a no good no hoper. On the Welsh side my Auntie Blodwen did the same and emigrated with him to Zimbabwe, what was then Southern Rhodesia. From there he wrote to my father saying he had high expectations prospecting for gold but needed some up front cash to get him going. Could my dad borrow the money from my grandfather and join him as a partner in the prospecting business? My father had served his apprenticeship as a millwright in Liverpool so he had a trade, but there was little if any work to be had in Wales or around and the thought of seeing a bit of the world and, more importantly, the lure of shiny gold nuggets, bars even, was too tempting, so what was there to lose if his dad did lend him the money? Well that's exactly what he did lose, every penny of it. Sister Blodwen's husband skedaddled with the lot never to be seen or heard of again and leaving my father stranded virtually penniless in Southern Rhodesia. He eventually made his way to Johannesburg, walked all the way according to his version.

What, through lion infested bush? Well, maybe he did, maybe he didn't, who knows and, however he got there, that's how he ended up in South Africa. I don't think his father ever forgave him though for losing that money, or probably himself for lending it in the first place. Neither a borrower nor a lender be. Aunt Ceridwen was the sole beneficiary of their mother's will, their mother having been the sole beneficiary of her husband's will, and when Ceridwen died in 1947 or thereabouts, she bequeathed everything to her accountant, much to my parents chagrin who, probably rightly felt there was a bit of shenanigan gone on there as well. Ceridwen was another who never married. Her fiancé having been killed in the First World War she never fell for anyone else. In a family album there were faded brown snapshots of her visiting his grave in France. Of Blodwen nothing further was heard though I believe she was another who might have died young, probably having had all she could take of her con man of a husband and dying being the only way to be rid of him.

Having arrived in South Africa, Llewelyn Idris, Lew to his friends, Welyn to my mother, got a job with South African Railways and Harbours and remained with the company all his life, and it was a strange twist of fate that led to their meeting. If it hadn't been for the intervention of that same Ebden Padday who officiated at aunt Grace's wedding, my mother would more than likely have remained in Port Elizabeth, a good Catholic daughter, got herself a job, married a local boy who Charlotte approved of, and I wouldn't be a Jones and who I am. Ebden Padday took a great shine to my mother. I don't believe it was sexual although she was a very pretty girl. I think, as he was a bachelor, he looked on her as a surrogate daughter. Anyway, he suggested to my grandparents that he would unofficially adopt their youngest daughter and make sure she obtained a good education. It meant her going to live with him when not at college and here came the sixty four thousand dollar question, would they allow her to become an Anglican? Well aunt Grace had gone over to the other side in order to get married and presumably my grandparents talked it over and came to the conclusion they had produced enough Catholic souls to get them into heaven and the loss of this one wouldn't go too much against them so they agreed, and Rosa Angela left Bullen Street for Natal and, from then on until her marriage, went under the surname of Ebden Padday, known to her 1920's chums as Paddy, always to my father as Ro. From Teacher Training College in Pietermaritzburg she

Mother and Father on their wedding day

eventually went to teach in Newcastle, Northern Natal. At least two of her junior school pupils were to achieve fame in their own way: Alan Paton, author of *Cry the Beloved Country*; and Sid James, star of the *Carry on Films*. Could two pupils have been less alike?

My father was working in Newcastle at the time. They met, fell in love, and married. How romantic. Actually it wasn't all that romantic. According to my mother my father's proposal ran along the lines of, 'All our friends are wondering when we're going to get married so how about it?' She never did tell me how she answered that but anyway it was in the affirmative. He was not a demonstrative man, my father. Kisses and cuddles were not for him with his Welsh chapel upbringing that ensured you never made an embarrassing display of emotion. And yet he was a very sensitive man underneath it all, something I never realised until he suffered the first symptoms of an impending heart problem. It took place on our farm, Blue Hills when, one morning, he had difficulty getting out of bed and, in fact, was partly paralysed down one side which made walking exceedingly difficult. We thought, if we could get him to walk, the paralysis might ease up, so I helped him out of the bedroom and on to the veranda that ran right around the house. He was fine until a friend of the family, courtesy Uncle Stan stepped out of his bedroom to appear on the veranda and my father immediately burst into tears. I couldn't remember ever having seen him cry before and it wasn't his condition that caused this, but the fact that uncle Stan witnessed his weakness and he had to be helped back to the privacy of the bedroom.

He might not have given physical examples of affection to his family but he couldn't pass a dog or a cat without stopping to make a fuss of it. During courtship the whinnying of a horse or the lowing of a cow in a neighbouring field would interrupt moonlit strolls down country roads and he would have to go off and make sure there was nothing wrong with the animal, leaving my mother standing nervously in the darkness of the road until he reappeared. His love of animals has been passed on to his children who cannot bear to see one suffer or be cruelly treated which sometimes makes living in Greece, where animals are too often maltreated, somewhat distressing. An animal though could have been the cause of his early demise when, one day on a picnic at a favourite spot down the south coast from Durban called Inyoni Rocks, he offered a piece of banana to a monkey. As the monkey, small and nervous, stretched out a paw to take it, a larger, more aggressive animal dashed in to grab the banana. Dad's immediate reaction was to pull back his hand resulting in a deep and painful bite. Monkey's teeth are not poisonous but neither are they clean and the result was acute blood poisoning that could have been disastrous. There were no antibiotics in those days. I don't know how the wound was treated but it took a very long time to heal and, at one point, it was thought he might have to lose his hand. It could have been even worse. King Alexander of Greece died of blood poisoning after a bite from a monkey.

From a story my mother told even a dead animal was accorded a certain sympathy. When a pet cat died my mother wanted to bury it in the garden but this upset my father who complained their dog, an Alsatian named Taffy, might dig it up. He suggested the nicest way to dispose of the cat was for it to be buried at sea. Why didn't my mother drop it in the Umgeni River, which would gently float the animal out to its last resting place in the Indian Ocean? The cat was placed in a brown carrier bag and covered with newspaper and, from home, it took two bus rides to reach the river. On each trip my mother placed the carrier bag under the stairs leading to the top deck and, on reaching the banks of the Umgeni, she tipped up the bag to drop the cat into the water only to release a small shower of cabbage, carrots, peas and potatoes. Every now and again for years afterwards she would wonder who tipped a dead cat onto their kitchen table. Why it was left to my mother to dispose of the body I really don't know and it probably wasn't a very good idea anyway because most South African rivers, those in Natal anyway, don't flow directly into the sea but form a lagoon behind the sand beneath which the water seeps out, so the cat would probably have lain decomposing on a sandbank.

As befits a Welshman my father had a fine tenor voice and was always being urged to sing at gatherings. It usually took a lot of persuading though and, when finally he agreed to perform, there was first of all the same bout of nerves I suffered as an actor. I used to see him trembling from head to foot but, once he got over it, he was well away with what the Welsh call 'hwyl' and there were always requests for an encore. His favourite rendering was the Victorian ballad *Somewhere a Voice is Calling*. Victorian ballads were standard in our house as my mother was more of a singer than her husband. She had a beautiful contralto voice and was occasionally employed professionally for concerts. She took singing lessons for many years with a man named Grogan Caney who had a nose that didn't point to his pocket, it pointed to his shoes and, if he opened his mouth to give an example of technique, he could be heard from one end of town to the other. When I was very small, favourite songs I loved to hear my mother sing, accompanying herself at the piano, were *Softly Awakes My Heart* from *Samson and Delilah*, *Handel's Largo*, *Caro Mio Ben*, *Love's Old Sweet Song* or was it called *Just a Song at Twilight?* And a song whose title I don't remember but which included the lines, "Tell me again you love me, kiss me on lips and brow," and I happily followed the instructions.

After their marriage a move to Durban followed when my father started work at the docks, in Shed 17 as I remember it, where he worked the rest of his life. He loved the sea and ships and, even when not working, would sometimes drive down to the docks to take in the scene and I would go with him. It was like a Sunday outing, though instead of going on a picnic or for a drive in the country, a truly great treat in those days, we went to the docks to look at the ships, the small boats riding the swell or beached on dry land, and the gigantic rolling cranes I found so fascinating. This was before containers when cargo would be hauled out of a ship's hold in giant nets that had to be unloaded before swinging back over the side to disappear into the hold. Some of the small boats, lying on their sides or in cradles on the concrete wharf out towards what was called The Point, had long since seen better days and lay rotting where they had been left. If I could manage it I'd climb aboard one to have a look-see, peep out through grimy little portholes or, hands on the wheel, the smell of tar in my nostrils, make believe I was sailing somewhere far distant. Sometimes we went on board a coaster or a freighter and visited crew members he knew, and we'd sit in a mess drinking strong tea with condensed milk and plenty of sugar to make it even sweeter. Or I'd leave them smoking and chatting and maybe drinking something stronger and I would stand on deck looking down at the filthy water as it eddied around the hull, at the flotsam and jetsam, the iridescent oil slicks. Or, if allowed, I'd venture down into the engine room taking great care on the steel companions as I went and, when on the lowest deck, gazing in awe at those, to a small boy, mighty engines. So I also inherited my father's love of ships and have always regretted that I am such a lousy sailor. I would often stand on The Point gazing at the horizon and wondering what I would find if I could sail out beyond it. *Red Sails in the Sunset* was for a time my favourite record. The closest I got to it though was on a fishing boat when the smell of fish and the motion of the boat on a choppy sea were making me distinctly queasy. It was also quite chilly so I thought I would go down to the engine room for a bit of warmth. Big mistake. The smell of that added to the fish was the last straw. It was back up on deck and heave-ho my hearties over the side.

On one occasion a purser friend of the family's, Ginger by name who came from some place in England called Cricklewood, I used to think Ginger a very funny name for a person and Cricklewood a very funny name for a place, and who had a son about my age, I was then thirteen, invited my father together with me and my sister, to lunch on his ship. It must have been a working day because I had to take Ceri two bus rides down to The Point to meet dad in Shed 17 before going on to Ginger's ship. Our father loved his kids appearing in Shed 17 where they could be greeted by all his workmates. When we arrived he was still working on a job and suggested we go ahead and he would join us shortly, as soon as he had finished. Ginger met

Chapter Two

us on board and, as we had to wait for the third guest, suggested he would like to show me a model boat he had made. Looking back on it from a life of much experience I don't think there was an ulterior motive when he led us to the prow, part of which had been portioned off for storage and hobbies and, indicating Ceri, he said, 'I don't want her in here fiddling with things.'

In a way I could see his point. She was only seven and seven year old's do tend to have itchy fingers. So he and I went ahead without her. When our dad arrived some time later he found the entire ship in a state of panic as Ginger, myself, and full crew hunted high and low for my sister. There was the possibility she had fallen overboard and some of the crew walked the side of the ship peering down into the filthy water, all of them, I imagine, praying this was not the case. Then one of them remembered that the previous day he had thrown a load of old rope into a hold close to the forecastle and hadn't closed the hatch. He shone a torch into the hold and there she was on the deck below, out stone cold.

The promised lunch of course was not forthcoming. She came to on a cabin bunk with a splitting headache and dad immediately drove us to Entabeni Hospital, but they refused to check her over without a doctor's admission, so the next step was to take her home and tell mom. She knew immediately that something had happened because dad was as white as a sheet and very nervous. Ceri was put to bed and, by the time the doctor arrived, was bouncing all over it so the doc didn't even bother to look at her, just turned tail and left. In her words when she tells the story she was furious at being told she wasn't wanted and decided to hide from us. She saw this big black square shape silhouetted against the light and went round behind it. The shape she saw was the hatch, held open against an upright beam, and down she went to the bottom of the ship. It was very quick she remembers. She heard a sound like "puff" in her head and knew no more. It was as well for her that she fell on the ropes otherwise she would have hit solid steel and the ending would have been a different story. Even on the ropes she could have suffered serious injury but luckily escaped unscathed, not even a concussion.

On another occasion some mates and myself were playing on a cocopan, a small wagon on a narrow gauge rail usually used in mines, but this one was on a steep hill and was being used for shifting earth. It didn't take too long before someone suggested we took a ride. We clambered aboard, the brake was released and the cocopan started its merry journey down the hill, which flattened out at the bottom before the cocopan hit some buffers. Ceri was with us and, as the wagon gathered speed, she fell off, to sustain nothing worse than a bruise maybe or a graze. I cannot help but think that, as children, we led charmed lives.

This was in 1944 when my mother bought a shop on the corner of Penzance and Bartle Roads in that part of Durban called Umbilo. It was opposite this shop that the hill with the cocopan rose up as far as Howard College, the Durban campus of the University of Natal. Most of the lower part of this hill was covered in bush and there was a plantation of mango trees where we would go scrumping and run like hell if we saw anybody coming towards us. There were two varieties of fruit; the Bombay mango, the one usually sold in European shops, very juicy and very sweet; and the sugar mango, which is longer in shape, not so juicy and not so messy when eaten in the bush. You can sometimes smell the turpentine in mango and if you get mango all over your face which, as kids, was half the fun of eating stolen fruit you had to wash it off fairly quickly or you were likely to break out in mango sores around the mouth, which happened to me only once and once was enough. I should imagine the bush and the mango trees have long since gone with the whole area being built up.

From that same bit of bush I collected a thorn in my foot that necessitated a doctor's visit when the foot swelled up like a balloon and I could no longer walk on it. The local anaesthetic in those days was ethyl chloride (I believe I've got it right) liquid held in a small compressed gas canister of the type used in old fashioned soda siphons so that, when a trigger was pressed, it was released as

Chapter Two

a spray cold enough to freeze the area requiring anaesthesia. It was also used for killing ringworm. Anyway, the doctor produced the anaesthetic and a scalpel and sliced into my foot which spurted out the most evil looking pus and my foot, just like that balloon, seemed to deflate on the spot.

The shop was bought with the proceeds from the sale of their first house in Umbilo, number 28 Fleming Johnston Road. I don't know why my mother bought this shop, actually two shops but one was kept shut and used for storage, but presumably it was a joint decision with my dad. My sister's reasoning is that, as mom liked her food so much and, as rationing was still in force, owning a shop, especially a grocery shop and "RoTom" as South Africans like to sign-post a tearoom, seemed a mighty good idea. Her claim to fame was once a week when her homemade brawn sold out in minutes. Nobody has ever made brawn like my mother. Brawn and shortbread were her specialities. Not that she didn't go in for a variety of things. Her date scones were pretty famous and she never forgave my friend David Scott Macnab who came to tea and picked out all the dates before eating the scones. She would have loved Crete with all her favourite nibbles: figs, olives, what we call Turkish delight, honey. I believe the word 'candy' is derived from the old name for Crete, Candia, because of the export of sweet things even in ancient times.

The problem with liking sweet things, something I've inherited, is that my mother always had a weight problem and was constantly trying to do something about it, never with any success. Whalebone corsets were used to hold everything in.

Our first house in Durban at 28 Fleming Johnston Road was a two-bedroom bungalow. It had a large enclosed veranda at the back which acted as breakfast room, day room, play room, party room, and during the war, when families who had the space were only too happy to offer their hospitality to troops passing through, it was bedroom to British soldiers, sailors, airmen, and marines in twos and threes, passing through Durban and with a few day's furlough, and convalescents from the military hospital outside Pietermaritzburg, and I fell head over heels in love for the very first time.

Outside 28 Fleming Johnston Road - Durban

    The house had a small, slightly sunken garden at the front separated from the pavement by a low brick wall with gates. There was a yard at the rear with a garage and a kaia: that is, a dark concrete box of a servant's room. It had no electricity supply and there was a separate section gained from the outside with a hole in the floor lavatory and cold water tap. The yard was reached by a drive down the side of the house and, in between these two outbuildings, there was an enormous avocado pear tree which, at the time of my first one-sided romantic entanglement had recently been pruned by my father, the sawn off branches left lying on the garage roof.

    Out of them all I have no idea what it was about this particular able seaman that made me fall in love but my behaviour, for the short time he and his mate were with us, grew quite wild and irrational. I remember one evening, possibly in a fit of jealous rage because he was paying me little if any attention, and there was really no reason why he should, I ran out of the house, down the back steps, across

Chapter Two

the yard, and climbed on to the garage roof to sulk, possibly to weep tears of unrequited love, though I really had no idea what this emotion could be that was churning me up. I was probably nine or ten at the time. In the gathering darkness I decided to hide in the lopped off avocado branches so that eventually the parents would grow anxious and think I had run away from home. I duly made myself a nest and, as I lay in my bower on the corrugated iron roof, I mentally ran through a few scenarios for the reunion, each variation growing ever more dramatic and, of course, my sailor, always the central figure.

Unfortunately reality, as it always does, intruded into my dream world. It was growing chilly and, as I moved my cramped limbs, I was suddenly stung by disturbing a nest full of virulent caterpillars. I fled my hideaway with a yell and, as the livid weals rose on my arm, I howled, I sobbed, I wanted to scream. Above all I wanted my sailor to take me in his arms and soothe away the pain. What I got was my mother sticking her head out the kitchen window telling me not to be such a silly boy and to come in at once. I am sure my sailor was soon forgotten once his ship had sailed. Out of sight, out of mind.

Many were the times we drove down to the docks to pick up our guests or take them back and wave them goodbye, together with the famous Lady In White who used to stand on the dock and sing à la Gracie Fields, *Wish Me Luck As You Wave Me Goodbye*, and nostalgic numbers from World War I like *Keep the Home Fires Burning* to the departing troopships as the troops, crowding the decks, joined in and cheered and we would watch the ship sail beyond the point before we turned away to go home again. The Lady In White was talked about for many a year afterwards.

My mother, together with a number of local ladies, started a concert party in aid of the war effort, whatever that meant, and gave concerts in a smallish old wood and iron hall called "The Shellhole" which I presume was built by some veterans' legion or other after World War I. It had a small stage and there were various relics from the war dotted about the walls: machine gun, steel helmets, tattered flags, bayonets, rifles, etc. It was used for dances and I remember having great fun doing *The Lambeth Walk*, lines of dancers all stepping in unison. The only thing I remember about this concert party was that it was all girls and the ladies had designed and wore patriotic costumes in red, white, and blue. My mother did a solo act playing a coloured waitress with an enormous padded backside on which was a large V for victory and she had the corniest of exchanges such as:-

    Diner: Waitress! Waitress! This egg is bad.

    Waitress: Not my fault, missus, I only lays the table.

Or words to that effect.

One night, when six years old, going on seven, I was packed off to sleep at a friend's house. What I remember most about that night in a strange bed in a strange house, was that light filtering in from the street and playing on top of a wardrobe made me think of goblins and I slept with my head under the bedclothes. I discovered the following day that I now had a sister, Ceridwen Gwyneth. The novelty of having a baby sister soon wore off and it wasn't long before sibling rivalry showed its face. I sometimes took her in her pram to the park or for a walk round the block but one day I went home without her, having left her in the park. Naturally I was sent back to fetch her and, this plot having misfired, the next time I took her out I stopped off at the local police station and said, 'This child is lost. Please can you find a home for her?' That didn't work either so I was stuck with her.

The fact that her niece was named after her did not soften my aunt's heart towards us. Humph! During the war and before the tree was so ruthlessly pruned, my parents sent crates of avocados to Wales. Everything else might have been rationed but avocados certainly weren't. As far as I know not even the avocados warmed her up and she remained as aloof as ever. I wonder what caused this coldness. We had a certain amount of rationing in South Africa but nothing to the extent of rationing in Britain. We also had the blackout just in case the Japanese got close and every evening we put up the blackout screens of plywood my father had made. Cars had their headlights dimmed by a black covering with a narrow rectangular slit in the middle.

Chapter Two

When I was four years old we had gone "home" as my father put it, on a visit, sailing in a ship of the German East Africa Line, the SS Watussi. Years later in a photograph of the Watussi I noticed the swastika flag flying at the ship's stern. Another photograph from that journey shows my father at the crossing the Equator fancy dress party, dressed as a fairy complete with star tipped wand! Grotesque make-up, overdone lips and heavily rouged cheeks and wearing a silky dress was one thing but he obviously wasn't going to go so far as having padded tits or hiding his hairy chest. I evidently went as a Christmas cracker all wrapped up in crepe paper. All I remember of the voyage were the paper streamers as we set sail, shuffleboard, and when the weather grew chilly, sitting in deck chairs with rugs over our knees drinking beef tea and nibbling little salty crackers. It couldn't have been that exciting being at sea for weeks but there was no flying in those days. Durban had no airport and the only planes I remember landing at Durban were Sunderland flying boats carrying the airmail. I loved watching them coming in to land in the bay, sending up a great sheet of water either side the keel as they touched down and then settling in and moving slowly forward, sitting in the water rather like a paddling duck.

My Welsh grandmother Mary Elizabeth was still alive at that time. There is a photograph of her sitting in a garden with me standing at her side but I really have no memory of what she was like as a person. Auntie Ceri had a nose even sharper than my dad's, a positive beak in fact, and a nature to match. One evening my parents went to the cinema and, on the way home, bought some fish and chips. By the time they reached the house they had finished their meal but dad's sister was waiting for them, arms folded across her chest, toes tapping the floor. A neighbour had telephoned to tell her about her brother and his wife eating fish and chips in public–and out of newspaper! Such behaviour was not to be condoned in North Wales, not in the nicer more respectable parts. I don't believe she went as far as to polish the coal but she was that sort of person. Maybe she did if she was in a real huff and it was a way of letting off steam.

Snapshots. Snapshot of me in the kiddie's paddling pool, Prestatyn. Snapshot of me in kilt and tam o' shanter and shouldering a toy rifle visiting Scottish cousins in Jedburgh. Snapshot of me sitting astride a cannon, Arthur's Seat, Edinburgh. Snapshot of me cuddling someone's pet spaniel, Jesmond. Snapshot of me feeding the pigeons, Trafalgar Square. No snapshot of me standing next to a table in a park enjoying a soft drink and, beneath the table, emptying my bladder at the same time. My parents couldn't work out why there was so much laughter at surrounding tables until someone indicated to them what was happening. They were mortified but at least I was peeing on grass. Memories of this trip, like so many childhood memories, are buried in the long distant past. It was my mother who told me these stories, usually preceded by, 'When you were little…'

Chapter Three

Ego est homo. Nihil humani alianum est. Have I spelt that right? My computer says no but then my computer doesn't speak Latin. Neither do I come to that, but this was the motto of my secondary school, Glenwood High in Durban, at least the second part, Nihil humani alianum was there on our school badge for all the world to see and I presume still is. For those, like me, who don't speak Latin the full translation is, "I am a man, nothing that is of interest to man is alien to me." Not being a linguist I just hate egghead writers who use classical or foreign quotations and don't give the translation, not even as a footnote. It drives me up the wall.

My Afrikaans master at Glenwood was a man named Lambrechts. By the time I went on from junior school to high we had moved from Fleming Johnston Road and were now living in a block of flats just around the corner from my mother's shop. Lambrechts also lived in Fleming Johnston Road, a few doors down from the Macks who lived directly opposite us and, coming and going from school, he would drive very slowly down the road. He always drove slowly which was just as well with all the kids playing about and, as he went by, I would shout something like, 'Hey, Lompy! How you doing, Lompy?' With various other infantile jibes added.

So here I was, a third former, a thirteen-year-old new boy at Glenwood and I'm walking along the passage leading to the almost subterranean refectory and who should be advancing in the opposite direction? My heart sank into my boots. Maybe he wouldn't remember me. Maybe he would forget. We passed each other. I almost heaved a sigh of relief which turned out to be premature as this voice barked out.

'Hey! You!'

I stopped and turned. He came towards me.

'What did you call me?'

'Me, sir? Not me, sir? It was never...'

I didn't get any further because the next second I was seeing stars as a very large and heavy hand gave me a stinging cuff alongside my ear. Lompy was a big man. Then he turned and walked away. Nothing more was ever said. Due to sit my Afrikaans exam for matriculation, Lompy, everybody called him that behind his back, bet me half a crown I wouldn't pass. You still owe me half a crown, Lompy. Of all the teachers I knew I admired Lompy the most: quiet, dignified, proud, and a very good teacher. I might not be much of a linguist but he got me through my Afrikaans exam, no problem.

Anyway, this quotation, our school motto, is from Terence and I wonder if the powers that be who chose it as such knew that Terence was not a Roman patrician, pleb, or any other old Roman by birth but a freed african slave. After all I grew up and went to school in a land where the book *Black Beauty* was banned because the authorities that did the banning hadn't read it and didn't know it was a story about a horse! Could a black girl be beautiful? Perish the thought, let alone have a book written about her. Little did we know at school, when we rejoiced over the change of government and the Nats[8] came to power in 1948, what it would lead to. Poor old General Smuts, wartime leader and always considered a traitor by hard core Afrikanerdom and German sympathizers, like his British counterpart, Sir Winston, was out of favour and out of office.

Of course apartheid existed before 1948 but it was petty in comparison to what it would become. By using that word 'petty' I speak as a White. For the rest of South Africa: Blacks, Indians, and what were

---

8 Nationalist Party.

known as Cape Coloureds, that is of mixed race; petty is not a word they would have used. Beaches were for whites only, benches in public places were labelled EUROPEANS ONLY–ALLEEN BLANKES, on double decker buses, four seats to the left, two to the right on the top deck at the back were reserved for Non-Europeans though European conductors didn't necessarily reserve them if the bus was packed. Blacks had to carry their pass at all times and woe betide them if they were found without. Blacks did not use white department stores. They couldn't use white restaurants and cafes, toilets, or stay in white hotels. There was no such thing as mixed marriages; miscegenation was illegal under the Immorality Act. If white boys wanted to have sex with blacks they had to go over the border into either Mozambique or Sun City which, from the stories I heard, they did in numbers. There were heartbreak stories of families and marriages torn apart by segregation. Who was black or coloured and who was white? Blacks in South Africa knew their place and stayed in it. Brought up the way we were, this was the way it was, and most of us didn't give it any thought. I cannot truthfully or honestly say I am now ashamed of my callous disregard for what was going on at that time and I am not going, like people decrying and somehow feeling personally responsible for something their ancestors got up to such as slavery or colonialism, to beat my breast over it. The simple fact is I just wasn't interested. I was too selfishly concerned with my own adolescent problems. Who was I? Was I different from others? How was I different? I was only ever ashamed at the time if I verbally mistreated one of our servants which I must have done on occasions because one day at Blue Hills our maid-servant, Priscilla, had had enough of my bad behaviour and, obviously much distressed, suddenly cried 'I have a heart too, Kosaan!' And I was immediately contrite and apologetic. White boys were addressed as 'Kosaan,' which means prince, and girls were 'Kosasaan.' Princes and princesses can behave very badly as we know.

Priscilla was with our family for a number of years and, like many domestic servants in South Africa, and despite the possible sneers of cynical liberals, really did become a part of it. I was already living in England when I was truly saddened at news of her death. Priscilla played the horses and invariably won. Where she got her knowledge of form from or what her system was, if she had one, no one knew, but it soon got around that she was something of a betting genius so others started to give her money to bet with. One Saturday even my mother, who never gambled more than a penny a point at bridge, asked Priscilla to put five bob on a horse for her and the selected horse just about made it to the finishing post. As Priscilla lost her own money on that particular nag she refused point blank ever to bet for my mother again. But betting, or the winning rather, was her undoing. Late one Saturday afternoon she was found lying in the road, unconscious with her head bashed in, her winnings gone. My brother-in-law carried her to his car and rushed her to the hospital where he stayed until she died. Maybe money is the root of all evil.

I don't know what percentage of people living in countries that are supposed to be more or less civilised, that is where murder is a phenomenon rather than a casual everyday occurrence, are touched by murder but I have had five friends that I know of die violent deaths at the hands of an assailant or, in one case, assailants. A neighbouring farmer to Blue Hills was the first. Sal Mineo was stabbed to death outside his apartment. The actor Michael Booth was a victim of queer bashing in South London and in 1973 I found an old school friend, Derek Spiers had been murdered on his farm outside Richmond, Natal. And then, of course, there was Priscilla of whom I have truly fond memories.

One day, coming home from school, I found her wailing on the back veranda. By now, 1946, we lived in an area of Durban called Morningside, at 111 Rapson Road. We called the house Prestatyn which was rather pretentious. There was even a painted sign on the gate. My mother said it should have been named after Lord Nelson: one eye, one arm, one ambition. It was on the other side of town to my school necessitating a tram ride into town and then a bus ride which is one of the reasons why, when I reached the sixth form, I asked my parents if I could be a boarder again to which they agreed.

Chapter Three

But this incident with Priscilla was when I was still living at home. From the noise she was making I thought something really dreadful had happened.

'Kosaan!' She wailed, 'the enemas, the enemas! They all have gone! All run away!'

What she meant was that the 'animals,' a word she never seemed able to say, in this case my sister's pet guinea pigs, had somehow escaped their cage and the wailing was because she probably thought she would be blamed. She wouldn't make an attempt to catch and put them back because she was terrified of them. They were nothing more or less than overlarge multicoloured rats and I had already played horrid practical jokes by creeping up on her holding one and sending her shrieking for safety. I went outside, recovered the escapees, one or two in next door's garden, and put them back in their cage. Priscilla did not get blamed much to her relief. Like "milnight" and "goom-bye", "enema" is a word still sometimes used in our house and it must sound really kinky to a visitor to hear something like, 'Have the enemas been fed yet?' Strange how some words can escape people. My father always referred to a commentator as a commenter and could never spell the word eleven. Sitting at the dining room table doing something like household accounts he would suddenly look up and ask my mother, 'Ro, how do you spell eleven?'

'E-l-e-v-e-n.'

Two minutes later, 'Glyn, how do you spell eleven?'

'E-l-e-v-e-n.'

'Hmmmn...'

And there it was, as sure as God made little apples.

"Elven," every time.

Two other memories of Priscilla: again, one day coming home from school and approaching the house, it really did sound as though murder and mayhem were being committed inside. I found Priscilla and my sister desperately clinging on to a doorknob while, on the other side of the door I could hear my mother yelling and banging on it. It turned out on hasty enquiry that there was a bat in the room, and as all three of them were terrified of bats, especially my mother who had been told as a child that they get entangled in your hair, Priscilla and Ceri weren't going to let my mother out in case the bat came with her. I managed to prise them away from the door and opened it. They fled for the lives down the passage to the relative safety of the kitchen and my distraught mother staggered from the room to collapse elsewhere before recovering and wreaking revenge on her tormenters. Why she never thought to open the windows and give the bat a possible escape route as it swooped around the room I really don't know. Sheer panic I suppose, with ghastly visions of the bat flapping about, trapped, and stuck like glue in her hair.

My mother tended to believe virtually anything she was told and I am equally naïve and will swallow most anything as gospel if it's not obviously too outrageous. When she was a child someone told her that if she planted a tin of condensed milk a cow would grow, so she dutifully planted one and conscientiously watered it until, one day, fed up with waiting for this cow that never appeared, she dug up the rusty tin.

The family, especially my father, loved rice pudding but, whenever my mother made it, he came out with the same dreary old line time after time. We knew it so well we could mouth it with him.

'Nice pudding, Ro, but not like my mother used to make it.'

Our mother usually took little notice. Her rice puddings were delicious and we walloped into them with relish, even my dad, despite the proviso. Then, one evening, the all too familiar line changed.

'Fantastic pudding, Ro! Just as my mother used to make it.'

And my mother got up from the table, threw the pudding at him, and marched from the dining room because that day Priscilla had cooked the rice pudding just as his mother used to make it.

When I went back to South Africa on a visit in 1973 I had to change planes at Rome and, queuing up to board were two giant, blonde, ruddy-complexioned rugger-buggers standing in line in front of me, and the one proclaimed in a loud voice and heavy Afrikaans accent,

Chapter Three

'Man, I don't care what anybody says, it's God's own country,' and I almost thought of turning back then and there.

Arriving at the immigration desk at Johannesburg before my onward flight to Durban, the officer looked at my South African passport, which I had kept and renewed all those years, and wanted to know what I was doing in England and when I intended returning to South Africa. I told him I wasn't and he shook his head and came out with those immortal words of Kitchener about my country needing me, though he didn't actually point the finger as in the famous poster. On my return to England, fed-up with having to stand for ages in the alien's queue at immigration and enviously watching the Brits passing rapidly through, arriving finally at the desk and having to explain yet again to a suspicious officer that I lived permanently in England and, in fact, now owned a house there, I decided finally to relinquish my South African passport and acquire a British one which would save all that hassle whenever I returned from a trip abroad.

But I discovered on that trip in '73 that petty apartheid was already breaking down. Of course the benches were still labelled for Europeans only but Blacks sat on them. In the block of flats where my mother lived the lift was for Europeans only but, one day when I was using it, some resident's African servant got in. Fine by me, no big deal, and no big problem. Next floor down though, this real stuffy, tweedy, colonel type gentleman got in. This is it, I thought, here comes the fireworks. 'Hey, you cheeky kaffir! (Cheeky was a favourite adjective) What do you think you're doing in here? Don't you know this lift is for Europeans only?' But, no. The colonel, if that was what he was, never said a word, just turned his back on us and leaned on his walking stick, gazing fixedly at the door in front of him. I looked at the black man and raised an eyebrow and he just smiled. Kaffir, an Arabic word meaning infidel or unbeliever, was a derogatory term for Blacks as was "Munt" from the Zulu, "Muntu" meaning a man. No one in South Africa today would dream of using the word kaffir, at least not in public, and they would be in a lot of trouble if they did. Of course racism still exists, it exists on all sides and I truly wonder if it will ever be eradicated or whether it is too ingrained in man's tribal nature. Of course in England "some of my best friends were black" just as "some of my best friends were Jewish" but any remnants of my own racist upbringing really seemed to end when I was on the faculty of James Madison University in Virginia and one of my African American, to use what to me is a pointless politically correct tag, you're an American or not an American: that is, unless you're a Virginian when you're a Virginian first and then an American. It's like being a Cretan. They're proud of being Greek but they're first and foremost, Cretans. But I have digressed. My African American student introduced me to her father, principal of a black college, and shaking his hand I said, 'How do you do, sir?' And immediately the thought ran through my head that here was I, a white South African born and bred, without thinking and quite naturally calling a black man sir!

A Lesson from Aloes - Liverpool Playhouse

In Durban I paid a nostalgic visit to Payne Brothers in West Street, the department store where my mother used to take me to buy my

Chapter Three

school uniforms: green blazer with badge; grey flannels, tie in school colours, green, red, and gold, (yellow actually but gold sounds better), white straw basher with band also in school colours. I found the store filled with blacks and remarked on it to the young white girl who was serving me. She immediately bristled. 'So what?' She said. 'Their money's as good as yours.' It took a little while to placate her, to tell her I didn't mean that I objected to it, it was just that in the 1940's any black daring to enter so hallowed a white establishment would have been made to feel more than a little uncomfortable. In fact would have been asked to leave or possibly been forcibly ejected. She found this a little hard to believe. Of course I knew what had been happening in South Africa in my absence. I knew about the ANC and Nelson Mandela. I knew about Soweto and Sharpeville. I performed in Athol Fugard plays, a playwright who stayed at home to personally cry the beloved country: *A Lesson from Aloes* which I played twice, the first time in Edinburgh and then at The Liverpool Playhouse with a wonderful actress, Valerie Lilley, and under the direction of Bill Morrison who I remember saying one day at rehearsal, 'Will you two stop being so bloody unselfish with each other? I can't stand it.' It couldn't be helped. It is that kind of play. It was a wonderful and thoroughly draining experience leaving us exhausted and hardly able or wanting to move at the end of each performance. In all the shitty work for all the shitty directors one has had to work with in a lifetime one is grateful for the few good directors one has known and the handful of plays that make it all worthwhile. I was asked to do Aloes a third time, at Sheffield, but I didn't think I could face the emotion again and turned it down. The other Fugard play was in Leeds when I played the small part of the policeman in *STATEMENTS after an arrest under the Immorality Act,* the sop to Cerberus, because the play is virtually a two-hander for the couple in love, being my reading extracts from Fugard's diaries in the first half.

Then, on television, I played the part of one of the lawyers in a play based on the Steve Biko trial. Nigel Hawthorne, later to really come into his own quite brilliantly with films like *The Madness of King*

George, another actor with South African connections, also played a lawyer. Part of the set consisted of a long sort of runway, caged in at both sides and overhead through which a number of actors playing Africans were herded at a run while policemen, played by security men, stood by with barking dogs. I couldn't help noticing one Alsatian was particularly vicious, almost hysterical as it barked and snarled and gnashed its teeth, lunging forward on its leash and its handler having a really hard time keeping it from actually attacking. I asked him afterwards how he got the dog to do that, the other dogs seeming almost playful in comparison. 'Oh, that's easy,' he replied, 'he hates blacks.' Good God, I thought, here we are doing a play about a man who was allegedly murdered in custody because of racist policies and it has meant absolutely nothing to this guy or he couldn't have said what he did with such a wide grin and such obvious pride. He would obviously have been in his element at Soweto.

Now here I have a problem because I have just come across a cutting from the *Radio Times* about a '*Play For Today*' called *Child of Hope*, concerning thirty-seven men from South West Africa (Namibia) being on trial for their lives in Pretoria and in which I played a character named Nami Philips. Nigel Hawthorne is also in it playing a Police Captain. But I am sure we were in a television play about Steve Biko or is memory playing me false?

Another South African piece I was in, this time in the theatre, was *Tsafendas* for a company called The Almost Free, a play about the assassination of Hendrik Verwoerd, the politician responsible for the 'homelands' policy whereby blacks were forcibly moved out of the cities into what were called Bantustans. Tsafendas, who stabbed Verwoerd to death, escaped the death penalty by reason of insanity. We played The Theatre at New End, Hampstead, and the production was also taken to Amsterdam.

There are times when sex with a stranger can be no more than an extension of masturbation, times when, no matter how fleeting the

Chapter Three

experience, it can be so intense it leaves a memory for a lifetime. In Amsterdam I decided one afternoon to pay a visit to the baths. This is not something I do without some trepidation because naked, even then, I never considered my body to be an object of masculine beauty and desire, no Praxiteles statue me. It was probably just as well I never did get a call to audition for James Bond. But there I was, seated in the steam room (steam hides a multitude of nature's errors) all on my own when the door opened and a slim, handsome youth slipped in and with a glance in my direction sat on the stone bench within striking distance. I froze and I remained frozen for some considerable time. Sooner or later I thought, this young Adonis is going to get up and walk out so, what the hell, he can only say no. With that I stretched out a hand and placed it on his thigh. The response was immediate and overwhelming. This beautiful head was slowly lowered sideways and came to rest on my shoulder. We made love; we made love, we made love. Oh, how, all afternoon, we made love, all afternoon until, reluctantly I had to leave to go to the theatre. His name was Alexander. He was Italian, twenty-four years old who, fortunately for me, liked older men. But it was the last day of his holiday and I would never see him again. Even as I was leaving the building he was already cruising his next conquest, making the most of his last hours before returning to his Catholic home where he would remain most firmly in the closet.

A similar moment of magic happened when Chris and I were on holiday in Munich. We spent the evening with friends in a club called "*The Green Goose*" where a kid called Gunter evidently took a shine to Chris. Chris didn't respond all that enthusiastically at first, I think the glasses were putting him off but I could see behind the glasses a very attractive youth so I did a *Suddenly Last Summer* and egged him on. 'Go on,' I said, 'go dance with him.' Then, having made the desired contact and Gunter obviously not averse to a threesome, I suggested we retire to "The English Garden" where in a mid-summer night's clearing we could continue the evening. Suddenly Chris whispered, 'There's somebody watching.' Now, if there's something I'm not, it's an exhibitionist. I get no kick from being observed in what I consider to be a private matter so I whispered back, 'Tell it to go away,' which was a totally irrational thing to say anyway. Chris didn't speak any more German than I did and why should he be the one to tell it to go away? 'No,' he hissed back, 'It's very beautiful.' I could see this figure standing motionless in the shadow of the trees at the edge of the clearing but I hissed back, 'How do you know? You can't see it properly from here. Tell it to go away.' Poor Gunter in the middle didn't have a clue as to what was going on and his head turned first one way then the other but then, and to this day I don't know why I did it, I stretched out my arm in the direction of the shadowy figure who stepped out into the moonlight to reveal the young Siegfried himself. He joined us, he enjoyed us, we enjoyed him, and when it was all over he touched each of us in turn lightly on the cheek and silently disappeared the way he had come. Not a word had been spoken.

A not so magical experience took place the following day when a friend of a friend, yet another young lawyer named Peter, (all our friends in Munich seem to be lawyers) took us for a drive. We stopped at a schloss for a delicious venison lunch during the course of which he casually mentioned that Dachau was a few more kilometres down the road. I suggested in that case we should visit it. At first he adamantly refused to take us but, eventually, he relented and we drove on. He did not enter the camp with us but waited outside as Chris and I went around. Inadvertently we had started off in the wrong direction and had taken in the worst, most horrific aspects of the camp first, ending up at last with the rather innocuous looking photographs of prisoners tending flower beds etcetera during the camp's early days. The only thing we missed were the ovens but we had seen so much of horror there was no way I wanted to go back to take a look at those. Before we left I said to Chris, 'Do you notice something very strange about this place?' I don't remember whether he had noticed it or not but I was struck by the total silence and the fact that, human visitors apart, there was not a single living thing within the camp perimeter: no bird song, no ants, no bees, no flies, no insects of any kind that I could see. The whole place was dead. As we stepped outside, the

Chapter Three

noise of the world intruded once more.

Pictures of Sharpeville and other atrocities in South Africa perpetrated during the apartheid era shocked the world but not all South African policemen were brutal or sadistic for the sake of it even though they certainly had that reputation. They also had the reputation of being as thick as two planks which in many instances was only too true, S.A.P. spells sap. So, when I was at university in Pietermaritzburg, the police advertised on campus for students to work with them during the long vacation, as they wanted to encourage a more "educated" type to join the force. Nihil humani alianum and all that I duly put in my application and was accepted but when I got to Durban and reported to West Central Police Station I was told that all the positions there had been filled. I was stunned.

'But I put in my application in Maritzburg,' I said, 'and I was accepted. It was down in black and white. Now I don't have a job for the vac.' To the captain, in front of whose desk I was standing, I must have been looking rather dejected, if not downright pathetic and he could have shrugged and said, so what, but he huffed a bit, shuffled some papers and then said, 'Well, all the jobs are clerical work with the CID but, if you really want to do this, I'll give you a job in the charge office as a special constable. Is that okay?'

Okay? I was sure clerical work with the CID would prove extremely boring and this sounded much more up my street.

'Yes, sir. Thank you, sir.' I didn't even think to ask what the going rate of pay was for a special constable.

'Okay, then,' he said, 'you start to-night.'

I looked at him as though he had suddenly grown two heads. 'To-night?'

'Night duty. Report here for...' and he gave me my time. I can't honestly remember what it was but probably midnight. There were three shifts of eight hours each and midnight to eight in the morning, eight to four in the afternoon and four to midnight would seem the most logical. Whatever time it was I duly presented myself in the charge office to be greeted from behind a long counter by an avuncular grey-haired sergeant, who looked up from the form he was filling in, carefully capped his fountain pen and said, 'So you're our new recruit. Okay, come around here.' He uncapped his fountain pen and went back to his form and, lifting the flap at the end of the counter and closing it behind me, I joined him and waited. Eventually, 'What do you want me to do?' I asked.

He looked up from his form but this time didn't cap his pen.

'Who do you see in this office?' He asked.

'You.' I said.

'And?'

'Well, me I suppose.' Though. I added rather fatuously, 'I can't actually see myself.'

'Anyone else?'

'No.'

'Then there's nothing for you to do is there?' And he went back to his form.

I could see he was smiling so I stood there and looked around. A police station is a grim, grey, and dirty place, at least this one was, and there really wasn't much to look at: desks, stools, cupboards, bulletin boards, pigeon-holes. I could hear chatter coming from the CID room next door and traffic from the street but otherwise it was strangely quiet. It wasn't long though before a much younger man came in, glanced in my direction, collected something, I don't remember what, and went out again without even a second glance. The charge office might have been grimy but this young police constable was anything but. Pristine would be the word for him if one can apply that to a human being. In time I got to know him pretty well. He was the exact opposite of the sergeant I met first who was a gentle man, and a kindly one, with a sense of humour and seemingly endless patience. The young one never greeted you or made any attempt at conversation. His uniform was always immaculate, his boots polished to a glassy shine. His hair was sleeked down and he was in the habit of constantly running a comb through it. He was forever washing his hands and cleaning his nails that were long and filed almost to a point. I can't recall his name but, for the sake of convenience and, as most of the men there were Afrikaners, let's say it was Kruger. I hope I don't do a real Kruger an injustice here by describing this man.

It wasn't long before he was back again and saying something to the sergeant, who capped his fountain pen, put it down and collected a bunch of keys which he held out towards me, holding one key separate from the rest.

'That's the one you want,' he said, and went back to his form, which seemed to be taking an awfully long time to fill in. 'Go with the constable,' he added.

I had a nasty feeling this was baptism by fire and I was right though it didn't turn out badly as I had imagined it would. I was almost at the door when the sergeant called me back.

'Have you ever seen a dead man?' He asked.

I shook my head. I think I might even have gulped.

'Well some advice then. Whatever you see, just never feel sorry. Okay?'

I nodded and trotted out after constable Kruger. This was definitely not clerical work with the CID.

Once out the back of the station you entered a long yard with a high wall that separated it from a side street on the right. Immediately to the left was a row of three cells; the largest one for blacks, one for coloureds, and one for whites. Each cell had a heavy metal door with a peephole. Every hour these cells had to be inspected, always by two policemen. Mayhem and murder could be going on in there but you never went in on your own. Apart from the danger, whatever happened you had no one with you to corroborate your version of events. But that first inspection was still to come. At this moment we were headed for the far end of the yard where I could hear a rhythmic purr that grew louder and louder as we approached. Once there, Kruger, without a word actually held out his hand and I gave him the keys. He opened the door, stepped inside and switched on the lights that, after the gloom of the yard, were very bright.

The mortuary was in two sections. From the yard you first entered the post-mortem section with its white enamel tables on central pedestals and in the centre of which were large drainage holes. There were glass-fronted cupboards containing surgical instruments and glass jars containing bits and pieces of human anatomy. There was a strong smell that I presumed from reading to be formaldehyde but, such was my ignorance, it could have been anything. This section was slightly separated by a short wall from the second half that held the fridges which were making the noise we had heard out in the yard, six doors in all in two tiers of three.

From this section double doors opened outwards onto the street. Once opened, the ambulance backed up and its doors opened inside the mortuary doors so passers-by couldn't look in and see what was happening. Kruger opened the double doors. The ambulance backed up and its doors were opened. My heart was thumping. What horror was I about to witness for the first time in my nineteen years? The ambulance men unloaded a stretcher covered by a white sheet with a red cross and laid it on the floor. They removed the sheet. On the stretcher lay a keshla, a very old Zulu in tribal dress. He wore a bechu, a kind of sporran made of leather thongs that covers the genitals; he wore his beads, and his keshla ring made of clay on his head. Why was he dressed like that I wondered. Perhaps he had been attending an indaba.[9] He still held his knobkerrie[10] in both hands against his chest and he was to all intents and purposes an old man who had fallen asleep. It was for me the gentlest introduction to death. My heart was no longer thumping. And I thought of ice cream.

Kruger had opened one of the fridge doors and there were only two sets of feet showing, each with a label tied to a big toe. The lowest narrow steel tray was empty and, as he pulled it out, I thought of ice

---

9   A meeting, usually of tribal elders.
10 A club

Chapter Three

cream. I thought of Fleming Johnston Road and the sound of the ice-cream cart's bell on a Sunday afternoon that brought all the kids running. A pony pulled the little two-wheeled cart under its canopy and a boy was the ice cream vendor. The boy was an African in his middle years. He wore a white cotton shirt with blue edging around the short sleeves and short white pants to match, just like a gardening boy or a house boy, or a boy who brought around the tray of drinks at the hotel. Why did it never occur to us how undignified it was for a middle-aged man to be called boy? His sandals were made from cut down pieces of old motor tyre.

The interior of the cart was kept cold with a large block of ice. In those days, before everyone had fridges, you could buy large blocks of ice. Like the little ice-cream cart, a full size horse-drawn wagon came down the road laden with blocks of ice covered with sacking to stop it melting too fast but still dripping all the way. A block of ice would be lifted off the cart and carried into the house using what I can only describe as a giant pair of callipers with very sharp tips. As for the ice cream you had a choice of two, either a rather tasteless white block, presumably meant to be vanilla, wedged between two wafer biscuits and which went down a treat tasteless or not, or an Eskimo pie; that is, a choc-ice. The ice cream boy walked beside his pony until there were enough eager kids hopping and skipping around to warrant stopping and moving to the back of the cart to serve them. The cart had doors there that opened like the fridges in the morgue and long tin trays which held the ice-creams in rows, each individually wrapped in paper, waiting to be taken out, unwrapped, placed between its wafers and accepted by eager young hands. One tray held the money. The steel trays that held the bodies in the fridges of the morgue, that's what made me think of ice cream.

Kruger filled in the necessary paperwork and the tag for the old man's toe. The kerrie and keshla ring were removed and he was placed on the narrow tray and slid into the fridge. There was no sign of a wound on the body. The door was closed. The ambulance left and the street doors were closed. We left, turning out the lights, and the yard door was closed.

It wasn't all going to be that easy. One busy night when I went down to the mortuary by myself I opened up and, as the ambulance men were bringing in the body, I opened the first fridge and saw the top place was empty so I asked them to 'put it up there.' One of the men pulled out the tray and, suddenly, I saw the feet of the corpse below jump six inches off its tray. To say I nearly had a laundry problem would be putting it mildly. What had happened of course was that the rubber coated handle from the tray above had hit the one below, making no sound but causing the corpse to come back to life. That was one time I couldn't get away from the mortuary fast enough. To make matters worse in my haste I left the paperwork behind and had to go back for it. The hum of mortuary fridges getting louder as you approach down a long dark yard does not make for a happy heart.

Naturally some of the bodies that were brought in weren't at all like the first one. There was the Indian lady found on a railway line for example and another taken from the remains of a house fire. This nineteen year old was getting quite an education but I managed to cope until one day I forgot the sergeant's original admonition. The ambulance brought in a little girl who had fallen down a storm drain and drowned. I looked at this little bedraggled, soiled, raggedy blonde doll her glazed blue eyes still open, and immediately felt so sorry for her. I was also immediately violently ill before I could even make it to a sink and my stomach kept on heaving even when there was no more to bring up.

That first night, after my visit to the mortuary, was hotting up. It had been unusually quiet up till then, maybe because it was the beginning of the week, but now vans arrived and prisoners were bundled out to be charged, fingerprinted, have their shoe laces and anything else they could use to injure themselves removed, and hustled off to the appropriate cell. They were given one thin blanket to sleep with on the concrete floor. There were no such things as beds. Who knew how many would be in there by morning when they would all be taken away to face their charges in court? Policemen came and went, plain clothes came and went, people off the street came in to lay charges, to make complaints. They came in bloodied from street fights. They were brought in so sozzled they didn't know night from day and I had my first indication of constable Kruger's sadistic nature when he tried to take one drunk's fingerprints. Every digit had to be inked on a pad and then placed on the appropriate form and rolled from one side to the other. It wasn't just a matter of putting the finger down flat and leaving it at that. Kruger put down the first finger and started to roll it. Half way through the process the man pulled his finger away, smudging the print. Kruger, apparently completely unruffled and without a word, screwed up the form, tossed it in the waste paper basket, took another, and tried again. The same thing happened. He screwed up the form, tossed it away, moved around to the front of the counter and tried a third time. Again the drunk pulled his finger away. Kruger turned him around and hit him with such force he literally flew through the air, slammed into the wall behind him, slid to the floor and pissed himself. And he spent the night in his soaking stinking trousers.

On one inspection of the cells, constable Kruger looked through the peephole and, hurriedly opening the door, moved quickly inside. Something was wrong and I entered the cell behind him just in time to witness Kruger's reaction. In each cell buckets took the place of a toilet but a drunk, instead of using the bucket, was pissing up the wall. Kruger took him by the seat of his pants and the scruff of his neck and rubbed him up the wall. The man screamed blue murder and no wonder, the cell walls were pebble-dashed. He was left crouching on the floor, moaning and clutching his wounded cock. Back in the charge office I wondered whether I should say something, maybe the man needed medical attention. Kruger wasn't worried in the slightest.

He had washed his hands, combed his hair, cleaned his nails and had other things to be getting on with and a later inspection revealed the man in the cell fast asleep. He probably woke up in the morning wondering what had happened to his shredded prick.

There was an African constable, let's call him Tefu, Tefu whose uniform was every inch as immaculate as Kruger's and whose boots, if it were possible, were even shinier. Kruger and Tefu played a game every time they passed each other, or were close enough, of trying to step on and scuff each other's footwear. Tefu didn't really stand a chance. He wouldn't have dared to inflict the tiniest scratch on Kruger's shoes anyway so he pretended to have a go and developed a remarkable agility in taking immediate avoiding action. I hate to think what Kruger's reaction would have been had a shoe actually been marked.

It's strange but I have no recollection of any cells for women, maybe because I never put away a woman prisoner. There must have been facilities for them but one evening just as I was prepared to go off duty a pathetic creature dragged itself into the police station; an elderly rather faded French lady beneath a faded straw hat who said her name was Madam Dumalain (I've spelt it phonetically) who was flat broke, tired, disorientated, said she had nowhere to go and wanted a bed for the night in the police station. Imagine an elderly Blanche Dubois seeking the kindness of strangers. She was told it wasn't possible and my mother got the shock of her life when I turned up at home with Madam Dumalain in tow. Our mother was used to stray animals being brought in but this was the first time the animal was human–and from the police station! I don't remember whether she stayed with us for just the one night or whether it was longer or what eventually happened to her. I have a feeling family eventually claimed her and all was well that ended well.

One of the corpses brought in to the mortuary was a coloured man who I was informed had died of a stab wound which rather surprised me as I could see no sign of it until one of the ambulance men with first and middle finger pulled the skin apart to reveal the

Chapter Three

wound. What surprised me was the absence of blood. I presume the bleeding was internal. I nearly caused a similar wound when I was at university. One evening at dinner, seated at the head of the table, I was expounding on something and growing more and more vehement about it when I became aware that at the next table they were all sending me up, urged on by one, Gerry Kollenberg. The Taurian temper took a strange turn. Quite coldly and deliberately I stood up, picked up a knife and taking aim for Gerry's ribs, let him have it. The blade hit where it was meant to but, fortunately, it was a blunt table knife and did no damage apart from possibly a minor bruise but the action, as can be imagined, was greeted by shocked silence. I don't know what the reaction was after I left because I immediately stalked out of hall.

The very first indication of my Taurian temper, at least the first I remember, happened in Fleming Johnston Road. The Macks who lived just across the road from us had a son, Warren, who was my age and my best friend. Well, I suppose he was called my best friend because, of my age group, he lived the closest to us. I don't think I particularly liked or disliked him at that time. He was just there. Another best friend was Rita Crooks, who lived in the house next to the Macks, but we had been barred from seeing each other for a while because we had been discovered in the wash-house tub playing touche-peepee, and didn't I half get a walloping for that one. Adults who don't believe, or refuse to believe children are sexual creatures, which they were themselves once, are living in cloud-cuckoo land. There are reasons for playing doctors and nurses, and milk the cow and they're not just voyages of discovery.

The Macks were a mean lot. If it was time for Warren's tea, his mother would say as much and tell me to go home, whereas in our house if it were tea time, friends who were playing stayed on and were invited to join in. Nobody really knew much about Mr Mack. He had a lathe in an outhouse and, when not on the golf course, spent his spare time turning wooden spindles in various designs.

No Official Umbrella

He must have turned hundreds, God and Mr Mack alone knowing what for. All the houses in Umbilo were bungalows and didn't need stair rails so to where did all these turned objects disappear? Maybe they were all table legs. The walloping I got for the Warren Mack incident was because I chased all his guests away from his birthday party, maintaining Warren was my friend and nobody else's. I really don't know why I did this. Possessiveness is one thing but this best friend bit was crap really. Maybe it was because I just wanted to play with all Warren's new toys and the other kids were getting in the way. Anyway, his mother gave me a good ticking off and ordered me home at which the Taurian temper blew. I must have been a psycho case at times because half way down the drive I picked up a piece of brick lying conveniently at my feet, turned, and hurled it at Warren with deadly aim, hitting him on the side of his head. His howling was probably heard the entire length of the road and Fleming Johnston was a long road. I was now in the deepest possible disgrace because he was recovering from a mastoid operation and the missile missed his stitches by an inch. He was screaming, his mother was screaming, and half the road came out to see who was being murdered. I fled and hid in the space beneath our house but I knew I had to come out sooner or later and face the consequences. Once I'd received my walloping I was frogmarched across the road to apologise, which I probably did with bad grace. I didn't visit the Mack household again for a very long time.

Whatever happened to mastoids? They seemed to be the in medical thing in the thirties and many a boy was seen with this long scimitar shaped scar and deep depression behind an ear. Tonsils and adenoids were also there to be excised at every opportunity. Mine were removed at the Entabeni, the S.A.R.&.H hospital in Durban. Employees working for Railways and Harbours, and their families, had free medical care so, not really knowing what was in store for me, there I was one afternoon feeling perfectly well, lying in a hospital bed, and no amount of assurance from my parents that the tonsils had to come out and there was absolutely nothing to it really, stopped me from being absolutely terrified. The following morning I was wheeled into the theatre, laid out on the table and this mask was placed over my face. The smell of the chloroform was horrendous, I felt I was being suffocated, choking, struggling, 'Just breathe in,' I heard a voice say before I started to see Catherine wheels and shooting stars in all the colours of the rainbow, circus noises like a distorted calliope and a loud buzzing sound filling my ears. It never went to black total non-being as it does with modern anaesthetics. The Catherine wheels and shooting stars and the noises continued unabated and nightmarish until I woke up back in the ward with a throat so sore I could hardly swallow. I wanted to cough but couldn't bring myself to do it. Consequently when the surgeon came to examine me and told me to open my mouth he was somewhat taken aback by what he saw in there. Sitting on a chair next to the bed, he withdrew the wooden spatula that had been holding down my tongue and said, 'Good God, boy!' I remember his words exactly. 'What on earth do you think you're doing? Cough that up at once, in here.'

He had a steel kidney dish on his lap and, having been urged a second time with a stern, 'Come along now,' I painfully yorked up a mixture of mucus, phlegm and blood the very second he moved the dish from his lap, and the trouser leg of his elegant expensive suit copped the lot. He jumped up, handed the empty dish to the sister standing next to him and, wiping the leg with a towel from my bedside cabinet, fled the ward. I don't recollect ever seeing him again. Sister, of course, accused me of being a very wicked little boy and somehow, after I'd got over my original cringing, I felt it was a just revenge for all the pain. I never did find out why I had to have my tonsils and adenoids out. Maybe the medical thinking was that, without them, my asthmatic condition might improve, perhaps disappear altogether. If that was the reason it didn't work.

At one time or another I contracted most of the ailments from which children suffer and catch from each other: mumps, measles,

No Official Umbrella

German measles, ringworm and, at two years of age, I suffered a really bad bout of whooping cough. It was this that led to my being an asthmatic, or so it was believed. I endured a number of allergy tests and took great exception to a lady doctor who wanted, goodness knows why, to look at my willy, as though that could have anything to do with my breathing. Well, sometime before this I'd been given a walloping for waggling that tiny organ as suggestively as was possible at my African nanny, Sophie, and I wasn't having this lady playing with my willy under any circumstances. So I got another walloping for being disobedient. Life was unfair, unpredictable, and confusing.

The Old School - Richmond Primary

My asthma attacks always struck precisely at three in the morning. You could take a bet on it, and the attacks lasted three, four, five days before disappearing as quickly as they had started. During those days though I was almost completely incapacitated. Movement requires breath and I had none to spare. I remember sitting in a deck chair in the front garden of 28 Fleming Johnston Road, eyes closed, chest heaving, wheezing away, even wearing a sweater while soaking up the sun and my mother, who had no idea what it could be like to be without air, (how could she?) kept trying to pull me out of the chair and demanding I do something, 'Don't just sit there. Go for a run. Go and play in the park. DO SOMETHING!' And the attack became even more chronic.

Eventually the doctors decided I should be living not by the sea but up country where the climate was drier and it was decided I would become a boarder at Richmond School, as the crow flies maybe fifty miles inland from Durban. Doctors were much-respected human beings in those days; a touch above the hoi polloi and their judgment was never ever in question unless they, themselves, wanted a second opinion.

So it was that one day I stood in tears at the top of a long drive watching my father's Chevrolet as it sped away downhill to disappear in a cloud of dust. I can't remember whether my baby sister was with us or whether she had been left behind and was being looked after in Durban. My weeping mother, beside a grim-faced dad, waved to me from the passenger seat. I was seven years old going on eight and this was the moment I had been dreading. The 'goodbyes' and the 'be goods,' the clinging hugs were over and, as the back of the car finally disappeared in a cloud of dust, this was probably the loneliest moment of my young life. Whenever adults say 'It's for your own good,' you can be pretty sure the 'it's' is going to be unpleasant but, in this instance, it didn't turn out to be so. Once I had grown used to the idea, being very young and malleable it didn't take too long I suppose, boarding school turned out to be not so bad after all. In fact, looking back on it, it was on the whole a happy and enjoyable experience even though three years up country at Richmond School did nothing whatsoever for my asthma. I still on occasion woke up on the dot as the clock struck three, struggling for breath, not only getting it into my lungs, but pushing with all the force needed to expel it, the bronchi were so constricted. I would leave my bed and move over to the window, open it and, with my chest heaving, my shoulders up to my ears, put my head out as though the air outside was healthier and easier to breathe than the air inside the dormitory.

No Official Umbrella

Asthma, in those days, was fairly rare, relatively speaking. I knew only one boy at Richmond other than myself who suffered with it and he seemed to be in a worse state than I as his shoulders seemed always to be up under is ears and he was forever puffing away at the inhaler he carried with him at all times, whereas I was on ephedrine tablets which had the unfortunate effect of turning my urine the brightest green but didn't do much, as far as I remember, to alleviate any symptoms of asthma. Much later on I was prescribed an inhaler that did help; it was a fairly large rectangular flattish rubber bulb that rhythmically squeezed expelled a cloud of vapour from a small glass container into which the medicine had been poured. When not in use the container was stoppered. It was pretty primitive come to think of it but I held onto it for years. At other schools and at university I was acquainted with no other asthmatics, though there must have been some. Today asthma appears to be endemic.

Richmond was, and most likely still is, a small sleepy town, the centre of a farming community. In those days it was surrounded by fields of maize, pastures for cattle, and plantations of wattle, the trunks of which were used as mine props and the bark in the tanning industry. We used to love eating the sweet tasting resin that oozed from the trees. I remember the very first drive as I was taken to my new school: entering the town over the railway tracks with the little station on the right, the Agricultural Hall and paddocks on the left, passed the Indian store with the large Mazzawattee Tea sign; a short way up the hill to the main street and turn left, post office up a flight of steps on the right and general store on the left where we used to spend our pocket money and, sometimes, I hesitate to confess it, do a little shoplifting, usually a tube of Smarties or a small bar of Cadburys chocolate. Then, passed the hotel on the left, turn and go downhill again, passed the cricket ground with its whitewashed pavilion and grass so dark it was almost black, a thatched house beside the road on the left and on up the drive to the school. The school building holding classrooms was undressed red brick, single story and three sides of

Chapter Three

a square. A little way further on the hostel was a large Victorian, or perhaps Edwardian house in two parts: a double storied section which held the girls' dormitories upstairs and, on the ground floor, kitchens and a large dining room. The boys' dormitories and bathrooms were in a single story section opposite, a covered veranda leading from one section to the other. Boys' lavatories were outside and some distance away. Night needs were served by chamber pots known as "chinkies."

We wore school uniform, the school colours being black and red and, for some reason, the school badge consisted of an anchor (so far from the sea?) with R on one side of the anchor and S on the other. We took it in turns to bath before supper and then, all scrubbed clean, we sat on the highly polished wooden floor of the dining room until the bell rang to call us to the tables. I have no memory whatsoever of the food but I do remember the spotless white linen on the long tables and stern-faced Matron watching over us as we fed. The first lesson in table manners was not to "alligate"; that is, eat with your mouth open. I don't recollect in real life ever seeing an alligator eat but presumably they do chomp away with open mouth and how I wish modern kids, and sometimes their wretched parents, had gone to Richmond school and been admonished at table for alligating. It's impossible to sit in a restaurant these days without seeing some brat or bratette stuffing their mouths and displaying for your edification everything they're chewing. And how I loathe those who chew gum with their mouths open, especially females chomping away, slobber slobber slobber. If I ruled the world, as Harry Secombe once sang, I would ban chewing gum, with the exception of travel gum which stops me being seasick and which, I may add, I chew with my mouth closed.

Everyone had to have a nickname which was all rather silly but the sort of thing boys do I suppose, so I became 'Bones,' and I gave my first public performance in the dormitory one night before lights out by sitting on my bed astride a plumped up pillow which acted as a saddle, playing a tennis racquet which acted as a guitar and singing as I rocked on my imaginary horse, 'Oh give me a home, where the buffalo roam, and the deer and the antelope play.' It didn't exactly go down a storm.

The next extra-curricular lesson, not at table of course, was masturbation: either as a solo, a duet, or in chorus; a circle of boys seated under trees well away from prying adult eyes all furiously wanking away. This ritual was usually led by an older boy by the name of Wiggy Moore who, to us smaller ones, was equipped with the most enormous dong that actually made spunk so he must have been a fair few years older than I and, in order to see the spunk, one or more of us was invited to do the hard work while Wiggy lay back against a tree trunk and enjoyed it. For a duet, my favourite friend, (we played with our Dinky toys together, no pun intended,) and wanking partner was a boy named Terry Terblanche. His mother, I remember her as a rather plain woman with thick glasses, was either widowed or divorced and later remarried to a man named Gold whose situation evidently suited his name, or his name to his situation. Terry became Terence Gold and a right little snob. After leaving Richmond I didn't see him again until high school when he was playing cricket for his school team, Maritzburg College as I remember, and he refused point blank to even acknowledge my existence as he left the pitch, bat in hand, walking passed me staring into the middle distance as if I were invisible.

Games more energetic than vroom-vrooming with Dinky toys were played; like building dens in the brambles and defending them with homemade bows and arrows. Shoes were something to be endured only on special occasions and, going barefoot most of the time, the soles of our feet became so tough we seldom suffered from thorns so trotting through the brambles was literally child's play. It was arms and legs that got well and truly scratched. The arrows were made from a plant called "stinkweed" that had a long straight hollow stem which, when cut down and dried, had a short length of sharpened wire jammed into the hollow at one end and weighted for flight with more wire wound around the outside. A notch was cut into the other end to take the bowstring. With our bows and arrows we also hunted field rats known as gundaane. These made runs in the long grass so

Chapter Three

four or more boys would sit with legs wide apart, toes touching so the legs made a wall, and part the grass in front of them until they found a run. An arrow was pushed into the ground beside each boy and one was fitted to his bow and the string pulled back ready to fire. A couple of beaters with sticks then started to herd the rats towards the row of seated boys and, as soon as a little snout and beady button eyes appeared the arrow was released, the second arrow taken up from the ground and the rat stabbed to make sure it was dead rather than just wounded. I really don't know why we did this and one rat had its revenge when I totally missed it and it ran up the trouser leg of my khaki shorts nearly causing me to have heart failure on the spot. Screaming in panic I leapt to my feet to shake the animal out while everyone else rolled about, hysterical with laughter. We also shot doves, either with air rifles or a .22 but at least we ate these. Disembowelled with a finger and cooked over an open fire they were a burnt offering really. Duiker, a small deer, and guinea fowl were also victims but at least these were for the legitimate pot. The last animal I killed some years later was a large iguana sunning itself on a riverbed. I tried to skin it but succeeded only in skinning my fingers and, I am glad to say, after the iguana, I lost any hunting instinct I might have had. Today, despite nature herself being red in tooth and claw and I am not sentimental about that, it is the way things are, I deplore the hunting and trading of wild animals. Species of buck were so decimated in South Africa that, when I was there in '73, I discovered you needed a licence to shoot one but they were still being poached with horrible wire snares more often than not leading to a slow and painful death.

As most of the boys at school were sons of farmers I spent many a weekend on a farm, sometimes walking a fair distance through the plantations to get to one. In particular this applied to a Mackenzie family who had three sons at the school and were not at all well off. There were no subsidies for farmers in those days. To get to their farm we had at one point to cross a stream and, on one visit, the eldest Mackenzie boy slipped and cut his arm on a rock whereupon I tore a strip off a shirt with which to bandage it. Wasn't that what they did in the movies? I don't remember matron's reaction when she saw the torn shirt.

It was generous of the family to feed another mouth even for just a weekend. The farmhouse was mainly wattle and daub and the section in which we slept was corrugated iron on a wooden frame. I had to share a bed with the youngest Mackenzie and one night I wanted to have a wank so I ordered him to turn around and go to sleep. As though he didn't know what I was up to. As I still wasn't old enough to make spunk and there was no need for something to wipe up the mess I had my orgasm and went to sleep.

In later high school years "guest farms", a way for farmers to augment their earnings and make ends meet, were favourite holiday venues and one was at a place called Creighton which was reached by train. When the train had a long stop along the way I found the Mackenzie family again, their Richmond farm lost and now living in a house near the railway line. They were in even more desperate straights than when I was at school with the boys. I was invited into the barely furnished house and given tea, and bread spread with condensed milk because that was all they could afford, and I saw hanging on the wall a plaque that read "What Is Home Without A Father?" When the train was ready to leave I said my goodbyes and I never saw the family again.

Memories I have of this particular guest farm at Creighton are of a parrot, an African grey, whose favourite trick was to whistle up the dogs for food and, when they arrived panting at their empty dishes, that evil bird would laugh its head off. We swam in the river and boated in a leaky old rowboat, and tried to blow up fish with carbide but it never worked. There was a Catholic monastery close by, I seem to recall it was called The Centacow Mission, where the monks produced their own wine and you were invited into the dark and damp cellars to taste. It was a red wine, very very dry and obviously

Chapter Three

of a high proof because, the moment you stepped outside and the sun hit you, you virtually keeled over on the spot. Three boys, previously strangers to each other, shared a room away from the main house. It had no ceiling so there were bare rafters under a thatch roof and beams from wall to wall. One day two of us killed a puff adder close to the building and decided to play a rather dirty trick on the third boy who was a real wet by hanging the dead snake over a beam above his bed. We let him go to bed first and waited outside for the inevitable screams but they didn't come. Eventually, more than a little worried, we went in and found him sitting up in bed literally paralysed with fright and the snake on the bed not two feet in front of him. And it was moving! He didn't even have the presence of mind to throw back the bedclothes, so covering the snake, and jumping out of bed. With a stick the adder was removed and thrown outside. It was a practical joke that could have had nasty consequences.

At Richmond school there was a superstition that if you killed a snake you had to burn its body before sundown or its mate would come looking for you seeking revenge. A rat up the trousers was one thing, a snake seeking you out for revenge was a terrifying thought. An elephant in the ear was almost as bad. Sitting on the grass one day a tiny beetle flew in my ear and, panicking, I shoved it in even further with my finger. A schoolmate, Jerry Nelson, who I saw on my visit to Durban thirty odd years later, remembered the incident and it was he who informed me that I had my hand over my ear screaming, 'It's an elephant! It's an elephant!' I was taken up the hill to the school doctor who syringed it out with hydrogen peroxide and wrapped it in cotton wool for me to take back as a trophy to school.

Poisonous snakes you knew about but didn't see all that often unless you went hunting for them at night with a torch and a big stick. Mambas were the exception. They had the reputation of attacking without provocation, and ringhals cobras that can blind you at a fair distance by directing a stream of spit at your eyes before attacking. Snakes would rather get out of your way than confront you. Once I had a run in with, and a hasty run away from, a boomslang, a long slender poisonous green tree snake. I thought it was a hanging vine and was about to push it out of the way when I saw it was looking at me.

John Lewis, a friend of long standing since high school days, tells a wonderful story about an uncle of his who owned a 'Tshininyama,' literally 'bread and meat' shop or general store in Swaziland which could only be reached along an avenue of tall trees. A black mamba decided to make his home there and was in the habit of dropping from a tree and attacking anyone walking to the shop with the natural consequence that trade dropped off alarmingly. Whenever the storekeeper went out with his gun there was no sign of the snake so eventually, in desperation, he put the word out that there was a fiver in the offing to anyone who killed it. One morning when he opened up to what was going to be another no customer day he found an old woman sitting on the stoop who asked him if it were true that he was offering five pounds to anyone who could kill the snake. He told her it was and, as if to confirm it, placed a five-pound note under a rock on the veranda. The old woman went away and the following morning was back with eight foot of stone dead black mamba lying on the veranda. How did she do it? She walked through the avenue of trees. African woman are used to carrying heavy weights on their heads, large paraffin tins filled with water and the like, and this lady had walked there with a black three legged pot on her head filled with putu. Putu is mealie meal porridge cooked and cooked until all the water has been boiled off so it attains a pretty high temperature. It is then, when cooler of course, rolled into balls to be eaten by hand. The snake launched itself from the tree, fell into the boiling porridge, end of snake and five pounds to the old girl, a great deal of money at that time. Needless to say she had padded protection between her scalp and the pot.

Another lovely story John tells of his uncle is when the Bishop of Zululand came to visit and was taking a bath in a tin tub on the lawn

Chapter Three

when he heard this slurping noise and noticed the water level in the bath receding. Turning around he saw an anteater, in Afrikaans an aardvark or 'earth-pig' drinking his bath water and gazing at him with those lugubrious brown eyes. He leapt screaming from the bath and dashed naked for the house much to the amusement of the Africans standing by.

One farm I frequently stayed on belonged to the father of my friend Billy Comrie. I don't remember a mother being around. The farm was called Hill Top and, unlike the Mackenzie's, the house was an impressive red-brick with open fireplaces in which, in winter, maize cobs were burnt giving off a terrific heat. Amongst the outbuildings there was one gigantic barn filled with a mountain of these cobs. It made a good battleground using the cobs as ammunition as, being fairly soft, they didn't cause too much damage when scoring a bull's eye.

Further on down the hill lived an aunt, a delightful elderly lady who lived in a truly romantic thatched cottage with thick crooked walls and low ceilings and windows with small panes so the rooms were cool and dark in summer and I'm sure warm in winter. This was Lower Hill Top and I used to enjoy my visits to her because, in front of the cottage was a large pond with an island in the middle on which stood a willow tree. There was a rowing boat and I could play at being a pirate, sitting with my back to the stern, watching the prow of my pirate ship approach the shore. Also, apart from cakes for high teas, she made the best butter fudge in the world and always produced a batch when she knew we were there. She had a small, flat, circular, white ceramic disc with grooves on the top that was placed in the pan and, by constantly turning, prevented the fudge from burning or sticking to the bottom. Naturally one day I had to pick this piece up from the pan and yell blue murder as the toffee on it, still liquid and boiling, stuck it to my fingers. As a kid my hands did seem to come in for an awful lot of punishment because, on another occasion at

Hill Top, Billy's dad had been to the horse sales and returned with a pair of mules. Billy, like most farm kids who could speak Zulu before they could speak their own language, had his own special umfaan, an African boy his own age who was supposed to be a herdsman but was there mainly to keep Billy company when he was at home, and this umfaan was told to name the new mules. Naturally the coal black one was named Snow White and the pale grey one was named Coal Black. In order to start training them to pull a wagon, a halter was placed on their heads and a long length of rope tied to either side. They then trotted along with Billy trotting along behind, one holding the reins, and me trotting behind holding the reins of the other. Unfortunately at some point along the road something spooked my mule which decided to bolt and, instead of letting it go, I tried holding on with the result that the ropes were pulled through my hands. Then I did let go. I was over a five-strand barbed wire fence, across a field, and plunging my hands in the cool water of a pond in Olympic Games time. When I took them out there were two red wheals of rope burn across both palms and it hurt like hell.

Further memories of farm visits are of days spent at gymkhanas sometimes standing in that soft misty drizzle so typical of the Natal midlands watching all the events: tent pegging, tilting the ring, leftover exercises of colonial cavalry with lances and flashing sabres. Horses could also have been the end of me, particularly one evil-minded hack who, at full gallop, suddenly swerved beneath the branch of a tree and sent me flying before I could take evasive action, fortunately with no ill effects except possibly a badly bruised bum. In fact, despite all the misadventures I suffered as a youngster, that wasn't the only nag to throw me, I have never suffered a single broken bone, which was sheer luck really. In later life when we were shooting an episode of *The Sontaran Experiment* for *Doctor Who*, in which I was playing a spaceman with a South African accent, we were filming on Dartmoor in the middle of a wet and chilly Autumn and, on one take, I tripped over a rock and rolled a goodly way down a steep hillside dotted with

Chapter Three

any number of jagged rocky outcrops and, again, got up without any injury. I admit that, due to the freezing conditions, I was well padded with tracksuits beneath my costume but I could still have emerged from that incident with any number of broken bones. Later when I watched the episode I couldn't believe I was so fat. I looked like the Michelin Man! And then I remembered all those tracksuits.

But it wasn't a horse that nearly did for me. It was a pig. On one farm I had a favourite sow, strange as that might sound, and one weekend going to visit her I found the pen in front of the sty empty, so I climb over the railings and went to take a look inside the sty itself. Sure enough, there she was, the big old white sow, but no one had thought to tell me she had just farrowed and, when I saw her lumber to her feet and the ten squealing little piglets tumbling about as they dropped off her tits, I hurriedly backed out and made a run for it, diving over the railings head first and catching my knee on the rusty barbed wire that ran across the top, put there to discourage poultry from roosting on it, pigs being great meat eaters if given half a chance, and oftentimes very dangerous when nursing. A pig's bite can be vicious hence my precipitous flight. So, okay, phew! Narrow escape. No harm done. Just a little cut on the knee.

Monday at school I sat behind my desk and fell asleep. The teacher shook me awake and had no sooner turned her back than I was nodding off again. This went on a number of times until, now rather worried, she left the room to call the headmaster. I remember Mr Kethro very well, a small fussy man with big teeth and a very large wife more than twice his height and built sideways to match. We kids used to speculate as to how they managed "to do it!" He was always dressed in a heavy tweed suit no matter what the temperature. He entered the classroom with the teacher and, so I was told later, marched up to my desk, pulled me upright and gave me a couple of slaps around the chops which evidently had no effect. My head rolled with the slaps and I didn't even open my eyes. By now the other kids must have been sitting around with their jaws on the floor as another teacher arrived, I was picked up and carried out and up to the hostel. The doctor was called, took one look at me and said, 'Get this child on his feet and under no circumstances let him go to sleep. Walk him about.' Something vile was forced down my throat. Liquid paraffin? That seemed to be one of the cure-alls in those days. Another considered necessary towards good health and delivered, as a standard weekly dose, was a spoonful of castor oil to ensure we didn't suffer from that horror of the Victorians, constipation. A sliver of orange to take away the taste followed the castor oil but, even well into adulthood, I could never eat a segment of orange without also tasting castor oil. I suppose it is the same syndrome as an amputee feeling the limb that's no longer there, or so I am told.

Whatever it was the doctor poured down my throat, the main treatment seemed to be to keep me walking and Matron, with the help of one of the African domestics, made sure I did. Every time my knees buckled and I looked like dropping off, the servant lifted me up and walked with me until, eventually, I don't know how it happened, I no long felt like nodding peacefully off into the next world. A few days later I broke out in the most horrendous weeping sores on my legs and had to take my bath after everyone else as it was laced on doctor's orders with sheep dip. It worked. It stung sensitive parts but the sores dried up and disappeared. Some old-fashioned rough and ready remedies would probably make a modern doctor's hair stand on end but they worked. My dad swore by horse liniment for muscular aches and pains and injuries like twisted ankles, Africans sometimes drank sea water for stomach complaints. Whatever happened to the warm soothing rub of camphorated oil for chest colds or the old Afrikaner remedy of bruised crushed apple for stomach ache? A sure-fire remedy for the collywobbles as my mother used to call it.

I have a little half-inch scar on my knee, hardly visible now but there nevertheless, to remind me of what was referred to as 'blood poisoning,' and of my youthful brush with death.

Chapter Four

My first professional acting job was in 1952 in Stefan Zweig's version of *Volpone* with what was then the *South African National Theatre*. It had no theatre of its own but ran two touring companies; one English, one Afrikaans. According to a letter I had later from one of the company, both were abandoned in 1962. Was it really true though or did I imagine it that in a production of *Hamlet* in Afrikaans I heard the Ghost actually say what sounded suspiciously like, "Omlet, Omlet, ek is jou pappies se spook."?

Also hard to believe, but true, I slept through my very first professional dress rehearsal, driving everyone frantic as, not being on the phone in my digs, no one knew how to contact me. I arrived, sweating, contrite and ashamed just as the rehearsal was coming to an end, made my grovelling apologies and told the truth. Well it was an extremely hot afternoon and I thought I'd just take a little doze, never thinking for a moment I would be out like a light for the next few hours. I got very wry looks from all, but nothing was said. What was there to say? You're fired? Hardly likely at that stage of the proceedings. I am capable of dropping off, dozing, cat-napping at the drop of a hat, and have even been known to sleep in television studios, particularly if playing a patient and lying in bed. Though once during a recording, having finished what I had to do and unable to leave the studio, I made my way into a Chinese opium den set and fell asleep on a pile of cushions. When it came to the scene in the opium den the camera passed over me and no one was any the wiser to the fact that there was an extra body on the set. I woke up to find the studio in darkness and everybody gone.

G.I.J. at University aged 19

Chapter Four

Stefan Zweig's very much cut down version of Ben Jonson's *Volpone* in which I was cast as The Doge was the first time the lake liner came into its own as the part really should have been played by someone at least twenty years older. Up to this time my theatrical experience had started at high school in that hoary old one act classic *The Monkey's Paw*. Then, at university, I played The First King in the *Coventry Nativity Play of the Company of Shearmen and Tailors*, and then came Hotspur in *Henry IV Part One*. I had always loved reading Shakespeare but this experience of playing it for the first time, the rush it gave me, was what made me decide I wanted to be an actor. Up until then I had waffled about with no real idea of what I wanted to do with my life. Even at this stage I never thought I would be an actor and a writer. Are there omens in early life that indicate future directions? When I was very young, I can't remember how old, but it was while we were still at Fleming Johnston Road, so it was probably just before my departure to boarding school, or during a school holiday, I wrote my first "novel": a dozen large, hand printed pages torn out of a schoolbook and held together with darning wool that I sold to my mother's bridge club for sixpence a copy. Ah, how cute! How could anyone possibly refuse? I wonder what it was about.

Starting at boarding school I also became a voracious reader, my first discovery being *A Christmas Carol*, followed by *Oliver Twist*, *Great Expectations* and *David Copperfield*. But my favourite was a nineteenth century novel called *Lost on the Prairie*, being an orphan boy's adventure on the Great Plains. I have searched high and low for this book ever since and would still like to find it. Many a tear was shed on the pillow over this one. The only reference I have ever come across to *Lost on the Prairie* was in an antiquarian bookseller's in Fremantle. Note: the novels are all about small boys being hard done by or suffering misfortune, except for *A Christmas Carol* but even that has Tiny Tim.

As for the acting, witness my playing at being James Mason after seeing *The Seventh Veil*. Any visit to the cinema saw me emerging after the film acting whatever character had taken my fancy, a habit that drove my mother to distraction, not knowing whether she was living with James Cagney, Howard Keel, Humphrey Bogart, or Donald O'Connor. He was a favourite even though I could neither sing nor dance. In high school I loved reading aloud and, when a volunteer was called for, I was the first to raise my hand. Poetry, prose, Shakespeare, whatever it was I really enjoyed it and I think my enjoyment transferred itself to the class because hot, sweaty, bored schoolboys suddenly listened and, I have to confess, I liked that. Yet previously at Richmond school when I was asked to conduct the percussion orchestra I suddenly became a shrinking violet and refused. My friend Billy Comrie took the baton instead and I was left holding a triangle.

I might have gone through life with no broken bones but that doesn't mean I have escaped unscarred. My third scar is the result of playing Hotspur. To die I had to fall back onto a ramp with Prince Hal's sword apparently doing for me under my upstage arm, but at one performance, as I lay there, the tip of his blade did actually stab me. I grabbed the blade with both hands and pushed. The harder I pushed, the harder Prince Hal pushed. I was a worm wriggling on a hook. It must have been the most convincing death scene ever, Finally I decided he wasn't going to give up until I was dead so I had better die and the writhing, pushing, and jerky legs suddenly ceased. Later in the dressing room I ripped off my tabard and chain mail (heavy knitted string painted silver) and, pointing to the blood running down my side said, 'You did that.'

'Did I? Sorry.' And he went on removing his make-up. To add insult to injury he won the cup as best actor. I swore he only won it because of his matinee idol good looks.

The second scar, after the pigsty incident, came about because of my love of swimming. A number of boys used to swim in the yacht basin at Durban and one of our favourite tricks was to dive off a jetty, swim

Chapter Four

under a yacht, and come up the other side. One day someone on the jetty said 'Where's all this blood coming from?' We all looked around and at each other and then I saw about three inches of flesh, a quarter of an inch wide on the outside of my right foot had been literally gouged out. I hadn't felt a thing. They say in water the sensation of pain is lessened if not deadened which, I suppose, is why Romans committed suicide in hot baths and I really had no idea it was my blood and that a sudden swell, more than likely caused by the wake of a passing boat, had lifted me up and I had been keel-hauled on the barnacles beneath the yacht.

My fourth scar, excluding dog bites incurred by petting stray animals, was when I tore a cartilage in my right knee and had to go into hospital to have it removed, a meniscectomy I believe the operation is called. I had to hitch-hike home to Durban from university in Pietermaritzburg and it was agony as the slightest wrong movement of the swollen knee caused the torn ligament to be nipped between the bones and my leg was permanently bent like a boomerang. Fortunately I did the journey in one ride. As I stood on the main Pietermaritzburg/Durban road, thumb in the air, a passing car pulled up a short distance ahead of me and I hobbled, hopped, skipped, and jumped for the passenger door while they waited. Goodness knows what was going through their minds, a husband and wife but, as I settled in the back seat I nearly told them that one day they would be proud of picking up so important a passenger. I'm glad I didn't. It was somewhat of a hollow boast.

This time around chloroform and ether were things of the past and I didn't even get to count to ten as I quietly went to sleep under the injection of sodium pentothal. I was expected to stay in hospital for at least two weeks, the first week in bed with my leg protected by a wire cage holding up the bedding. These days I believe you're in and up and about the next day. The second week I made myself useful to the nurses by fetching and carrying, emptying and sluicing bottles and bedpans, freshening up the vases of flowers, rubbing patients with methylated spirits to prevent bed sores, and anything else they thought I could be entrusted to do.

So first of all I thought I'd like to be a doctor. After all I'd played at being a doctor many times as a child and, although that was mainly sexual exploration I did later feel, though still as a child, there was a certain glamour attached to the profession. Then, when my dog, Casey, died of distemper, my howls of anguish and my love of animals made me decide I wanted to be a vet so that no dog would ever die such a horrible death again. But unfortunately, to start a degree in these professions, you had to take scientific subjects in the first year; maybe it was even for three years for a BSc degree, before going on to medicine or veterinary science, but for me science was definitely nihil. Out! Maths I loathed, with the possible exception of a slight bias towards trigonometry, I have absolutely no idea why. Algebra went right over my head. I just couldn't get my mind around all that χ equals γ stuff. Geometry was equally of no interest. Chemistry and physics? Uninterested in either, unless really dramatic reactions were involved, preferably explosive. Botany and zoology were interesting because they involved living things. Glenwood was basically a technical school and, apart from English and Afrikaans, all the subjects were scientific so how I managed to matriculate in all and go on to university is a mystery. At university I fiddled and farted about for two years, taking courses, dropping them and starting others not knowing what I wanted to do and obviously and unfortunately wasting my parents' money but keeping on because, according to my mother, with a degree, one could always become a teacher if nothing else.

No disrespect to the teaching profession but it was an alternative and, as part of my education, I even had to take practicals in a real classroom. It was at a primary school for boys and one day, disgusted with a child who adamantly refused to understand something I was striving to drum into him, I took his ruler out of his hands to smack him over the head with it–lightly I hasten to add–but he had been sucking the end and I do not like saliva in the wrong place, that is

Chapter Four

out of the mouth. I dropped the ruler as if it were a live snake. The next day when I entered the classroom every single boy was sucking something; an eraser, a pencil, a ruler, a thumb. It was actually very funny but I decided teaching small boys was not the way I wanted to spend the rest of my life, especially remembering some of the masters I had had at my own schools. Many many years later I would teach and thoroughly enjoy it but my students were that much older. There was always my love of the countryside and farming of course. That was another alternative. I could go to agricultural college instead and become a farmer.

I joined the university Ballet Club, God alone knows why. I couldn't make a dancer in a million years. As a kid playing in the park I got giddy on the roundabout, sea-saw and swings so two turns on stage and I would be flat on my face. Fortunately for me the only ballet I danced in I wasn't required to turn or leave the ground, merely make grotesque shapes playing one of the four horsemen to a Rachmaninov prelude. I don't remember which horseman. It couldn't have been famine; I was too bulky for that. It could have been war I suppose. I found making grotesque shapes not too difficult at all but that was my one and only shot as a dancer.

With the Dram. Soc. I had played a tiny part in the play *See Naples and Die*, which involved me sleeping on a bench throughout the entire evening with a straw hat over my face, a guitar across my chest, then waking with a start and dashing offstage in six directions at once as it were, which always brought the house down, much to my satisfaction. I'm very much surprised I didn't actually go to sleep. And then came Hotspur. "My liege, I did deny no prisoners, but I remember when the fight was done." The decision was made.

Having been an ignominious failure at university, academically that is, for two years running I approached Pearle Celine in Durban to discuss the possibility of training with her *Masque School of Theatre and Ballet*, a big title for a very small outfit. I auditioned for her,

Hotspur of course and, when it came to the questions of fees, my heart sank. My parents weren't going to put any more money into my education, especially into one they were so dead against, as they raised the usual objection many a budding thespian has experienced. The theatre is a parlous profession with absolutely no security. Little did my parents know that one day even being a bank manager, that most staid and secure of positions, would no longer be as secure as it once was.

'Why don't you get a proper job?' My mother would say, 'and get your acting out of your system as an amateur. I get pleasure from my singing but not always as a professional and you could do the same with your acting.'

But this argument cut no ice with me. I wanted to be a professional actor and that was an end to it. Fortunately Pearle was obviously interested in me and said I could join the school as a sort of scholarship student; that is, she would waive the fees if my parents were willing to keep me. They were talked into it. After all, that was a generous gesture on Pearle's part and she wouldn't have made it if she thought I was a hopeless case. But the parents were determined to see if I would stick it out so all I received from them, apart from board and lodging of course, was my bus fares to and from the studio and a packed lunch. Money for anything else was simply not forthcoming. I couldn't even afford to go to the bioscope any more.

I stuck it out. Under Pearle I learned a great deal and, at the annual Eisteddfod, a show for show-offs, I made off with a couple of gold certificates for extracts from *Richard II*, "this sceptred isle" and Caliban "all the infections that the sun sucks up" from *The Tempest*. No Hotspur this time, I wonder why. I was also able to extend myself with performances in amateur productions, playing Hibbert in *Journey's End* and Salvatore Ferraro in *A Man About the House*.

But my year with Pearle came to an end and the question was, so what now? Openings for work in the theatre at that time were few and far between. There was the Brian Brooke Company in Cape Town and The Repertory Theatre in Johannesburg, and then there were the

Chapter Four

two National touring companies. A rep was started in Durban at one stage but quickly collapsed. The only people to keep theatre alive in my hometown, and that in an amateur capacity were members of the Jewish community, and that included my drama teacher, Pearle, who remained a friend right up to her death in England a few years ago. Durbanites were simply not used to or interested in theatre. Rugby, football, cricket, golf, the country club, bridge, social dances, the beach, cinema, the braaivleis,[11] these were leisure hour activities. Of course little girls from better off families took ballet classes. That went without saying. Not boys of course. That was too sissy for words and a boy interested in that sort of thing was highly suspect. The only live theatre I remember seeing in Durban was a South African National Theatre production of *Hassan* and an evening with the English comedian Nat Jackley. In that same cinema cum theatre, the *Alhambra*, just after the war I sat through a special film showing the Nazi death camps which, Belsen and Dachau in particular, I never dreamed I would one day visit. In a way the awful pictures were almost too much to take in but they stayed with me for a long time afterwards and, to this day, I can still see the face of Josef Kramer with those heavy jowls and that black five o'clock shadow, and those dreadful hulking female guards. It's strange but their images are imprinted on my mind as though I had known them intimately.

So, if theatre work in South Africa for a nineteen year old was virtually out of the question, where was the entrée into theatre to be? Why, in England of course, so one just had to go to England. Easier said than done. To get to the Promised Land you needed money and of money there was none. This meant I had to find some kind of work, any kind of work, in order to save enough to make the journey. I had heard that good wages were paid on the copper mines of Northern Rhodesia, now Zambia, so decided that was where I would make my pile. For a while I worked in a bottle store, an off-licence, in Durban until I had saved enough for my train fare to the mining town of

---
11 Barbecue

Ndola where I ended up after a fairly uneventful journey through miles and miles of nothing but miles and miles but which did take in the Victoria Falls, a truly amazing sight, and just outside a mining town called Wankee, a rogue elephant standing on the line, trunk swaying from side to side, ears flapping and refusing point blank to move. When he finally did he'd added a few hours to the journey time.

Ndola was for me a very boring place to be, a small town in a flat landscape of scrubby bush, those miles and miles of nothing but miles and miles. There was the club for company employees, white of course, the only place of recreation where you could drink and play billiards. I worked as a clerk in the mine's office and I lived in a house with a mad Irishman named Bay whose wife and children were, for some reason, elsewhere. Every morning two pints of milk and a bottle of whisky were delivered to the house and, by nightfall, Bay had emptied the whisky bottle. I used the milk. A couple of times I had to lift him, spark out, off the lavatory seat, his head on his arms resting on the cistern, and put him to bed. In the morning he remembered nothing.

So, good wages or not, Ndola didn't last very long. I collected what I had earned and set off to find work on a tobacco farm where wages were also reputed to be high. Ending up in a little place called Fort William in the centre of the tobacco growing industry I checked in at the one and only hotel to start my enquiries and wait for developments. Seated at the bar I noticed a bottle high up on a shelf labelled "PPP" and asked the owner what it was. He took down the bottle, which was obviously his own puerile private piece of whimsy because the label on closer inspection read PURE PANTHER PISS. Ho, ho, ho, big chortle just to keep him happy and, as I sat there, the hoped for developments arrived in the form of a singularly unexpected partnership; an American by the name of Alex and an Armenian by the name of Dmitri who could never pronounce my name and called me "Greeno." They had come up from Southern Rhodesia to pick up and

Chapter Four

take back illegal labour from Mozambique.

No, sorry, they had no work on their tobacco farm for such as I because it was the end of the season and casual workers were no longer required. The illegal labour would be doing backbreaking stuff for peanuts. The same would definitely apply anywhere in this neck of the woods, but I could travel south with them if I wanted. So, as there seemed little point in hanging around with nothing else in view, I climbed into the cabin of their truck and, seated between them, we set off for Southern Rhodesia, partly back the way I had come. In the back of the truck, protected by a tarpaulin, there sat a dozen or more rather dejected Mozambicans together with a haunch of high venison that made its presence felt whenever the wind blew in our direction.

Half way home and late at night we stopped at a traveller's rest house. This consisted of four walls and a roof, a number of beds with bare mattresses and mosquito nets, and cooking facilities in the shape of a wood-burning stove. There was a hole-in-the-ground loo some distance away. The Africans of course slept outside or in the back of the truck and cooked their, by now, stinking venison over an open fire. If game is truly meant to be consumed high, this was certainly high enough for any gastronome's taste. I can't remember what we ate. That good old stand-by, corned beef, more than likely, or baked beans, or both.

In the early hours of the morning I was wakened by the urgent call of Mother Nature so, gathering up my hat, my hurricane lamp, and the rifle with which I had been supplied, I trotted out into the dark and to the wooden shack that was the loo. Opening the door I lifted up my lantern and peered all around to make sure there were no unwanted visitors in residence. After all one doesn't want to be disturbed in the middle of meditation and a satisfying movement by the sudden appearance of something awkward like a poisonous reptile. I laid my lamp on the wall to wall wooden seat, rested my rifle against the wall behind the door, made sure there was paper, torn up newspaper as it happens which was a pretty regular thing and, satisfied that all was

No Official Umbrella

hunky-dory, lowered my shorts and sat down. The very next second I leapt to my feet and I think my scream could have been heard in far off Johannesburg. Forgetting the lamp, forgetting the rifle, holding his hat on with one hand, and his trousers half way up with the other, the intrepid hunter fled into the night. Alex and Dmitri had come out of the house with rifles cocked. Surely a lioness had grabbed me and at this very moment was carrying me off into the bushes to finish me off. The Africans, all awakened by my scream, were staring wide-eyed in my direction. Rather embarrassed, I pulled up and adjusted my shorts and explained to the guys that, when I sat down, something cold and clammy had flapped against my bare backside and naturally I had nearly died of a heart attack. Dmitri went to investigate and came out carrying my lantern and rifle. He was trying very hard not to laugh. 'It's okay,' he said in his heavy accent. 'It was a bat.'

Of course, as is their wont, it had been hanging upside down beneath the seat and my mother was right, bats are horrid creatures and, if I had a hairy bum, it would probably have stuck there! Or such were my thoughts as I went back to bed. There were no longer any symptoms of my wanting to use the toilet but I suddenly got a fit of the giggles. In more youthful years we used to devour comics, both American and English. I remember spending weekends down the South Coast with a family named Webber. The boys slept on an open veranda and we used to sit on our beds devouring comics by the dozens. The English ones like *Beano* were pretty twee on the whole but the American ones were full of action and exciting characters and I lay there in the traveller's lodge that night thinking, if that bat had stuck to me I wouldn't be known as *Batman*, I would be known as *Batbum*. It was a stupid idea to go to sleep on.

The next morning I woke to find the rest house was situated on top of a very high hill. Way down below was a river, the banks of which were covered in crocodiles and, before breakfast, we took pot shots at them, knowing full well they were too far away for us to do any damage. We were on the border of three countries: Northern and Southern Rhodesia, and Mozambique. Having taken in the view I was called to the truck to set off and, at least now, we didn't have that stinking venison to keep us company.

I can't remember the name of the hamlet that was home to Alex and Dmitri but, when we arrived there, Dmitri insisted I stay in his house which, I discovered, consisted of one large room and a kitchen. The room was divided by a curtain, behind which was the matrimonial bed, and I slept in the front portion.

There was an aged grandfather, three small children and a Spanish wife who was a ball of fire. She never said anything but it didn't take long for me to realise, every time those black eyes flashed in my direction, that she resented my presence and I told Dmitri as much. He immediately went into the kitchen where I heard him verbally laying into her in no uncertain fashion. Not wanting to be the reason for domestic discord I told him I was leaving and, despite his protestations, I moved in with the local butcher, an Afrikaner, and his wife, in a nineteenth century house crammed with Victorian bric-a-brac.

It wasn't long though before I was on the move again, not because of the wife's displeasure this time, but because I just wasn't cut out to assist in the slaughter of animals. In the butcher's yard there was a concrete floor about four metres square in the centre of which was a large iron ring around a staple imbedded in the concrete. A length of rope was passed through the ring and a loop at one end was placed around an ox's horns. Africans at the other end pulled on the rope until the animal was on its knees in front of the ring, its forehead on the concrete. Then, in the manner of a matador, a long sharp knife was thrust between the shoulder blades and the animal died instantly. This was not done by me I hasten to add. I was far too squeamish and would probably have botched it anyway. Then, one day, it was not an ox that was slaughtered but a magnificent bull. Who knows why? Maybe he just wasn't up to strutting his stuff but it finished it for me and I was on the road again thumbing my way back to South Africa. Arriving in Durban I phoned home and my mother answered.

'Mrs Jones?'

'Yes?'

'I'm a friend of your son's from Rhodesia and he suggested I give you a call and maybe you could put me up for a couple of days till I find somewhere to stay.'

Of course, any friend of the still absent prodigal was only too welcome to stay and, having told her where I was phoning from, which was quite close to home, I was ordered to wait there and she would come and pick me up.

When she saw who was standing by the phone booth the car practically mounted the pavement and almost hit a lamppost and, after the big welcome home, she said: 'Well? Where's this fortune you've brought back?'

I handed her one Rhodesian penny with a hole in the middle and, to tell the truth, that was all I had.

So, after the financial fiasco of the Rhodesian adventure, and with still no hope of making it to England, the second alternative to teaching became a fact when my parents bought a "guest" farm called Blue Hills at Manderston not all that far from Richmond and close to the main railway line at Thornville Junction. A branch line ran from Thornville to Richmond and as a schoolboy I had travelled that line many times going home for holidays

The train from Richmond consisted of a small locomotive, one passenger coach with one each of first, second, and third class compartments, and a guard's van. The rest was made up with flat beds to take logs, milk churns, sacks of farm produce, caged poultry, and anything else that needed transporting such as a plough or other farm implements. The journey started at an early hour, about seven-thirty I seem to remember and in winter the ground was hard with a heavy frost which also made the rails slippery so that the train would chuff-chuff forward two lengths and slide back one. On steep hills we sometimes jumped out and walked beside it till it reached the top. Added to this it stopped at every siding to pick up whatever needed picking up, all of which took a considerable amount of time so that

Chapter Four

the twelve mile journey to Thornville took something like four hours. The train was known as "The Galloping Snail."

When I went back in '73 The Galloping Snail was still in use, sitting in the station just waiting for me to go over and relive fond memories. I might even have wanted to take a ride in it but, on looking into the compartments, I discovered it no longer took passengers as that

The Galloping Snail - 1973

coach was now in a terrible state and obviously acted solely as a goods van. The journey to Durban from Thornville Junction, less than fifty miles, took the rest of the day because there was a long wait for a mainline connection, then another change at Cato Ridge, also with a very long wait, so you didn't arrive home until almost dark, having spent a greater portion of the day sitting on your suitcase on station platforms. At Thornville Junction there was a trading store we youthful travellers made a beeline for the moment the galloping snail pulled in. Shopping for sustenance for the rest of the journey and mooching about for a while inspecting the goods helped a little to pass the time. When I went back the old store had been demolished and a brand new one built. Another disappointment. I discovered progress had also caught up with Richmond school as the old hostel had gone and a smart new building stood in its place. I didn't have the heart to take a close look. I should have realised in all those years there would have been many changes when, on the way there, I saw the fields of maize had given way to sugar cane, previously grown only at the coast.

Well, I thought, the little Anglican church we attended, St Mary's right at the top of the hill, they couldn't have messed about with that surely and, indeed, there it stood, exactly as I remembered it when we used to walk up that hill to attend morning service with the sun blazing down on our black blazers and serge trousers, shoes and long socks. Well, we left the hostel wearing shoes and socks but, the minute we were out of sight, off they came, the socks were stuffed in the shoes which were tied together by their laces and slung around the neck and, barefoot, we walked to church where the shoes and socks were put on again to go inside. As soon as we came out, off came the footwear once more. In the churchyard there was a large family grave beneath a cement block. Part of the edges had given away leaving slight gaps and we used to drop some of our collection pennies down there to hear them bounce on the coffins. I dropped in a coin for old times sake but, alas, heard nothing. Everything must have got pretty mouldy down there. We told each other as kids never to pick up anything from a grave, like a chip of marble for example, and take it back with us or at night the ghost whose grave was robbed would come to collect it. It was really just a variation of the revenge-seeking snake.

I visited the post office, which hadn't changed at all. I didn't recognise the lady behind the counter who must have been well into her sixties if not older but she looked up at me and, without hesitation said, 'You're Glyn Jones.'

This was quite incredible, that she could look at a man of forty plus and see a child of ten she once knew but had never seen again since that time. Maybe it was all the tuck boxes I collected, my letters home always including a request for the inclusion of a tin of condensed milk. Ah, to punch two holes in a tin of condensed milk, throw back

Chapter Four

your head and suck out all that sweetness. Why I didn't just use my pocket money to buy condensed milk in the village store I really don't know. Maybe from home it tasted sweeter. *Tate and Lyle Golden Syrup*, the green tin with the picture of the dead lion and the buzzing bees was another request but not as often as the condensed milk. On the syrup tin was inscribed a motto which read something like "Out of the strong came forth sweetness," or words to that effect. I haven't seen a Tate and Lyle tin for a very long time so I may have misquoted.

I drove out to the farm of a high school contemporary, Derek Spiers, and was met on the driveway by a pack of about six or seven dogs all wagging their tails in joyous greeting, or so I thought. Anyway, reassured that they were friendly, I got out of the car, walked to the house, mounted the three steps up to the veranda and knocked on the door. There was no answer. I tried again, turned around and looked at the dogs all sitting in a circle watching me. There still being no answer I started to leave the veranda. There was an immediate snarling and baring of teeth. What happened to all those nice friendly welcoming doggies? This was canine Jekyll and Hyde! I moved slowly and surely towards the car not daring to show the fear I felt as these damned dogs circled me, all snarling like crazy and, I felt sure, about to attack on mass. I made it to the car, slowly opened the door and slipped into the driving seat. As I slammed the door they went berserk. Too late, babes, I'm out of here. So, unfortunately, I never saw my friend and the next news I had of him was of his murder.

To drive to Thornville Junction and on to Richmond I had to pass Blue Hills and saw it had been turned into an aloe farm. I suppose I could have gone in and said hello to the current owners and talked of old times but I drove on.

When my parents bought it and I moved there, Priscilla was transported from Durban to attend to my needs. I can't recall she ever made me a rice pudding and I don't think she was too happy being a country girl. It wasn't within reach of a racetrack for starters and she couldn't play the horses so back to Durban she went and I was left to my own devices that consisted mainly of trying to get the place back on its feet it was so sadly neglected. The only livestock were two dogs, a cat, and a number of chickens, which at least provided me with eggs and the occasional roast dinner, though I didn't wring their necks as my uncles used to do. A sharp axe on a block of wood finished them off.

The farm was very small by South African standards, a mere sixty odd acres and a lot of it was covered with wattle saplings that had taken root, sprung up, some to quite a height, and which had to be cleared. That was the first job. The house was large and in fairly good condition but I preferred to use a rondavel, a round hut of wattle and daub under thatch, as my bedroom. There was a tennis court that was a mass of weeds but restoration of that would have to wait. A generator that kept breaking down supplied electricity in erratic fashion. I don't know why the farm was called Blue Hills. Someone with a Hollywood mind must have named it because I certainly never noticed any hills that were blue. There was one long low-lying hill quite a way off called Ngomnkulu, which sounds very romantic, but, like Kilimanjaro in Kenya that merely means "white hill", the former translates as "big cow." Not so romantic.

I once thought of writing a short story called *The Spirit of the Pioneer* that was to be about my neighbour at Manderston, Betty Nel. I don't think I got further than typing out the title so now here is my memorial tribute to a remarkable lady.

Sitting on the veranda one day I watched as this battered old Pontiac approaching up the dusty driveway to stop in front of the house and this rather large dowdy lady stepped out, fingering a long necklace of heavy amber beads. I got up to greet her and she introduced herself as Betty Nel and she farmed close by. From an Afrikaner family, she never had much to do with her neighbours except for an Indian family who kept a store, so why she decided to call on me that day and why

Chapter Four

we became such good friends I really don't know, especially as she was even less keen on men than she was on neighbours. Maybe it was because I wasn't married and she felt more at ease without another woman about the place. I noticed she walked with a decided bias to one side and later, on closer but hopefully discreet inspection, I saw this livid scar running in an inverted U virtually the full length of her calf. She knew I was intrigued by this and told me her story. It appeared she was having trouble with a tractor and, as she did any repairs on the farm herself, she set about putting it to rights. Unfortunately, while she was under the tractor, it rolled and it rolled over her leg, severing the calf muscle almost from the bone so that it hung loose behind her. Holding it up with one hand and with blood dripping over the running board she managed to drive as far as the Indian shop where the wound was bandaged enough to stop the flow of blood and for the Indian friend to drive her into Maritzburg and hospital. Rushed into emergency, she was laid out on the operating table and the surgeon informed her as kindly as he could that the leg had to come off, at which Betty Nel got up and started to limp from the theatre, presumably trailing blood as she went. She only agreed to return on condition she was not put out, so that she could keep an eye on proceedings and that, instead of amputation, the muscle would be stitched back on. It was agreed, the leg was saved, but she would always walk with a decided limp.

I don't know how old she was when I knew her. I wasn't very good at guessing women's ages. She could have been anything between thirty and late forties but she was a great help and companion to me the short time I was on the farm. Unfortunately, or fortunately, I don't really know which, Blue Hills was a short-lived episode in my life, which came to an end with my father's first stroke, and the farm was sold.

I was in England, living at Goldhawk Road, when I had news of his death and I remember I was playing *Porgy and Bess* on the record player and even today, if I hear the song *Jesus is Walking on the Water* my father comes to mind. He died in November one hour before his sixtieth birthday which meant my mother then had to live on a reduced pension, One Hour! No allowances made. Wasn't that sick?

The Manse,
Plas Avenue,
Prestatyn, N. Wales.
December 15th, 1959

Dear Mrs. Jones,

The sad news of the passing away of your dear husband, Mr. Llewelyn Jones has reached us through Mr. and Mrs. Aneurin Williams. I write personally and on behalf of the Church at Nant Hall Road, Prestatyn, to convey to you and to your dear ones the heartfelt sympathy in your great sorrow.

At our Sacrament of Holy Communion on Sunday Evening, December, (sic) *I referred to your sorrow and the congregation stood in silence in tribute to one who was brought up in our church, christened there, and was the son of the founder and builder of our sanctuary, Mr. Thomas Jones. May I ask you then to be assured that the thoughts and prayers of our people are very near you these days, and although great distances of land and sea separate you from us, our sympathy is no less sincere. May God grant you every strength and comfort in the knowledge that your dear one has passed not in darkness or in void, but into the glorious company of God's elect in heaven. We understand that Mr. Jones suffered much during the last weeks and that every medical care was brought to him. Now he lives in a realm where pain and death can no longer touch his spirit.*

I had the privilege and pleasure of meeting him on his last visit to Prestatyn, following the death of your sister in law, Miss Ceri Jones, whom I buried some years ago. It was easy to see how glad he was to make contacts with his old friends and to visit the scenes of his home town.

Chapter Four

Next year we celebrate the Diamond Jubilee of the founding of our church, and no occasion of that kind can pass without grateful reference to your dear husband's family who were the founder members. Much has happened since those days of small beginnings and I am pleased to tell you that our church is now the biggest in membership of all the Presbyterian Churches in North Wales and the churches in Prestatyn. Many of the old families have passed away, but there are a few who still remain and recall the early days.

Should you ever return to the Old Country and find yourself in Prestatyn, please do not fail to call to see us at the Manse. We shall be more than glad to meet you. Meanwhile, accept again our tenderest condolences as a church.

Yours sincerely, R.B. OWEN (Minister).

But I have digressed again. Another story I heard about Betty Nel was how she dealt with a hitch-hiker who tried to steal her car. Evidently she stopped to pick this guy up just outside Maritzburg and they hadn't gone very far when he produced and aimed a pistol at her and ordered her to stop, at which Betty produced her .38 from the pocket of her door, cocked it and, pointing it at her passenger, said, 'Who shoots first?' She then slammed on the brakes and the guy made a run for it.

Betty Nel's cure for asthma was a mixture of sheep-dip and honey but fortunately I never had to try it because, while at university I had my very last attack. It was unusual in that, instead of happening at three in the morning, it hit me in the middle of a hot, bright, sunshiny day as I was walking back to university from a rugby practice. I suddenly had to sit down at the side of the road, shoulders around my ears, my chest heaving. At tortoise pace and with frequent stops I eventually made it to the hostel and to my room where I collapsed on the bed. The attack went on without let-up and nothing helped, not even my spray. I couldn't get to sleep and, as I had done when a small boy, I sat leaning out of the open window above the bed desperately trying to get air both in and out of my lungs. Finally I felt I couldn't, didn't want to struggle any longer, and I quite simply consciously and peacefully gave up the fight. No longer struggling and no longer caring I dropped back on the bed and fell asleep. The asthma never bothered me again.

As with Priscilla, I was in England when my sister wrote and told me of Betty Nel's murder in the course of a robbery, her house having been broken into and the police discovering her body in the boot of her car. A tragic end for a feisty lady.

Chapter Five

My second summer rep season was in Ventnor on the Isle of Wight, 1957, and I actually got to play in *The Seventh Veil!* Not Nicholas unfortunately, though I would have probably played it like James Mason, but as Max.

In John Penrose's office overlooking Cambridge Circus I was interviewed for that forthcoming season by the producer, today he would be called the director, Carl Paulsen. Again it was play as cast and stage manage, not assistant stage manager this time but stage manager working with, so Carl informed me, a first class stage director, another title that's been jettisoned and the person now concerned probably designated the "production manager", who really knew his stuff. For some unknown reason I was reluctant to say yes, I don't know why. What had I been doing since New Brighton? Working as a barman and then a doorman at the Leicester Square cinema, all togged up in a concierge's uniform and peaked cap, standing there in all kinds of weather watching passers by, looking at the square and getting very sore feet. The only highlight of that pounding of the pavement was one day seeing John Gielgud passing by. I was still stage-struck enough to get as excited as a kid seeing a great actor in the flesh, as it were. The same thing happened when I saw Alec Guinness emerging from a theatre on Shaftesbury Avenue.

'It's Alec Guinness! It's Alec Guinness!'

Maybe I should have stopped Gielgud and asked if he knew of anything going for an out of work actor.

Perhaps it was the weekly bit that was putting me off accepting the Ventnor engagement, but here I was being offered a whole summer of theatre work and thinking of turning it down. Was I out of my mind? I was a beggar in no position to be a chooser and Carl talked me around without actually having to break my arm. So off to the Isle of Wight I went to be introduced to a nineteen-year-old Kenneth Alan Taylor as the stage director who "really knew his stuff." That line, sold to me by Carl, was on a parallel with "the cheque is in the post" or "I won't cum in your mouth, I promise."

It was a long season, from the middle of June until the 22nd of September, starting with *Death and Brown Windsor* by Michael Pertwee and ending, for three days only, with a play called *Fly Away Peter* by A.P.Dearsley in which I played a character named Arthur Hapgood and about which I have no memory whatsoever.

I do remember *Death and Brown Windsor* though, because in it I played Detective-Sergeant Forsyth and, at one point had to make an entrance to break up a fight between Geoffrey Wren (playing Mark Anderson) and Trevor Richins (Squadron-Leader Tim Mantel) and one night, standing behind the set gradually becoming aware of an awful racket coming from on stage, I realised I should have made my entrance. I flung open the door and dashed on to find two dishevelled sweaty actors clinging to each other like boxers who have gone twelve rounds, having exhausted themselves prolonging the fight and improvising like crazy, even to throwing the furniture around.

'DON'T YOU EVER DARE DO ANYTHING LIKE THAT AGAIN!'

I did it again, the very next night, probably through sheer exhaustion though, despite the amount of work in the theatre, I still managed to find some time for the beach and to write a very bad play called *Enter Anthony*. Any play with a title like that just has to be bad. I fondly hoped it was "commercial" instead of which it was just dreadful theatrical Mills and Boon.

Over the years an actor works with such a multitude of folk it's too often ships that pass in the night and inevitable that a great many will be forgotten, but certainly not all, and some remain friends for life. Anyone having read this far will no doubt have come to the conclusion that I'm a bit of a scatterbrain with a tendency to go off into my own little world and, as I grow older, that memory is not my strongest point which can lead to embarrassing situations, like the time an actor was talking about a play of mine and I blithely asked if he had seen it. There was a slight pause before he said, 'I was in it.'

I remember sitting on the top deck of a bus one day going down the Marylebone Road and my friend, Peter Mackie, sitting beside me was going on and on about a couple of characters who didn't ring any bells at all so, finally, we were just passing St. Pancras Station I remember, I turned to him and asked who he was talking about. His answer was simply, 'You wrote the play.'

Geoffrey Wren had been a member of the Tivoli company so Ventnor was a reunion but after that we met only in passing when, good actor though he was, he gave it up and became a manager for the Alberys. So many young talents who feel they're never going to make it or that the rat race is just too much hassle and the disappointments too many, give up early. I almost felt like giving up myself once when, standing in line at Chadwick Street, an actor in front of me who I had met doing walk-ons on television turned to me and said, 'It's my thirty-fifth birthday and what have I got to show for it? A tin of sardines.'

I had to admit at the time I didn't have very much more though I had gone beyond the time when I had alternate eating and smoking days. But there comes a time when it's too late to think of giving up. What else can you do? You're well and truly in and there's nothing for it but to plough on. When I was teaching I would say to my students, 'When I was a young actor going to an audition there were at least twenty other young actors just as suitable. Whether you got the job or not didn't always depend on talent but whether the producer, director, casting director or, in the case of commercials, agency, or clients liked you enough. Today there are probably two hundred who could fit the bill.' But still the drama schools proliferate and the universities run drama departments and where are all these young hopefuls expected to find work in what has always been an overcrowded profession?

In the intervening years since that summer season in Ventnor many have died and, looking at one Ventnor programme today, out of eleven names, I know of the death of five, with the certainty of a couple more due to age but which I don't know about. Two of the five, Dudley Stevens, and a lovely actress, Nona Williams who unfortunately also gave up early, but in her case through illness, remained friends until their deaths. One, who is still with us and a yearly holiday visitor to our house in Crete, so is well known by the taverna owners on Kalyves beach, is Vicky Clayton who acted under the name of Vicky Lind. The four of us worked together again after Ventnor, namely at Buxton and I with Dudley in *Irma la Douce* and on tour in Sweden in a show he devised and wrote. Originally called *Dugout*, according to the script on my shelf, but changed to *When the Lights go on Again*, a number that was sung in the show which, as the title suggests, was obviously all about the Blitz and in it I played "Dad" yet again. Pip Hinton, who drove me mad in Stockholm insisting that I go shopping with her, played "Mum". I hate shopping at the best of times and that is not a contradiction. I love mooching about in antique stores, bookshops, record shops, even stationery shops, (at junior school if a volunteer was wanted to collect something from the stationary store it would invariably be me because I just adored standing in that windowless room; smelling it, touching the books, examining the pens, pencils, erasers, inks) the same as I enjoy museums and art galleries, but actual shopping I dislike. I go in, I get what I want, if possible, and I come out. I hate shopping for clothes when I have to change to see if things fit just as I used to hate wardrobe calls as an actor, and trailing around stores with Pip Hinton was torture so it only happened once.

Noel Coward's *London Pride* opened the show, after which Dudley had made sure he and Derek Parkyn, veterans of Old Time Music Hall at The Players Theatre, would carry most of the musical numbers, all

Chapter Five

songs from World War II. The show was sponsored and managed by the Riksteatern. It opened in Stockholm for a week and then, looking at the schedule, I see we played, mostly one night stands, fifteen Swedish towns. I was amazed in the Stockholm metro to see glass cabinets holding costumes from Swedish films and thought to myself, in England they wouldn't last five minutes. Athens underground too has the most beautiful stations, immaculately kept and some of them almost walk around museums with ancient artefacts in glass cases.

I liked Gothenburg but, apart from that, I found Sweden a pretty boring place, with apologies to our beautiful friend, Ulf Larsson for denigrating his home country. The coach journeys along miles and miles of straight roads through endless forests consisting of the varieties of trees you had already seen when you came in to land at the airport hardly raised any interest though the pit-stop meals, in comparison to British motorway cafes, were cordon bleu and reasonably priced. The hotels were all overheated and you couldn't remember which town was which by the hotel you stayed in they were all so alike. Was it the one with the green painted corridors, or the blue, or the yellow?

The Swedes themselves must find Sweden a rather boring place because I believe the suicide rate is pretty high and, although liquor was horrendously expensive and jealously guarded by the government, Saturday night was "get pissed out of your mind" night. I remember looking out of my hotel window in the early hours of a winter morning to see, on the opposite side of the road, slightly sheltered from the icy wind in the entrance of a large store between the shop windows, a hot-dog stand around which a number of young men dressed in shirt sleeves were grouped. I don't know what the temperature was but I do know it could get down to minus 26°. However, feeling peckish, I put on my greatcoat, thick scarf, woolly hat, and gloves and ventured out into the night and the street, deserted except for this little gathering. My nose immediately turned to a block of ice. I ordered my hot-dog and, noticing the lads were not only enjoying theirs but were taking frequent slugs from various quarter size bottles, I decided to engage in conversation, knowing all Scandinavians speak English, in many instances better than a lot of Englishmen. 'So what are you guys doing here?' A somewhat ridiculous question one might think. Obviously they were eating hot-dogs, drinking from hip flask size bottles and, by the look of it, they ought to have been turning blue and freezing to death. The one nearest me turned his blonde head slightly and said, 'Ve're vaiting for vimmins.'

His English, at least his accent, was not so hot.

'Oh, yes?' I queried, 'And where exactly are these vimmins, er women, coming from at this hour of the morning?'

There was an eloquent shrug and he took another slug before thrusting the bottle in my direction. I declined his offer by shaking my head as I munched on my hot-dog, meanwhile wondering, if they had to wait for their vimmins in the freezing cold, did they have anywhere to take them or did they risk losing their bits and pieces by exposing them to the arctic temperature? Maybe their bits and pieces were accustomed to the arctic temperature.

'And, if no women arrive, what are you going to do?' I asked.

Another shrug and another swig, 'There vill be some boys from the next willage.'

My mind boggled. In the absence of women were they going to double up and have a gangbang with the boys from the next village? 'And then?' I said.

'Ve beat the shit out of them.'

It was quite a common sight to see someone standing stock still or swaying ever so slightly suddenly, almost in slow motion, either tip forward on his face, or backwards like a felled tree, to disappear into the snow, out like a light, and for the police from a passing patrol car stopping to dig him out, pick him up and cart him off, presumably to hospital where he could sober up. I disappeared vertically myself one day, but not because I was drunk I hasten to add. In one of the towns in which we played I saw what I thought looked like an interesting little church and, going to take a closer look, missed the

Chapter Five

path, disappeared into five feet of soft snow and had to be hauled out sopping wet and freezing.

Led by Derek, who was pretty good at it, we hired boots and skis and went on the piste. I hated every minute of it. Firstly I wasn't wearing skiing gear so that every time I fell over, which was quite often, I collected another sopping wet patch somewhere and, secondly, because I felt the whole time that those damned boots pressing against my shins were going to break my legs. So, as I stood there, more or less hapless, three year old's were whizzing past me at the rate of knots as if they had popped out of the womb on skis. The après-ski was fantastic.

I will say in Sweden's favour that wherever we went the welcome was tremendous and the audiences fantastic, singing with gusto, *Roll Out the Barrel* and *Bless 'em All*, the lyrics being the only words in English, apart from our names, in the programme. But then, if you live in the middle of nowhere where nothing much happens, I'm sure a visiting troop of performing chimps would be welcomed to relieve the tedium. I thought of watching television one free Saturday evening but, after I had watched ten minutes of a rather plump adolescent girl discussing her acne, a boring nature programme, and a medical discourse on something else, I gave up. And this was a Saturday night's entertainment.

We made it as far as the Arctic Circle and saw herds of reindeer and that was Sweden.

At Ventnor in a play called *Ring for Catty* by the actor Patrick Cargill, Catty being a nurse and the play set in a hospital, I'll never forget Dudley sitting up in his bed eating chocolate. The business he invented turned a simple bar of chocolate into a three-course meal. Firstly it was removed from his locker and the label studied. Then it was turned upside down to be carefully unwrapped, broken into portions and offered around to the other patients, all of whom had to decline it. Then a piece was slipped lovingly into the mouth while a look of rapture spread over the face. While being savoured, the remains were offered around once more, once more to be declined. Another piece was broken off to be delicately nibbled around the edge before finally disappearing into the mouth. The remaining chocolate was then carefully re-wrapped and placed on top of the locker. Then, on second thoughts, it was put back inside. The fingers, one by one, were licked clean of chocolate, with particular interest in the right thumb, wiped with a handkerchief, which then also had to be disposed of. Talk about milking it! I don't remember what dialogue or what action was supposed to be happening while all this was going on but no one in the audience would have been watching anything or anybody but Dudley and his chocolate. An actor should be inventive but a good director would have rapped Dudley across the knuckles for so monstrous a piece of upstaging. Many years later I saw the same thing happen but this time in the West End by a big star, Alistair Sim no less, and this time the object used was not a bar of chocolate but a cigar.

At Ventnor Vicky Lind met the musician Kenny Clayton, playing piano on the pier at lunchtime to entertain the old ladies having their coffee and cakes, and in the evenings playing with a band at The Winter Garden. They married and have one daughter, Alex, who I used to baby sit back in London when they lived in Ladbroke Grove and who now has two growing up daughters of her own.

Kenny and I worked on two musicals together written so many years ago. The first is an adaptation of the Cupid & Psyche legend suggested to me as a possible musical by another South African, the dancer Rex Rainer. I once shared a flat in the Goldhawk Road with Rex and another South African Ernest Weston, both of whom alas died young. I inherited a beautiful pastel portrait of Rex by the actor Keith Michel, another ex-pat, this time from Australia, but I digress. I took up Rex's suggestion, resetting the story in Edwardian London so that Cupid becomes a young man about town: Psyche, who in the

Chapter Five

legend is a princess, becomes the daughter of a pearly king and queen and is a chorus girl at the Olympic Theatre where Venus is the star. Mars is naturally a general, Juno a society hostess and Jupiter a retired statesman and a legend in his own time, which he pretends to find very boring. Neptune is a retired seaman now a cockle vendor and head of a gang of spivs, the Tritons. Neptune's wife, Salacia, helps run the cockle stall but is constantly eating the profits and, as Neptune says, 'You know what fish does to you.' Now I was always under the impression that the word salacious came from her name as shellfish were once considered to be aphrodisiac, but I read in Collins English Dictionary the following:

Salacious adj 1. having an excessive interest in sex. 2. (of books, etc.) erotic, bawdy, or lewd. (C17 from Latin salax, fond of leaping, from salire to leap. *(Well, apart from leaping into bed to have it off, what does leaping have to do with sex unless it is a form of eroticism I know not of?)*

In the musical, Pan is a pimp and his sheep are ladies of the night. I tried a few years back, when I was directing musicals with amateur societies, to get them interested in Cupid but they all thought it was too rude. Oliver Bayldon, a designer with the BBC, loved the idea and rendered some beautiful costume and set designs. Kenny's music is so melodious and catchy but, alas, it is another work languishing in the script cupboard. A couple of years ago I took it out again and did some rewriting, mainly tightening it up and I would still dearly love to see it produced. Once upon a time a very young Cameron Mackintosh came around to our house in Hackney to hear Kenny play the music but he didn't bite.

The second musical I wrote with Kenny is called Black Maria. I read somewhere that the Black Maria was named after a lady named Maria Lee so I did some research and came up with:

"Maria Lee was a Negress of immense stature and strength who lived some years ago in Boston, Mass. Whenever the police were having too much trouble with recalcitrant criminals, the cry went up, "Send for Black Maria!" and she promptly came to lend a helping hand. Such was the regard for her abilities that when the first wagon was introduced into the police force they named it the Black Maria in honour of Maria Lee."

"Black Maria–a popular name for the covered van, usually painted black, in which criminals are usually conveyed to and from jail. The name is said to have originated in Philadelphia during the anti-slave riots of 1838 or the nativistic riots against Irish Catholics in 1844–A dictionary of names, nicknames, and surnames of people, places, and things by Edward Latharn (N.Y. Dutton 1904)"

"The Boston City Directories between 1790 and 1860 do not list any Maria Lee. Neither do we find her listed in the Boston Vital Records or any of our histories about Philadelphia–Mrs Sarah W. Flannery–Coordinator of the Humanities, Boston Public Library, Massachusetts."

Don't the Americans simply love titles? Define a coordinator of the humanities.

"The Black Maria was named after a Negress who kept a sailors' boarding house in Boston and helped the police in handling violent cases–The Encyclopaedia Americana Volume 4."

Ah, good! That's where we'll set it, in a sailors' boarding house. We'll give Maria a pretty daughter who one of the sailor's falls for and… and here we go again. It is said that, like the eight notes in an octave, there are only eight basic stories and, on rereading Black Maria it is simply a variation of the Cupid and Psyche story; boy gets girl, boy loses girl, boy gets girl. There are some jaunty numbers in the show but, unlike Cupid and Psyche, which I feel has withstood the passage of time, I think *Black Maria* in style is very much dated.

Chapter Five

Some time in the sixties at The Commonwealth Institute Theatre in Kensington I assisted in the production and compared a Jazz & Folk Concert in support of a multiracial project sponsored by the South African Students' Union. The concert was the idea of Pearl Prescod, then a member of the National Theatre Company who had just received rave reviews for her performance as Tituba in *The Crucible*. The aim of the project was to enable a coloured student from Basutuland (Lesotho) to study at a British university for three years and the concert was the contribution of Hull University to the project. It starred Johnny Dankworth, Cleo Laine, Adelaide Hall among others and, among the others, was Pearl herself, a lady with a voice to make the angels weep. Pearl was my Maria Lee if ever it were to happen but it never did and Pearl died not long afterwards. If I believed in heaven I'd say she'd be up there singing fit to bust and knocking the socks off every archangel around.

While on the subject of musicals, I also wrote the book and lyrics for an adaptation of Ronald Firbank's novel, *Prancing Nigger*. This one was written very early on and I never found a composer for it but anyway, after Sandy Wilson's *Valmouth*, a certain Colonel Firbank who was then the copyright holder of Firbank's work, refused permission for any more adaptations. I wonder what the title would be if it were produced today. It certainly couldn't be called *Prancing Nigger* although that was the perfect title for it, coming from the term of endearment Mammee in the book uses for her husband. I don't know why Sandy Wilson didn't choose this one for his musical rather than *Valmouth*, which is so slim he had to add to it extracts from *The Eccentricities of Cardinal Pirelli*.

I also wrote a version of *The Pickwick Papers* with the composer Malcolm Sircom, who had written incidental music for my play *Oh Brother!* at Ipswich, but Harry Secombe put paid to that effort, especially as there were two other versions going around at the same time.

No Official Umbrella

At least I have seen one musical produced, my version of J.M.Barrie's *Peter Pan* with music by Andy Davidson, which was presented at the Playhouse, Weston-Super-Mare for the Christmas season 1994/5 with Peter Dean from *Eastenders* as Captain Hook and Melissa Bell from the Australian soap *Neighbours* as Peter. I couldn't blame the director this time for anything going wrong as I was the director. I have to

Poster for Peter Pan - Weston -Super-Mare

Chapter Five

admit that, because of Equity's safety rulings, the fight arrangements were pretty obvious and about as exciting as a sugarless jelly but, as soon as the fight director left, I rearranged them and my fights were just as safe and at least had some life and authenticity in them.

I was also directing a musical with a Peter Pan who couldn't, or wouldn't, sing. Melissa, in fact, has a very pretty voice that, with amplification, would put her on a par with any pop singer who can't be heard beyond the first row without it. But she refused point blank to believe me when I tried to persuade her she was capable of carrying Peter's songs. This meant that another member of the cast had to sing from the wings while Melissa mimed, an arrangement that brought the wrath of a theatre mother down on us, there being no credit for her daughter in the programme. I also had, quite frankly, a television actor who, lovely man though he was, as an actor on stage was simply a no no. Getting closer to opening night the producer, Garth Harrison, complained to me that Dean was terrible and what did I think I was doing?

'Trying to get a performance out of a block of wood,' was the answer, 'and, if you don't believe me, come to rehearsal tomorrow and watch. I've called him by himself for the entire morning.'

Garth came, he sat, and he went away without another word. I had even read the lines to Dean the way I wanted them, something I hate and never do, but he still couldn't pick it up. He had no sense of rhythm and no sense of timing and his voice was monotonous. He was also another who couldn't manage his songs, particular a laundry list number I had written for Hook, called *Soggy Green Cake* and here is the list:

HOOK: Cake, Smee, Cake.
SMEE: Cake?
HOOK: Cake.
        DEVIL'S FOOD CAKE AND ANGEL CAKE,
        CHOCOLATE ECLAIRS AND DOUGHNUTS,
        THEN NO MATTER WHAT ELSE IS AT STAKE,

          ANY SMALL BOY WILL GO NUTS
          FOR JUST THE PROMISE, JUST THE THOUGHT,
          OF APFEL STRUDEL AND LINDE TORTE.
          EYES LIGHTING UP FOR ALMOND FLAN,
          LICKING THEIR LIPS AND SIGHING,
          CUSTARD SLICES ARE NOT IN MY PLAN,
          SOON THEY WILL ALL BE DYING
          FOR JUST ONE SLICE OF WHAT I BAKE,
          A GIANT, FATALLY TEMPTING CAKE.
          Green I think.

SMEE: Green?

HOOK: Yes, green. What boy can resist green?
          THEY'LL COME UNSTUCK,
          THEY'LL COME UNGLUED,
          AND KNOWING MY LUCK
          I'LL NEVER BE SUED,
          WHEN THEY DIE,
          WHEN THEY DIE
          WHEN THEY DIE
          DIDDLY AY DI DEE DI DI DEE DI,
          'COS I'LL BET A DUCKET,
          THEY'LL ALL KICK THE BUCKET,
          AND THAT'S HOW MY PLAN WILL CONCLUDE,
          AND THAT'S HOW MY PLAN WILL CONCLUDE.

SMEE: It's the wickedest, prettiest plan I ever did hear of.

HOOK: BATTENBURG CAKE WITH MARZIPAN,
          STRAWBERRY TABATIERES.
          SIMNEL, MARBLE, AND DUNDEE WILL FAN
          FLAMES OF GREED IN LITTLE DEARS,
          BUT FOR SOMETHING REALLY MEAN,
          THERE'S NOTHING GROSSER THAN CAKE THAT'S
          GREEN.

SMEE: What about a nice plum-guava latticework tart?

HOOK: No no no no!

Chapter Five

TIRAMISU FOR ME AND YOU
BUT THERE'S NOTHING A BOY LIKES BETTER
THAN DAMPLY RICH
RICHLY DAMP
EVER SO TASTY,
NICER THAN PASTRY,
DELICIOUSLY SCRUMPTIOUS,
SPLENDIDLY SUMPTUOUS,
SOGGY GREEN CAKE,
SOGGY GREEN CAKE,
OI!

You would have thought any seadog worth his salt would have made an Edwardian banquet out of this one but no, in the end I had to give most of the lines to Smee. The following year *Peter Pan* went on at The Gaiety Theatre, Douglas, Isle of Man with Debbie Lee Harrison a delightful Peter and a real actor, John Spooner, rather than a star name, as Captain Hook. Not only could he sing all his songs he approached the role with imagination and impeccable comic timing. I also had the most delightful, beautiful, and talented Wendy in Susan Tummon, a local girl.

The strange thing is that the review in Weston was good, even going so far as to praise Peter Dean's acting and, in Douglas with a more talented cast, the review was poor and I took the flak as evidently, according to the reviewer, the production "looked amateurish." The Frank Matcham theatre in Douglas is beautiful, though with an awkward backstage because of the shape of the site on which it is built. Odd sightlines had to be masked with blacks creating dark entrances and, with hardly any wing space, the stacking and moving of large flats was carried out almost by numbers.

The town itself, especially during a bitterly cold, wet and windy winter, is rather gloomy. The front is, or was when I was there, lined with tall houses that were once holiday boarding houses but holidaymakers don't seem to go there anymore. Most of the buildings were empty, some of them boarded up, and it was truly depressing, like the centre of American towns where the malls and supermarkets on the periphery have killed off the old heart in the centre. I was a rat. I couldn't wait to get away from Douglas and be home for Christmas so I bought the adult members of the cast a crate of wine to help them celebrate, wished everyone good luck and a merry Christmas, made for the airport and fled home to Yorkshire.

In working on Barrie's play I tried to simplify it as much as possible to make scene changes and the job of stage management that much easier. Of course there is no way one can do without the flying and who would want to? That is so much part of the magic, but I did manage to reduce it slightly. Traditionally the parts of Mr. Darling and Hook are doubled (did Barrie know his psychology?) and I thought, if that is the case, why not give Mrs Darling something to do in the middle of the play, other than sitting in her dressing room? So my one innovation of which I am quite proud is I doubled her with the Crocodile who, as a man-eating vamp, shimmies into view belting out a torch number, *I'm a Fancy Crocodile*, accompanied by tap-dancing baby crocodiles, The Crockettes.... if required.

And, would you believe it? Advertised in the Weston programme for *Peter Pan*, was the Christmas show at The Bristol Hippodrome: a revival of Harry Secombe in *Pickwick–The Musical!*

Earlier in 1994 I saw in Writers' News an ad by someone wanting a collaborator to work on a musical based on the exploits of Garibaldi and, remembering the man's portrait hanging in the house in Bullen Street, I answered the ad. Garibaldi was an incredible character, mainly responsible for the unification of Italy and very popular with the workingman in England, especially in the North where, when he visited England, he was received by adoring mobs. The British government was a trifle on edge in case he started a revolution but the worst that happened was having a biscuit named after him. My mother used to call them "fly cemeteries". Before Garibaldi came along the Austrian chancellor said of Italy that it wasn't a country, it was a geographical expression.

Chapter Five

The writer was a London lawyer who informed me he had been living with this pet project for twenty years or more. That should have produced an amber light, but I have lived with pet projects myself for twenty years or more so it didn't. He went on to say that this person and that person and every other person had seen the script, made suggestions, and generally fiddled about with it, and this should really have turned the amber to red but, more fool me, I took home a big fat script as Basil Boothroyd would have said, and a tape. He had, some time previously, paid singers and musicians to do a recording that must have cost him a pretty packet. He couldn't write music himself but hummed or whistled his tunes for someone else to write down. I was told Lionel Bart was the same, I don't know how true this was I hasten to add before I get sued. These days of course there are fantastic computer programmes that will do all the work for you, even to transposing and copying. Anyway, I read the script, I listened to the songs, of which there were enough to make the evening last five hours or more even without the book, and most of them terrible. The book itself was awful enough. But, muggins here, listens to one supremely beautiful, haunting melody, wonderfully sung by a young man with a golden voice, (he was evidently a Cantor) and agrees to go to work, purely on spec of course.

I rewrite the book, I cut the worst musical numbers, I rewrite lyrics for the better ones and I also write new lyrics for our lawyer friend to put to music. I get a letter from him saying he and his family are on holiday in Weston and how much they all enjoyed their visit to *Peter Pan*. They thought it was super. I keep writing, I complete and present him with the new act one, at least my first draft of how I feel the show should go. This one also has a laundry list number and, as it is an Italian subject, it's all about ice cream. I can quote it because it is my original lyric so I am not breaching any copyright but I later found out he was incapable of writing music to someone else's lyrics anyway so he had, without my knowledge at this point, put a red pencil through it.

During my research I discovered there was a famous ice-cream parlour in Paris called the *Café Procope* so I wrote that, in Turin, Signor Bottone's parlour was more famous still:

IT'S A DEFINITE REQUISITE,
WHEN YOU'RE IN TURIN YOU VISIT,
THE COOLEST PLACE IN TOWN,
BOTTONE'S ICE CREAM PARLOUR,
AN ESTABLISHMENT OF RENOWN.

And the laundry list included:

THERE'S CHOCOLATE, PISTACHIO, APRICOT,
CARAMEL, VIOLET, CHESTNUT AND CHERRY,
ORANGE AND LEMON AND WHO KNOWS WHAT?
ROSE AND EVERY KIND OF BERRY.
THERE'S WALNUT AND PEACH, BANANA TOO,
HONEY AND GINGER, THERE'S RHUBARB AND COFFEE,
ALMOND, VANILLA, TO NAME A FEW,
MELON, PEPPERMINT, APPLE AND TOFFEE.
OH WHAT JOY! OH WHAT RAPTURE!
TASTE BUDS TAKE FLIGHT AS EACH FLAVOUR THEY CAPTURE.

"Some time later," as the caption would read on a silent screen, I receive a phone call from someone who tells me our lawyer has approached him about doing the orchestrations. Why did this man keep bringing people in at this stage of the game? It was much too early. My first draft of the full script wasn't even finished let alone being a polished version. There is a saying that a musical isn't written, it's rewritten and this one was certainly living up to it. Our lawyer friend was another Jack Le Vien and worse, totally hopeless and totally opinionated. Anyway, this musician gentleman whose name I'm afraid I have forgotten, tells me he's read the first act and how much he likes it. Okay, so? I leave the script with our lawyer-cum-playwright and

Chapter Five

start thinking of the second act, which, as it involves the invasion of Sicily, is a wee bit, more complicated but more dramatic with tremendous possibilities. "Some time later" it is while I am working on a scene where Garibaldi is hiding in a nunnery (shades of *Sound of Music*? But a true incident in his life never the less) that I receive another phone call from our incipient orchestrater. Bad news. Our man has just come back from yet another holiday, this time in Devon I think it was and, while lounging on the beach no doubt, he had gone over the script with the result that there was red pencil everywhere. Not only that but he had put back some of the worst lines of his original lyrics, lines that rhymed okay because he made sure they rhymed but that's as far as it went. They simply did not make any sense, had hardly anything to do with English, and nothing whatsoever to do with what was going on story-wise. I went berserk. This was not what I called collaboration. As far as I was concerned he had wasted a year of my life and I was out. I returned his books on the subject and his tapes and wrote him probably one of the angriest letters I have ever penned, and got back a rather bland reply which simply said I was no longer involved "due to an unsatisfactory first act."

Eleven years later I wonder if he is still pushing his pet project and if it will ever come to anything. But be warned: if it is, and any of my material is in it, I'll sue him to kingdom come, lawyer or no lawyer.

On my first visit to the states twenty odd years ago, staying with our friends, actor and writer, Lionel Wilson, and choreographer, Paul Glover, in their apartment on East 71st, I mentioned I was thinking of writing a musical about Victoria Claflin Woodhull; the nineteenth century advocate of free love, champion of women's rights, Wall Street broker, and the first woman to put herself forward for the presidency of the United States, finally marrying a scion of the Martin banking family and retiring to Gloucestershire where, having become respectable, she entertained the Prince of Wales to tea.

'It's been done,' Paul said. 'Called *Onward Victoria* it was on and off in a night.'

The following day he waltzed into the apartment with a copy of the record, evidently produced before the big flop and which cost me fifty dollars as a rarity. Fifty dollars! I'd never paid fifty dollars for a record in my life. I played it once. There was no need or desire to play it again until 2004 brought us the US presidential elections and a whole lot of speculation as to the plans of Hilary Rodham Clinton next time round, in which case would a musical about Woodhull be a good idea at this time, knowing the modern American's propensity for choosing the worst for president? So I played the record for a second time, that's twenty-five dollars a throw, reread the biography *Mrs Satan*, which was what she was called in a famous cartoon, and decided against it. The woman lived too long, changed her colours whenever it suited her, and the beliefs she stood by in her younger days are no longer relevant. Besides which I have at last, after many years, achieved one ambition here in Crete, and that was to write book and lyrics for that musical on the life of La Belle Otero, the Spanish courtesan and chanteuse of La Belle Époque. This project only finally came about because the composer Christopher Littlewood came to live in Gavalahori, a village about four kilometres away and it seemed like fate and an opportunity not to be missed. I hope one day it will be produced but, even if it isn't, I at least have the satisfaction of having completed it.

Like Cameron Mackintosh I was hooked early on by the musical *Salad Days* and decided to try my hand at writing one. This was when I was still working for the newspapers. I didn't have a subject; I didn't even have a title, so I pretentiously gave it the working title of *Opus One*. I remember part of a lyric went:

I WASN'T BORN I WAS COME ACROSS,
AT BREAK OF DAWN NEAR CHARING CROSS,
SOMEBODY FOUND ME NEATLY FURLED,
SNUG AS A BUG IN THE NEWS OF THE WORLD.

Chapter Five

SIGHING SO PEACEFULLY ONCE OR TWICE,
SLEEPING IN SEX CRIMES, MURDER AND VICE.
HAPPILY, HOPEFULLY, CAREFULLY TRUSSED,
WRAPPED UP IN WICKEDNESS, LEWDNESS AND LUST,
HAPPILY HOPEFULLY CHEERFULLY LEFT,
LYING IN HOMICIDE, ARSON AND THEFT

What was all that about I wonder? Another opened with the line, "We're the dumb belles of Allison's gym," not a pun to please the modern feminist. The work, thank god, is lost, half of it anyway.

One door closes, another door opens. There may be no business like show business like no business we know but in show business a long time can elapse between closing and openings.

The clichés flow, running concurrently with the misquotes. Or should I say they come with the territory? Like Stephen Sondheim, for whom my admiration knows no bounds, I like to play with words though, alas, I have nothing like his genius. I find it hard though to forgive him his line in *Into the Woods* "the end justifies the beans." It ranks on a par with Tim Rice's rhyming of "farmers in their pyjamas". I shudder every time I hear Mr. Sondheim's line and I have heard it a lot as *Into the Woods* is a great favourite in this house as is, I might add, *A Little Night Music*, *Sweeny Todd* and *Pacific Overtures*. The only Sondheim show I've not been able to take to is *Sunday in the Park with George*. Pointillist painting does not for me transfer to pointillist music. When Cameron Mackintosh endowed the chair of drama at Oxford University and Sondheim accepted it and advertised for would-be writers of musicals to enrol in his class I immediately applied, sending off a CV, examples of lyrics, a script, and a tape. I was not accepted. Too old? As well as untalented? It was only one of a stream of rejections over the years but it was disappointing enough, even though I had held out only faint hopes to start with.

Dudley Stevens too had ambitions as far as musicals were concerned, that is apart from performing in them. I remember he wrote a version of *Lysistrata* called *Nothing Doing Tonight* but nothing doing came of it. I'm surprised no one seems to have come up with a sure-fire smash-hit based on that play. It would seem the perfect choice for a musical. So salacious!

Another good old rep stand-by at Ventnor was *The Ghost Train* by Arnold Ridley who made such a delightful late come-back as Mr. Godfrey in *Dad's Army*, and I particularly remember a play called *Dark Victory* because, at one point, Dudley onstage had to throw a very heavy silver trophy to me, standing offstage. As this was, of course, a borrowed prop and valuable we had been told to take particular care with it, but Dudley was totally useless at throwing anything. Sometimes I had to leap up to catch it, sometimes I had to go down on my knees or rescue it as it bounced off the tormentor, (a permanent masking flat.) I'm surprised it never went into the audience and one night I missed it altogether and caught it with my crotch. I don't know what the audience made of the agonised yell that emanated from the wings. Could have been a really nasty moment. I remember in Brentwood going to an open air school production of *Julius Caesar* during which corpses, of which there are many, were borne off by a couple of stretcher bearer Roman soldiers and, in one instance, the corpse's helmet had fallen off, at which one of the soldiers picked it up and tossed it onto the corpse. Naturally it hit the spot and the corpse jack-knifed back into life with a particularly loud yell before falling back again desperately clutching the offending helmet with both hands.

When I was a pupil at Glenwood High the school had no swimming pool and on certain afternoons and for competitions we used the municipal baths on the beachfront. The morning following one of these outings Lompy strode into class, put his books on his desk and, looking straight at me, said, 'Jones, what did you do to Mousy Johnson?'

'Me, sir? I didn't do anything to Mousy Johnson.'

'He says you kicked him down at the swimming pool and he's in

Chapter Five

the hospital.'

This was the first I knew anything about kicking Mousy Johnson at the baths so, as soon as school was over, I made my way to Addington, the government hospital down by the south beach and there, sure enough, was Mousy Johnson prostrate.

'What's all this about my kicking you?' I asked.

For answer he threw back the sheet beneath which he was lying to reveal a scrotum the size of half a football and dark blue, almost black in colour. It looked horrendous. I couldn't believe it! I caused that? Evidently I did. What had happened was I took a running dive off the side of the pool and Mousy took a running dive right behind me so that as I went in he was in a position where one of my heels caught him in the groin and broke a blood vessel. The blue colour and swelling of his scrotum was all the blood that had flowed into the sac. I had been totally oblivious of this and gone happily swimming away to the other end of the baths and knew nothing about it until Lompy's accusation the following day. Fortunately Dudley's throwing of the cup during *Dark Victory* didn't have the same result.

When we came to do *Doctor in the House* Dudley did throw something - a hissy fit! It was obvious that all season he had been looking forward to being cast as Simon Sparrow, definitely his part but, when the cast list went up, who was down to play it? Kenneth Alan Taylor. A worse piece of miscasting couldn't be imagined and, what is more, Dudley was down to play the rugby playing Doc, another piece of ridiculous casting. I had words with Carl.

'Carl,' I said, 'I don't know what you think you're doing but this casting is ridiculous. Dudley must play Simon Sparrow and I should be playing John Evans, that's obvious. Kenneth will have to play the hospital porter. You can't leave it like this. Not only will you have a truly rebellious Dudley on your hands but Carey Ellison from Spotlight, (the actors' casting directory), is coming down to see the play and what will this do to your reputation as a director?' The following day the new cast list went up.

That Saturday night, after the last performance of the previous play, the cast, including a very happy Dudley, went home to their digs and stage management which meant Carl, Kenneth, two assistant stage managers and myself started to strike the set ready to put up *Doctor in the House*. By 1 a.m. I had had a bellyful of them all, including our director, and our stage director who really knew his stuff. I stopped whatever I was doing and said, 'Look you lot go home. I'll put up the set by myself. That way I'll at least get home for some sleep tonight.'

They took me at my word. The next thing I knew, Carl was prancing out of the theatre toting his shoulder bag, followed by Kenneth, followed by the two girls. When they returned in the morning the set was up ready to be dressed.

Carl went on to become Artistic Director of The Coliseum in Oldham, taking Kenneth Alan Taylor with him. He remained there until his death and Kenneth stepped into his shoes. I take it by then he really did know his stuff. I never again worked for either of them. In 1974 I sent a play to Kenneth called *Little Footsteps on the Petals*. It was a flat cap North Country comedy I wrote especially for two marvellous performers, Sheila Bernette and Frank Marlborough, a real comedy actor, and I thought it would go down a treat at Oldham. It came back of course, not really suitable, in fact "an unsatisfactory two acts."

My big faux pas at Ventnor, and this really is my last story about that season, was when suddenly one evening I couldn't dim the houselights. I tried everything to rectify the fault. Houselights that go out instantaneously are disruptive because it gives the audience the giggles and it takes time for them to settle down again. Finally, after a couple of nights and in desperation because I simply couldn't trace the fault, I telephoned Strand Electric in London who sent a man all the way down to the Isle of Wight to investigate. He took one look at the board, one look at me, flicked a switch, and went back to London.

Chapter Six

So Blue Hills was no longer. I was back in Durban and at a loose end. Maybe I had to give up my acting ambition and somehow find a job I could settle down to, possibly even enjoy. I wrote to African Consolidated Theatres, owners of the biggest chain of cinemas in South Africa, was taken on as a trainee cinema manager and sent to a town called Boksburg, just outside Johannesburg. I remember nothing of Boksburg except that I became addicted to koeksusters, a double plait of fried dough soaked in sugar syrup. I also grew quite fond of muscatel, a sweet and conveniently cheap wine. Did I put on weight? Do fat puppies fart when you squeeze them? I wasn't long at Boksburg; my next stop being Springs on the Rand. I don't remember the name of the cinema. In fact, like Boksburg, I don't remember much about Springs at all except that the cinema was new, very clean and very large. The only film I remember showing was *Captain Hornblower* with Gregory Peck and every week, as the manager had passed the task on to me, I wrote the weekly report and sent it off to head office. Naturally I informed head office how wonderful I was, one of the few occasions I've been able to sell myself, I suppose because the praise was ostensibly coming from somebody else. So it wasn't too long before the Springs manager called me into his office to inform me I had been given my own house, the Tivoli in Fordsburg, a suburb of Johannesburg. Visions of a cinema similar to the one I had been training in rose in the mind. The reality, alas, was a very different proposition.

I stood on the pavement opposite, lowered my suitcase to the ground and, for a long while, regarded my new charge. It was most definitely jaw-dropping time. The Tivoli was a tiny, grimy, graffiti daubed, dilapidated slum. Fordsburg was an area of poor whites, noted for its toughness and its teenage street gangs. Naturally this piece of information had not been passed on to me. Oh, well, in for a penny, in for a pound, I picked up my suitcase and, crossing the road, made for the hole in the wall, or that's how I thought of it, which was the cinema's entrance. I stood in the foyer, big enough for three bodies at a pinch, and peeped through the tiny grille-covered opening into the box office, big enough to accommodate two and doubling as the manager's office. The about to depart incumbent came out and introduced himself. He had a black eye, a bruised and swollen lip, and a cut on his forehead. It turned out he had been beaten up by some of his young patrons and that was why he was being hurriedly replaced, and being replaced by this wonderful new assistant manager from Springs. Hoist by m' own petard! Critics could have a field day with this, the way the clichés flow, but then I have always maintained the world runs on well-oiled clichés anyway and what's wrong with that? As we were talking a couple of youths emerged from the cinema.

'Hello, Mr. Manager,' they yelled in unison.

'Fuck off!' He growled, just loud enough for them not to hear.

It's little wonder he got beaten up, I thought. He went back into his office, collected his briefcase and, wishing me luck but not really meaning it, left me to it.

The box office lady, probably in her late seventies, or that's how she appeared to my all of twenty years, had worked in that cubby hole since the year dot and, as far as she was concerned, she owned the Tivoli Cinema; lock, stock, and barrel. There I go with the clichés again. Later in life I came to find out that this is a common delusion amongst box office ladies, that the theatre they work in becomes theirs by right of occupation. She eyed me with distrust and murmured something incomprehensible before turning back with a loud sniff to her ticket roll. It could have been a greeting of welcome or it could have meant something like, "they come, they go, and I can see this one won't last long". She weighed all of five and a half stone, which was definitely an advantage in that cramped space and the veins in her hands were her most prominent feature. Sadly, as we became quite good friends, I don't remember her name. I decided to take a look at the auditorium.

I pushed aside the soiled, faded, once maroon curtain and the usherette, in soiled, faded, once matching maroon pageboy cap and uniform with a number of buttons missing, rose from her sprung, push-down wall seat against the back wall and flashed her torch at my feet.

'I'm the new manager,' I whispered.

She switched off the torch and went back to her seat. For a while I stood in the gloom, peering through the cigarette smoke at *The Lone Ranger* "Heigh ho-ing" Silver on the not very large screen, toward which half a dozen still alight cigarette stubs arced their glowing way. Then I left. The place stank, mainly of stale cigarette smoke.

Continuing my tour of inspection, I went around to the back and stepped into the outside roofless disgusting men's toilet. A group of youths were drinking cheap wine, smoking, and playing cards where the floor was dry. They looked me up and down, decided, whoever I was, I wasn't worth bothering about, and went back to their gambling. I went back to the cubbyhole.

For the next couple of days, before every performance, I went up on the stage and made a little speech which went something like this:

'You know who I am. I'm the new manager, okay?' That is very South African, ending a sentence with "okay?" 'There are two things I want to say to you. Firstly I have noticed that a number of seats in this cinema have been slashed or damaged. I couldn't care less. You're the ones who have to sit in them, not me. If you want to be uncomfortable that's your business so go ahead and slash as many as you want. They won't be replaced. The second thing is more serious.

I have seen lighted cigarettes being flicked up here…' At this point, first time round, one landed at my feet and I stubbed it out with my shoe. '…Like that,' I said. 'Now I'm sure none of you have ever seen what a fire can do in a building like this. I'm sure none of you have ever seen or smelled a charred body…' giggles at this, they probably had no idea what the word charred meant, '…well I have,' I continued 'and believe me it's not a pretty sight.' The giggling stopped. 'I am sure none of you want to end up a charred body. The next person to flick a burning cigarette up here will be thrown out and will never, I repeat, never be allowed in again. Is that understood? Right… whose first?' Dead silence, nobody moved. I signalled to the projectionist to start the film and left the stage.

No more seats were ever slashed and no more cigarette butts were flicked at the screen, except for once when the culprit was immediately set upon by those around him. 'Mr Manager says you don't do that hey.' He never did it again. After a couple of weeks the boss of the Fordsburg gang, a scrawny nondescript looking lad who couldn't have been more than fifteen, came up to me one day and said, 'Mr Manager, if you have trouble with anybody, you let me know and we'll sort them out, okay?'

I thanked him and said I would do that. I now had gang protection. Later I even managed to persuade them to leave their weapons in my office before they went into the cinema and quite often there would be a pile of knives, coshes, bicycle chains etc., in a corner of the cubbyhole. What they got up to in the lavatory was their business and I never interfered.

I knew I was accepted by the box office lady when, one day shortly after my arrival, she brought me in a couple of her special rock cakes for my tea. When I say rock, I mean rock, but I ate them anyway and she was pleased.

For the kids of Fordsburg, the Tivoli was a social centre as well as a place of brief respite from the harshness of their deprived lives. One afternoon the usherette hauled a small boy into the office by keeping

Chapter Six

a firm grip on his ear and giving it a good twist if he tried to get away. I suppose he must have been about eight or nine, a handsome child with spiky blonde hair, dressed in filthy singlet and khaki shorts, barefooted as most children were, and with grubby hands and face, let alone feet. I had got used to usherettes dragging misbehaving brats into the office for a ticking off from the manager so, 'What's he been doing?' I asked.

'Mr Manager, he's been pulling a little girl's pigtails. He's made her cry.'

I tried desperately to get everyone to call me by my name but, with the exception of the box-office lady who used it far too frequently and sometimes with a coyness that belied her age, I could never get them to call me anything but Mr. Manager.

'Why doesn't the little girl just change seats?' I said.

'She has, Mr. Manager, he just follows her and does it again.'

'All right, leave him with me.'

The usherette hurried out before her absence in the auditorium could be noticed with the possibility of pandemonium breaking out. I looked at the child, putting on my severest face.

'What's your name?'

'Karel?'

'So, Karel, you like pulling little girls' hair, do you?'

No answer.

'What did she do to you?'

No answer.

'Why don't you take on someone your own size who can hit back, hey? Pull a boy's hair. Then he can give you a good smack in the mouth and see how you like that.'

No answer. I resisted mentioning that there were girls in the cinema who were quite capable of giving him a good smack in the mouth. He could go back in, try his luck, and the result wasn't worth thinking about. 'Well what are we going to do with you?'

He shrugged, lower lip thrust out.

'We can't let you back in there, you'll just do it again, won't you?'

The bottom lip was pushed out even further, mouth turned down at the corners. He sniffed loudly, which was what he needed to do anyway, because his nose was running a rivulet. He wiped it on the back of his hand and wiped his hand on his pants.

'So you'd better stand in the corner.' I pointed. The blue eyes opened wide. This was totally unexpected. 'Go on,' I ordered, 'stand in that corner.'

He turned, took a step or two, and faced the wall. There he stayed, every so often peering over his shoulder to see what I was doing. For a while I ignored him but, after about ten minutes or so, I relented and told him he could go. Five minutes later the usherette brought him back, it seems willingly, because this time there was no holding him or ear tweaking.

'What's he done now?' I asked.

'Nothing, Mr. Manager. He says he wants to stand in the corner.'

I told him I didn't particularly want him standing in the corner but if he went home and cleaned himself up, the next time he came to the cinema I'd let him in free. This didn't really mean very much because he more than likely sneaked in for free anyway but it was a gesture. Home he went and the next time he appeared he was not only scrubbed from top to toe, even his clothes were clean, and his spiky blonde mane was slicked down, all but one stubborn bit that remained upright like a faun's horn and that, for all the world is what he reminded me of. All he needed were cloven hooves and a panpipe.

My employment at the Tivoli didn't last long either. My weekly reports were probably decidedly more sober but the powers that be decided I was worth something better and, at twenty, I became the youngest manager of a major theatre, The Opera House, Pretoria. And that only lasted three weeks because I finally, finally got that call that made me a professional actor.

Volpone was rehearsed and opened in Pretoria and then toured all four provinces, playing one night stands in small towns and villages with longer stays in larger towns and major cities. I saw more of my

Chapter Six

home country in those short months than I would otherwise have seen in a lifetime. Those members of the company with minor parts had secondary jobs, mine being to share with one other, Teddy Darrell by name, driving the mini-bus transporting the actors from one venue to another. The set, costumes, lights, and stage management went in a pantechnicon.

I loved the driving. I could happily sit behind the wheel for hours. I did tend to like speed a bit too much and, at various times in my life, there were some pretty hairy incidents but, if there is a patron saint of drivers, he, or she, has definitely been on my side, like late one night in Johannesburg I was alone in the bus and lost, and driving full tilt down a dark road, suddenly in my headlights I saw this metal barrier across the road. I slammed on the brakes and stopped, tyres screeching, literally six inches from the barrier. I got out and went to look at what was the other side: a forty foot drop or more to a crossroad and moving traffic. On an earlier occasion, driving from Thornville Junction to Manderston, I had to cross the main railway line at a point where the road turned sharply left and you drove up a short steep blind rise cut into the bank beside the line before exiting the other side. As I almost reached the line I had a sudden vision of a train standing in Thornville Junction and slammed on the brakes just as it came through at full speed. I turned to my sister sitting beside me. 'Did you hear that coming?'

She shook her head. I knew there was a sign on the line warning train drivers to signal their approach, I knew he knew he had done me wrong, as the old song goes and, if I cared to report him, he would have been in very deep trouble. I had a great drive one night in Virginia when I was with the Wayside Theatre there and a young member of the company, David Harwell, fell ill and had to be taken to hospital. I really put my foot down, hoping and praying a patrol car would pull me over and I could yell something like 'Emergency! Hospital!' and get escorted in accompanied by wailing sirens and flashing blue lights: very dramatic it would have been, but no patrol car appeared. There's never a policeman around when you want one.

There's always a policeman when you don't want one. I was given my very first speeding ticket when I was in my late sixties in Crete of all places where there are some of the worst and most reckless drivers in the world.

Another near miss happened after the Christmas I spent with our friend Susan Burrell's family in Richmond, Virginia. On, what in England would be Boxing Day; we went to Williamsburg for the day and were walking around in shorts and shirtsleeves and eating ice cream. That evening I had to drive north back to Harrisonburg and, as I drove over the mountains and hit the crest at a fairly decent speed, my windshield in a split second went opaque as the snow hit it. How I never left the road on that steep bendy downward stretch I'll never know. I'd seen the signs warning one about deer crossing the road. There was nothing to say you'll suddenly hit a blizzard so beware! Snow in Virginia does strange things. Driving from Baltimore-Washington International Airport, this time travelling south to Harrisonburg, it happened again. I had been to the Airport to pick up Tom and Kay Arthur, both faculty members at James Madison, and in whose house I was staying. Tom at that time was head of the theatre department and the man responsible for my being there, and Kay, Professor of Art History in the school of art. I arrived at the airport about thee o'clock but naturally their plane was late and it was dark by the time we left the airport. Kay insisted we stop at the first MacDonald's we came to so she could have a REAL AMERICAN burger. We drove along quite happily until, suddenly, about thirty miles from Harrisonburg we hit a blizzard head-on. The snow, driven straight towards us by the wind, was hitting the windscreen at such an oblique angle, virtually horizontal at times, and at such a speed the optical illusion it created was that the car was almost going backwards. After a while of painfully slow going and taking into account any number of skids, 'Maybe we ought to stop,' Tom suggested nervously from the back seat. 'We can put up at a Motel.'

'No,' I growled. 'I said I'd get you home and I'll get you home.' My Taurian heels were well and truly digging in.

Chapter Six

'We're going off the road!' Kay suddenly shrieked, seated next to me.

'How do you know we're going off the road?' I yelled back. 'I can't see the fucking road! It's covered in fucking snow!' Shows you how tense I was behind that wheel, straining to analyse a surrealist landscape where the road signs looked as though they were receding and my stomach was beginning to complain. I had to shoot one red light or the car would have ended up in a ditch when I applied the brakes no matter how gently, and when we got to the bottom of Campbell Street and I turned the wheel to go up the hill and home, the car just carried on in a straight line. However, we eventually made it, but what a homecoming. Kay marched straight into the house and, yelled at Adam, their son, who hadn't done a thing, and started without even taking off her fur hat, to vigorously clean the cooker, one way to relieve tension I suppose.

A cup of coffee was all I wanted and I thought of apologising for my language but decided not to bother.

The fact that I loved driving but couldn't care one iota how a car actually worked used to infuriate my father who loved tinkering. He would spend a weekend pulling his car to pieces, first the Chevvie, then the Plymouth, and putting it back together again. The strange thing was, every time he did it there always seemed to be a part left over, and yet the car still ran. I can't envisage that happening with today's computerised vehicles. If anything goes wrong they have to go for an electronic diagnostic test to find out what the trouble is. I have to admit that sealed batteries that never need water are a distinct improvement but it would be nice to think you could restart a stalled engine with a crank handle.

Driving along in the company bus I remember an actor as camp as a row of tents called Gerrit Wessels sitting with his knitting, glancing out of the window every now and again to tell us which husband we were passing. 'Oh, look, there's my wine-making husband.' Then came a waggle of the fingers at the window. 'Oh, there's my sheep farmer husband, there's my policeman husband,' and so on. He left the theatre to run a restaurant at 3 Anchor Bay presumably with his restaurateur husband.

The actor, Frank Wise, large and of florid type complexion, tried to seduce me but, sorry, Frank, you just weren't my type. 'You don't know what you're missing,' he declared huffily pursing his Oscar Wilde type lips. He played the part of Volpone and, when speaking on stage, he produced an awful lot of saliva. Sitting upstage on my Doge's throne with the lights behind him I couldn't help but see the spray and was glad I never had to work close to him. He too left the theatre and, after a spell in a home for alcoholics, went to work in a department store. Mosca was played by a very well known South African actor, Siggy (Siegfried) Mynhardt. Leontes was played by a rather bad English actor who was also stage director and another compulsive spitter, especially when living up to his name and ranting, which he did most of the time. Vivienne Drummond, who also performed later in England, was in the company but I don't remember the name of the character she played. I do remember she had a large 69 supposedly tattooed but actually done in greasepaint on one bare shoulder. I shouldn't think any of the audience in the hinterland of South Africa got the message. Apart from entrances and exits, I sat up on that Doge's throne looking very self important, so it hadn't taken much rehearsal to block my part.

The set consisted of three sections and I was told it was a snitch from an earlier English production. Could it have been the RSC? There was a circular rostrum in the centre, over which was a domed canopy and, on either side of this, two long rostra like curved wings, also with canopies, but flat rather than domed. Curtains could be drawn around any of these sections when the action changed. Lights were fitted to cross bars on two very tall metal stands downstage, one on either side.

The routine as I remember it was, first thing after breakfast to herd everyone, bags and baggage, onto the bus and drive from the previous night's venue to the one for that evening, drop off the actors at the

Chapter Six

hotel and go on to the venue to sort out costumes and dressing rooms. We played in all sorts of places including at one town a hall where, in what we had to use as dressing rooms, they had been keeping the pigs for an agricultural show, so the pig shit had to be cleaned out before we could do anything else. If we played more than one night the days were our own and I remember sitting in a deck chair on the lawn of some hotel in the Cape, reading a book, when I heard a strange sound coming from some nearby bushes. It went something like a soft "ha… ha… ha… ha" as though someone was forcing out their breath in staccato bursts, and then "ssssssssss" followed by repeats of the pattern. Intrigued, I got up and went quietly over to the bushes, behind which I found two large tortoises mating, and the noise was coming from the male as he steadily made his way up the mountain that was the female's shell, 'ha… ha… ha… ha' and the sssssssssssss was as he slid back down again. A tortoise having it off is a tortuous business. I'm sure they don't get to do it very often.

At another hotel, also in the Cape, the owner kept an African grey parrot in the bar and when one of the company asked him if the parrot spoke, the man said, 'Go over there, hold your glass over his head and tilt it as though you're going to pour your drink over him.' This being duly done the parrot cocked his head to one side, regarded his would-be assailant with a beady eye and said, 'Fuck off you dirty Scotch bastard.'

It turned out this particular bird was previously kept on the veranda and he had a very large, very dirty vocabulary which he used with relish every time a female walked by until, finally, the police, fed up with a stream of complaints, insisted he be taken inside. From that day the "Scotch bastard" line was all he would say. He would have been happy being a theatrical parrot like the one Bernard Miles had at The Mermaid Theatre; a bird that came to exuberant life whenever Christmas approached and he knew it was *Treasure Island* time, and who went back into doom and gloom when the run was over. All year he skulked on his perch in the green room, now and again pulling out his feathers in frustration until he looked like he had a nasty disease but then, as soon as rehearsals started, he was a totally different bird: a lively, luvvie, stage-struck parrot. 'Pieces of eight! Pieces of eight!'

I loved Cape Town and stayed in a wonderful old Victorian house, at Sea Point I think it was, belonging to an artist so it was sort of *La Boheme* time or pre-hippy hippy, a free and easy, come and go as you please sort of existence and a new experience for me. The tour ended in Johannesburg and there was a short break before rehearsals started for *Twelfth Night* in which I was due to play the sea captain but I didn't do it and a young actor named David Rich took the part. He too became an ex-pat in England and a staff director at the English National Opera. I often used to see him when attending the opera at The Coliseum but he never acknowledged me (probably didn't remember who I was) and he carried himself with such an air of snootiness I never acknowledged him.

In Jo'burg I was staying with my good friend, Dorothy Spring, a journalist, a wonderful woman, and a devout Catholic who tried her best to convert me. When I left she gave me a small prayer book and a rosary. Remaining unconverted I've never used them but I have kept them to this day. Her son Tim was in the company on the stage management side. While sitting in Dorothy's flat reading the morning paper I came across an article about a Bud Flanagan Jnr. and a Rhodesian girl companion about to set out hitch-hiking to England. It took no time at all to get to their hotel, meet up with them and invite myself to the party, and that is why I sold most of my meagre belongings, bought a rucksack for the necessities I kept and didn't play the part of the sea captain.

Bud Flanagan Jnr. was not really a very pleasant character. In fact I marked him down as a bit of a shit. He did suffer from some apparently incurable ailment that might have explained things but he was the apple of his father's eye and his father's biggest disappointment. He died quite young in New York. When I got to London I called on Bud Flanagan Senior at the Victoria Palace where he was appearing with

The Crazy Gang but we really had very little to say to each other, a short exchange at the stage door, and I only saw him the once. For some reason or other, for the life of me I can't remember why, Bud Junior had taken charge of our passports but we had only just entered Southern Rhodesia when we came to a parting of the ways and I demanded mine back. From then on I never saw the others again. I was on my own. Sitting beside the road one day, my rucksack in front of me between my legs, enjoying a cigarette, very cheap in those days, I think the ones I was smoking were called *Zimba*, cost two old pennies for ten and the quality was slightly above dried cow dung rolled in newspaper, a young Afrikaner lad passed me on his bicycle.

'Gooie more, oomie, vaar gaan jy?' Good morning, uncle (an often used but polite form of address to an elder), where are you going?

'London,' I said.

He thought for a moment and then said, still in Afrikaans, 'And I'm going to Russia. Have a good journey.' And off he pedalled.

Have a good journey. I was sure it would be and I actually arrived at Dar-es-Salaam, the seaport of what was then Tanganyika, now Tanzania, with little trouble and here a letter I wrote to my mother can describe my journey from there.

"My dreams of a couple of weeks idling in Dar-es-Salaam to recuperate after the tiring journey that far were rudely shattered when Bud Flanagan turned out to be not all he made himself out to be and I found myself penniless and homeless in ye foreign city. This was about 8.30 in the morning, I can't remember which morning, and I do mean penniless. I paid a visit to the Port Captain to enquire into the possibilities of working on a ship. He politely informed me that he had just about had a skinful of South Africans asking about ships. It was then that I began to realise that it is no novelty to meet hitch-hikers en route to Europe from South Africa.

Later in the morning I met a young man by the name of Simon. I got talking to him because he looked like a seaman. He was thinking exactly the same thing about me. He had just finished working with

M.G.M. in "Snows of Kilimanjaro" being paid seventy five pounds per month for holding up nails for another seventy five pound a monther to hit with a hammer but now, having diminished his seventy five pounds to five he was at a loose end. The pair of us decided to try our luck with the shipping in Mombassa. Until our departure I slept on his veranda. The problem now was how to get to Mombassa. The following story will illustrate the old cliché about how small the world is. I met a young Welsh artist in Dar who invited me over to his flat for supper and to look at his etchings[!] We talked about all sorts of things until ten and then tootled over to Maison Blanche for a cup of coffee after which he walked part of the way home with me, home being the fourth floor veranda under the sign "Nazim Mansions." After he had left me to continue alone a car drew up and out stepped Simon and a woman's voice called to me from the car. It was an old friend from home now married and living in Dar. What is more her husband was at university with me. They had picked Simon up at the new Africa Hotel because they said he looked so lonely. He could not help looking lonely. It was the way he always looked: besides which he was writing poetry. They invited him home for dinner and my name cropped up in the conversation. Val decided there couldn't possibly be two G.I.Joneses from South Africa (not two like me anyhow) so after dinner they set out to look for me. They managed to trace me because of my beard, everyone in Maison Blanche having seen the big man with the red beard. The result of this little reunion was that John lent me ten pounds and Simon and I flew to Mombassa, in a Dakota of all things, which I swore I would never travel in. We stopped at Zanzibar and Tanga and after much bumping and bouncing arrived at Kenya's premier port. Another ten minutes and East African Airways would have had to lay in a new supply of brown paper packets.

We landed about four-thirty and I decided to look around the town. Simon meanwhile visited a real low dive inhabited by sailors, prostitutes, etc., where a native band played rotten music and black and white mixed freely. He said he wanted to contact sailors.[!] I wandered down the main street until I arrived at Fort Jesu. After inspecting the fort I

Chapter Six

strolled aimlessly through the Arab quarter, through narrow picturesque streets until I arrived at the dhow harbour. I seemed suddenly to walk out of the twentieth century and back to the days of pirates and corsairs. Even further back as some of the Arabs could have stepped out of a Bible picture book so little have they changed. I went down to the wharf and engaged in conversation with the only European in sight. We chatted about the dhows and the upshot of the conversation was an invitation to spend a few days with him. This was a very handsome gesture on his part and I don't think he realised just how broke I was for I had said nothing to him about my financial position.

He is a teacher at the M.I.O.M.E (Muslim Institute of Education), a graduate of Cambridge. We went home to his flat. The school itself consists of a number of large pink buildings of eastern design, a style of architecture most suited to the climate of East Africa. The humidity of Dar-es-Salaam and Mombassa had already given me "prickly heat", a painful rash up both legs and the insides of my arms. I left a note for Simon at The Anchor Hotel (12/- per day) where we originally deposited our belongings, to meet me the following morning. I never saw Simon again. He was a peculiar chap, very lonely and quite bitter that he had never had a home life or decent upbringing. His father being in the army and posted to various places he never had a chance to acquire a decent schooling. He detested his mother and his parents are divorced. He was evidently the black sheep of the family as he had strict instructions never to go home again, what there was of it. He was intensely grateful for any interest taken in him or any favour done him and I cannot to this day understand why he disappeared so suddenly. Looking back on it now could it have been he felt I had deserted him?

The following afternoon my host and I visited the dhow harbour again sailing down the creek in an outrigger canoe. We took with us a young boy, his mother was a native woman and he belongs to the Royal Household of Zanzibar. He was to act as interpreter, which was not very successful as he could speak very little Arabic and the Arabs could not speak Swahili. The dhows themselves are the most fascinating craft, some of them having magnificently carved sterns. I learned the names of the various craft, booms, sambuks etc., and also that a dhow today costs somewhere in the region of three to four thousand pounds so some of the skippers must be fairly wealthy men. I would have liked to have sailed in one, the fare from Mombassa to Aden being four pounds and if you have plenty to read and can stand living on shark and dates for a few weeks it should make quite an interesting journey. However they only travel with the monsoons and the winds do not change until the beginning of April.

We went first aboard an Indian dhow from Calcutta. It was surprisingly clean [!] but as none of us could speak Hindustani we soon left and made for an Arab craft from The Persian Gulf. We went up to the captain's quarters. Unfortunately he was away in town but the crew made us very welcome. The whole crew sleep on deck and, after taking off our shoes, we sat down on the most handsome Oriental carpets. The crew were the most piratical band of human beings I have ever encountered especially one huge fellow with very pale skin, blue eyes and a vivid red beard, his hair cropped close to his scalp".

I leave my letter here to write about how I remember it today.

My fondest memory of Mombassa was my trip out to a dhow, one of those beautiful Arab ships built entirely of wood and with the large triangular sail that take the trade winds, moving south with them, returning north with them. My friend took me out in a dinghy to where this particular dhow was moored and, when we bumped against the hull, a hand came down and hoisted me up on deck as if I were no more than a ten year old stripling and there, facing me with a huge grin across his face was a giant, the biggest Arab in the world. Not only was he the biggest but his face was pockmarked, he had bright blue eyes and flaming red hair and I swear his mother must have said something like 'Fuck off, you dirty Scotch bastard,' because from where else could he have got that flaming red hair? I loved him on an instant, not sexually, but we spent the entire afternoon glancing at each other every now and again and grinning for all we were worth

Chapter Six

as though we had known each other for years and there was some wonderful secret between us. I can still see his face all these years later. Back to the letter.

"During the conversation a hookah was lit and passed among the crew. I intimated that I would like to smoke it and immediately a fresh pipe was lit. The smoke was quite tasteless and has to be sucked with great force directly into the lungs. The Arabs say this makes for a healthy chest. There was now a general hurly-burly among the crew all vying with each other in offering their hospitality. One brought the most delicious dates, which he kept pointing to and insisting they came from Beirut. Another brought biscuits, a third brewed coffee. With the Arabs one always accepts food with the right hand as they perform their toilet with the left and it is considered an insult to take food with this hand. Being left-handed I found it quite difficult to keep on the right side of etiquette. When one has finished one's coffee the cup is given a gentle shake as an indication that no more is wanted. Not knowing this I drank about six cups and wondered why the boy stood before me obviously expecting to pour more. On leaving we had to shake hands with every member of the crew, as they feel deeply hurt if you shake hands with one or two and ignore the others."

They say if you drink coffee together you are friends for life.

"For four days I haunted the Kilindini docks in the hopes of finding a ship. As the school is about three miles out of town and the docks are another two miles you can imagine how I felt having to walk everywhere and virtually without the price of a cuppa in my pocket as I felt what I still had needed to be hoarded for any emergency. I went aboard Norwegian ships, Danish, Finish, French, British, Italian, Greek and American. After two or three efforts I went straight to the first officer's cabin but the answer was always the same. They were without exception very charming and considerate but I still didn't get my ship. On the Friday night I spent my last ten shillings on a motor launch to take me out into the stream where I went aboard a Norwegian ship, the S.S. Gol. The captain was quite sympathetic and, as he was discharging a fireman, he told me to call around at the agent's the following morning. As he still had not had his sailing orders he asked me to call again on the Monday. I duly turned up on the Monday morning to be informed that he had discharged his fireman and would sign me on. I was jubilant; a ship at last, my ten bob was well spent. At one o'clock he still had not arrived (presumably the captain at the agent's). In his place came a young man who said that at ten o'clock that morning a ship had berthed and discharged a fireman and at eleven o'clock with her new fireman the S.S. Gol had sailed for the United Kingdom. I could have sat down and wept I was so disappointed but weeping would not help. There was nothing for it but to try again.

There were five new ships in port but none of them would take me. I did not want to go back to Gordon's as he thought I was by now well on my way so I collected my rucksack and without any plans started walking down the street. I hadn't gone ten yards when I felt a tap on my shoulder. A young chap was standing next to me. 'Excuse me,' he said, 'but are you a hitch-hiker from South Africa?'

He was with another and they introduced themselves as fellow hitch-hikers from Rhodesia. They had read an account of two young South Africans hitching to Europe. I told them they had got hold of the wrong chap but we discussed our experiences and that night the three of us slept in the churchyard. I slept fully clothed, but not those two. They cleaned their teeth at the garden tap and went to bed in pyjamas using convenient trees to hang their clothes on. The following morning we deposited our goods at a hotel, had breakfast, [with what?] and wandered down to the docks again. I felt better now having company again. We wandered down to the dhow harbour where we watched a film unit filming a scene from "West of Zanzibar" starring Anthony Steele and Sheila Sim.

I then insisted we pay a visit to the editor of The Mombassa Times and tell him our tale of woe saying it was evident we were to be in Kenya quite a while and would like to take a hand in the emergency. He sent us

Chapter Six

first to the police reserve and then to the D.C. [District Commissioner?] but everyone was so vague that one would have thought there was no such thing as an emergency and we were not going to Nairobi on the off-chance our services would be required. He finally decided to send a message on the teletype, and as the answer was not expected until the following day, Alistair and Ting (his name was Bell) retired to their churchyard and I, feeling like a bath and a shave, walked out to Gordon's. He was naturally surprised to see me but when he heard my story he asked for the first time what my financial position was like. I told him quite truthfully that I had but ten cents to my name. I also informed him that I was leaving for Nairobi the following day. The next morning when I went to breakfast he had already left for school and on my plate was a cheque for five pounds.

We duly left for Nairobi with instructions to report to The Elector's Union. We had to split up after a while, Alistair and myself going ahead, Ting following. That night we slept on a veranda at a sisal estate at a place called Voi (about ninety miles from Mombassa). Alistair let me share his flimsy blanket that was much too small so arms and legs were sticking out all over the place. It was a bad night and at about four in the morning the mosquitoes put in an unwelcome appearance. At about seven we picked up a lift in the back of a van (an open truck). Passing through the game reserve we saw wildebeest, giraffe, Thompson's gazelle, buffaloe [sic] and zebra. We indulged in a good breakfast, wash and shave at Mack's Hotel sixty miles from Voi [presumably I had somehow managed to cash Gordon's cheque] and then resumed our journey. The sun was blazing hot and I was wearing shorts. After a while I had to borrow Alistair's hat. The only part of him that got sunburnt were his lips so before we started he plucked a fair sized leaf and held it in his mouth throughout the journey.

On arrival at Nairobi we went to the Queens Hotel where we had to meet Ting. I was beginning to feel bad and, after a hot bath, unknown to the management, and some lunch we rolled up at the Elector's Union. At four-thirty Ting arrived and they put us up that night at the police reserve camp about fifty yards away from a compound of Mau Mau prisoners. By this time I was beginning to feel really wretched. The warmth from the pavement even in the evening hit my burnt legs agonisingly. My head was swimming so I left supper and went to bed. Lying on my back my legs felt as though they were on fire and the top half of my body was as cold as ice. A dull pain throbbed in the back of my head and I shivered with fever. I kept on saying I would feel better in the morning and I did for a while.

The young lady at the Union was most efficient and hearing that Ting had ranching experience and that I too had farming experience she sent us both around to the Board of Agriculture as there are many farmers up here wanting assistants and managers. The secretary there decided we should see the Land Settlement Board the next morning. Meanwhile we saw Alistair off to do a spot of farm watching. That was the last I saw of him but I hear he is in the Nyeri district which is rife with Mau Mau. Meanwhile I had begun to feel bad again. The pain in my legs was almost unbearable and I couldn't stand the sun for more than a few seconds at a time. The giddiness and the headache had returned so I staggered back to the camp and spent the rest of the day and that night on my back. I knew now that I was violently ill but I daren't let anyone know for fear of not getting a job and having nowhere to go.

The next morning we saw Brigadier Channer, of the Land Settlement Board who said he could fix us up but not until Monday. The police, having grown tired of us, we went back to the Union to volunteer as farm guards for the weekend. As we were there I suddenly broke into an uncontrollable fit of shivering. My teeth chattered madly and my whole body shuddered violently. I hurriedly left Ting to make the arrangements while I sat downstairs.

That afternoon we were sent to Naivasha where I was posted to a Captain Todd. I sat up at night with a .45 next to me but by about two a.m. I could take it no longer and went to bed. Sunday I noticed my urine was dark brown in colour and my stomach was upset. I ate nothing all day. Sunday night I sat up until about one. Monday morning a lift had been arranged for me to Nakuru where I was to take up a post with a Mrs Cooper. Brigadier Channer had asked me

Chapter Six

what I know about farming and I told him dairy, crops, pigs, poultry and fruit, trusting to my luck.

'You know the drill on this, do you?' He asked.

'Oh, yes!' I said.

'Do you know anything about flowers?' He asked.

'Oh, no!' Said I.

Monday morning Captain Todd called me for breakfast. I couldn't lift my head from the pillow. He came up to the bed and peering at me intently said, 'You really are sick, aren't you?'

I grunted.

And that is the last thing I remember until I woke up almost a week later in a very comfortable bed in a very pleasant bedroom from whose door I could see the lake and a thousand thousand flamingos. I was starving. If you want to lose weight in a hurry, go into a coma. The good lady of the house brought me some breakfast and I couldn't touch it. I had lost ten pounds in weight and felt as weak as a kitten but for the first time in ten days my head was clear. It turned out I was suffering from sunstroke, malaria, and jaundice all at once and it took a few more days before I was back on tottering feet and ready to go. It seemed that while I was out cold the doctor at one point was almost ready to give me up. I still had a slight pain in the liver and spleen but was well on the way to recovery. That afternoon, still shaky, I set out for Nakuru.

Captain Todd is a cripple and has great difficulty getting around but he and his wife were both good to me. So also was the doctor who knowing that I was pretty flat refused to be paid for his services. Friday night I staid [sic] with the Channers who took me to a performance of "Off the Record" by the Nakuru Players. It was a good production and I had my first real laugh in weeks. I also taught Brigadier Channer how to prune a peach tree and he was most impressed."

If this letter didn't put the wind up my mother nothing would.

Some reminiscences as I remember it all these years later: The architecture of the school buildings was Arabic in design, the exterior walls built with blocks with designed apertures to allow air to circulate. Despite this, the humidity was such that, when you put on a shirt it immediately clung to your body and clothes in a closed closet developed a mould overnight, even if the closet was ventilated with louvre doors. Prickly heat was caused through excessive sweat and loss of salt. On board ship one was issued with salt tablets to ensure against it.

Even as we took off from Dar es Salaam, through the window I could see the rivets popping out of the wing. As we circled and approached Mombassa airport coming in to land I saw the runway literally ended at the edge of a cliff. As we straightened to descend we hit an air pocket and dropped like a stone. There were shrieks from the couple of ladies on board but, strangely enough, it didn't bother me. I just thought, 'Well St Peter, here I come' and the next moment our wheels hit the tarmac.

I don't know why in the letter home I say the plane was a Dakota. I seem to remember it was a DeHaviland Dove, seating seven passengers.

Leaving Nakuru I was taken further up country to Njoro where I met my new employers: an ex-Indian Army major and his wife, a very pleasant very middle class lady who seemed to float everywhere. The first time I saw her at dinner I thought she was ready for bed but it turned out she was wearing her best evening gown. She looked like a little brown hen. One still dressed for dinner in this colonial outpost but, because I had very little in the way of clothing, I was excused. Dinner was served at an exquisitely laid table with patterned cutlery, silver condiment cellars, crystal glasses, folded white linen napkins, in a dining room where all the windows were shuttered and next to each side plate there lay a pistol. It was bizarre. The couple had two young sons away at school in England.

There was a well-stocked bookcase and plenty of records so I

Chapter Six

wasn't going to be short either of reading matter or music. I had my own room and bath a short distance from the main house. The farm produced gladioli for export and I didn't have much to do with the working of it except each afternoon to help carefully pack the cut blooms in long flat boxes and take them down to the railway station in an old Fordson van. I waited at the station to see them safely away before driving back. I had been issued with a pistol which lay on the passenger seat, had been instructed under no circumstances to ever stop on the road, and to be back at the farm before dark. I obeyed the instructions implicitly until one night I had my one and only brush with the Mau Mau. It was evening, the train was late and, by the time the flowers were loaded, it was growing dark. I started off for home. The road was heavily rutted and, in daylight I could see my way, weaving between the ruts and potholes but in the dark I had to take it much more slowly and on reaching a steep hill with trees on either side the old Fordson decided it simply wasn't going to make it unless I dropped down into first gear. I had to stop to do this and, at that moment, I heard the shot, and had I imagined I heard the bullet whistle passed the windscreen? I let go the steering wheel, I let go the brake, I was still in neutral and the van ran backwards and swerved off the road. Had I not stopped to change gear I swear it would have been a bullet through the head because, whoever he was, he was a very good shot. Now came my John Wayne bit. I picked up the pistol, safety catch off, always awkward for a left-hander and, resting my right arm on the door, held the gun over it with my left hand.

And I waited. And I waited. But nothing more happened. I gathered that, unsure of what was going on, the safest thing for my assailant or assailants would be to quietly retire. It was quite a while before I put the van into gear and drove on.

Arriving back at the farm, I was soon luxuriating in a hot bath, pistol in holster hanging on the side of the bath. It was reckoned if you couldn't draw and fire in three seconds you were a dead man. That's what I was told anyway. I went to the main house and found that the local police captain and his wife were guests at dinner. In the lounge we had sherries and the talk was all about "the situation" and recent developments and then we went into dinner. Soup was served. I lifted my spoon, I dipped the spoon in my soup, I lifted my spoon again, I dropped my spoon, spattering the clean white linen and all around me with soup, and I sat there quivering from head to toe, in total shock. The captain looked at me and said, very calmly, 'You've been shot at.'

One evening, enjoying my sherry before going in to dinner, I was going through the bookshelf in the lounge and noticed a copy of Gore Vidal's early gay novel *The City and the Pillar* which I had read whilst at university, and when the major came in I mentioned it. He blew. Steam came out of his ears. Somebody had given him the book; he didn't even finish reading it, he threw it aside in disgust. The whole thing was sordid, revolting, filthy, and he couldn't understand it. I apologised for mentioning it though, if he felt like that I wondered, why hadn't he thrown the book away? We were joined by the wife and went into dinner. It remained in the bookshelf but was never referred to again.

In England a few years back, I think by then we must have been living in Yorkshire, I was watching a programme on television called *The Flame Trees of Thika* all about a pioneer woman starting her coffee plantation in Kenya, and I was enjoying it when, almost towards the end, the penny dropped. I knew this lady. I had stayed on her neighbouring farm and she was nothing like the character being portrayed. That was understandable as Hayley Mills was playing her young and when I knew her she was an elderly lady. Her name was Tilly Grant and she was Elspeth Huxley's mother and, because she hated guns and would feel safer with a man in the house, I was asked to go and stay with her one weekend. I arrived to find her at shooting practice, which involved turning her head away from the direction in which she was firing and pulling the trigger. Servants who were around crouched very low to the ground in case a bullet headed in

Chapter Six

their direction. Seeing me, she stopped, introduced herself with a hearty handshake and, relieving herself of the gun by handing it to me, marched me into the house for a welcoming drink. That was the first time I heard the expression 'What's your poison?' My poison, was a long cool beer. Her poison was a compote glass filled to the brim with gin, a few drops of bitters added, and gone in a couple of gulps. She was short and a little on the roly-poly side and by dinner she had gone through half a dozen poisons with no apparent ill effect. There was a dog for every seat and every cushion in the room; dogs of every size, shape, and colour and, in order to sit, an animal had to be moved.

'No, don't move that one, he doesn't like it. He'll probably snap. No not that one either. Here, sit here.' She shoved some miniature animal off a chair and I sat down. The miniature animal immediately jumped on my lap and stayed there. Dinner was called and the first course was the inevitable soup. I don't remember in Kenya ever having any starter to a meal other than soup but this particular soup was one I had never come across before. It was a consommé with an egg poached in it. I poked at the egg, which was a mistake because I broke the yoke and, as the yellow goo spread across the clear soup I felt my gorge rise. I would never be able to eat this stuff. Eggs is eggs and soups is soups and never the twain should meet. Somehow, out of politeness, I managed to swallow it without puking but I really had to work hard to hold it down and please, never again!

Because of the Mau Mau there was no Kikuyu servant you could totally trust, (one of them could just happen to forget to close the latch on a shutter for example), and you never knew for certain where their sympathies lay. Someone in the night could disappear never to be seen again or be found murdered in the bush, as happened to the husband of a domestic who came crying to the house one morning saying men had come and taken him away. She thought the men were police because they were wearing boots and indeed they might very well have been. Whoever it was who took him he was never found and, in searching for him in the bush, we came across hamstrung cattle which was a sight I will never forget, those poor creatures unable to walk, their back legs slashed with pangas[12] lowing in agony until a bullet put an end to them. I also saw the remains of burnt out huts in which people were not allowed to escape the fire or, if they did get out, were panga'd on the spot. I suppose, thinking of Rwanda, there have been worse times in Africa, but that was not a good time to be a Kenyan, and the atrocities were evidently not all on the African side.

At the end of March I handed my gun to the Major, packed my rucksack, and headed back to Mombassa. My parents, on their way to England, were due there on the Braemar Castle. I said I was going to try again for a ship but, if I failed, I would be back. They wished me well and hoped I would be back.

The Braemar was already in dock when I arrived and I went on board to greet a cheerful dad and a tearful mom who had my fare stashed under her bunk and was all for paying it then and there.

'No, mom,' I told her, 'I started this thing on my own and I'm going to finish it on my own.'

If things hadn't turned out the way they did I don't know whether I would have lived up to this youthful, over-the-top dramatic boastful declaration. As it was I stayed with the parents until it was time for them to take lunch when I trotted down the gangplank and waved a cheery goodbye. I wonder if my mother had any appetite for her lunch.

'But if you go back to the farm you'll be killed!' She had almost wailed. Well, if it had been someone else it would have been a wail but she was made of sterner stuff, it was almost a statement of fact. After all they had brought me up from earliest days to be as independent as possible.

'I won't be killed,' I assured her. 'I've nearly been killed half a dozen times in my life and I'm not going to be killed now.'

They had no sooner disappeared than I was up another gangplank

---

12 A machete

Chapter Six

Braemar Castle

and asking to see the purser who happened to be standing close by going through some paper work. He turned to me and I made my request.

'I can only take you on as a bathroom steward,' he said. 'A man jumped ship at Beira and I need a bathroom steward. Okay?'

Okay? Okay! I could have yelled and punched the air, instead of which I solemnly said, 'Yes, sir, thank you, sir.'

'Right, this man will show you where to go and instruct you in your duties. Formalities can come later when I'm not so busy.'

I was led to the stern and the crew's quarters and shown a lower bunk in a cabin for four, given a general tour and told which were my bathrooms and exactly what was required of me. I would also on occasions be serving afternoon tea on one of the decks. I was fitted out with black trousers and shoes and white steward's jacket and, as the Braemar pulled out of Mombassa harbour I was all set for duty. Inner cabins on a lower deck were not en suite. There were separate bathrooms some of which were my responsibility. This included at set times running a passenger's bath. At five o'clock I knocked on my mother's cabin door.

'Yes?'

'Steward, madam. Your bath is ready.'

She opened the door and nearly keeled over.

My dear naive mother came into contact with an obviously gay character for the first time in her life because the other steward in my section was as camp as a row of tents. Actually it was the second time though she wasn't aware of it. The first time it was Noel Coward who she met in Durban and complained that when she shook hands with him he 'stank of scent.' In those days deodorants for men were a totally unknown quantity.

'Glyn, what's wrong with that young man?' She asked of the steward.

I took her into her cabin and explained. It never really sank in but, from then on, she observed him as though he were some specimen to be studied and pondered over. As for the steward himself, one night two young crew members decided to indulge in a spot of queer bashing and got the surprise of their lives when they ended up in the sick bay. As my Swedish friend would have put it, they had the shit beaten out of them. Our minnie gay steward was an ex-marine and they gave him no problem.

We passed through the Suez Canal, an amazing experience, seeing ships sailing through a sea of sand. The heat was totally enervating and it was a relief to enter the Mediterranean. Soon we passed south of a large island with a beautiful range of snow-covered mountains and someone said, 'Those are The White Mountains of Crete.'

Now, many years later, I live in the shadow of those mountains. *The Lefka Ori.*

Part of my duties on board also lay in the galley where there was a mountain of crockery and cutlery always waiting to be cleaned. Noise and steam filled the place and I couldn't believe how the guy in charge of cutlery, tea services, coffee pots, salt and pepper cellars, etcetera, and known as "the silver king", if he didn't feel like cleaning something in his wired-off cage, simply tossed it out the open hatch. I suppose at the end of the voyage the loss could always be blamed on souvenir hunting passengers. Food too was thrown out by the ton, food for the fishes except when we docked in Genoa and the nuns of

Chapter Six

charity came on board to be given as much as they could carry away.

Disregarding my brief visit to Great Britain as a four year old, it was in Genoa, my chitty stamped by the Italian police, that I first stepped ashore in Europe. As we entered the harbour I couldn't believe the number of ocean going vessels docked there. Huge, beautiful, multicoloured ships were everywhere. Could it still be like that I wonder or does it now, like Cape Town, once such a busy port, berth only the occasional solitary cruise ship?

I couldn't wait to get ashore and my first surprise was to find a man's urinal imbedded in the wall of a building in full view of the street and passers-by. Boy, these Italians were pretty cool about having a piss in public. I had to use it and did, feeling marvellous as I shook it off, but disappointingly no one took any notice. I wanted matches so the next stop was a wonderful old tobacconist with an array of smoking paraphernalia the likes of which I had never encountered before. Then, accompanied by one of the nurses from the ship, we visited the cemetery. This was not an auntie Grace type visit. The cemetery in Genoa is amazing and a must for anybody visiting that city and it is also visited by the city's inhabitants. At the gates there are flower sellers, stalls of religious articles, fast food stalls. Because Genoa is built on hills there isn't room for the cemetery to expand so after a certain number of years you're dug up to make room for someone else. That is, unless you're from a great family or very rich in which case you're probably going to lie in a mausoleum. There is even one there for the Capulets, or was it the Montagues? Maybe both.

Here in Crete we have purchased our burial plot in the local cemetery so we know exactly where we're going to lie when the time comes. The ground here is rock so you're not actually buried six feet under but lie in a concrete sarcophagus faced with marble which we haven't had built yet but will eventually get around to, not too late I hope or we will be put elsewhere. After your coffin has been cemented in as it were, the marble facing with inscription can be laid. Funerals in Crete happen fast, unlike in England where days can elapse before you're buried or cremated, here you die tonight, and tomorrow you're buried. It's amazing how quickly "The Final Office" as it's called can set it up, ready at a moment's notice. There is no cremation. You might turn out in future years to be a saint and where would the relics come from if you've been rendered into ash? Our neighbour, Eleftheria, who helped organise the purchase of our plot, is delighted with it. She's even said she'll have a telephone line installed so we can chat to each other. Presumably that will be for the first forty days because, according to Greek Orthodoxy, it takes forty days for the soul to reach heaven. Telephone calls after that might prove rather difficult.

Apart from the mausoleums, the cemetery in Genoa is filled with statuary of every kind, large and ornate, small and simple. There is one of a little old lady with a basket in front of her and a bread ring in her hand. The story goes that for years she saved up her pennies selling her bread until she could afford her monument and, before her death, she used to visit the cemetery to sit and look at it. The most beautiful statue of all for me was that of a young angel with wings outspread protectively over the deceased below and who I fell instantly in love with.

At one point we were wandering through a sort of arcade and, turning to my companion, I said, 'Do you realise where we're walking there are corpses below us, on either side of us, and above us?

She thought that was too creepy for words. We found ourselves in a large, gloomy, cave-like stone chamber stacked with coffins, presumably awaiting burial, where workmen, by the light of a hurricane lamp, were having their lunch and downing their Chianti seated around one of the coffins being used as a table. They waved for us to join them but we didn't think that was a good idea.

We left Genoa and the Med, passing Gibraltar, and entered the Bay of Biscay, a two day journey from our destination. Each morning throughout the voyage, the crew's steward I think he was, would pop his head through the cabin door and wake us with the same cry,

Chapter Six

'Hands off cocks, hands on socks!' But once we entered the Bay his command was greeted by a chorus of groans as half the crew and most of the passengers went down with mal de mer. I have never been so ill in my life and it was going to last for two days which was the same as saying it was going to be never ending. The surface of the sea was like a mirror it was so flat but beneath that deceptive surface there was a swell that caused the ship, despite her stabilisers, to roll continuously. I was leaning over the aft rail puking for the umpteenth time when an old salt passed by and said to me, 'Put some food in your stomach, boy. Go down to the mess and put food in your stomach. You'll feel better.'

I did as he suggested but it didn't make me feel better. I just went back on deck and puked it all up again.

There were hardly any passengers at dinner. They were all confined to their cabins feeling wretched and, needless to say, not a single bath was run. Our cabins were right over the propeller shafts and we always went to sleep with the sound of the screws' rhythmic turning but, to make matters worse that night, the ship began to pitch, so much so that when the stern lifted out of the water the propellers were revolving in mid-air with a terrific "vrooor-vrooor" sound. Then the stern dropped and hit the water with a thud. It did nothing for my body that, due to my constant heaving, was one big ache. Would it never be over?

On the 28th of April 1953, a day after my twenty-second birthday, I stood on deck and looked from George V docks out over the rows and rows of chimney pots of London's East End.

Chapter Seven

After my cycling trip around North Wales I returned to London. It was a beautiful sunny Spring day I remember and I found myself, rucksack on my back, walking from Victoria, across Green Park to Piccadilly where I indulged myself by stopping to be shaved in an expensive gentlemen's hairdresser. The rest of the day is lost but I obviously had to find somewhere to stay, and seeing a small ad in a newspaper for someone to share a bed-sit, I telephoned the number given and found myself sharing a large and pleasant first floor room in a house in Norroy Road, Putney with a hairy Welshman by the name of Graham Philips.

Another tenant in the house was a young Australian named Donald Copp, originally from Port Lincoln. We knew each other for only a very short time as he had already decided he'd had enough of England and was about to head back to Australia. When he left he gave me two volumes of Thurber, the one inscribed "To a Taurian with Taurian patience" and the other "From a Capricorn with Capricorn impatience." He was currently working at Swan & Edgar's, the large department store on Piccadilly Circus and had previously been a footman at Buckingham Palace. Giving in his notice at the Palace had been a bit traumatic he said because, once taken on, you don't then tell them you want to quit, but a certain princess was making his life hell. It was the time she was having her affair and wanted to marry Group Captain Townsend and Donald put his foot in it well

Chapter Seven

and truly by opening a door and coming across them in flagrante delecto as it were. Evidently, or so he informed me, the protocol was to knock on the doors of private rooms and wait, but public rooms where decorum is supposed to reign, you knocked and went straight in, that was, unless Margaret was in there, and no one had told him that. She never forgave him and never let him forget he was unforgiven, making life difficult for him in a hundred small ways.

I think Princess Margaret was quite a goer from an early age. When George VI and Queen Elizabeth with the two princesses visited South Africa in 1947, the mansion in Durban called King's House used for visiting VIPs was in Morningside, so they attended matins in our parish church of St James where our whole family were in the choir. During the service, though not supposed to of course, I naturally took a few surreptitious peeks at the four figures in the front row pew just a few feet directly opposite me. After all it would probably be the one and only time I would be so close to royalty and, on one more audacious glance, and my last, I was greeted by a very broad wink from the diminutive figure at the end of the row. I immediately dropped my hymnal, much to the obvious annoyance of choirmaster cum organist, Mr Reginald Woodroffe, who glared at me in his mirror, and our parson, The Reverend Austin Giles, who glared at me as he made his way down the aisle between the choir stalls to give his sermon from the pulpit.

The two shows I most wanted to see on my arrival in England were *The Innocents* with Flora Robson and Jeremy Spencer, and *Porgy and Bess*, and both came off a day or so before I arrived. With Donald, before he left for Australia, we took in a number of shows, two of which I remember being the musicals *Paint Your Wagon* and *The Two Bouquets*.

Graham and I spent the night, wet and chilled to the bone, in Hyde Park in the company of hundreds so that we would have a good place from which to watch the coronation procession the following day.

But my only other memory of Graham is how he used to drive me mad first thing in the morning, standing in his underwear at the fireplace with a bowl on the mantelpiece shovelling huge spoonfuls of cornflakes and milk into his mouth and grinding them very loudly with very large teeth. As I wasn't working I was still in bed and there was no way I was ever going to get to sleep again.

But I wasn't out of work for long. Due to Donald's and my visits to the theatre I had to get myself something decent to wear anyway and it was a toss-up between Burtons and 50 Shilling Tailors for the cheapest suit in town. I don't say it was decent or in the best of all possible taste as Kenny Everett might have said, but at least it was respectable if somewhat dull and thus, suitably garbed, I presented myself for an interview at the Piccadilly office of *The Sunday Times* advertising department, having replied to an advertisement in their very own paper.

I had decided, in order to make my mother happy, I would get a nine to five job and hold it down for two years just to prove to her I could do it. Two years would be my limit. So it was that I was taken on as a "rep" selling advertising space in *The Sunday Times* which was a bit silly really because at the time newspaper was still rationed so there was no space to sell anyway. Maybe they were looking forward to the day when newspaper would come off ration and I would have to go out and really earn my salary. That day didn't arrive while at *The Sunday Times* because I was transferred to Kemsley Newspapers' building in the Grays Inn Road to represent two of Lord Kemsley's provincial papers, *The Sunday Mail* and *The Sunday Sun*. I think one might have been in Glasgow and the other in Newcastle. I still didn't really earn my salary. I was there under false pretensions and I got by, as the song goes, with a little bit of luck: quite a large slice of luck really. For example, my immediate boss said to me one day, he wanted me to try and get the advertising account for Canada Life Insurance. This particular company advertised in *The Observer*, Kemsley's great rival owned at the time by Lord Camrose, and the

Chapter Seven

insurance company placed their advertising themselves rather than using an agency. The person for me to see at their office just off The Haymarket was a certain Colonel, or Major, or something. So I duly telephoned and spoke to the ex-military gentleman's secretary and made an appointment for the following day. Before leaving the office I informed my boss the appointment had been made.

The following day however, before I set out, the secretary at Canada Life called me, said she was awfully sorry but the ex-military man had to cancel our appointment and could she make it for another time? I told her not to bother and set off with my two friends in the office, Michael Sutton and John Cutts, to the Kardomah Coffee House in Southampton Row, usually our first port of call where we sat for an hour or so talking movies. John wrote for a screen magazine and later went to the states where he achieved his ambition of becoming a producer. I saw an episode of something he produced which was part doctor series, part police series, part lawyer series, a little bit of everything really and, I seem to remember, shot in Canada. After the Kardomah we went our separate ways, I to the Y.M.C.A. to use the weights in the gym, to swim, and then have a snack lunch with friends after which I may have made a call or two before wending my way back to the office where I would pretend to be frightfully busy until going home time. I still occasionally have dreams where I am in an office sitting at a completely empty desk, the boss is approaching and, as I am doing absolutely nothing and have nothing to show him, not even a scrap of paper, what am I to say and what will his reaction be? I suppose it is a variation of actor's nightmare and serves me right. Nothing was said about Canada Life and, in fact, I don't believe I even thought about it again until a few days later when a beaming boss bustled over to my desk burbling, 'You got it! You got Canada Life!' There were awed congratulations all round.

Evidently a large order had come in from the colonel, or major, or whatever, to that effect and I was for a while the golden boy, the red-hot salesman of Kemsley Newspapers. I never let on that I was a total fraud.

I didn't stay in Norroy Road very long. I grew more and more irritated with the ways of the hairy Welshman, apart from his shlurping crunching noises in the morning, and was driven to find digs elsewhere, elsewhere being a large gloomy house in Cleveland Square, Bayswater where I had my own large gloomy room. After I had settled in, I decided to explore the neighbourhood and went marching down the Bayswater Road in khaki shorts and barefoot, as I would have done in South Africa. Bayswater Road then, from Marble Arch to Queensway, was lined with working girls who sent me up something rotten with wolf-whistles, cheers and remarks such as 'Great pair of legs!" "Nice bum!" I didn't do it a second time. Telephone kiosks were plastered with the girls' cards. One in particular I remember read, "Patient with old gentlemen."

There was a sort of house mother at Cleveland Square who had a very pretty daughter named Cherry whose cherry one night I was about to pick when mother hammered on the door and put a stop to that little bit of naughtiness. A breakfast of sorts was included in the rent and mother, the next morning, let her feelings be known in no uncertain terms as she slammed my burnt sausage down in front of me. Cherry was kept well out of my way. Two other tenants were the sculptor, Nigel Konstam: two of whose bronzes we own; a statuette of a standing female nude, and the mask from the full sculptured head of a Negress. The artist Michael Leonard was the other. For some years we received hand crafted Christmas cards from Michael until he faded away as so many do. I recently read a letter in *The Athens News* from a Michael Leonard living in Rhodes and wondered if it might be the same. Quite possibly, as the astrologer Patrick Walker, whom I knew in London in my early days, had retired there before he died. When I knew Patrick, intimately, he wasn't the big shot, syndicated, fashionable astrologer but ran a gay club called The Spartan. It's interesting that when journalists don't want to out one of their own the obituary usually reads something like, "He remained unmarried," or words to that effect.

Chapter Seven

My club in those days, with gym and swimming pool, was the Central Y.M.C.A. known disrespectfully as "young men chasing arseholes" with some truth in many cases, and some cases not quite so young, and in some cases even elderly, and rather sad. There was this weird Irish doctor who, presumably after morning surgery, would appear in the lounge and just sit there for hours on end gazing into the middle distance, occasionally offering someone the glimpse of a watery smile. I never saw him actually talk to anyone. Another head case was a dyed-in-the-wool young communist who used to come in with carrier bags full of magazines, presumably scrounged from the Russian embassy or bought from the communist bookshop down the Charing Cross Road and, regaling the virtues and wondrous achievements of the USSR, he tried to convert us, not with any success as I recall.

The real head case was a very plain young man with pebble glasses and a face terribly scarred from acne who continuously ranted and raved and drooled at the corner of the mouth about filthy homosexuals and how they all deserved to be put to death. The height of frustration must be a footballer who scores the winning goal and no one in the team wants to kiss him. Did anyone ever want to kiss this raving homophobe?

I'm going to digress here. Every time I write "who", my computer tells me I'm wrong and it should be "that" but I learned at my school-teacher mother's knee that "that" applies to animals and objects and "who" applies to human beings. "The man who…" "The dog that…" It's like hams are hung but people are hanged. Every time I see "that" for "who" I feel the writer should be hanged by his thumbs. Also whenever I hear journalists say "aparthite", pronouncing it as though it were German, instead of "aparthate" which is the Afrikaans pronunciation I wish they'd check it out. Goodness knows there's no excuse, it's been said often enough. Digression over.

I first met a lad at the Y who hailed from Birmingham, Tom Austin, who has remained a friend all my life. We used the gym together, playing handball, and I would get him to throw a heavy medicine ball onto my stomach while I was lying flat. This wasn't masochism, though it might have seemed like it, but an exercise for strengthening the stomach muscles. How come when I wrote to audition for that first James Bond movie I didn't even get a first call? Another friend from those days was a German from Hamburg, Peter Oeser, whose father was in shipping. Peter was in London perfecting his English that, as with so many continentals, was pretty near perfect anyway. We spent a week in Paris together, neither of us speaking a word of French, and stayed in a small hotel just off the Rue du Rivoli. One day at The Louvre we were walking up a gallery, he on one side, I on the other, and he came trotting across to me to say, 'Interesting picture that.'

'Oh, yes?' I replied, 'Who's it by?'

'It's by Catal,' and off he went to his side of the gallery.

After a while he found another interesting picture also by Catal.

Catal? Catal? I'd never heard of a painter by the name of Catal, and seeing an El Greco over the far side I sent him off to find out who the artist was. No one can mistake an El Greco so, when he came back to tell me it was also by Catal, I had to go across to inspect it. Sure enough, on one bottom corner was the artist's name, El Greco, and on the other corner was Catal: short for catalogue, I presume.

There was Roy Miles; the young crimper with a pair of golden scissors who later became a well-known London art dealer and who has had his own autobiography published entitled *Priceless*. Roy too is still occasionally a part of my life, if a distant one, and I have to say this, for which I hope he will forgive me, he is the most priceless of snobs and an inveterate social climber. If you read his book, you will realise the truth of what I am saying by the constant name-dropping and references to any number of lords, ladies, and members of the royal family. I remember him saying to me once in all seriousness, 'Glyn, all I want are the simple things in life, like a Rolls Royce,' and he got one too, in fact more than one.

In my usual impoverished state, life with Roy around could be fun

Chapter Seven

though. Thanks to him, I spent a Christmas day in the Chelsea flat of a multimillionaire manufacturer where the dinner was served on gold plates and I was looking across the table at an original Vlaminck, one of my favourite artists. Also in Chelsea we went to a party taking place in a not very large, rather dingy and crowded bed-sit. There were any number of Chelsea "types" there, as the saying goes, both male and female, a continuation of the Bloomsbury set possibly or who imagined they were, but they were no more strange than the occupant himself, an odd little middle-aged man with purple hair who was introduced to me as Quentin.

Quentin Crisp, who became the most flamboyant of gay icons and made himself famous with the publication of his autobiography, *The Naked Civil Servant*, later beautifully and movingly filmed for television with John Hurt as Crisp.

Another party was at Chiswick. I don't know whose party this was but Beverly Nichols, sitting in a corner like the queen on her throne called Roy over and, waggling his fingers in my direction, said, 'Roy, who is that very interesting young man?'

The interesting young man in question pretended not to have heard and edged off to a far corner of the room. There's an old song that goes, "No one loves a fairy when she's forty," and in the brashness of youth anyone over the age of twenty-four or five was to me way over the hill.

At yet another party, this one in the home of some lord or other in Little Venice, my evening was made and broken in an instant when Michael Redgrave arrived accompanied by two Americans; Gore Vidal and his friend, Austin. After being introduced and stuttering something utterly banal like how much I admired Mr Vidal as a writer, I retreated to the library where I sat myself down with a drink and a magazine. It wasn't very long afterwards that a voice behind me said, 'I hear you make the best curries in London.' Someone else had been making enquiries about that interesting young man.

'I do.'

'When can I try one?'

Well, this was when I was at *The Rose and Crown* and I certainly couldn't ask for the use of the pub kitchen and invite an internationally famous author there to dine. Though, come to think of it, it could have been an experience for him. It was Roy who came to the rescue by suggesting his Chelsea flat and so it was that I made Gore Vidal a curry and fended off his interest by boringly wanting to talk literature all evening while he boringly wanted to regale me with the size of various Hollywood cocks, both ancient by reputation, and modern, by rumour and hearsay more than likely, possibly some from personal experience. As he left he turned at the door and said, 'It's sad isn't it? That we fill our Pantheons with our very own idols only to realise our gods have feet of clay.'

I think he enjoyed his curry though.

When Roy started his first gallery I bought a small picture from him; a mill scene, school of van Ruysdaal he told me, and at his last gallery when he was importing Russian art I would have loved to have bought a small painting of Chekhov's country cottage but, in my usual impecunious state, though it was only catalogued in three figures it was nevertheless out of my price range. Whenever a rich period has come my way, rich being very much a relative term, I have bought paintings, including five by the Irish artist, Padraig Macmiadechain– phonetic spelling, he signs his paintings in Gaelic, but with Padraig, buying was made easy as he let me have them on the never-never.

I do have a full size photographic print of Lord Leighton's *The Hit*, a painting with obvious homoerotic overtones, the subject being an almost naked seated man teaching a practically naked boy to shoot with a bow. After its exhibition at The Royal Academy in eighteen something or other it was bought for a private collection and never seen again until one day there it was in Roy's office. I couldn't believe it. This was another memory of my childhood. I first saw a reproduction of this picture as a sepia print in a book of knowledge and had never forgotten it, and now to stand there and see the real thing was magical. It was for sale for only the second time and Roy had two photographic prints made, one for himself, one for me for the princely sum of £32.34 including VAT. It's a great pity that over the years the colour has faded so the picture is once again in various shades of sepia. It is still a beautiful picture. The story goes that the models were two Jewish boys from London's East End, the elder being in Leighton's employ, and the young one being his brother.

Women Around - designed by Hans Christian - Worthing

It was also Roy who helped to produce my play *Women Around* at the Connaught Theatre Worthing because, as an outside production, a certain amount of finance was needed and he put in £200. I directed this one as well and it had a good reception and local notice but never went further. I was watching a ballet at Sadler's Wells one evening when the idea for the play popped into my head, I don't know why, and went on developing throughout the rest of the evening. What was the ballet? I don't remember but basically *Women Around* is about a pretty boy who all the women in his life are in love with and who spoil him rotten: his mother, his aunt, his sister, the au pair. Two strangers, at that time they were hippies, break into the house and his cosy domestic set-up is upset. There is, as in all my work, a darker side and layers beneath the surface and a psychiatrist would have a field day with this one. The boy keeps pet snakes in the basement, toys in the attic, (nothing is thrown away,) and his dead grandmother lies in her coffin in the room in which the play takes place. Sound like fun? It was, but what ballet could it have been that inspired it?

This was also the play in which, during rehearsals, I reluctantly had to fire Anoushka Hempel. As time went on it became obvious she had a habit that was never going to be eradicated, no matter how hard she and I tried, and that was she couldn't open her mouth without prefacing every sentence with a 'Tch,' a click of the tongue against her top teeth. It was almost as if she were a Xhosa or a Zulu whose languages have these clicks and it was driving the rest of the cast crazy. Finally, as the play's director, I had to take the decision, hateful as it was. There were floods of tears of course but Anoushka was replaced by a delightful actress, Caroline Dowdeswell who, in the time we had left, waltzed into the part no trouble at all.

Who knows? It might have been the best thing for Anoushka. Her list of credits is long and seems pretty impressive even if some of her film work appears to be a little on the edge as it were, so obviously she managed to overcome her little drawback. Wealthily married and, apparently an astute and successful businesswoman and designer with hotels for the rich and celebrated, what need has she for show business? Unless of course she lives with regrets. Hopefully not.

It's annoying when actors have personal idiosyncrasies that get in the way of both performance and play. I went to see a play in Washington D.C. that is a complete blank in my mind except for the set which was on two levels, very modern with masses of supposedly plate glass windows, and a damned actress whose head was continuously bobbing even when she wasn't speaking. It almost got to the point where I wished it would bob right off and go rolling across the floor.

Michael Denison I called the "toe actor." On stage with him it was difficult not to be continuously looking at his feet as his toes in his shoes went up, his toes went down, his toes went up, his toes went… Pearle Celine would have killed me.

And at the Y.M.C.A. I also met and became friends with Peter

Chapter Seven

Mackie who, at the time, was a student at RADA but who never went on to make the theatre his career. At the Y he and I also used to indulge in vigorous games of handball though I don't recall any exercises with the medicine ball though there might have been. It's sad in a way that I fell so very much in love with Peter as one of the first things he said to me was, 'I hate queers.' This was evidently in response to someone trying it on when, as a child actor, he was in a production of *The Wind in the Willows*. If he stayed overnight at my place he would sleep with me, both of us stark naked, but definitely no touching. Many years later he confessed to Chris that I was the only man he could ever have loved. Too late.

Peter also writes but, in the early days of our friendship after leaving RADA, he was more a jack-of-all-trades like being a builder, which he maintained, was a doddle as all you needed was a bit of common sense. With most of the builders I've had to deal with I'd say common sense was the last thing they possessed.

When I was a kid at Fleming Johnston Road I must have done something rather stupid one day because, with a ticking off, my mother finished up by telling me to go down to the shops and get some common sense. I thought it very generous of her to give me half a crown with which to get it. Our next-door neighbours were a family by the name of de Jongh and Mister de Jongh was a shoe repairer. He had his workshop in what was actually an old lock-up garage a quarter of a mile away just before you reached the row of shops and I went in and gathered up a handful of sawdust that he spread on the garage floor to keep the dust down, borrowed one of his empty tobacco tins, filled it with the sawdust, then I went home to present my mother with a tin of common sense. I felt even more of an idiot when my smart-arse gesture backfired (no pun intended) as she laughed and said she really did want a tin of *Commonsense*, a product for cleaning or for some other domestic use. Maybe it was a cockroach powder.

When I was very small I never used to eat breakfast at home but always slipped through a hole in the hedge to have it next door because I firmly believed, erroneously no doubt, that Mrs de Jongh made better porridge than my mother. She was a large hearty woman who wore pince-nez that kept me wondering how they stuck to her nose and, although I loved her and her porridge, I loved her daughter, Olga more. There were three children in fact; Hubert was the eldest, followed by Millie and then Olga. I even ironed my socks to go to the movies with Olga.

'What on earth are you doing?' My mother asked, 'you don't iron socks. You just put them on, and nobody's going to see them.'

In the Roman Catholic cathedral in Durban, Olga married one of the visiting English sailors, Dennis Godfree, and moved to live in Croydon. They had one son, David, who unfortunately suffered meningitis as a child, which left him handicapped. Olga died sometime in the mid-seventies and I never saw Dennis or David again. I hope I never allowed my antipathy to show but I never took to the man right from the beginning and, once Olga had gone, I didn't feel I wanted to keep up with him.

I remember, during one of my out of work periods, helping Mackie on a job where we had to lay a pavement light outside a shop in Kensington. My but those little square glass panes all together in their metal frame don't half weigh a ton. It took us virtually a whole morning to manoeuvre and set it in position. We used to lunch just off Kensington High Street in a vast Fred's caff: real chips and H.P. sauce with everything type meals. Peter did his National Service as a Military Policeman and was posted to Northern Ireland as I remember. At one time I stayed in his mother's mansion flat in Barnes, just over the bridge from Fulham and later shared the attic bedroom he created in his mother's house in Upper Richmond Road. In the height of summer, right under the roof, it was like an oven in there.

I went to The Vanburgh, RADA's old theatre to see him in a production of *Hobson's Choice* and was most surprised to see him lift off the stove with a bare hand an iron pan in which sausages had supposedly been frying and whose handle would in reality have been red hot, and I thought, 'this is England's premier drama school?' Many years later I saw another student open a French window by putting her fingers through a, of course nonexistent, pane of glass.

When I was in a play called *Who Goes Bare*, in 1972, the play in which I met and worked with Sheila Bernette and Frank Marlborough, the couple for whom I wrote *Little Footsteps on the Petals*, someone on the management team had referred during rehearsals to "a theatrical moment" and Sheila and I would stand backstage during performances spotting supposed theatrical moments in order to keep sane, we both hated the play so much. Joking aside there are theatrical moments, good and bad, that stay forever in the mind, and Peter's lifting of the frying pan is a small example of the bad.

After my arrival in London it wasn't long before I was haunting the Gods, the only theatre seats I could afford and it was at the, alas, long since gone, King's Theatre in Hammersmith that I had the good fortune of seeing Donald Wolfitt's *Lear*. Stories about Wolfitt are legion, told with relish by those who knew or worked with him and those who never did but enjoy telling the stories anyway. That highly diverting and moving play *The Dresser* may or may not be about Wolfitt but ham or no ham, for me his *Lear* was definitive. I can still in my mind's eye see, far below me, that tiny figure as Lear enters with Cordelia dead in his arms, and still hear the words that are actually written down, "Howl, howl, howl, howl." Wolfitt said those words. He didn't scream or shout, yell or cry. There is no way of describing how he said those words. They came from the mouth of a man who had seen his own vision of hell. Each howl seemed to have been torn from a gut so twisted with pain it's a wonder any sound came out at all. I felt the prickling of my scalp as my hair stood on end, the goose pimples on my arms and legs, that awful feeling in the groin when you are suddenly confronted with something you might wish you hadn't seen, and I gasped out loud. I left the theatre still trembling; such was the impact he made on me.

The only other time I can remember gasping out loud was when I directed the play *Orphans* at James Madison University and the young student actor, Ron Copeland, playing the character 'Treat' seemed incapable at the end of the play of giving me the emotion I felt the moment needed. Then, on the last or maybe it was the penultimate performance, he gave out such a cry of anguish it was a primal scream as he hurled himself over the couch and, involuntarily, I gasped. The whole theatre must have heard it because I was standing at the back of the auditorium and, when I went back stage, he said, 'I heard you.'

Another example, still in Hammersmith, this time at the old Lyric Theatre, a house that gave us some notable theatre in the fifties: Gielgud in *Venice Preserved*, Trevor Howard, pissed as a newt giving his all in *The Cherry Orchard* and the Cambridge Marlowe Society's *Edward II*. Edward's death scene is enacted thus: two men enter with a table. The executioner, all in black, follows them. Edward knows what is about to happen. He is desperately afraid. The executioner lays Edward down and, kneeling beside him, takes the king in his arms, rocking him, stroking him, soothing him as if he were a babe, before gently laying him on his back. Quickly the table is inverted and placed across the king's body, the red hot poker is produced, the two assistants jump on the table, Edward's leg is raised, the executioner thrusts in the poker, Edward screams and screams and screams and screams. The executioner steps back, letting out a long shuddering sigh, framing his genitals with both hands in the shape of a heart and it was at this moment that I swear I saw the semen stain his breeches. 'Was it not marvellously well done?' Talk about suspension of disbelief! It was shattering.

Another such moment came in Seneca's *Oedipus* at The Old Vic when Jocasta pierces her vagina with Oedipus's sword only, here, the action was symbolic, the sword being represented by an obelisk rising a sword length from the stage. But as Jocasta, with splayed legs stood behind the obelisk and lowered herself behind it with a series of jerks, such is the power of imagination that symbol became reality and it was almost impossible to watch.

Chapter Seven

A bad example came during the production of *The Power and the Glory* starring Paul Schofield at The Phoenix Theatre. Schofield had developed this extraordinary accent that was presumably meant to be Mexican and which, after a moment of shock, one accepted quite happily. He has this gritty offbeat voice anyway. The setting was a barred cage in which a number of filthy, ragged, tormented prisoners huddled, with guards patrolling outside. The priest character played by Schofield is unceremoniously thrown into this prison and for a few seconds he stands looking around. Some of the prisoners, curious, eye him in return, others ignore him. I am totally gripped by the illusion of heat and stench, of dirty, sweaty, tortured bodies, of pain and fear, despair and desolation. After a moment he spots in a corner this disgusting, shit-encrusted bucket, walks across to it and, looking down, says very quietly, 'Is there water in there?' And from somewhere amongst the huddled masses comes this cut glass, county, pink cardy and string of pearls voice saying, 'Why? Are you thirsty?'

That one brief moment, those four cut-glass little words, and the whole carefully built-up atmosphere went down the tubes. End of play, at this point we might as well all go home.

At the Y I went back to being an amateur to play my first part in England, Harding in *She Stoops to Conquer*, and then I joined a group called The Taverners who, as the name suggests, took plays into pubs and, in holiday times, went as far afield as Great Yarmouth where I had my freckles tickled. It started to rain while we were on the beach one day, typical English summer, and we made a dash for the pier to stand beneath it. I felt these fingers run down my back and, turning around, saw this young girl who jumped a mile and said, 'All those freckles!' Maybe she was just wondering if they were real.

Naturally I suppose everyone had to take his or her holiday at the same time, which must have been quite an achievement. The group was run by a man named MacCarthy, simply known as Mac, and the two plays I remember in which I performed were one called *The Fifty Mark* and Andre Obey's *Noah* in which I played the bear, my one and only skin part and, my god, it wasn't half hot in there. I always remember that play because, for Noah's big climactic speech, Mac used the finale to Stravinsky's *Firebird* as incidental music and it was very moving.

It was also while working at Kemsley's that I wrote my first play, *The River of Sand*, a play naturally, as it was my first, set in South Africa. The action takes place shortly after the Boer War and the leading character is an elderly Boer woman. The play couldn't be produced in South Africa because there were Africans in the cast and a mixed cast couldn't play together on stage. I sent the play to Flora Robson who was ideal casting for the lead. She sent it back with a letter saying thank you but no thank you, "What would my fans say if I played a part like this?" A part like what may I ask? What on earth did she mean? There is nothing unsympathetic about the role. The woman is a strong character, as Boer women had to be at the end of a war in which their men folk were defeated, when women and children died in concentration camps and saw their homesteads burnt to the ground. But to what could Miss Robson have taken exception? To this day I have no idea. Actresses are strange creatures. They continually wail about playwrights not writing parts for women but, when they do, they refuse them. I have written three plays with all women casts, only one of which has been continuously played for a good many years, mainly in Germany professionally, but all over the world by amateurs. I sent *The River of Sand* to Granada Television way back in the fifties and their reply when they returned the script was, "Who's interested in South Africa?" Timing can be everything in this business.

I think the nicest rejection I ever had, if a rejection can ever be called that, was from Beryl Reid. When I was at The Haymarket in 1982. Beryl Reid was at The National Theatre and I sent her my play *Red in the Morning*. I addressed it to her direct at the National stage door with a covering letter to say I was doing that because I didn't really trust agents. She immediately gave it to her agent complete with letter as I realised when, about a week later, I received a phone call from him saying he had read the play and was passing it on to Beryl with his recommendation but not to expect an early reply as she was dyslectic and it took a long time for her to read a script. Also, despite his recommendation, he didn't think she would do it and, when I enquired as to why not, he said he felt she would be afraid of it. Sure enough and, again within a very short period for a dyslectic, the play came back with apologies.

A short time after I was at Acton rehearsing a television for the BBC and one lunchtime in the canteen, having served myself, I was waiting at the cashier's desk when I heard this voice behind me say, 'I know what I've forgotten, I've forgotten the darling little pats of butter.'

That's Beryl Reid, I thought and, turning around, sure enough it was she. So I waited where I was and when she arrived at the cashier's and had paid her money I said, 'Excuse me, Miss Reid, you don't know me, my name is Glyn...'

I never got any further.

'The play!' She shrieked for the whole room to hear, 'The Play!'

She insisted I sit at her table, introducing me to her director and the six or seven people seated there with, 'This is Glyn Jones and he's written this simply marvellous play I'm not going to do.'

When I asked her why she wasn't going to do it, she said.

'Oh, I couldn't, my dear, I simply couldn't, What if I wanted to *GO?*'

I had always wanted to write a piece of Grand Guignol as produced at that little theatre in Paris before it folded but I soon came to realise why their plays were literally one-acters. You cannot do a whole evening of Grand Guignol. Each playlet had one specific piece of horror, so I decided to write the well-made full length two act play with moments of Grand Guignol, and the gore that was engendered obviously terrified her.

In the fifties there was a lovely actress named Janet Barrow who had a "salon" in her studio house in Notting Hill where I would later start directing in a small way with a group of young actors, and *The River of Sand* was performed there as a reading. The patron of the salon was Flora Robson. Did she attend the reading to hear how what she had turned down actually sounded? She did not. The irony of it being that she was in South Africa at the time.

The only more mature person in the group was an actress by the name of Rosemary Matthews, who received a rave review for a performance she gave in a production at a theatre club when she was eighteen. The revue was in *The Daily Mail*, and she lived off the memory of it ever after, but she never achieved anything. When I knew her she was working for a small-time educational publisher

Rosemary Mathews

Chapter Seven

getting the occasional walk-on on television. I wanted for many years to write a play about Rosemary, her story being so typical of the many who never make it, but it wasn't until she died and I had news of her death whilst teaching in Denmark that I sat down and wrote it. Like Coward, who could rattle something off in record time, it wrote itself and was finished in five days, quite a difference from my very first, *The River of Sand* that took two years. Naturally it is just called *Rosemary* and is yet one more waiting to be done. I thought Alan Aykbourn in Scarborough might take to it but his letter on returning it said he was afraid his aged audience could be upset by it. It was performed as a play reading at JMU, which enabled me to see its faults and rewrite. Now it sits in the cupboard, still unwanted.

When I think of the number of plays I've written that have never found a home and I see London theatres packed with musicals that run for ever, and revival after revival, I think of a man called Paul Butters who I knew in the early sixties, not engaged in the theatre but a solicitor from Stafford, with about twenty plays under his belt, one of which called *Daggers Drawn* I was supposed at one time to direct, a plan that as usual came to nothing. But reading Paul's plays I knew they were never going to get anywhere they were so terribly old-fashioned, as though he hadn't actually seen a play since before the war, but I wonder how many thousands of better scripts are out there looking for a home. I don't know whether it is an apocryphal story or not but it is said that a manager had a play running in London which was coming off and he wanted to keep the theatre for another he had out on tour, so he needed to put in any old rubbish just for a couple of weeks. Consequently he merely reached out to his manuscript shelf and pulled down something that had been lying there for months, unread and gathering dust, threw it to his producer and said, 'Here, get this on.' The play was *Dial M for Murder*.

I entered my play *Twilight of Aunt Edna* in a competition at the West Yorkshire Playhouse and it came back with a highly complimentary letter and two readers' comments which, had they been newspaper revues, would have been raves. Three plays were chosen out of two hundred for readings and *Edna* was one of eleven, finalists I suppose you'd call them. Shortly afterwards I received a letter out of the blue from another playwright who was evidently one of the judges and her letter read:

> *Dear G Jones*
> *Excuse my presumption in writing to you.*
> *Your play was short listed but did not make it to the last three–whatever gets chosen is always so incredibly personal. All of us found favourites out of the 200 or so plays entered. I only skimmed through yours but if you'd like to talk about "Aunt Edna" or I can help in any way, would you like to ring me? I know of no way to help but appreciate those who entered and are good writers will be, as I usually am, screaming with frustration.*
> *Sincerely.*

It was extremely good of her to take the trouble to write an encouraging letter but, as she only "skimmed" through my play in the first place and as she knew of no way to help, I think I wrote and thanked her and left it at that.

The interesting thing is that not too long afterwards I sent *Rosemary* to the West Yorkshire Playhouse and this one they did want to do something with, as a reading.

> *Dear Glynn* (Name spelt wrong).
> *Re: Reading of 'Rosemary'*
> *Just to bring you up to date on plans for the reading. I have had to change the date of the reading since last time we spoke–the new date is Monday March 21st. The reading will take place in the afternoon. We should meet for a chat before hand [sic] to discuss the play and the reading.*
> *I will ring you on Tuesday next week to confirm this date as we are waiting to check actors' availability. If this date is not good for you do let me know.*

Best wishes.
This was from the "Literary Co-ordinator."

The next letter, still from the "Literary Coordinator" read in part, "I have had the play on hold in the hope of doing a reading but unfortunately this looks less and less possible as time goes by due to the pressure on the time of the actors in our companies."

In other words, as the Americans would say, they just couldn't get their shit together. Back came the script.

In 1993 the Royal Court put it about they would like to do more "well-made" plays so I sent them a bunch, five in all. The following reply came back with the plays:

Dear Glyn Jones,
I am finally returning your plays, which have now all been read by our Literary Department. We found them all interesting, but have decided not to take any of them further.
You may wish to know that Rosemary and Generations were especially highly praised, the former because of its unsentimental treatment of the play's subject, and the latter because of its atmosphere, tension, and characterization.
I am sorry we are not in a position to work with you any further on this, and we wish you all the best in getting them staged elsewhere.
Yours sincerely,
Stephen Daldry - Artistic Director

Well, if they liked *Generations* so much at the Royal Court, and if the theatre faculty at Carnegie Mellon in Pittsburgh thought the play was written by a black lady from the Deep South instead of a white fella from England, I wondered if the ethnic and feminist approach might possibly ring a few bells with The Royal National Theatre, so I sent it to them with an altered title page and a covering letter saying it was by a student of mine in the states by the name of Pijama Brown. It didn't work. Back came the script, this time not from the

"Literary coordinator" but the "Literary Manager" saying *'there were many things in it which he enjoyed but was afraid he couldn't really see a way forward for it at the National. Nevertheless thank you for this introduction to Ms Brown's work. Do wish her luck with the play in the States. [sic]'*

You really would think that, by this time, any sane person would have given up and become a shelf stacker in B & Q but, no, we plough on, ever hopeful. The problem is there have been so many close decisions and near misses that, even with all the disappointments and put downs, thousands and thousands of words later, one is still at it.

During the days of the salon I did a walk-on in a BBC TV production of *The Trojan Women,* and one of the two directors was Casper Wrede. I gave him *The River of Sand* to read. He was enthusiastic but got nowhere in trying to get it produced, but that was probably one of the first near misses. Then I wrote a play called *Between Two Sighs*, inspired by a poem by W.H. Audin in which an unwanted child, the result of a quick shag, is born divinely fair, and a wanted child conceived out of love is born deformed and ugly. There was a close call this time at The Belgrade Theatre, Coventry but no, the final reaction was, what if there were people in the audience with such a child? How would they feel watching the play? And then of course along came *Joe Egg*, which answers that question.

If no one wanted to do my plays at least I could take off my writer's cap and put on the actor's.

It was the production at the Beeb of *The Trojan Women,* renamed for some reason, *Women of Troy* that made me a believer in an Equity closed shop, as all the extras in the studio were medical students. So, okay, students need money just as much as anybody else, but they were doing legitimate actors out of work. Later when I was in half a dozen episodes of a musical offering by Associated-Rediffusion, not doing very much I hasten to add, directed by Joan Kemp Welch, the star was the South African born singer, Dickie Valentine, and one episode his drummer wasn't needed so was given a part. Again this

Chapter Seven

meant an actor wasn't working. We all know about producers' and directors' lovers, male or female. What I didn't expect and didn't approve of though when it was brought in, was the closed shop being so stringent that students graduating from drama school found it almost impossible to enter the profession, with provincial theatres rationed as to the number of cards they were allowed, and no going straight into a London theatre. Witness the hullabaloo that was set up when Kenneth Branagh was cast in *Another Country*. He did get in, and what great publicity with which to open your career.

While I was still at Kemsley Newspapers a familiar face from Glenwood High turned up in London, John Lewis, who had come over on the *Llangibby Castle*, her last voyage before the breaker's yard. He was staying in a poky little hotel near Russell Square station and did something that never occurred to me when I first arrived, which was to pay a visit to the South African Embassy to enquire after former friends who might be around. He got my address in Cleveland Square and found lodgings for himself in Earls Court before its popularity led to the great Australian invasion and it became known as Kangaroo Valley.

Bed-sits were inexpensive then but often pretty grotty with their shilling in the meter gas fires and rings for boiling kettles or heating baked beans, and a chilly bathroom half way down the stairs, so we decided to share a flat and found a very comfortable one, reasonably priced at 68 Holland Park. It had a back gate onto Holland Park Avenue almost opposite the underground station and we were in residence until one morning I woke up to find John gone. It turned out he had got up in the middle of the night and, without a word, had slipped out and made his way by cab to St. Mary Abbott's Hospital where he had a tube thrust down his throat to regurgitate his dinner and was operated on for acute appendicitis. As a week in the hospital left him flat broke we could no longer afford the flat and moved into a fairly decent first-floor bed-sit in Onslow Gardens.

If blue plaques were to be put up outside all the places in London where I have lived they would amount to at least twenty. There were two different bed-sits in Onslow Gardens and another just opposite South Kensington tube, and after my spell with Peter Mackie in Barnes and Upper Richmond Road I moved, with Tom Austin and my sister, into a ground floor flat in a house in Fulham, Townmead Road right opposite the power station. The house was owned by two of Tom's friends who had the flat upstairs dolled up with black and purple flock wallpaper like an Indian restaurant. I'm led to believe the house was bought with funds from a dog racing scam: feed the champion dog to lose every race until the stakes are high enough and then starve it to win. Whether this is true or not is anybody's guess. I don't remember their names but the younger of the two was called 'Erwith.' It was the writer Stanley Miller who named him that as he was never seen without his dog on a lead so Stanley called him "Er with the dog," which became Erwith, and the dog's name was Derf: Fred backwards.

It was while living in Fulham that I had a letter from my mother enclosing another from Kenya. Not having been in touch with Njoro since my departure, the Major had written to my South African home address, and the letter was to tell me he was coming to England and he would like to see me again. In fact he had already arrived and was staying at a large hotel in Victoria. So I rang and we arranged a rendezvous at Piccadilly underground after I'd finished work the next day. There he was, waiting for me, looking very handsome and, with his dark tan, standing out from the pasty-faced, scurrying, rush-hour crowd.

After a sumptuous Chinese meal we went to view the newest thing in town, *Cinerama* at the Casino, now the Prince Edward. Throughout the film he kept coming out with the remark, 'Oh, didn't they have fun?' This was said in such a school-boyish way the amber light should have at least flickered but, as I have already stated, I am the greenest of greenhorns. I've lost some wonderful opportunities because I didn't realise what was expected of me and I've been caught in awkward situations for the same reason. We came out of the cinema and he

Chapter Seven

asked where we could go for a drink. It was now late, I was tired, I wanted to go home. I had my one and only nylon drip-dry shirt to wash for the following day and, if I waited much longer, I would miss my last bus.

'Sorry, but you're in London.' I said, 'Specified drinking hours and all that and we've passed them. All the pubs are shut by now.'

There were clubs we could have gone to but I didn't think he would appreciate that kind of club so I kept my mouth shut. But I didn't get away that easily. He suggested we went back to his hotel. Well, he'd given me a wonderful evening so the least I could do, as he was alone in London, was accept his hospitality and keep him company for a while.

We arrived and went up to his room where, evidently, or so he informed me, he was within the law to order drinks which he proceeded to do. It must have been about half an hour later that I announced it was very late, I had to go to work on the morrow, and it really was time to be heading home.

'Stay here,' he said.

That took me by surprise. I looked at that huge double bed, pristine white with masses of downy pillows, and for a moment I was tempted. After all it was a long walk from Victoria to Fulham and by this time I really was very tired, but all in all I didn't think it a good idea and politely turned down the offer. As I almost got to the door, the bombshell dropped.

'Do you remember in Kenya there was a book in the bookshelf?'

I turned back to look at him standing in the middle of the room. To say I was shocked is putting it mildly. He was the one who had gone on about filth and disgust and non-understanding and, if I had come on to one of his sons, he would have had me clapped in jail without a second thought.

'Why didn't you say something earlier?' I asked. 'I could have taken you to half a dozen places where you could have found someone to bring back.'

'No, that's not what I want. It's you.'

I was almost speechless. I burbled apologies. I thanked him for a wonderful evening but I was sorry, this was not on, and good night. I closed the door behind me leaving him still standing in the middle of the room.

I walked home to Fulham, thinking all the way, and the most stupid thought that ran through my head was, "what would I do with a man with a moustache?" This was before the day of the clone when it became the fashion to wear one. I lay in the bath still thinking; only now I was thinking I could have been a little kinder. I didn't have to leave him as though I were being chased by a swarm of bees. He would think he had made the most ghastly mistake and be worried sick. I kept on hearing 'Oh, didn't they have fun?' and thought, he must have missed out an awful lot when he was younger. Had he been bottling up this desire all these years and what was in me that I was the one to trigger it? This was the first time a married man had come on to me and, in my mind, I kept on seeing his little brown hen wife. I've had my full quota of rejections and unrequited love so I wasn't exactly ignorant of the way he must have been feeling, having dreamt for months of the moment that didn't come true, that I just couldn't make true for him. Neither, and this was my one real regret, did I get in touch with him to set his mind at rest, and I never saw or heard from him again.

It never ceases to amaze me that people still can't bring themselves to believe there are those in their neck of the woods, family members or friends, who deviate from the mythical one hundred percent heterosexuality that is supposed to be the hallmark of the real man, or that so-and-so, surprise, surprise, is bisexual. The Freudians are right, all men are bisexual, only to different degrees, and the sooner this Judeo/Christian idea that it is abnormal, sorry David and Jonathan, is given up, the better, and there can't be many men between the ages of sixteen and sixty who haven't at some time in their life been attracted to, fallen in love with, wanted sex with, played around with, been fascinated by, had erotic or romantic feelings, not necessarily leading to anything physical but romantic nevertheless, for another man. After all, as Goethe said, amongst the many things he did say, "How can you call anything in nature unnatural?"

So why the big brou-ha-ha when it was suggested that Laurence Olivier had an affair with Danny Kaye? Why the shock when it was revealed Rock Hudson was gay and dying of aids? The shock wasn't because he was dying of aids but because this handsome, apparently "normal" matinee idol film star was gay. Why isn't it possible that Cecil Rhodes was in love with his male secretary or that Baden-Powell had these nasty feelings lurking way way down, or that Kitchener had an emotional hard on only for his aide de camp? A recent storm in a teacup has been from a group of Greek lawyers who objected to Alexander The Great being portrayed in the latest film as bisexual. Was Hephestion Alexander's lover or was he not? It's interesting that African dictators and the like, wanting to put down potential rivals, immediately accuse them of being homosexual and in the financial scandal that has rocked the Greek church, the spectre has risen again, an archbishop being accused of sexual advances towards a young cantor, and it certainly isn't the first time that whispers, rumours, and innuendo, or downright accusation have helped to destroy lives and careers. Now it is being suggested that Howard Hughes had affairs with a number of big Hollywood stars. I can't help but think that Gore Vidal was right when he said there are no homosexuals, there is only homosexuality. I think it's a terrible pity the terms "homosexual" and "heterosexual" were ever invented in the nineteenth century. The homosexual appellation is so overused by journalists and others it is sheer tautology and only helps to continue the isolation of the gay community. If Jim and John are having an affair is it really necessary to say it is a homosexual affair? It couldn't be anything else. After all, they don't write that Jim and Jane are having a heterosexual affair do they?

Hollywood is at last, in some cases, beginning to come to terms with the fact that faggotry need not be a turn-off except in the very centre of the Bible belt where God hates gays and, in the words of a Christian Ku Klux Klansman, 'I hate Jews, I hate Niggers, I hate faggots. I hate them because they're there.' What a boring mess though was made of *Troy* because Hollywood simply couldn't allow that Patrokles and Achilles were lovers, so they made them cousins. Cousins? Achilles is so low-key about death in battle including the possibility of his own but, when Hector kills his "cousin", he goes totally ape-shit. For a brother maybe, for a lover, definitely, but for a cousin? Absolute nonsense unless love was involved. The problem with most homophobes of course is that love is never involved in a relationship. As far as they're concerned it is simply sex, nothing more.

Of course, after the labelling and persecution that came about during the eighteenth and nineteenth centuries, culminating in the trial and imprisonment of Oscar Wilde, (presumably once a happily married man), and continuing well into the twentieth century, being brought up and educated the way they are, unless she is lesbian with her own way of life or of a very strong, forgiving character, it would come as a shock for any woman to discover her husband straying in the homos direction, but it happens much more frequently than is admitted.

On Ceri's second visit in 1958 I had moved into 63 Nevern Square. She arrived unexpectedly, so unexpectedly that I came home one afternoon to find a strange woman sleeping in my bed. I was only grateful that she didn't find anyone else sleeping there which could easily have been the case. This was the time of the coffee bar. They were opening up and closing down everywhere and Ceri went to work as a waitress in the Norrland in South Kensington where I could sometimes be found of an evening washing dishes or peeling potatoes. Then I was cast to play Herring in *Grab Me a Gondola* and Ceri moved into my room to keep it for me till I got back from the tour. Tom Austin and John Lewis also lived at one time in 63 Nevern Square and an aspiring young actor named Bruce Timson, but the only other character I remember was an ex-pat Australian and failed actor by the name of Peter Latrobe, known as "the widow". Evidently he never took acting jobs because they either didn't pay enough or the

Chapter Seven

parts weren't big enough. His grandfather was Governor of Tasmania which, I think, gave him ideas above his station. He was first called the widow by Stanley Miller who seemed to have a knack of giving people the name they would always be remembered by. The last I heard of the Widow Latrobe, and this was of course many many years ago, he had moved to Holland where he worked as a tour guide. I borrowed money off him once and he was forever telling everybody how I never intended to pay him back. When I eventually managed to actually do so I think he rather regretted it. The widow, like Anoushka, had a speech, I can't call it an impediment because that implies something like a cleft palate, so let's call it a bad habit, and that was he would sniff loudly virtually between every word he spoke. It was a large nose and I think now and again he even pinched it between finger and thumb. His face was a bit prune like and he had masses of black hair that he brushed twice a day, a hundred strokes each time. He also, at one time, had been tutor to Mussolini's children.

I worked my two years at Kemsley Newspapers and have no doubt it could have been a job for life but the stage still called and I handed in my notice. The only problem was I was still no further in my theatrical ambition and I still had to earn a living, so I had this brilliant idea of working nights, and the place to work nights was Cadby Hall, Joe Lyons' enormous bakery in Hammersmith. At that time the Corner Tea Rooms were still to be found all over London and they, together with shops, hotels, posh garden parties and the like, had to be supplied from Cadby Hall. The plan was that, the days being free, they could be used in visiting agents and hunting for work theatre wise.

My first job was blending the mix for swiss rolls, not as easy as it sounds. On a high platform, reached by mounting a set of steel steps and situated above a conveyor belt, the ingredients; flour, powdered egg, sugar, etcetera were poured into a large stainless steel hopper and were then blended by hand and arm using a circular paddling motion with wet mix up to the elbows. The hopper was then tipped up to empty its contents via a chute to the conveyor belt below. The hopper was cleaned out with a flexible rubber paddle; you washed your arms and started on the next load. It was tiring work, so much so, that it was a short period on, a period off. Meanwhile your previous mix was on its way to be baked before it would emerge to be jammed, cut, rolled, and move on to be wrapped in cellophane, sealing the wrapping on a hotplate and, finally, to be boxed.

The job of mixing lasted until I started to develop dermatitis so I was taken off the hopper and put to work with the cellophane and the hotplate. This demanded total concentration because the rolls came through at a steady pace and if, like me, you tended sometimes to have your head in the clouds, you could suddenly find yourself with mutilated swiss rolls mounting up and even falling off the belt. You were not popular if you allowed this to happen; bonuses were involved.

Lunch was at two in the morning and was the only truly interesting part of the night as the eight or nine people around our table, excluding me as I have no university qualification, had so many degrees between them from so many universities the conversation never lagged. As for the plan of seeing agents during the day, that went for a complete burton as, by morning, I was so knackered I flopped into bed and knew nothing more till the evening and it was time to go back to work. Something else was called for and, seeing an ad for an opening with a publisher in South Kensington, Robert Hale & Co, I applied and was taken on. The job didn't live up to its description. I was sold a pup, being nothing but a stamp licker and office junior. I did read some quite interesting books though via an open desk drawer that could be quickly closed should anyone pass by. There was one particular story about a Pharaoh who had a secret treasure chamber built in his palace, so secret that those involved, including the master builder were of course put to death. But the builder had installed his own secret passage to the chamber from the outside and passed the secret on to his two sons who were soon merrily helping themselves to the Pharaoh's treasured baubles. Noticing what was happening, the Pharaoh set a trap and one of the brothers was caught. Unable

Chapter Seven

to escape and, in order to save his brother, he ordered his sibling to cut off his head and take it away so the Pharaoh wouldn't be able to identify him. The Pharaoh, discovering a headless corpse in his trap, put out a proclamation containing the usual fairy-tale rewards: half the kingdom and his daughter's hand in marriage if the culprit gave himself up. Whereas he could have gone on enjoying the secret passage to wealth, instead the ninny presented himself at court and Pharaoh said, 'The Egyptians are the cleverest of people and this man is the cleverest of Egyptians,' and promptly cut off his head. Or maybe he threatened to cut off the robber's head but the princess had fallen in love and begged for his life so that they lived happily ever after. What a wonderful story for a play I thought and started work on it. I was busily scribbling away with the radio playing when I heard an announcement which went, 'We now present a play by the South African author (I have forgotten his name) *The Two Brothers*' I knew before the first word was spoken that this was my play and, adding insult to injury, written by another South African. Ideas get in the air, which is why it is inadvisable to talk about them. Peter Mackie said to me one day he had a marvellous idea for a television series. 'Oh, yes?' I said, doubt in my voice. Everyone has at least one TV series inside him or her. 'And what might that be?'

'*Colditz*,' he said.

So, the next time I was in Television Centre I put it to a director I had worked for and knew well, and I was laughed out of the building. I was used to being laughed out of the building because I wanted to write a version of Italo Calvino's *Baron in the Trees* and I was laughed to scorn over that one. Too difficult, can't be done. Can't be done? Crap! A couple of years later what did the BBC come up with? *Colditz!* A happenstance perhaps? And what did they come up with after that? Could it have been *Baron in the Trees?* No I believe at one time Richard Gere held the film rights for it but he obviously never got it off the ground. Pity. It's a great story.

I had a bete noir at the BBC. I don't know what I did to him that he stymied me so but, as far as the writing was concerned, after he had read a couple of scripts I offered him, *Baron in the Trees* being one of them as I had already written a first episode purely on spec, he told me I would be better off as a street cleaner. Those were his exact words. Then, when BBC2 started and the mandarins were looking for production staff and I applied, who should be sitting as one of the interviewers but my bete noir. He never said a single word throughout the entire interview, which I honestly believed was going extremely well until, just as I was getting up ready to leave, he opened his mouth and said, 'You're a writer aren't you, Glyn?'

What could I do but say yes, indeed, I wrote?

'And television always needs writers,' he added with a crooked little smirk, and I knew the whole interview had been a total waste of time.

His name was Elwyn Jones and, for some reason, he was indeed my bete noir. Another in whose eyes I could never do right was Bob Swash who was a member of the Sydney Box Organisation but I think the reason for his animosity was my closeness to Sydney, which he resented. Sydney looked at me one day and said, 'Twenty years too young and twenty years too late.' Now what could he have meant by that do you suppose?

Chapter Eight

In between visits to Chadwick Street, 1958 started with a number of television walk-ons, thanks to the lugubrious Eric Blythe, an agent who specialised in them and who, I would have thought, made a pretty decent living from it. His decrepit offices in Great Newport Street near Leicester Square, arrived at up a very narrow flight of stairs hardly wide enough for two people to cross, consisted of two rooms; the outer one, whose walls were lined with bentwood chairs, was where you sat together with all the other hopefuls, voices never rising above a whisper, until Eric appeared at the door of his inner office, looked around, and with a finger beckoned you in or shook his head and said, 'Nothing today.'

The first production he sent me to was a period piece, *Lady of the Camellias*. The studios were in North London somewhere, Highbury I think, an area I didn't know at all then. I remember on the set there was a huge table laden with real food as opposed to the normal dressing of artificial flowers, prop fruit made out of wax, and chickens made out of rubber. I was in my usual impecunious state, very hungry, and forbidden by watchful eyes to go anywhere near anything so inviting. I don't think I was the only one to regard that splendid feast with belly button almost touching my spine.

There followed two days on *Murder Bag*, then an episode of *Joan and Leslie* (Leslie Randall and Joan Reynolds). *Diary of Samuel Pepys* came next, the first time I worked for Chloe Gibson who, in two later episodes gave me the small part of Roger Palmer, Lord Castlemaine.

I remember her saying, 'He's supposed to be rather ugly, dear, but I'm sure make-up can do a good job on you.'

More walk-ons followed: *You Are There, Hotel Imperial, Boyd QC, The Jack Hylton Show, Charlie Chester, Dickie Valentine* and a part in a children's adventure serial for the BBC, *Queen's Champion*, nine days work in all on that one, unheard of! I did quite well out of this sort of programme which required swordsmanship as I had for some time been taking fencing lessons in Hammersmith with a man named Gordon who, I was told, had even fenced in the Olympics. Another was *Three Golden Nobles* in which a young Michael Crawford appeared. This was the only one I remember in which someone was hurt during a fight. The scene took place in an interior, the hall or kitchen of a castle, and one of the extras panicked and fled for cover into the huge fireplace where he promptly knocked himself out on a hanging witch's pot and had to be ferried to hospital for stitches. Then there was a series about the war of the roses called *The Golden Spur*. I was only another soldier in this one, cast because, when asked if I could handle a sword, the answer was a positive and truthful yes. We were bussed out to Epping Forest to film the battle scenes and I had hardly got into my costume when the fight director, Terry Baker, came up to me and said, if he arranged a special fee, would I do all the principal fights for him, as the other extras, all of whom said they could handle a sword had lied through their teeth and didn't know their arses from their elbows and he didn't want to be responsible for any injured principals. So all day long with my back to camera, in chain mail and a constant change of tabard, I fought and died in a dozen fights or more. It was a long day and, by the end of it, I hardly had a thumb my hand was so swollen from wielding a broadsword. When I watched the transmission I wondered how many people noticed there were a lot of left-handed soldiers dying that day. Actually, so I am told, cameramen usually like left handers because they can get more open shots but it didn't apply in this instance because I was always shot from behind.

There was a young actor in *The Golden Spur* playing a royal duke.

Chapter Eight

I put him down at about nineteen but in fact he was twenty-three at the time, and was without doubt one of the most incredibly beautiful men ever to appear on television: ever to appear anywhere for that matter: not handsome but so beautiful; tall and slender with a flawless olive complexion and great dreaming eyes. Even the sweaty, hairy, big butch cameramen and crew ran rings around themselves to be noticed by him. He was very quiet and unassuming and responded courteously to anyone who approached him. Could it be that all that attention was the reason I wonder, to dispel any doubt about his sexuality, why he went on to become a gross, ugly, scarred, brawling, drunk, dying before his time? His name was Oliver Reed.

If ever I had to ask an actor if he could handle a sword and the answer was yes, I merely held out a weapon, hilt towards him and watched how he took it. If he took it palm up, thumb out I was inclined to believe him and a few thrusts and parries could confirm it. I auditioned for the Royal Shakespeare Company once and was asked that question.

'Yes,' I said, and then added as a joke, 'I ride a horse too.'

There was lengthy silence before a voice said,

'We don't use horses at the RSC.' Feeble joke it might have been but they'd no sense of humour that lot. I went to see an RSC production of *Peter Pan* at the Barbican because a wonderful actress by the name of Katy Behean who I had directed at RADA was playing Wendy. I really found it difficult to believe that Katy could ever give a bad performance but what she gave here was not what I expected of her. Thanks to London's traffic we took our seats just as the house lights went down so I didn't get a chance to look at the programme. Edward Petherbridge, who I had worked with many years before at the old Queen's Theatre, Hornchurch, was in it and I kept wondering who he was meant to be and why he was using an American accent? It took a while but finally the penny dropped. Oh, of course, he is the great J.M.Barrie himself telling us what is going to happen next and the accent isn't American it's meant to be Scots, I think. During the interval, which didn't come too soon, I had a chance to catch up on the programme and saw the character was listed as "The Storyteller". Great, I thought, Barrie's play, which has stood the test of time, been a perennial favourite for decades, turned into more than one movie and more than one musical, is so incomprehensible we need a story teller to let us know what it is all about. Or maybe the director doesn't want us to get too involved (in this he succeeded admirably) in case we get carried away and actually start to believe in fairies, or maybe become too distraught at Tinkerbell's imminent death, so how about a spot of alienation? Brecht comes to *Peter Pan*. I don't know whose brilliant idea this was but I noted in the programme that the directors were indebted to Andrew Birken for his invaluable and expert help with the text. Now, as Andrew Birken wrote that masterpiece for television, *The Lost Boys*, how could he, if it was he, think that the storyteller device would work? All it did was hold up the action and, as we had already been told what to expect next, the consequent action held no surprises. There was a comedian who, when asked the secret of his technique in setting his audiences roaring, replied, 'First I tells 'em what I'm going to tell 'em, then I tells 'em, then I tell 'em what I told 'em.' Fine for a stand-up comic: disaster for *Peter Pan*. I did not even have the consolation of a brilliant performance from Katy. Even she couldn't lift this mess off the floor. Talking to her afterwards as we took tea in the bowels of the earth beneath the theatre her first words to me were, 'Oh, God! I can't wait to get out of here!' She wasn't made any happier by my reaction to her performance as I am not the kind of person who can go backstage and say 'Wonderful, darling! Marvellous!' unless I truly mean it, but I hope whenever I have criticised it has been without malice or insensitivity.

The programme at The Barbican contained what must be the most absurd credit I have ever read in any programme anywhere–"Canine movement by…" Does someone honestly mean to tell me that good sponsorship money was wasted on having someone teach an actor to move in a skin? No one thinks of Nana as being a real dog any more than they believe the pantomime cow is a real cow. Imagine a programme note that read "Bovine movement by…" Could you take

Chapter Eight

it seriously? And how come the poor ostrich didn't get any tuition?

I now had an agent, Laura Stevens of Perry and Stevens, but the TV's seemed to dry up after a while so it was with relief that, when I auditioned for *Grab Me a Gondola*, I was cast as Herring, the bos'n. Interviews I could cope with, and quite often was given a job from across a desk or from a reading in an office, but I always loathed auditions. Even late in life when I said to myself before I even left the house that I either had the job or I didn't, I still found them nerve wracking. There's a lovely apocryphal story about an actress who auditioned and auditioned and was rejected so many times with those fatal words, 'Thank you, we'll let you know,' that when one day she was finally offered a part she said, 'Oh, I don't act, I only audition.'

National Tour of Grab Me A Gondola with Jasmine Dee

At this particular audition I galumphed around the stage and managed to dry in the middle of my song but I knitted my way back and evidently the management decided I would be either very good or very bad and they'd take a chance on it. I was probably not very good and not very bad. A reviewer not knowing what to say about me would more than likely have said I was "competent in the part", the kind of observation that sends most actors up the wall. There was one opening night on the tour though, I seem to remember it was

Nottingham, when I was completely thrown by a totally unexpected very loud sound coming from the pit on the intro to my number. Evidently the score at this point included an electric guitar but no one had ever mentioned it, we had never had one before this, and the sudden amplified to one thousand decibel twang took me totally by surprise. This was still the time when a touring company picked up a new orchestra at each venue. For a few seconds I had no idea where the hell I was musically but I managed to bring myself in more or less on time and the number went off okay. It was a hairy moment though.

This was also still the time when managements did a deal with British Rail whereby whole coaches were booked for a travelling company with the sets and costumes stowed away in the guard's van and carriage windows plastered with signs reading "Reserved For..." and the name of the company. Some cast members of course preferred to use their cars if dates were close enough to London and they wanted to get home for a Sunday. For the rest of us, travelling up and down the country, Crewe Junction was where you might catch up with friends heading in different directions on different tours. Many were the cries of greeting that rang out over Crewe railway station's platforms and exchange of gossip. I suppose the railway employees were used to it. Strange people these pomping folk.

It was while playing in Manchester that I met a stage struck kid who even came over to Leeds to see me again. He invited me to his home in Oldham where he lived with his mum in a tiny terraced house with scullery and a shared privy out back. A letter from the agent A.P.Watt & Son from 1959 reads:

A CORNER FOR DREAMS: There have been so many plays about boys in industrial backgrounds who want to go into the theatre. The glamour and glitter of the show business world has been set against the humdrum workaday life of the mass of people. It is therefore hard to take such a theme and make something fresh of it. In this play the picture [sic] of the boy's home is well drawn, but the conflict does not excite us the way it should. I would call this a near miss.

Chapter Eight

Now an extract from a letter from the boy himself dated 1993:

"Remember the thin and callow youth I used to be... Do you still write? You once wrote a play about me–do you recall? A CORNER FOR DREAMS–you were intrigued, dismayed, horrified by my humble home–my dear, dear mother (unmarried till the day she died, God bless her) and my grandfather in a stroke–is that right? Why ever did I take you home? Where did I find that sort of courage?"

His name is Jimmy Chinn and a much more successful playwright than this playwright who tried to encourage him all those years ago.

"Shakespeare was wrong, you know, the fault does not lie in our stars, nor in ourselves, it lies somewhere in between. There is a place for dreams, as there is a place for everything and the place for dreams is in a corner. Let them out of the corner and they run wild. When a kid's finished playing with his toys they must be put away, or he is liable to forget where they where left and one of them will take him by surprise. Bang! Crash! Wallop! Over he goes. If he isn't hurt someone else is. You scatter your dreams about and sure enough one day they trip you up. When you finish with your dreams you should put them away somewhere, in a corner.... where they'll be safe."

Definitely a young man's writing.

It was after *Grab Me a Gondola* that I went on to the Library Theatre in Manchester to play Cinna the poet in *Julius Caesar*. I stepped out of the station to be greeted by an almost solid wall. This was before the clean air act and the smog was so dense you literally couldn't see your hand in front of your face. So here I was in a strange city not knowing what lay in front of me or whether I should turn left or turn right. The acrid yellow cloud muffled sound; it caught at your throat and burned your eyes. It was like being in a ghost town. Eventually a figure loomed out of the dark and I managed to get directions and make my slow way to the bus station and head for my digs, a freezing uninviting room with a thin lumpy mattress on the bed and ice-cold linoleum on the floor.

The play was directed by David Scase, one of the few directors for whom I had the utmost respect. Many years later when I was playing Doctor Seward in *Dracula* at the Forum, Wythemshawe, under another director I enjoyed working for, Roger Haines, he came to a performance and, in the bar after the show, he reminisced about *Julius Caesar*.

'Did we ever invite you back?' He asked.

'No.' I said.

'That was unkind.'

It certainly was because, although the play took me well into 1959, it was back to Eric Blythe and walk-ons: *The Charlie Drake Show*, Charlie Drake working so hard I thought he would have a stroke. He was almost purple in the face. *The Arthur Askey Show*, Arthur Askey the most terrible ad libber. At one point he took my chin in his fingers, turned my face full on to camera and said, 'What a lovely boy, who's your agent?' *The Frankie Howard Show*, Frankie Howard, impatient, irritable, and bad-tempered *Hancock's Half Hour*, Hancock a quivering bundle of nerves, worse than me. This was before he had to resort to idiot boards, *The Army Game* amongst others. But it wasn't all walk-ons. I now did a play *Act of Terror* for Granada in which naturally I played a South American rebel who gets pretty shot up. When I went into the canteen for lunch the girls behind the counter nearly had heart attacks when they saw my make-up. In fact the one serving me pointedly refused to look at me, saying she was likely to be sick. Anyway, Cliff Owen directed the play and I must have done a good job for him because he very kindly contacted the casting department saying they should consider using me more. They did. One more *Army Game* with nothing to do and that was it. I was then cast in an episode of *Softly Softly* for the BBC, and a part in *The Expert* starring Marius Goring, and then Chloe Gibson came to the rescue again with parts in *No Friendly Star, The Secret Kingdom*, and *The Infamous John Friend*.

Chapter Eight

In 1960 I auditioned for Orson Welles for his *Moby Dick*. I was interested as to whether he would think what a number of people remarked on, that I bore a resemblance to him, but I don't think he did and I wasn't selected for the company anyway. I had moved by now and was living in my two rooms in Well Road, Hampstead. I did something on television called *The English Captain* about which I have no memory whatsoever, and still taking fencing with Gordon before starting rehearsals for a play called *The Little Saint* by Roberto Bracco being produced by Papa Rietti at the Institute of Contemporary Art. This was a nonpaying engagement and the second time I was in the same cast with the young Michael Crawford, who this time was playing a deaf and dumb youth and doing it brilliantly. Papa Rietti, who was Jewish, was a wonderful old man who adored playing Catholic priests. Being Italian maybe they were the only parts that appealed to him. His two sons were both in the profession, Ronald in management, and Robert forever appearing in British movies as an Italian policeman. Robert also started an upmarket theatre magazine called *Gambit* but I don't think it lasted any length of time. At the end of the run Papa sent me a card thanking me for my wonderful performance, wishing me the best of luck in my career and, if I still had a copy of the script, could I let him have it back.

In between the minimalist acting engagements I registered with a cleaning agency and was engaged to clean other people's houses, an illuminating experience. There was the Irish lady in Belsize Park who believed implicitly in "the wearing of the green". Her clothes were green, her house was green, the curtains and the furniture were green, the crockery and, where possible, the kitchen utensils, were green. It was like working in a fish tank. One day when I had finished my four hours there was no sign of her. I waited at the front door and eventually she came scurrying up the area steps, all out of breath and saying, 'I had to go back to the bank. They gave me blue pound notes instead of green ones.' What did she do I wonder when the green ones went out of circulation?

There was the lady in Mill Hill who insisted I use the dirty water from the washing machine to clean the floors and I insisted just as strongly that I would do no such thing. It was clean water or nothing. She was a knickknack lady whose mantelpiece and every available flat surface was covered in china and glass ornaments. I moved them to dust and she followed me, quite certain I wouldn't put them back in exactly the right place. To prove her point, she moved them a millimetre this way, a millimetre that, each time giving me a little frown and, now and again, a sigh of vexation. Then one morning she appeared in half-open negligee and provocative Hollywood pose at the top of a very Hollywood staircase. It was actually not a very pretty sight and as I took no notice she changed her cleaning man. If my replacement gave her the satisfaction she required maybe she stopped having to move ornaments around.

There was the Jewish family in St Johns Wood, two spinster sisters and a bachelor brother. They really had no need for a cleaner because they kept the house spotless. It was one cadaverous sister who followed me everywhere watching everything I did. Half way through the morning there would be a cup of weak coffee and a single biscuit waiting for me in the kitchen and she would stand in the doorway with her watch timing my break, I believe to the second. I was asked to clean bedsprings, those old fashioned beds with the spiral springs uncovered. I ran my finger around one of the springs and held it up to her face. There wasn't a speck of dust on my finger, nevertheless the springs all had to be cleaned with a rag dipped in paraffin. One day it was requested that I wash down the kitchen walls. Like the bedsprings, the paintwork was pristine: no dust, no cobwebs, not even a splash of grease. By this time I'd had a bellyful. I didn't want to just walk out. There must have been some subtle, unknown to me, reason for my being there in the first place, and this terrifying obsession with cleanliness, and I just had to get out of that depressing place. It was just before Passover. The cutlery had been taken outside to be buried in the sand and I did the one thing I knew would get so far up her nose she would practically faint. I stood on her kitchen

Chapter Eight

table with no protection between the tabletop and my shoes. For once she didn't seem to be around but she eventually came in and literally reeled backwards when she saw me. I was out of that house so fast I practically hit the pavement running and I believe she was already on the phone to complain of my behaviour. What a joyless gloomy household it was, those two elderly dry as dust spinsters and that bachelor brother probably all eating each other's hearts out. How come I never wrote a play about it?

I "did" for the journalist, Arnott (Lady) Turner in a beautiful Georgian House in Hampstead and we got on famously, so much so that I voluntarily did other odd jobs for her on the side. We were practically neighbours after all and she had no man about the house, just a pretty useless son who never seemed to be around, his presence felt by the total mess that was his room. I also did for one time famous cabaret artiste, Douglas Byng in his flat in the West End. All his available surfaces, especially on the grand piano, were covered in framed photographs of all the servicemen he'd had ding-dongs with during the war. Byng was definitely tri-sexual: soldiers, sailors and airmen.

Also in Hampstead I cleaned the flat of another Australian ex-pat, one Charles Osborne who I think originally wanted to make it in the theatre, didn't, and was making a success as a writer and music critic. At the time I had applied for an Arts Council bursary and Charles knew it. I had submitted no fewer than eight plays but I did not get the bursary. Charles, who was on the selection panel, and whose floors I was scrubbing in order to keep paying the rent, had the insensitive gall to inform me to my face that he had voted the bursary be given to a young West Indian who wanted to go home to Jamaica for a holiday! Maybe it was revenge for his lover staying home on one of my cleaning days in order to seduce me. Not much cleaning was done that morning.

The result of my application wasn't known until the following year when I received the following letter from the Assistant Drama Director, Dick Linklater who I think was disappointed for me because he kept up quite a friendly correspondence for a while afterwards.

Dear Mr Jones,
I am very sorry to have to tell you that the Drama Panel has decided not to recommend you for the award of a bursary under the Arts Council's New Drama scheme. Obviously this will be a disappointment to you [the understatement of the decade] *but I want to assure you that the Drama Panel's sub-committee held detailed and prolonged discussions of your work and financial circumstances* [like I was dead broke, scrubbing floors, and about to be thrown out of my flat?] *before reaching this decision. Those members of the panel who read your plays–and they were all read of course–were glad to have had the opportunity of doing so, and if at any time you think we could be of use to you in some way* [Yes, yes! Like right now with some loot!] *please don't hesitate to get in touch with us.*

Although fairly cold comfort perhaps, we are anxious to give you every possible help towards the production of your plays. If you want me to do anything to help specifically or mention your name to any particular companies, please let me know.

I am returning under separate, registered cover, one copy each of THE NARROW LANE, BETWEEN TWO SIGHS. THE RIVER OF SAND, BAY RUM, OH BROTHER! PARADISE ROAD, MY LOVELY TRUMPETER *and* PRANCING NIGGER."

Of the play *Paradise Road* I have no memory whatsoever. There certainly is no play of that title in the script cupboard. I wonder what happened to it.

My other very small source of income at the time was from the Institute of Psychiatry at the Maudsley Hospital, South London. For example:

"*Mrs Treadwell* (Isn't that wonderfully Dickensian?) *wondered whether you would be able to come here for some further nitrous oxide testing for one day. The tests are similar to those you took part in before, and the payment is the same (30/- plus an allowance for lunch and fares). If you are willing to help us again, could you please telephone me on extension 103 or write to me, and we can then arrange a convenient day."*

Christmas saw me at the Belgrade Coventry to play the baddy strong man in *Circus Boy* by Michael Redgrave. The boy, Ludo, was played by a young actor straight out of Drama College by the name of Brian Stanyon. We became friends and, when I was later at Northampton, he and his family would come over on a Saturday evening to see a play and I would go back to their home in Leicester for a pleasant weekend. Brian was later cast in a movie and I remember us all going for a Chinese meal in Soho and then to the premiere in Leicester Square. I have no memory of the movie but maybe Brian didn't like what he saw because shortly afterwards married to the actress Antonia Pemberton he gave up the theatre and became engaged in social work.

But my life was about to change because in April 1960 I went down to The Queen's Theatre, Hornchurch to play Morocco in *The Merchant of Venice* and Boris Kolenkhov in *You Can't Take it With You*, and in the workshops at a pound a week was an "apprentice", a stage-struck youth by the name of Christopher Beeching who cycled to the theatre every day from his home in Romford. When even younger, still at school and playing with his home-made puppet theatre, he had written to MacQueen Pope, author of many books on the theatre, asking for his advice about the theatre as a career: advice which turned out to be the usual; forget it, it's an overcrowded profession, the chances of success are negligible, etcetera.

I would arrive at the theatre and go straight to my dressing room. There I would make my presence known by singing or generally making some kind of noise and then start counting. I never got to more than fifteen or twenty when who should appear at my door with a breathless 'hello' but this skinny, spotty, bespectacled youth who became my lover, friend, companion, help, critic, significant other, other half, whatever you want to call it. It nearly didn't happen. Some of the company, during a break in rehearsals, were enjoying the sunshine outside the theatre one day when quite casually I asked him how old he was. When he answered that he was sixteen I decided jailbait was not for me. But Chris had ideas of his own. MacQueen Pope didn't put him off and I wasn't going to either. I heard Michael Caine some years back in a television interview say with a smile that he could not imagine sharing his life with another gentleman. It was a charming and gentlemanly way of telling the world exactly where he stands. I have been sharing my life with another gentleman and that is where I stand, no pun intended, not for forty years as the Albert Chevalier song has it, but forty-five years and, to misquote another song, we're still here.

I waited until almost the end of the run of the second play when, as it seemed to him he was getting nowhere and desperation was setting in, then I asked him if he would like to come up to Hampstead on the Sunday. Why did I bother to ask? From a window I watched him, coming down the street at a run, pulling off his tie as he came. The joke for many years was that, by the time he reached the second floor, he was stark bollock naked. Come to think of it, it might not have been a joke. There were other Sundays after that and his mother, highly suspicious, was getting more and more worried.
'Is he funny?' And, 'But he's so much older than you.'
I was twenty-eight at the time.
In order to call me he would tell his parents he was going for a walk and would then phone me from a call box. It got to a point that, one evening when he called, he was in tears and desperate, the parents had been getting at him to such an extent.
'Put the phone down,' I said, 'and go home. I'm going to call your mother,' which I did.
She answered the phone.
'Good evening, Mrs Beeching, this is Glyn.' (A very audible gasp at the other end). 'Chris has just called me and he's in a bit of state

Chapter Eight

because you've been saying things about our friendship that have upset him.' (Another gasp) 'So I'm coming down to Romford to talk to you.'

This time there was almost a shriek on the other end.

'No, no! There's no need for that! You don't have to come down. I'm sure everything is all right,' and so on.

I nicknamed her 'Hysterical Mum' shortened to Hyst Mum, and the name stuck. So much so that thereafter she signed her cards, first night telegrams, and letters that way.

The upshot of all this brouhaha was that I did go down to Romford to be greeted with, 'Oh, you're not as old as you looked on stage,' and not much more was said as I become more and more a member of the family. She did attempt to brooch the subject to Chris's elder brother, Roger with, 'Do you think Chris is funny that way?' The answer to which was, 'What does it matter so long as he's happy?' And nothing more was ever said until I went to Northampton for a season and Chris came to the railway station to see me off which elicited, 'You're nothing but his little black boy carrying his bags.'

He would come up to Northampton for week-ends, after one of which he went home with the present of a rather beautiful mohair sweater he never wore, and a book, *The Pictorial Book of Philosophy* which he has never looked at and which is still a joke in the family.

'Read your book on philosophy yet?'

She went up to his bedroom and watched him unpack and, when she saw the sweater, she flipped.

'What's that?'

'A present from Glyn.'

'Why is he giving you such expensive presents? I knew there was something going on. Send it back at once.'

'All right. I'll send this back too.' And he produced a woollen scarf I had bought for her.

'Oh! Oh, isn't it beautiful?' She said, 'I must write and thank him.' End of conversation.

But, before Northampton, I had gone up to Glasgow in August

to join the Citizen's company, firstly to play two parts, Phylax, and Odoaker, in Durrenmatt's *Romulus the Great*, opening at the theatre and then moving on to the Edinburgh Festival, "Of the Citizen's cast, only Glyn Jones as Odoaker and Joe Greig as Romulus caught the subtle flavour of this intriguing play" then to stay on for a number of plays including *Hamlet* in which I played Laertes. Local boy made good, John Cairney, returned to his hometown to star as Hamlet. The director was Callum Mill and Cairney ran rings round him getting his own way with whatever he wanted. 'Oh, Callum,' he would whine, 'if I give up these few lines here can I have that speech back?'

We were walking through the Gorbals one day on our way to rehearsal when two infants accosted us, the one saying, "'Amlet, 'Amlet! Gie us some o yer patter" (How do you write "patter" in a Glaswegian accent? Pa-ha?)

The trap at the Citizen's which was used for the grave scene is very narrow and, when lowered, with nothing on either side you had to be extremely careful where you put your feet because it is a hefty drop to the stone floor beneath. Having to leap into the grave and lift the dead Ophelia in my arms took great care to avoid any mishap and so it also took a few moments longer than just rushing into it. At a school's matinee, when the dead Ophelia was lifted up there was a gasp, the kids got restless and Cairney, who I don't think had ever done a school's matinee before, hissed from behind the tombstone where he was hiding, 'Hurry it up! Hurry it up!'

Naturally I did no such thing and later, in the green room, he flew at me. The stage manager who was also in the cast had to literally hold him off otherwise a right old ruction would have occurred because I certainly wasn't going to take that from our local hero.

Later, on Hamlet's line, 'Give me your pardon, sir, I have done you wrong,' instead of the usual handshake as rehearsed, Cairney took my hand in both of his and squeezed hard, gazing at me as much as to say, this is my apology for what happened earlier; and I nearly fell for it. Then I thought, bugger it, he's had his own way ever since he got here and I'm not letting him get away with this. I had arranged the fight and at one point I had given *Hamlet* a movement diagonally right across the stage with a running flèche, balestra, which is automatically followed with a lunge and which *Laertes* parried in seconde. This time I brought my blade across his knuckles and immediately regretted it because it did hurt, there was a sharp intake of breath and, looking at his eyes, I knew he knew I had done it on purpose. "Forgive me, sir I have done you wrong." I don't recollect he ever spoke to me again after that.

From the Citizen's I went on to Coventry for Christmas and then another period of cleaning other people's houses, a single television, *Amelia* and on to Northampton.

The director there was Lionel Hamilton, not the most brilliant of directors but a delightfully pleasant man and, competent, I suppose, would be the right word. Even if they lacked imagination, his productions were clean, professional and at least he didn't always abide by French's acting editions. There's a wonderful story about a director, who looking at his French's script, says to his actor, 'You move downstage here,' to which the actor replies 'I am downstage,' to which the director says, 'I don't care, it says here you move downstage,' and the actor falls into the orchestra pit.

A director to be aware of is one who uses reverse direction. In other words he turns everything in the acting edition arse about face so that if an entrance is marked stage right he has it placed stage left. Everything is rearranged accordingly and all the moves are reversed. This he fondly imagines makes it "his" production.

I enjoyed working with Lionel and the audiences for the most part enjoyed coming to the theatre. The one play which practically emptied it was Harold Pinter's *The Caretaker* in which I played Mick. Theatres are not always designed with actor traps in mind. The Belgrade, when I was there anyway, had a concrete cyclorama which meant if you had to exit one side of the stage and enter the other you had to go outside come wind, rain, or snow, in order to get around. The stage of the Royal at Northampton, a much older theatre, hadn't that much depth so that, once a set was up, there was only a narrow passage between the back of the set and the back wall of the building, what actors call a rat-run. On the opening night of *The Caretaker*, making an entrance via the dark rat-run, I trod on the sill iron that runs across the bottom of a door flat minus its door. It had the same effect as treading on a rake. The flat sprung forward and I was hit across the temple and literally saw stars as, for a second or two I couldn't figure out what had happened. If the flat had hit me any harder the performance would have ended then and there. I pushed it back against the wall and made my entrance. When the performance was over the air backstage turned blue. Up until this point in the season no one in the company had heard me so much as say boo to a goose but this particular evening that all changed.

"What stupid **** left that ******* flat backstage? I could have been knocked **** senseless. Too ***** lazy to take it and put it where it ****** well belongs. You do that again and I'll have your **** guts for **** garters!" And more to the same effect until my rage abated. Everyone leaving the theatre took avoiding action in case the volcano was still simmering.

The designer was Osborne Robinson who had been there for a hundred years but was extremely well known in the profession and whose work was much admired. He hated actors for cluttering up his sets. Also in the company was an actress of many years by the name of Vera Lennox. Her dressing room had to be constantly searched for gin bottles. On stage she teetered on skeletal pins. She wore spectacles that weren't jam jar bottoms, they were double jam jar bottoms behind which her magnified eyes flickered and swivelled like those in old flat-faced rag dolls I remembered from childhood. Her teeth didn't fit so that when she spoke the top set sometimes dropped to the bottom or the bottom set rose alarmingly to the top. It was most disconcerting when you were facing her close to as I was, when continuously positioned to do so in *The Tiger and the Horse* as she was, believe it or not, playing my wife. Maybe disbelief was suspended from out front but it certainly wasn't on stage. With the sometimes added effect of the contents of an undiscovered gin bottle, holding our scenes together became a nightmare. It almost got to the point where I was seriously thinking of saying something to Lionel but then a strange thing happened. The company went across to Birmingham to record an adaptation of *Jane Eyre* and, as we stepped off the coach outside the BBC studios, the commissionaire almost ran forward virtually rolling out an invisible red carpet.

'Miss Lennox! Miss Lennox! How wonderful to see you again!'

We went inside and everywhere it was the same. She was greeted enthusiastically, almost with bows and curtsies, and her response was quite regal as she basked in the pleasure of all this recognition. I remembered in the Stanyon's house in Leicester seeing a copy of *Who's Who In The Theatre* so the next Sunday I was over there I looked up Vera Lennox. My God! As I remember it she had been a star in London, New York, and Paris with columns of credits to her name and I never thought again of saying a word to Lionel. Let her enjoy her gin, I thought. Let her eyes roll in their sockets and her teeth behave like a set of castanets. She hasn't much further to go and really what does it matter?

The television companies had a director's training scheme whereby they paid the salaries of promising young people who were sent out to various provincial companies for a period to start learning their craft. So one day this mousy little thing appeared to join the company. He was introduced as Ken Loach and his first directing assignment was an Agatha Christie. Agatha is known amongst actors as "Agony" because playing in her plays is exactly that. You learn her lines parrot fashion, there really is no other way and it has been known for many an actor, especially playing a police inspector, to leap from one act to another without realising it, and everyone having to knit like crazy to get back on track, especially if some vital piece of information has been omitted in the jump. One year I was offered an audition for *The Mousetrap* so thought I had better take a look at it first. I did and immediately called my agent and said forget it, and I was once offered a whole summer of Agony Christie in Rhyl and I said forget that one too. I think by the end of the summer I would have been a nervous wreck. Well, we started rehearsals and Ken wanted to analyse poor old Agatha to death and motivate every sentence and I would stand in a corner and say, 'Hang on a minute, Ken, I'm just motivating this bit here.'

I don't think Ken was amused and I certainly never worked for him when he became so famous a film director. They say you should be careful how you treat people on the way up, you never know who you'll meet on the way down but up or down I don't think I would have worked for him anyway, even if I hadn't taken the mick so much. My outlook on life may be a little on the pink side but it's certainly not a deep-dyed red. Human nature being what it is, I'm too much of a cynic for that.

I know I thoroughly enjoyed the musical *Salad Days* when I saw it in the fifties but now we did it at Northampton, I had to perform in it, and I really came to loathe it. It is the ultimate in English whimsical tweedom. I don't think Sandy Wilson's *The Boy Friend*, from the same period, being a pastiche, need ever date and the songs are still a delight to listen to. But would theatre goers in this day and age still want to sit through *Salad Days* having had the blockbuster musicals and shows we've had in the last twenty years or more? I have to admit *Salad Days* did fill the theatre back then and a few years later when we produced it at Buxton. This time I had nothing to do with it but Chris with his dancing training was wonderful as the mute, Troppo, even making it a two-hankie job for the little old ladies in the audience who didn't want him to be parted from his beloved piano. And I still hated it.

My digs in Northampton, just a warm comfortable bedroom, was a short walk from the theatre and the rent included an evening meal, most of which I'm afraid went down the lavatory pan or, if not suitable for that method of disposal, such as including bones, was spooned into a large coffee jar and taken away to be dumped elsewhere. Lovely lady though she was, my landlady was also the world's most abominable cook.

Chapter Eight

Finally at Northampton I played Baron Hardup in the pantomime *Cinderella* looking all of my thirty years despite the lake liner and with stepdaughters older than I. It was fun though, my one and only pantomime. Ken Loach was in the chorus and I can still see those skinny little legs in his wrinkled tights. He hadn't learned the actor's trick of twisting a coin in them to keep them from wrinkling and he looked as comfortable on stage as if he had an itch in a secret place and couldn't scratch it in public.

I'm not a great devotee of Mr Stanislavski, Mr Brecht, or the "method." Neither do I go for all the academic crap that's taught about "acting." Professors of theatre make up courses sometimes to satisfy their own intellectual egos or make sure they look good to ensure tenure. You cannot teach anyone to be an actor. They either have it or they don't. They can either do it or they can't. They either have the talent for it or they don't. Yes, you can teach stage techniques, yes you can correct bad habits, but that is a different thing altogether. Of all the students I had in my acting classes in Virginia there were maybe a couple of the girls I believed to have real talent and who I would have

On stage as Baron Hardup in Cinderella at Northampton with David Lyn & Lionel Hamilton as the ugly sisters

encouraged to go further if they had asked but I never went out of my way to tell them that. I believe anyway if the question has to be asked then the answer is no. But at a downtown eatery, called The Little Grill, used by students for improvisational evenings and doing their own thing, I went to see a play a group of them had produced, *Scenes and Revelations* by Elan Garonzik and in it was a young man playing no fewer than five different parts who I had never seen before and who just swept you away he was such a natural. When the play was over I asked one of the kids who had been sitting with me to tell this boy I wanted to speak to him. A little while later he duly came over and I told him who I was to which he replied he already knew who I was and that his name was Scott Harrison. He was a psychology major and this was the very first time he had ever attempted anything on a stage. I asked him if he had ever thought of going into the theatre professionally. He hadn't of course but the seed was planted and he has worked in theatre ever since. He came from Washington D.C. his father being a big-shot in the US army, and when he graduated from James Madison he asked my opinion about acting teachers in Washington. I couldn't give him any help there. I only prayed silently he wouldn't find some charlatan who would mess him up. We still keep in touch and, as I write, his last email to me reads:

"New Mexico update – Things here have been good. I started a theatre production company in September called Ironweed Productions and we have our first production in March. We are doing *Fool For Love* at a warehouse space in Santa Fe. I'm acting in this one and couldn't be happier with the group of people we have. A terrific director, great cast. I've always been a fan of Shepard's "family" plays and have really enjoyed this process. It's been a sometimes tough but ultimately rewarding path Lisa and I have been on since moving here. We're enjoying it a lot. How are things with you? I hope our paths can cross again soon. I think of you often. Scott."

It really is gratifying to know one has been a positive influence in

Chapter Eight

other lives.

When my play *Generations* was performed at Carnegie Mellon University in Pittsburgh, before I went over the director called me in England to introduce herself. Sure enough, the first thing she said to me was she was an MA in directing. Wow! I am truly impressed. At rehearsals she kept on asking me where "the spine" of the play was. I replied I didn't have a clue where the spine was. If she wanted to know that so badly she'd best hunt for it herself and did anyone ever ask Eugene O'Neil where the spine was in his plays? Then she went on about the "beat". Well, the story I heard about "the beat" was that a Russian lady at the Actor's Studio in New York who had a thick accent talked about "this bit" and "that bit" but pronounced it "thees beet" which the awestruck Americans recorded as "beat". True or false? I don't know. Could be apocryphal I suppose but sounds very close to the truth to me. When I was directing at RADA a movement teacher called Toshka said to me, 'Darlink, I danced weeth Max Reinhardt in a veelchair and he said to me, "Toshka, von day you vill be a star!"

I never found out who was in the wheelchair, Toshka or Max.

Pittsburgh was not a happy experience for me. I had four professional actresses courtesy of Actors Equity Association and one MA director all on my back, all knowing how to better this not so good play they were engaged on, and who kept moaning and criticising until it got to the point where I could stand it no longer, simply walked out of rehearsals and left them to it. I couldn't by then give a toss what the end result might be. The atmosphere degenerated to such an extent the head of the department invited the director and myself to lunch at a restaurant in town to try and calm things down but I recall the atmosphere remained icy and I still didn't go back to rehearsals. The play went on, it played to full houses, the audience reaction was wonderful, I had little notes of "thank you for your wonderful play" from actresses who only a short time before thought it was shit.

I did enjoy meeting James McLure whose writing I had come across and admired at James Madison. He had his play *The Haircut* entered in the festival and we shared a few beers together bemoaning the vicissitudes of writers in general.

At Northampton we performed Somerset Maugham's play, *The Noble Spaniard*, which the company also took to Leicester, a city that didn't have a theatre at that time. Maugham is another writer whose dialogue I found you virtually have to learn parrot fashion if it's going to stick in your head and, during the course of the action in this particular play, my character had to be challenged to a duel by having his face slapped with a glove. Unfortunately the actor doing the slapping was not only a little too enthusiastic but also not very good at aiming and a finger of the glove whipped across my open eye which meant I played the rest of the evening half blind.

Acting is a dangerous occupation. My eyes are extremely sensitive which made filming difficult for me. It was always a case of keep the dark glasses on until ready to roll and then quickly whip them off and hope the eyes don't start watering before the end of the shot. Bright sunshine kills them and, when being made up in film or television studio, I always told the make-up girl to do whatever was necessary (though I simply loathed spirit gum and crepe hair) but when she got to the eyes to tell me what she wanted and to let me take over. One girl was adamant she was going to do the lot so I let her get on with it and, sure enough, the minute her brush came to within striking range of an eyelid, the tears flowed, smudging what she had done and necessitating a good half hour's delay before business could be resumed. When I was a kid having my hair cut, so small the barber placed a plank across the arms of the chair for me to sit on, so I was within reach of his scissors. When he combed my hair forward to create a fringe that he would snip across my forehead, I closed my eyes and invariably couldn't open them again for a long while afterwards and had to grope my way out of the chair and sit elsewhere until they stopped streaming. The same thing happened in a movie house once watching a Tom and Jerry cartoon. Tom had been out on the tiles all night, and was warned that if he didn't catch that mouse he

Chapter Eight

was for the chop so, in order to stay awake, he resorted to all sorts of tricks like drinking gallons of black coffee, trying to hold his horribly bloodshot eyes open with band-aids, then with matchsticks, but his lids were so heavy the matchsticks bent and snapped. By the end of the cartoon I was totally blind and missed half the following picture. So being slapped across the open eye during a performance was almost a disaster.

It was almost a disaster too when *Who Goes Bare* opened a brief tour at The Wyvern in Swindon before going on to play a season of twice nightly in Bournemouth. I was playing a mobster in this farce set in a health spa and my costume consisted of a fedora, a pair of dark glasses, a shoulder holster with gun, and a towel. Just before the dress rehearsal the stage manager, a lovely girl by the name of Tina Steele, passed me in a corridor and said, 'Your gun is on your dressing room table.'

What she should have said was, 'Your gun is on your dressing room table, it's loaded, and the safety catch is off.'

It was one of those unexplainable moments. For some inexplicable reason I still cannot fathom, I picked up the gun and pulled the trigger. I was brought up with guns and I treat them with the greatest respect so why did I do it? The muzzle was facing away from me but this was a sporting pistol and the charge is released at the top so I got the force of the blast full in the face. I dropped the gun and, with elbows leaning on the dressing table, held both hands over my burning face. Blood was running onto the floor and the company manager with whom I was sharing the dressing room was being very cool, calm, and collected but, inside, he must have been frantic. He kept quietly urging me to take my hands away from my face but I just couldn't bring myself to do it. Eventually he took my wrists and gently prized my hands away. I looked in the mirror. The cardboard cap from the blank had cut my chin, which was where the blood was coming from. (Scar number five?) The rest of my face was pitted with little black specks of gunpowder. The eyes! What about the eyes? I peered in the mirror and breathed a premature sigh of relief. Nothing there...

No, wait a moment… Yes, gunpowder was imbedded in one eye. Shit! I had a closer look, hoping it wasn't true but it was, and this meant an immediate visit to the hospital where I was given an anti-tetanus shot and then, while drops in the eye were taking effect, the very charming motherly Scottish matron started to pick the gunpowder from my face. The doctor then arrived to pick the powder from my eye and I flinched. More drops. More flinching.

'Be brave, Mr Jones,' crooned the motherly matron.

'Matron, you don't know how brave I'm being,' I replied.

So much medication had been dropped in my eye nothing could be seen but one enormous pupil. Eventually it was all over and my costume that evening and for the next few days included an eye patch with the dark glasses.

This was the second time in my life I had surgery in this area. When I was still at school I developed a cyst beneath a lower eyelid and our doctor in his surgery gave it a jab with some instrument at which I yelled blue murder and pulled back my head at which he yelled blue murder, telling me I was a stupid boy and he could have cut my eye open. Did he really expect me to calmly sit there and let him excise it without an anaesthetic? I wasn't going to give him a second go at it so, once again, I found myself in the Entabeni only this time it was all over in an afternoon. With, presumably, my good eye, I watched the whole process in the mirrored light above my head and somehow it didn't seem to be me but a stranger the surgeon was working on.

It was while I was at Northampton that I learned my literary agent, Laurence Fitch, had sold my play *One Candle for Jenny* to Associated Rediffusion. Was this finally going to be the breakthrough towards which I had been working so hard? Of course not–what could have given me such a ridiculous idea? It was never going to be as easy as that. I know I keep harping on about crappy directors but unfortunately it is only too true that they far outweigh the good ones. I am sure there are actors who don't rate me very highly as a director

Chapter Eight

but the fact is that in over fifty years in the theatre the number of directors I would want to, would happily, work for again can probably be counted on my fingers, maybe add a toe or two if you really push it. One of them was the remarkable Paul Watson, the only TV director I worked with whose crew were willing to put the union rule book to one side and that says an awful lot.

In a letter to Laurence, head of drama at A-R described the play as one of the most talented scripts the company had received and so they gave it to a director who hated it, didn't understand it, and didn't want to do it. His name was Mark Lawton and he demanded so many rewrites the whole thing became a mess.

"Regarding the rewrites of ONE CANDLE FOR JENNY, I do feel that this bears little resemblance to what we discussed when we met in Northampton. For instance I still feel that there is a lack of different character background, Mamma could be Jewish or Cypriot, the girl English and the boy apparently a Cockney."

[Am I writing a version of West Side Story here relocated to London's East End?]

"The whole dialogue is rather old fashioned with the characters saying lines but without very much meaning. The new scenes do not portray this feeling of loneliness which Johnny is suffering. Also I do feel the scene with the barmaid has no real connection with [sic] and is therefore rather boring."

[The inclusion of the barmaid was at his suggestion and as I based her on Ivy from *The Rose and Crown* I knew exactly what I was writing about.]

"I repeat what we discussed previously, that this play must rely on simplicity of dialogue and thought."

[What on earth is that supposed to mean?]

"Perhaps you would look at the play again and let me have your comments."

Thanks to you Mark Lawton this most talented script Associated-

Rediffusion had received was shelved and that was that.

In the meantime my mother, sister, and my first nephew, Mark, a babe in arms, arrived in England on the Edinburgh Castle and stayed with Olga and Dennis Godfree in Croydon. Ceri was now Mrs Wiercx. I remember this barefoot youngster by the name of Dennis Wiercx, whose family lived further up the hill, standing in the middle of Rapson Road grinning at me and never thought he would one day be my brother-in-law. Well, at our respective ages there was no reason why I should.

My mother was on a bit of a globe trot as she was continuing her journey to Australia to visit all the relatives there, sailing on the maiden voyage of the S.S. Canberra. I went down to Southampton to see her off and I must admit the liner was state of the art for the period. Strange to think the ship's life was over so fast. How many years does a luxury liner have before she's outdated and scrapped? I was to be no bathroom steward this trip though. Sitting with my mother in one of the lounges I asked a young steward tripping by what time visitors had to go ashore.

'Why? Are you a visitor then?'

'Yes.'

'Pity.' And off he waltzed. So I was no wiser but it didn't matter as later public announcements soon made it clear.

I'm surprised my mother didn't say something like 'Glyn, what did that young man mean?' or words to that effect but maybe she didn't hear. Maybe it just went over her head.

Ceri and Mark took the train to Liverpool and then the Empress Of Canada for Quebec to join her husband Dennis.

I took the train to Stafford to discuss *Daggers Drawn* with Paul Butters.

Chapter Nine

In 1962 Kenny Clayton was musical director to Petula Clark so Vicki and Alex went off to France to be with him. This meant them giving up their flat above the tobacconists at 116 Ladbroke Grove and I moved in. The flat was on the second floor and consisted of two decent sized rooms; the front overlooking Ladbroke Grove, the back overlooking a school and the Metropolitan Line. It was noisy to begin with but after a while you got so used to screaming kids and to the trains, you no longer saw or heard them. There was a small kitchen and, off that, a tiny room no more than seven foot by seven. Later, when it became available, we expanded to a spare bedroom by taking a room above. The bathroom though was still chilly and still off the landing, half way down the stairs. A madam and her girls inhabited the rooms on the first floor and I would quite often get annoyed at punters who rang our bell at all hours asking for one of the girls.

After two stints working at the Queen's Hornchurch and an intervening one in Cheltenham, Chris had decided he wanted to be a dancer, so I said, if that's what he wanted to do to go ahead and do it. He'd left it a bit late and the big question was how would his parents react to the idea but, strangely, this time they put up no objection and paid for him to start training at Bush Davies in Romford and then with Ballet Rambert.

He was still living at home and attending classes at Bush Davies when I was offered an Arts Council tour of Wales with The Welsh Theatre Company, playing Henry VIII and doubling Cardinal Wolsey in Robert Bolt's *A Man for all Seasons*. I had already played Henry at Northampton so it was an interesting double for me. I was to play Henry a third time on a tour for Charles Vance, taking over at the last minute for someone who had dropped out, or been dropped, and Ben Hawthorne, who was in the Northampton company and knew I had played Henry, called and asked me to meet Vance with a view to filling the gap. This was three days before opening but, as I knew the part, that would be no problem.

Chris came up to London to see me off to Wales, which turned out to be not such a good idea because on the train I slept through the entire journey. Arriving in Cardiff and, after settling in the digs, some of us took in a movie, which happened to be *Plein Soliel* with Alain Delon. I remember it well despite the fact I kept nodding off during the film. A bit strange I thought as I'd slept all the way over on the train and shouldn't be tired. Back at the digs my head hit the pillow and I went out like a light. The following morning I woke up feeling great, sat up, swung my legs off the bed stood and almost fell over as the room spun around me and my bum hit the bed again. Then I looked down at myself and, horror on horror, I was covered in angry red spots.

I got to the theatre and the doctor was sent for. He was most concerned because Cardiff, being a seaport and a seaman having been found to be infected with smallpox, he was worried at the time about a possible epidemic breaking out but, after examining me, he said, 'You're not pregnant are you?'

'Not that I know of,' I replied.

'Good, because you've got German measles. Very dangerous to ladies who are pregnant.'

'Well, then, I'm glad I'm not pregnant,' I said, keeping up the merry banter.

Evidently a number of students at Bush Davies had gone down with German measles and, though he didn't catch it himself, I suppose

Chapter Nine

Chris must have passed it on. Can someone be a carrier of German measles? I can't see how else I got it.

'Can he go on to-night?' Peter Penry Jones, a very concerned company manager asked.

'Don't see why not,' said the jovial doctor, much relieved it wasn't smallpox, and off he went.

What he neglected to say was that, the hazard to pregnant women apart, bright light is dangerous to someone suffering German measles so the moment I walked on stage and faced the lights I virtually blacked out and, quite honestly, I remember absolutely nothing of that opening night. I did it all on automatic pilot. The performance went all right because nobody in the audience knew there was anything amiss and some of the ladies afterwards were "oohing" and "ahing" over my beautiful mellifluous Welsh voice. What? How come I've never been given a voice-over in my life? Just to think of all those products my mellifluous Welsh voice could have sold and no one ever thought of using it. I did do a couple of plays for BBC Radio using my mellifluous Welsh voice (though to be truthful the accent was a wee bit wobbly. I'm not sure which part of Wales it was actually meant to come from) and a couple of South African plays using my guttural South African voice, accent okay, I was even hired by an independent television company, Yorkshire, as dialect coach to an English cast playing South African. I remember Andrew Ray was in the cast.

Playing Henry VIII on tour for Charles Vance, my costume consisted of doublet, hose, and slashed breeches and one evening, sitting on my stool and unbeknownst to me, my bosun's whistle and lanyard somehow became entwined in the slashes so that, when I stood up to roar in anger 'I have no queen!' the line came out as more of a soprano like squeak as I was suddenly doubled up with the lanyard, tight between neck and breeches, pulling my head down towards my crotch. Then, instead of just improvising and making a joke out of it, facing the audience to undo the whistle and the damage, I turned upstage to do it surreptitiously, or so I thought, but that for all the world looked as though I was playing the hunchback of Notre Dame

As Henry VIII in A Man for all Seasons with William Roderick - Welsh Theatre Company

desperately trying to have a pee. How Sir Thomas More kept a straight face I do not know.

This was the year I attempted a rewrite of *Enter Anthony* but I needn't have bothered. It remained a mishmash of trash. A bad play is a bad play and no amount of fiddling is going to improve it. This was the result of my trying to write something "commercial" and totally against my natural inclinations. It's when fiddling turns a good play

Chapter Nine

bad that anger sets in, especially when some actors believe they're better writers than the playwright and feel obligated to improve on his work.

This was also the year I saw one of my plays on stage for the first time when *Oh Brother!* was produced at Ipswich, directed by Bob Chetwyn who, as far as I was concerned, did a really faultless job. Laurence Fitch, who was sitting beside me on the opening night, said afterwards how delightful it was to see a playwright smiling happily all the way through.

'Were you not watching the play, Laurence?' I asked.

'Of course I was,' he said, 'and enjoying it too, but I have excellent peripheral vision.'

The play never went further than Ipswich despite at least two very good notices and the praise of at least one West End manager who ended with the rider 'but who wants to go to the West End to see a black actor in the lead?' How times do change. Now we even have a black actor playing an English king.

"ELOQUENT PLEA FOR WEST END SHOWING"

The Ipswich Theatre Company's current production *Oh Brother!* by Glyn Jones might be taken as an eloquent plea that this lively new play deserves a West End showing.

In theme and structure, *Oh Brother!* fits almost too neatly into the contemporary theatrical scene: five guilty characters are huddled together on a bomb site where they talk about the church, superstition, themselves, and politics, and finally prove either useless or treacherous even to each other.

But Mr Jones' dialogue has a verve and good humour which turns what might have been a depressing and pointless evening into a rewarding and oddly exhilarating experience. He does not just pity people; he likes them.

"PHILOSOPHY AND COMEDY"
New Play at Ipswich Is Good Theatre.

No Official Umbrella

Once in a while into the placid by waters of local repertory is dropped the challenging pebble of a premiere production. Too often the resultant ripples peter out in the pool of local interest. Not so, one would think, in the case of *Oh Brother!* which, even if it does not establish a bridgehead of new ideas, should at any rate make reasonable impact on the wider contemporary theatre.

Robert Chetwyn, Clifton Jones & G.I.J. discussing set model - Oh Brother!

Amidst the groping characters, the dominating force is a coloured ex-seaman (and murderer) whose dynamic playing by Clifton Jones gives tremendous power to this sensual, aggressive bully. He makes his own rules of life as he goes along and thus clashes violently with Joe, an ex-shop steward who lives in the vernacular of the political and trades union text-books (in which role Patrick O'Connell is particularly well cast).

A third escapist is Rob, the ex-priest, a refugee from temptations of the flesh and seeking redemption in the conversion of others (a part acted with devoted sincerity by John Southworth).

Through the first act this trio revolve around Bill the tramp who, with no apparent axes to grind, lives only in the present and gently pours philosophic oil on the troubled waters around him. Robert Gillespie's quietly spoken interpretation is effective.

RACY ANECDOTES

So far so good. Glyn Jones' easy flow of philosophy, racy and colourful anecdotes interlaced with rich comic relief all add up to very good theatre and one was quite content to settle down to a second act of the same brew.

The author however has other ideas and at this point introduces a teenage delinquent, Mike, and a plot. However, after Mike has fallen the wrong side of the knife-edge of decision, we were rewarded with a dramatic and intensely moving final curtain, which suddenly underlined the significance of much that had gone before.

Robert Chetwyn's meticulous production must have pleased the author.

Indeed it did.

Although I never expected anyone other than a psychologist perhaps to get the deeper meanings of the play, because I didn't realise them myself until some time later when, 1962 being Mental Health Year, I was fortunate to come across a book *Fear, Anxiety, Neurosis and the Wolfenden Report* and it all became clear to me, so I wrote an essay on *Oh Brother!*

It was at Ipswich that I met Malcolm Sircom who wrote a lovely piece of incidental music for the play and with whom I would later collaborate on *Pickwick*.

1962 was also the year John Cutts and I were nearly caught up in a Nigerian money scam with a man named Alfonso who asked us to be directors of a company called *Pan African Films*. Fortunately for both of us the continual promises never seemed to be forthcoming

Patrick O'Connell, John Southwark, Robert Gilespie & Clifton Jones
On the set for Oh Brother! - Ipswich Theatre Company

and we resigned before letters from the bank asked us to reimburse them for the amount Alfonso had overdrawn from the account and, surprise surprise, who appeared to be no longer available!

The rest of the year seemed to be taken up with writing: a new play *Beautiful For Ever,* and I rewrote as a novel a screenplay I had written called *Angel*. It got a couple of complimentary remarks from publishers on its return before being put back in the cupboard, and I started writing *Early One Morning* which I note, in my appointments diary, was completed on the 9th December.

Samuel French published *Beautiful For Ever* and I see in the script it is copyrighted 1978, sixteen years after I wrote it. To the best of my knowledge it has only ever had two productions and those were by amateur groups in South Wales. When I say amateur I really mean amateur. I saw the first and it couldn't have had a worse production. Dear, sweet ladies, they were over the moon that I went all the way

Chapter Nine

down to Wales to see the result of their efforts and, despite the production and the acting's total inadequacy, the play stood up remarkably well to the mauling it received which delighted me. If it were a bad play it would have sunk me in a pit of gloom. As it was I was quite chuffed. I really did think others would pick it up but apart from a second production, also in Cardiff I don't think it has ever been done again. Professional actresses who have been approached have turned it down flat. Could it be the two leading characters are both so unsympathetic? Unattractive even?

In April 1963 I received a letter from a gentleman called Bob Norris who, I'm afraid all these years later, I don't remember but he must have had a theatrical "in" and the letter reads,

Dear Glyn,
Thank you for your letter. My apology for not answering before but I have been waiting developments.

I tried Tottie Baddeley but she is going to stay in America. I think that possibly Peggy Mount might be an idea, but then linked with Esme Cannon the public might think it a comedy.

I told you of the reply I had from Sonia [Dresdel presumably] *and it is enclosed so you can see for yourself. I think they are rather niggling things* [her objections?] *so I have not bothered about them.*

I know Martin Landau as he worked for us once when we did a play at the Garrick. I think Warren Jenkins might be an idea for a producer, but I would like to get the play to John Gielgud and get his reply. I have made arrangements for Graeme Evans of the Tennant Organisation to read it. He produces their plays for television and is a friend of ours, and he rang last week to say that they have agreed for him to produce one play a year on the stage for them so have suggested he reads Beautiful For Ever.

I must say I am surprised to the replies to the leading part. I would have thought any actress would have jumped at it.

Have been speaking to Disley Jones at the Lyric, Hammersmith, and he has suggested we meet over the holiday and talk about Beautiful For Ever as he is very interested in doing the set.

No other news. Will make a date to go and see the play at Cambridge [?] when it opens so let me know nearer the date.

Despite this flurry of activity, it never went further.

The play is based on the true story of a fraud, or robbery if you wish, perpetrated by one Sarah Rachel Leverson in 1867 on a lady by the name of Mary Tucker Borrodaile and is written for five or six women. People have asked me why I wrote it as an all female play but, the subject being what it is, the beauty biz, I felt the presence of a male would be a mere intrusion. The supposed courtship of Mary Borrodaile by Lord Ranelagh was carried on by correspondence so there was no reason to introduce him in person. Giving evidence in Madame Rachel's trial, he said, 'I stand in rather an unenviable position. I have been so embroiled in this public scandal that I am glad to tell you. I had the same curiosity as any other gentleman to see the prisoner who, I understand has been able to get a large sum of money out of a lady. Curiosity led me to the shop. You don't suppose I went there to be enamelled. I think I saw Mrs Borrodaile once in the shop. I have no recollection of being introduced to her.'

Mrs Borrodaile's evidence included, 'I asked her to do something for my skin, and she promised that, if I would follow out her course of treatment in every particular, she would ultimately succeed in making me beautiful for ever. And, Madame Rachel told me how to word it and I wrote out this receipt: "A receipt for £800 being balance of £1,000 received from me for bath preparations, spices, powders, sponges, perfumes and attendances, to be continued till I (Mrs B) am finished by the process." And, Madame Rachel said we were to be married by proxy, and that it was to be done by letter-writings.'

Of Mrs Borrodaile, Montagu Williams, Q.C., has this to say, 'I do not wish to appear unkind or ungallant; but how the witness could have been led to believe such a consummation possible–if she had consulted a looking glass and seen what nature had done for her–I was, and always will be utterly unable to comprehend. She was a spare thin, scraggy looking woman, wholly devoid of figure; her hair was dyed a bright yellow; her face was riddled with paint; and the darkness of her eyebrows was strongly suggestive of meretricious art. She had a silly, giggling, hysterical way of talking, and altogether gave one the idea of anything but the heroine of such a romance.'

At her first trial, when the jury failed to reach a verdict, Madame Leverson was heard to say in a loud voice, 'Sensible fellows!' But at her second trial a month later she was found guilty and sentenced to five years in prison. Perhaps the most incredible part of this incredible story is not the fact that Mrs Mary Tucker Borrodaile fell for one of the greatest confidence tricks of all time but that, when released from prison, Madame Leverson, having been completely discredited, revealed as a rogue, a fraud, her reputation in tatters, she set up once again in business and once again attracted much custom this despite the publicity. Such is the gullibility of human beings who believe simply because they wish to believe and for whom a belief, no matter how outrageous in appearance, is the only thing that can make life bearable.

The Music Hall entertainer Arthur Lloyd wrote a song on the subject. It was titled.

MARY PLUCKER SPARROWTAIL or BEAUTIFUL FOR EVER

I AM CALLED WIDOW SPARROWTAIL,
OFT FOR THE LOSS OF MY GOOD LOOKS I'D WEEP AND WAIL,
BUT THOUGHT IT WAS OF NO AVAIL,
TILL I PERCEIVED ONE DAY,
TO MY UTTER ASTONISHMENT,
IN THE NEWSPAPER A FLARING ADVERTISEMENT,

SAYING AS HOW MADAME BRACHEL SHE COULD PREVENT
BEAUTY FROM GOING TO DECAY. SO

LADIES I PRAY TAKE EXAMPLE BY ME,
CAN I FORGET MADAME BRACHEL, NO NEVER,
ALTHO' SHE GOT FROM ME,
A VERY LARGE FEE,
IN RETURN I GOT BEAUTY FOR EVER.

I believe two plays about Madam Rachel and Mrs Borrodaile were written at the time.

There is a strange coda to this story. I am an atheist. I do not believe in an afterlife. As far as I am concerned, when I die, that is it, it's ashes to ashes and dust to dust. And yet I smell ghosts. That is the only way I can put it. When Chris and I were hunting for our first house we were sent by an estate agent to one in Englefield Road, Islington. The house was empty and he gave us the key to let ourselves in which we duly did. It is one of those Victorian houses built on the Georgian model of basement and three floors with two rooms to a floor, the kind of house that made the French say the English lived in birdcages. We inspected the two rooms on the ground floor. The house had been empty for a while and had not been updated since before World War II by the look of it. Nothing to worry about. It would require total rewiring but that could be expected of many a period house. We climbed to the first floor and I opened the door to the back room and was assailed by the most nauseating stench that almost made me vomit. I said, 'She died in here,' and slammed the door shut.

We stood for a moment and then went to look at the front room. There was nothing untoward in there. We went up to the next floor: back room, front room, all fine. Above that floor was a creepy little wooden-lined area with a filth-encrusted glass roof light and an old-fashioned zinc sink and if any place in the house harboured ghosts that was surely it. Bodies could have been cut up in there such was the atmosphere and yet I sensed nothing. We went back downstairs. We paused in front of the closed door on the first floor but nothing would allow me to open it. We went outside and sat in the car. According to Chris I was as white as the proverbial ghost. After a while, I said,

Chapter Nine

'This is ridiculous. We're going back in.'

'Are you sure?'

'I'm sure.'

So back in we went and explored the entire house again except for that room on the first floor, which was left to last. Eventually I plucked up the courage to open the door and once again the putrid smell hit me.

'Can't you smell it?' I almost yelled at Chris as he walked into and around the empty room.

'No. There's nothing here.'

'No smell?'

'Nothing.'

'Come away, come away!'

We left that house and there was no way I would ever think of buying it. I only mention this experience because it brings me to the next, which is the coda I mentioned.

One of my students in Denmark was a Norwegian boy by the name of Morten Leine and I went to visit him in Norway. His mother's boyfriend (his parents were divorced) lived in a beautiful old farmhouse on the edge of a lake, a house which they told me was haunted, that no one would sleep in the very large attic bedroom, so I volunteered to do so. We drove from Lillehammer to the farm. It was early summer so there was never going to be very much darkness, in fact hardly any at all. However, they all insisted I wouldn't last the night in that room.

We entered the house walking straight into a large kitchen come breakfast room and the first thing I noticed was the scent, a scent I was familiar with but couldn't place. I asked where the flowers were. There were no flowers. Then, simply because I couldn't place it and was still curious, I asked what kind of scented spray had been used in the room. No one had used a spray. I asked what then was the scent I could smell? They said there was no scent.

'Oh, come on,' I said, 'can nobody smell it?'

They all shook their heads in bewilderment.

'The thing is,' I went on, 'I know this scent but I can't think what it is.'

They decided to show me the rest of the house and we went into a very long, low-ceilinged, dark, dining room with a massive mahogany table and chairs and the scent in there was overpowering and, at last, I recognised it.

'I know what it is!' I said, 'I know what it is! It's Madame Rachel face powder. My mother used to use it.'

The boy friend's face had gone ashen.

'Oh, my God!' He said. 'My mother. She died in this room.'

Later on I went upstairs and slept like a log in the attic room. There were no ghosts up there, not that I could smell anyway.

In the train on my way to Wales to see the production of *Beautiful For Ever* I got chatting to a Welshman by the name of Karl Hawker, an artist and the boy friend of Sir Michael Tippet. We got to know Karl well and bought one of his paintings, a strange but striking piece mainly in shades of grey of the blind seer Tiresias painted as both male and female. We were invited to visit Sir Michael's house in Corsham and the great man came to tea in humble old Ladbroke Grove. I realised we didn't have a single piece of his music on record and, before he arrived, hurried up to Notting Hill Gate to see what I could find, managing to get a recording of the *Concerto for Double String Orchestra*. I have to admit Tippet is not high on my list of favourite composers. His music is too linear for me. I prefer music either extremely romantic and melodic or gutsy with balls: Simpson, Hoddinott, Havergil Brian. As it turned out he wasn't really interested in whether we had any of his music or not but he was interested in buying back the picture of Tiresias and as we were, as usual, short of the readies, back to Sir Michael it went. One Christmas, to pay for the festive season and with much regret, we had to sell another painting, a Paris scene by Darton Watkins.

In August of 1962 Chris and I took our first holiday together, five whole days in Swanage, Dorset. We went there because he had

Chapter Nine

previously holidayed there with his family. Also because he liked the beach at Studland where he could prance about in the nude. I hated it because there was no shade and I burn to a frazzle in minutes. Too many times as a child in South Africa I overdid it and had to have my burns soothed with calamine dabbed on with cotton wool. We took an inexpensive room and in the evenings we visited the Mowlem Theatre where H.L.W.Productions welcomed us to *"Each Evening at Five Past Eight, A Holiday Entertainment."* The Mowlem wasn't really a theatre, it was an ex-library, and the entertainment was devised and produced by a man named Alec Hastings. There were three different bills during the week, each signified by the colour of the programme, blue, pink, and green, and it was all wonderfully wonderfully, gloriously tatty. For example for the finale line-up, always the same song written by Alex, *"When each evening, party time is over,"* the boys would be in evening suits and bow ties but wearing khaki shirts! That year it was the seventeenth consecutive season.

We went into Bournemouth to see uncle Nin, arranging to meet him at the bus station. When we got there we discovered there are two bus stations so I stayed at one and Chris went off to the other with instructions to look for someone who I would look like in forty years and, in no time at all, he was back with uncle Nin.

Padraig Macmiadechain had his studio in Swanage and I bought the first picture from him, one of two he painted in Poland and called *The Red Abbey*. I had also become a photographer, having bought a second-hand Rolleicord for £12 from my friend Peter Reddy, and was taking pictures of anything and everything that took my fancy, all black and white. Back at the flat I had set up the smallest room as a writing room and dark room and was really getting into developing and printing my pictures. I first met Peter at the YMCA and at one stage we were living in separate bed-sits in the same house in South Kensington and both washing dishes at The Norrland Coffee Bar. He was older than I and from Mauritius so spoke fluent French and was a qualified pharmacist. The last time I saw him he was working at Boots in Piccadilly. His background otherwise was always a complete mystery but I mention him because he introduced me to Michel Morvan, another friend who died tragically young, and although we haven't seen her for many years, we are still in touch with his widow, Charlotte, who never remarried, bringing up their two daughters, Anne and Anaïs, on her own. When we were in Paris during the filming of *A King's Story*, Michel took Harry Booth and myself around the city in his French sardine can on wheels, ending up at Les Halles at five in the morning for onion soup and calvados. I didn't take to the calvados but the soup was delicious. Like Covent Garden, the market of Les Halles was moved out of Paris. Such is progress.

Christmas saw Chris in pantomime at Harrogate and it was my turn to go visiting. I have never been so cold in all my life as I was in the digs there. We had everything piled on the bed including greatcoats and still spent the night shivering. In the morning there were stalactites of ice on the inside of the windows. With all the shillings dropped in the gas meter the bed just shouldn't have been that cold so I stripped it, including the mattress, slotted more shillings in the meter and set all the bedding up in front of the fire. We must have got six pints or more of water out of it. No wonder it wouldn't get warm. Harrogate must be one of the coldest cities in England. That was the first Christmas I came across the eating of Christmas cake with cheese. Queer folk these Yorkshire folk I thought, but I tried it and it was good.

After the tour of *A Man for all Seasons* for Charles I performed in a number of plays for his "Company of Three", moving between Weston, Cambridge, and Wolverhampton, *Kill Two Birds, Breaking Point, The Unexpected Guest*, playing the Inspector of course in that one, though I don't think I jumped from one act to the other. Another five day break in Swanage, another large Macmiadechain painting and then to Chelmsford to rehearse *A View from the Bridge*, during which Charles read *Early One Morning* and decided to put it on. Of course, despite high praise, I was at least ten years too young to play

Chapter Nine

Eddie Carbone in *A View from the Bridge* but I got another stab at it when the right age.

A student at James Madison, Brian Bolt, approached me one day saying he had been given a slot in Wampler, the Experimental Theatre, and could I suggest a play for him to direct so I said yes, indeed, if he cared to do *A View from the Bridge* I would play Eddie for him. He could have said thank you but no thanks instead of which he leapt at it, which I suppose was only natural. Putting any talent I might have as an actor aside, he was being given the opportunity of having a man of the right age to play Eddie rather than a young student and would be directing a member of his own faculty. What nineteen year old would turn away from such an opportunity? As it turned out he was a very good director. He designed the set himself and he knew exactly what the play needed in that black box of a space. His directing was clear, he listened to suggestions even if he didn't always go along with them, his manner to all was exactly the same, no one (meaning me) pulled rank. I took his notes without a murmur and gave him no trouble at all whereas I gave the fight arranger, now called a choreographer a whole heap of trouble until one day during a break he came to me in tears.

'Why are you giving me so much stress, Glyn? Is it because I'm so young?'

'Of course not. You're the same age as Brian and he's not complaining.'

'So why are you picking on me then?'

'I'm not picking on you. I'm teaching you.'

'What?'

'How old do you think I am?'

'I don't know.'

'Well how old do you think I am?'

'Fifty maybe?'

'Actually I'm well over that and you are choreographing a stage fight for a twenty year old. You really haven't given it enough thought, have you?'

'Oh.'

'Do you want me to have a heart attack? Go away and think about it.'

He did and everything from then on went smooth as clockwork. The fight in such close-up had the audience practically out of their seats and one night, as Marco's knife went into my back, a black student of mine in the writing class, no more than three feet in front of me, uttered a little shriek and froze in her seat. Afterwards she said, all breathless.

'How did you do that? How did you do that? I thought there'd been an accident! I thought the knife had really gone into you! I thought for sure you were dead! And how can you motivate yourself to do that?'

This last was uttered with disgust and total disbelief.

'Motivate myself to do what?' I asked, knowing full well to what she was referring.

'To kiss Ron Copeland!'

I forbore to tell her I really enjoyed kissing Ron Copeland. There was no need for method acting in that beat of Mr Miller's play. But it was something she couldn't comprehend in a thousand years.

I even got an all American buddy hug and a thank you from the fight choreographer.

Chapter Ten

I'm sure it is all changed now but, when I was a boy, if you took the South Coast Road from Durban you passed a flour mill on your right and found the road continued on through an industrial area and then passed the smallholdings of Indian farmers. We were told as kids never to eat fruit or vegetables bought from an itinerant "coolie", or "churra", as we used to call them, without washing them thoroughly first. Indian women in their colourful saris would come around to white people's houses with a laden basket at each end of a long pole they carried on their shoulder and, squatting in the back yard, would haggle over the price of whatever they were selling; bananas, pawpaw, mangoes, vegetables, sometimes lychees, always expensive.

Coolies were dirty. They chewed beetle nut that made their teeth all red as though they had perpetually bloodied mouths. They blew their noses between their thumb and finger and flicked off their fingers any mucus that hadn't hit the pavement. How could they think we were unhygienic blowing our noses into a square of cotton and putting it in our pocket? They fertilised their vegetable plots with their own faeces! But I was fascinated by them, by the strings of marigolds, an evil-smelling flower, that were strung across their doorways, by the red marks on their foreheads, by the colourful festival wagons that were hauled down to the river to be burnt, hauled by cords attached to hooks imbedded in flesh, by the walking over red hot coals with apparently no ill effect.

After the smallholdings you came to a long bridge across a river, long because on either side of the river were wide tracts of reedy marshes. Never go barefoot near any of these marshes, you'll get bilharzia[13] and be pissing blood before you know it. Once over the bridge you came to the foot of a long steep hill known as Jacob's Ladder. Carrying on for some miles from the top of Jacob's Ladder and passing through thick groves of bamboo–never go into bamboo groves, they're full of mambas both black and green and the deadly mamba is one snake that will attack without provocation–you came eventually to a place called Hillary. All this, knowing how cities expand, must now look completely different from when I was a boy, but how well I remember puffing and panting on my bicycle, making my way up that hill, my calves aching, to get to Hillary and the house where Alex lived. There, hot, sweaty, and thoroughly exhausted, I would lean my cycle against the garden wall, sit and wait, and hope for a glimpse of him. Not that I didn't see him at other times because he was my patrol leader in the Sea Scouts and I was, without really knowing what it was, head over heels in love. He was maybe two or three years older than I, had large red hands and mushy eyes like pissholes in the snow and I can still see him to this day, standing under a tree by a river bank gazing dreamily into the far distance at nothing in particular. Mind you, I was in love with the film star June Allyson at the same time because she too had those same mushy eyes and I loved her gravelley voice.

What was it made me join the Sea Scouts? I must have been out of my mind, knowing my allergy to wool and having to wear that rough blue seaman's jersey. Getting dressed for scouts was a production number. I would lay everything out on my bed and, having taken my shower, I would then stand staring at it for a good few minutes as if to hypnotise the jersey into behaving itself. I would then put on socks, shoes, pants and a shirt whose sleeves could be pulled down low over the wrists and whose collar could be pulled up high. Then,

---

13 Disease of the urinary organs caused by a river parasite.

Chapter Ten

in one swift movement, on went the jersey and, before it could start pricking and giving me goose pimples, on went the scarf, hurriedly knotted up tight with the toggle. Finally on went the sailor hat. I then had to stand still for a while in order to calm down.

My mother told me that when I was a baby a friend had knitted an outfit for me in that very soft baby wool with the silver thread. My mother dressed me in it to go out and then went on with her own preparation. After a minute or two she wondered why I was so quiet and discovered the wool had tickled me to sleep. That was her story anyway. On one camping weekend as we were breaking camp it started to rain quite heavily and, instead of the usual production number and wanting to get away in a hurry, I put the jersey on over my bare skin, nothing between me and it in the cold and the wet. By the time I got home my whole upper body looked like broiled crayfish. I didn't last too long in the Sea Scouts. Another episode with wool happened in London when I went for a fitting for *The Army Game*. I remember the fitting was in a mews in South Ken, could it have been Bermans? Anyway, I said to the guy doing the necessary, would he please make a note when sending off the costume to make sure it was with a cotton shirt. What arrived at the studio? Wool! Rough army regulation wool! Fortunately I had with me the right shirt to wear beneath it.

Sometimes on my excursions to Hillary I would hear Alex playing the piano and it was one work in particular which I romantically associated with him and which led to my love of classical music, the Chopin Nocturne in E Flat. Up to that time I had been taking piano lessons with a Mrs Lethbridge, a tall, formidable woman whose favourite colour was grey, whose fingers were adorned with numerous enormous rings, and who scared the shit out of me. Her studio was on the top floor of Cuthbert Chambers in West Street, a building that fascinated me as it was built on four sides with an open well in the centre and all that stopped you from toppling into that well from the fourth floor was an iron handrail. When I made my visit in 1973

I found that Cuthbert Chambers no longer existed and a new office block had gone up in its place. It was one of a number of inevitable disappointments. Under Mrs Lethbridge I was learning "syncopation."

'Why don't you take piano lessons?' My mother had suggested. 'You could learn syncopation and then, like Donald Grieves, you could play in a dance band and make some money.'

Donald Grieves was the second son of a courtesy uncle and aunt. Uncle Alex and Auntie Ethel. Uncle Alex had suffered an industrial injury to a hand which left him with a couple of mutilated fingers, used to play suggestive party games on unwary maidens. Auntie Ethel helped out sometimes in the shop and Donald did play in a popular dance band.

So, under the tutelage of the redoubtable Mrs L, I had managed to reach the stage of being able to play a tango or two with some panache. But now, although Alex was never to know the influence he had over me, syncopation and making money playing in a dance band were of no interest to me whatsoever, if ever they had been. I arrived at my next lesson with my music case bulging with my mother's music.

'What on earth is all this?' Mrs Lethbridge gasped.

'That's what I want to learn from now on,' I said.

'Don' be silly,' she snapped. 'This isn't piano music. These are songs.'

'Well of course they are,' I replied. 'My mother's a singer, isn't she? But look, there's some good music here,' and I rifled through the pieces, *Handel's Largo, Gypsy Moon*…What's this? *Softly Awakes My Heart*… Better than syncopation,' I added airily.

Mrs Lethbridge visibly bridled.

'If you want to play the classics then bring in some piano music,' she said, 'not your mother's songs,' and she slammed the offending pile of music down on top of the piano with a loud thwack. The rest of the lesson was spent in rehashing a couple of tangos and the following week I arrived with the complete score of the *Tchaikovsky Piano Concerto* I had borrowed off a girl who, when I visited her house, would play the first few crashing bars on the piano downstairs before we ended up snogging on a bed upstairs. It was a strange

Chapter Ten

house, right on the edge of the bush. I never saw anyone else there. I remember the top of the piano was covered in a green chenille runner and it was the first time I ever saw lustre ware of which there were any number of jugs, bowls, and vases. The bedroom upstairs were we snogged had large sash windows on three sides and no curtains not even nets, and the only furniture in it was the bed, standing on bare floorboards. She was pale and thin, wraith-like, with blue eyes and washed-out blonde hair and I don't remember her name.

If she had been made of lesser stuff, Mrs Lethbridge would probably have keeled over on the spot when I handed her the score. As it was, she fiddled with her bejewelled fingers and gently, for her, suggested we come to a parting of the way and I take my lessons with someone else, which was how I came to start with Cecil Noakes who had his studio at the top end of town, in the same building as The Stardust nightclub, just opposite the Roman Catholic cathedral where Olga got married. And it was because of Cecil Noakes that I first learned about queers.

I had been taking lessons with him for some years by the time I was seventeen and reaching the end of my school days. In that time I had progressed from tangos to being semi-proficient with a Mozart Sonata and very clumsy with a Brahms Rhapsody. I could also play the slow movement from Beethoven's *Moonlight Sonata* and, whenever anybody sits down at a piano and starts to play that, I know they've taken piano lessons but never got very far. Much as I loved the music and could sometimes persuade Cecil to play for me instead of my trying to play for him, I was never going to make anything of a pianist because in those days I was just too bone idle to practice and too lazy to learn the theory. I have always regretted it.

Alex was now a distant memory and there had been interim loves of sorts, all unrequited and none serious. Not that there hadn't been sex. From the age of seven there had been plenty of that, either alone for comfort or with others for the simple pleasure of it. But, except with girls, it was always restricted to the genitals and unaccompanied by any feeling associated with being in love. If I did believe I was in love it was usually with a girl and usually to the sound of music. One episode involved my dreaming of her to the sound of Ravel's *Pavanne Pour Infanta Defunte, Pavanne for a Dead Princess*, still one of my favourite pieces of music, I declare one of the most beautiful melodies ever written but what a strange piece to accompany feelings of love–a dead princess?

Girls could sometimes be a terrible turn-off though. A neighbouring family with a daughter my age had bought a smallholding up country were they went for bucolic weekends and once or twice I went with them. In the woods down by a stream was an ideal place for a bit of hanky panky and, one day half way through, she suddenly said, 'Glyn, if you're not serious, I'll never forgive you.' Guess who lost his erection on the spot.

She was a horsey girl, as many a girl of that age is, and I enjoyed more our riding bareback at full gallop along the beach first thing of a morning with the salt spray hitting me in the face. Better than snogging halfheartedly by a stream and being asked if you're serious.

Then there was Monifay and Monifay was different. Her name was Monica Fay Henwood, hence the diminutive to Monifay. I first met her on a schools educational course in that same town, Newcastle, where my parents first met and fell in love. I remember I bought her a rhinestone pendent. Students from different Natal schools boarded in a Newcastle school for a week, boys in one dormitory, girls in another and, as I remember it, visited factories and went down a mine. I can't think what else we did. Of that group I remember Monifay, her friend, Ruth Nicholson, and a boy from Maritzburg College, Alistair Murray who I also got a bit of a thing about without truly realising it. I spent weekends at the Murray house in Pietermaritzburg, most of which seemed to be spent playing ping-pong and Alistair asking everyone to admire his beautiful feet. The rest of Alistair was not as beautiful as his feet but he had a certain elfish charm that was very attractive. He visited us in Durban, borrowed a towel from my mother to take

Chapter Ten

to the beach, returned without the towel and was never forgiven. I last saw Alistair in Luton of all places. He saw me on television and wrote care of the BBC and I visited his home. Married with children he had grown very fat and, as he never liked his name, had changed it to John. He was now a teacher and eventually emigrated to the states where he taught at a school in Nevada. A couple of letters winged their way across the Atlantic and then there was silence. Ruth I visited on her farm near Richmond when I was there in '73. She had hardly changed, a larger than life very jolly lady. When I was working Blue Hills I seriously thought of proposing to Monifay but subconsciously I must have known it was not a good idea. On that '73 visit I caught up with her as well, having dinner with her, husband John, and family in their Durban North home. As I looked around the dining table did I feel just the tiniest twinge of jealousy? I think I did. And I fell in love again, this time with the youngest who had that gravelley June Allyson type voice.

Up to this point in my life, my final school year, I had made love to a number of girls and would probably have continued to do so. Well that is what a boy is meant to do, isn't it? Have girl friends? People had been asking for years, ever since I could remember, 'And do you have a girl-friend?' And no point in having a girl friend if you don't make love to her. But I had never made love in the truest sense to a boy, and then came Jay.

The next few paragraphs might read like bad romantic fiction except for the fact that instead of boy meets girl it's boy meets boy and it does not end happily ever after. It happened almost sixty years ago and I see it in my mind's eye as if it were yesterday.

Glenwood High was principally a school for day scholars and the boarding establishment, known as the hostel, was a smallish, two story, red brick building holding, I suppose, no more than fifty boarders and set some distance from the school proper. You approached the front entrance from a main road but you could get in the back way through the changing rooms by crossing two playing fields, known as upper and lower, a transverse road separating them. One afternoon, school over, I was returning to the hostel via this route and, on crossing the road and entering on the path that ran down the side of the lower field, I saw a game of cricket was in progress. A batsman had just driven the ball nicely on the offside and it rolled to a stop at my feet. I bent down to retrieve it and, straightening up again, raised my arm to lob it back. My arm remained in the throwing position and time stopped. Whoever loves who loves not at first sight? The nearest fielder, waiting expectantly for the ball, was a boy I had never seen before. I don't know how long it was that I stood there, probably no more than seconds, before I gradually became aware of sound, that everyone on the field was yelling at me to throw back the ball. I don't know why, probably so that he would have to turn away, I threw it over the boy's head. The game resumed and I continued on my way. My legs were like rubber. My mouth was dry. My heart thumped. I glanced back, hoping he would be looking at me, but he was once more engrossed in the game.

I had my bath, dressed for dinner, and went downstairs to start some prep but my mind was on nothing but that face. That face! Who was he? Where had he suddenly appeared from and so late in the term? I looked for him in every green blazer that entered the room or went past the doors. Maybe he wasn't a boarder. Maybe I would have to wait till the next day to see him again. Then how would I approach him? What excuse could I find for striking up a conversation, if I even got a chance? And then he walked into the room and, once again, my heart was thumping and I couldn't take my eyes off him until the dinner bell rang and there was the usual general noisy exodus to the dining room across the way.

As luck would have it there was no room for him at the fifth form tables and a place had been set for him at the foot of the sixth formers' table right next to me. As he was their junior, the others at the table ignored him, the schoolboy pecking order dictating that sixth formers

Chapter Ten

did not hob-nob with fifth formers. That made it easier for me and I soon learned his name, that he came from a place on the South Coast and had, up to then, been at an Afrikaans school in the Free State and was to spend his last two years of school at Glenwood. His father's reasoning in sending him to an Afrikaans school first was to make him fluent in that language as being bilingual was a distinct advantage in the work stakes. It also meant he lived in the shadow of the strictly Calvinist Dutch Reformed Church which immediately showed as he was decidedly prissy when he first encountered schoolboy ribaldry in a less restrictive atmosphere. Not that our masters didn't try to keep some control over us. Once during a rugby match when someone's boot was a little too familiar with my head I yelled at him to get off, calling him a "basket." The master refereeing the game, a young man hardly out of training college whose name was Slater and who went by the nickname of "Chicken" a name he loathed, literally tore the scrum apart and hauled me to my feet by the scruff of the neck. His face was puce with rage. Lips quivering, he glared at me through his glasses and berated me soundly. 'I will NOT have that kind of language on my playing field! Understand? Do you understand? I will not have it!'

It was difficult to keep a straight face, not only because his own face was a sight to behold, but because some of the other boys had gathered around behind his back and were mimicking him.

We once sent a request in his name, Mr Slater of Glenwood High, to a radio programme for a song, *There's Nobody Here But Us Chickens* and he went totally bananas trying to unmask the culprits. The nadir of our schoolboy humour though was to sprinkle the bottom of his chamber pot with crystals of potassium permanganate and Andrews Salts so that, when he got out of bed for a piss in the middle of the night, he would hear the fizz in the darkness, switch on the light and discover his urine was a deep purple. We could have given the poor man a heart attack. As it was we never had the satisfaction of finding out whether it worked or not. I don't know why he was called "Chicken." He walked more like a duck with splayed out feet and, when he ran about the field, they sort of flapped. He later became headmaster and then headmaster of a prestigious school, Hilton College, so I was told.

Jay and I soon became close friends. Looking back now I realise there were sexual opportunities offered me by others on a level above jerking off. For example, travelling back to Durban by train from Pietermaritzburg after a rugby match I climbed onto the top bunk in the compartment for a sleep and was soon joined by the captain of the team who puts his arms around me and it could have happened right then and there had I been interested. On another occasion a boy named Gerry Moolman who slept in the row of beds on the opposite side of the dormitory to mine, for some unknown reason one night after lights out, suddenly took it into his head to cross the floor and leap into my bed. Before I could do anything about it, like kick him out, I froze as the door opened and there, framed in the passage light behind him, stood Chicken. He stood there quite still for a long time. This was expulsion for sure I thought as I watched him through half closed eyelids. Gerry, behind me, lay absolutely still, hardly breathing. He obviously couldn't be seen from the door and his empty bed was probably out of sight behind the row of lockers in the middle of the room. Eventually Chicken stepped back and closed the door and Gerry was out of my bed and into his own faster than a bullet.

It was Jay, not me, who precipitated the romantic aspect of our relationship. I got back to the hostel late one afternoon; hot, sweaty, and dirty after a rugby practice and flopped down on a bench in the changing room prior to taking a shower. I'd hardly had time to remove one studded boot when he appeared at the inner door. After an initial greeting and some desultory chat while I unlaced and removed the other boot he suddenly said, 'Are you going to the sixth form dance?'

I said I was.

'Who are you taking?'

He was not acquainted with whichever girl of the moment was to

Chapter Ten

be my date but I told him who it was anyway.

'Will you take her to the stands?'

The grandstand on the upper field was a favourite petting spot. I said that more than likely I would.

'Will you kiss her?'

'Of course.'

'How?'

The question took me by surprise. I looked up at him. He was looking straight into my eyes and his gaze never wavered.

'How? Do you mean where? On her mouth where else. What do you mean, how?'

'How will you kiss her?'

'Have you never kissed a girl, Jay?' He shook his head. 'Well,' I went on, 'you put one arm around her shoulder, and the other around her waist, and you pull her towards you, and you kiss her.'

'But how?'

'I've just told you how. You put one arm around...'

'Yes, but how?'

I stared at him. The inevitable was about to happen and suddenly I knew it. Once again I could feel my heart racing. I was trembling. I tried to make a joke of it.

'Oh, come on now, Jay!' I laughed. 'You don't really want me to show you.' Silence. 'Do you?'

He did not move. He did not answer. He was still looking straight into my eyes. I got to my feet and slowly I put one arm over his shoulder, the other around his waist, and I didn't have to pull him towards me, he was already there. Our lips met. At that moment wild horses would not have dragged us apart. We were standing in a public place. At any moment someone, master or boy or servant, could walk through and it did not matter. It was his first kiss. It was the first time I had ever kissed a boy and no girl kiss had ever given me what I was feeling at that moment.

As an American student was to say to me many many years later,

'Sex with a girl is okay, but sex with a man is INTENSE.' Or as the Eastern proverb has it, 'A girl for a boy, a boy for a man, and a melon for ecstasy.' Sometimes goat replaces the melon.

In a strange way what was happening with Jay wasn't really sexual. I liken it to that beautiful scene in the film *The Color Purple* when the two women, both in need of comfort, start to explore each other; tentatively at first with a hesitant touch and moving on to more intimate caresses. For me this scene wasn't about sex but had everything to do with two human beings desperately needing tenderness and affection and, yes, love.

After that first coming together we were as inseparable as our situation allowed us to be. We embraced in corridors. We walked home from church on a Sunday evening hand in hand in a crocodile of boys. We sat at table with our legs entwined. We touched each other at every possible occasion. In our innocence propriety was the last thing we cared about and I don't think we ever realised what a dangerous path we were treading. He stayed in my home, I stayed in his and that was really the first time we were actually able to make love.

It is difficult to describe the place Jay came from. One couldn't call it a village because it consisted of nothing more than a dozen or so houses in a row separated from the beach and the Indian Ocean only by the dunes and reached by a dirt road through bush and fields of sugar cane. The railway line cut off the houses on the other side. I spent wonderful weekends there. I never took to fishing but, after a swim, I would sit on the beach and watch him casting with such expertise, sending the lead flying far out to sea, standing in the surf and raising one leg like a stork whenever too large a wave threatened to bowl him over if he remained standing on both legs. Hanging beneath the roof of the veranda that ran around the house were sharks' jaws, mainly his father's trophies. Once I lightly ran a finger across a shark's tooth and the weight of my finger drew blood. (I used this in my play *Red in the Morning*; no experience is ever wasted.)

Chapter Ten

We collected mussels from the rocks and cooked them over a driftwood fire on the beach, in an old paraffin can filled with seawater. We made love on the beach. We made love under the trees. We made love in the bedroom. Nothing but a thin partition separated the headboard of his parents' bed from ours and still we made love. It never occurred to us that what we did when no one else was around actually had anything to do with anyone but ourselves.

Despite the natural and long lasting erections engendered by all this erotic activity, neither of us ever made a play for the genitals. Bodies pressed together we never made love naked and, in fact, never went as far as orgasm that, for me, was an entirely new experience but one that seemed perfectly natural at the time. I was satisfied with what we had. Sometimes in the showers at school, seeing him naked, I would feel the stirrings of an erection which, had I not been able to conceal it, could have proved embarrassing. How I never suffered an attack of orchitis amoroso acuta or, in the vernacular, lover's balls, or in the American, blue ones, I'll never know. I suppose I must have saved myself that agony by carrying on solo. It wasn't until the very end when, one afternoon at my house, it was chilly and we were lying beneath a rug. He had his back to me, my arms around him and, for the first time, I started to caress him through his shorts. The action was very slow and gentle and, feeling his erection through the material and finding myself becoming really aroused for the first time beyond being able to stop, I slid my hand inside to feel what I had seen but never felt. That's all it took. The reaction was instantaneous. I felt the wet on my hand and, at the same time, he went rigid.

'What's happening? What's happening?' There was a note of panic in his voice.

I realised then that this was his very first orgasm. To someone who had been having orgasms from the age of seven and who had lost his heterosexual virginity at an early age, it had never occurred to me that a sixteen year old had never come in his life. He slipped off the bed and looked down at himself, and then at me. Realisation had dawned.

'You made me spill my seed,' he said accusingly, almost crying.

'That is the sin of Onan.'

The Dutch Reformed Church had never left him and, although I didn't realise it at that moment, it was the end for us, not only as lovers but also as friends.

But sometime before this, for him, cataclysmic event, while we were still in our David and Jonathan period, with no apologies to the religious, I was returning to the hostel one day after my music lesson and a schoolfellow came and sat next to me on the top deck of the bus. He asked me where I had been and I told him, indicating my music case.

'You're not still learning with Cecil Noakes are you?' He asked and, when I said I was, he went on, 'You want to be careful there, you know. He's a queer.'

'A what?'

'A fucking queer!'

'What do you mean? '

I was more than surprised that he even knew of Cecil Noakes let alone anything at all about him but in a parochial town like Durban gossip spread fast. I was later to learn how fast. There was an organist who used to play between films at one of the cinemas and many were the jokes about his rising organ. Eventually he threatened to sue anyone who persisted in spreading rumours about his sexuality. The rumours persisted.

'Cecil Noakes is a homo,' my companion went on. 'Don't you know what a homo is?'

Feeling a real ignoramus, I shook my head.

'Where've you been all your life?' And he went on to explain. I was genuinely astonished. Horrified.

'You mean to say there are men who actually prefer other men rather than women?'

Evidently there were. They weren't exactly thick on the ground but they were around, and Cecil Noakes was one of them. The whole idea was preposterous. And yet, sitting alone on that bus before my schoolfellow joined me, all my thoughts had been on a blonde youth back at school from whom I had been away too long and who I couldn't wait to get back to. In fact, even as we talked, his image never left me and it never occurred to me for a second to equate our feelings and what we were doing with the knowledge I had just acquired. It was, as Tom Robinson once said, his parents warned him against certain people until one day he realised he was one of the people his parents warned him against. My schoolmate didn't go on to tell me about lesbianism. Maybe he didn't know about that. And maybe, like Queen Victoria, I wouldn't have believed him anyway. That was too impossible. But certain things about Cecil Noakes began to make sense for the first time. Though paedophile was a word not yet in my vocabulary, paedophile was what Cecil Noakes was rather than homosexual. I remembered the hand on the knee, stroking the thigh when I was younger, the constant invitations I never took up to go sailing on his yacht, the uneasy feelings I sometimes had by the way he looked at me, the references to boys before they shaved. My innocence had been my protection. Now I no longer needed any warning to take care with Cecil Noakes. I'd started shaving.

Despite indications to the contrary I have never thought of myself as being particularly sexually attractive and am always taken by surprise when someone, especially a beautiful someone, finds me so. Until my pants are down around my ankles, metaphorically speaking, more often than not I don't realise it's happening. I think it started when I was about six or seven. My mother walked into her bedroom one day to find me seated in front of her dressing table mirror gazing intently at my reflection, the side mirrors at right angles so I could study both profiles.

'What are you doing?' She asked.

'Mother,' I replied, without taking my eyes off my image, 'by any stretch of the imagination, would you call me handsome?' She burst out laughing and when she had recovered enough breath to talk said, 'No, son, not by any stretch of the imagination.'

That hurt, to hear your own mother laugh at you, and yet I suppose she couldn't help but laugh, at the syntax if nothing else. It's a droll child who uses an expression like, "by any stretch of the imagination." On the other hand she had denied I was handsome.

My courtesy relations, auntie Dolly and uncle Stan Lambon arranged, when I returned to South Africa for that brief visit in 1973, a big party and get together. They hadn't seen me for over twenty years and their greeting was effusive. That is, auntie Dolly's was with a huge hug and kisses. Uncle Stan was too Anglo-Saxon for more than a handshake and a beaming smile. After the hug, auntie Dolly stood back and said, 'And do all the girls still go'… she heaved a big sigh … 'when you walk into a room?'

To be perfectly honest I was never aware they did.

I left Glenwood and went to university in Pietermaritzburg and I saw Jay only once more. He too had moved on and was now doing his national service. Back in Durban during a vacation I was walking through town and I saw him standing outside a department store called Bon Marché. He looked so handsome in his uniform. Naturally I went to say hello but it was obvious from the moment he saw me that he didn't want to know me. He too had learned about queers, either during his last year at school or, if not there, definitely in the army. There must have been a great deal of talk and what had once been something beautiful between us was now considered dirty. His embarrassment in case he was seen with me was acute. He never once looked me in the eye as he used to do but shifted his gaze all around as though expecting someone to approach who he hoped would not. I left him there. I don't think I even said goodbye. With Jay I had started to find my place. For Jay it ended in the wrong place. I heard some years later he had married and, by now, he must be a grandfather; and yet, in my mind's eye, I still see that youth on the cricket pitch waiting for me to throw the ball back to him.

"At school friendship is a passion. It entrances the being; it tears the soul. All loves of after life can never bring its rapture, or its wretchedness; no bliss so absorbing, no pangs of jealousy or despair

Chapter Ten

so crushing and so keen! What tenderness and what devotion; what illimitable confidence; what infinite revelations of inmost thoughts; what ecstatic present and romantic future; what bitter estrangements and melting reconciliations; what scenes of wild recrimination; agitating explanations, passionate correspondence; what insane sensitiveness, and what frantic sensibility; what earthquakes of the heart, and whirlwinds of the soul, are confined in that simple phrase, a schoolboy's friendship."–Benjamin Disraeli. 1844.

But now the real world had to intrude. I had a friend by the name of Ned Mayer. His family came from one of the French colonial islands and French was his home language though his father, with the same reasoning as Jay's, sent him to an Afrikaans university, Stellenbosch. Before that, Ned was at the most prestigious Church of England school in Natal, Michaelhouse, so though we saw each other only in the holidays we were good mates. I often slept over at his house even though it was no more than four hundred yards from ours and never once did I try anything on with Ned, despite the fact that he was a handsome blonde with sparkling blue eyes and an athlete's body. It just never occurred to me and, in fact, I had rather a thing for his young sister. I told him and he thought the whole idea was ridiculous, as he couldn't imagine anyone really fancying her. But I did. Was it just an older bother's reaction on his part or was there something else? Ned used to come on picnics with my family and we were really good buddies until one day, one day that is almost obliterated from my mind he suddenly said to me, 'Fuck off, you fucking queer!'

That is the total sum of what I remember of the incident: that, and the look on his face. Had he suddenly lunged out and punched me without warning I could not have been more shocked or more hurt. I don't remember where it took place, somewhere in the middle of town, or what the occasion was that we met, or what my reaction was to his verbal assault, or what happened afterwards. What did I say in reply, if anything? Where did I go when I left him? Or where did he go when he left me, if he left me? It's a total blank. Virtually everything about the incident, except for what he said, has been wiped. Now I can think that there had been a lot of gossip, most of it unfriendly, and he was only protecting his own reputation. I hope this was the reason for his attack because that is understandable. It is the reason for many an attack when one's own well-being is in danger. Naturally our friendship was over from that moment and, naturally, from that moment, I kept myself more to myself. The closet door had closed.

It opened again in London when I confessed all to David Scott Macnab who was studying at The Slade School of Art at the time. It was on the corner of Baker Street and Marylebone Road. Without a word, David Scott Macnab, up till then one of my closest friends, turned on his heel and walked away. I was so astonished I couldn't even call after him. This was the man whose idols included Noel Coward and Oscar Wilde. I never saw or heard from him again until my visit to South Africa in '73 when he admitted to me that his reaction was something he had always deeply regretted.

Chapter Eleven

1964 was the year of the Sydney Box contract and the first time in nine years I had a regular and, for that period, quite handsome income. Apart from starting the year writing the screenplay for *Brigadier Gerrard*, I was now also earning miniscule pennies as a portrait photographer because one day out of the blue, an unknown actress, unknown to me that is, called and said she'd seen some pictures I had taken of Ben Hawthorne while we were out on tour and would I take some of her? She would of course pay me. I took the pictures and charged her the magnificent sum of three pounds, or maybe it was guineas to be posh. Guineas were still in use then. Actors need photographs and actors are always skint so why charge more? The result was someone else saw her pictures, and the next thing I knew I was spending quite a lot of time both taking the photographs and developing and printing late into the night. I even went so far as to buy lamps, reflectors and large rolls of backing paper both black and white for indoor shots.

What put an end to this merry-go-round was not lack of time or lack of sleep but lack of sympathy when I was asked to photograph an actress of extremely plain features with a personality and manner to match. With an instant antipathy towards her, I found I simply could not take a decent picture. The first thirty-six frames were crap so I tried a second time but still with no success and told her to try someone else. There would be more like her and I had other things to do so, before those others came along, I gave it up, despite now having bought one of those new Japanese toys such as the Beatles had acquired, a single reflex camera, a Pentax. Later I also bought a Russian camera, a Practika and, with the Rollei, still have all three, though now of course digital is the thing but I haven't got around to that, although Chris is brilliant with his.

When it comes to modern technology I am a complete nincompoop. Like the three year old's flying past me on the ski slopes, three year old's leave me standing when it comes to computers. My first attempts at using a computer were in Virginia when I was staying with Allen and Anne Lyndrup in Harrisonburg. Allen had an "Apple" and I tried using it but it seemed like every few seconds I was howling for their son, Jens, to come to my aid because I'd lost whatever it was I was working on. Heaving sighs he'd come schlepping upstairs to his dad's study where I was working and say, 'What's the matter now?'

'I've lost it again, Jens. It's somewhere in outer space and I can't get it back?'

'Have you trashed it?'

'No.'

'Then it's still there.' With which he would press a key and, lo and behold, back on the screen flashed my lost work. But it wouldn't be long before, 'Jens!'

So I gave up and went back to my trusty borrowed typewriter.

I can't even manage mobile phones, or cell phones as the Americans call them, kinita in Greek. Chris was always going on about how useful they are, particularly in an emergency and we really should have one but the suggestion was firmly resisted. Then, on his sixtieth birthday one arrived from one of those Munich friends of many years, Wolf Kern, so there was nothing to do about that except to say thankyou. While I was in Athens the damn thing died on me in the middle of a conversation so, thinking it had run out of money, I took it to a local periptero[14] where, although I always start off a request in Greek, if the guy speaks English, he'll come back in that language which makes life a lot easier and I bought a 20 euro card, asking him

---

14 Kiosk

Chapter Eleven

to do the necessary. But he needed our pin number so a call back to Crete secured that and we then discovered there was a total of 78 euro credit. Why the phone had died he was unable to figure out. The following day I could not get it to behave. I wanted "menu" and kept on getting all sorts of wonderful things, everything except "menu". It didn't help that it was a freezing cold day and I was getting more and more uptight with the damn thing. I stopped in a snack bar and ordered a coffee and then realised all I had on me was a hundred euro note. The girl behind the counter was not a happy one but, in typical Greek fashion, left the bar and her till unattended to go out and get change. On my way home I walked through an arcade and there was a Vodafone shop so in I went. It was pretty busy but one young lad appeared to be free. I went up to the counter and, in no mood to attempt my sub-standard Greek, said, 'Do you speak English?'

'Yes.'

'Well there's something wrong with this phone. I can't get it to go back to menu.'

He took the phone from me and like Jens, and like the man from Strand Electric, he pressed a button and handed it back. Genuine amazement on my eyebrow sat.

'How did you do that?' I squealed, loud enough to get the immediate attention of the entire shop.

'I pressed this.' He showed me. 'You were pressing the wrong button, that's all.'

'I'm stupid.'

'No you're not.' This was said softly and came with a little smile and a twinkle in the eye. Cute? He was so cute he could have died of it as the saying goes in certain circles.

'Have a nice day,' he said as I left the shop. Time to show him I speak Greek.

'Epeesis,' the same to you, I said.

The Greeks are crazy for mobile phones. Television programmes are overloaded with ads for mobile phones. Everyone has one. When I was at university I used to light my pipe with a Zippo lighter. It was called an arsehole because everybody had one. Nowadays I think mobile phones should be called arseholes. I hate them. I hate seeing people in the street chatting into them. I hate people in buses and trains chatting into them; in restaurants, on the beach, whilst driving, in cinemas, or anywhere else for that matter. It used to be a Walkman that was glued to someone's ear, now it's a mobile phone. Where once people had to worry about their children growing up deaf due to the number of decibels in the music they listened to, now it appears people are worried about brain damage due to the microwave emissions from mobile phones.

It's amazing to think how science and technology have advanced in my lifetime. When I was a kid at Richmond School, if my parents wanted to phone me, from a distance of forty, maybe fifty miles as the crow flies, they had to book the call in advance and the matron would say something like, 'Your mother will be calling you at six o'clock Saturday evening so be there.' The "there" was the dining room where the telephone was situated and at ten minutes to six, better be early rather than miss it, I would be sitting on the wooden floor in the dining room, ready to leap up and lift the earpiece off the telephone fixed to the wall above my head, as soon as I heard the school's call. All the phones were on party lines and everyone had a call signal of so many short and so many long rings rather like the Morse code. Nosey parkers weren't backwards in picking up the phone to listen in to other folks' conversations so very little, if anything, was said on the telephone that shouldn't be said or could be misconstrued. But for kids being in touch with home we would try to get as much news in as we could before we heard the operator's voice saying, 'Your three minutes are up, do you wish to pay for a further three minutes?'

Please, mom, please say yes. Your little boy is homesick and about to cry.

Now there are DVDs and CDs, including portable ones, and even more advanced technology than that, the I-Pod with, no doubt, more

Chapter Eleven

wonders to come. How many pieces of music do you need to carry about with you all in one tiny gadget? If we wanted music on an outing back in the good old days it was the portable gramophone in its big heavy black box with a handle to carry it, a crank to wind it up, and you could stash half a dozen records in a pocket in the lid. You had to make sure you had the right needles which, when worn, were put away safely in a little metal tray that slid out from the base. The records were heavy, easily breakable 78's on labels like *His Master's Voice, Decca, Parlaphone,* and *Brunswick*.

"*I'm sitting on top of the world, just rolling along, just singing a song!*" It might have sounded tinny but it went well with sun, sea, and sand and 'Who wants a drumstick?'

'Me! Me!'

It's also hard to think, what with Kentucky Fried, chicken nuggets, chicken this and chicken that and all the chicken loading down supermarket shelves, that at that time chicken was an expensive luxury to be enjoyed only on special occasions. My mother's favourite was the parson's nose. No one would dream of denying her that titbit. She ordered a chicken from the butcher once and took it back immediately saying, 'I ordered a chicken, I didn't ask for Ghandi's brother!' I know I'm digressing again but this is reminiscence after all.

This was the year, 1964, it was all happening as they say. Firstly Ben Hawthorne came to me and said he had the chance of producing a summer rep season at Buxton in Derbyshire but needed finance to get it going, would I put up the money?

'You want to direct, don't you?' He said, baiting the trap nicely, 'well here's your chance.'

'How much do you need?'

'Six hundred pounds.'

Six weeks wages from Sydney Box. Well, the money either goes to the tax man, or I buy a couple more paintings, or I can spend it giving fellow actors some work and, if I lose it, it's not that much skin off my nose so, okay, let's do it.

We formed a company, Durwell Productions Limited: the Dur from my home town, Durban; the well from his home town, Wellington, New Zealand. The company directors were Ben and myself and the three Directors of Production were Ben, myself, and an actor by the name of David Rayner who was a friend of Ben's and who, I'm afraid, I did not take to at all. He was more self-opinionated than was good for him, totally lacking in charm, and abrasive with those around him. On top of which I never considered him to be a particularly good actor. He played Ricard in *Rattle of a Simple Man*, which I directed and, when it came to the fight, he refused point blank to follow my directions, maintaining the way he had thought out was much better.

'All right, David,' I said, 'show me your way.' And he did. Then, looking at me for approval, 'What do you think?' He asked.

'I think it looks like shit,' I replied, 'but if that's the way you want to do it, then you do it.'

Brian Gilmar, who was playing Percy, looked at me as though I had taken leave of my senses. Everyone knew perfectly well the fight, as arranged by Mr Rayner, looked like the worst amateur shit. It wasn't too long though before he was doing it the way I wanted.

Reading through some of his business and publicity letters now, to begin with and early on that summer his head was certainly in the right place. Why he eventually went off the rails, unless it was that cock of the walk conceit, I really don't know. I was beavering away in London when I received the following letter from a member of the company and all I could do was have a quiet chat over the phone with Ben. I don't think it did any good. David was Ben's friend, Ben had brought him into the company and Ben's opinion of himself was also up in the stratosphere somewhere so he never took too kindly to criticism, though he could dish it out when he felt like it.

Dear Glyn,
Certain very disturbing things have been happening here and, since I feel sure you know nothing of them, here goes. On Friday lunchtime I went into the office to be paid and was confronted by Mr Rayner. His

Chapter Eleven

words were roughly as follows. "The stage management have been told if they can't keep up with the pace they must give in their resignations. Now we feel that you can't keep up the pace and since we don't intend to let the standard slip, I have no alternative but to give you two weeks notice."

I was rather dumbfounded as you can imagine but merely said it was a disgraceful and appalling way to behave and left it at that—no scene, no fuss. Now Ben was not present at that interview and up to date has made no mention of it and given NO sign that it took place. Not wishing for any unpleasantness and having two more shows to get through I have carried on as though NOTHING had happened. What makes it worse is that about ten days before, Ben, quite unsolicited said that I would probably be getting a rise for Private Lives.

Item No 2.

George O'Gormon who came down for the "Music Hall" was offered a part in "P.E & P.E,[15] rang his agent for the o.k. and accepted, learned a couple of days later second-hand that they had changed their minds. He was first offered the part by Mr Rayner and finally told "no" by Ben. Now, whether they know it or not, they are legally bound by "word of mouth" contract to pay George that week's salary.

Are you also aware that the stage management have been working on Sundays without remuneration? That initial wonderful pioneering spirit seems to have been killed and been replaced by the hideous whispering in corners routine. Twixt you and me I think Mr Rayner is mostly to blame with rather a lot of help from Mr Job [one of the actors in the company]. I also feel that Ben, as senior member here must bear the responsibility. I suppose you know that Sara and Anastasia have given in their notice?

And the letter goes on. I don't think it was written because he had been given his notice or to spite David Rayner. I do believe he wrote

---
15 Private Ear and Public Eye.

it because he honestly thought I should be aware of what was going on. He admitted the strain of playing large parts week after week was beginning to tell on him but the answer to that should have been to give him a week out to rest or at least a couple of weeks playing minor roles, which I'm sure he wouldn't have minded, not to dismiss him in so brutal a fashion, a loyal actor who had been in the company from the beginning.

Durwell's proposed Buxton season of fourteen weeks opened on the 15th June with the play *Marriage Go Round* by Leslie Stevens, directed by Ben Hawthorne, with Brian Gilmar, Nona Williams, Margo Evans and David Rayner in the cast. It was followed by *The Lodger*, which I directed. We were back to weekly rep but it was felt that longer playing periods were just not viable. There were three seat prices, the top being 5/6, twenty-seven and a half pence in decimal coinage, and there were concessions. Pensioners could sit anywhere in the house for 2/6 (Thirteen pence). Everyone in the company, including directors, was paid the same salary, £16, which wasn't bad for that time. After *The Lodger* came *Rattle of a Simple Man*. Moving into July we had *Two for the See-Saw* by William Gibson, a play that caused great consternation with a group of seventy Methodist holiday-makers whose spokesperson wrote a strong letter of protest to the management, condemning the play:

"We desire to make a protest in the strongest possible terms against the performing of this play. We offer no criticism of the good standard of performance by the cast, but express our utter disgust at the dialogue of the play. Our protest is against the immoral suggestion throughout which is injurious to all, and especially to young people. In a day when it is necessary to strengthen the life of the nation by upholding sound moral principles, it is deeply to be deplored that such a sordid and degrading view of sex should be paraded before the public. Many of our young people walked out in protest, and those of us who remained to the end were nauseated buy its theme. It is our belief that theatre managements

could do much to strengthen our communal life by refusing to perform such kinds of play which inevitably tend to lower moral standards by degrading sex and the sacred vows of marriage, and help to undermine the true and pure foundation of a strong national life."

Attached was a petition signed by seventy members of the group, led by the Reverend Frank E.Reedman and the Secretary of the Willersley Castle Holiday Centre, Miss June Lamb.

It's amazing how sex is considered the sin above all others with the followers of Wesley and Calvin. I remember seeing an interview on television in which Mary Whitehouse said with great pride that in a questionnaire to university students, ninety percent of them condemned sex before marriage. But Mrs Whitehouse left out one important word; she neglected to say that the university concerned was a Methodist one. A sin of omission methinks.

Rex Rainer back in the fifties danced in a series for American television, the Xavier Cugat show I think it was, in which the male dancers all had to have their chests bandaged beneath their costumes lest the sight of a boy's nipples caused offence or arousal in the Bible Belt.

What would the Methodists who kicked up such a fuss over an innocent little play like *Two for the See-Saw* make of to-day's offerings in the entertainment industry? What would the Lord Chamberlain make of them? In 1964 his office was still in existence and I have in front of me the licence issued for *Bay Rum*, a fascinating document in beautiful flowing copperplate script, with the exception of the details of the play and date inserted by hand. It is numbered 4337.

Beneath a large facsimile of the Royal Coat of Arms it reads,

LORD CHAMBERLAIN'S OFFICE

I, the Lord Chamberlain of the Queen's Household for the time being, do by virtue of the Office and in pursuance of powers given to me by the Act of Parliament for regulating Theatres, 6 & 7 Victoria Cap. 68 Section 12. Allow the Performance of a new Stage Play of which a copy has been submitted to me by you being a Play in 3 Acts entitled

"Bay Rum"

with the exception of all Words and Passages which are specified in the endorsement of this Licence and without any further variations whatsoever.

Given under my hand
This 16th day of July 1964
Cobbold
Lord Chamberlain
To The Manager of the Playhouse, Buxton.

Attached to this imposing document is a memorandum that reads,

Memorandum

Any proposed alteration or addition to this Play, or alteration of title must be submitted for the Lord Chamberlain's approval. Failure to observe this Regulation may endanger the continuation of the performance of the Play.

And on the reverse side yet another,

Mem. The particular attention of the Management is called to the following Regulations, which refer to all Stage Plays licensed by the Lord Chamberlain. The strict observance of these Regulations is to be considered as the condition upon which the Licence is signed.

- Any change of title must be submitted for the Lord Chamberlain's approval.
- No profanity or impropriety of language to be permitted on the Stage.
- No indecency of dress, dance, or gesture to be permitted on the Stage.
- No objectionable personalities to be permitted on the Stage, nor anything calculated to produce riot or breach of the peace.

- No offensive representation of living persons to be permitted on the Stage.

All a bit draconian when you come to think of it. I don't recollect any lines being cut in *Bay Rum* but when the licence was issued for *Early One Morning*, one of the lines I do remember receiving the red pencil was a reference to guardsmen's boots on the stairs. Everyone knew at that time that guardsmen followed a long tradition of being rent but the Lord Chamberlain didn't particularly want it broadcast.

Bank Holiday Attraction
Premiere of a new comedy
by
Glyn Jones.

BAY RUM

"It is with great excitement that Durwell productions present their first premiere of the season," etcetera. This was how the blurb started in the previous week's programme and, in actual fact, *Bay Rum* was the one and only premiere of the season. The blurb, after a few lines about myself, went on to give a résumé of the play, which went:-

"It is set on a tropical island in the Pacific Ocean. A young and attractive widow, Millie Watson, arrives to take up residence on the island. She is greeted by four of the local European inhabitants. They all become immediately infatuated with her, and her charm and frankness is (*sic*) quickly misconstrued into relationships of a more serious nature, much to her amazement. One bewildering event follows another and the easy charm and humour with which the play unfolds ensures a gay evening in the theatre.

Bay Rum is a play to sit back and enjoy. It is pure entertainment value. Nona Williams makes a welcome return to the company to play Millie, and audiences will have the opportunity to see new faces as well. At last Ben Hawthorne has the opportunity to direct this play, an eagerly awaited event."

I see the sets were designed by Anastasia Wade-Brown and executed (what a terrible word for it) by Christopher Beeching. He had in fact already "executed" a design for the play and built a model but Anastasia was the company's designer and her designs took preference. When Chris was working on his design I told him I wanted plenty of a vine called Golden Shower that grew in South Africa. Don't know whether it grew on a South Pacific island but what did that matter? Nobody else would have known either. I kept on trying to describe to him what the flowers looked like and eventually, in frustration, I smacked my hand down on a biscuit tin on the table between us, "Three Ring Biscuits" from South Africa and what was the design on the lid? Golden shower. By the time *Bay Rum* went into rehearsals Anastasia had left and Chris took over the design department.

Bay Rum duly opened on August 3rd with Nona playing Millie and Dudley Stevens as the romantic male lead. Vicky too would arrive shortly afterwards to play in *Salad Days*. Shades of Ventnor.

The first act of *Bay Rum* went like a dream. The audience loved it. The second act had me so embarrassed I could have slid off my seat and hidden on the floor. It was awful: not the production; not the performances, it was the writing. How did I ever think I could get away with it? The play is a sort of cross between *The Little Hut, My Three Angels*, and a ghost story and has joined *Enter Anthony* in the deepest recesses of the script cupboard never to see the light of day again. One patron suggested I turn it into a musical, a suggestion I dismissed out of hand.

The summer season went exceptionally well. Ben added *Old Time Music Hall* to the plays during the week of the Buxton Music Festival which evidently was enthusiastically received, and *Salad Days* was extended a week playing to capacity. I directed two more plays before the end of the season, *Trap for a lonely Man* and *A Doll's House*, the sets for both plays designed by Chris.

With a healthy bank account Ben asked if he and David could carry on with an autumn/winter season and of course, with that, everything

Chapter Eleven

was lost. There were no holidaymakers in Buxton that time of the year to swell spare audiences and it was the end of Durwell Productions. I did try to get a theatre in Malta to take us in but without success and I also tried to get a play on in Ghana. This was called *Wind Versus Polygamy* and was by a Nigerian by the name of Obi Egbuna. Julian Grant, for whom I had written a couple of short films on the Scottish clans, passed the play on to me asking if I could place it. It was pretty dreadful simply because, if nothing else, in playing time it was longer than an uncut *Hamlet*. Ghana was not interested but I did some considerable work on the play and it was bought and produced by the BBC. Did I get an acknowledgement from Mr Egbuna? Did I even get a thank you from Mr Egbuna? No, I did not. But that's the way it goes.

Before the summer season at Buxton even started, a letter was received from a girl by the name of Nina Webster asking if she could be of any use in helping to start a Theatre Supporter's Club, adding as a postscript that she did have a typewriter, and Nina soon became part of the company. At the end of the season Ben asked if I could take her on as my secretary as she was now out of a job. Although I really didn't have need of a secretary, being the lazy git that I am I took her on and she stayed with me until The Royal Ballet Touring Company advertised for a secretary. With a little help from me in the form of an enthusiastic (and truthful) letter of recommendation, she got the job.

This was also the year Pearle Celine, in England via the Middle East and Cyprus, started another drama school, this time in Ealing. I went out there a few times at her request to take classes and met a young Australian student, Ray Bluett, actually from Tasmania, who has remained friends to this day. He returned to Australia to continue as an actor before going on to teach. I visited him in his shack in Tasmania a couple of years ago: as far south as you can go, next stop Antarctica. It's a beautiful country, except for areas of thick forestation very much like parts of England, and unfortunately it also seems to have English weather at its wettest. Through Ray I met another Australian, Ron Southcott from Melbourne and he and his other half, Doctor Ian Chenoweth, living in Melbourne, were also visited. They couldn't believe, after all the years and, countless invitations, that I had actually made it. Australian joke about Tasmanians, not one of cousin Bertie's this time: 'If a Tasmanian couple get a divorce on the mainland are they still brother and sister?'

In 2003 I travelled the full length of Australia by train, from Perth to Melbourne and I did not see one specimen of wild life. In Tasmania at night I caught a glimpse of wombats, or small furry buggers as Ray called them, but I didn't see a single kangaroo until I went to Perth zoo on my return to that city. Bert's wife, Janet, asked one day what I would like to do and was most surprised when I said I wanted to go to the zoo, but I had a reason for it. I wanted to see a tiger snake. Perth zoo is beautifully laid out and well kept. It covers a large area and the animals are not confined but have plenty of room to roam. We made for the reptile house where, of course, they are confined and I hunted in vain for my first sight of a tiger snake. I saw lots of other snakes and the biggest crocodile in the world, twice the size of any I had ever seen in Africa, but no sign of a tiger snake, so I asked an attendant if they had any.

'Yees.' Why do Australians say 'yees' instead of yes? 'We do have one but he's in quarantine at the moment.' So I still haven't seen the scaly poisonous little bugger and the reason I wanted to see him was because Ray had told me at length about how poisonous these reptiles are and they are now a protected species so, if you see one guarding your front doorstep as he has done, you don't send it into snake heaven, you go around to the back door and hope he goes back to the bush.

1964 was also the year when I did sell something to television that was actually produced, *Doctor Who and The Space Museum*. It came about because Trevor Bannister and his wife, Kathy, invited us to

Chapter Eleven

dinner and the other guests that evenings were David Whittaker and his wife. David was at the time script editor for the Doctor Who series and, during the course of the evening he told me that if I had an idea for the show to send it to him and, if he liked it, he would commission it. A few days later I sent him an outline and he commissioned four scripts. I was fortunate in meeting him when I did because he was on the point of handing over the editorship to Dennis Spooner who certainly tightened up my scripts but denuded them of all humour, which was a pity. William Hartnell was the Doctor and, at a pretty advanced age, was really getting past it. He had great difficulty in remembering his lines and at times that is evident as he hums and haws his way through a scene. The other point of regret for me is that the group of rebels in the story were all boys. Were I to write it now, or even at a later date from when it was first written, I would have included girls, which would have made it a much rounder piece. As it was, the only two females in the show were the two principals. It

William Hartnell as Dr Who in A Space Museum with Ivor Salter & Richard Shaw

wasn't a deliberate choice at the time, just the way I happened to write it. I'm really surprised Spooner didn't pick up on it. Shortly afterwards I came up with another story for the series but Spooner rejected it and, when I was told in 2004 that a new series was on the cards, I sent in another idea through a friend of a friend of a friend but to date have had no word as to its reception. The problem with friends who tell you how much they love your work and how they just know somebody who can do something with it, is that invariably it leads to disappointment when that is the last you hear of it. More scripts have gone into outer space that way never to be seen again. W.H.Allen later published *The Space Museum* as a book after I had given them a sample of my prose writing. The firm was later taken over by Virgin who seemed to be totally uninterested in *Doctor Who* as sales dried up completely even though, when I was in America, people kept asking me for it and I had to tell booksellers of its existence. But that wasn't the end of it. The BBC brought it out on cassette as a special edition in conjunction with a couple of episodes of *The Crusaders*, the other episodes of that one having been lost.

When I was playing at Derby in 1980 a kid came to the stage door with a copy of a sci-fi magazine and asked me if I was the Glyn Jones who had written *The Space Museum* and, if so, would I autograph his magazine because in it in comic form was the complete story. I duly gave him his autograph and, as I knew absolutely nothing about this publication, I phoned my agent who also knew nothing about it but immediately got on to the publishers for the fee they should have paid in the first place had they asked permission to publish.

But more was happening in 1964. I started work on *A King's Story* and met the editor, Harry Booth with whom I was to be associated for a few more projects, both those actually produced and those that weren't. He and a producer, Roy Simpson, were partners in a production company called *Century Films* and they asked me if I could come up with anything for the *Children's Film Foundation*, an

Chapter Eleven

organisation financed by the big distributors. The C.F.F. contracted filmmakers to produce movies for kids' matinees, Saturday morning showings that were supposed to build the audience of the future.

When I was very young there was no such thing as television and going to the bioscope on a Saturday afternoon was a real treat for which you got all dressed up. If the film you went to see was on at the Playhouse you gave yourself plenty of time so that you could have an ice or a milkshake in the front of house cafeteria before the movie started. The décor there was mock Tudor to set the imagination rolling and when you went into the cinema itself you were in a medieval town, the walls being lined with the facades of buildings, their diamond pane windows lit with a golden light. What, I used to wonder, went on behind those windows? The ceiling was a dark blue sky full of stars. The golden light began to fade and if you heard the music for *Loony Tunes* or any other cartoon there would be howls of joyful expectation from the audience. There were also the newsreels of course, television not having arrived, and maybe a *Pete Smith Special* or a travelogue, or *The March of Time*. Finally came "the big picture" as it was called. I don't recollect it ever being called the main feature.

There was radio of course and I never missed an episode of *Michael Strogoff* whose theme music was the overture to *The Flying Dutchman*. I don't remember as a kid ever being bored. I had a Meccano set with which I was supposed to build cranes and similar constructions but all I did was make swords and daggers with which to have fights. I particularly liked daggers with the guard shaped like wings such as they had in *The Corsican Brothers*. My father also bought me an 8mm projector and a few little reels of film and we would hang up a white sheet in the dining room and have showings for neighbourhood kids. Did they never get tired of seeing the same old movies over and over again? There was Mickey Mouse and Pluto and Donald Duck, Popeye and Olive Oyl and a couple of movies of *Our Gang*. The gang consisted of half a dozen slightly offbeat, slightly crazy American kids and a dog with a black eye. They got up to all sorts of tricks and, no matter how many times we watched them and knew exactly what was coming next, we would always fall about with laughter. So I put it to Harry and Roy that we should do a modern version of *Our Gang*.

'Who were they?' Harry asked.

'You've never heard of *Our Gang*?'

They both shook their heads so I set about giving them a quick low-down on the various characters and the dog. I wish I had a tape recording of that conversation which led to so much because it was thus that *The Magnificent 6½* was born and, after that, *The Double Deckers*.

There were two series of *The Magnificent 6½*. I was totally involved in the first and did some co-writing and ghosting in the second. I notice now the credits on a flier include "Based on an idea by Henry Geddes." Henry was head of The Children's Film Foundation at the time and obviously wanted a credit somewhere down the line and this was the only one I presume Roy and Harry could come up with. The last episode in the first series was called *Peewee's Pianola* and was simply about the gang being discovered and chased by an irate farmer while out scrumping, whereat they throw their ill-gotten gains over a hedge and, hearing this musical sound as the apples bounce on something, they discover an old abandoned pianola which they take back to town with them by means of lifts on an assortment of vehicles, all singing as they go. They end up getting a ticket from an irascible old parking attendant and then I think the pianola rolls away downhill creating mayhem. I'm not too sure about this last bit. It was a long time ago and I no longer have a script to verify it but I think that's how it ended.

'It's got no story,' Harry complained on reading my script.

'Of course it's got a story,' I said.

'No. It needs a complete rewrite. It won't do. There's no plot.'

'Harry,' I said, 'I've written and rewritten for you and given you exactly what you want with every script even if I've sometimes disagreed with it. This is one I would like you to shoot word for word

Chapter Eleven

"THE MAGNIFICENT SIX AND $\frac{1}{2}$"
(2nd SERIES)
(EASTMAN COLOUR)

A series of six short stories presented in serialised form

MADE BY

CENTURY FILM PRODUCTIONS LTD.

FOR THE

CHILDREN'S FILM FOUNDATION

Made on location and at Shepperton Studios, England

DISTRIBUTED BY

CHILDREN'S FILM FOUNDATION LTD.

6-10 GREAT PORTLAND STREET, LONDON, W1N 6JN

TELEPHONE: 01-580 4796

Programme cover for 2nd series of The Magnificent 6 ½

please, exactly as it's written, because I am not changing a word of it.'

To say Harry was taken aback is putting it mildly so I pleaded a bit more. 'Please, Harry, believe me, trust me, it will work. Just go ahead and shoot it.'

It took a lot more argument to convince him but, in the end, he did what I asked of him and I believe it won what was called the "Chuffy Award": that is, the kids voted it as their favourite Saturday morning film. Harry never stopped boasting to all and sundry about 'HIS' *Peewee's Pianola*.

The Daily Cinema film review reads, "*First class comedy both visual and verbal, acted with remarkable ease by the seven children and with enthusiastic solemnity by the adult cast. To see this series is to be convinced that the art of making knockabout comedy as good as that of the old silent days is not dead. Lucky, lucky juniors to have this gorgeously funny series to look forward to for six successive Saturdays.*"

But before this, while we were still in Wardour Street working on *A King's Story*, Harry said during the course of a chat that a movie set in a girls' school would be a big hit, so I went off and wrote a screenplay initially entitled *The Magpie* later changed to *Finishing School*. An article in *The Sunday Express* dated May 25th, 1969 with a photograph captioned

'NOW SUE PRESENTS SUE'

"Actress Sue Lloyd (above) has decided to be a film producer. She has set up her own company and hopes to start making her first picture at the end of July. It will star Sue Lloyd–"Naturally," she says. "The film will be a psychological thriller set in a girls, finishing school. I'm very excited about it because production is something I have very much wanted to do for a long time." Miss Lloyd, 29, will be co-producer with her friend and fellow company director 25 year old Jo Martinez. And the film will be shot entirely at Dibden Manor the

Chapter Eleven

Hampshire home of his father, wealthy engineer and design consultant Mario Martinez. Jo's parents will take a two-month holiday abroad during filming." Very wise.

I was introduced to Sue Lloyd through our lawyer and lifelong friend, Andy Moore and I really don't know what eventually happened to this one. Sue called in another of those "I know it all" directors by the name of Ray Austin who, off his own bat, did a whole heap of rewrites and gave it the ridiculous title of *It Happened on Tuesday* or was it Monday? Whatever day it was, it didn't happen on any day and that was the last I heard of it. Or did it happen without my knowledge? Because some years later Andy said 'You were done on that one.' And I wonder what he could have meant? A Spanish film with the same title came out shortly afterwards but it bore no resemblance to my script. I thought of rewriting it as a book but gave up when I realised there is no such thing as a finishing school in England, leastways not to my knowledge.

Also in Wardour Street I met Arthur Ferriman who was the accountant on *A King's Story* and who had bought the rights to a series of books by Herbert Jenkins written between 1916 and 1924 about a fictional Cockney character called *Bindle* who was to be played by Alfie Bass. Arthur asked me if I would write the first script, which I did. I went out to, Mill Hill I think it was, somewhere in North London anyway, to meet Alfie for pre-production talks but all I can remember of that meeting was gazing in wonder at a room of rich velvet and brocaded furnishings and curtains literally torn to shreds by a pair of Siamese cats.

Alfie was not a good choice for *Bindle* and, here I go again, neither was the director. When I saw on the set beside Bindle's bed a statuette of the Madonna I had my doubts and, when Alfie proceeded to drop lines and make up his own as he went along which he fondly thought were witty, and a weak director who did nothing to put a stop to it, I knew disaster was looming. Poor Arthur, he had put his own money into this project and he lost it all. I can sympathise with him even though he still owes me my final payment. I never had the heart to harass him for it. I doubt he could have paid me anyway.

While filming the Windsors in France, Le Vien put us up at The Hotel Raphael in Paris and, although my room was a little on the pokey side, it was more than comfortable. When luxury does come my way I can appreciate it though it isn't the be all and end all for me. I don't know what I would do if ever I became what is euphemistically known as stinking rich. I don't want a fleet of cars or even a single Rolls Royce. I don't want a yacht or a private jet. I don't want an entourage. I don't like champagne, it's too dry for my palatte, and I loathe oysters. Caviar I do like but one could get sick of that I suppose if one over indulged.

Chris and I went to Swanage for another five days and bought two small Macmiadechain, as Padraig sometimes signs himself, pictures from what he called his Looe period. It was no train journey this time as I had hired a car so we followed up Swanage with a tour around Dorset and Cornwall and I was no sooner home when Harry was on the phone again.

Chapter Twelve

The reason for Harry's call was because he had a request for his services by another American, Milton Lehr, who wanted to produce a TV special in Madrid with Xavier Cugat and his orchestra and was I interested in writing it with him? Writing with Harry meant me writing and Harry watching, with an occasional interjection. I really mustn't denigrate Harry Booth. I owed him a great deal at that time for the work he and Roy gave me and, above all, for the faith they had in me, but sometimes I wondered if he suffered from short man syndrome. It became a bit of a joke that Harry wanted every aspect of a film credited to Harry Booth and if he could have got a credit for the ice-cream sales in the intermission he would have had that too.

He was certainly no writer although many a script is partly credited to him but that is hardly unusual in the world of films. As a director I would rate him for the most part as no more than competent, though sometimes even there I had my doubts. Take for example a scene from *The Double Deckers* in which the owner of a flea circus was putting the fleas through their paces for the benefit of the gang of kids. After shooting a master of the entire scene, Harry then went on to shoot the whole scene again eight more times, each time from the point of view of one of the participants, seven kids and one adult. Now Harry I believe, and this was before I met him, had a wonderful reputation as an editor, and I may be wrong but, as an editor, surely he was knowledgeable enough to know what he needed for cutting purposes without so much waste of both time and footage. Why was he suddenly so unsure of himself I wonder? Perhaps he should have stayed an editor. As for hogging the credits, every tin pot director these days likes to see on the screen the credit that says the film is his; "A So-and-so's Film" whereas in fact the film belongs to everybody who works on it. But that's the way the egos go and it's rather pathetic really even if it's felt necessary for the sake of career.

I went with Harry to the Hilton Hotel in London to meet Milton Lehr and soon after was off to Madrid for eight days to write the Cugat script. A pleasant airy apartment was put at my disposal where I could sit on the porch, sip pina coladas, occasionally look up to admire the view over the city and type away, Harry at my side making occasional noises. In the evenings it was tapas and dining out at Milton's expense. I thought a solid hour or more of Senor Cugat's orchestra on television would probably be a bit boring in the end so I tried to spice it up with a bit of variety. For example, there was a handsome young bullfighter of the day who went by the name of El Cordobes, a sort of James Dean of the bull ring and, despite the criticisms of the aficionados as to his style (or lack of it) in the ring, he had all the glamour of a young film or pop star and a following to match. I wanted to do a scene with him in the Prado[16] strumming his guitar and making a few passes at nubile young ladies playing at being bulls. A bit of gender bending there but it could have been fun. It was immediately red-pencilled. When I come up with these outré ideas they always get shot down in flames as with Henry Thynne, Marquis of Bath when I wrote (Harry directing) a documentary on Longleat which I titled *Bathtime*, hardly original I admit. Longleat is a magnificent house approached down a wide sloping driveway half a mile or more long and I wanted the credits to be superimposed over the Marquis, coronet on head, sitting in a hip bath at the top of the drive scrubbing his back with a long brush or loofah, even better to actually have the credits on his back and scrubbed off or washed away with each rinse to disclose the next, but Henry would have nothing to do with it.

16 Museum & Art Gallery–Madrid

Chapter Twelve

'Good God, boy! What would they say in my club?'

Working on the film in Madrid was a young American expat by the name of Arnold or Arnaldo Taraborrelli who had a small apartment in the centre of the city and later that year Chris and I would return to Madrid for a holiday, staying with Arnold and gadding about: Toledo, Aranjuez, Allegre, Alcala de Henares. I will never forget Toledo because in the early hours of that night I woke up in Arnold's apartment as sick as the proverbial dog. I really thought I was at death's door it was so bad, as bad as my experience in The Bay of Biscay. My ribs were one solid ache as my stomach kept heaving even when it was empty. The following morning we went through everything we had eaten the previous day. Could it have been the strawberries at Aranjuez? No, Chris had eaten the strawberries as well as I. Could it have been the lunch? No, we both had exactly the same. Then I hit on it. It had been a boiling hot day, Toledo is hilly, I was dying of thirst and was the only one to drink from a street fountain, and it was the water that did it.

I didn't stay for the shoot of *Cugat in Madrid*. My job was done: so well done that Milton tore it up and wrote a script of his own, in rhyming couplets so I was told. It probably played Argentina and that was that.

Arnold came to England to work on *The Double Deckers* and stayed with his friend, John Perry, an artist from whom I bought two pictures, a large oil and a small pastille of Arnold's apartment in Madrid. Arnold is also an artist and he wittily illustrated a book of children's poetry I wrote called *Hildegarde H and Her Friends*. Hildegarde is a hippopotamus and her friends are an assortment of African animals. Some years previously I met a young couple from Canada, Alex Teck and Caroline Humby. They lived in St Charles Square close by Ladbroke Grove and, as they were on their uppers when I first met them, they had tried to sell a picture to Roy Miles but Roy wasn't interested. When he heard they were interested in writing and film, he suggested they meet me and we became close friends.

Caroline designed a chart showing the lineage of the Royal Family that they sold virtually door-to-door and which became a really big seller. So much so that they formed a company, Abydos Publishing that later became a company manufacturing items for museum gift shops. The business expanded at a terrific rate but unfortunately in 1984 Alex developed a brain tumour and died. I was just in time on my return from America to attend his funeral. After his death Caroline became a real workaholic and continued to go from strength to strength, the company producing the most exquisite calendars and souvenirs etcetera for museum customers all over the world. While still in early days as Abydos they published *Hildegarde* but made the fatal mistake of ring-binding it which meant that libraries would not buy it as little fingers can easily tear out favourite pages from a ring-bound book. Unfortunately it was also the end of our friendship with Arnold who took great umbrage over his name being misspelt and he disappeared from our lives.

*The Belicose Buffalo from Hildegarde H & Her Friends
Illustrated by Arnold Taraborelli - Abydos Publishing*

Chapter Twelve

Hildegarde H once lived in style,
On the reaches of the upper Nile,
But being the kind to follow her star
She doesn't mind
What was left behind.
Mud is mud, wherever you are.

One of the poems was about *The Bellicose Buffalo* and the six year old son of a friend went around for days warning people not to be bellicose with him or else!

Also for Abydos I worked out a possible scenario for the true story of King Arthur. This was going to be developed as a poster, the first of a series on mythical, or so-called mythical characters, such as, for example, Robin Hood and William Tell. I started my research in Bournemouth library while playing in *Who Goes Bare*, reading everything they had on King Arthur, then followed it up with further research on my return to London and came to only one conclusion as to the true identity of Arthur, and that is he was a Welshman, the grandson of King Llyr. Yes, there was an actual King Lear who with time has also become a part of Welsh myth. The Welsh name for Arthur is Arivagu, meaning a bear and Arthur's Roman name was Caractacus. Unfortunately I no longer have my notes but everything I unearthed at the time pointed to this conclusion. Just, for example, it was said that Arthur defeated the great boar at Caledon, which, at that time, was near Chichester, and the great boar was symbolic of the invading legions of Claudius who was of an Etruscan family whose shield was embossed with the head of a wild boar. Arthur was espoused to Boadicea but turned her down for Gwenhwyfar and, as a woman scorned, Boadicea betrayed him to the Romans. Taken to Rome he made such an impression, instead of being sold into slavery he was freed and given a villa that I believe exists to this day, The Villa Arthur. Sent back to England by the Romans to control unruly tribes on their behalf he eventually became sickened by Roman atrocity and turned against them once more only to be killed in his Welsh stronghold. The first legendary stories of Arthur did not come from Britian but emanated from Italy, spread by troubadours across the Alps to France and Germany and only from there did they return to England by which time he had become the mythical king, Medieval writers writing about his exploits as though they happened in their own lifetime which is why later writers were confused by the dates. It's possible that Stonehenge gave rise to the myth of The Round Table and Merlin was simply a Druid with, as was their custom, a bird's name, "Nightingale." Sir Lancelot du Lac was a French knight; son of a Roman governor of Gaul and his personal struggle was between spirituality, exemplified in his quest for The Holy Grail, or temporal satisfaction in his love for Gwenhwyfar. There were so many more examples that added up I became convinced, and still am, that this was the true Arthur. What I would have liked from the art director at Abydos was to have, on one side of the poster the legends, and on the other side the historical reasons which brought those legends into being. Unfortunately he just wasn't interested in that idea at all and designed a swirling psychedelic piece that really said nothing about Arthur except that there was a sword in the stone and a crown and a boat with a sail and … and … and nobody liked it so the whole thing was shelved.

Back in London from my eight days in Spain I met, again through Roy Miles, an Indian gentleman by the name of Ronnie Singh who was interested in film and who wanted to tell me various stories about India that he had come across which he felt would be good film material. One of them was the mutiny of The Connaught Rangers in India in 1921 when the last soldier in the British army to be executed was a Private James Daly. I was fascinated by this episode in military history that very few people seemed to know about, but put it aside momentarily as I was finishing up writing my all women cast play, *Thriller of the Year* as well as *Finishing School* and another original screenplay, *The Master Craftsman*, all purely on spec. Crazy or what?

Chapter Twelve

But ideas come and they say, 'write me' so you write them. I was told that trying to sell an original screenplay was almost an impossibility, which in my case it certainly proved to be, but it didn't stop me from trying.

In March I was cast in an episode of the BBC's *Softly Softly* which brought in a little money and Chris, after Buxton, went on to Coventry to dance in the pantomime *Cinderella* followed by *The Spring Show* starring Frankie Vaughan, Des O'Connor, Jack Douglas and a positive newcomer, a young comedian by the name of Jimmy Tarbuck, and Chris was now a dancer with Sadler's Wells Opera.

One night, when he was due home from the theatre, I was in the tiny kitchen and I heard these slow heavy footsteps as he mounted the stairs and I thought, "Oho! Something's wrong." So, opening the door, there was this pathetic figure who, the moment he saw me, burst into tears.

'Good God! What's the matter? What's happened?'

This just had to be a major tragedy. The sobbing increased.

'I fell over ... TWICE!'

I'm afraid I laughed but, after comforting him for a while, got the whole story. He was dancing two characters, dragonfly and ash, in Ravel's opera *L'enfant et les Sortileges*. As dragonfly he had to leap onto a rock fluttering his dragonfly wings. Unfortunately the stagehand who placed it had neglected to lock it in position so that, on its castors, it slid away from beneath him and he landed heavily on his coccyx. During rehearsal the artist playing the enfant terrible, on pulling down the wallpaper made sure the remnants lay on the floor close to the wall, but on opening night she left it lying across the stage. As ash, Chris's costume consisted of yards and yards of grey net which limited his vision so, dancing on his usual spot and not noticing the wallpaper lying there, he tripped over it and came another cropper. It was interesting that one of the critics mentioned, "at least two characters fell over," never realising they were one and the same person. The unfortunate aspect was that he neglected to enter it in the accident book. He swears there was no such thing as an accident book at that time but he has suffered on and off from back problems ever since and it all stems from those two horrific falls on stage.

One night he returned to the flat after a performance bringing home with him a young stage door Johnny in evening dress complete with scarlet lined opera cloak, medallion hanging from a ribbon (which turned out to be his father's), a bottle of champagne, strawberries, and a huge bunch of rhododendron. This florid gentleman's name was Jeremy Nightingale and a lawyer by profession who would remain one of our closest friends until his death in 1987 His father was Sir Geoffrey Nightingale, a hereditary baronet, psychiatrist, and head of the Warley Mental Hospital in Essex. Adjacent to the hospital and in its own grounds was "Greenwoods", a large beautiful house with a tennis court–unused, Jeremy was not the sporting type–a rose garden, and surrounded by dense bushes of purple rhododendron. Father and son lived in this idyllic setting with an enormous Great Dane named Hera and a manservant named Albert, a burnt-out schizophrenic who I used as the model for a character in my play, *Rosemary*.

Jeremy unfortunately was an alcoholic, the first of three in our lives and drunks may be funny on the music hall stage but in real life they are a tragedy, Jeremy's youthful death being a case in point. Although the subject never came up we surmised he was born on the wrong side of the blanket and therefore, being illegitimate, could never inherit the title that went to a cousin, much to Jeremy's chagrin. His mother, who was in another institution for a mental disorder, was Catholic and Jeremy was brought up in that faith much to the fury of his father who could not tolerate Catholicism so, much as he loved Jer, or said he did, there was always that antipathy between them. Goodness only knows what Sir Geoffrey thought of the friends Jeremy brought to Greenwoods of which there were many and various. Father kept himself mostly to himself, listening to recorded music of which he had a fair collection or speeding around the countryside in his E-Type

Jag. He sounds like a character Tom Sharpe might have dreamed up.

"Greenwoods" was a house that, with the warm scents of an English summer was full of people, the sounds of Gilbert and Sullivan, Jeremy's favourites, champagne, strawberries and cream and, in the evenings, possibly a stand up buffet. I remember one particular occasion, standing at the table wondering what to help myself to first, I suddenly heard this loud "shlurp" beside me and looking down saw half a smoked salmon disappearing into Hera's mouth. My reaction was immediate and instinctive. 'Hera!' I bellowed, and I have a pretty stentorian bellow that brought the dining room to a complete standstill as I gave her a cuff across her chops. I'll never forget the look on that dog's face. She had never been smacked in her life. Geoffrey meekly led her from the dining room and shut her in his study.

This was the night Jeremy, drunk as usual, decided to do a jeté down the passage that led from the kitchen to the front hall and, in so doing, hit his forehead on the lintel of the door creating a nasty and very bloody gash and knocking himself out cold. The first we knew of it was when we heard Albert from the kitchen door shouting, 'The dog! The dog! The dog's eaten Jeremy! Eaten Jeremy it has! Eaten him! The dog!'

Hera came to a sad end unfortunately. After Geoffrey retired from the hospital, Greenwoods was his to use no longer and he bought an Elizabethan house not too far distant named "Gents Farm." It was an amazing house with floors that lay at all angles. You could start at one end of a room with a ceiling height of say ten feet and find yourself at the opposite end with a height of seven feet or even less. But it was small and there was no room for Hera. Jeremy couldn't have her because he had by then bought a house in Hackney, just down the road from where we were now living, so one of the Essex lads, Robin Farnham, took Hera in only to have his father shoot her, accusing her of chasing sheep. None of us believed it as that dog was so timid she was frightened of her own shadow and a sheep would have scared her half to death. Not that she didn't in her time do her own amount of scaring. Strangers to the house, seated comfortably in the lounge, would suddenly leap out of their chair with a shriek when a large heavy head and slobbering jowls came from behind to rest on an exposed shoulder.

Some of the parties included boys from Brentwood school, among them one who was to make quite a reputation for himself as the writer of the *Hitchikers Guide to the Galaxy*. His name was Douglas Adams.

After our week in Spain, Chris went out on tour with the Sadler's Wells Company and Harry Booth called again. He had a film to direct for the C.F.F. It was called *River Rivals* and he wasn't happy with the script, would I do some more ghosting for him? As well as that, I wrote myself a part and we shot the film on location and at Shepperton. This was the first time I had serious doubts about acting as a profession though the doubts must have been fleeting as I continued to do it. It happened because of a scene being shot on the river when a crowd on a largish boat laughingly watched the baddy and his sons, having been dumped in the river, floundering in the water before they scrambled to the bank. Harry had his camera set up on the deck of the boat and shot the trio doing their stuff in the water. Then, while they were carted away to be dried and warmed in blankets and given hot drinks, the camera was set up on the bank for a reverse angle taking in our reaction. Harry informed us that our eye line was where the rope mooring the boat to the bank trailed in the water and on 'Action' we all started laughing uproariously at this rope in the water, and I thought to myself as I was doing it, what a bloody silly thing it was for a grown man to be doing, laughing at a rope in the water.

Eighteen years later in the kitchen of the Lyndrup house in Harrisonburg Virginia, I was having a cup of afternoon tea, the television was on and a movie came up called something about a dragon or a dragon something, I forget what the American title actually was but I seem to remember the houseboat in *River Rivals* had dragon in its name. I called Jens and Carrie into the kitchen to come and watch it and waited for their reaction when they saw me on screen. They were totally unimpressed.

'You were much younger,' Jens said and went back to whatever it was he had been doing.

I was involved with one more movie that year. I had become a director of yet another company, Oracle Productions, the other director being one Mark Peterson. He produced and directed a short feature without dialogue; the story based on an attempted assassination and the film was called *Stop*. Trevor Bannister took a small part in it and even put some money towards it, which he probably knew he would never get back. I also took a small acting role in it and much of the film was shot in our flat but it would seem the only outcome of all our effort was to provide an audition piece for Mark who became a well-known director of commercials. I was never offered a part in any of his commercials though. His small son, Christian was in the film and at a certain point had to have his face slapped. He wasn't forewarned and it was Mark himself who did the slapping. I'll never forget the look on that child's face. There was a gasp of total disbelief before the howling started and then Mark picked him up and told him he could hit daddy as much as he wanted, an invitation the child took up with gusto.

1967 saw me on my way to Leicester as a member of the company of the Phoenix Theatre that, like the mythical bird it was named after, had risen from the ashes of the old. The director was a man named John Hales, a protégé, God alone knows why, of John Barton of the RSC, or so we were told. Prematurely balding and full bearded with absolutely no sense of humour whatsoever, Hales was another of that legion who rely on the talents around them to get them through.

The first play was *Billy Liar* in which a very talented actor named John Trigger played Billy and I played the father. Trigger did not have a happy time at Leicester and by the end of it he had totally lost confidence in himself. The first thing John Hales said to us as we gathered in the theatre to start rehearsals was, 'Yes … well … I haven't set the furniture … because I thought we'd just kick it around a little.'

As far as I was concerned and, possibly, the other actors as well, this quite simply meant he hadn't an idea in his head, hadn't done his homework, and it was up to us to produce the play. The furniture, after we'd kicked it around a little, ended up in the most peculiar configuration. I played most of my scenes in a high backed wing chair facing upstage, away from the audience! The Phoenix was not a proscenium arch theatre but had a thrust which was really no more than a platform about six inches high. After three weeks rehearsal we sat on this platform with Hales seated in the auditorium facing us and we waited for notes. There was a long silence as he stroked his beard while gazing into the middle distance over our heads and then, very slowly, as if each word was produced with supreme effort, he said, 'Yes'… pause … 'well' … pause… 'then'… pause… 'we've done some very good work' … an even longer pause… 'what we must realise now is… this is a comedy.'

A whole set of actors' jaws hit the floor. We'd rehearsed for three weeks and this was all he could find to say? Nevertheless, and in spite of Mr Hales, *Billy Liar* played to excellent houses, over ninety percent I believe and with only the top of my head visible I even managed to get my laughs.

The second play was *Look Back in Anger*, the play rescued from oblivion by Kenneth Tynan and whose production at The Royal Court is credited with being a turning point in the history of British theatre, but I'm afraid I personally think the play's reputation is a tad over the top. I still think Osborne's best play is *Epitaph for George Dillon*, which he wrote in collaboration with Anthony Creighton. Naturally I played the Colonel in *Look Back in Anger* and this was followed by *Inadmissible Evidence* in which I played Hudson, the two plays running in rep. For Hudson I was bought a suit by the management, agreeing to buy it from them when the play was over. But as we were getting towards the end of the Osborne's, Hales, passing by in

Chapter Twelve

a passage, said to me, 'Glyn' ... pause ... 'I don't think I've got' ... pause ... 'anything for you in the next play.'

'What you mean, John, is you don't want to have anything for me in the next play.'

He mumbled something through his beard about boring actors to which I replied that boring actors were made by boring directors, a remark that certainly didn't go down at all well.

'Well what about the suit? You are buying it, aren't you?' There were no pauses while this request was being made.

'No, I'm certainly not buying it. You've just put me on the dole and you expect me to spend money on your suit?'

'But you said you would! What about my budget?'

'Fuck your budget.'

In the programme for *Look Back in Anger* I see someone, of whom I have no memory whatsoever, named Trevor Vibert directed it. I can't even put a face to the name, most unusual. I was a trifle upset at not staying on as I wanted very much to perform in a John Whiting play, one of the reasons I went to Leicester in the first place and *Penny for a Song* was scheduled, but apparently it didn't stay in the schedule so in the end it really didn't matter.

The houses for the second play were not as good as for the first. For *Inadmissible Evidence* they were even worse and, by the time it got to John Arden's *Live Like Pigs* I was told the house was virtually empty which meant the end of John Hales at the Phoenix.

Before going up to Leicester I had started my research on the Connaught Rangers and was not getting very far. The War Museum was no help at all, neither was the Ministry despite a letter of complaint written by Jeremy to Number 10. The Regimental Association dismissed my request for information out of hand. The official history of the Connaughts, an Irish regiment, the 88th of the line, glosses over the mutiny in a sentence. I suppose they couldn't get away with obliterating all memory of it. Over breakfast one morning I was telling my landlady about it when she said, 'Oh, yes, I know all about that. My husband was there.'

Unfortunately her husband wasn't around to talk to me about it but it turned out he was a schoolboy in India at the time and she told me even the schoolboys were put under arms; in case the mutiny spread was the official reason given. This was a fact I might not have known if it hadn't been for that fantastic coincidence of taking digs in that particular house in Leicester.

In the meantime I had written yet another play that wouldn't be produced called *Are You Sitting Comfortably?* And in July a play was actually produced. *Thriller of the Year,* starring Heather Chasen and with Gabrielle Hamilton, Judith Harte, Kathleen Moffatt and Elizabeth Weaver making up the cast. Directed by Ben Hawthorne, it opened at the Golders Green Hippodrome and, having seen it on its way, I went down to Southend to play in *Irma La Douce.*

Thriller of the Year was immediately published by Samuel French and has been a source of moderate income ever since. Unfortunately Ben took a scythe to the third act, cutting it to about fifteen minutes and who wants to come back from an interval to a fifteen-minute act? I was not at all happy about it but Ben insisted that what he cut was repetition so I went along with it. I still don't know whether he was right or not as the original third act is lost but, with the cuts, this was the version published and in production there has to be at least an act drop between acts two and three or one loses a good curtain and audiences never seem to mind sitting in the dark for a couple of minutes, though no more than that or they get restless. There is a rewritten version that I call my American version as it was done at the request of a group of American actresses who wanted to produce it in Hollywood. In the end they never actually got around to it but, as part of a trip around the states by Amtrak, I stopped off in Los Angeles to do the rewrite.

After Golders Green I didn't see much of Ben Hawthorne. He suddenly got religion. In his case it was Sufi and he was told to change his

Chapter Twelve

name to Raymond. Raymond! There's absolutely nothing wrong with the name Raymond, it's a good old name, some of my best friends are called Raymond, but changing to Raymond for religious reasons? What kind of quackery is this? To me he was still Ben and always will be. There was no way I could call him anything else. Anyway, he returned to his homeland to be a big fish in a little pond and that was the last I saw of him until the opening night of *The 88* at The Old Vic twelve years later, and it was far from being a happy reunion.

In October a new magazine hit the news-stands. This was ZETA, Volume 1 No 1 described as a

"PHOTOCOLOURACTIONMAG"

It was in fact a soft soft porn magazine describing the adventures, through storyboard with accompanying not very well shot photographs, of three girls named after the Fates of Greek myth: Atropos, Lachesis, and Clotho, and they had a young sidekick by the name of James Word. Why do writers think the name James carries connotations of male sexiness? Anyway, James he was called so James I was stuck with. The publisher was Michael Gassman. The first number had a Script Editor but from number two it had a Script Writer and that was me for the next six or seven issues. How this came about I don't remember. Presumably someone recommended me to Mr Gassman. Issue number two was described as "THE ALL-COLOUR PHOTO FANTASY" and the title of the story was *Come into the Coven Maude or Lost in the Harem* and I do not think for one moment I came up with that one. It has all the touch of a Michael Gassman. I found it hard to believe that anyone would spend hard earned money on this stuff but it seemed to have quite a circulation, not only in England but also all over the continent where, if you couldn't read the English text, at least you could look at the pictures. Reader's age group, according to letters received, seemed for the most part to be late teens, early twenties, who got it off ogling plenty of tit with a frisson of masochism. There were invitations for girls, or for boys who knew a girl, to send in their photographs so they could stand a chance of being chosen to pose with professional models, and there were story writing competitions and teasers like cutting out pieces of a photograph and keeping them in a safe place until the next issue when, together with another photograph, they would make "a most interesting picture." It came to an end for me though when I started to disagree with the Art Editor for the simple reason that the choice of photographs was beginning to take preference over and to make no sense of the storyline. If he happened to like a particular picture, even if it didn't fit in anywhere, he liked it so he was going to use it. His word was law and, after a number of arguments, I quit. Michael Gassman withheld my last payment. Oh, dear, here we go again! This time I didn't have to fight for my rights. I had a secret weapon. I marched into his office with Jeremy. Gassman looked up with some surprise from behind his desk.

'Who's this?' He said.

'My lawyer,' I replied.

There was no more than a two second pause before payment was forthcoming.

I then made my first appearance in a London theatre, The Mermaid, in *The High Bid* by Henry James. It starred Fenella Fielding, Edward Woodward and Laurence Hardy and, for me, it was back to walk-ons again as an American tourist. But it was work and I wasn't going to be fussy. Also Harry came back into the picture because he was working out at Elstree. I don't know quite what his position was but he had something to do with *The Avengers*. Working at the Mermaid gave me time to sit down and write *A Model's Lot is Not a Happy One* which I duly presented to Harry to pass on to the powers that be as a possible episode for the series: shades of *Zeta* maybe except all the girls in my story were trained assassins. It certainly wasn't a pastiche on Gilbert and Sullivan despite the title and Harry had no idea where that came from but it was rejected anyway, so back in the cupboard

Chapter Twelve

it went. Many years later I rewrote it as a novel; unpublished. It was never meant to be great literature but I thought it would do well in airports and railway stations. As I write this, Douglas has taken it out of mothballs and it is once again starting to do the rounds, now called *Dead on Time*. It is currently with agent number five. (Finally published in 2007.)

Towards the end of the year I travelled to Belfast where Michael Emmerson who was currently director of The Belfast Festival had asked me to give the Guinness Lecture, which I duly did. My first meeting with Michael was when he was a lowly assistant stage manager for Charles Vance. The lecture was called *Success is Always Overnight*. Irony. From Belfast, using my speaker's fee, I took a train south to Dublin for the sole purpose of continuing my research into *The 88*. That is the title of the play because, not only was the regiment the 88th, but 88 men were brought to trial so what other title could it possibly have? Evidently the Connaughts were also known as "The Devil's Own" which is a better movie title maybe, though a bit clichéd. There is no copyright in titles, witness my play *Oh Brother!* and the later BBC series of the same name, but *The Devil's Own* must have been used, or certainly something like it.

In Dublin I stayed with a friend of a friend who also very kindly lent me his car so that I could get out of town. I loved Dublin. I don't know how much it has changed since I was there but it was a city I felt very comfortable in, even so far as to drinking Guinness at breakfast time. Ah, but there's no Guinness like the Guinness in Dublin, black cream it is. I'm told it's the waters of the Liffy that does it. I met up with Chloe Gibson again, having lunch with her at Telefis Eireann where she was to spend the rest of her working days, and I'm sure she didn't miss London one little bit, which was a pity for me because I would never be working for Chloe again.

I was told that if I went to a place called The Bog of Allen I would find a pub called Roche's Bar and there I would also find one of the survivors of the Connaught mutiny. I duly set out in the borrowed car and, in the dark, came across a herd of cows in the middle of the road so I stopped; the car stalled, and wouldn't start again. I tried, I waited, I tried again. It was as dead as a doornail. The beasts that were the cause of the trouble in the first place had meanwhile moved on, pausing to rip up tufts of grass from the verge, giving me sideways glances as they passed, and the road was clear which wasn't much use to me at this point so I got out of the car, had a wank at the side of the road, got back in the car and she started at the first touch no trouble at all. It's what I called my little bit of Irish magic.

Out of the blackness of the night and truly in the middle of nowhere, well in the middle of The Bog of Allen I suppose, I saw this enormous red neon sign, big enough for a ten story building, which read ROCHE'S BAR and, parking the car, into the bar I went. The first thing I noticed was the wonderful smell of the peat fire. The bar was small, one room divided into two. In the first section behind a counter there were some wooden shelves on which stood a few tins of peas, possibly a few other items as well like baked beans and corned beef maybe but for some reason, it was the peas I noticed, possibly because they looked as if they'd been there a very long time. In the second section that was the bar itself, seated in a corner by the fire, was my eighty-year-old mutineer. There was no mistaking him. At the counter I enquired from Mr Roche himself what the old guy was drinking and with two glasses and a packet of rolling tobacco I went over to his table, put down the glasses, introduced myself, and said, 'I want to write something about the mutiny of the Connaught Rangers in India. I believe you were there.'

'I was that.'

'Do you mind talking about it? Oh, here's some tobacco for you, and cheers,' as I lifted my glass.

'And here's health to you, sir,' he said, lifting his own glass and, from that moment, never stopped talking except to pause when I went back to the bar for refills and he rolled himself another cigarette. By this time Mr Roche, who had probably heard the stories many times, still came over to the table to listen in. If only I had had a tape recorder

Chapter Twelve

with me. As it was I just listened and made mental notes. Who could resist a story like?

'Did I never tell you about Biddy McCann? Wait till I tell you. "Here I am" says she, "I can fuck, fight, chaw tobacco and play the melodeon all at once," and by God she could too.'

The "fuck" in that story is the only time in the play the word is used and I'm very proud of the fact that, in a military play, when its use could be frequently expected, its absence goes unnoticed. Another line he gave me was when I asked him if he was married. He thought about this for a while and then said, 'I was a little bit once, but not much.'

And there was also his story about his visit to a whorehouse that ran, 'I made an amadain[17] of myself in the bullring one night there. Ten bob was all I had in the world and there she was. Wait till I tell you. I chose the little thing for myself. She was young. She was white. She was everywhere. Ten shillings I had and I never knew where I was. Got me legs around me neck and damn near choking me and me ten bob gone. I was a fool to have give it her in the first place. Didn't know whether I was there or not I can tell you.'

All these stories I used verbatim in the play.

Mr and Mrs Roche very kindly asked me to have supper with them and, as it was late, to spend the night. From the bar you reached their house across a wooden walkway laid over some very muddy earth and the house itself seemed sparsely furnished. The dining room was that: a table and chairs. The bedroom was that: a bed. But the cold meal Mrs Roche set out was sumptuous, the centrepiece being a home smoked ham. I was introduced to the sons, one of whom was the most angelic little Downes syndrome boy and obviously the spoilt, and rightly so, darling of the family. I spent a very comfortable night and in the morning when I was preparing to set off, one of the sons was watching me and I asked him if he knew anything about cars. He thought for a moment and then said, 'Now I don't. But if I did, sure enough I'd embrace them as my hobby.'

17 Fool/idiot.

And one of the London critics, Steve Grant in *The Observer*, had the nerve to say I "indulged in some rather fanciful language". Did he really think the Irish talk like the English or perhaps he thought that I should reduce the fanciful for his benefit? What English boy would use the word "embrace" in that context?

This is as bad as the critic who ticked me off for dressing pageboys in my production of *The Old Batchelor* at RADA as Redskins: sorry, Native Americans. If he had done his research as well as I had done mine he would have known that ladies of fashion of the period dressed their little pages as Redskins – Native Americans – thanks to the newfound colony of Virginia.

From the Bog of Allen I moved on to Mullingar to see James Daly's sister, Teresa Maher. I found the modest little house, walked up the short pathway and knocked on the front door. It was opened by a quite formidable looking lady and, when I told her what my intentions were, she retorted that too many people came seeking information, wanting to write about her brother and, sorry, she wasn't interested. I didn't push. I merely thanked her, wished her good day and turned to leave. I hadn't gone half way down the garden path when she called me back.

'What is it you'll be wanting to write?'

'A play.'

'A play is it? Hmn ... All right. Come on in.'

I spent the next hour or more with her, looking at photographs, reading letters, and listening to her memories. It was very moving. Then she told me the local shopkeeper was a sort of historian on the subject and had a mass of material so, thanking her; I made my way down the garden path a second time.

'The best of luck to you!' She called after me.

I turned and waved a thank you before visiting the local historian.

'Good day to you, sir, and what can I do for you.'

'I hear you have a lot of information about the Connaught Rangers.'

'I may have.'

'Would it be possible for me to see some of it?'

'I'm not too sure about that.'

'All right, I'll just sit here and have a cup of coffee.' Refreshment was served in this establishment and he went off to make my coffee. Half way through he suddenly reappeared at my side. 'And what would you be wanting it for?'

'I want to write a play about it.'

'A play is it? Humph!' And off he went only to return a few moments later to place a thick folder on the table.

'You'll not be taking any of it away now.'

'Wouldn't dream of it.'

And so I continued my research as he produced folder after folder and this time, prepared with pen and paper, I made copious notes. Perhaps the most moving piece of all was Daly's last letter to his mother.

When I returned to London I was ready to start work on *The 88*. It would be twelve years before it was produced and it would come off in less than twelve days thanks to the London critics.

Chapter Thirteen

Although the Sunday evening ritual at Glenwood was for the boarders to attend the nearest local church, it was either Methodist or Presbyterian I forget which, Sunday mornings we could attend our own church as individuals. Mine was Church of England: St Cyprians; a large modern building that seemed to put many people off, and those who weren't put of by the building were put off by it being High Church, and those not put off by either the building or it being next to Rome, were put off by the vicar whose personality was rather abrasive and who liked to be called Father; Father Ramsden. I wonder what his Christian name was. The congregation never amounted to more than fifteen or so in that vast building. I attended St Cyprians during the mixed-up murky waters of my adolescence when religion was a boon and a blessing and I took it very seriously. It was in the book-lined vicarage that I went for tea, scones, and confirmation classes. Then, after my confirmation, I became an altar boy and incurred Farther Ramsden's wrath one Sunday when I absentmindedly forgot to set out various necessities for Mass. Yes, for Father Ramsden it was Mass, not Holy Communion. Christian forgiveness was not in his nature. He scowled menacingly throughout the rest of the service and afterwards I got the severest dressing down for my carelessness. Naturally the rhythm of the ritual was somewhat spoilt by my forgetfulness when I had to go back to the vestry, twice, to collect what had been forgotten but it wasn't such a big deal and I'm sure Father Ramsden's God wasn't that upset.

Chapter Thirteen

He liked to take confession in the Lady Chapel but, being an Anglican church and not a Roman one there was no confessional as such, no screen here between confessor and the one confessing, and he was particularly interested in naughty sexual goings-on, which I think, as a bachelor and most probably an aging virgin, gave him a vicarious thrill because he always got a bit agitated at these revelations.

At St. James' in Morningside I would don cassock and surplice again as a member of the choir but this was not because I was still in religious mode but because I enjoyed the music and singing and being in the choir was a family affair as both my mother and sister were in it as well. '*Hear my prayer, Oh, Lord, incline thine ear, from my petition do not hide*.' Traditional English church music is very beautiful. There was an occasion when the choir visited another church that had a few black members in the congregation and we all felt like real brotherly Christians in shaking hands. What has happened to the church since those days? The Church of England was always a moderate gentle persons club but now we get happy-clappy hearty rugger bugger vicars who don't wear dog collars and insist you call them by their first names, pop hymns sung to twanging guitars, hugs all round and the kiss of peace, dumbed-down Bibles and order of services that have lost all sense of poetry and beauty, mystery that has become demystified, and it's all totally embarrassing or totally boring. Once I moved on to university attendance at church dropped completely except when on visits home.

To begin my religious education while I was very young and we were still living in Umbilo, my parents sent me to Sunday school at the Congregational church, the closest religious establishment to home. I don't think quite frankly either of them was particularly religious at that time but they obviously felt their children ought to start having some dealings with the Almighty and, as professed Christians, with His one and only begotten son, and it didn't really matter what denomination brought it about. Sunday School was tedious and I loathed having to go to it, but we were given little scriptural cards with pretty pictures, which I quite liked. One Sunday

No Official Umbrella

I handed back the one they gave me of Jesus, saying I had Whiskers Blake[18] the previous week and I would like someone different this time. Later at a C.of E. church there was always Palm Sunday as well and this is an extract from my play *Twilight of Aunt Edna*, a father bemoaning the behaviour of his errant son.

ERIC: Strange? STRANGE! Strange is hardly the word I would use. No. Why? I keep asking myself. Why does he deliberately turn his face from the light? It seems to me like a perverse act of defiance. And with his mother a shining example it is beyond my comprehension. (*A cry from the heart*) He went to Sunday school didn't he? Oh, how I remember his little piping treble rendering 'All things bright and beautiful.' How I remember him coming home and kneeling on the carpet right there to paste his pretty scripture cards in his little scrapbook. And how he came home on Palm Sunday proudly bearing his little palm cross. He won a prize! What went wrong?

What went wrong was, having got over the neurosis and turbulence of his adolescence, religion no longer held any meaning for him. Here in Crete we have been to church more often than in all our time in England despite the fact that to me religion is still all superstition, mumbo-jumbo and mystical claptrap, and I don't believe a word of it. When you're dead you're dead. The light goes out and that is it. No afterlife, no life eternal, no resurrection. If these possibilities existed, what happens to the soul when someone goes into a coma, maybe for years, and then regains consciousness without having had a near death experience or any memory of the soul existing elsewhere? So where was it all the time the brain had switched off and the elements of life only continued because of external support? Though Peter Pan might have thought of death as being an awfully big adventure it is in fact a great big nothing. Actual pain suffered in the act of dying is another thing altogether. The best prayer the Catholic church ever

---
18 A well known wrestler at the time.

came up with is "grant me a peaceful death."

As we try to be part of the Greek community rather than simply expats who have moved to Greece to live the good life, we go to church for weddings, baptisms, funerals and memorials of which there have been any number, but it is mainly Easter that is the big festival in Greece, much more important than Christmas which is only recently coming into its own, mainly because of commercial interests, and we attend the Easter service as a bonding with the community rather than as a held belief in the resurrection. After all, there is nothing original in the resurrection myth. Gods have died and been resurrected before Jesus came along but we dutifully kiss our Greek neighbours and say 'Christ is risen' to which the response is 'He is truly risen.' Hypocritical? I suppose it is but is it any more hypercritical than the phoney American fundamentalist preachers who coin a fortune out of the unhappy and the gullible: the "Give five dollars to Bob and God will save you from cancer," brigade of hell-raisers who, when found out for their very human failings (sins to the religious) confess all and tearfully repent on television. Then, their tears having cleansed them of their sins, they go on to make another fortune.

On my first visit to America to teach staying in the house of Tom and Kay Arthur while they were away, I shared the house with two post-grad youngsters, Susan Senter and Cindy Marshall who I used to follow from room to room switching off lights after them as they moved on. I don't know what was so bad about drinking Guinness at breakfast in Dublin except, if I had stayed in that city any longer I would have probably put on a lot of weight, but I used to watch Susan every morning standing at the open fridge in the kitchen noshing away on Doritos and Cola. How she kept her figure so trim I really don't know. I mentioned it to her and then found the following on a piece of paper taped to the fridge door:

SUSAN'S DIET

> Monday–Dorritos (½–1 bag) / 1 -2 beers / 7 Choc. Chip cookies
> Tuesday–Pizza / 1–2 beers
> Wednesday–Wendy's / NO BEER / 2 bowls ice cream
> Thursday–Burger King / 2 Beers / cookies
> Friday–Peanut butter sand & Dorritos / bananas / Danish / cookies
> Don't have to diet on weekends

On a Sunday morning I sat in the basement playroom watching, one after the other, the Bible-thumping hell-fire preachers, their dewy-eyed spouses at their sides, sometimes with the backing of enormous robed choirs, rousing the faithful to hallelujahs as they packed into their lavish temples erected to the glory of God and themselves, and I honestly wondered if they believed in what they were saying or whether it was just God making a lot of money for a canny privileged few.

Another way of spelling God of course is P–A–I–N: the pain of illness, the pain of loss and bereavement, the pain of the loveless and the downtrodden, the pain of death, the pain of not knowing; and do those preachers know how to twist the knife! Their showmanship, like that of snake-oil salesmen, I have to admit is brilliant. Their veracity I cannot help doubting. And, anyway, what do you make of a God who suggests you're very special to Him by having part of your willy chopped off? Couldn't He have come up with a better idea than that? Especially as others were doing the very same thing.

The only time I went to church in America was for weddings, one of which was Susan's and that was the last time I saw her. The ceremony took place in a church in Arlington, Cindy sang at the wedding, accompanying herself on the guitar, and the reception was held at The Fort Myer Officers' Club. When I enquired as to how I got there, I was driving Tom's car, I was told to just follow the others. That was fine for a while until we hit a street light and all the cars in front got through leaving me stranded as the light turned to red. So there I sat, watching the last car disappear around a corner, totally lost, unable to find The Officers' Club despite making a couple of enquiries with locals who hadn't a clue, so I decided to head for home. I was getting quite hungry by this time not having eaten since an early breakfast and for a while I drove around in circles until, eventually I found myself in Washington proper.

Washington D.C. with its grid and one-way system is not a city to drive in if you are a stranger. I was going around again, not in circles this time but in blocks, up one street, across another, down the next, up the first street again. Eventually I found myself in quite a high position and I could see across the Potomac way below the road I wanted to get me back to Harrisonburg but how the hell did I get there? I also saw a parked patrol car just ahead of me and, going up to the driver's door, I looked inside where a trooper was sitting paring his fingernails with an enormous flick-knife.

'Excuse me, officer,' I said. He didn't even look up, just went on with his manicure. 'Could you please tell me how I get to Route 66?'

There was a long silence as he was now busy cleaning his nails with the tip of the knife. Eventually he looked up at me and said, 'Way-ell now...' gave me explicit directions and in a few minutes I was well on my way home. But it was now early evening, I was starving, and unless I wanted to take the chance of deviating from the main highway and probably getting lost again, there was nowhere to stop and get something to eat. I could see them all as I drove on, all those fast food eateries on side roads, but not a single one on mine.

In 1987 Douglas Foote, who has already been mentioned, came into our lives. A semi-pro production of *West Side Story* in Newcastle at the beautiful New Tyne Theatre which was celebrating its 125th anniversary had run into trouble when, in the middle of rehearsals, there was an artistic difference of opinion between Jack Dixon the director and Yair Vardi, the Israeli born choreographer who walked out taking a third of the cast with him. We had previously got to know Jack when Chris was on tour with *Oliver*. As assistant director he went in advance of the company to each venue to rehearse a new set of boys and rehearsals in Newcastle took place in the Tyne Theatre. Chris had also directed and choreographed the pantomime *Babes in the Wood* for Jack so, when he received a phone call one morning asking if he could step in and take over *West Side Story*, he immediately agreed despite the fact that he was already committed to a number of Music Hall performances that meant commuting between London and Newcastle. Douglas was stage manager for *West Side Story*. Originally he had wanted to be in but, as he tells it, when he saw the queue of young hopefuls stretching right around the theatre block all waiting to audition he didn't even bother to get off the bus. He had worked with Yair Vardi previously and did consider leaving with the others but being the loyal person he is, decided he should stay with the show and, as such, was a pillar of strength to Chris who, in the circumstances, was grateful for someone who was so professional. Had he left with Yair the last nineteen years would have been a different history.

We were also at that time in the process of packing up house in London prior to moving to Yorkshire, and my shortly leaving for the states so altogether it was a pretty hectic time. As a thank you to Douglas he was invited down to London to stay for a few days with visits to the opera: *The Pearl Fishers* and *Pacific Overtures* at the Coliseum and *La Boheme* at The Royal Opera House.

After I left for the states, Douglas moved down to Yorkshire. The following year, as I was reaching the end of my second teaching stint at James Madison: in fact I had asked for it to be cut short as I had been invited to play Dysart in *Equus* at Furman University in Greenville, South Carolina and, as I had just directed that play at JMU, I thought it would be an interesting experience to now play in it. Unfortunately the director was not all that imaginative and directed virtually from the printed edition. I would have enjoyed "kicking it around a little."

Douglas joined me in Virginia for my last week there before we were driven by Ron Copeland down to Greenville. I did most of the driving as Ron had been partying the night before and slept on the

Chapter Thirteen

back seat most of the way and Douglas, who hadn't yet learned to drive, spent the journey balancing gummy bears on his prick. You can imagine how they took to him at a conservative protestant university when he walked around the dressing room naked, having been roped in to play one of the horses, a cast member having sprained an ankle the day before we arrived. Nobody else showed so much as a nipple or a pubic hair let alone the full monty and, of course, there could be absolutely no nakedness in the play. *Debbie does Dallas* would hardly go down well in this neck of the woods. Neither Douglas nor I can remember what happened in the scene where the boy has to try having sex with the girl and we have decided it probably didn't even happen. What we do remember is my drying one night and having to knit my way back. The whole cast sat there aghast wondering how I was going to do it. They knew immediately I had gone off the tracks when I said, 'Alan, you like playing games, don't you?' Which is not a line in the script and they all thought my improvisation was marvellous. Douglas, who knew the whole play off by heart as is his wont had to keep a tight ring piece until I got back on course.

I don't know whether this is yet another apocryphal story but it is said the first university football team was called the *Furman University Christian Knights* and, at the inaugural dinner, the serviettes were printed with these initials but were hastily replaced when someone realised what they had come up with. The team's name was then changed to the Furman University Paladins.

During the course of rehearsals Douglas and I were told about this other university in town, the "Bob Jones," a truly fundamentalist college whose most famous alumnus is probably the Reverend Ian Paisley which says a lot about this particular establishment where a bowdlerised Shakespeare was produced once a year and was, in fact, currently in rehearsal. The story we were told was that the founder, the original Bob Jones was informed by his son, Bob Jones Junior, that Bob Jones Junior wanted to be an actor but Bob Jones Senior, as a good Christian, refused point blank to countenance his son going into the theatre, so the theatre was brought to him in the shape of a New York building, purchased by Bob Jones Senior, pulled down brick by brick, packaged, transported, and re-erected exactly as was in Greenville, South Carolina on the campus of the Bob Jones University; and what a magnificent theatre it is.

When we had the time we went over to the Bob Jones University to find out if we could possibly see a performance or a rehearsal of whatever Shakespeare it was they were doing because it has been declared that Bob Jones Junior, I think it was Bob Jones III by this time, was (is?) one of the three greatest Shakespearian actors alive. Presumably the second of the three was Olivier but who was the third? Could it have been Gielgud?

Well behaved, well showered, and well scrubbed young men and women, all decorously dressed, were wandering around the beautiful campus. They could have been extras in *Invasion of the Body Snatchers*. We found the theatre and, on making enquiries of the young lad behind the box office grille, we were disappointed to discover times clashed and we weren't going to be able to see the Shakespeare after all, so we asked if we could take a look around the theatre. He wasn't too sure about it but, at this point, a faculty member happened to walk by and we were told to ask this gentleman who turned out to be head of the film division. Of course he was only too delighted to show us around and, from the foyer that circled the stalls, the walls lined with photographs of previous opera productions and Shakespearian plays, all very Victorian looking, we entered the vast auditorium with seating for three thousand. We were told that for the yearly opera production principals are hired from the Met. We mounted the stage half the size of a football pitch complete with revolve, traps, lifts, and flies that were three or four stories high and, looking back into the auditorium, the rear of the upper circle and the gods were so far away they were in darkness.

We were then taken to see the wardrobe and the well-equipped film studios with separate facilities for animation. Religious films are produced here which are hired out at no small fee. Throughout the tour this gentleman never stopped talking and, as neither Douglas

Chapter Thirteen

nor myself are religious, the message being pushed home was growing just a wee bit tedious but I suppose we should have expected it. Proselytisers don't give up easily. He produced a couple of tracts that were thrust upon us and then he mentioned that we might have noticed there were no coloured folk on the Bob Jones campus. This, he said, using the exact same Biblical arguments used by the Afrikaner to justify apartheid was because, as the children of Ham etcetera, etcetera, and on he rambled quoting chapter and verse. Of course he ended up by saying the IRS had withdrawn the university's charitable status because of the refusal to take in black students and, since then, applications for places coming in from all over the states had increased five times over. The strange thing is that in the photograph on the front of their information handout, there is a happy smiling black face among all the other happy smiling faces. But now, seeing the look on Douglas's face I decided it was time we high-tailed it out of there before an unseemly argument broke out so, having thanked him politely for his trouble, we headed for the exit doors. But as we were going he mentioned there would be a prayer meeting soon in the ampithorium (seating seven thousand) if we cared to attend we'd be most welcome. We said we'd think about it and lingered just long enough to be given directions before making our hurried way out.

Heaving a real sigh of relief, cliché or not, I said to Douglas, I couldn't care less that it was a no-smoking campus; I needed a cigarette badly and duly lit up. There are times when tobacco, as Mark Twain knew, is a real comfort. Then I saw my first pair of chipmunks, cute furry little buggers Ray Bluett would have called them. It was the chipmunks scuttling along the base of a wall that led us to the entrance to the Bob Jones art gallery and this we just had to see.

Protestants, particularly fundamentalist Protestants do not do art, so how come Bob Jones went in for it, housed in a special building with quite an extensive number of galleries; thirty rooms housing over four hundred paintings? Naturally the pictures were all on a religious subject including quite a few effete St Sebastians and one or two very good pictures, a Tintoretto; "Christ With A Book" by Titian, "Christ Cleansing The Temple" by Giordano, pictures by Rubens and van Dyck, all of it of course Catholic art. The situation was surrealistic and to cap it all we saw our one and only black face on that beautiful campus–the janitor.

When we had a few days off from rehearsals we had the use of a university car and drove down to Charleston for a break. In the market there we came across a small bookshop where we found a card on the outside of which was written, "Jesus may love you", and on the inside "but the rest of us think you're an asshole." We sent it to Bob Jones Junior.

Speeding merrily along on the return journey to Greenville there was a loud bang and the car started to wobble alarmingly. With a huge Mac truck practically tail-gating me I managed to manoeuvre onto a grassy island in the middle of the highway, there to get out and survey the damage. The offside front tyre had gone. We changed with the spare that for some reason was smaller in diameter but, fortunately, the blowout had occurred right by a hamlet just off the road where we found a garage and an eatery in which to while away the time as the damaged tyre was being replaced. The university paid for the new tyre but that was another close call with the reaper. Maybe it was God putting on the frighteners for our being so irreligious with Bob Jones.

An institution similar to the Bob Jones University is the CBN University in Virginia Beach, founded by the televangelist, Pat Robertson. A flyer from this establishment gives ten good reasons for you to consider their M.A. program (American spelling) in drama. The first two are 1) A Biblical View. Committed Christian performing artists, critics, scriptwriters, and art managers develop a Biblical [!] perspective of the drama field. 2) Reclaiming The Arts. Become part of the unique mission of reclaiming the performing arts for the glory of God. So the theatre is obviously still wicked wicked wicked but if you can't beat them, join them.

Chapter Thirteen

In London one day two young Mormons came to the door, clean, handsome young men in their smart grey suits, collars and ties and wanted to know if I had found Jesus.

'I didn't know he was lost,' I said which didn't go down at all well. 'But, if I do find him, as he doesn't seem ever to have mentioned it, I'll ask him what his views are on homosexuality.'

They were off down the road as if the devil himself was at their heels. I used a variation of this incident in my play *Third Drawer from the Top*.

This word homosexuality can really create knicker-twisting torment for some people. I was standing in line at Drury Lane Theatre one day waiting to book seats for *A Chorus Line* and I overheard the man in front of me, holding a fistful of tickets, say, 'I booked these seats for my daughter's birthday because I was led to believe it is a wholesome family show, but I have since learned it contains ho... ho... ho... ho...' He couldn't even get the word out and then, all in a rush out it came, 'homosexuality! And I want to cancel them.'

Money is usually nonrefundable once you have bought theatre tickets but the guy was obviously so distressed he was given his money back. I used him as a model for the father in *Twilight of Aunt Edna*.

When the House of Commons was debating the Wolfenden report as to whether or not to legalise homosexuality between consenting adults, I wonder how many of those politicians knew there is a statue outside the house to an English hero known as The Lionheart who was much given to these sort of fun and games, who was the lover of the French Dauphin and who was abjured by his Bishops to give up sodomy and evil practices before he brought the wrath of God down on his kingdom. Long before that the Emperor Justinian banned homosexuality because it causes earthquakes and there are still religious fanatics today who solemnly believe it is the cause of natural disasters.

The proselytising Jehovah's Witnesses can be a nuisance, usually rapping on your door just as you're enjoying watching sport on television. Douglas doesn't bother with niceties. He merely slams the door in their faces something, I suppose, they're more or less used to. I usually make a polite excuse before closing the door in their faces, but one day I was sitting on the wall outside the house in Yorkshire when two members of the church came by and stopped to ask if they could talk to me about Jesus. I think they were rather taken aback when I said of course they might and even more taken aback when I confessed to being a very happy human being who had no need of God thank you, not right at that moment anyway. That, according to them, was an impossibility. Without God no one could possibly be happy. Oh yes they can, I argued, I have everything I want in life and I made a pact with God a long time ago. I'll leave Him alone if He'll leave me alone. And it's no good quoting scripture at me, particularly the Old Testament. Those books were written a long long time ago by men, warts and all. They were not dictated by the Almighty and written down with a heavenly gold plated ballpoint to the sound of angelic trumpets… by which time they'd had enough and, proffering a Watchtower, which I generously accepted, they left me to my atheist devices. We never saw them again.

December 1975 saw me in Liberia, West Africa where I had gone as part of a film unit hired by an Indian gentleman and led by my friend Lionel Ngakane who was to direct a fictional picture but set in the real event of the marriage of A.B. Tolbert, son of the Liberian president, to Daisy Marie Suzanne Delafosse, the daughter of the president of the Ivory Coast, a union of dynasties as it were. William R. Tolbert Jnr's family originated from Charleston, South Carolina. He was an ordained Baptist pastor and former president of the Baptist World Alliance and was known as the Preacher President.

Manu Naranj, the Indian gentleman producing the film, was obviously loaded because, before we left, he took us to dinner at a

Chapter Thirteen

Japanese restaurant in St. Christopher's place where the bill came to £600, he tipped a £100 and he bought a bottle of whisky to take away at the inflated price of £60. At today's values that's well over £5,000 if not more.

Flying to the capital, Monrovia, for some reason or other we had to first touch down in Guinea. Maybe it was to refuel though it could have been political as Guinea, Liberia and Sierra Leone had just agreed to share each other's air space and, as we started the descent, I began to experience an earache that grew worse until it was so intense it virtually had me at screaming pitch. I almost begged a hostess to get me something but, apart from handing me a boiled sweet to suck, there was nothing she could do. I tried holding my nose and blowing hard to release the pressure in my ears but that just increased the agony. I was literally squirming with the pain. The African gentleman seated beside me turned and said, 'You had better see a doctor in Monrovia. You have an infection in that ear. You shouldn't be suffering such intense pain.' It turned out he was himself a doctor so I thought I would take him up on his advice. What I was dreading was the fact there would not only be a second landing but a third and a fourth and a fifth as we flew from Monrovia to Abidjan, back to Monrovia and then back to the UK and each time I would be going through it all again.

We touched down in Guinea and the captain made an announcement to the effect that no one was to leave the plane and, under no circumstances was anyone to be seen with a camera. As we taxied along I looked out of the window as we passed dense green jungle littered with burnt out planes, destroyed jeeps, armoured carriers and other remnants of war. This was indeed a dark place. The plane came to a halt and, after a while, the doors opened and a couple of soldiers in green fatigues and with automatic weapons entered the cabin and, in dead silence, swaggered up and down the aisles looking at every passenger before standing at the door again to flirt for a few moments with the hostesses before leaving. The doors were closed and a short while later we took off for Monrovia. Coming down the pain was as bad as before but there was nothing for it but to hope it wouldn't last long.

At the airport cars were waiting to transport us to our hotel at Caesar Beach and, while they were being packed with our personal belongings, and all the paraphernalia required for filming, I had a look around. The main reception area was pretty bare and bleak and where a sign read TELEPHONE I noticed there were only bare wires hanging from the wall but Abie, as he was known, had two telephones in his car. Driving to Caesar Beach we passed wooden signs at the side of the sandy road roughly painted with the names of the property owners: The MacDonald Residence, The Lee Residence, The Adams Residence, and one sign which read "God's Little Acre." It was only when I saw that particular sign that I thought, "Hey, I am, for the first time, in black Africa as opposed to what had been white colonial Africa and all these names, adopted from former owners, are names of the descendents of freed slaves."

Caesar Beach Hotel was a collection of thatched buildings with all air-conditioned, (what would now I suppose be called climate controlled) rooms, sensibly not over-furnished but very comfortable. It took a matter of seconds to walk down to the wide beach facing the Atlantic Ocean or to a small bay that, as in Natal, was separated from the ocean by a sand bar. The first thing I did was unpack my swimming costume and head for the sea where I dived in and luxuriated in the warm water, every now and then staying beneath the surface to get an earful of sea water. I didn't have to see a doctor and never had any trouble with earache again.

On the way to the hotel we had stopped by a beach for Abie to buy freshly caught lobster. He actually paid the fisherman, which was unusual for him. Maybe it was because we were around. Normally he just took what he wanted as we discovered when, for a party at his well guarded house, he ordered a load of alcohol from a nearby Indian shop and, when the shopkeeper had the temerity to ask for his money, he got beaten up by Abie's goons. Later that first evening we were driven back along the dusty road to a house belonging to one

Chapter Thirteen

of Abie's friends where we feasted on lobster till we literally could not take another mouthful. I am particularly partial to shellfish, especially lobster, and it isn't often one gets to make an absolute pig of oneself on what in Europe is an expensive luxury which is probably why Abie didn't mind paying, the cost for twenty lobsters or more in Liberian dollars coming to the equivalent of about five shillings, (twenty-five pence).

I found Monrovia fascinating with its assortment of architecture from modern hotel to old colonial style houses and gaudily painted ramshackle shacks. I thought I might stop my peregrinations and step into THE AUTOMATIC MEAT PIE RESTAURANT for a bite but had second thoughts, probably just as well. Shades of Mrs Lovatt? I was also intrigued to see a sign that said the "Holy Temple Church of God in Christ" ended with an "Inc". Incorporated into what I wondered? Heaven? There were tin shanty slums a plenty and some corrugated iron houses not slums at all but substantially built three stories high, standing on brick piles presumably to keep termites at bay. I took photographs wherever I went and didn't realise I was putting myself in any danger until one day as I was photographing a particularly picturesque house I heard this voice yell, 'Hey, you!'

Gods Little Acre - Liberia

I turned around to see a group of four or five Monrovians sitting on the grass on an island in the middle of the road all eyeing me and one getting to his feet where he stood looking very menacing.

'What for you photograph my house, man?'

Taken aback rather, 'It's a very nice house,' I said, somewhat lamely.

'Fock you, man! Who you bullshitting? Don't you bullshit me!'

'Okay, I'm sorry, if you don't want me to...'

'Fock off, man. Jes' fock off.'

I focked off, realising this guy had a suspicion I could have been a plain-clothes cop and that this country, although maybe not quite as dark as Guinea, was also virtually a dictatorship and suspicion was always present.

Anybody who wanted to be anybody, with the exception of Abie of course who was already somebody, being the great man's son, wore a sort of safari suit. The story behind this being that, taken by surprise when his predecessor, President Tubman, died in a London clinic in the middle of the night, Tolbert, from his home in the country, hurried to the presidential palace to take over, not even stopping to change his clothes. Tubman had left Secretary of State Rudolph Grimes in charge while he was away and, when Grimes received the telegram informing him of Tubman's death, he tried to get himself installed as Acting President but Tolbert beat him to it and was installed as President dressed in his safari suit. Everyone took this as a sign that what was right for the new President was right for him so from then on safari suits it was. No doubt with the uprising that saw the bloody end of Tolbert, Abie, and their cronies, the mode of dress changed. Tolbert's presidency lasted nine years and, although benign to begin with, gradually earned a reputation for nepotism and despotism, such is the corrupting influence of power even on a good Christian and Baptist pastor.

Abie's wedding took place in Abidjan, capital of the Cote D'Ivoire. There were crowds, motorcades and guards sweating it out in fancy dress uniforms. We didn't, at least I didn't, watch the lavish ceremony, but the reception in a vast conference or banqueting hall seating well

Chapter Thirteen

over a couple of thousand guests looked spectacular and, mingling with these well-heeled revellers was our actor fugitive, looking so ragged and out of place it just wasn't true. In fact it was total nonsense. Ordinarily he would never have been allowed in, let alone left to wander around. Security would have had him out on his ear in seconds. Never mind, it's all for the camera and I am supposed to write something around this scene.

We had had a script conference of sorts before this but nothing concrete seemed to come out of it by way of a story line so I was really floundering from the beginning.

'What was he meant to be doing in there, Lionel? '

'Looking for the person he's supposed to assassinate.'

'And who might that be?'

'I don't know. You're writing it.'

Great. This really is the way to make a film; tack it together as you go along, keep your fingers crossed, and hope for the best. Back at Caesar Beach I did spend some time at the typewriter but I have to confess not much. In order to get ideas I was either in the sea or floating in the lagoon mulling things over. It would have been a better story, and with this one I definitely would have spent more time at the typewriter, if we had our man a courier for diamond smugglers from Sierra Leone who was desperately trying to avoid pursuers out to get him because diamond smuggling in Sierra Leone could mean a bullet in the head without the necessary formality of a trial. Also with that there was opportunity for double cross and double double cross and all the other clichés of an adventure movie. But I only discovered this too late when, sitting in a hotel lounge in Monrovia towards the end of our stay and already having shot a whole load of rubbish in the bush, a Sierra Leonean, if that's what they're called, engaged me in conversation and said, 'Do you want diamonds?'

'What do you mean, do I want diamonds?'

'Get yourself a shed at Heathrow and I'll send you all the diamonds you want.' Note: Get myself a shed if you please: not a hut, not a left luggage locker, but a shed. Diamonds, and here I digress again because this is the point I'm at; diamonds are the biggest con in the world, the con perpetrated by the Russians in cahoots with the South Africans, at that time anyway. Sierra Leone has so many diamonds they're as common as pebbles. They have even found one pure white diamond there the size of half a brick and what can you possibly do with that? You bury it. At the mouth of the Orange River, it is said, there is a channel cut into the sea by the flow of water that stretches out for half a mile, the bottom of which is inches deep in diamonds, and this area is verboten with speedboat, helicopter and camel patrols keeping everyone away and the beach concreted over on either side of the river mouth. So my newfound friend informed me, and seemed a little disappointed that I wasn't immediately going to phone Heathrow to rent a shed. Anyway, get caught smuggling diamonds from Sierra Leone and endangering the economy and the market and you are in deepest doo doo. My measly contribution to smuggling from Liberia was a gold nugget ring I bought for Chris.

Back to the wedding: Monrovia is a low-rise town, Abidjan is a high-rise city looked at from a distance, very similar in appearance to Perth in Australia. In close-up of course vastly different because, outside of the skyscraper city centre with its modish shops and magnificent French patisseries loaded with fresh cream goodies, there are the inevitable African slums.

Our twenty story hotel with its swimming pools, huge conference hall, stylish lobby, restaurants, atrium, promenades, bars, lounges, shops and foyers was an architectural wonder; beautifully and stylistically decorated in the public areas with variations of ethnic art and bas relief figures even on some of the ceilings. There were gardens with the inevitable palms and manicured lawns and, driving up the circular drive to the entrance, you passed a sort of totem pole a good hundred and sixty feet high also colourfully decorated African style The en suite room Lionel and I shared was large, airy, comfortable, and with a magnificent view over the countryside stretching away.

Naranj's wedding present to the happy pair, if that's what they were, was a pair of beautiful antique Indian thrones, fit for a prince and

Chapter Thirteen

princess. She was like a princess too, one of the most beautiful young women you can imagine, delightful and charming with it, and we all thought Abie a very lucky man. But, would you believe it, on the night of his wedding he was trying to make it with our continuity girl? She made it pretty clear she thought him a complete shit, and how right she was.

Christmas Eve at Caesar Beach there was a party with the "Police Women's Federation of Liberia Rock Band," five trumpets, five saxophones, three electric guitars, bongos and percussion. Had Wagner written rock, this would have been it. Christmas Day and Abie's chauffeur appeared at Caesar Beach to say that as I was a "real cool cat" would I like to spend the day in his village? The answer was an immediate yes as the alternative was just to hang around the hotel with the rest of the gang whereas this would be a new experience and give me the chance to see something of the countryside. So we set off in one of Abie's smaller cars and we hadn't gone very far when we stopped to pick up one of the chauffeur's cousins. This was definitely "a real cool cat", a young man wearing dark glasses, a little moustache and goatee beard, his loose shirt decorated in colourful African motifs, his legs in white flairs and feet in white boots: gold ring on finger, gold bracelet on wrist, gold medallion hanging on a gold chain around his neck; a lady killer if ever there was one. He also had this idea I was a real cool cat. Maybe this was because most of the time I don't usually say very much which gives a false impression of hidden depths. A few miles further on we stopped at a village where, at a garage shed, the chauffeur and the cousin stopped to join a local lad tinkering with a white truck. Here we picked up the twins, two young ladies both in identical floral frocks and wearing similar hats. The hats were made of some white open-weave material, heavily wired to keep their shape, especially the wide brims, one of which was edged in blue the other in pink, that was the difference, so you knew which twin was which.

With the cousin and the twins lodged in the back we were once more on our way on a good road through miles of rubber plantation until, eventually the good road stopped and we were on a dirt track in the bush. We picked up two more male passengers, all five squashed in the back for the final stretch of the journey we never finished by car. The road was rough and getting rougher and, as we hit a donga[19] there was a loud crack and that was it; the back axle was in two pieces, the wheels sloping in at the top at quite an alarming angle. It was time to walk. We eventually arrived at the village in time for a very late Christmas lunch that consisted of a green orange. Well I could have had more than one green orange, there were half a dozen in the basket but I declined even the one.

I met the chauffeur's mother who, as a native Liberian, spoke only the local dialect, but I gathered from her tears and the way she spoke to her son that not everything in the little village of mud huts in the middle of the jungle, far away from the neurosis of civilisation was, as I had fondly and naively believed; peaceful, harmonious, and all that it should be. Every society creates its own conflicts and the cool cat cousin soon put me in the picture as to what was going on. It appeared the inhabitants of the village resented the fact that this woman's son was chauffeur to the high and mighty Abie and was earning good money by Liberian standards, part of which he sent back to his mother who consequently was better off then her neighbours, so out of jealousy they were accusing her of witchcraft. Her son, the whispering went, only got his job because she put a spell on Abie and, 'They are saying,' he told me, 'that she can get a snake at night while you are asleep to climb inside your arsehole and bite you from the inside so that nobody will know how you have died.'

So much for all the work of every missionary who ever attempted conversions in this part of the world. The belief in magic, voodoo, and witchcraft has never gone away.

Towards evening we started our walk back towards Monrovia. It grew dark and the stars came out in their millions. With no light pollution to diminish their intensity the night was ablaze with them

---
19 South African, a ditch.

Chapter Thirteen

and the occasional shooting star flashing across the sky to be suddenly extinguished. Walking through the jungle there was not a sound and, looking up at that night sky, it was suddenly as though I had never left Africa and all the intervening years were no more than a dream, that once Africa is in your blood it is there forever. We hadn't gone too far when a little hand was slipped into mine and, looking down I saw it was pink twin who wanted to know when I was going back to London and would I marry her and take her with me at which a little hand was slipped into mine on the other side and blue twin wanted to know the same. Fortunately I was able to inform them I couldn't possibly marry them both so they were better off staying where they were.

Getting on for midnight we were finally assailed by ear-blasting music as we approached a small collection of lights and I saw we were in a hamlet where a reed and mud walled, thatched building was heaving with a dance in progress. On the wall was written, "This is a quiet place" which was the last description I would have given it.

We went over to a trading store owned by a Lebanese where at last I got to put something in my stomach, a meal consisting mainly of a sort of pilaff, it went down a treat and then, utterly exhausted, I was escorted back to the quiet place where the owner had prepared a bed for me in his best bedroom. I don't know where he and his wife slept that night if they slept at all but the room was adjacent to the dance floor with only a thin partition separating them and, even with the music going full blast I hit the pillow and went out like a light.

In the morning the first thing I needed was to empty a very full bladder so I stepped outside to find a number of men all sitting around a table and drinking home brewed fire-water. On enquiring as to where the necessary was I was pointed to a little hut a short distance away. Entering it I found there was nothing but a sand floor. This was meant to be a loo? I went outside and looked back at the table for confirmation but they all nodded positively so, back into the sand floor loo I went. Later I had another go in there. It was pristine: a magic African loo. Whenever I tell anyone this they always want to know how it worked but I never did find out.

It wasn't long, news having got back to Monrovia as to my whereabouts, before a military vehicle arrived to pick up both the chauffeur and myself. I don't know what happened to him for the damage to Abie's car, probably nothing as Abie could well afford to buy, or more probably be given, a dozen more. But, for taking me into the bush without telling anyone where we were going I think for that he must have been severely rapped over the knuckles. I hope he didn't lose his job on account of me. Evidently the police and even the army had been scouring the countryside for me and the film unit were at panic stations.

Being very chary of our Indian producer and remembering events of the past, on arriving back in London I immediately bearded Naranj in his den and got a cheque off him, which I hurried around to his bank and cashed. I don't think he expected this, probably believing I would put the cheque through my own bank account and, if that were the case, he had plenty of time to cancel it. I had warned Lionel to do the same as me but he ignored my warning and it wasn't long after that I received a letter from his lawyer asking if I would be a witness for Lionel if Naranj was taken to court for non-payment of fees due. I never heard anything else so presumably it didn't come to court but I know Lionel never got his money so it must have been that Naranj did a neat disappearing trick.

Many months later I had a phone call from the Liberian Embassy asking if I knew where he was and also if I knew where they could find the film. I could truthfully say I knew nothing of either but didn't add that, whatever film did exist, it would be so embarrassing I hoped it would never see the light of day.

I also sincerely hope that, in all the turmoil of civil war that overtook Liberia, Abie's beautiful wife remained unscathed, that "God's Little Acre" is still there, and the "Holy Temple Church of God In Christ Inc." still exists to bring comfort to those who need it.

Chapter Fourteen

The big event of 1968 was our move on August 1st from Ladbroke Grove to a flat in Highbury Grange, north London. This was a distinct improvement. No longer was the bathroom half way down a flight of stairs and chilling to the bone in winter. The flat was owned by an elderly Jewish couple by the name of Wolf who lived in Chelsea and who only appeared on rare occasions just to check all was well. The rent was paid by post. The flat was on the top two floors of a large house with two spacious flats beneath and four flats in a modern extension at the side but all sharing the same flight of stairs. I used to complain that every other resident was an avowed socialist who never bothered to clean the communal stairs, change a light bulb, empty a bin, or tidy the garden but who never failed to vote Labour, which was hardly surprising as Islington was known as The Soviet Republic of. Our friend of many years, Ray Peters, who was a teacher in that borough gave up in despair and took early retirement once the trendy lefties moved in, education was turned on its head, and political correctness gradually assumed ridiculous proportions.

The flat was entered via a short passage with a window on one side, overlooking an unkempt garden. You went up three steps to a door that opened into a large hall we used as a dining room. Off to one side of this was the bathroom and on the other side, down a short flight of stairs, the door to the lavatory. When we decorated we used a large patterned William Morris style floral wallpaper in yellow, orange and browns that also covered the door to the outside passage and we used to watch people who weren't in the know, trying to get out by going down the short flight of stairs to the loo and coming out looking totally bewildered.

'How do you get out of this place?'

It was surprising how sometimes such a small moment of disorientation could cause quite a large amount of panic. Sometimes, when shown the way out, a tradesman would stand opening and shutting the wallpaper clad door a few times and shaking his head before departing. Whether this was in wonder at the ingenuity of it or thinking what crazy people lived in this place I don't know: probably the latter. It certainly wasn't an innovation but one he had never come across.

From the hall/dining room, four doors led off from a long passage: the first two, one on either side, to bedrooms; the second two to the living room and a large kitchen. At the end of the passage was a narrow curved staircase that led to what was virtually an attic floor that included my study and a large studio that became Chris's workshop. We had all this for a magnificent eight pounds a week exclusive and the rent never increased, but we would only spend three years in Highbury Grange and, when I bought our first house in Hackney and terminated our lease to move on, the Wolfs offered to sell us the entire block of seven flats for £42,000! If only we had had that money! But it wasn't meant to be.

A month after having moved in I was invited to Chesterfield to direct *Come Laughing Home* by Keith Waterhouse and Willis Hall, a play of which I am afraid I have no recollections whatsoever.

This was also the time, exploring the neighbourhood and quite by accident we stumbled on the empty and almost derelict meeting house that was the Almeida and thought to ourselves what a wonderful theatre it would make. Say no more. Had Douglas been with us then I'm sure we wouldn't have just said, 'Ah, well…' and left it at that. He would have said, 'Come on, let's do it,' and found the ways and means,

Chapter Fourteen

as he did when it came to raising the money to buy the house in Crete.

This was the year I completed writing *The 88, Women Around*, a play for television called *King Demon* and co-wrote with the producer the first episode of *The Gold Robbers* for London Weekend Television. What that meant was I wrote it and John Hawkworth rewrote it according to his lights. Everyone has his or her own ideas and there's no arguing with your producer when his mind is set.

A scene from ITV 's - The Gold Robbers - 1969 starring Richard Leech & Peter Vaughan

It was also the year of *Bathtime* and, in writing it, I wanted to steer clear of the straightforward guided tour around the house bit so concentrated heavily on the library, the Thynne family, unlike most noble families who go in for paintings, fine furniture, and other works of art, having been great collectors of books, including a Caxton Bible plus other extremely rare editions. Also the house is reputedly haunted by a number of ghosts; what stately home isn't? And I decided to use their stories in the various parts of the house they haunted. One is supposed to walk the great hall where a jealous rival killed him in a duel and I arranged a fight scene with swords all shot in shadow for which the hall was an ideal setting. Shades of Errol Flynn in *Robin Hood*. The swords were actually broom handles. In shadow play sword blades would not have registered. It was this film that incidentally led to the purchase of our first house. Some time later one of the producers of *Bathtime* and his wife invited me out to dinner and we arranged for me to meet them at their flat in Islington near The Angel. They weren't quite ready to leave when I arrived so, while they were still dressing, I was left to entertain the kids, one of whom was a small boy who stood in front of me in his pyjamas and very seriously, if not slightly bellicose, said, 'What do you like?'

It isn't often one is faced with questions as loaded as that so what to reply, especially confronted by an infant with hands on hips and a no nonsense protruding lower lip?

'I don't know,' I said, hedging. 'What do you like?'

He thought for a moment and then said, 'I like soldiers, dressing up clothes, and milk bottles.'

And there was definitely no answer to that.

During dinner I was asked, as someone who had a bit of experience fencing, whether I would be willing to go to a school for autistic children in the East End and play swordsmanship with them to give them a feeling of spatial awareness. I said I would be delighted and so one day found myself driving through Dalston on my way to the school. The only thing I knew about Dalston previous to this was from a line by Harold Pinter about the 38 bus passing through it. It wasn't how I expected it to be and I was amazed to find, once you got beyond the junction, that it was a very pretty area, not at all what one had always imagined the East End to be. I immediately thought about the possibility of buying a house there but, at the time, it was no more than an idea. Chris was in Paris playing in *Sweet Charity* and I remember writing to him and saying, "How would you feel about living east of here?"

The reason I was able to drive to the school is that one day I went out to buy some strawberries and came back with a second-hand–sorry, pre-owned in modern parlance, maroon Rover 3000 Coupé automatic which I bought for £600. This was my very first car and,

Chapter Fourteen

while it lasted, it was an expensive love affair. I also one day went up to the chemist's for a tube of toothpaste, the chemist was next door to an antique shop and I came home with a stripped pine chiffonier. I seem to have a habit of doing that. In Yorkshire we went out looking for a bath and I bought an enormous carved oak fire-surround and over mantel ideal for our barn conversion. It wasn't till it was delivered that we wondered whether it might not be too tall but the over mantel slid into place below the ceiling with half an inch to spare. The whole thing was so heavy it took five men to put it in place.

Sometime previously Sydney Box had introduced me to a gentleman by the name of Philip Ridgeway: a moustachioed, Harris Tweed, soft fisherman's hat without the flies, suede shoes, cane carrying type of slightly eccentric English gentleman, evidently quite well known in the world of British film studios and whose letterhead read "From The Desk Of Ridgeway." He had various ideas for television series and I wrote two scripts for him.

One of his ideas was to tell the stories of various works of art sold at auction at Sotheby's, for which he had the co-operation of that famous house, and I wrote a script about the smuggling out of Holland of some antique paintings under the noses of the Nazis. I can't remember what the other idea was or even what the script was about but the one I wrote for him was entitled *The Hump of the Camel* and, not having a copy of it, which is most unusual, it is a complete mystery. I never heard anything more from the desk of Ridgeway so must presume he was unable to sell anyone his ideas. At least Ridgeway was honest in saying there was no money in the kitty and anything I wrote for him was purely on spec, whereas another producer who wanted to do a series on musical instruments with Bernard Haitink and the Concertgebouw of Amsterdam asked me to write an outline for a pilot. I did so, the instrument I chose being the violin and the piece I called *Air on a G String*. He read what I had written which was a pretty comprehensive document to begin with and asked for more. In other words he wanted virtually a completed script without payment of any kind, an invitation I declined. I even took away what I had written. It wasn't that I knew everything there is to be known about the violin but there is always something called research and research takes time and time, as they say, is money.

I once wrote a documentary on computers for J.Arthur Rank though, at the time, I knew absolutely nothing about computers. I still don't if it comes to that. I called it *A Hard Look at Software* and was taken to Putney, a large building just over the bridge, and shown a computer that took up an entire factory sized floor. When the Fax first came out I was also asked to direct a seminar and promotional video praising this wonderful new invention. Out of the blue through my acting agent Errol McKinnon, and why he was particularly chosen to recommend someone I really don't know, I don't recollect there were any directors on his books, but I found myself happily directing the product launch at The Holiday Inn, Croydon of British Telecom's new gadget. The show starred Stanley Unwin and, as the script was by someone else and all I had to do was put it together, it all worked out beautifully. One of the stage crew was standing around looking a bit awestruck and, when I asked him what he was gawping at, he said he was just flabbergasted at the easy way I seemed to be putting it all together which was a very nice compliment to say the least but it didn't require much imagination on my part as everything seemed to just slot into place. Compliments don't come that fast and furious, especially as I hadn't a clue as to how a fax machine actually worked.

Our lawyer friend, Andy Moore tells a lovely story about a case during which the Judge said he had unfortunately left a vital document at his home in the country and one of the prosecuting lawyers said, 'Fax it up, my lord.' To which the learned Judge replied, 'Yes, it does rather, doesn't it?'

Jeremy Nightingale was with the Prosecutor's office for a while and, during one case, the court was brought to a standstill when, over some detail, he turned to the bench and said, 'Legally speaking, my lord, I am the queen.' 'Quite so, Mr Nightingale, quite so,' was the response.

Chapter Fourteen

On another occasion a policeman took advantage of a convenient moment in court to whisper, ''Ere, you fancy me, don't you, Jer?' And Jer, having agreed this was indeed the case, the man then said, 'Well, if you can get a recess you can 'ave me,' and they had it off in the nearest available broom cupboard. This is the way Jer told it anyway. Sex in a broom cupboard is mentioned in *Rosemary* though not in a court of law.

This was also the year I finished with *Zeta* by delivering script number eight so, writing wise, it was quite a prolific year. *Thriller of the Year* went out on tour, bringing in some welcome cash. Laura Stevens had given up the agency so I had my new agent, Errol McKinnon, an expat Canadian, and the only acting that year was when I was cast in another episode of *Softly Softly*.

Engagements for the year 1969 are neatly laid out in the front of my Letts Desk Diary. January is a blank but in the book itself it says I wrote something called *The Magician* that I had to deliver to Mount Street. What was that about I wonder and who in Mount Street? I have no memory of it at all. This is the problem of my not having kept a full account of what I was doing at the time. In February I was involved in a film called *Strange Report* shot at Pinewood which the family in South Africa saw but hadn't a clue as to what I was talking about on the screen as it was dubbed into Afrikaans, and like me, they're not great on languages.

In March Chris was on tour with the Wells and I travelled in the train with the company up to Newcastle and saw their production of *Samson and Delilah*, a production Chris thoroughly enjoyed, throwing himself into the orgy scene with abandon. But his role with the Wells in which he broke a few hearts, including that of a randy Rear Admiral who sent a note around to the stage door inviting him to dinner at the club, was as Bacchus in Offenbach's *Orpheus in the Underworld*.

The Ashes of Thebes by Moris Farhi - Mercury Theatre

Back in London I started rehearsals for a play *The Ashes of Thebes* by Moris Farhi, ex-RADA, ex-actor, ex-playwright, published novelist. Of Turkish origin, I first met Moris during *A View from the Bridge* at Chelmsford when he played the lawyer, Alfieri. *The Ashes of Thebes*, in which I played Diomedes, went on at The Mercury Theatre under the auspices of something called The International Theatre Club and was not well received by the critics, mainly I think due to Rio Fanning's direction that was described quite rightly as slow and ponderous. Also in the cast were John Trigger from Phoenix days and a charming man, Kevork Malikyan, from Armenia, who went on to appear in a number of movies usually playing Middle Eastern baddies.

In May I had two meetings with the director Michael Bogdanov who wanted to do *The 88* but the size of the cast defeated his efforts to get it on. Then, I see, I had eight days filming at Shepperton, I know not what for, after which I made a commercial for Guinness, directed by Terence Donovan. This was a solo effort consisting of me playing at being a brewer and coming up in the end with this wonderful goblet of Guinness. It was indeed a wonderful goblet because, half way through

Chapter Fourteen

the morning as I was holding it up to the light to admire my brewing expertise, Terence suddenly said, 'Careful with that goblet, Glyn. It's a borrowed antique, it's priceless and irreplaceable.'

He might even have said it came from The Victoria and Albert Museum but I can't be too sure of that. Whatever, it was a great piece of information for creating nerves had one given way to it, which fortunately I did not. What was really disappointing though, as everyone involved seemed more than pleased with the result, was that the commercial never went out. The reason for this I was later told was because Guinness were changing their agency and the ones making the commercial were simply using up their budget, a pointless exercise I thought, and bang went my dreams of a country cottage. I made a number of commercials: Go to work on an egg, Danish Bacon, Sharwood's Curry, Whiskey Flake Tobacco, Mother's Pride bread and more, but none of them made me a fortune in residuals. Douglas maintains he knew me before he met me because of the film I was in for the Ministry of Information about smoking in bed, and then the BBC play *Breakaway Girls* in which I played a father yet again.

I'm surprised the two tobacco films didn't put me off smoking then and there. The Whiskey Flake commercial was shot on location at a football ground somewhere in South London. It was freezing cold and the day did not start well when it was discovered that nobody had thought to bring the film and someone was dispatched post haste back to town to fetch it, while we all hung around, stamping feet and rubbing hands to keep warm. After filling and smoking my pipe goodness knows how many times my tongue felt burnt to a crisp and I was heartily sick of the taste of tobacco. In the smoking in bed film the director wanted to get a big close up of the ash on the end of my cigarette and eventually, after lighting up and puffing away on half a dozen cigarettes one after the other I told him, 'If you don't get it this take, you don't get it at all, because I'm not going to light one more cigarette.'

He got it.

July saw me working in an episode of *The Expert* and then going on holiday with three friends, yachting on the Norfolk Broads. It was not a great success because the one I shared a cabin with had the same problem with his feet as the guv'nor at *The Rose and Crown* and, in the confined space of a tiny cabin it was truly horrendous. Also he was a city lad from Manchester and the open countryside, especially with so much wet around, did not appeal to him at all, so he was desperately unhappy and couldn't wait to get back to the big city. Chris was working.

While all this was going on Roy Simpson had been beavering away setting up *The Double Deckers*, a follow on from *The Magnificent 6½*, and having the go-ahead, from September we were ensconced in offices at Elstree. Although I would write a number of the scripts I wasn't going to write them all and, bearing in mind how difficult it is to break into writing for television, as Script Editor I advertised through The Writer's Guild and I think possibly in *The Stage and Television Today*, for writers to submit ideas. Those who contacted us were given a full breakdown of the kids' characters, format, and what was required story-wise. Also what wasn't allowed for American television: no sharp instruments such as scissors, no disrespect shown for the American flag and a whole list of more don'ts. I received half a dozen ideas out of which there was only one I could commission. It was disappointing to say the least. Even the one commissioned had to have a virtual rewrite.

In October auditions were held at the studios and it seemed as though, always the inevitable way when prospective fame beckons, there was a never-ending queue of kids to be seen. Gradually they were whittled down until we had four groups of seven, then two groups and, finally, our seven kids. Peter Firth who hailed from Pudsey in Yorkshire and had the strongest Yorkshire accent played the leader of the gang. He was my choice from the beginning. The Americans were dubious over the accent saying no one in the states would understand a word he said but we pointed out that that was what dialogue coaches are for. Peter, I could see, was getting more and more disgruntled with the whole process and I was silently willing

Chapter Fourteen

him just to hang in there, the part was almost his, as it eventually was. But I find auditions nerve wracking even from the other side of the table. It's awful having to turn people down, especially young hopefuls. One girl who nearly made it to the last two groups burst into almost uncontrollable floods of tears when told she wouldn't be wanted and it was not because she wasn't talented but simply that, at fifteen with budding breasts she was too mature. It turned out that was her third rejection in a week. But it's not just turning down kids that can be distressing. When I was teaching in Denmark we flew to Norway to take auditions for places at the school for the following term and were faced with an elderly woman who had flown all the way down from the north of the country to Oslo to show us she had no talent whatsoever either in speaking or singing and, of course, she was much much too old to be interested in dancing. How did she happen to be there? Was Mickey, the head of the school, out of his mind? When she had boringly delivered her pieces we said thank you very much and there was a long silence as she stood looking at us: Mickey, myself, and the musical director, Roger Davidson and she said, 'Is that all?'

I think, having been inwardly squirming with embarrassment a short while before, I could have burst into tears myself at that moment.

In New York I attended an "audition class" at "The Actors' Center" held by our friend Jeffrey Dunn. What Jeff doesn't know about musicals isn't worth knowing. There were probably thirty or so actors, singers, artistes, budding artistes, all there with their music. One by one they left the body of the room and came up to the table where we were sitting, handing their music to the pianist on route. Then, stepping back, they did their stuff and Jeff would tell them what he thought of their choice of song and their rendition. He knew every number sung that evening. He knew which show it came form, which act it came from, who sung it in the original production, even songs that never made it mainstream. Was the number upbeat or a real downer? Was it the kind of number the auditioners had heard twenty times already that morning and didn't want to hear again? Did it suit a person's voice? Did it suit their personality? Was it within their range? Had they done their homework and tried to find out what was required at the audition? Were they putting the number over in the right kind of way? All his remarks seemed to me to be spot on and very helpful and there was only one embarrassment, an Oriental girl, Vietnamese or Korean, I don't know which, who was totally and embarrassingly hopeless. Otherwise, as I remarked to him afterwards, I had never heard so many beautiful voices and so much talent gathered together in one room. He looked at me, one eyebrow raised and said, 'There wasn't one I would engage for a Broadway show.'

'Why not?'

'Not good enough.'

Such is the competition in New York.

It's amazing how insensitive, even downright rude, producers and directors can be at auditions. I have always maintained the theatre is a vocation that demands the utmost sensitivity from its adherents and at the same time does its best to destroy it. It would seem there are some directors who wittingly or unwittingly, are part of the destructive process, such as those who feel they need a whipping boy they can vent their spleen on. Such a one was Ed Steele at the Wayside Theatre in Virginia who used young David Harwell in this way to such an extent he reduced the boy to tears. Anthony Quayle was another, directing at the Haymarket, only his was a whipping girl, a young actress to whom he was so abusive one day that it was all I could do to control myself and he suddenly knew it because he looked at me and backed right off. I didn't rate him as a director anyway. He divided the company into two; the stars such as toe-acting Michael Denison and Dulcie Gray were darlings, the rest of the company were hardly worth the time of day. He seemed to have an enormous chip on his shoulder, what with all his contemporaries being knighted and made lords and here he was still just plain Anthony Quayle.

We did a new play by Ronald Millar called *A Coat of Varnish* star-

Chapter Fourteen

ring the Denisons, Peter Barkworth, and the great man himself. The play, to put it kindly, was not a very good piece. Before it opened, in his dressing room one day, Quayle asked me what I thought of it so I started to give my criticisms until he yelled, 'Stop! Stop! There isn't time!'

But after its London run it went out on tour and was evidently a great success, I should think due to the presence of Peter Barkworth. While still in London the company manager came to me and said, 'Glyn, you don't really want to go out with this play, do you?'

'No I don't,' I said. 'I've been as miserable as shit in it in the West End, why would I want to be as miserable as shit out in the Styx?' Or should that be "sticks"?

Anthony Quayle never spoke to me again. I would pass him in a corridor and greet him and he would walk by without so much as an acknowledgment. As I disliked the man so much it really didn't matter.

Many years ago my agent sent me to the Prince of Wales Theatre to audition for Durrenmatt's play *The Visit* starring the Lunts and directed by the internationally famous Peter Brooke.

'Is this an individual call or a cattle call?' I asked.

'Oh, individual, your call is ten-thirty.'

Just before ten-thirty I arrived at the stage door to find every actor in London was there. We waited, and we waited, and we waited. The morning went by. The afternoon started to go by. At about three-thirty, having hung around for five hours, we were called to the stage en masse and Mr Brooke addressed us from the stalls as follows,

'I'm not looking for talent,' he said, 'I'm looking for types.'

The Taurian blood boiled. I stood at the front of the stage and said, 'Mister Brooke, you may think you're God's gift to the theatre but I've got news for you,' and giving him the finger, I turned and left to an astonished silence. How not to get yourself a job.

When I was at Birmingham rep in *Are you now?* he came to visit as his wife was in the other company playing in *Anastasia*. They had recently returned from Africa where they had been teaching African

359

kids how to act like lions, another pointless exercise I would have thought, and so patronising. We had to sit through a boring amateur film of this escapade in futility to which there were a few sycophantic ooh's and ah's and I wondered if he would recall the incident at The Prince of Wales but obviously he did not, and why should he? It was that long ago and he wouldn't have remembered me among all those faces.

Another example of rudeness was when I auditioned for Roger Redfarn for a production of *Hobson's Choice*. I had just done that season at The Haymarket during which I understudied Anthony Quayle and Gordon Kaye in that very same play and, as I stood on the stage at this audition working with a stage manager, script in hand, which was like working with a dummy anyway, I could see out of the corner of my eye that Redfarn was taking absolutely no notice of what was happening on stage but was busy chatting to those around him. I stopped and asked him if he was interested in what I was doing or should I just go home? I went home. He has to be one of the rudest men in the business. Comparisons aren't odious when I compare him to Olivier and Ian McKellen both of whom I have auditioned for and both of whom could not have been more genuinely charming or welcoming.

It was during *The Double Deckers* time that my agent called to say I had an audition for The National Theatre. Isn't it typical of this business? There hadn't been a call for me for an eternity, well a year or more, but the minute I was ensconced out at Elstree three came in one week: for a commercial, an enquiry from a rep, and The National. I told him it was pointless my going as I wouldn't be able to take up an offer even if it were made seeing as to how I was busy with the series and would be for quite a while. It really is a stupid business.

'I still think you ought to go,' Errol said. 'Every now and again they clear the books and, if you don't, you mayn't get another chance for a couple of years.'

'All right, I'll go. Will God be there?'

'No, he only goes to the third audition.'

Chapter Fourteen

'Okay, in that case I'll do Hotspur.'

I was reluctant to do Hotspur in front of God because I had always believed this was one of his great roles early in his career.

I arrived at the Nissan Hut behind The Royal Court Theatre where the audition was being held to be met by the director Bill Gaskill who said, 'What are you doing here?'

'I've come to audition.'

'What for? I know your work.'

This was mainly because I had been taking his acting classes. I know, I know, I said you can't teach people to act but there is always room for improvement.

'Oh, well, now you're here, you might as well get on with it. What are you going to do?'

'Hotspur.'

'Hmn-hmn, and?'

'Davis, from *The Caretaker*.' A bit long in the tooth now to do Mick.

'Fire away.'

So I fired away and later got a call from Errol to say I had a recall. Was there any point in going? Errol insisted there was so, 'Will God be there?' I asked.

'No, I told you, he only goes to the third.'

'Okay, then I'll do Hotspur again.'

I arrived at the Nissan hut to find God and all his archangels there, Gaskill, Dexter and all. My heart sank.

Sir Laurence, as he was then, got to his feet, shook my hand, smiled and said, 'Thank you for coming, Mr Jones. What are you going to do for us?'

'Hotspur,' I gulped. Did I see a twinkle in his eye? Did I notice a little smile around the mouth?

'Yes? And?'

I dried totally. I stuttered. In desperation I looked at Bill who said, 'Davis, *The Caretaker*.'

'Oh, yes! Davis, *The Caretaker*.'

A short while later a call from Errol told me I was being offered a contract with The National.

So, unfortunately, I never got to work with Olivier in any capacity, not even as a spear carrier, unlike Senator John Warner who I met at The Boar's Head Inn in Charlottesville. I was there with Su Burrell, Gray's mother, Shirley, and her then boy friend, George Riley, later her husband, and Gray was playing piano when Senator Warner walked in and all the girls in the room went "Aaaah!" He came to our table and, during the course of the conversation when naturally it came out that I was in theatre, he asked if I had worked with Olivier to which, of course the answer was no. He then said he'd worked with both Olivier and Gielgud.

'How?' I exclaimed.

'I was married to an actress once,' he said.[20] Sometimes, sitting in an office at a Television Company being interviewed by some young lion of a director I've thought, I wonder what would happen if, at the end of his questioning, I suddenly said, 'Now tell me about you? What have you done and are you really good enough to direct me?'

The answer to that of course would be, 'Good morning. Next please.'

There is the apocryphal story (another one) of the actress, I think it is attributed to Athene Seyler, who when asked by a young director what she had been doing, as she was removing an elegant glove, looked up at her interlocutor and said, 'You mean today?'

I was at the studios writing for the remainder of the year and Chris, playing King Rat, opened Christmas Eve in *Dick Whittington* at Watford.

January 26th 1970 was a red letter day, being the first day of shooting of *The Double Deckers* and I was visited in my office by the ACTT[21] shop steward who wanted to know why I was not a member of the union because my not being a member was grounds for a walk-out. Now I had previously applied to join this union and been rejected

---

20 For those who do not remember as I didn't it was Elizabeth Taylor.
21 Association of Cinematographic and Television Technicians.

Chapter Fourteen

Bruce Clark, Gillian Bailey, Debbie Russ, Peter Firth, Douglas Simmonds, Michael Audreson, & Brindsley Forde On the set of The Double Deckers

so I informed him that I was a member of The Writers' Guild and as such had no reason to join the ACCT. Being a member of The Writers' Guild simply wasn't good enough he argued, in my position as Script Editor I had to be a member of ACTT or else. In my mind's eye I had this picture of Peter Sellers in *I'm Alright Jack* and I allowed this argument to go on for a while, playing hard to get with crossed fingers behind my back, but eventually allowing myself to be persuaded to join the union.

From now until July virtually every weekday was spent at the studio and this was what we called my second rich period, having a weekly salary as script editor topped up by fees for the scripts I wrote. On the strength of *The Double Deckers* I decided to go ahead with trying to buy a house as I thought, even when work on the series came to an end, the residuals would be coming in and for a while we would be fairly secure financially so it wouldn't be a burden to take on a mortgage. Unfortunately Twentieth Century Fox, the studio at the top of the production ladder, had different ideas. No one received a penny

Michael Audreson, Charlie Pinner, Douglas Simmonds

in residual payments from them. The series never went into profit they maintained which simply couldn't be true as it cost peanuts to make and was a huge success, selling all over the world, syndicated in the states, broadcast first by the BBC in the UK and then by independent stations. I received some money from the Performing Rights Society for the four songs I had in the show so I know how it sold. Equity tried to get money for the actors, the Writers Guild tried to get money for the writers according to our contracts. The West Coast Writers Guild tried. All came up against a brick wall. Eventually Roy Simpson went personally to Hollywood and was told by an executive of Twentieth Century Fox, 'Roy, why don't you just take a beating and fuck off?'

There's the charm of the high-powered mogul for you. Anyway that is exactly what Roy told us on his empty-handed return. I was surprised a short while ago to receive a small cheque from France of all places, nothing to do with Fox, everything to do with new technology.

The Sun ran an article (I don't have a date) headlined,

Chapter Fourteen

KIDS–THE VERY LATEST TREND

British and American TV have made an amazing break-through in entertainment. They are beside themselves with joy. The discovery? Why, children! Real live kids, who can dance, sing, and act. Today we see the first fruits of this discovery–the first of a series called Here Come The Double Deckers (BBC1, 4.55)

The programme will not come as a surprise to Sun readers. They were given the exclusive news about it last July, when we introduced them to the six British and one American unknown child-actors who are now about to become internationally famous.

For this comparatively cheaply-made British product (with no American TV "advisers" to tell producer Roy Simpson and director Harry Booth how to do it) [Not quite true and what about the poor old writer?] *is now running on a major American TV network and getting rave notices. It has already been sold to Finland, West Germany, Holland and Italy and negotiations are going on with nearly all the other Western TV nations.*

Chris had left Sadler's Wells, now the English National Opera. He had wanted to do two seasons with the company on its transfer to The London Coliseum and now, in April, he was dancing in a new musical, *Nell* that opened at the Richmond Theatre. I had been approached by Pan Books to write *The Double Decker* stories in prose which I was busy doing so all seemed to be going well and, with no idea of how Twentieth Century Fox's creative accounting was going to let us down so badly, we went ahead to look for a house. We saw one beautiful Georgian house in the country we both fell in love with. It was called "Shepherd House" and was in Marden in Kent. The asking price was £12,000 and, try as I might, I just couldn't raise the money. Roy Miles came down once in his latest Rolls Royce to take a look at it with us but he wasn't impressed because it had no land. The back of the house looked directly, I should say looks, as I am sure it is still there, over the graveyard next to the nearby church but it was a peaceful country scene and we would dearly have loved to have bought it. I still have the plans I drew of it. With prices of English property now in the realm of fantasy I should think Shepherd House is up in the millions somewhere.

Back in London and still house hunting in 1971 we concentrated on Islington and Hackney and viewed a number of properties including the haunted house in Englefield Road. Driving around we passed a house painted pussy pink and elephant foreskin grey and I said were that the last house in London I wouldn't buy it. I bought it. A Victorian house of four floors with a small front and a large back garden at 162 Richmond Road, Dalston, cost £6,500. Rex Rainer lent us £1,500 for the deposit and Nationwide provided the rest thanks to a friendly creative accountant of our own.

Another friend advised us against buying in Dalston as Hackney Town Council was planning to compulsory purchase and demolish the whole area of Victorian houses known as Mapledene in order to erect high-rise council flats. We decided not to take his advice and, having bought the house, we got together with other residents of the area to form the Mapledene Residents' Association with the specific purpose of taking on Hackney Council that had come up with this scheme because they were afraid of the "gentrification" of the area. Everyone pooh-poohed our chances of success. Members of Town Councils, especially those like Hackney, were accustomed to steam-rolling their way over objections, but we hired legal help and we won; proving statistically that by carrying out their ridiculous political proposals, because that is all they were, for an outlay in the millions they would gain exactly four bed spaces in the jargon of the time.

Before we left Highbury Grange, Jeremy appeared late one evening totally smashed. He was literally green around the jowls. I had never seen that before and it certainly wasn't a trick of the light. I sat him down in the kitchen for a cup of strong coffee and asked him where he thought he was going. When he replied that he intended driving

Chapter Fourteen

to Brentwood I told him he was doing no such thing. He was almost paralytic and would either kill himself, some innocent, or possibly both. And, even if that didn't happen, he would be sure to be pulled over by the police, breathalysed and lose his licence. He could sleep upstairs in my study where there was a single bed.

Before we went to sleep I asked Chris if he knew whether Jer had gone to the loo or not before going upstairs. The answer was he didn't know so I thought, leave it be, he's going to sleep so heavily he won't know anything till morning. I was deep in sleep myself when I heard a thud somewhere in the flat. I also heard myself bellow like a bull as, in one leap, I was over the bed, then out the door, down the passage, switching on the light as I went, and half way up the stairs where I had Jeremy by the throat before I was even fully awake. He had come groping his way down in the dark heading for the loo, slipped on the polished wood of the stair and landed with the thud on his backside. I had totally forgotten he was in the flat and he now had no need of the loo. He had pissed himself right then and there. Maybe he even sobered up a little.

When we viewed the Richmond Road house every room had a family of West Indians in it and the heating was by paraffin stove which, with all those kids around, was extremely dangerous, especially as the stoves were all much too close to bedding some of which was on the floor. So, inexpensive as the house might have been to purchase, the first thing to do was install central heating and rewire from top to bottom. We had a true Cockney electrician who said, 'You got ter 'ave yer laterals in pyra,' and I thought of writing about the experience of buying and refurbishing the house and calling it, *Yer Laterals in Pyra*. I never got around to it though. To save money we made a deal whereby we would do all the hard work like lifting floorboards, drilling holes, chasing walls and replastering, leaving him to wire and join up. I also got Peter Mackie in to lend a hand at £20 a day, not a bad salary for that time. He had been working on a house the other side of town where six puppies were looking for a home and asked if we would take one. In my youth when I fondly believed I would one day be exceedingly wealthy, I thought I would keep four Great Danes: a fawn, a black, a harlequin, and a brindle. I also decided on the first two names, Ninian and Nathan. The other two names never came to mind, possibly Nobby and Niblick. This puppy, a cross Labrador/German Shepherd wasn't exactly in the thoroughbred class but I said yes, we'd take him. I drove over to Fulham to pick up Peter and the pup, stipulating that I would only take it if it were a dog, having always been led to believe bitches to be a nuisance. Picking up the puppy, belly facing me, I discovered it was a bitch.

'Peter, it's a bitch.'

'It never is.'

'It's a bitch, Peter. What do you think that is?'

'It looks like a boy to me.'

'Good grief, you're a married man with kids and you can't tell the difference between a prick and a twat?'

'Don't you want her then?'

I looked at the little black bundle of fur in my hands and all I said was, 'Of course I want her.'

We never regretted it and, from that moment, all the dogs we have owned have been bitches.

She could hardly be called Ninian or Nathan (or even Nobby or Niblick) so she became Natalie.

We already had a cat from the Ladbroke Grove days. One freezing winter night as we were letting guests out after a dinner party, one of them bent down and picked up this tiny shivering tabby, literally with snow on its whiskers, corny as that may sound, handed it to me and said, 'Look what's come to visit you.'

As our visitor's name was George, 'We'll call him George,' I said. Then, discovering George was a queen, George became Georgina.

That was the dinner party when I cooked a lamb casserole for twelve people and, there being so little room in our tiny kitchen, I had put the cooked meat in a large plastic bowl that, without thinking, I placed on top of the gas cooker. The irons of course were still hot

Chapter Fourteen

and they melted the plastic. Within seconds lamb fat had spread everywhere, not only all over the cooker but all over the floor and the kitchen was like a skating rink for days. We had to let the guests in through the bedroom door and place the kitchen out of bounds as we slithered and slid trying to dish up without an accident. It's a wonder a few vertebrae weren't put out in the process. That was not the only incident with fat. While still a puppy, one night when we were out, Natalie ate a pudding bowl full of hard fat, a large portion of Christmas cake and half a bar of Fairy Soap. When we got home there was this furry ball on the kitchen floor with four feet sticking out at right angles. She was sick on and off for the next couple of days and, apart from the bubbles, at least everything she brought up was solid due to the fat. On another occasion, for a dinner party, Chris had prepared a chicken from a medieval recipe, the dish evidently served at the coronation of Henry IV in 1399 and the recipe taken from *Seven Centuries of English Cooking* by Maxime McKendry, published by Weidenfeld and Nicolson: the ingredients consisted of sugar, honey, cloves, raisins, lemon peel, egg yolks, and finely chopped cooked chicken but Chris went a step further and used this to stuff and reshape a boned chicken which was then 'endored,' that is gilded, and somehow this wonderful creation just happened to disappear. I can't remember what replaced it.

Keeping a cat in a flat was fine but now with a house and garden Natalie was our very first happy dog, a fairly large one at that. It's unfortunate that when you get a pup you know you're also going to get heartache somewhere down the line but, in the meantime, Natalie was everybody's favourite despite the fact she had a particular penchant each time she was left alone for chewing up every citisus plant we bought to replace the ones she'd already chewed up. She never destroyed anything else. The last time she did it I was so angry I went to give her a smack and she ducked. Result, one badly dislocated finger the shape of a brace with the middle bone pushed down below the other two, caused by hitting the edge of a door straight on. A visit to E & R in Mare Street to put it right had the Indian doctor hold my wrist in one hand and pull the finger with his other. All it did was make me yell so loud that, two or three injections later the finger was back as it should be, except for the hand looking like a rubber glove that's had air blown into it.

She also developed a taste for fruit and we would watch from behind a window as she walked down the garden, turned to look at the house making sure the coast was clear, and then gently pick a strawberry or two. On holiday once she discovered an apple tree and would pull down a low branch with a paw to bite off an apple whenever she felt like it. Georgina on the other hand was a sucker for curry, the hotter the better.

The word "park" became taboo. Any reference to parking the car, Natalie immediately assumed you meant London Fields where we took her for runs and she was at the door, ball in mouth, ready to go. For a while the word was spelled out but it wasn't long before she twigged what P-A-R-K meant so park, when walkies were involved, became the botanical gardens, and the car was never "parked" it was "left". Both at Richmond Road and later when we moved to Farleigh Road in Stoke Newington, we would sometimes eat in the first floor drawing room whilst watching the television and Natalie would carry the cutlery up from the kitchen in a paper bag and then, having delivered that, make a second trip for the condiments. When it was time to dish up she would appear at the drawing room door, bell in mouth and give it a good ring to tell you dinner was ready. Sometimes, if it were a party and guests took no notice, she would become quite frantic, standing at the door and ringing her bell until someone had the nous to say, 'Natalie's calling us for dinner, we'd better go.' And she would lead the way downstairs.

In the morning she waited by the front door for the postman and, if you were still in bed, she would bring the mail up to you. Once or twice a letter slipped and finished up under the bed, which was unfortunate if it contained a cheque and we didn't find it for a while.

Apart from the central heating and rewiring, 162 had to be repainted inside and out–that pink and grey had to go–which meant

Chapter Fourteen

burning off old paint going back fifty years or more. A new bathroom was installed and we opened up the beautiful Victorian fireplace in the first floor drawing room and the kitchen fireplace in the basement. By this time Jeremy, through a couple called Tom and Beth Bishop, had bought himself a small cottage at Wood Norton, a tiny hamlet in Norfolk. We spent many a week-end there, only each time we drove up in the Rover the road seemed to get longer and longer. Natalie had the same problem as I; motion sickness. From the vet we acquired tablets and the first time we used them, following the vet's instructions, the dose was too much for her and she missed the whole week-end, falling asleep in the car and not really waking up till we were back in London.

Tom and Beth lived in Aylsham, a short distance from Wood Norton and apart from dabbling in a little real estate they dealt in antiques. Two huge barns were crammed to the rafters with furniture, old farm implements and bric-a-brac. Their stock overflowed into the yard with building materials salvaged from demolished houses. We never visited Tom and Beth but we didn't come away with something and the mantelpieces and surrounds for both fireplaces in Richmond Road came from Aylsham, together with the old station clock and a bench from the platform. Lord Beeching had closed the line. One of our friends from Munich, Wieland Brandt, gave us the drawing room fireplace as a truly generous house-warming present; polished wood with caryatids holding up the mantelpiece. The kitchen surround was much older and, according to Tom, was probably made from a broken up chest. It was carved oak and in the top section below the shelf was a roundel with a figure, presumably the great dictator himself, and the lettering, "God Bless Oliver." The carving in the over mantle was different and looked of a later date.

There was a lane in Wood Norton where we used to go to pick sloes, for sloe gin what else? Natalie was always with us, ferreting away in the hedgerows, and in my play *Red in the Morning* there's mention of a "Natalie's Lane." I thought it a nice gesture of remembrance for a very special dog.

From the Bishop's barns we also bought corner cupboards and other stripped pine pieces, stripped pine being the rage at that time. Included was a very tall cupboard with double doors, the back of which we took off and placed the cupboard in front of the lavatory door that, unfortunately, faced the front door and the street, so it was now masked. New guests were slightly nonplussed when they asked for the loo and were told it was in the cupboard. They would sometimes stand there a long time before opening the doors, wondering if they were being taken for a ride. The same cupboard, with its back replaced, is now the wardrobe in my bedroom in Crete.

A select purchase from Tom was a series of six pornographic cartoons by Rowlandson. It was a case of not knowing whether they were genuine Rowlandson or copies but we took a chance on them for twenty quid with the intention of hanging them in a bathroom but they remained in their plain brown wrapper until just recently when we had them framed and they now hang in the flat in Athens. I wondered how our framer in Chania would respond to them but he thought they were wonderful, not because of the subject matter, but the quality of the paper and the drawing. We used to hang a lustre plaque behind the cistern in the loo which read "Prepare To Meet Thy God" but I'm not sure if anyone, as they unzipped, got the joke or not.

Through the lawyer who did the conveyancing for Richmond Road I was introduced to Greville Wynne, an English businessman who was imprisoned behind The Iron Curtain, eventually released through a prisoner exchange, and who wrote a book on his experiences, *The Man from Moscow*. He was looking for someone to write a treatment. I read the book and liked the story so much I decided not to bother with a treatment and presented him with a virtual shooting script, although it says "First Draft Screenplay" on the cover.

'I don't understand it. I don't understand it at all,' he informed me. 'And I gave it to my accountant and he couldn't understand it.'

'Tell your accountant to give me an audit,' I said, 'and I won't understand that. Why the hell should an accountant be able to read a film script which requires above anything else a visual perception?'

Chapter Fourteen

I think what really confused them was the fact that I gave the film three different endings–one of my bright ideas–because it ends with "whatever happened to the Russian Colonel, Oleg Penkovsky?" At that time his ending was a mystery. Now, with so many archives from the Soviet era being opened, maybe the mystery is no longer a mystery.

I now had to fight once more for my pathetic fee of £200, which is what we had agreed on for a treatment. Why are people so reluctant to pay up? It wasn't until I threatened him with a lawyer that I got my measly payment.

Paul Glover and Lionel Wilson were our first American guests at Richmond Road. Paul was a choreographer and assistant to Bob Fosse on the New York production and film of *Sweet Charity* and he reproduced the show in Paris (in which Chris played) at the Gaité Lyrique. It starred Magali Noel, a wonderful Charity, and Sidney Chaplin. We have the Paris recording of the show and poor Sidney could be the male equivalent of Florence Foster Jenkins when it comes to singing off key. Paul's partner, Lionel, actor and writer, appeared to have had his great moment sharing the spotlight with Mickey Rooney in *A Midsummer Night's Dream*, or so the photograph taking pride of place in their apartment at 308 East 79th seemed to indicate. The apartment, according to Lionel, was our home from home in New York and he couldn't wait to show me Times Square. Unfortunately, when I did get to look at it, my reaction was, 'Is that it?' Like Piccadilly Circus, when you actually get to see it, it's a bit of a letdown. I found, as it was then, naughty naughty 42nd Street much more interesting. They had a Dachshund bitch named Anastasia, usually called Stassie who had the unfortunate habit of peeing she got so excited whenever she saw you.

My accountant… that sounds very grand but it seemed, if I were to save paying unnecessary income tax, I needed an accountant, and he did help us get the house, in the end proved to be more costly than the Inland Revenue, charging me a whole lot more than I would actually have paid in tax. It was very nice of him to invite me to lunch in the office but I hardly expected to be charged for his time while we enjoyed the Stilton and water biscuits. He introduced me to Sal Mineo who was looking for someone to write a treatment of Robin Maugham's book, *The Wrong People*. I wrote the treatment for him, parts of which he liked, parts of which he hated but as it was yet another project that never got off the ground it didn't matter, and I was paid for the work, my accountant naturally taking a cut as his "introduction fee."

More importantly, we became good friends with Sal and his significant other, Courtney Burr III. The first night they stayed in Richmond Road, despite being buried under a pile of duvets, they had all the bars of two electric fires going the whole night. Wintry London is not California. We went on to enjoy a memorable snowball fighting traditional English pre-Christmas winter weekend at Wood Norton.

There were visitors a plenty at Richmond Road, dinner parties and, especially when Chris was in *A Little Night Music*, Sunday afternoon teas. At one dinner someone brought and introduced his new boy friend who was princess prissiness personified and objectionable with it. So, the next time they were invited, Chris served up a ham and chicken pie, decorating his pastry with two ejaculating penises and the lettering, "Make date for cock fun." We never saw the boy friend again. One Sunday afternoon, our friend Chris Gay, electrician at the theatre, brought two sarf London lads, Dave and Steve, to the house and a very young Michael Jenn. Steve grew up, married, and emigrated to South Africa but South Africa didn't suit a south London lad and he was soon back. Michael auditioned and gained a place at drama school in Bristol and has become an established actor, (*Maurice, Another Country, Quills*, RSC) and Dave we more or less adopted and he came to live with us in Stoke Newington, remained a close and treasured friend until we moved to Crete when, for some reason best known to himself, he disappeared out of our lives. In fact his disappearing trick has been so good no one seems to know where he is. The first girl friend he brought back to Farleigh Road was named Barbara, surname Pooley so known as Poo, a delightful girl who we loved and who complimented Dave completely. Poo was into horticulture and when we moved to Yorkshire, she came to live with us for as while, working at a local nursery. She was always fun to have around but eventually she and Dave split and the last we heard of her she had taken up with someone else and had a son they named Zac. After that Dave had a succession of girl friends, all very different, but none of them ever lived up to Poo.

Chapter Fifteen

1972 started off with an immediate engagement, playing the tiny part of Torlini in *Reunion in Vienna* by Robert E. Sherwood. The production starred Margaret Leighton and Nigel Patrick and had been previously seen at The Chichester Festival theatre. Directed by Frith Banbury it was now scheduled to go into the Piccadilly in London. Also receiving top billing in a cast of twenty-eight were Michael Aldridge and Beatrix Lehmann but the cast member who was to have a profound effect on our lives was a young man by the name of Charles Pinner, assistant stage manager and playing a waiter. He had previously been cast in an episode of *The Double Deckers* and although I had nothing to do with him then, he now introduced himself and, during chats, it transpired that he wanted to start a film company and become known as the youngest producer ever. He asked if I would be interested in writing something for him. As he was nineteen or twenty at the time and as I was gainfully employed as they say I thought why not encourage such youthful enthusiasm? I wonder how different things would have been if I hadn't made that decision.

I don't know how we actually arrived at the story but I ended up writing a script about a young man from a rich upper class family who wanted to be a Formula One racing driver but who got mixed up with drugs and came to a sticky end. At first I thought of calling it *Images* pronounced the French way but, when written it would just look like "Images" the English way. Then I rather fancied the title *Torque*. That was most apt for the subject but, when spoken, it would sound like

Chapter Fifteen

"Talk" so that was out. I finally came up with *Speed*, which was also apt having to do both with racing cars and drugs. This was before the American film of the same title came out and Charlie even had very expensive rugby shirts and woollen sweaters made with *Speed* knitted in. I've never worn mine because it is, for me, that abrasive wool similar to my jersey of Sea Scout days and the rugby shirt is far too small anyway. I think Charlie thought everyone was his size, which was skinny.

He went ahead as he intended and formed his film company, Halpin Film Productions with an office at Pinewood, and suddenly he started appearing in immaculate Saville Row suits, expensive shirts, ties, and footwear and telling me a Dutch bank was putting up the money for the film, the money currently being in escrow which was why he couldn't start paying me for the writing. Escrow? This was the first time I had come across this word but like a fool I believed and trusted him. Time moved on, as they say and we asked Roy Simpson, as someone having the most experience in actual production, to become involved.

Reunion in Vienna had come and gone. My one and only real memory of it apart from Charles was one night standing in the wings behind Margaret Leighton, waiting to go on, I suddenly re-enacted that gesture the young girl had performed on my freckles many years before in Great Yarmouth. I stretched out my hand and ran my fingers down her naked back. She turned to look at me "Oh, shit!" I thought, "Here I am, a bit part player molesting a star! Say something quick."

'Sorry, Miss Leighton,' I whispered, 'I couldn't help it. You have the most beautiful back.'

Which, in truth, was the reason for my impulsive familiarity.

'You're welcome to it, darling,' she whispered back, 'and you can have the pain that goes with it.'

She turned back to face the stage and then I noticed for the first time how she stood first on one leg then the other trying to ease the pain. But when she heard the cue for her entrance "Doctor Footlights" came into his own and she glided on to that stage as graceful as a swan, a star in every sense of the word.

Chris went into the musical *Gone with the Wind* at Drury Lane, playing Brent Tarleton, his twin played by the dancer Andy Norman. Sal and Courtney attended the opening night and Noel Coward was there who evidently said the best performance of the evening was from the horse when it shat itself centre stage. This was the first time we met Bonnie Langford who was playing the Bonnie of the story and I hate to say it but she was a theatre brat because her mother was a theatre mum, albeit a very pleasant one. She appeared one evening with a birthday cake for her darling, pieces of which Bonnie took around to every dressing room on paper napkins inscribed with the legend, "From The Real Bonnie." But there was no denying the child's talent and stage presence and, offstage, she was a charmer who grew up to be a wonderful artiste and was always totally professional, even as a bratette.

We have the double disc Japanese recording of the show, Japan being where it started, and it really must be a fact that the Japanese can't pronounce their L's because every time Scarlet is mentioned it comes out as Scar-ret. I was allowed into the dressing room on this occasion because I did in fact enjoy the show with some jaunty numbers and great production value although I felt the second act a let down. How do you follow the burning of Atlanta? But my criticism of Chris was that, when he waved his rifle (carbine?) in the air and said, 'We're going to fight the Yankees!' he waved it about rather like a handbag. 'Do you know how much those things weigh?' I said. 'Do it like this.'

The following night he did as I suggested and Joe Layton went to the dressing room after the show and tore him off a little strip.

'Someone's been giving you directions,' he said. 'You go back to the way I want it.'

Never gratuitously interfere in another director's production.

Chapter Fifteen

The summer came and went with *Who Goes Bare* with a cast of mostly TV faces, and with researching King Arthur, then Bob Philips, a lawyer friend of Andy Moore's, asked me to write (on spec of course) a pilot for a projected series he had in mind called *The Image Makers*. This was to be about sports-men and women and those agents and managers who make big commercial stars and big money out of them. I wrote a pilot and, as I was still hanging about waiting for something to happen to *Speed*, I wrote it about motor racing and Bob and I went down to Snetterton to watch some races and take in the atmosphere. I've never been to a horse track or to the dogs and this was the first time, television viewing excepted, I watched racing cars. I can't say I was over-excited by it. In Durban I used to attend motorcycle meets, which I did find exciting, but I've never ridden a motorbike except pillion and guess I'm a bit too old for that now. As a young teenager I dreamt of one day owning a Velocette. What happened to the Velocette, and the BSA, and the Triumph? The Japanese happened to them.

Whenever I think back on the actors I have understudied my stomach still turns over because understudy rehearsals conducted by stage management are usually on a take it or leave it basis and I was never fully prepared to go on. I have to admit it was partly my fault for never taking it seriously enough and trusting to luck. Understudying at The Haymarket for instance I spent most of my time in the basement playing chess with a young stagehand by the name of Robert Alge. But if anything had happened to cause an unexpected absence, I dread to think how abysmal I would have been. This especially applies to someone like Alistair Sim who I understudied in a play called *A Private Matter*, nicknamed *A Matter of Privates* because it was the first time an actor, Derek Fowlds, stripped off to appear completely nude and full frontal in a straight play. It was not a great play by any means but evidently Alistair had promised to appear in it and, as Alistair's name was bound to put bums on seats, on it went, opening for try-outs in Brighton and Edinburgh before moving into the Vaudeville.

No Official Umbrella

In Edinburgh Alistair took us all out to dinner and chortled gleefully at table about how he managed to find the cheapest restaurant in the city. It might have been the cheapest but the meal in fact was very good. Maybe he was just kidding, playing up the mean Scot bit. On the other hand, maybe not. On the opening night we were all presented with a ceramic goblet inscribed with the title of the play.

It was also in Edinburgh, where they live, that I met my cousin, Robin Hendry the youngest of three brothers for the first and one and only time. He came to the theatre one evening and although, at the time, he must have been in his thirties, he looked like an old man and a not very attractive one at that. One of the stage management passed us by at the stage door and the next day I asked him how old he thought my cousin was. He guessed somewhere in his late fifties, maybe sixty. I can't remember where we went that evening, either a bar or a café, but across the table he opened up to me possibly in a way he had never done with anyone before. Maybe he had an idea he would never see me again. His father had been employed by the Irish Linen Bank and wanted Robin to follow in his footsteps that, after doing his national service and as a dutiful son, he did. But he hated every minute of it. What he wanted more than anything else in the world was to be a shepherd and that is what he should have been. So, whenever a youngster tells me his or her ambition is to do something out of the ordinary I always tell them to go for it no matter what anyone says, like the kid in Harrisonburg who told me he wanted to be a potter but everyone was against it. I told him if he wanted to be a potter to go and be a potter. I thought it a wonderful ambition to have, to create something both beautiful and useful. What did it matter what anyone else thought? It was his life. I later learnt he did exactly that, went to Japan to study and became a resident of California where I am told his ceramics are very much sort after.

But Robin had other problems, mainly sexual, and confided that he could not have sex except with a prostitute and then only if she wore a plastic mac. Robin died shortly after and I am sure he would

Chapter Fifteen

have forgiven me, and I hope his brothers will, for using that bit of him as part of the son's character in my play *Twilight of Aunt Edna*.

A Private Matter was directed by Ian McKellen, who asked me to understudy and at a later date he asked for me again, again to understudy. I apologised and turned it down saying understudying wasn't really what I was about and, believe it or not, he actually apologised for asking me.

There is no doubt that audiences came to see Alistair and, had I gone on for him, I think at least half of them would have walked out by the interval. No one, but no one, could possibly come up to an audience's expectations taking over from such a character. West End managements are miserly when it comes to understudies and you usually have to cover at least two parts, both major. In this case my other understudy was to cover Peter Cellier. Mister Cellier is not the most charismatic of actors and if I had to have gone on for him I would have probably been able to take a stab at it fairly successfully, even unprepared as I was. But Alistair? Follow that act if you dare. It was in this play that he indulged in that really naughty piece of upstaging knowing exactly what he was up to. In one scene Peter Cellier as a prospective Conservative MP had a long speech that was the high point of his performance, or meant to be, but Alistair, playing a professor visiting this particular family in the course of researching the family patriarch's life and death, had other ideas. At this point he was positioned standing in front of the fireplace and, as Peter started on his monologue Alistair picked up a silver cigar box off the mantelpiece, opened it, selected a cigar, closed the box, put it back on the mantelpiece, sniffed the cigar he had chosen, rolled it in his fingers, decided he didn't like it and picked up the box to put it back and choose another one, going through the same routine with maybe a little variation such as, when rolling it between his fingers, holding it to an ear. Then he had to hunt for the matches but, before lighting his cigar, he had to roll it between his lips to wet the end by which time not a single person in the audience was looking at Peter or hearing a word he was saying. It really was totally outrageous and, of course, Peter was quite rightly upset and complained to Ian. But what could Ian do? He evidently tried to have words with Alistair, who simply gave him that characteristic Sim look of bewildered innocence and said, 'Me, dear boy?'

This was the year Natalie became a mother. We had decided she would have one litter before being spayed and the time had come. We found her a suitable mate a few doors down from 162 on the opposite side of the road and it was a tiring and sweaty business which bored us all silly, including her, so much so that at one point she decided to lie down. This elicited a howl from the dog as his prick was bent backwards and we had to hurriedly hold her up on all fours and keep her there until he eventually withdrew by which time arms had become almost numb from her weight. We then, as she shook herself and started to spray semen in all directions, lifted up her back legs and gave her a good bouncing to make sure at least some of it was well and truly where it was meant to be. The result? Seven beautiful pups all given Wagnerian names. We had made a whelping box in the area at the rear of the basement where she was perfectly happy until, as Chris and I both had theatre commitments and couldn't stay with her, I telephoned Caroline and asked if she and Alex could come over and keep watch which they did and Natalie, hearing them at the front area, sped across the kitchen to greet them, dropping a pup as she went. Tristan and Isolde were the first two to appear followed by Brunnhilde, Siegfried, Gunter, Gutrune and Flosshilde. We found good homes for them all and I doubt, with the exception of Isolde who we kept, any retained their Wagnerian names. I know for a fact that Siegfried, taken by Peter Mackie, was renamed by his children, Mr Plod. Snowy white Isolde was the most beautiful of them all with the sweetest nature.

After my trip to South Africa it was back to the Labour Exchange for the rest of the year. There was still no progress with *Speed* and money was getting very tight. My mother had paid my air fare to

Chapter Fifteen

South Africa and this was a fare I gladly accepted as she was getting on in years and not in the best of health and I felt I had to make the effort to see her. In a way it was a two-edged sword because she died the following year and it is possible our brief reunion hastened the end.

1974 started well. I did a programme for the BBC called *Books, Plays, & Poems* and then went straight on to the Mermaid to understudy yet again in a quite ridiculous play called *Something's Burning* by Ronald Eyre. It starred Bill Fraser and, as there is no mention of me in the programme, I assume it was he I understudied. The play was not at all well received, though Bernard Miles went round all the dressing rooms the night after the reviews came out saying, 'Best play we've ever done. Here, have a toffee.'

Presumably it was the best play because of the grants system which meant if you spent your entire allowance you could have it again the following year and perhaps a little bit more but if you ended the year in profit your grant would be cut. Not a very good system and a certain invitation to waste money along the lines of my Guinness commercial.

There now came an opportunity to possibly quit Britain and try a new start in Australia when a television company called Crawford's who produced the *Homicide* series advertised for writers. A meeting was held at The Europa Hotel where the prospective writers already selected, amongst whom I was one, were given a briefing and shown a number of episodes, all of which bar one, were pretty run of the mill crime stories. The exception was a really beautiful, gritty, in-depth film in the manner of *Hill Street Blues* they were obviously very proud of though unbeknownst to me, but which I found out later, hated at the same time because it was evidently the least popular among viewers. This was the one I decided to model my required audition script on and my script came back to me with a reader's report saying I was a "B class writer." A "B-class writer"! That's how I was labelled and I wrote a letter asking for justification. In reply I was told that, were I

As Billy Bones in Treasure Island - Mermaid Theatre

living in Australia they would probably have considered using me but they didn't feel justified in going to the trouble and expense of taking me over there when they could employ someone local instead, so that was the end of that.

Bernard must have taken a liking to me when he gave me my toffee because he now cast me in a play called *The Great Society* all about Watt Tyler and the peasants revolt of 1381; severed heads on pikes and in bloody sacks starring Pete Postlethwaite. During a break in rehearsals he suddenly asked me if I sang to which, naturally, I replied yes but I had no idea why he would ask such a question unless he was thinking of putting on a musical. Well, yes, in a way it was a musical, and November saw me back at The Mermaid to play Billy Bones and a pirate named O'Brien in Treasure Island. Bernard as always played Long John Silver. Jonathan Scott Taylor, later to be Damien in The Omen was Jim Hawkins, William Rushton played Squire Trelawney, and Spike Milligan was Ben Gunn. At one performance, enacting my death scene half way down a trap, my foot slipped on the stage blood previously spilled on a step and I hit my elbow on the side of the trap as I disappeared below. It hurt for a few minutes but I thought no more of it until, at breakfast the next morning, Natalie gently pushed at my elbow with her muzzle and I let out a yell as I nearly hit the roof. Fortunately we had friends a few doors down the road, Daphne and Martin Knight and Martin was a doctor so down the road I went for a quick consultation. He touched my elbow where Natalie had nuzzled it and again I let out an involuntary yell as the pain shot up my arm.

'Martin! What are you doing to Glyn?' a concerned Daphne called from the kitchen.

Evidently, in just hitting the edge of the trap I had chipped off a tiny sliver of bone that would soon mend and nothing to worry about, provided nothing touched it for a while to aggravate it. So I went to the theatre with my arm in a sling and told them I couldn't possibly go on that night, not with a broken arm. I gave them a minute's worry before telling them, no, it's all okay, and took off the sling. The joke didn't go down too well but the accident did go down in the accident book, just in case.

When I was directing *Orphans* at James Madison, during a break in rehearsals one night I went off to relieve myself and when I returned I found one of my actors, Pat Dooley who was playing Phillip, lying all twisted up on the auditorium floor just below the stage with my stage manager, Kim Russell, and Jim Anzide who was playing Harold standing by looking sick, and Ron Copeland kneeling solicitously beside him.

'He fell off the stage,' Ron said. 'I think he's broken his leg.'
I nearly had a heart attack.
'April fool!' They shouted.
Payback time.

One evening Jeremy appeared at the front door of 162 with another waif and stray, human this time, our Swedish friend Ulf Larsson who had been staying in an artist's studio down beside the Thames so cold he was literally freezing to death. Jeremy brought him in for a warm and he stayed for more than a year. When he left to return to Sweden I was rehearsing *Under Milk Wood* at Colchester and our trains crossed, his heading for Harwich, mine for Liverpool Street. I opened in Colchester in that piece of old Welsh moody by Dylan Thomas and shortly after received a card from Sweden saying, "Somewhere I lost your Colchester address–that's why you did not get a first night card. Sorry. I know I'm a naughty boy. Hope everything is all right with you, Richmond Road, Speed, and your typewriter. I'm okay but missing you, thinking about you, with love from your Swedish au pair." Which gave me the idea for yet another as yet unperformed play, *Au Pair*.

There was still no progress with *Speed* and I seemed to be wasting my time with rewrites suggested by both Roy and Charles who informed me that he had lined up Peter Finch, Bradford Dillman, Charles Aznavour, and Mia Farrow for the cast. Guy Green was roped in to direct. I had a meeting with both him and Mia who had actually read the script and who was now demanding massive rewrites, namely to increase the size of the part she was being asked to play. Had I acquiesced, the whole thing would have been thrown completely out of kilter so I went away and fiddled a bit here, tarted up a bit there. tweaked a bit elsewhere, and the next time we met, she gave me a glacial stare and said, 'Do you take me for a complete idiot?' And that was the end of me and Mia Farrow, a lady I must say I did not warm to.

In '75 work came intermittently. After *Treasure Island* I stepped onto the stage of The Royal Opera House, Covent Garden for my one and only brush with grand opera and it just had to be Wagner

Chapter Fifteen

when I stood in for the tenor Richard Cassilly while Eleanor Fazan choreographed and rehearsed the Venusberg scene in *Tannhauser*.

Roy Simpson then asked me to write a pilot script for a proposed animation series called *The Henry Eggins Show*, later renamed *The Eggspert* for which Judy Dench did the narration. We went shopping together and this time it wasn't a chore as she was such a delightful companion, also a generous one I discovered, as for no apparent reason, when she emerged from the Scotch Shop where she had gone to buy a sweater, she handed me as a present, a beautiful paper weight of clear glass, imbedded in it a white crystal flecked with silver. It was a lovely and totally unexpected gesture. The proposed series unfortunately was another that never saw the light of day. The paperweight sits on my desk in front of me.

A stage play of mine was produced. Originally called *How Do You Like Your Wagner*, and retitled *Tell Me You Love Me*, it went on in Perth under the direction of Joan Knight and with the backing of Peter Saunders. Of all my plays this was my agent Laurence Fitch's favourite: also the favourite of Peter Saunders' right-hand girl but it never went further than Perth. When Laurence sent it to Samuel French for a possible publication, the reply was, "This really is a rather good play, is it not? We have found it intelligent, moving and dramatically sound with good dialogue, good roles, a solid intellectual framework and the right blend of comedy. However, in truth, this play must have some sort of good professional exposure before it can work as a commercial proposition for us. Plays with difficult themes such as this one has do not appeal to amateurs unless there is a professional history. More's the pity. I am returning the script herewith and hope that in a year or two we will have an opportunity of talking seriously about it. Many thanks for letting me see it."

Chris went into *A Little Night Music* and I, for a short period at The Open Space to play Escalus in *Measure For Measure* under the direction of Charles Marowitz. Richard Mayes was playing the duke. Many years later I was walking down a side alley in Kalyves, Crete, and this couple were walking towards me. I stopped them and, addressing the man, said, 'You're English, you're an actor, and I've worked with you.'

'Quite right on all counts, old chap. Richard Mayes, and this is my good wife, Beryl,' the actress Beryl King who he usually refers to as BK.

We then spent a great deal of time fruitlessly searching our respective pasts wondering where and when we had worked together. Now, sitting here, if I look up to my right, hanging on the wall is a framed programme for *Measure For Measure* and the first name on the cast list is Richard Mayes. Of course neither of us wanted to remember *The Gorky Brigade*. Richard had wiped that from his memory as well.

This trying to remember when and where you met any of the people you have worked with can be truly aggravating. Working with Melvyn Hayes on *The Double Deckers* we both thought we had worked together but it wasn't so and yet we knew we had met somewhere. Yes indeed, it was in passing at a stage door in Manchester.

A Little Night Music was our introduction to Stephen Sondheim. I listened to a recording of the show and was not impressed. In fact I remember being distinctly disparaging about the whole piece, saying something to the effect that all the queens in London would go to see it and then it would come off. I never thought I would come to love it, as well as becoming an avid fan of Mr Sondheim.

Chris fell in love with Jean Simmons and got off to a bad start with Hermoine Gingold by calling her "Ma'am" which she heard as "Herman", her nickname, and only very close friends, not uppity young actors, called her that. Later, when it was explained to her what he had really said, she grew quite fond of him.

Unlike me, who hated the very thought of understudying, Chris could go on at the drop of a hat or jump into the breach even with something he hadn't rehearsed which he did on a number of occasions, not only in *Night Music* but in *Cole* and in *Cats*.

At The Open Space I waited apprehensively for the dreaded Marowitz improvisation sessions but they turned out to be highly

Chapter Fifteen

imaginative and enjoyable. After one morning rehearsal when everyone was heading off for lunch Vanessa Redgrave and cohorts suddenly appeared at the door to spread the good news that the Workers Revolutionary Party were up to something or other and volunteers and supporters would be needed on the big day! Unfortunately everyone had seen her coming and dodged out leaving me to face her. She rabbited on and on while I tried without success to escape until finally, in desperation, I said, 'Oh, Vanessa, stop being so bloody aggressive. I want to go to lunch.'

'I am not being aggressive!'

'Stop being so fucking boring then.'

'Well do you have a car? Can you give people a lift?'

'I don't have a car.'

'Well what's your phone number?'

'I don't have a phone,' with which I managed to flee. Whoever heard of an actor who didn't have a phone? Half an actor's life is spent sitting on the phone.

There was a young actor at The Mermaid, a member of the Workers Revolutionary Party who was forever trying to sell the rest of the company the party's newspaper. Finally one day I bought one just to get him off my back, flicked through it and left it on my dressing table. At the time the party's big scare was that the government had tanks lined up in tunnels beneath the Thames ready to roll out and mow down the masses should there be an uprising and this kid kept going on about it. It was the time of the miners' strike and the three-day week. My purchase didn't do the trick. He kept on and on with his sales pitch until a few weeks later when he tried yet again to foist another newspaper on me my patience ran out. I asked what the point was of my buying it when it would be saying exactly the same thing as the previous edition? I picked up the old paper, for some reason still lying on my dressing table, and compared the word for word headlines. 'What do I want to buy your bloody paper for?' I said. 'Look! Look at the headlines, they're the same in both papers, virtually the same bloody headlines week after week. And the copy is the same as well. Every week I'll read the copy in the one I've got and save money, okay? It's all crap anyway. You come in here with your Harrods's shopping bag...'

'What's that got to do with it?'

'You can't possibly be a member of the Workers Revolutionary Party, not when you live with mummy in Mayfair..."

'Knightsbridge.'

'Wherever, and walk about carrying a Harrods's shopping bag. If you really want to do something for the revolution why don't you go down to the Thames and flog your stupid paper to all those tank commanders before they come out and blast the shit out of you?'

He never tried to sell me another paper. In fact I'm not sure he ever spoke to me again.

As *Measure For Measure* was drawing to the end of its run, Marowitz asked me if I would like to play the Ghost in his version of *Hamlet*. Like an idiot, instead of asking to see the script, I automatically assumed the Ghost to be as small a part as in the original and turned it down. I later learned that in fact in Marowitz's version it was a part well worth doing.

There followed an unpaid lunchtime run of *Don't Walk About With Nothing On*, a rare Feydeau one act farce at the Maximus Club in Leicester square which John Dalby directed, asking both Chris and myself to be in it; and then a radio engagement for the BBC, *People Are Living There* followed by another radio broadcast, *Robben Island*.

New York, Wednesday, May 19th, 1976–The show biz paper *Variety* on its International page, published the following:

Halpin Film Prods. To Roll
Speed
Next Fall In Britain

"Speed", actioner with an auto racing backdrop, is planned to start here in the fall by indie Halpin Film Productions for worldwide release

Chapter Fifteen

by London distrib Scotia-Barber. Guy Green is to direct for producer Charles Pinner, with Roy Simpson as exec. Producer.

Set thus far are Charles Aznavour, Bradford Dillman, Peter Firth and Dinah Sheridan. Original screenplay is by Glyn Jones.

Peter Finch, who we had originally envisaged playing the father suddenly died...

...and Charles disappeared.

Later, for some reason, I was asked to make a statement as a witness in the matter of bounced cheques, the statement reading:

"I first met Charles Pinner when I was in a play called "Reunion in Vienna" in the early 1970's. Later he asked me to write a script for him concerned with motor racing called "Speed". I am now shown a cheque drawn by Charles Pinner on the National Westminster Bank Claygate Branch, 109 Hare Lane, Claygate, Esher, Surrey dated the 1st October, 1977 and marked refer to drawer. This was in respect of fees due to me for the script. It was in fact an on account payment. Shortly after having sent the cheque to my bank I received a letter from them, dated the 10th October, returning the cheque marked refer to drawer. It has been put to me that at the material time I knew that the cheque would be dishonoured that I had asked for the cheque for reason of my own. One of the reasons suggested to me was that my bankers needed the money for my account. This is not so and I have continued to use that account. I remember this in particular because prior to his departure to South Africa Charles Pinner said to me on the telephone that he had arranged with the Finance Director of his Company for me to be paid £300 in cash and he had left his post-dated £500 cheque. Needless to say the £300 did not materialise and the Finance Director knew nothing about it."

So that was the end of *Speed* with a producer hotfooting it to South Africa presumably to get as far away as possible from some angry creditors, including me. I did feel terribly sorry for his parents though

No Official Umbrella

whom I think really came to grief over all this. And it wasn't the last I heard of Charles Pinner as I was landed with a bill for £120 from a firm of solicitors, let's call them Cherubini & Partners, and once again Jeremy came to the rescue. It is a true saying, "have lawyers for friends but never go to law."

> Dear Glyn,
> re: *Cherubini & Partners and yourself.*
>
> *I have written to Cherubini & Partners about the bill they sent you and one of my clerks, M.F. had a conversation with the partner there who drafted the bill.*
>
> *They are being decidedly unhelpful. They maintain that the advice was given to you and that you are responsible to them for payment of the account. They say they are highly competent and expert tax lawyers with special knowledge of the entertainment business, and that the time taken to prepare the letter to you and the time taken in conference on the telephone fully justifies the charge of £120 which they have made.*
>
> *It is your right to require them to obtain a certificate from the Law Society that the work done by Messrs Cherubini & Partners justifies the charge they have made and if the Law Society feels that the work done does not justify the charge they will certify what in their opinion is a fair and reasonable charge should be.* [£120 was quite a sum in 1978 for a letter and a phone call]
>
> *This is, of course, Without Prejudice to your claim that you are not responsible for the bill at all.*
>
> *Enclosed a copy of our letter to Cherubini & Partners.*

The enclosed letter reiterates the above and concludes with,

> *Mr Jones does maintain that it was really Charles Pinner who sought your advice in connection with the bill in which Mr. Jones was to be involved and that therefore you should be looking to Mr Pinner for payment. Perhaps you would care to let us know what Mr. Pinner has to say about this.*

Chapter Fifteen

And that, as far as I remember, was the last we heard of it, whatever Mr. Pinner had to say.

1977 for me was mainly an acting year both on television and in the theatre: something called *Marcia* for the BBC, of which I have no recollection, one episode entitled *Alison* in the series *Breakaway Girls*, *The Windscale Affair* for the BBC and an episode of *The Liver Birds*. In the theatre *Statements After an Arrest* in Leeds and in Aberystwyth a summer of a new play, *The Day the Welsh Rose* directed by Gareth Jones. By now I was driving an old Austin station wagon and I tried to save some money by not taking digs in Aberystwyth but driving up into the mountains after every performance and sleeping in the back of the car. I took a couple of flasks of coffee with me but didn't save very much because I had to have the exhaust on the car replaced.

While I was there Chris and I found a delightful country property near Knighton. The house was literally on the English/Welsh border so that you slept in Wales and had your breakfast in England. That part of the country is very beautiful and the house, or the ruins rather, called Vron Mill had a good piece of land with a long river frontage. The price was £1,500. At Colchester I met the actor Lloyd Johnston, a genuine Welshman, not a phoney like me, and he and his parents, Fray and Betty came up from Cardiff to look at the house. Fray was at one time a builder though they now kept a little newsagents/tobacconist shop. We all marched into what would have been the kitchen to be confronted by a bull that not only looked very irate but also lowered its head so menacingly that we all fled for our lives. Bellicose just wasn't in it. Fray evidently told this story until his recent death. I didn't know where I was going to get the £1,500 from but the purchase never went ahead anyway because the estate agent called to say that the land was no longer included in the deal to which I replied that without the land the deal was off.

Returning to London at the end of the season I picked up two young hitchhikers who turned out to be German boys who had been "tenting" as they put it in Wales. I don't know why it was but Cheltenham was the only place in England I was ever stopped by the police for some minor infringement and it happened with the two boys in the car. This driver behind me was blinding me with his lights so I drove faster. He kept up with me. I drove faster still until suddenly the blue light came on. I pulled over. He pulled up behind me, got out of his car and came to my door.

'You're driving very badly,' he said. 'You're all over the road. Are you tired?'

This was because it was in the early hours.

'I have to admit I am a bit,' I said, using the excuse he had given me.

He looked in the back and saw the two wide-eyed youngsters staring at him, taking note of their haversacks. 'Hmn... Dad's been to pick up the boys after their holidays, huh? Well, in order to get them home safely I suggest you pull over and take a rest before you go much further. There's a lay-by not too far on.'

I thanked him for his concern, said I would do that, and drove off. I pulled into the lay-by and watched as his patrol car went passed and, when I thought he was sufficiently far away, I drove on. We got to Hackney about four in the morning and the boys thanked me politely for the lift and started to move away from the house.

'And where do you think you're going at this hour of the morning?' I asked. 'You don't even know what part of London you're in, do you?'

The answer was two big shrugs.

'Come on,' I said, 'there's a bed in the house you can have.' So they stayed what was left of the night and their big excitement came at breakfast the following morning when they heard that our next door neighbour was Mike Ratlidge of the rock group *Soft Machine*. They practically flipped. Could they meet him? Well, why not? They were introduced, they got Mike's autograph, they went away two very happy German boys. A couple of months later a box was delivered to us containing a dozen bottles of superb German wines as a not so small thank you.

I went to the Old Vic to see a stunning production of *War Music*: words by Homer and Christopher Logue, music by Donald Fraser,

Chapter Fifteen

all about the Trojan War and, at one point, a line-up of boys turned upstage to reveal twenty or so bare bums and I thought, "large company, all male, *The 88.*" The following morning I telephoned Laurence and asked him to send the play to the Prospect Theatre Company at The Old Vic.

'What for?' he said. 'A waste of postage.' But I managed to persuade him and Toby Robertson accepted it.

Then Leslie Lawton cast me as Sergeant Cokes in David Rabe's play *Streamers* at the Liverpool Playhouse. *Streamers* was one of the very few plays for which you couldn't wait to get to the theatre and at the end of each performance you didn't really want to leave. As usual the critics were divided, some disliking the play, others virtually raving over it.

With Don Mckillop in Streamers - Roundhouse London

"Drop everything. Get out your superlatives and go and see "Streamers". Seldom does a play hit an audience with such a high emotional blast that the nerves are tingling from the first to the last moment, but Leslie Lawton's tender and soaring production of David

No Official Umbrella

Rabe's Broadway hit receiving its British premiers at the Liverpool Playhouse sends one away mentally winded. Two drunken war veterans Sgt Rooney and Sgt Cokes (Don McKillop and Glyn Jones) sing in a sweet and sour episode 'Beautiful Streamers' a song to fend off their own 'streamer' a non-opening parachute. Glyn Jones is especially moving in the long final soliloquy searching for his friend. His tipsy ramblings lull us through the calm after the holocaust. – The Stage."

Erlend Clouston in *The Liverpool Post* was decidedly on the side of the negatives.

"Lesson in futility"
'Don't tell anybody you saw me do this,' the barmy black (Don Warrington) whispers hoarsely after knifing two men. The audience tittered, confirming that they were hopelessly lost and perhaps thinking the line a fitting epitaph or a mysterious but relentless failure.

David Rabe's Streamers, which had its British premiere no less, at the Playhouse last night, comes trailing the stardust of New York plaudits. It takes on London in three weeks time. One's only prayer for the company and director Leslie Lawton is that the Roundhouse audiences are better drilled in futility than Northerners.

What baffles is how Mr Rabe has managed to mess up the marvellous scenario he has drafted for himself. We are in a US Army barracks room. To our right is a homosexual, to our left a bright college boy, around the back are two shades of black, and somewhere in the future lies a posting to Vietnam. Plenty of meaty stuff there but somehow Mr Rabe contrives to slouch round every issue. The war is just something you say "shit" about, when not grinning amiably at a pair of improbably drunk and jovial sergeant Bilkos.

Homosexuals are an excuse for childish jokes. The persistently inebriated (and occasionally inaudible) nature of Mr Warrington's black rather cancels out his role as some sort of Caliban of the Ghetto. And of course everybody swears a lot to demonstrate that they are (a) American; (b) military and (c) soulful.

Chapter Fifteen

I am reluctant to blame this disappointment on director and cast. Menace is absent, perpetually relationships are awkward, tears forced, laughter hollow–but these are brick builders struggling with rotten straw. I'll remember some of James Aubrey's mincing, some of Mr Warrington's power and Glyn Jones' valiant assault on a witheringly boring drunken soliloquy. Beyond that, nothing.

But Diana Harker, writing for *The Daily Telegraph* had a different perception of the play, a complete contradiction of the above.

'What are you crying about soldier?' 'He's crying because he's a queer.' When Sgt Cokes asks the question it is near the end of the play. He is looking for his friend Sergeant Rooney and instead finds two enlisted men. So, while waiting for the missing soldier, he tells very drunkenly, a horrifying tale of their exploits together earlier in the day when they smashed a Chevy, a Buick, and a Triumph in their intoxicated drive around town.

What Sergeant Cokes does not know is that previously Rooney and another enlisted man, Billy, had been brutally and pointlessly stabbed by a coloured soldier, Carlyle who, fresh from the "cat-house" outrages the others by his intentions to physically possess the queer soldier.

Leslie Lawton's production of the prize-winning American play "Streamers" at the Liverpool Playhouse is as horrifying in its visual brutality as that last speech is in its words.

David Rabe's writing is strong, and yet has moments of sheer poetry. The inter-relationship between the three soldiers in the barrack room in Virginia in 1965 who are befriended by the lonely Carlyle is beautifully constructed.

When "Streamers" goes to The Roundhouse in London later this month I am sure it will be as widely acclaimed as it was in New York and David Rabe will be recognised as a major American playwright alongside Albee and Miller.

The *Telegraph* review in London by John Barber was also positive and I note I was one who particularly distinguished himself which, complimentary as that was, it was nothing like Peter Bennett referring to me as "the superb Glyn Jones." Never in my professional life had I ever been called superb. Yet, perhaps the nicest compliment I was paid was some time after the play had closed and I was entering the British Library to go to the reading room when a young man, an American, stopped me and said, 'Excuse me, sir. But weren't you in *Streamers*?'

I said I was and he said how much he had enjoyed it, etcetera and then added, 'But you're not an American!' And that really was a compliment.

The entire cast were devastated to learn that the play was not going further than the Roundhouse and, after the last performance it was like a wake. I thought I would like to write to David Rabe to thank him for a wonderful experience but never got around to it. I should have done it. It would have been a nice gesture.

And then who should turn up like the proverbial bad penny, all boyish, bouncy, and ebullient, as if nothing untoward had occurred, but one Charles Pinner, tanned by the southern sun? And what had he in mind? Why, another writing assignment of course. This was the year the Winter Olympics were held in Canada and he had this bright idea of a two-part musical TV spectacular to go with it. Fine. And who had he in mind to write the music? Why, Elton John of course. Could you get better than that? The mind boggles or, at least, boggled at the time until he informed me he was now employed in some capacity or other by no less a person than Elton John and, as if to prove it, we drove in one of Elton's swish cars to the house in Windsor where, entering through the large kitchen, we passed through a room lined with Elton records and awards and I was given a guided tour of the entire house. I was also presented with a couple of hundred quid as a sweetener and I thought, Oh, well, and *Alice in Winterland* was born. Of course, as it was Charlie Pinner, it naturally turned out to be a case of still birth. I doubt very much whether Elton even knew anything about it and Charles' association with him didn't continue for very long. The last news I got of that young man, as he was then, was that this time he'd fled to America.

"SHUBERTIANA"

LILAC TIME AND LINDENBAUM,
THE ALPINE HUNTER'S SLAYING.
SYLVIA'S SWAINS DON'T COMMEND ANYMORE,
AND THE TRAPP FAMILY SINGERS ARE BRAYING.
YODEL-AY-AY-EE,
YODEL-AY-AY-OO,
DOESN'T IT FILL YOU WITH WONDER?
GRETCHEN'S AT THE STEERING WHEEL
AND THE ERL KING'S RIDING A HONDA.
ON THE RIVER QUAILS CRY,
ALINDE ISN'T COMING.
DON'T DESPAIR FOR THE HILLS ARE ALIVE
WITH THE TRAPP FAMILY SINGERS STILL HUMMING.
YODEL-AY-AY-EE,
YODEL-AY-AY-OO,
DOESN'T IT FILL YOU WITH WONDER?
GRETCHEN'S AT THE STEERING WHEEL,
AND THE ERL KING'S RIDING A HONDA.
NORMAN MOUTH YOUR DREARY DIRGE,
NO WEDDING BELLS ARE RINGING,
SHEPHERDS LAMENT BUT YOU'LL KEEP THE URGE,
WHILE THE TRAPP FAMILY SINGERS KEEP SINGING.
OH LEDERHOSEN YODEL-EE,
OH LEDERHOSEN YODEL-OO,
KEEP AN ALPEN ON YOUR STOCK,
KEEP A CUCKOO IN YOUR CLOCK,
KEEP A BUCKET IN YOUR WELL,
AND A FLOWER IN YOUR LAPEL,
KEEP A FEATHER IN YOUR CAP

AND BEFORE YOU KNOW IT–ZAP!
YOU'LL BE SINGING LIKE ONE OF THE FAMILY TRAPP.
EDWELWEISS?
NICE.

One of the lyrics Elton never set to music.

Chapter Sixteen

From the Elstree Studios of Associated British Productions Limited I received the following letter dated the 7th July 1970.

Dear Glyn Jones,

Re: The 88

I am sorry I have kept you waiting well over a month for any sort of personal reaction to your kind submission. During the interim of course I had received very enthusiastic and complimentary reports from my Scenario Department and I finally succeeded in finding a quiet hour or two last night to read the script personally.

I think it is an extremely fine piece of writing and construction and held my interest from beginning to end. I will be totally honest, and without qualifying my admiration for your craft and obvious ability, I do firmly believe that it will make a very fine stage play and not a very good film–and the very things that commend it as a play, would, in my opinion, work against it if expanded into screenplay form. I sincerely hope that you do find a stage management for it because if produced with imagination and cast with imagination I would think that it could have a big success.

I have no idea whether or not you have concluded any arrangements for a stage presentation, but if you haven't and would care to send this letter to Lindsay Anderson at the Royal Court, I would be more than

happy to lend any support you might need. You obviously write with extraordinary authority and economy and I congratulate you very much indeed.
Kindest good wishes,
Yours sincerely,
Bryan Forbes.

So where do we start analysing the failure of *The 88*. Toby Robertson, head of the Prospect Theatre Company obviously felt the same way as Bryan Forbes or he would not have accepted the play. Admittedly it had already been turned down by the Abbey in Dublin and by Tyrone Guthrie among others but that is par for the course. It was an expensive play to produce but, sponsored by Trident Television, the company at The Old Vic did it proud in production value. Opening at the same time as *Amadeus*, what made the one a runaway success and the other, an abject failure in the eyes of the critics? I say in the eyes of the critic because the reaction from the audiences was totally different, and not just from those still directly connected with the events of 1920.

A lady by the name of Anne Morley-Priestman was as vicious over *The 88* as Malicious McCarthy was over *Early One Morning*. To quote a small section, "the lacunae in the way the narrative is carried itself forward appeared like moon crevices," and "Tension in this play is apparent only in stage effects, usually noisy ones."

Dear little lady, the play is about soldiers, soldiers have guns, soldiers use guns. Did you expect them to be equipped with silencers? Milton Shulman, a critic I had always admired, later gave away the reason for his dislike of the play when he admitted to hating loud noises on stage and, at the end of *The 88* he was faced with a volley from a firing squad of twelve. There is little point in quoting too much from obviously biased reviewers but how did B. A. Young of *The Financial Times* come to write, "I must say in conclusion that this hardly seems the most discreet time to put on a play about Irish

Chapter Sixteen

G.I.J with the cast of The 88 - The Old Vic Theatre

disaffection in the British Army, when the British Army is trying to keep the peace, with great difficulty and hardship, in Ireland today." In Ireland, Mr Young? To the best of my knowledge the British Army has not been in Ireland for a very long time. But here we do come to the nub of the matter because "How dare they?" was heard at least twice in that theatre. The first time was from a nasty little creature, a member of The Old Vic Trust Limited, by the name of C.S.K. Benham OBE who I renamed Mr Venom and who was heard to say in a very loud voice, "How dare they put on this play in my theatre?" My theatre? Presumably he considered The Old Vic to be his personal fiefdom. If he were a character in a Restoration play he would be called Sir Puffedup Pomposity. The second was at a press reception when one of the critics, also in a loud voice was heard to say, "How dare they put on this play so soon after dear Lord Louis' murder? I am going to tear it to pieces." At which he was firmly put in his place I am glad to say by the theatre's Press Representative, Jane McCulloch. This didn't stop him in his review from damning the play with the faintest of faint praise.

My one gripe with the actual production was that, yet again a know-all actor, in this case, Ronnie Stevens, was hell-bent on doing rewrites that unfortunately the director Chris Selbie let him get away with. He came in for some good reviews for his performance but he lost all respect from me when an elderly actor dried on stage and Stevens, who could have come to his aid, as most actors would do if possible, stood there instead with a smirk on his face leaving the obviously embarrassed man to stumble on as best he could. It was a bad moment.

After the opening night the papers were full of the fact that the sponsors, Trident Television wanted the company name taken off all publicity and the theatre bigwigs were really getting their knickers in a painful twist. Why? Did none of them know before the play went on what it was about? Did none of them bother to read the script? Did none of them bother to read or look at the publicity material that was put out? Did none of them see the two page spread in *The Observer* about both the mutiny and the play? Where were they all, in cloud-cuckoo land, that they didn't think to stop the play before it even went on? They had every opportunity to do so.

There were a couple of critics who had decent things to say, chief of whom no doubt was Felix Barker in the long since defunct *Evening News*.

"There are occasions, rare and important, when the theatre clasps hands with actuality. This happened last night in this play about the last peace time execution of a man serving in the British Army. Many interesting questions tumble over each other demanding answers but first the facts."

He then goes on to say what the facts were before continuing, "Out of this little known drama Glyn Jones has fashioned a fascinating play with topical overtones. We see the mutiny grow out of intense stubborn Irish nationalism. One fascinating question is how, in a place so far away in the early days of the "troubles", young men should have felt so passionately committed. The story is told within the framework of the court marshal where the tight-lipped prosecuting officer (Ronnie Stevens) presents the case against Daly (Mark Buffery giving

Chapter Sixteen

a fine performance as a smiling, resolute, but not unduly fanatic soldier).

In Christopher Selbie's admirably unpartisan production we see the squib of revolt ignite briefly and fizzle out tragically. Was it all just a futile waste of a young life? Not when you realise that a rebel may die in semi-obscurity yet find himself presented as a martyred hero in a play 59 years later.

The author has done a fine job but was denied access to court martial records. This means that his scrupulously fair play must lack some clarity, depth and the quality of absolute authenticity. It remains utterly absorbing and particularly painful in today's political climate. But why official secrecy? Do we fear the repercussions of the whole truth about James Daly's trial and death?"

10 Downing Street,
Whitehall,
October 2nd, 1967.

Dear Mr Nightingale,

The Prime Minister has asked me to reply to your letter of September 14 in which you ask if some way could be found of permitting you to have access to the proceedings of the Court Marshal of James Daly.

Courts Marshal proceedings are public records and access to them is governed by the Public Records Act 1958. In accordance with Sections 5(1) of that Act, the Lord Chancellor has prescribed a closed period of 100 years for them and this is strictly applied to all such proceedings.

I am sorry you were given a misleading answer when you telephoned the Army Records Centre. There is a rule, which in some circumstances enables relatives to obtain a copy of court marshal proceedings within a limited period after the trial. The person dealing with your enquiry was obviously thinking of this rule as you have since been informed, it does not apply in the present case. I regret therefore that the proceedings relating to James Daly must remain closed.

Yours sincerely,
S.H.Andrews.

No Official Umbrella

Farnham College,
Surrey.
10th November 1979.

Dear Mr Robertson,

I am a teacher at the above college and last night I brought a group of students to the Old Vic Theatre to see a performance of Glyn Jones' play, 'The 88.'

I wanted very much to write and tell you what an immense impression the play and the production made on both the students and myself. They are aged between 16 and 18 and they were, in their own words, moved and disturbed by an experience the like of which they have never had in a theatre before. They found the play mentally and emotionally stimulating, could talk of little else on the journey home, and felt that the experience had opened their eyes to the aspects of our history about which they are kept in complete darkness.

I believe that the production also made them aware of how simple and effective theatre can be in bringing to the public (particularly the young public) issues, concerns and characters contact with which is either through the media (at best) or text books (at worst).

Finally, I would like, personally to say how good it is to see new work of this calibre at the Old Vic, and to thank Mr Selbie, his production team, and his excellent acting company for making our visit so memorable.

Yours sincerely,
Stephen Rawsthorne.
Head of Drama.

Chigwell, Essex.

Dear Glyn,

I am the old Connaught Ranger who had the honour of meeting you last evening. You have produced an excellent play and I would like to congratulate you for the very hard work that you have put into it. It must have entailed much research after all the years that have gone by. I have a very good memory myself and your play as far as I am concerned could not be faulty (sic), because it was so authentic and

Chapter Sixteen

true. The cast was well drilled and disciplined. Outstanding of course was Mark Buffery as Pte James Daly. (God bless him.)

Paul Toothill was excellent as Major Payne (who was exactly that type of officer.) The whole cast was very good indeed and I was thrilled to meet them after the show. I had a lump in my throat all the time. I trust that "The 88" will be well supported and I wish you the best of good luck for the future. In conclusion I would express my sincere thanks for a very enjoyable evening.

Yours sincerely,
George Byrne.

Chigwell, Essex.

Dear Glyn,

I am so sorry to hear that the English critics were so unkind to your play "The 88". To me it was a gem and I am sure that those who saw it were of the same opinion. I have recalled one scene that may be worth putting in and would not take too long. One morning in Jullundur during the mutiny about a hundred of us were lined up with our backs to a wall when in marched Major Payne with an armed party of South Wales Borderers who formed a line facing us. Major Payne addressed them as follows: "When I give the order to fire, any man who lingers I will shoot like a dog." An old R.C. priest came between the lines and cried, "Stop! You are shooting innocent men. These men have not had a trial." Whereupon Major Payne marched his men away, but not before a mutineer (who held the Military Medal) punched him (Payne) in the face. This man was Pte Gallagher of B Company. Personally I always thought that Payne was mad. I loved the old regiment and I shall never forget such fine officers and men I soldiered with.

Yours sincerely,
George Byrne. (44 Byrne of the 88th)

This incident is actually in the play, remembered slightly differently by another mutineer.

> *Norwood Green,*
> *Middlesex.*
> *8th November 1979.*
>
> Dear Mr Jones,
> My husband and I saw your spellbinding play "The 88" at the Old Vic last evening. We both lived in India for many many years and considered ourselves 'experts' on all that had happened in the Sub Continent past and present though we were amazed to see your play. We found the story utterly fascinating–And I am wondering if you can tell me whether or not a book has been written on this subject. I would be most grateful, etc.
> Yours sincerely,
> (Mrs) P. D'Arnaud Taylor.

If Kenneth Tynan could save *Look Back in Anger*, Bernard Levin I thought might be able to save *The 88*. He could have hated it as well but I was prepared to take the chance so I wrote to him at *The Times* newspaper using Chris as a cover and received the reply:

> Dear Mr Beeching,
> Thank you for your letter. I shall try to get to the play if I can.
> Yours sincerely,
> Bernard Levin.

He didn't make it.

> *Old Trafford,*
> *Manchester 16.*
>
> To Glyn Jones
> I want to write and thank you for the great joy you gave me my family & sister for the play you put on regards my brother Jim Daly it was great to see it all replayed god what them poor lads suffered and all political prisoners are still suffering give me regards to mark and all the people that took part in it also the lady who read the letter thank ye all so much it will be some thing to tell the people of Tyrrellspass when I go home. So I hope it pays for itself and ye had full houses every

Chapter Sixteen

night it was lovely to see Jims photo outside the Vic it was worth going to see even that,

Now regards money been made on it me, or my family do not want any of it as we call it blood money and if any one else try to claim we object so refer them to me

Thanking you so much,
Yours Sincerely
Teresa Maher.

From *The Irish Press*, Monday 12th November 1979.

BACKERS BAULK AT MUTINY DRAMA.

A play at London's "Old Vic" dealing with a mutiny by an Irishman in the British Army has sparked a behind-the-scenes rebellion–by its financial backers. In an astonishing snub, sponsors Trident Television, who shelled out an estimated £20,000 to launch the production have labelled it politically controversial. After attending the first night performance, angry executives demanded that the company's name be taken off all advertising for the play.

Now its author, Glyn Jones, has accused the TV chief of "small mindedness."

"I just don't feel that men like these should be on the board of a media company responsible for the entertainment of hundreds and thousands of people," he said.

The row erupted after Trident's chairman, Mr Brian Ward-Thomas, and three fellow directors and their wives watched the opening performance last Thursday night.

Mr Jones' play tells of a true-life incident in 1920 when a number of Irishmen serving in the British Army mutinied in the Punjab.

The soldiers–men of the Connaught Rangers–refused to help Britain rule India when Irish patriots were fighting the British back home.

"The atmosphere was like an iceberg on the opening night. The party from Trident Television would have been invited as a matter of courtesy. I think it was their wives who were more indignant than their husbands. They made their protest to the theatre administrator the following morning, asking that the name of the company be withdrawn from the programme. The telephone wires from the Trident boardroom where white hot," said Mr Jones.

He thought the reason for the protest was part of an anti-Irish feeling. "The fact seems to be you've only got to mention the word Irish and some people get cold feet and all last week the newspapers had mentioned the IRA and the Panorama episode," he said.

"Perhaps the reason for withdrawing had something to do with the Mountbatten murder, but I didn't murder Mountbatten. The play was written 12 years ago, well before the start of the Northern Ireland troubles," he protested.

He pointed out that the script had been sent to Trident months before the production and if the executive did not receive it they had only to ask for another copy. "Leaflets were sent out something like four months ago, stating unequivocally what the play was all about. But we didn't receive any criticism."

The author thought another reason for the complaint may have been coupled with official embarrassment over historical incidents. He dismissed the accusation that the play was politically controversial and pointed out that members of the British Troops Out Movement demonstrating at the theatre complained it was not controversial enough.

In the audience was Mrs Theresa Maher, the 76-year-old sister of James Daly, executed for his part in the mutiny. Mrs Maher from Tyrrellspass, Co. Westmeath was accompanied by about 20 other relatives.

"I thought the play was very accurate. Of course, I found it emotional and a lot of us were in tears," she said afterwards.

Mr Jones said the money provided by Trident had already been spent but he was unsure of the future of the play.

Ethelbert St.
Balham.

Dear Mr Jones,

I hope your play "The 88" will be a huge success and trust America gets to see it in due course. Dublin should give it the rousing acclaim,

Chapter Sixteen

as *The Bishops Bonfire* so obtained at *The Gaiety Theatre* in Dublin on its opening night.

Dalys Company of the Connaughts were in the trenches in 1918 and in 1919 were in the occupation army in Europe. But the Colonel Blimps instead of sending them back to Ireland or England selected the worst shit-hole in India to send them to. So "The Devils Own" The 88th struck, not alone against tyrannical Tans in Ireland, but against their own condition in India. The Flower of Connaught, the finest Regiment in the British Army. Why Sir, the Pay of Tommy Atkins those days were one shilling per day. The Pay of the Murderous Tan in Ireland was £5 per day! L.G.[22] was the Tan Qr/master.

The little man from Tyrrellspass Co-Westmeath, will be long remembered, while Irishmen live. His near neighbours the Col. Boyd-Rochforts, are almost forgotten with contempt.

The Leinster Regiment, Munster Fusiliers, Royal Irish Regiment, Connaught Rangers, and the Royal Dublin Fusiliers are disbanded and gone. Many of their graves lie in France, Gallipoli (sic) Africa and India.

But Jim Daly of "The Devils Own" the 88th will always be remembered. I hope to see your play.

Yours faithfully,
Patrick McDonnell.

Janet Maw read the letter Teresa Maher refers to. This was the only female voice heard all evening. The letter is copied verbatim from the actual document.

"October, Saturday. 1920. My address is in Heaven along with John– and God. My dearest mother, I take this opportunity of writing to you to let you know the dreadful news that I am to be shot on Tuesday morning the 1st of November but what harm it is all for Ireland. I am not afraid to die but it is thinking of you I am that is all if you will be happy on earth I will be happy in Heaven I am ready to meet my doom the Priest is along with me when needed so you need not worry

---
22 Lloyd George.

over me as I am going to my dearest home in Heaven but I wish to the Lord that I had not started getting into this trouble at all I would be better off but it is done now and I have to suffer out of 62 of us I am the only one to be put out of this world but I am ready to meet if God bless ye all hoping to see ye all in Heaven one day. I hope mother that you won't be put about but keep a good hart I know it is hard for you but what can be done now I am writing to Kitty and Doly to let them know the Priest will send these letters to yous all right I have not much to tell yous it is no good this is my last letter you will get from me and may God bless you Mother dear and the Bird (his sister Bridie) and Frank. Tell Father I forgive him…"

[The letter here has been destroyed by time]

"… I hope Paddy is well. Kisses to all."

[There are nine crosses]

"I hope mother you will get a mass ready for me pray for a happy rest of your fond son Jim taking from you for the sake of his country Ireland. God bless Ireland and also you all at home. From your fond son Jim to dearest mother."

As they were leaving the theatre, the wife of one of the Trident directors was heard to say in an exceedingly loud voice, 'They should have shot all eighty-eight of them!'

Ben Hawthorne, who happened to be in London at the time, slunk passed me muttering something unintelligible but obviously not complimentary as he went to join the mockers. So much for friendship.

It was obvious, by resurrecting this episode in British history, I had trodden on a lot of painful corns, not least of all my own. Up to that point in my life I considered *The 88* to be the best thing I had written but such was the venom flying about that night, even from some of the company, it shattered me and it was more than two years before I could bear to even think of writing anything again. Even today I can choke up when I think of it. But there is nothing new under the sun. When D'Urfey's *The Banditti* or *A Ladies Distress*, given at Drury

Lane in 1686, was damned, the author dedicated the printed quarto to "The Extreme Witty and Judicious Gentleman, Sir Critick Cat-call whose prejudice took vent even before the play began."

Eleanor Road,
London E.8.

Dear Glyn,

Thought you would like to know that a friend of a friend saw 'The 88' and thought highly of it, even though expecting less because of the critics. There is no doubt you have been the victim of a hatchet job based on outside considerations rather than an honest assessment of the play. The cast have also been unfairly treated in my opinion. Perhaps the next production in a few years time will produce a true valuation of its worth.

Yours sincerely,
Alex.

There's no denying how deep the deep hurt was at the time and even if I do sometimes still think about it, what the hell? Time and life move on and at least I only suffered the abuse of the London critics, unlike poor Euripides who was torn to shreds by unleashed hunting hounds. Now that really is criticism.

Chapter Seventeen

With the failure of *The 88* and nothing coming of *Speed* or the *Alice* project, although we were both working in the theatre, Chris doing a not very well paid tour of *Beauty and the Beast* and I rehearsing in Derby for the first of three plays I was contracted to do, money was a big problem. In fact it was an overdraft problem of £20,000 the bank had allowed me on the basis of Charles' spurious contract for £40,000. I was now paying interest on the interest and it was time to pull in our horns and down size as the saying now goes, so 162 Richmond Road was put on the market. It had been a wonderful home and it was only dire necessity that forced me into giving it up. Strangely though I was not nearly as upset as Chris who was quite devastated by the turn of events.

In the meantime it was to the Derby Playhouse I went for three good roles: the Inspector in Priestley's *An Inspector Calls*, Van Helsing in *Dracula*, and Truscott in Joe Orton's *Loot*. Once the play had been blocked, the director, who shall remain nameless, retired to the auditorium where he sat throughout rehearsals with his eyes glued to the book and whose idea of notes to the cast consisted of, 'That was much better everyone. You knocked two and a half minutes off that act,' and 'Glyn, on page eighteen, third line down, you'll see the first word is "but" not "and".'

Fortunately most of the cast were all experienced actors and, despite the hunched silent spectre seated out front, just got on with it.

Chapter Seventeen

As Inspector Trusscot in Loot - Derby Playhouse

An Inspector Calls was well received on opening night but, on the second night, I was nearly thrown when one of the front of house lamps suddenly started to pulse quite noticeably. I mentioned it to the stage manager after the performance and then forgot about it until the following night when it happened again. Some members of the audience as well as the cast were a little disconcerted this time so again I told the stage manager and asked him to look into it. He in turn asked me if I'd noticed which one was the offending lamp. So, when it happened yet again, I glanced out front, made a mental note and passed on the information with a rider that, if something weren't done about it pretty damn quick, *An Inspector Calls* would be going on without the Inspector. He promised to look into it but at the very next performance it happened again, even more noticeably than before. I'd had enough. My proverbial Taurian patience was wearing decidedly thin so I collared him backstage, though he tried to avoid me, and demanded to know why nothing had been done.

'Well,' he stalled, looking a bit sheepish. 'You see, it's like this, we've had a new dimmer system installed and, after a while, it tends to overheat and when it does that, there might be some pulsing and there's nothing we can do about it really.'

'You mean you've known the reason all along and kept quiet about it?'

He shrugged.

'And you mean to tell me the theatre's paid thousands of pounds for a new dimmer and the fucking thing doesn't work?'

He shrugged again.

'Show it to me.'

'There's honestly no point, Glyn. I told you, there's nothing we can do about it.'

'Show it to me!' I guess I sounded pretty aggressive by now if I hadn't sounded it before so he turned and led me along a passage, through a door and up a narrow staircase. The room with its banks of dimmers was, still is I guess, small, and he was dead right–hot. I looked around while he stood there obviously feeling justified and smiling with self-satisfaction. Here was just another prat of a conceited actor. What did he know about the technical aspects of theatre?

'Have you thought of opening the window?' I said.

The smile disappeared and we had no more trouble with pulsing lights.

We had a lighting problem with *Dracula* as well but one that was quickly solved. During the tech[23] I wandered into the auditorium to have a look at the set. The director was sitting there. I moved over to him. 'Is that the lighting?' I asked.

He nodded.

---
23 Technical rehearsal.

'It's pitch black.'
'It's atmospheric.'
'So is my arse. What are we doing here, a radio play?'

The levels were raised. It might not have been quite so atmospheric but at least the actors could be seen as well as heard.

But the main problem with *Dracula* came in the shape of a lovely young actress fresh from drama school named Sandy Miller. Actually Sandy wasn't the problem. It was the direction or, rather, the lack of it. With the experienced old-stagers in the cast it didn't really matter all that much as they had already proved. We had all experienced directors who relied on the talents of their casts to get them through but for Sandy, here rehearsing the part of Mina, her first major role as a professional actress, and getting no help whatsoever, she was beginning to seriously worry and her anxiety was becoming painfully obvious.

Actors on the whole, professional or amateur, no matter how talented they might be, are insecure vulnerable creatures who appreciate a little cosseting, let alone those who say, 'I really can't get the hang of this character at all. I just don't understand him. I'm going to need a lot of help.' Yes, it's not only amateurs who give you this line. Do I not speak from personal experience as both actor and director? And, even though aware of this, it was brought fully home to me when I directed *The Rivals* at RADA.

Daniel Flynn, who was playing Bob Acres was a natural for the part and was galloping away with it from the start. Great, I thought, no worries with this one. Gives me more time to work with those in trouble. One day, returning from lunch, I found Daniel sitting alone in the rehearsal room in floods of tears.

'Hey, Daniel. What's the matter?'

'You… sob sob… sputter sputter… sniff… you… sob… don't like meeeeeeee!' The "me" coming out in a heartfelt wail.

'What on earth are you talking about?'

'I… I… I'm… s… s… so bad… sob… you don't even t-t-t-talk to me. I'm so… howl… terrible… you have… have… haven't… given me a… single' … another howl… 'note.'

Which was quite true, I hadn't. Like Sandy before him, apart from having been given his moves, he had received nothing. I really did feel bad.

'Daniel, the reason you haven't had any notes is because you haven't needed them.'

Howl!

'And the reason you haven't needed them is, quite simply, because you are absolutely splendid in the part.'

'No I'm not! I'm bloody terrible!' His normally ruddy complexion was now crimson lake and his red hair went a bobbing as he burst into another bout of sobbing. The others would soon be returning from lunch. I didn't want them to see him like this and I eventually managed to convince him I meant what I said. He calmed down then and I never ignored him again. Even if what I said was only a token encouragement at least it kept him in the picture and he was, as I knew he would be, a wonderful Bob Acres.

As the opening night of *Dracula* drew closer and closer so Sandy's apprehension grew until one day she approached me and asked if I would watch her performance and give her notes. I don't know why she chose me and never thought to ask but my response was that I didn't feel it to be a very good idea. No matter what you may think of them, it isn't ethical to meddle in someone else's production, though there are any number of actors who are only too fond of giving fellow actors notes. Nigel Patrick was a good example. During the run of *Reunion in Vienna* he was at it constantly, 'Why don't you try it this way?' 'Why don't you try it that way?' But Sandy went on pleading until finally I agreed provided she and I were the only two to know about it. So I surreptitiously took over the direction of Sandy.

I also went on to partly direct the following play, *Loot*, openly this time and at the director's own request when he was suddenly called away to his father's funeral. He had done what he wanted with the first act so it was a matter of directing the second from scratch. It would happen during *Loot* wouldn't it? I'm sure Orton would have

Chapter Seventeen

had a field day if he'd still been around. It wasn't the best thing for the play though as it was obvious how different the two acts were but I couldn't bring myself to redirect the first act which was his, of my performance as Truscott, the local reviewer said, "Glyn Jones adds to his Derby successes with an outlandish caricature of the detective who claims to be a water board inspector–because they have right of access without a warrant–and he tops the role with a clipped delivery and a springy walk."

The upshot of all this was, standing in the wings with Sandy one evening, she suddenly turned to me and said, 'Have you ever thought of directing at RADA? No? Well you should. You'd be absolutely marvellous with students. Why don't you write to Hugh Cruttwell? He's a very nice man and terribly approachable.'

'Maybe I will,' I said.

The play scheduled, or as the Americans say, "slated" to follow *Loot* was *Blithe Spirit* and I came up with an outrageous idea that I took along to the director's office to put to him. 'Look,' I said, 'I've come up with what is either going to be the most brilliant piece of casting or a complete fiasco.' Perhaps outré or bizarre may have better described the idea than brilliant. 'Are you prepared to take a chance?' I said. By the look on his face he wasn't, but I was ready to plough ahead anyway and, when he asked what it was, the tone of voice reinforced my belief that my chances of success weren't exactly in the high probability range. 'Well,' I said, 'I've played three inspectors in a row, van Helsing being an inspector of sorts, how about letting me play a fourth, of sorts?'

It was obvious he hadn't a clue as to what I was talking about so I went on with all the enthusiasm I could muster.

'Madame Acarti,' I said. 'I want to play Madame Acarti.'

He went quite white and almost fell off his swivel chair. So I didn't get to play Madame Acarti and with that door slammed firmly in my face I wrote to Hugh Cruttwell using Sandy as a reference. The letter in return was short, polite, and to the point. He had contracted all his directors for the forthcoming term but would bear me in mind for the future. Oh, how often had one seen those words, or variants thereof, because seldom if ever did the promised future arrive.

"Thank you for sending us your play which we enjoyed reading and which gave us such a good laugh." (What at? The humour in the script or my temerity in submitting it?) "The play has warmth, pathos, and humour," (Ah, that's okay then) "and the story is beautifully told." (Good) "But, alas, it is not what we are looking for right now." (Shit!) "Have you tried the television companies?" (Not that hoary old fucker again. If it's a TV company they'll want to know if you've tried the theatre) "Wishing you every success with your work and we do hope you manage to place your play somewhere." (Where had they in mind do you suppose? Don't answer that).

So, convinced I would never hear from him again, I put Cruttwell's letter away and, thinking no more about it, mounted my trusty bicycle and headed for my vandalised, litter-strewn, filthy, disgusting slum of a local Labour Exchange that I now envisaged visiting once a week for possibly months to come, wending my way through the slough of discarded social security bumph, standing in a long line with the dead beats, the druggies, the winos, the absolute no-hopers, the mentally unstable, the forever unemployable; keeping a wary eye on my cycle even though it was chained to a railing, and running the gauntlet of the grotty members of the loony left flogging their rabid views and their newspapers. This was the nuclear free zone of Hackney adjacent to the nuclear free zone of Islington, both hotbeds of Marxist-Leninism where the councils were so far to the left they'd done a complete circle and come around to the right again, vying with each other in their march to Moscow. Any opposition to their ideas of political correctness was met with scorn and derision if not outright hostility. If you weren't black, incapacitated, a single mother or Lesbian you didn't stand much of a chance if requesting something like a grant. We tried to get the council interested in the one-man show I wrote for Chris, *Champagne Charlie* to take it around old people's homes and the like, and made the fatal mistake of saying it was in no way amateur but really an excellent entertainment at which we were informed by a snarling harpy in a council office, 'We don't believe in excellence. Excellence is elitist.'

At least it's not all bad; at least they promote gay rights.

Anyway, having worsted the council over their Mapledene plans and with them now seeing how the area, as they had feared, was becoming more and more gentrified, I don't think they wanted anything to do with anybody obviously white, middle class and not from an ethnic minority. But the middle class was definitely moving in. Jeremy had bought a house not three minutes walk away close to London Fields and when we told our friend Ray Peters, the ex-school teacher, of one going a few doors down from us he went ahead and bought it. Once we moved out of London, Ray's house became, as Lionel Wilson would have said, our home from home. So it is for a number of people who accept his hospitality and he is, without doubt, the most hospitable person in the world. How he manages it on his income I really don't know but he buys handfuls of concert, opera, and ballet tickets for parties of friends, some of whom unfortunately don't bother to reimburse him, and a dinner party at Ray's is not complete unless there are lots of presents to go with the meal. Every now and again we get a lengthy letter complete with newspaper cuttings of articles he thinks would interest us and we always maintain he should be a writer; the letters are witty, beautifully written and of much interest. In his straightened circumstances Hackney Council informed him by post that they had underestimated his rates bill for a number of years and he had to stump up a four figure sum immediately or else!

We thought we had a ghost at 162 Richmond Road; a friendly ghost, female, and we called her Hortense. It was all imagination of course but she would flicker lights next to the room you were in. Never in the same room, always next to it, and why would lights flicker in a house newly rewired? I saw her twice. Once while sitting in the drawing room in a position where I could see the hall and stairs I said to Chris, 'Hortense has just walked by.'

'Where'd she go?'

'Towards the front door. Or she's gone to the loo.'

'What'd she look like?'

'A grey shape, very Victorian, full length skirt, high bodice'

The second time I saw her I was working in the garden and happened to glance up at the house and saw the same grey shape standing behind the stairs window on the landing between the first and second floors. The moment didn't last. All imagination of course. What wasn't imagination was Natalie's reaction one night in my study, which was a small room right at the top of the house. I was typing away and the dog was lying in front of the fireplace fast asleep. This was a fireplace that was never used. Suddenly she sat bolt upright, looking at a spot in front of the fireplace and, getting to her feet, she backed away towards the open door, snarling as her hackles rose. Then she started to bark. There was nothing there, nothing a human being could detect but something in that room had scared that dog rigid and I was goose bumps from head to toe and I could feel my own hackles rise, that is the hair on the back of my neck. She stood at the door and no coaxing on my part would induce her to re-enter the room. I don't think I did anymore writing that night.

These are all memories of our time in that house. Chris's brother Roger and his wife, Jean, came to dinner one evening. I had been at a studio all day and, when I got home, I found Chris had lit a fire in the kitchen. A fire? A conflagration! The flames were roaring up the chimney to such an extent you could have roasted an entire ox. The next morning I was working in the garden and again I glanced up at the house only this time I didn't see Hortense. What I saw was a wisp of black smoke rising out of a chimney. As the fire had died out the previous night this looked ominous and I returned to the kitchen to investigate. Standing in front of the now cold fireplace I saw large red globs occasionally falling from above and was on to the fire brigade in seconds. Three large engines arrived generating enough excitement to bring the whole street out and half a dozen men marched into the kitchen. They had a quick look at the fireplace and then went up to the drawing room and felt the chimney breast, then up to the first floor bedroom for the same procedure. I preceded them to the top floor where Ulf was sleeping and woke him up with, 'Ulf, half a dozen men in boots and helmets are going to come in but don't worry, they're just trying to trace the source of a fire so stay where you are.' By the time I'd finished my speech in they trooped all wishing Ulf a good morning as they passed his bed.

'Good morning.'
'Good morning.'
'Good morning.'
'Good morning.'
'Good morning.'
'Good morning.'

Sure enough, the chimney breast here was red hot so out they trooped and down the stairs back into the kitchen where they moved all the furniture away from the fireplace, laid plastic sheeting on the floor and then gave a whistle to those outside. The ladder on one of the engines went up with a man holding the nozzle of a hose and water gushed down the inside of the chimney and, of course, all over the plastic on the kitchen floor. But they cleaned up beautifully after them and you wouldn't have known they'd even been. I couldn't thank them enough.

'It's what you pay your rates for,' one said, 'there's no need for thanks.'

Ulf built a sort of retaining wall in the back garden. It was only two or three courses high but became known as "The Great Wall of Ulf." He would work on it in the early morning wearing nothing but a very short flimsy pale blue silk dressing gown borrowed from Chris that more often or not didn't cover a thing, much to the excitement of Beryl next door whose eyes were out on storks every time the gown flipped open and Scandinavia came into view. Beryl was the wife of our Cypriot neighbour, Tony Fizentsou, car mechanic and father of at least a dozen kids, so Beryl was obviously no stranger to the male anatomy though Ulf's was obviously a continuous source of fascination and, probably, wishful thinking. Tony owned an enormous Mercedes Benz and a white caravan and once a year drove and ferried the family back to Cyprus for a holiday. He also saved us a lot of money working on the Rover that, when I really couldn't afford to run it any longer, I eventually sold to one of the stage staff at the Mermaid.

I could never understand why Tony always called me Mister Glyn and not just Glyn or Mister Jones. I tried to get him to change but it was always Mister Glyn and, it wasn't until I came to Greece and discovered this is the normal form of address that I realised why he did it. He was a lovely generous man who had a bit of legal trouble once and I introduced him to Andy Moore who settled it for him. Years after leaving Richmond Road we were truly saddened to hear from Andy that Tony Fizentsou had died of a heart attack. He was only in his early fifties.

At an earlier date, Beryl had walked out on him and the kids and was never heard from again. Maybe the vision of Scandinavia had given her ideas.

It was at Richmond Road that the hiatus hernia, which was obviously a malformation of the stomach from birth, really began to play up. Most of my life I remember suffering from occasional heartburn. After church on a Sunday evening my mother used to make a batch of what in South Africa we called pancakes but which are probably best known as griddle scones or flapjacks, and invariably they were followed by milk and bicarbonate of soda. For years I had been taking antacids of one kind or another but now, for the first time, the oesophagus decided it had had quite enough acid from my stomach and closed up as tight as a duck's arse, and that, as they say, is water tight: so tight it was even impossible to swallow saliva and, after a short period, if I had been trying to swallow it rather than spit it out, I would regurgitate half a cupful of it as clear as spring water, though viscous of course. While you are able to swallow you simply do not realise how much saliva you are constantly producing. Any attempt to swallow anything else resulted in a sharp pain and a reflux reaction that brought back up whatever it was, even a small sip of water. Sometimes the closure lasted only a short while and, with a click, the gullet would open up again. Sometimes it lasted a day or two, finally opening up again during sleep. It wasn't too much trouble if it happened at home and there was nothing on the calendar. Food might not have been that important for a while but you eventually found yourself longing desperately for a hot drink.

There had to be a number of occasions elsewhere though when "being stuck", as Chris called it, was both awkward and highly embarrassing because I would suddenly look like a startled squirrel with a mouthful of nuts. One such occasion was dinner at Joe Allen's after a performance of *Cats*. Chris immediately asked, 'Are you stuck?' Knowing full well I was; well and truly. I couldn't even talk. All I could do was nod and, leaving the table, head hurriedly for the toilet where, even though I brought up the obstruction, the oesophagus remained closed. It was quite a while before I rejoined the group and obviously I couldn't do anything more with the food. The evening was spoilt as the others at the table had never come across this before and even if sympathetic were made ill at ease by it. On another occasion it happened during a performance of a play I directed at RADA, I don't remember which one it was but I spent most of the evening in the loo drooling saliva into a toilet bowl. I managed to go around backstage afterwards to say nice things to the cast and left them unaware there was a problem but the bus trip home was a nightmare and by the time I got off at Dalston Junction my handkerchief was wringing wet.

Jeremy opened a law office just off the Mile End Road and threw a celebratory opening night party. Ulf having left, we had a new house puppy at this time by the name of Roland and he and Chris had gone down early to do the catering. I was to follow after feeding the animals. But I grew a bit peckish and there were the remains of a leg of lamb in the kitchen so I cut myself off a piece and hey presto! An immediate protesting gullet was the result and no party for Glyn.

It happened the night prior to my having to take the train the following morning for Edinburgh to start rehearsals for *The Elephant*

Man and we had to call the theatre to say I might be a day or two late. Fortunately my role in this play was not a major one and the delay would not be serious but I hated having to do it nevertheless and decided to take a chance on the trouble clearing up.

Whenever I had previously visited Edinburgh I always stayed with a delightful lady by the name of Pearl Pink. Everyone tried to get digs with Pearl so, as soon as you knew Edinburgh was on the itinerary, you got in first with a booking if you could. Once she was so full she put me in a space practically under the stairs. This time I stayed with another delightful lady, Agnes Ness, and her two young sons, Greig and David. I still hadn't fully recovered from the hernia episode and on my first night, of all things a grown man, I wet the bed. Shamefaced I confessed to Agnes who wasn't phased one little bit.

'Well, you have been sick,' was all she said and that was that. We are still in touch all these years later.

Twice in America it was the cause of extreme distress. The first time was in New York just before I was due to fly to Washington. In the company of Laurence Senelick, professor of drama at Tufts University, I was having lunch in an Italian restaurant in Thompson Street just off Washington Square and enjoying my osso bucco when zap, it happened, and this time it was a really bad situation. I didn't like to say anything to Laurence and, after lunch, as there was time before I had to leave for the airport; we strolled around to my favourite bookstore, "The Strand". Although this is one of the first places I head for in New York (graffiti in the loo–"A Smurf is a giant herpes virus") I certainly didn't feel like book browsing on this particular day although I did pick up *A History of the Liverpool Playhouse*, a book impossible to find in England at the time and it cost me all of two dollars. I also didn't feel like sitting in a plane although there was at least a paper bag to spit into, because by now I was again possessed of a wringing wet handkerchief. From Washington it was an uncomfortable car trip to Harrisonburg and it was well into the afternoon before, with a click, the oesophagus suddenly opened up again.

The second occasion was when staying with the Lyndrups. Alan's parents Luther & Carolyn were visiting and took us all out for a splendid meal in a Chinese restaurant. I startled the whole place when, on breaking open my fortune cookie, I burst into a roar of laughter reading, "You will be attracted to the glamour of the theatre." Now into my fifties my fortune tells me that? I also startled the Lyndrups on the way home when my gullet closed up. They had to stop while I was sick at the side of the road and they all remained firmly seated in the car. It was not a good ending to an otherwise delightful evening and all I could do was apologise.

The strange thing is that in all the years it never once happened to affect a performance but it wasn't until we were living in Yorkshire and it closed up for a longer time than usual, that I finally decided the time had come to do something about it. So I went down to the Health Centre in Hebden Bridge, our nearest town, and saw my crusty old doctor who was sitting in his surgery waiting for retirement, and told him my problem. He sniffed loudly and said, 'You're an actor aren't you?'

I knew exactly what he was thinking: another one of these squeamish, ultra-sensitive, nancy boys. Needs to pull his socks up and get on with things.

'Humph! Sounds like globus hystericus to me. Well, I'll send you off to Halifax for an x-ray. See what they come up with.'

Obviously nothing in his opinion, as it was all in my hysterical mind anyway, but the hospital at Halifax did come up with something. The x-rays revealed an oesophagus which, though no longer actually blocked, had the lower couple of inches or more with a diameter narrower then an HB pencil. The next stop then, after a morning of nil by mouth, was the Bradford Infirmary where I had to undergo deep throat, the operation performed by Mr Mears who was the specialist in gastric disorders. There was no counting to twenty this time either; I was out before I even hit five and woke up back in the ward, not in pain but definitely aching all over; presumably from fighting the anaesthetic. That night I slept sitting up in a chair, next day I was more or less fine except for a sore throat and guttural speech.

At the time we were in the middle of rehearsals for *The Queen and the Rebels* to be performed at Hebden Bridge's Little Theatre and in which I was playing the General. Being a rather sick puppy at the time I have to admit I was hell to work with, but what does one make of a director who, although she knows you have been for an operation involving the throat, makes no solicitous enquiry as to how you are feeling and is insensitive enough on hearing you speak, to say, 'Is that the voice you've adopted for the role?'

I had to return to the hospital for an interview with Mr Mears who wasn't at all like Doctor Kildare or Richard Chamberlain but a little roly-poly gentleman with the broadest of broad Yorkshire accents whose opening remark was, 'Well, Mr Jones, you have a bloody awful gullet.'

'I'm very aware of that,' I said. 'Apart from the constant trouble it's given me I've seen the x-rays and they didn't look too healthy to me.'

'So do you want the operation or don't you?'

This took me aback rather. I thought I'd already had the operation. 'What operation?' I asked.

'It's called Henderson's Procedure. I cut you from here to here,' indicating sternum to belly button, 'and open you up and then I put a sort of, like a rubber band around the bottom of the gullet to stop the acid rising. Well?'

'Er, why don't we just play it by ear and see what happens?'

I then got a call to return to the hospital for an examination which consisted of the usual hanging about in a waiting room for an hour or more before being called in to be done and then having a tiny instrument at the end of a wire shoved up my nose and down my throat which immediately made me want to vomit. I panicked. As a kid you are constantly warned about putting anything in your ears or up your nose and this, as far as I was concerned, was positively barbaric. What is more it was going to be done three times, each time while I drank a glass of water and the third time left in for twenty-four hours while my stomach acid was being monitored on an instrument hooked to my belt. No thank you.

I managed to take the first one and swallow the water but 'Pull it out!' I yelled as the sister tried to insert number two. My eyes were streaming and I just knew I was going to puke any second. 'Pull it out!' She did and that was the end of the session though she made no bones about what a big cry baby I was. At my next consultation with Mr Mears all he had to say was, 'I hear we gave you a very bad time.'

I nodded.

'You wouldn't like to do it again would you? For fifty quid?'

'What?'

'There's a new drug I want to test. It would mean carrying it around for twenty four hours but fifty quid's all we can afford to pay you.'

'Thank you,' I said, 'But if you don't mind, I'd rather not.'

'All right.' And, as I turned to leave his last words were, 'You know you have no peristalsis, none whatsoever.'

I underwent deep throat twice more before my doctor, a new one, Doctor Williams: not the crusty old bugger who had at last vacated his chair; prescribed a new wonder drug which for more than ten years, touch wood, has kept the acid at bay. Had it not been for that particular drug I doubt I would have had the courage to move to Crete. What did amaze me each time I went to Bradford were the number of patients all suffering the same thing lined up for the afternoon's surgery. It was like a conveyer belt. It is obviously quite a common condition and I came across an illustration in a book on inventions showing a man in the nineteenth century with an incision in his stomach and a tube with a funnel at the end inserted, through which to pass nourishment. I showed it to Mr Mears who was fascinated. It was something he had never seen before and I think he would have liked me to have given him the book but I was too mean.

Chapter Eighteen

Much to my surprise and delight I wasn't destined to spend months signing on at the labour exchange because about a week after receiving his letter, Hugh Cruttwell telephoned to say he had lost one of his directors though illness and was I available? The play he wanted me to direct was Ibsen's *Pillars of Society*, did I know it? Know it? Of course I knew it. Was I not familiar with the whole Ibsen canon? No, I did not know it. The only Ibsen play I was familiar with was *A Doll's House* because I had directed it at Buxton. But Ibsen's collected works were on my bookshelf and it was a matter of moments before I was engrossed in *Pillars of Society*.

I arrived at the Royal Academy of Dramatic Art in Gower Street at the appointed time and, after a brief chat with Hugh in his office, went to face my cast. At RADA you had no say in casting. Cruttwell presented you with the cast list and, though you might think some of his choices bizarre to say the least, he knew his students and had his reasons. It was up to you to get performances out of them and I never knew him to interfere once a production was under way.

Bruce Payne was cast as Karsten Bernick and playing the part of Olaf, a young man who I predicted would do very well for himself. Staff members pooh-poohed my prediction and in turn suggested someone who has never been heard of since. The young man I thought so talented was Paul McGann.

In Greece where every television station at some time or other, and

Chapter Eighteen

often more than once, will show the same film, I keep seeing Bruce's name in the paper as starring in a film called *Flight 59*. We have in fact watched the movie in which he plays a real dyed in the wool villain. We've also seen him in two or three other schlock-horrors but at least, in going to America, he seems to have opened the Hollywood door. I think his first movie was *Privates on Parade*.

Paul I saw in another production at the academy, *Tis Pity She's a Whore*, a production full of effects but, with the exception of Paul, not a memorable performance in sight. I can't remember what I was directing at the time but lunching in the canteen one day, a member of the other cast took a seat at my table and said, 'You'll never believe what our director has just said to us.'

He was obviously dying to tell me so I expressed an interest with a look and he went on, 'He said, "I am one of the three best directors in England and I believe it is my duty to come here and give you students the benefit of my talents." Can you believe that?'

I don't now how true this story is because, as I said, it was relayed to me, but I see no reason why it shouldn't be, and it could be the reason why Adrian Noble became big white chief of the Royal Shakespeare Company. Up to that moment I had never heard of Adrian Noble, let alone knowing he was one of the three best directors in England, but sometimes I wish I had had that kind of chutzpah instead of being a shrinking violet when it came to selling myself. I have often wondered whom he had in mind as the other two best directors.

Also in my cast was a young American, Rick Lusby who, I was warned by practically everybody on the staff, was a nightmare to work with and would be giving me a great deal of trouble. 'You've got the dreaded American,' was the phrase used or sometimes 'the mad American.' Rick was a misfit at RADA and as I discovered when I got to know him, hated the place, virtually everyone in it, and was desperately unhappy. He was labelled a rebel, reputed to be unruly and violent, having in fact landed a neat punch on a previous director's jaw and stalked out of his rehearsals. Forewarned is forearmed however (another cliché) and, perhaps because I took a great deal of trouble

No Official Umbrella

over him he gave me no trouble at all. In fact we became good friends and he kept in touch for a while after returning to America. Rick's forte was a magnificent baritone voice. When he was practicing in the building you heard him practically everywhere. When the time came for goodbye's, in front of an astonished class he said 'What the hell!' and gave me a kiss full on the mouth. The last letter I got from him was to say he was singing with an opera company in Israel. He then returned to the states and became very ill. Chris had a phone call from him while I was away in which he said he had Hodgkin's Disease and later we had a letter from him.

"It's been nearly six years since I last saw you. This is simply too long. You have never left my thoughts though. I wish we were sitting together in your kitchen and could spend the afternoon catching up. My last conversation with Chris probably seemed a little loaded–emotionally, that is. Let me see if I can fill you in. Last year was really like a one-night stand with death for me. One Thursday morning, after an audition on 57th Street, a specialist here in New York took a quick glance at a bump on my neck and told me I had cancer. He said it as if he were asking me whether I liked cream in my coffee. Until then I had felt perfectly healthy. Anyway, after the shock wore off, I quietly proceeded to have a nervous breakdown. Waiting for the results of tests and biopsies was literally a question of waiting to see if I would live or die. As it turned out I couldn't have been luckier. I suffered through ten weeks of radiation therapy but it would be extremely unlikely for the cancer to recur.

So much for bad news.

Let's see. Good news. Well, I had a terrific trip to the Orient last December. Performed in Tokyo, Singapore, and Hong Kong. Singapore is overflowing with Hindu temples and Buddhist shrines where I spent the bulk of my free time. Also I drank Singapore Slings. Loathsome stuff. Both Singapore and Hong Kong have a strong British influence. I was very relieved that we could communicate without speaking through translators as we had done in Tokyo. Heard the Brahms B-minor clarinet quintet for the first time and fell in love. Music always loves you back, for which I am grateful.

Had a wonderful job in January. I was the baritone understudy in William Bolcom's setting of William Blake's 'Songs of Innocence And Experience.' It sounds sort of like a cross between Alban Berg and Dolly Parton. Anyway, it got marvellous reviews.

How is London? What's going on with the one-man show [Champagne Charlie] Will you be coming to the states soon? Of course one of the biggest changes in New York since I moved here is that nobody has sex anymore. What is the status of aids in London? Several of my friends and acquaintances have died, some of them quickly and some of them not so quickly, but all of them too young. What a strange experience, to have lived through the sexual revolution, beginning with the raiding of Stonewall in the sixties and escalating to such a horrible climax, like a giant 20 year joke.

Well, I miss you both sorely, but surely we will see one another before too long. Until then, remember I love you."

It was unfortunate we never did meet up again but so much for the American who was going to give me so much trouble.

The American who did turn out to be the dreaded one for me was one Mario Arrimbide. He might have been forgiven for his truculence and bad behaviour had he been a better actor.

Hugh obviously liked what I did with *Pillars of Society* although a couple of students told me they didn't approve of the ending at all, it was much too Hollywood. Maybe it was. Nevertheless I was invited to direct William Congreve's *The Old Batchelor*. At the first rehearsal the young man playing Sir Joseph Wittoll stepped out empty-handed onto the marked floor.

'Where's your book?' I asked.

'Don't need it.'

'You mean you've learnt it?'

'Yes.'

'What happens if I make changes, cuts?'

'I'll learn them.'

This was a young man very sure of himself but instead of praising him I'm afraid I was rather curt. Unlike Mr Coward who evidently liked his cast to arrive at a first rehearsal dead letter-perfect, I believe it is much better to learn your part through the rehearsal process. If you come to it already learnt you come to it with preconceived ideas that might be totally against the director's vision of the play or even the author's intentions and how your part should develop in conjunction with the rest of the cast. By all means study the play and study the play and study the play, not just your own part, but do not deliberately set out to learn it. That way it is easier to dry and that way it is easier for a critic to say so-and-so seemed to be appearing in a different play to the rest of the company. There is a difference between a performance that grows out of the rehearsal process and one that could start off on the wrong foot by being pre-learnt. However, the young man had learned his part, he was dead letter perfect and that was that. His name was Kenneth Branagh and this was a young man I knew would go far but little did I realise quite how far and how quickly.

When I was invited to play the psychiatrist, Dysart, in *Equus* at Furman University, I was unavailable for the first weeks of rehearsal being still engaged at James Madison and a student stood in for me, so the director asked me to arrive word perfect. I told him, I couldn't work that way and, anyway, I knew the play pretty well having recently directed it myself. Strangely though, despite knowing the play so well, I had great difficulty in studying Dysart. Right up to the first public performance I never seemed to know which scene followed which. It was weird and perhaps, for once, I should have broken the habit of a lifetime, done a Branagh, and learned the lines before I got there.

I don't know why the English have to denigrate success. Americans love little magnetised pieces of kitsch they stick all over their fridge doors and I have a piece, this one made in Canada, which reads, "Success does for living what sunshine does for stained glass." Now

Chapter Eighteen

you couldn't get cuter than that but I don't think an Englishman could write it and what is it about success that make an Englishman's hackles rise? Someone in the states once asked me what I thought the big difference was between Americans and the English and I replied that I thought the Americans are a race of up lifters whereas the English are a race of put downers. You come up with an idea in America and their first reaction is–great, go for it! You come up with an idea in England and immediately any number of reasons are given as to why it's no damn good and it seems to me, I know this is a generalisation, that the English are seldom generous about or happy for someone else's success. There was a time when Kenneth was never out of the papers, never off somebody's chat show, was most definitely flavour of the month in a big way. Then, suddenly, the snide remarks, the cutting articles starting to appear. It seemed like a case of, "Hey! This guy's getting too big for his britches, maybe it's time to pull him down a peg or two." The modern version of the Roman 'Remember you are mortal.' Within the profession it could have been jealousy that started the sneers but why did the media do a sudden volte-face? What did Branagh do to go from the plaudits to the hiss and boo? So he wrote an autobiography while he was still virtually wet behind the ears. So what? So he decided to direct and star in a film of *Henry V*, so what? Why shouldn't he? Was Olivier's film the definitive version? The media couldn't at one time do enough to build him up and, suddenly, it seemed they couldn't do enough to pull him down and put him in, what I suppose they thought to be, his place.

Kenneth was not the only talent in that particular production of *The Old Batchelor*. There were also Mark Hatfield as Sharper and Katy Behean as Laetitia. Mark has a truly remarkable sense of comedy and I admire him enormously as an actor. I don't think to my dying day I will ever forget his performance at RADA as Chandebise in *A Flea in Her Ear* when he had me literarily aching with laughter. And I saw him later as Grumio in *The Taming of the Shrew* at Sheffield's Crucible Theatre where he had the same effect.

I think it was after the opening night of *The Old Batchelor* that

I went backstage to congratulate and thank my cast: to the girls' dressing room first.

'Are you decent? Can I come in?'

Squeals and shouts of 'No! No!' So I said what I had to say from the door. Then I moved on to the boys' dressing room on the other side of the theatre and didn't bother to say anything as I walked in. I was used to this in the professional theatre but hadn't taken into account that these were students and the big wide world was still out there waiting for them. They were all in the shower and as one man they turned to face me and I could see by their attitude and looks exactly what they were thinking, defying my eye line to drop to crotch level which it didn't. I nearly said it aloud, 'Too bad, babies, but there isn't one of you I fancy,' but I merely said my thank yous and congratulations, turned and left. I never went into their dressing room again but waited for them in the canteen to say what I had to say.

I directed half a dozen plays in all at RADA, the others being *The Rivals*, Edward Bond's *Saved*, and *Paradise is Closing Down* by Pieter-Dirk Uys, finally *The Questioning of Nick* by Arthur Kopit. I think Hugh gave me *Saved* because of my liking of Bond's work and the Uys play obviously because of my South African upbringing. I don't know why the Kopit turned out to be my last production there. Perhaps Hugh felt I was getting tired, though I never gave anything but my best, and sometimes I felt I was almost living in the place. Perhaps he felt I'd had a good crack of the whip and it was time for me to move on. Perhaps it was internal politics, I don't remember which play it was but, on one occasion, my first day back, I walked into the foyer from Gower Street to be greeted by the receptionist with a very loud, 'Why, hello, Mr Jones! How nice to have you back. Come to set the standard again?'

A generous compliment it might have been but hardly the thing to say just as two members of staff are walking by.

Perhaps it was because I opened my big mouth too wide at staff meetings, expressing my opinion on matters of school policy when

Chapter Eighteen

it might have been politic to keep my mouth shut. I did not like, for example, the fact that students on the acting course were actively discouraged from taking an interest in stage management. As I said to Cruttwell, not all the acting graduates were going to go straight into the National or the RSC. Some would be out of work, possibly for a very long time, and when they were finally offered a job it would most likely be as acting ASM in which case they ought to at least know the basics of what happens behind the scenes. Also it might teach them to appreciate all that is done for them. When we did *The Rivals* I wanted the staging to be as close to the 18th century style as possible so the set I got Chris to design was a simple box, plainly dressed, and with sliding screens for scene changes. Simple though it was it still entailed a great deal of work but one of the actresses stood centre stage before the dress rehearsal, surveyed the set and said in tones of deep disgust, 'Is that it?'

Of course she wasn't my only critic. If we set ourselves up to do this kind of job we set ourselves up to be criticised. This might sound like stating the obvious but it is surprising how many people resent criticism of any kind. The professional criticism of *The 88* was a whole different ball game and I had every right to resent that but, if ordinary members of the audience didn't like the play, I'm sorry for it but I can buy that. I've been a critic myself when a play or a production hasn't absorbed me. For example I went to see a production of *Three Sisters* during which I was so bored I started counting the books in the bookshelf. And the reason for my boredom didn't lie with the play but because all the cast came on stage with a huge invisible sign over their heads which said "I am in a great classic" and that, unfortunately was the way they acted it. Yet I am sure there were many in the audience who were thoroughly captivated by it. No two people sitting side by side in an auditorium witness the same play. Audience participation does not only happen in pantomime, 'Oh, no I'm not!'

'Oh, yes you are!'

'Oh, no I'm not!'

An audience sitting more or less in silence is still participating and their reactions can really affect a performance, which is why actors say after a lengthy spell of rehearsing, 'What this play needs now is an audience.'

Each member of an audience brings to a play only what he or she is capable of bringing at that particular moment, and takes from it only that which they are capable of taking. As a very young man when I first saw *Who's Afraid of Virginia Woolf* all I saw were four people drinking themselves to death and yelling at each other and I dismissed the play out of hand. When I saw it again after thirty or more years of living, even though directed and performed by a not very good student cast, I realised just how wrong I had been. And when I came to play George a few years later, the play simply grew on me with each succeeding performance. I couldn't work on it enough. Even in the very last week I discovered things I wished I had discovered earlier. We give different interpretations to what is there and sometimes we see or hear things that aren't there at all. There is a story (apocryphal?) about John Gielgud when he was playing Hamlet, taking a bet with a fellow artiste that the audience always hears what it expects to hear and, in proving his point, he went on stage at a matinee and said, 'To be or not to be, let us have a cup of tea.' And not a single member of the audience so much as stirred. As I say, I don't know how true this little fable is, but I wouldn't be at all surprised if it were. The theatre is full of weird stories, like the wonderful one concerning Dame Edith Evans at The Old Vic. She was to take tea with the actress Mary Kerridge and had quite forgotten about it so, when an ASM knocked at her door and said, 'Dame Edith, there's a Miss Kerridge on the stairs.' Dame Edith in her fruity voice replied, 'Don't bother me with it, child. Wipe it up.'

I remember, after seeing the film *The Servant*, discussing it with John Lewis who saw it with me and, talking about the fight on the stairs between Fox and Bogarde, I said that I thought the figurine in the niche half way up the stairs was bound to go for a burton and I was most surprised it hadn't. He was surprised as well.

'What statuette?' He said, 'what niche? There wasn't any statuette.

Only at the bottom of the stairs and that did go for a burton.'
'There was another one towards the top. Are you blind?'
Who was right? Until I see the film again I won't know.

Whatever the reasons were for ending my invitations to direct at RADA I was destined never to work there again. Hugh Cruttwell retired. I sent a cheque towards his retirement present, a small measure of thanks, and a letter to his successor telling him what I had done and how much I would like to work at RADA again. I received in return the usual "We will bear you in mind for the future" reply and naturally never heard another word.

I thoroughly enjoyed working with the students and I believe they enjoyed working with me. Also I felt the end results of our work together justified Hugh's faith in me. Did any of them register a complaint against me as happened at James Madison on my second visit, when a girl complained I shouldn't be teaching there because I actually "shouted" at one of the students? Perhaps, though I can only think of one who may have done so, Mario Arrambide, a young man of moods, usually introspective ones, so I was totally taken aback one day when, passing him in a passage, I said, 'You were late for rehearsal this morning.'

He stopped, flushed, glowered at me and, without a word, strode angrily by. I turned to watch him go and called after him. 'Mario!' He was about to disappear around the corner so I said to his departing back, 'An apology might be in order.'

He swung back; his face contorted with rage and, at the top of his voice, hurled a stream of abuse and obscenities in my direction. I had absolutely no idea what I had said or done to Mario Arrambide to warrant this vituperative attack and, while it was happening, I stood there absolutely speechless. It might in fact have had little to do with me. Actors unfortunately do not always leave their problems and their neurosis at the stage door. As I had no particular desire to be liked by Mr Arrambide it really didn't matter though I was quite shaken by it at the time.

I had two black students in *The Old Batchelor*, a boy and a girl. The boy was playing a servant and he came to me one day and said could he put in a piece of business cleaning and polishing his master's shoes to which I replied, why not? The following day he put the business in and, out of the corner of my eye I saw the girl gather up her belongings and leave the room. I didn't see her until the following day when she came to me and apologised, saying she thought I had given him that piece of business, though she found out later the idea had come from him. I accepted her apology but I'm afraid I was very short with her over the way she had behaved and she left the room again, this time in floods of tears.

The last time I set foot in The Royal Academy of Dramatic Art was to see, at his request, Kenneth's *Hamlet*, that most demanding and continuously controversial of roles. But Kenneth was never one to avoid a challenge and, although I wasn't totally enamoured of his interpretation, he had a good stab at it.

Meanwhile Chris had gone into *Cats* at The New London and this was to lead to my working in America. Shortly after I arrived in Harrisonburg I did an interview with the local radio station and the first question I was asked of course was how did I come to America to which I replied, 'On a virgin and a pair of yellow socks.'

There was moment's shocked silence before I explained. Virgin is not a word to be used on American radio. At least it wasn't at that time anyway, so I went on to explain that the Virgin was the first ever Virgin Airways flight into America and the yellow socks belonged to Andy Leech, an alumnus of James Madison University who was a fan of *Cats* and who had seen the show at least four times, always sat in the same seat, and always wore yellow socks so in the dressing room the saying was, 'Yellow socks is in again.' Then one night after the show he was found standing at the stage door and Chris got talking to him. It wasn't long before he visited us at home and, through Andy, we met Tom Arthur who was then head of Theatre at JMU and currently in

Chapter Eighteen

charge of the university's London semester whose students of course included Andy. They spent Christmas Day with us and, when Tom heard I had directed Restoration plays, he asked if I would like to do the same at JMU. Evidently they very much wanted to do one but, as none of the faculty had any real experience of Restoration drama except in theory, no one was volunteering to do it.

These things always take time to arrange and I went into the season of plays at the Theatre Royal, Haymarket: *Hobson's Choice* to understudy Quayle and Kaye, *Captain Brassbound's Conversion* to play Osman, and of course, *A Coat of Varnish*, playing a detective called Reece. *Captain Brassbound's Conversion* starred Penelope Keith as Lady Cicely Waynflete. I found a programme for the first night of the very first production of the play at The Royal Court and gave it to her as a first night present. I don't think to this day she knows who gave it to her because she was in such a state that night she probably thanked a bemused somebody else. She certainly never said anything to me. Once the plays were all up and running they remained in repertory so when I arrived home from the theatre one night to hear there had been a phone call from Virginia with an invitation to take part in the university's Arts Festival, it was obviously impossible for me to accept. Chris took an early holiday from *Cats* and went in my place. As he was performing in the then hottest show in town he was feted left, right, and centre and had a wonderful time. He gave a talk on *Cats*, a classical ballet class, and one on Elizabethan Dance. The Americans can be so welcoming. One Spring break I flew to Illinois to stay with David Harwell who had graduated form his university in Alabama and was then working at a small university in Decatur and the head of drama asked me to give a talk to his students. When I saw the invitation announcing the talk pinned up on a notice board I was quite taken aback to see it headed, "PRIVILAGE, PRIVILAGE, PRIVILAGE."

Coming down to land at The University of Illinois Willard Airport at Champaign was quite magical as this part of America was still in the grip of a decidedly hard winter and, as we taxied along the runway, the trees on either side, glinting in the sun, looked for all the world as if a Hollywood set dresser had decorated them with frost and ice. It was quite spectacular, the flat shimmering landscape stretching away for miles. The result of my visit was a play, purely fictional, my imagination sparked by the milieu and which I call my Neil Simon play, *Third Drawer from the Top*. If it is ever produced I will have to ensure it is prefaced with the usual disclaimer, "any resemblance to persons living or dead is purely coincidental."

David and I went to see a production of *Little Mary Sunshine* at the University of Illinois Krannert Center for the Performing Arts. It's always interesting to see what other university drama departments produce; also what their facilities are like and the University of Illinois has an Arts Centre second to none with a stage for opera, one for theatre, a studio, restaurants, even an indoor car park. It really is a magnificent building. The production was fun although it was unfortunate the director's choice was to send the musical up which, considering it is a pastiche and already a send-up, was the wrong decision.

The JMU invitation was the second I had to turn down because I couldn't leave the theatre. The first was while I was understudying Alistair Sim and Harry was still in my life. He called one day to say he was to write and direct a film in Holland starring the Dutch comedian Wim Sonneveld, the money being put up by Philips, could I go with him to Wim's villa in the South of France for a conference? I would have loved to have gone to the South of France for a conference but of course it was impossible, though Harry, like uncle Nin's landlady, couldn't understand for the life of him why. I told him to bring back with him any material he could on Mr Sonneveld: recordings, photographs, articles from newspapers and magazines which he duly did and, when we met and I went through this material, I said,

Chapter Eighteen

'Harry, this guy is another Jacques Tati and that's the sort of script that's needed.'

I adored the film *Monsieur Hulot's Holiday* until someone decided it needed more dialogue and a new sound track was added which ruined it.

Harry blew. Jacques Tati? No way. Jacques Tati's films lost money. They were all owned buy the banks. The man himself was bankrupt. The last thing we wanted was a Jacques Tati type comedy. So during the following days I paid umpteen visits to Harry's house where patiently under Harry's direction I put together a typical English end of the pier type comedy script. He went off to Holland with it, came back, and called me.

'Bad news, Glyn, they don't like the script.'

'Oh? Did they give reasons?'

'Yes. They said what they wanted was more of a Jacques Tati type script. There was a long silence while I tried to breathe, and then it was my turn to blow. Harry emphatically denied I had ever even mentioned Jacques Tati.

A new script was produced by a couple of fairly well-known writers of comedy and Harry made his film which was so bad evidently Wim refused to attend the opening night and died of a heart attack shortly afterwards. Harry made another film in England, *Go for a Take*, a comedy that, as the title implies, was all shot in a film studio and thus cost next to nothing as everything was at hand. I attended the premiere at the Astoria in Charing Cross Road with Roy Simpson and even Roy couldn't hide his embarrassment. I don't remember that I ever saw Harry again after that and the last news I had of him was that he was in Australia.

Meanwhile, back at the ranch, still in the process of selling Richmond Road and looking for another house, one weekend at Wood Norton we discovered close by a Church of England rectory for sale, a magnificent half Georgian, half Victorian house with land and a walled orchard, and suggested to Jeremy that we buy it together leaving him to bid for it when it came up for auction. The house had so many rooms, including eight or more in the attic, it was plenty large enough for us to share. There was an entrance hall that was a room in itself with a magnificent stone fireplace, an enormous dining room to one side, and on the other an equally spacious drawing room. A large flagstone kitchen led on to a dairy and pantries. A separate garage and stables had more rooms above. Of course the house, having stood empty for quite a while, required a great deal of work as did the land but, like "Shepherd House" in Marden, we really fell head over heels in love with it. Nicknamed 'The Rectumry' we waited for the day of the auction.

Unfortunately there was something going on that neither Chris nor I knew anything about and this was that Jeremy was getting himself into a whole heap of trouble by using money from his clients' accounts, something lawyers, agents etc., simply do not do, and he had no way of paying the money back. At the same time the second of our three unfortunate alcoholics entered our lives. I performed a second time in *Treasure Island* at The Mermaid where a young electrician latched on to me in no uncertain terms. I won't mention his name in deference to his wife and family and I had no idea he was not only an alcoholic but also an habitual liar. His home was in Yorkshire where, so he informed me, he owned several hundred acres where he had grown chrysanthemums under glass until an import of plants from Holland brought with them some disease that wiped him out. The truth was, as I discovered when I happened to go to Yorkshire, he lived in a small semi-detached house with a tiny back garden that held no more than three or four cloches and no way was he in the business of growing flowers.

But, before knowing this, for the last time I became a director of a company that was dead in the water from the very beginning. It was registered at Companies House as Akenglen and was to be a practical supplier of anything and everything from A to Z required in film, TV, or theatre. I spent fruitless hours traipsing around London looking for suitable offices because, let's call him Simon, had managed to

Chapter Eighteen

put up enough money to form and register the company and pay for the printing of brochures and, as yet, I had no suspicion of his true financial state. By now he was using 162 Richmond Road as his London base and, despite a flow of letters from The Yorkshire Bank, presumably letters of demand, I still remained trustful and blissfully unaware of the situation. What brought matters to a head was the way Jeremy and Simon were seen whispering together in dark corners as it were which I found highly suspicious and my suspicions were confirmed when it turned out that the first bankrupt alcoholic was trying to borrow money from the second bankrupt alcoholic to get himself off the hook. Unfortunately the second bankrupt, being the liar he was, said of course he could lend the first bankrupt the money and a cheque that bounced higher than a helium filled balloon was the end of Jeremy Nightingale. It would have happened eventually anyway, this merely brought the disaster forward and he lost his practice. He was reduced to working as a clerk for another solicitor and eventually he lost both Wood Norton and his home in Hackney, in fact virtually everything he owned. It also opened my eyes at last to the shenanigans Simon was capable of.

One evening he came home and retired to his bed in the spare room saying he was ill. I took one look at the state he was in and called an ambulance. The men walked into the room and it didn't take them more than one look, before one of them turned to me and said, 'He's drunk.'

I felt like a complete idiot. They carted him off to hospital anyway and a few hours later he was back but, not for good. I had had enough and, after a temporary reprieve, that was the last we saw of him. All letters from the Yorkshire Bank were returned unopened. Eventually they stopped coming.

As for The Rectumry, Jeremy didn't even attend the auction as he had promised to do and told us later the property had gone for £35,000 which, with the increase in value of 162, was well within our range even after paying off debts and even without Jeremy's participation. Still, it was obviously never meant to be so it was back to house hunting in London and we eventually found a terraced house in Stoke Newington at 36 Farleigh Road. While we waited for the exchange of contracts on both 162 and 36 we took a holiday in Sicily, flying from Luton to Palermo.

Sitting beside us on the plane was a young Italian, a waiter in one of London's many trattorias, now returning home on holiday and petrified of flying. At Palermo it was too late for him to continue his journey to his hometown of Caltanissetta so we let him share our room at the hotel and, when he left the following morning, it was with a firm invitation, an order even, to visit his family. I doubt we would have thought of visiting Caltanissetta otherwise but that was how we came to see the wonderful collection of Greek artefacts when we had the local museum all to ourselves for an afternoon, his uncle, who turned out to be of an age with his nephew, being the curator, and the museum officially closed that day. After a spaghetti meal (what else?) in a local restaurant, we spent a delightful evening in the uncle's flat with his wife and bambini, and our young friend, the conversation made possible with a good wine, a few words of Italian, some German, some French, some English and a whole lot of gesture. The following morning as we were getting ready to leave our hotel there was a knock at the door and there stood uncle and nephew in their best suits and with hats in hand come to see us on our way to Taormina.

Our compartment in the train, which we had to ourselves, was a museum piece in perfect condition with its high backed plush buttoned seats, polished wood, carpet, framed pictures, the rich curtains with their bobbles and tassels. Although train travel is my preference above any other form of transport I am not a railway buff so I have no idea of the coach's age, but it must have been manufactured somewhere near the turn of the twentieth century. Our newfound friends in their best bib and tucker standing on the platform waving goodbye with their hats, and the wonderful compartment; then the hot, dry, pale yellow, almost African landscape of Sicily passing by made it feel as though one were in a period movie. All it needed was

Chapter Eighteen

a couple of peasants with shotguns and maybe a priest with egg on his cassock to complete the picture. We passed through Catania, birthplace of the composer Bellini, and on to Taormina, booking into a moderately priced hotel and, going in the lift down to the beach; braving the onslaughts of brawny German ladies with very sharp elbows they knew how to use.

We stopped off in Palermo on the way home and, among our explorations discovered what looked like a garage in which was a traditional puppet theatre. Chris, having always been mad on puppets, naturally we had to see a performance which consisted mainly it seemed of the crusader Roland decapitating Saracens. After the show we were invited backstage and I was amazed at both the size of the puppets and their weight.

Farleigh Road to begin with was a disaster. Moving a week before Christmas was fraught. The ubiquitous "they" say, next to birth, marriage, and death, moving is just as stressful and it was made even more so by this empty neglected house devoid of heating and in a freezing winter the dampness making it even colder. It was another house that was going to require a lot of work and for a few days while trying to settle in, with furniture everywhere and anywhere and umpteen boxes to sort out, we lived off mince pies and toasted sandwiches.

As with Richmond Road, heating, wiring, and a bathroom were the first priorities. Later an extension was built enlarging the dingy miniscule kitchen and creating a breakfast room. But that was further down the line. What drove us almost to nervous breakdowns from the beginning was the noise. We had double-glazing fitted at the front of the house to reduce street noise but unfortunately it augmented the sound from the houses on either side. Victorian terraces were not built to withstand noise. When these houses were built there were no vacuum cleaners or television sets to worry about let alone music centres with speakers that could fill the Albert Hall. To one side of us we had a charming Jamaican couple, Gladstone and Daphne, who unfortunately liked to eat in the kitchen at the back of the house while watching television at the front of the house, which meant their TV might just as well have been on in our house. We politely pointed out the problem to them and they did turn the volume down, enough to make it at least bearable. What was unbearable came from the house on the other side. This was owned by a Housing Association and a number of West Indians were living in it. We never knew how many they were, there was so much coming and going. Cars came and went throughout the night and people hung about in the street. The problem was they were running an illegal club, a shebeen, charging admission for illicit booze, probably engaged, although I have no proof of this, in drug deals, and playing their music through those huge speakers until five in the morning. In our bedroom upstairs what we got was a continuous deep bass thump thump thump vibrating through the walls until it drove us almost mad. Direct complaints got us nowhere. I was actually taken into the room on their ground floor in which the gigs were held and proudly the huge speakers were pointed out to me. Complaints to the Housing Association got us nowhere. Calling the police resulted in ten minutes of quiet and then it started up again. It almost affected the rhythm of the heart and we were seriously beginning to suffer from sleep deprivation. Then one night a black girl, all bruised, scratched and bleeding, and trembling violently, came scrambling over the back garden wall asking us to take her in and to call the police, which we did. The Housing Association now started to finally sit up and take notice and shortly afterwards the house was emptied of its occupants.

Then the builders moved in. Mind you we were having enough trouble with builders of our own let alone having to put up with those next door. We engaged a builder who lived a couple of doors down from Jeremy and who had worked on his house, evidently to Jer's satisfaction. Had we known what a klutz he was he wouldn't have been allowed within a mile of us. Together with his knuckle-on-the-ground assistants, they became known collectively as "Ron and his merry men." They had a habit of disappearing for days on end, presumably to work on other jobs or, in Ron's case anyway, his real job which was for Hackney Borough Council. Usually they left at the most inappropriate times more often than not leaving a crisis of some sort behind them. For a while I was in Edinburgh and got a distraught phone call from Chris who had been left for nearly two weeks with no water in the kitchen and who wanted me to lambaste Ron over the phone. Was there any point? This coming and going could be a universal habit of builders because the same thing happens in Crete. Another characteristic they possess, apart from cutting corners and botching jobs, is to be totally oblivious of their surroundings. For example the builders next door had their cement mixer running while facing our newly painted side wall, which of course was immediately spotted with cement and would eventually have been totally splattered had I not seen what was happening and yelled blue murder, at which they turned the machine sideways to face down the garden, the position it should have been in in the first place.

As far as botched jobs were concerned, a leak in the extension roof was never repaired because no one, including another builder, could discover from where it was originating. We also discovered that copper pipes had been laid without lagging in corrosive cement. I only hope whoever is living in 36 Farleigh Road now doesn't suddenly find the floor getting very wet as the pipes disintegrate, if they haven't done so already.

One day an assistant, an infant of about seventeen summers, walked by, stopped, and said, 'What's your dog's name, Glyn?'

'Which one? There are two dogs.'

'The White one.'

'Isolde.'

'Oh.'

He stood there for a while digesting this piece of information and moved on. A few minutes later he was back again.

'What did you say your dog's name was?'

'Isolde.'

'Oh.'

And, later in the day, the question was put a third time. This was getting a bit like my father's, 'How do you spell eleven?'

There was even a fourth time of asking before I heard him calling her, 'Isarold! Isarold!'

On another occasion while we were out and the merry men had the house to themselves, on our return the infant came running out the front door complaining, 'Isarold bit me!'

'What did you do to Isarold that she bit you?'

'I didn't do nuffink.'

I don't believe she bit him. There were certainly no discernible marks on his supposedly injured ankle. She probably gave him a good lick.

'Well you must have done something,' I said. 'Isar...Isolde is the gentlest and most timid of dogs. It's all we can do to get her to bite her breakfast. I shouldn't think she'd find your ankle very tasty.'

That was the last we heard of that though I never heard him call Isarold again.

There was another problem with the house: the smell of Daphne's cooking. It wasn't until we stripped six or more layers of wallpaper off the party wall in the stairwell and discovered a six-foot long, quarter inch wide crack that the source of the smell was revealed. Inhabitants of the house had been wallpapering and painting for decades without stripping first and it was fascinating as layer after layer were uncovered going back to the original Victorian paper which fortunately wasn't green. Green wallpapers and some pigments of the period contained cyanide until it was finally realised they were the cause of a number of deaths including ladies and artificial flowers and scenic artists in the theatre using green paint.

The coving and centre rose in what was going to be the dining room, but was never finished in all the years we lived there, were so thick with paint including a top coat of gloss that the egg and dart design coving was totally obscured and the rose just shapeless lumps. Seems to me there was always one room in a house that was

Chapter Eighteen

never finished. At 162 it was the lower ground floor room behind the kitchen that was also going to be a dining room but, as with 36, all it ever remained was a storage space. If we had lived there longer I suppose we would eventually have got around to making it what it was meant to be at 36. We did get as far as to install a handsome pine fire surround and over mantel with bevelled mirror supported by Ionian columns. In Yorkshire the unfinished room was going to be a second loo and shower but when we left it was just a space for storage although it had in place, over a sink, when the sink would eventually be installed, a beautiful Victorian mirror with shelves and a half-dome canopy. Chris picked this up in a junk shop in Hackney for five pounds and it was moved from the bathroom in Richmond Road to the bathroom in Farleigh Road and finally to Yorkshire where it stayed.

The exterior also had to be stripped and, while I was in Denmark, I received a letter from Chris, all excitement, saying he had stripped the paint over the front door and that 36 Farleigh Road had a name. It was called "Ragnall House." As they say in Wales, "There's posh."

It was at Ragnall House that Chris went back to his origins in the theatre when Raymond Gubbay commissioned him to design and build sets for *Trial by Jury* and *HMS Pinafore* for performances at the Queen Elizabeth Hall on The South Bank. We built half the sets in the back yard and half in the abandoned fire station that had become available for use by the community. I was his assistant together with a local lad named Laurence who Chris one day reduced to tears; he is such a perfectionist and demanding taskmaster. For some unknown reason Laurence also got the idea I wanted to have sex with him. Not only that but that I wanted it "dirty", telling me in confidence he hadn't washed for a couple of days. I told him in confidence that not only did I not want to have sex with him, had never even thought of having sex with him but, if I did, dirty was the last thing I had in mind.

Chris was now engaged as an assistant director for that long tour of the musical *Oliver*. Starring Roy Hudd as Fagan the tour in Britain was in two parts, divided by the engagement in Toronto at The Royal Alexandra. During the first half of the tour while the company was in Birmingham, Chris's brother, Roger called me to say their father, Hugh, had died. According to Hyst Mum, he came in from the garden, leaned against the kitchen door for a moment and then silently slid to the floor and that was that. Roger wanted to know whether he should call the theatre. I didn't think this a very good idea and said I would do it myself. Consequently I telephoned the theatre and spoke to the stage doorkeeper, giving him the news and telling him not to say anything to Chris until after the show, by which time I hoped I would have been able to get a train for Birmingham and would be there soon after the final curtain. It was actually very late when I arrived but Roy, and his girl friend Debbie were wonderful, taking Chris back to their hotel to comfort and keep him company until I arrived.

After the company had left for Toronto on the 3rd June '83, I got myself an American visa and booked a flight in plenty of time to fly to New York a couple of weeks later. I stayed at our home from home on 79th and Paul and Lionel took me to a restaurant in the Village called *Clydes* where, due to jet lag and the time difference I almost fell asleep. The following day Courtney Burr and Marc Lutsky both visited and then went off with each other, which turned out to be a bit of a disaster as, later, each accused the other of passing on the clap! This was fortunately before the advent of AIDS. Paul and I meanwhile went for dinner at a fish restaurant called Squid Roe where they had pussy rather than doggy bags. I had a good time in N.Y. that trip though it ended with the oesophagus episode over the osso bucco in Ticino's before flying down to Washington and motoring on to Harrisonburg to "case the joint" as it were, and meeting most of the theatre faculty. I returned to New York from Washington by Amtrak and then flew to Toronto where Chris was ensconced in a pleasant furnished apartment. Naturally, like good tourists, we had to do Niagara Falls and, wrapped in our sou'westers take a trip on *The Maid of the Mist*, the boat that goes almost to the base of that

Chapter Eighteen

thundering water. After Niagara On The Lake we passed a farmers' market at the side of the road where the fruit looked so wonderful we bought apples, peaches, nectarines, pears, and god know what and after one bite at each threw the lot away. Everything was not only tasteless; it all had exactly the same texture, cotton wool.

That evening I went to the "Toronto Free Theatre" to sit through a wonderful production of *March of the Falsettos*. The cast were uniformly brilliant and afterwards I went back stage to congratulate them and tell them how much I enjoyed the show. Now this was something I had never done with a company in which I was personally unacquainted with any member so it says something about my appreciation. I also wanted to apologise for the audience that night being so few in number, even though that hardly had anything to do with me.

The summer was hot and we spent days at Hanlan's Point Beach and Kew Beach and swam in the Weston Hotel pool where Roy was staying. We also had to do the C.N. Tower and I went out to Stratford to see a production of the Scottish King in which our friend Nicky Pennell was playing the lead. He had been in Canada a while by then, playing seasons as one of their leading actors and, out of season, teaching in Chicago. He had been at RADA at the same time as Peter Mackie, which is how we first met and is probably best remembered in Britain, if he is remembered, for his part in the TV series, *The Forsythe Saga*. He was very good in the play and couldn't believe it when I walked into his dressing room at the end. His embrace, still in full costume, was very sweaty I remember. I asked him if he had any regrets about leaving England and his answer was why should he have? He was playing leading roles in a wonderful company in a wonderful country and was perfectly happy. There was nothing about England that he missed. Unfortunately Nicky was another one to die young.

Naturally I also saw a performance of *Oliver*, not the one when one of the kids, Stephen Mostad, got his leg caught between two revolves moving in opposite directions. In the wings he kept calling for Chris, 'I want Chris! Where's Chris!' so Chris had to go with him in the ambulance to hospital while the rest of the company got on with the show. We still get yearly greetings from the Mostad family and Steven, visiting Europe some years later, stayed with us in Yorkshire, bringing as a present a piece of the Berlin wall. A few years back we had an invitation to his wedding in New York which, being one of our penniless periods, we had reluctantly to decline.

The climax of my visit to Toronto was probably the open-air concert at Ontario Place featuring the divine Ella Fitzgerald. Unforgettable. Chris returned with me to New York because he particularly wanted to see the show *Merlin*. Apart from puppets and scenery, acting, dancing, directing, and stained glass, Chris's other love even from childhood is magic and illusionists, and in *Merlin* he finally saw on stage for the very first time a Victorian illusion he knew all about called *Moth to the Flame* involving the instant disappearance of a lady moth from within her silken wings, and the wings as well, all in a flash. The following day we took in Radio City Music Hall, that amazing building that covers an entire block, and then he flew back to Toronto.

I had a couple more days in New York so of course I had to visit the Strand Bookshop and the "Actors' Heritage" shop and, in the evening saw *Torch Song Trilogy*. The following day it was The Lincoln Centre to do some research and then, after dinner with Lionel, Paul and Jeff at Ichabods; Jeff and I went to Madison Avenue Presbyterian Church where we watched a group of young actors playing James McClure's *Bourbon and Laundry* and *Lone Star*. They had produced the plays themselves and invited prospective agents, producers and casting directors. They were a great bunch of kids and both they and I regretted I couldn't join them for their last night party the day I had a plane to catch. 'Stay, stay! Put it off. Take a later plane.'

Back in London I wrote another play, *Hear the Hyena Laugh*, which started its long history of submissions and regular returns in stamped

Chapter Eighteen

addressed envelopes.

The *Oliver* Company came back from Canada and started the second leg of their British tour. I arranged to visit Chris in Newcastle and on the preceding Saturday booked my train ticket at King's Cross. I don't know why I stayed up so late that night but I was working at something in the breakfast room when I heard this very strange noise in the passage where I last saw Natalie lying and I knew immediately what it was. She was already dead by the time I reached her and all I could do was kneel down and bawl my eyes out. I was very Greek about it because I talked to her for a long time before I finally got up and went out into the garden to dig her grave. She was a big dog and the hole needed to be deep. When I went to pick her up, her mouth was open and she had already begun to stink. I buried her wrapped in an old greatcoat with a mock fur collar that once belonged to Peter Mackie and, with her, her "passport" that is, her record of inoculations etcetera, and her favourite toys. Not her bell for calling people to dinner. We still have that. In my diary for Saturday the 10th September I recorded, NATALIE DIED. 2.15 AM. AGED 12 YRS 4 MONTHS.

I wasn't going up to Newcastle for another five days and I said nothing to Chris but, once we were face to face he knew immediately that something had happened and I blurted out, 'Natalie died!' And it was the cue for another bout of sobbing.

The *Oliver* tour ended with the company ensconced in the Aldwych Theatre, Ron Moody taking over the part of Fagin from Roy, and I went into understudy mode again, this time at the Albery in a not very good play by Charles Dyer called *Lovers Dancing*. It was a very good cast, Paul Eddington, later to become very popular in *Yes Minister*, and Colin Blakely, who I understudied. No doubling up this time. Perhaps because of the smallness of the cast everyone had their own cover. The ladies were the delightful Georgina Hale and Jane Carr.

It never ceases to amaze me how directors and designers ignore directions in the script. *Lovers Dancing* was supposed to be set in a country cottage and the set was more a country mansion, and modern with it. I remember going to see Michael Jenn in a play at The Crucible theatre in Sheffield where the setting was described as a luxurious palace and what we got was dull grey concrete and sparse stainless steel tubular furniture. At the University of Virginia I went to see a production of *A Midsummer Night's Dream* directed by George Black and he had set it in India during The Raj. Why? It worried me all evening, especially every time Athens was mentioned. It would have been better to have set it in an American Athens. Was his decision because of the little Indian boy? As there are millions of little Indian boys in India that would seem a non sequitur for starters. There is also the problem of positive casting. It is really pushing suspension of disbelief when a black actor is cast as an English king and in circumstances like that I don't believe it is doing the actor any favours. That particular actor in an interview defended the choice by quoting white actresses playing Cleopatra. Wrong example I think as Cleopatra, being a Ptolemy and the Ptolemys being Greek, was white anyway. He would have done better to have quoted all the white actors who have played Othello. There are plenty of roles in which black actors can be cast without being quite so political. I wonder if anyone will ever cast Cleopatra as a dumpy frumpy saggy baggy critter or will she always be Elizabeth Taylor?

So I think George would have been better advised to have located his *Midsummer Night's Dream* in Athens, Georgia, if that is where there is one, and given himself plenty of scope for casting African-Americans though I don't recall seeing too many on the UVA campus. I always wondered why Americans referred to cities like Paris, France, or Birmingham, England, until I went to America and realised just how many place names are repeated. I used to laugh as well at the pronunciation of herbs as 'erbs until I discovered the American pronunciation is correct. It was the snobbish middle class Victorians in England who added the H, not wanting to be mistaken for the working class who dropped their haitches. Moral, don't show up your hignorance.

Chapter Eighteen

Chris was now dancing for the choreographer Geraldine Stevenson in Raymond Gubbay's Strauss Galas and various period televisions and had taken to performing in Old Time Music Hall. One of the songs he sang was a number called *Gilbert the Filbert*. It was a little on the short side so I wrote him an extra verse which ran;

IF I SPORT A FLOWER IN MY LAPEL,
IT IS NOT BECAUSE I'M A FRIGHTFUL SWELL,
BUT IN CASE I MEET WITH A LADY COLD,
I CAN WARM HER UP WITH A GESTURE BOLD.
WHEN I MAKE MY BOW AND I RAISE MY HAT,
THEN I MURMUR 'NOW?' OR A PHRASE AS PAT.
SHE SEES MY BLOOM,
SHE STARTS TO SWOON,
THE CRY GOES UP–'HOW'S THAT?'
Spoken: What one might well call a wicket maiden, old chap, what?

Of course an obscene gesture with the bloom was what made the maiden swoon. Another music hall artiste, Larry Barnes copied it and went around telling everyone it was something he had discovered. He passed on this piece of information to our friends Annabelle Lee, and her husband, the writer, Richard Carpenter, who passed it on to us; not that it mattered. If Larry wanted to be known as the discoverer of this hitherto unknown piece of magnificent period writing so let it be.

One evening after a performance for The Hackney Festival in Stoke Newington Town Hall we met the then chairman of the Music Hall Society, Ellis Ashton, who said whenever he saw Chris perform he always imagined that was what George Leybourne must have been like, to which we replied in unison.

'Who was George Leybourne?'

'Why, the man who was Champagne Charlie of course.'

It was decided then and there that I would write that one-man show for Chris based on Leybourne's life and we immediately started our research. This was a fascinating time. In the Liverpool public library I discovered in a local paper the first announcement of his appearing at the old Parthenon Music Hall in that city under the name Joe Saunders. Something which has baffled writers for years is the question of his name, was it Joe Saunders which he changed to George Leybourne or was his name really Leybourne? Chris's meticulous research has established without any doubt that his real name was Leybourne. All anyone had to do was find his birth certificate and there is a letter from his wife published in *The Era* after his death which states categorically that her husband's name was Leybourne. Tommy Trinder starred in a movie, *Champagne Charlie*, produced by Ealing Films, which opened with the lines, "In the year of Grace 1860, two brothers set out from the mining village of Leybourne for London town." When Chris did a show with Trinder he queried it and Trinder loyally maintained the writers had been most diligent in their research, so how they managed to come up with two brothers and the village of Leybourne is anybody's guess and the film was full of anachronisms. Most writers, failing to do their own research and following hard on each other's heels, simply taking as true what had been written previously and copying it, wrote that his name was Joe Saunders and he came from Stourbridge near Birmingham when in fact he was born in an area then called Stourbridge, but no longer so named, in Gateshead.

We discovered he is buried in Stoke Newington Cemetery, a short walk from the house, and went in search of his long neglected grave, first going through a book of numbers and then, oh, the excitement when, together with the workers who had joined in and who became infected with our enthusiasm, we finally ripped away years of neglect, the mass of ivy, brambles, and tangled weeds that had until then totally concealed it.

'George Leybourne? Who was he then?'

The labourer, a redheaded Irishman, leaned on the handle of his rake and spat, the tone of his voice implying something of a disappointment at our discovery, especially after the sense of ex-

Chapter Eighteen

Christopher Beeching as Champagne Charlie - Mayfair Theatre

citement that had built up during the search. He looked around at the small group who stood staring at the simple white headstone, now stripped of its heavy blanket of ivy and revealed in almost perfect condition to the world for the first time in God knows how many years.

'Well, who was he then?'

The repeated query broke the silence that had descended on the group; two eager researchers and five cemetery workers who we had nicknamed 'the stagehands.' Well you can't stop theatricals from being theatrical and the situation was pretty theatrical. Victorian monuments to death were all around us, many of them imposing indeed, even in their broken and neglected state with their tall columns, urns and angels. Around and over the graves the jungle of weeds, ivy, nettles, elderberry and bramble in the lushness of summer had simply taken over and many of the smaller memorials, long double rows of graves with headstones back to back, had been totally obscured. It was in one of these double rows that we eventually found what we had been looking for. It had taken a long time and the stagehands may have been a little disappointed but to us each letter on the gravestone as it was unveiled was a moment to cherish. And now the whole stone stood revealed in its simplicity. The inscription read:

> IN LOVING MEMORY OF
> GEORGE LEYBOURNE
> Who Died September 15th 1884
> Aged 42 Years
> God's Finger Touched Him And He Slept
> ALSO OF FREDERICK CHEVALIER
> (Grandson of The Above)
> Who Died November 26th 1909
> Aged 22 Years
> GOD KNOWETH BEST
> ALSO IN LOVING MEMORY OF
> ALBERT CHEVALIER
> THE BELOVED HUSBAND OF FLORENCE CHEVALIER
> Who Died July 10th 1923
> Aged 62 Years.
> DEATH IS THE VALE WHICH THOSE WHO LIVE CALL LIFE
> THEY SLEEP.... AND IT IS LIFTED
> ALSO THE ABOVENAMED
> FLORENCE CHEVALIER

HE FLIES THROUGH THE AIR WITH THE GREATEST OF EASE,
A DARING YOUNG MAN ON THE FLYING TRAPEZE,
HIS MOVEMENTS WERE GRACEFUL, ALL GIRLS HE COULD PLEASE,
AND MY LOVE HE PURLOINED AWAY.

As a very small child this was definitely my favourite song, not just because it has a catchy tune but because my father would sing it and at the same time, taking both my hands would swing me almost horizontal in a circle while I shrieked with both delight and apprehension. What if he should lose his grip and let me go? Would I

Chapter Eighteen

Christopher Beeching as Champagne Charlie - Mayfair Theatre

be a daring young man and fly through the air with the greatest of ease? How far would I fly before I hit the earth with a painful thump? Or perhaps my arms would come out of their sockets! There was a fearful thought. But, as soon as he put me down, there would be a cry of, 'Again, daddy, again!'

That small child growing up in South Africa might have been able to sing, "A daring young man on the flying trapeze" but he had never heard of Music Hall or George Leybourne so it was strange to think that almost half a century later, strands of my life would come together in such a way that, together with the man who was to represent Leybourne on stage, five years of my life would be partly taken up with researching and writing about a man, once famous, now almost forgotten. And, when I mentioned *Champagne Charlie* to my acting class in Harrisonburg and they all stared at me blankly, I said 'I'll bet you a hundred dollars to a penny I will sing you one of his songs and you will know it.' They all thought this was holarious, as Andy Leech would say, (Andy's pronunciation sometimes was most peculiar. He kept on telling me about a musical called *The Rubber Bridegroom* which I thought rather kinky until I realised he meant robber.) So I started to sing, 'He flies through the air…' and that was as far as I got before the whole class took it up.

We started rehearsals for *Champagne Charlie* in the breakfast room at Farleigh Road and one evening the strangest thing occurred. There was a line in the original script that read, "If I were the ghost of George Leybourne, I wonder what I would say?" And, as Chris said the line, so the light above us flickered quite violently. Shades of Hortense. When rehearsals in the breakfast room were no longer viable because of lack of space we moved to the rehearsal rooms belonging to The King's Head in Islington and our friend, Michael Jenn sat in on the book for us.

As well as the scenery, consisting mainly of a very large ornate screen, Chris made most of the costumes himself, recreating the originals from the illustrations on the Victorian music covers. The whole show: screen, table, chair, costumes, props and bits and pieces fitted into and on top of a Mini and *Champagne Charlie* opened at The Intimate Theatre, Palmers Green on the 24th July 1984, the centenary of Leybourne's death.

Shortly afterwards I left for the states to start my first stint at James Madison University in Virginia.

Chapter Nineteen

My first attempt at procuring work in America was a letter I wrote in 1981 to Earle Gister, Head of the Acting programme, Yale School of Drama. Nothing like starting at the top. The reply was similar to one of many I was to receive when, as my year at James Madison was coming to an end, I sent off numerous applications to universities, schools, colleges, theatres, hoping to stay longer in the states. The Yale reply was brief and to the point. "Unfortunately we do not have an opening on our faculty at the present time."

Hanging on my bedroom wall is a framed print, the artwork by someone named Dick Richardson. Anne Lyndrup gave it to me after my first year at JMU. Decorated with a water colour of apples on a leafy branch it reads:

To be a Virginian, either by birth,
marriage adoption, or even
on one's mother's side, is an
introduction to any state
in the Union, a passport
to any foreign country,
and a benediction from
the Almighty God.
Anonymous.

Not quite politically correct I suppose (even on one's mother's side?) but this is indeed, I think, how the Virginians see themselves.

No Official Umbrella

The Country Wife - James Madison University 1984

One of my English set books at school was *The Virginian*, a book I thoroughly enjoyed though, apart from it being an American state, I had absolutely no idea where Virginia was; somewhere out in the wild wild west I imagined as it was all about a cowboy. I suppose had I been interested enough I could have looked it up in an atlas. But now I was seeing it for real and I loved it. I loved the Shenandoah Valley, The Blue Ridge Mountains, Skyline Drive and the rolling countryside around Charlottesville. I loved the towns, the villages, the beautiful farms and I loved the southern hospitality of the people. Of course there were rednecks a plenty but they hardly impinged on the milieu of academe and the student body. I believe in a town called Elkton a pair of brothers thought their day hadn't been worth getting out of bed for if they hadn't been shot at at least once. There was the farmers' market with its fresh produce and antique stalls and the unusual sight of black clad Quakers driving by in their horse drawn buggies. On occasions there was "The Book Fair", way out in the middle of the countryside where, in an enormous barn, you could rummage through second-hand books, old periodicals, newspapers, sheet music,

Chapter Nineteen

ephemera, and new books kept in a separate building. When the fair was open one of the fields was parking lot to a hundred cars and they kept on coming and going all day. There is the beautiful campus of the University of Virginia in Charlottesville with its famous redbrick crooked wall and rows of students' rooms with winter firewood neatly stacked outside each door. Founded by Thomas Jefferson whose own son could not attend the university because his mother was a slave, perhaps its most famous alumnus was Edgar Allen Poe. At James Madison I was introduced to American football, which found a new fan as my companions explained the intricacies of the game to me, and I still find it extraordinary that a quarter back can throw that ball such distances, and with such accuracy. I was also introduced of course to cheerleaders and the marching band and the JMU Marching Band was really something both to watch and, more importantly, listen to. Marching Bands are a big thing in the states and, when I was at the Wayside Theatre I suggested to David Harwell, who was into music and knowledgeable about marching bands that we write a musical together but he wasn't all that enthusiastic and we never pursued the idea. I'm surprised it hasn't been done. The first game I saw was against William and Mary and JMU lost 20-10.

The Country Wife was not my choice. My first suggestion to the faculty was Vanburgh's *The Relapse* but this was considered too rude for the Shenandoah Valley, as were a few more suggestions I made. Even *The Country Wife* was near the knuckle but, performed in the Latimer-Shaeffer, the main theatre, with a delightful colourful set by Allen Lyndrup and costumed by Pam Johnson, and with a young cast who took to it like ducks to water ('I never ever want to hear from you the word "motivation"' said the director) it was well received both by students and townsfolk. I had a lot of hassle from the music department trying to borrow a harpsichord but eventually managed to persuade them it would be well looked after.

To costume the play necessitated a visit to The University of Virginia in Charlottesville, JMU wardrobe being small and more than a little short on period stuff. Pam drove me over.

'We'll take the scenic route,' she said, 'Route 33.'

The scenic route it certainly was and we passed a clapboard house set well back from the road and with its veranda almost obscured by laundry hanging out to dry. 'I'm going to write a play set in that house,' I said. Over the years the house has become quite a landmark in that neck of the woods with folk writing to the editor of the Harrisonburg newspaper about it and the paper itself coming out with an article, possibly more than one. But did they realise it was also going to be the setting for a play? The big question on the minds of passers by seemed to be; did the laundry ever change? It always seemed to look exactly the same every time anyone drove by.

So I had my setting for a play but what was the play going to be about? A few days later I was standing in line in the faculty dining room when Tom Arthur's then secretary who was standing in front of me, turned and asked if I would like to spend Thanksgiving at her house, an invitation to which I immediately said yes. The Dean and his wife had already invited me but I made my excuses there as I thought this second invitation would prove more interesting, and so it did. The secretary, who was a young white girl, lived with her coloured boy-friend and his family, including a wonderful man who hardly said a word and who, without objecting, seemingly had boisterous, none too gentle kids clambering all over him through most of the day. He doesn't actually feature in the play, it is an all women cast, but he is a catalyst and described in detail.

Then Tom Arthur took me to a restaurant out of town; real southern cooking by a great lady, Ma Thomas. She walked with the aid of a cane and, during the course of the meal she came and sat at our table where she told us the story of how, when her sister died, she brought her body all the way back from Tennessee and how she had given what money she had left to the church in memory of her. My southern fried chicken, sweet potatoes and corn went cold on the plate and, if my mouth wasn't hanging open, it should have been because here I was listening to pure unadulterated Tennessee Williams. As with my mutineers and their tales, Ma Thomas's speech went wholesale into the script. It is not my writing. It is hers.

The restaurant walls were hung with the most amazing collection of plates from all over the world and when Chris visited her she took a great shine to him, inviting him into the inner sanctum (more plates) and even allowing him to play her precious piano.

At the time the two big issues in America were child and geriatric abuse. Add to this some southern redneck racism, and how about that for thickening the plot, Missy McCarthy? In fact the criticism from one of my students was that too much was happening but *Generations* almost wrote itself. When it was produced in the experimental theatre with four talented young actresses and beautifully directed by another student, Christian Holloway, a local schoolteacher attended the first night and then each subsequent performance, every time bringing different friends with her and, of course, everyone recognised the house but, what was more important, everyone recognised the themes in the play. It took some persuasion before Christian agreed to direct it, feeling with all of his nineteen years that he wasn't up to it, that it was too big a responsibility, but I had seen and enjoyed his production of the musical *Once Upon a Mattress* at a school outside of town and I knew he could do it. So, after a little arm-twisting, he finally agreed and although I was technically his supervisor I more or less left them all to it. During those rehearsals I did look in on I never once heard any of the technical jargon academics and MFA directors are so fond of. They just went straight for it and they got it right. Unfortunately reviews are not encouraged in the experimental theatre. Neither were there any reviews when the play was later done at Carnegie Mellon so nothing has ever been written about it.

Tom and Kay, having returned from Europe, I had moved to the Lyndrup house on Franklin Street and, while sitting in my broiler house loft bedroom writing *Generations* on a typewriter borrowed from Allen, Chris in London was beavering away on *Champagne Charlie*, cutting and pasting, reshaping, rewriting. Really and truthfully the posters from then on, instead of reading "Written & Directed by Glyn Jones" should have read "Written by Christopher Beeching & Glyn Jones." After the opening night at Palmer's Green, what I had fondly thought to be a brilliant idea was immediately cut. Leybourne had a rival who went by the name of "The Great Vance", born Alfred Peck Stevens, later Alfred Glanville, finally The Great Vance. With the success of Leybourne's champagne song, Vance sang one of his own, *"Cliquot Cliquot! That's the wine for me,"* after which they went alternately in song through every alcoholic drink they could think of ending rather lamely with beer and ale. So the idea I came up with was to have two glove puppets, on one hand Leybourne and on the other, Vance; and Chris would sing a medley of the songs delightfully arranged by the musical director, Jeff Clarke. It was greeted by thunderous silence. Another occasion when I wanted to crawl under my seat. It wasn't because of Chris's performance or Jeff's arrangement that it didn't work but because the faces of those damn puppets, handsome as Chris had made them and no matter how they were manipulated, were totally lifeless. All right, Punch and Judy can't change their expressions but Punch and Judy are seen in virtual close-up, as are most puppet shows unless the puppets are fairly large. On holiday in Munich we went to a puppet performance of Mozart's *Il Seraglio* and it was fantastic. If a puppet show is successful, after a few minutes, you have forgotten puppets are what they are. Pinocchio becomes a real boy. We followed this visit with another performance of the same opera a few days later, this time performed by humans and it wasn't nearly as enjoyable because the humans couldn't do what the puppets could. For example, as a puppet, Osmin in his anger would rise high in the air waggling his arms and legs vigorously and it was very funny. Not something any human singer could do. So puppet Vance and puppet Leybourne went into mothballs, never to perform again.

 I knew my brief for James Madison was to direct *The Country Wife* and to take an acting class but I got rather a shock on arrival to find I was also taking a class "Writing For The Media."

Chapter Nineteen

Not only that but the class was full and there were students still hoping to be enrolled. I did take a couple over the limit but felt more than that would be detrimental to the class.

To be honest I have few memories of this class except that it must have been successful or at least acceptable as I was asked to take it a second time when my stay was extended. First time around I had a student; a young man who sat at his desk and hardly said a word. Most of the time he appeared to be glowering at me, now and again shaking his head as though I was talking absolute nonsense. I was certain he spelt trouble so, when it came to an assessment of my work, I was most surprised to hear what he had to say of me. "He's rough and he's tough but absolutely fair and knows what he is talking about. I advise anyone who wants to write to take his class." This about someone who has enough rejections not just to paper the loo but to paper the entire house.

There was a girl with, in my opinion, great talent and the kookiest sense of humour whose writing reflected it. Whenever I had an assignment to mark I would take hers out and put it to one side, knowing that if I became too depressed at what I was reading, I could turn to her submission and have my faith restored. Unfortunately due to some family reason she dropped out of college before the semester ended.

On another occasion a girl presented me with work so abysmal it really did upset me. It was as though everything I had tried to teach her had gone in one ear and out the other. I held out her script and said, 'Do you know what would happen to this mess if you submitted it to anyone?' Pause for effect. 'This is what would happen,' and I threw the piece across the room. 'Straight into the trash can with it. It wouldn't even be read.'

They all trailed out of class at the end and, as I was leaving, I noticed one of the boys, Steven Schwab, was lingering by the door. He stopped me and said, 'Mr Jones, if you don't mind my saying it, I think you're taking this much too seriously.' Much too seriously? Was *he* serious? These kids and their parents were paying good money for an education and he thought I was being too serious? I thanked him for his concern and went on being serious.

One of the first things of which I had to take note is the difference between American English and English English. I believe George Bernard Shaw had something to say about that if I could remember the quote. At the very first class I asked if anyone had a rubber, a request that was greeted with hoots then, as the penny dropped, I said, 'All right, all right, has anybody an eraser?'

On my return visit to JMU in 1988 Professor Tom King invited me to be after dinner speaker at an evening with the Shenandoah Phi Beta Kappa Association, the faculty fraternity. The invitation included the title of my talk, which was "*Words, Words, Words" (Some Amusing Twists of the English Language).*" How I ever had the chutzpah to accept this invitation I'll never know. I had already agreed when I discovered Phi Beta Kappa was the fraternity of academic eggheads and my audience would consist of more doctorates gathered together than could be good for one but there was no backing out.

Also on that return visit, one evening I was crossing the Latimer-Shaeffer car park when a white van pulled up to a screeching halt and a young man leaped out yelling, "Mr Jones! Mr Jones!" Then came a vigorous handshake and, 'You remember me?' To be truthful I didn't but it didn't matter because he went on, 'I heard you were back and I just wanted to thank you.'

'Thank me? What for?'

'Well, first of all for what you gave me in your class and then for your advice to go west. I did, and I'm writing for one of the studios.'

Did I really say, 'Go west young man?' I must have done and the reason for it was that I felt too often academe takes a hold on someone and they can't let go. It isn't enough to have a Bachelor's degree, it has to be a Master's and then maybe even a Doctorate, and then maybe a degree in another discipline, meanwhile time is slipping by and instead of getting out there and starting a career, it seems a metaphorical umbilical cord simply won't be cut.

Now I was invited to extend my stay for another semester, an invitation I jumped at. Money was still something of a problem. It wasn't that the remuneration was miserly but I certainly wasn't earning mega bucks. My contract with the university did not include medical insurance so I was a member of Blue Code/Blue Cross of Virginia, a not inexpensive package; particularly as every month I seemed to get notice of two or three more medical conditions which were suddenly excluded and for everything else they paid 80%. There would also be rent at the Lyndrups, day-by-day living expenses, and expenses back in London. For one thing, although we had downsized moving from Richmond Road to Stoke Newington I had still taken out a £10,000 mortgage that required monthly repayments. In the Spring semester I would again be taking an acting class and repeating the writing class but, before then, there was a break so what was I going to do about Christmas?

We first met Susan Burrell through Andy Leech. They were fellow students at JMU and Susan has remained a friend to this day, popping up every now and again when least expected, like visiting us in London, me in Liverpool, in Harrisonburg, spending a wedding break together in North Carolina and visiting Tangier Island where the natives, (sorry, inhabitants,) still speak (or did then) Elizabethan English when the tourists aren't around, Virginia Beach which was a big disappointment and where in *The Jewish Momma* we weren't sure which of us the waiter fancied he was so tactile with both. Maybe he was like that with everybody. I went down to Richmond specifically to see Susan, or Garrison as she now calls herself, playing in *Educating Rita* and, apart from an excellent performance, was amazed at the accuracy of her Liverpool accent, a whole lot better than mine in *The Liver Birds* I must confess.

In Richmond I saw that wonderful actress Mercedes McCambridge in *Night Mother* by Marsha Norman, a play that won the Pulitzer Prize, a Tony nomination and other awards, God alone knows why because I didn't believe the premise for a single moment. I also saw Susan at The Wayside in *A Christmas Carol* with Allen and Jens Lyndrup playing father and son. Christmas 1984 was spent in Richmond, at

Susan's family home.

Having been thrown in the deep end with my writing class and survived, it seemed in the second semester I was now to be thrown off the high board when Tom King cast me as Dodge in *Buried Child*. This was my American debut. Could I really get to grips with a mid-Western accent? I have never been good with accents but with the help of the cast who corrected me every time I said "record" instead of "rekid" and "been" instead of "bin" I guess I made a passable shot at it. Accents aren't always what one expects. I drove with Cindy Marshall to visit her grandmother in a little village high in the hills that still flew the reb flag and was surprised to hear her say 'tomahtoes' rather than 'tomaytoes.' No one questioned my accent anyway and, in front of my own acting students, I had to give a performance or else… The revue in the campus paper *The Breeze* read

"Glyn Jones is outstanding as the gruff Dodge, a retired farmer in his seventies. Dodge is sick and weak but never without spunk. He continuously growls and argues like a senile recluse but arouses sympathy. The audience cheers as he argues with his dictatorial wife, uses his illness to control his son, and flirts with his grandson's girlfriend."

The revue in the Harrisonburg paper was most flattering:

"Jones Sparks Child" was the headline and the text read, *"The fine acting is highlighted by guest artist Glyn Jones, who portrays the lead of Dodge. From the moment the lights go up, Jones, playing an aging, drinking eccentric, is on stage for the duration. The entire time he plays on his audience by stroking, teasing and manipulating. All the while he is the spoke of the wheel for the rest of the cast. All cues are taken from his awesome presence."*

Not being contracted to do any directing this semester I made a bid for a slot in Wampler to direct Edward Bond's *Narrow Road to the*

Chapter Nineteen

Deep North. The great thing about academic theatre is you can get to do plays you wouldn't stand a chance of directing in the commercial theatre. The policy in Wampler was simple; anyone connected with JMU, though it was mainly students, could do anything they fancied

As Dodge in Buried Child - James Madison University

provided they could justify their reasons and their budget. Reading Bond's play I was intrigued by the young monk with his head stuck in the pot and thought it a shame one couldn't see his reactions as he tried to remove it. Then I thought why not see his reactions? Just get rid of the pot. But if I got rid of the pot I would have to carry the concept through the whole production, even to the sword fight and the loading and firing of a cannon. If nothing else it would give the kids good practice in mime so that was what we did. There were no props, no set, There was a simple circle marked out on the floor and a long curtain down one wall open at one end which served for entrances and exits and from behind which the sound team covered the mime when needed, for example during the sword fight, every time the nonexistent blades clashed, two boys behind the curtain produced the sound with metal bars. As with puppets, after the first few minutes of bewilderment, the audience became totally absorbed in what was going on. I was truly delighted with the result.

Letters From America.

20th August 1984

The McConkys *(Don McConkey and his wife, Martha-Ann. Don was Dean of The Department of Communications which included theatre)* were on holiday in West Virginia last week so god knows how I would have got to Harrisonburg if Andy hadn't brought me down. I don't know where Tom got it from that they were going to come up to Washington to pick me up. Martha-Ann certainly knew nothing about it when I called from N.Y. I haven't met Susan Senter yet but the other girl in the house is Cindy Marshall. Yesterday she made me drive Tom's car (which is automatic) and we went to the pool for a swim. Then, last evening, she went off to the beach for a couple of days so I have the house to myself. I'm getting used to driving here [on the wrong side of the road] and the car being automatic helps.

I only went to the theatre once in N.Y. to see *"Brighton Beach Memoirs"* which I enjoyed, though not as much as I thought I would. Wish I'd seen the original cast. Andy took me to Dinner Theatre to see *"Best Little Whorehouse In Texas"* which was fun and, in Washington at The Source Theatre; we saw a new play called *"River Rats"* which was TERRIBLE!!! *[I sent a programme back to England across the front of which I had written "Terrible–ghastly–too awful for words. Terrible script, bad bad direction, hideous performances." One of my future students Ramsey Midwood was in it.]* We also saw the film of *"Another Country"* so if you speak to Michael Jenn, tell him I saw him in Washington. He has a nice part, better than he led me to believe. One of my ex-RADA's was also in it. I can't believe I've only been away not quite twelve days–it seems an eternity. I'll have to tell you more in my next letter. Stay well and happy. Hope the problems aren't mounting. Wish I could be Champagne Charleying with you. Love to our Dave and the girls and you.

Always… Meece. [Nickname].

21st August.1984

I suppose I really should have started at the beginning when I wrote before but it would have taken too long so here's some more. First the flight was A.O.K. Anne met me at Newark Airport. Their house is on a new estate which is still being built so we were surrounded by Kake book construction workers all beavering away in their tin hats, boots, and shorts! "Hi, there, how are you today?" 'All the better for seeing you.'

They also have a very dolly son of 21, home from Cambridge for the vac, a sort of cross between James Dean and Robin Farnham and with all the charm in the world.

[John and Anne Laughton were friends from Durban days. John and his younger brother, Harold, lived with their parents in a huge house near Mitchell Park (virtually opposite the zoo) where they were expected to dress for meals, collar and tie and jacket, and call their father "sir". Anne also came from a well off family. Once I left Durban we lost touch but I had heard she and John were married. Then, one evening Chris and I went to a concert at the Festival Hall and in the interval we were leaving the auditorium, turning right to go out when, for no reason at all, I suddenly turned back to go out the opposite side and, in doing so, passed John sitting in the first row above the aisle. Was that intuition or coincidence? He and Anne were living in Hull at the time and I visited them there before John was transferred to the states and they were living in New Jersey.]

Friday Anne had more English visitors to meet at Newark so I took the airport bus into N.Y. and so to Lionel and Paul's. What a downer! Sadie, Lionel's mother, who is 86 or 91 or something had fallen and broken her hip and Lionel is doing the full Jewish angst "what a lousy son I've been" bit, living on tranquillisers and looking 86 or 91 or something himself. So the pair of them are like a couple of very soggy rags. It was no fun though I did my best to cheer them up. Jeff wasn't answering his phone and when I finally got him I found out why–he and Chuck had just split up and he was doing the full Jewish bit on losing his lover. Oi vay! On my life! So I did my best to cheer him up. Fortunately Len [Calder] was a lot more fun (although he and his lover are also splitting up but that is taking a long time so, unlike Jeff, he is getting used to it.) We had a very pleasant lunch and he is beavering away trying to get *Red in the Morning* on. They have already had a reading! I had a lunch at The Gaiety, the deli with that wonderful Ethel Merman type waitress where you and I went. Also called in on Janice Fishbein, my Brooklyn Jewish agent and her associate, an elderly skinny queen in shorts named Wendell would you believe? No, not the shorts, the queen–split infinitives again. So I packed my bags and took a New York Air Shuttle from La Gaurdia to Washington where Andy was waiting for me. At least he was smiling and happy. And so to Gaithersburg and the next instalment. Will Andy stay smiling and happy? Stay tuned in to this channel, folks for your next episode of "CAMPBELL STREET" Your favourite soap. In the meantime, "Have a good day, you hear?"

27th August 1984

Episode 3 of "Campbell Street"–Your favourite soap.

Two days of meetings. First the new faculty "orientation" meeting: forty odd new members all introduced individually; all Masters and Doctors with a string of academic qualifications behind their names. "What," I thought, "is Doctor Rex Fuller going to say about me when it comes to my turn?" Well, he did pretty well boosting my reputation beyond its natural limits. Then full faculty meeting, more introductions, and more speeches. Then school meeting (Fine Arts and Communications) and more introductions. Then department

Chapter Nineteen

meeting (Communications). Then finally section meeting (theatre). In the evening the President's "pig-roast", eaties, drinkies, and dancies at the Convocation Centre. The McConky's picked me up for that and, afterwards, I went to their house for a quiet drink and a chat. They already want me to skip a class ("Oh, send them to the library") so they can take me to Washington for a day and show me around. More orientation in other words. Very nice of them though. Next Saturday they're taking me to my first football match of the season and afterwards to the "Newcomers" party, and if all this sounds as if I haven't been working I assure you such is not the case. Have sorted out my (Tom's) office, written out the syllabus for the acting class and have done more reading in a week than in years. Registration is Monday and classes start on Tuesday. I have one class a day, five days a week. M.W.F. scriptwriting. T. Th. acting. "*The Country Wife*" is scheduled for November 13 – 18th. Having my first meeting about that on Monday. Did a lot of work on it while I was at Andy's. He is still having trouble with his legs and going to therapy twice a week, Rehearsals for the tour of "*Seven Brides*" start in about a week's time. I hope he is ready for them or he is going to be one very disappointed boy. It is a nationwide tour so he is going to see a whole lot of country, right across to the West Coast. A lot of people keep asking how you are and what you're doing so you are a well-remembered person. I'll have to tell you about Andy's ménage in another episode. Do you remember the third act of "*Torch Song Trilogy*"? The rabbits? Well with them it's bears! The enclosed is my first fortune cookie in the states. [Temptation awaits you] Too true–it keeps appearing and disappearing, like the blonde, blue-blue-eyed beauty that came to mow the lawn today. Oh, my gawd! Kniption time. Big bucks! Big bucks! No whammies! [TV game show, Wheel of Fortune?] Su Burrell is coming up from North Carolina tomorrow to stay a couple of days. Stay well and happy and love to all. That's it, a wrap for today.

4th September 1984

Where do I start? I meant to bring my diary to the office so I wouldn't forget anything, but forgot. So, first of all, Su spent a couple of days here, which was great. She wanted to see a lot of people of course so threw a tea party at the house and among the guests was William who came up from Houston. He's still working in the Opera House down there. Anyway, I have sent him back to Houston with strict instructions to get a good theatre company started and I will come down and be its first artistic director. He said he'd talk to his sister who is down there and evidently a fundraiser. I meant to write to you yesterday but my writing students handed in their first attempts after class and I spent the rest of the day assessing them ready to talk tomorrow. Final analysis of their work 2 A's (Exceptional), 4 B's (Excellent), 7 C's (Very good), 5 D's (Average), 3 F's (Fail). The three F's are only because those three didn't submit anything so fail the buggers. The writing class is now 26 and the acting 15. Oh, by the way, Houston is only an hour away from Galveston so that's pretty close. *[I once had a crazy idea that I'd like to live in Galveston]* It is one of the top (richest) cities in the states and, after the opera, has no theatre, just little not very good (according to William) struggling fringe or off-off-Broadway type companies. Which is why I told him, now is the time to do something about it. Today I got my assistant director/stage manager for "*The Country Wife*", Greg O'Donnell who is really on the ball. Within five minutes he was arranging audition notices, audition times, audition rooms, etc., so, after days of nebulous nothings, everything suddenly started to happen.

Before I forget, would you call up Paul Day and ask him to extend my insurance cover please? It seems to be cheaper from that side than this at the moment and the way we have worked things out money wise I won't be covered by what they call "workmen's compensation" as I won't be paying US Social Security. The university will pay me an "Honorarium"–that is a professional fee, the full amount with no deductions. I suggest we make the insurance till the end of December. Now, if I don't get this up to the campus post office together with your parcel I'll never get it off today. Also I want to get up to the library, not that there's any hurry for that. It stays open till midnight seven

Chapter Nineteen

days a week and, I am told, till 2 am during exam time. Can you imagine English libraries doing that? This place never ceases to amaze me. I wish you could have been with me during the football game. It doesn't seem right having all these experiences and not sharing them. Miss you, miss Dave, miss home, miss the girls but am having a marvellous time.

25th September 1984

Here I am at last with a real letter. I've forgotten what episode we're on but then so much has happened. I've cast *"The Country Wife"* and am pretty pleased though had to disappoint a whole lot of kids in the process, which I suppose was inevitable. Will start rehearsals next week as soon as I get my ground plan from Allen. Within five minutes of sitting in my office Greg had my whole life organised–as far as the play is concerned that is. Sad news about Andy, his legs are a complete mess and he has lost the tour of *Seven Brides*. He has had to take a job in a shop and the doctor has told him he shouldn't even drive for six months let alone dance. I was told all this last night by his old friend John who I bumped into at a rehearsal for *Waiting*. This is a new musical written by a girl student and is a student production in Wampler (the converted turkey shed). The *Virginia Woolf* I saw on Friday was also a student production and I was very very impressed with what they did with it considering the average age is about nineteen, including the director. Unfortunately most of my cast are in *Waiting* or *Crimes of the Heart* so I am having a difficult time getting a rehearsal schedule together.

Skyline Drive is where we went for the picnic on Sunday and it was wonderful. Also the Sunday before Cindy and I drove out to TUTTLE & SPICE. The museum was fascinating. You would love it with all the Victoriana. The shop itself is tourist and the fudge a horrible disappointment as well as being expensive. In fact anything with sugar is expensive in the states: candies, chocolate, jams, cakes, bread (£1.30 a loaf?), biscuits–sorry, cookies. After TUTTLE & SPICE we went to New Market and had lunch in a "diner". Actually it was named "The Battleground Restaurant" but it was a diner–meat loaf and potato salad. It was good though. Then, me being me, I discovered an antique shop and we went in for a browse. I bought you a cravat pin and Cindy can bring it over when she comes. Wednesday last the McConkeys walked me off my feet in Washington, especially Martha Ann. She's like you and goes for it hell for leather. *[It says something considering in Leeds I walked a sixteen-year-old John Tabert off his feet and in Paris did the same thing to a young Dave]* Washington is beautiful and we had a really great day but more of that another time, as I have to go to my costume class in a minute. Did I tell you I'm sitting in on Pam's costume class? It's fascinating. We've done the Sumerians, Egyptians, Cretans, and we're now on the Greeks. She's doing the costumes for *The Country Wife* and I had a session with her yesterday afternoon on wigs and costumes. She has some great ideas and a wonderful capacity for detail. She's not satisfied until she's gone into colour psychology, complimenting colours, dissenting colours, etc. For Horner she wants to give him a wig with a phallus hanging down the back. That is the hair tied like a prick, so we've come up with this idea that we will wire it, then before he goes into the closet to fuck Lady Fidget it will be standing up and when he comes out it will be drooping. I am going to be very naughty with this production–don't tell Tom.

26th Continued.

Yesterday afternoon Cindy and I drove down to her parents' place for dinner and we drove through the Appalachian Mountains. It is indescribably beautiful. We drove up Mount Shenandoah playing *CATS* on the cassette player. Can you imagine that combination? Williamsville, which is where her home is, consists of a church, two stores and about four houses. The night before I was watching Public Television, a programme called POPS with the Boston Symphony. John Williams was conducting and, in the programme was–guess what? Of course, *ET*. Then, after POPS, they transmitted the film of *La Clemenza Da Tito*, based on the Stuttgart production so I had a

Chapter Nineteen

real feast of music. Fortunately the JMU radio station plays a whole heap of classical music, especially in the morning, so it is almost as good as having the Third Programme…sorry, Radio Three.

27th Continued.

I WILL get this letter finished. I got that far yesterday and then remembered there was a theatre meeting at three o'clock. By the way, it is by no means certain that I am going to do a second semester here. It is a question of them finding the money to pay me and they are trying to sort it out at the moment. Please don't be upset. I am doing my best to share it all with you. Last night I went to a run-thru of *Crimes of the Heart*, the first main stage production and, I am afraid, it is too awful for words. I'm afraid everyone knows it is too awful for words but, boy, am I going to have to be diplomatic today. Also yesterday one of the girls in my class asked me if I had written a play "Champagne Something" because she had just had a letter from a friend of hers on the London semester saying it was "just great!" I have also had a letter from Michael Sawyer, Lionel and Paul's playwright friend in New York, giving me the names of three agents who could be interested in it. The other idea I had was to write an article on it and try and get Ezra to publish it in DRAMATICS.

If you see Tom and Kay tell them everything in the house is fine. You would love Cindy and Susan, the two girls in the house. They are both great fun and hysteria reigns supreme. Dave would especially love Susan: small, slender, twenty-four and beautiful. Unfortunately for Dave she is getting married next year to another Dave she has been seeing for seven years. She's a real doll. "How can you be a good ole Virginny boy, Gleeyun, if yew all doan like tomaytoes?" I tell you, they grow tomatoes in this state the size of balloons and eat them non-stop. Cindy has hysterics every time I pronounce "ate" as "et". Since starting this letter have gone [in Pam's class] from the Greeks to the Romans and are now in the Dark Ages. The weather has gone from the eighties down to the fifties and suddenly today everyone has appeared in sweaters. Some of the northern states have had up to fifteen inches of snow and, although it isn't cold indoors, the wind is chilly so maybe it's a comin offin that thar snow. Oh, I meant to tell you, up on The Blue Ridge, although the trees are only just beginning to turn, the blueberry bushes (I picked and et wild blueberries) have to be seen–every colour from dark green to pale green to cream to yellow to orange, pink, scarlet burgundy and purple. Amazing! Talk about Joseph and his dreamcoat!

PS: Don't be unkind to Bella. She's a very loving dog and it's not her fault she can't get her act together.

6th November 1984

Dear Richard [?]

At last I've actually got some spare time to sit down and write a letter instead of merely sending you postcards. *[Just around the corner from the Harrisonburg post office was (is?) a little shop specialising in coins, stamps, and period postcards, wonderful early Americana and Victoriana: 19th century city scenes, vistas. Valentines, Christmas, Easter, birthday cards, cartoons; and I was constantly buying them quite cheaply to send to people.]* I'm glad your meticulously researched show went so well. Sorry the audiences were lousy. Still, as co-writer you must have been pleased, especially being so clever as to leave "*Champagne Charlie*" right to the end. I wonder who directed it! Only kidding. The tape is lovely. Hugely enjoy the play-in music, especially with my favourites clumped together. *Ting Ting* might be a silly song lyric-wise but that melody is so haunting, especially the way it is played. Presumably it is Jeff on joanna. When the other tape arrives I'll listen carefully to the opening and see what I can do with it though, as co-writer, I don't know whether I really dare. Do I? Played the first bit of the Strauss *[Memories of Covent Garden by Johann Strauss the younger, which includes snippets of Leybourne songs, Champagne Charlie of course, Flying Trapeze, The Mousetrap Man and Sweet Isabella]* to Andy over the phone. "It's *Champagne Charlie* and I've only heard it once!" He said. He was going to come down this weekend but got an audition for *Baby* at a local dinner

Chapter Nineteen

theatre and has a recall for Saturday, although he thinks the show is pretty much precast. He was going to come with Susan and me to the Wayside to see Anne Lyndrup in *The Gin Game* so had to go without him. Had a fantastic meal in The Wayside Inn, very old and full of antiques and obviously very popular. Waitresses in 18th Century costume (Laura Ashley by courtesy of). Su had turbot steak and I had game pie (venison, pheasant, quail, guinea fowl etc.,) and a bottle of Piesporter. And, before you yell blue murder, it was my first time out in weeks and my first expensive time out since I got here. The show was v. good. Anne was lovely. How glad I was to be able to say it. Ed greeted me like a long lost friend so hopefully he's thinking of me for the summer. The Americans still like me and guess what? They spell my name write. (*sic*) At the moment, for *The Country Wife*, I am billed as Glyn Jones of London–makes me sound like a department store. The theatre ticket at The Wayside included sweet and coffee and I had a Boston cream pie which was delicious, just a very light sponge with cream filling and the thinnest layer of chocolate on top. The kids here eat so badly. They get up in the morning and the first thing they do is reach into the fridge for a coke. They come to rehearsals with packets of carbo rubbish such as you wouldn't believe and one of their favourites is something called "moon pie" which looks so revolting I haven't even asked what's in it.

The cold weather has arrived but the sky is cloudless and the sun shining brilliantly. I've had to go out and buy a pair of sunglasses. I told you, didn't I, that I lost my glasses in the costume shop at Virginia University? They haven't come to light yet and I suppose soon I ought to do something about it. We went to see the film of *The Dresser* on campus the other night. Finney gives a wonderful performance. I couldn't believe it. *[Unlike everyone else who saw the young Finney fresh out of drama school playing "Billy Liar" I did not rate his performance in the least, feeling it was no more than a big bundle of drama school tricks. But that was then and this was now. At that performance of "Billy Liar" I gave Chris a little mascot mouse and, when he was in "Gone with the Wind", a little mouse dressed as a reb and, waving his carbine. 'We're going to fight the Yankees!' And that is how I came to be called Meece.]* It isn't as funny as it was in the theatre [getting back to *The Dresser*] but takes on a whole different dimension, which is understandable if you compare Finney with Freddy Jones. It's a lovely film and you should see it. Because of all the theatre stories I've been telling my kids in class–including how I saw Wolfitt's *Lear*, they went to see it and couldn't stop talking about it. Must go now. Promised to drop over to the costume shop. They're all totally amazed over there. They've never had a director who not only takes an avid interest in what they're doing but who will actually discuss style and colour with them and come up with ideas. So far, so good.

You had best give this letter to Hyst Mum to read. I just haven't had time to write to her properly.

12th November 1984

Dear Dave,

Where does time fly to? I can't believe we're almost into the middle of the month. Anyway, I'm in my office and I've a few minutes to myself and don't feel like work (are you surprised?) so here is that long awaited reply to your letter. Had to get up extra early this morning as one of the English professors asked me to talk to her class before they all came to the play. I hate getting up early. Got to do it again Wednesday, only even earlier, as I have to go to Strasburg to talk to a High School and Strasburg's about an hour's drive away. They expect me there for eight which means getting up at six. It's okay for you bus drivers, you're used to it. How are the buses by the way?

Like I said, I didn't think this letter would get finished yesterday so here I am again taking another shot at it. Dress rehearsal last night went okay except for a couple of stage management fuck-ups. They can be an undisciplined lot sometimes. You wouldn't believe how casual everything is, though underneath the casualness they can be like spoilt babies and their quicks get hurt faster than you can say cock Rubenstein. I couldn't believe it, yesterday during my writing

Chapter Nineteen

class I criticised one guy's script and read out to the class how I would have written it. Now this guy is one of my favourite students, a great big hulk built like the side of two shithouses but, when I came out of class, he was standing in the hall and, would you credit it, almost in tears? The thing is he is good, he can write, but he was upset because my script was so much an improvement on his. "But, Dave," I said (yes, his name is Dave) 'that's what I'm here for and, anyway, I've had thirty years more experience than you.'

"Well I just hope … sniff sniff … that I can learn."

"That's what I'm here for, Dave."

"Yea …well… sniff sniff" Exit slouching down corridor… sniff sniff. "Come on, Dave," I said, 'I'll buy you a beer.'

"Yeah… sniff sniff."

I've got another one, Patti, a real kook but, boy, can this little girl write. She's terrific. The first couple of scripts she handed in were written by P. Hayden. Then it became Patti Hayden. The last one I note was written by Patterson Hayden and her name's not even Patti. This girl just can't stop inventing. The class for next semester is booked full and I have gone five over. That is IT. No more! I am not going to listen to one more sob story as to why they just HAVE to take my class. Sorry.

Wednesday.

Okay, I'll really get it finished now. Just got back from Strasburg. The drive was lovely. The trees haven't lost their leaves yet and are still all the colours you can think of so, instead of heading back down Interstate 81, I took Route 11 and then 42 through the hills and it was beautiful. Now all I want to do is go to bed and sleep. *The Country Wife* went very well and everyone is saying nice things so that's okay. Chris's (your) first night greetings arrived in time–right on the day in fact. One nice thing about writing letters here is that, if you've got the right postage, you don't have to go to a pillarbox or post office as the postman picks up the mail as he delivers it. Isn't that great? You just leave the outgoing mail in your letterbox with the flag up.

No Official Umbrella

Andy and family are coming down from Washington this evening to see the show.

> Next letter to Hyst Mum.
> 24th November 1984

Here I am, letter time–not that I've run out of postcards but I thought you might like something a little longer for a change. Can't believe it is almost December and the semester has only three weeks to go. Good grief! Do you know what's just started on the radio? The recording used in *LOVERS DANCING*. Small old world. Memories of St Martins Lane in the wet, catching the number 6 every night.

I spent Thanksgiving with a poor black family and you've never seen so many kids in one small room, kids of every hue and screech. We played Trivial Pursuit (I came second), and had the obligatory turkey, sweet potatoes, corn pudding etc., followed by pumpkin or mince pie and I will tell my writing class on Monday all about the new characters I've found. There are only five more writing classes left, and six acting. Next semester I am doing the writing course again and "Experimental Theatre" whatever that may mean. Actually I'll use it to start rehearsals on the Edward Bond play. I never thought I would ever get the opportunity to direct *Narrow Road* especially the way I want to do it, all in mime. They're going to have to sword fight without swords, load and fire a cannon without a cannon. Should be interesting, no? Did I also tell you I am making my American acting debut playing Dodge in Sam Shepherd's *Buried Child?* There's laying your neck on the chopping block, playing an American in an American play with an American cast in front of an American audience. Think I'll get away with it? Oh, I knew about the black family before I got there by the way because from June's (Tom's secretary) kids I knew she was married to a black. I didn't know though that she had a black foster mother, a most charming woman.

Andy got an ensemble part in *Baby* and is covering one of the leads. I'm so glad as I think he was getting pretty mizz not working, though putting a brave face on it. He came down with his folks to see

Chapter Nineteen

The Country Wife and I didn't think he enjoyed it much as he seemed noncommittal, but I had a letter from him Wednesday saying, "I just wanted to write and tell you how very much I enjoyed the show the other night, I've seen very few shows at JMU where every actor seemed to understand his lines, others lines, and the point of the show and then communicated all of that to the audience. I think I heard every line–no small compliment. I really enjoyed the show and was so glad to have gotten down to see it." So there, I was worried for nothing. I'd have been most disappointed if he hadn't liked it, as it was his yellow socks that got me here. I had dinner last night with John Lee and Robin (Haigh) and told them that story. They pee'd themselves.

Allen and I had a long meeting Wednesday to discuss *Champagne Charlie*. He thinks we should go ahead on our own [without an agent] and cover colleges and universities in Virginia, Maryland, West Virginia and North Carolina. He is trying to find out whether it is possible to get grant aid from various Virginian institutions and I am trying to put together a brochure. We are in a magazine called "*SING OUT–The Folk Song Magazine.*" Chris Simmons did an article on British Music Hall, which included naturally enough a piece on Leybourne and "*The Tailor and The Crow.*" (Thanks to Chris Beeching and Glyn Jones for providing a copy of the original sheet music from which the following transcription was made.) He also sent a videotape of his last bill, which isn't bad all things considering, except for the chairman who is so laid back he's almost not there. *[This is sometimes known sarcastically as "telephoning in your performance"]* Interesting to see Chris himself doing ROLLICKING RAMS and the audience certainly seemed to join in. I'll send the tape over with Cindy. She flies to London on Monday and can't contain her excitement. Here is a list of things for her to bring back

- Half a dozen copies of *BEAUTIFUL FOR EVER*. There are a lot of all-women colleges around. I enclose a letter to Samuel French.
- 2 copies, if poss, of *HEAR THE HYENA LAUGH*.
- *CHAMPAGNE CHARLIE.*

- My white address book—make sure it's got Laurence's new address in it, also Robert Alge's. You'll find it in the personal correspondence file.
- A copy of a play called *BETWEEN TWO SIGHS*. I want to look at it (it's very old) and see if I can rewrite it for America. (Up on the shelf. Brown cover.)

The enclosed photograph is of Harcourt, Horner, and Dorilant rehearsing. Greg is the one who stands like a dancer. He leaves at the end of the semester. I was thinking he might make a good understudy for Leybourne, no? This is a problem. I can't see us undertaking a long tour over here (presuming we do) without understudies–too much at stake. I am also joining an organisation called The Alliance of Resident Theatres/New York. It only costs $30 and, if we try to go off-Broadway, being a member will be very useful. Hope Ezra publishes the article. That will be a great help.

8th January 1985

My first letter to you in 1985 Happy New Year. Here are some more photos. The pictures of Williamsburg were taken last year when I went down with Mitzi. We went down again after Christmas and you wouldn't have believed it! 75 degrees and people walking around in shorts and shirtsleeves. First of all we went down to Hogs Island, a nature reserve. The Burrell's are keen on birds and are great conservationists. We then took the ferry across to James Town, the first settlement, had a picnic lunch before going on to Williamsburg because Mel (Sue's dad) wanted to see the Christmas decorations, the traditional decorations made with greenery, pine needles, cones, fruit, berries, and nuts. We also watched the lowering of the colours (Union Jack) and beating the retreat with the drum and fife band, all local kids and very good too, playing French, German, English and Scottish military music of the 17th and 18th centuries. Sue's family, friends, and neighbours couldn't have been nicer, more welcoming or hospitable if they tried which is why I was there for ten days. They

Chapter Nineteen

wouldn't let me go. Their best friends are a gay couple, Roger and Bob who have a large house and yacht on the tidewater. *[During the course of the conversation at Roger and Bob's I kept on hearing references to the "Mary Yacht" and wondered to whom that belonged until I realised they were talking about the "Marriott Hotel".]*

Had lunch with Sue and a friend of hers, Alis in a restaurant called "Bus Stop" and who should walk in but Greg, my assistant on *"The Country Wife"*. Well! I nearly slid under the table. He had shaved off his moustache and here was this pretty pretty boy. All I can say is, just as well he had his moustache while we were working together and I was too stupid to see beyond it.

Oh, I didn't tell you, I'd got the Burrell's a couple of bottles of champagne and Pat (Su's mum) decided to make sure they were chilled so put them in the freezer. When we came to open them–well! Have you ever seen a champagne bottle having a slow shit? We had hysterics as half frozen champagne oozed slowly out. Then the second one, after it had had its slow shit, suddenly went berserk and champagne spurted everywhere, a good half bottle of it. By this time we were in agony from laughing so much.

Andy and Kenny gave me for Christmas a pair of slippers. Each slipper is a pooch with huge eyes and wearing a pink and white nightcap. They are the size of boats. You put your feet in the bodies and the eyes look up at you. Definitely the campest present I've ever had. Kirk gave Addy *[Andy's parents]* a train set for Christmas. She's always wanted a train set! Cindy gave me teas and a bottle of Fanny & Mary's *[Fortnum and Mason]* whiskey marmalade. The Burrells gave me home made jam and crackers, and Susan gave me an antique smoking jacket from the thrift store.

Allen's been talking about *Mazeppa* most of the evening, *[production at Sadler's Wells]* apart from how absolutely wonderful you both are and what a fabulous time they've had.

Please check with the bank that the draft for $1,100 I sent before Christmas has arrived. After all the trouble with the last one, which arrived AFTER I put a stop to it, (what a mess!) this one was sent registered. *[When the previous draft didn't arrive and I reported it at the post office I was told they had to wait 60 days before instigating any enquiry.]*

16th January 1985

Here you are then, firstly your money to come over to the good ole US of A. Secondly some money for Her Majesty, Betty Guelf. *[Income Tax]* Please put in a covering note saying it is "on account." You will find the relevant crap in my correspondence tray–I think. Will you see that the bank gets its share, and the cheque is for the house insurance. The Bloom County I just had to send you. I showed it to the girls in the bank and they all shrieked. I didn't tell you my branch has a completely female staff. Boy, the Dominion is the unstuffiest bank ever. Wish the Midland was as much fun.

We go down to Tampa, Florida on March 6th and come back about the 11th. Flying down and coming back in the van with the students. I want to see the DEEP south. Semester started again this week. First week is a bit draining, getting into the swing again, meeting new students. Tom is still disorientated and Kay has nerve ends sticking out of every pore. Today was thirteen degrees Fahrenheit but beautiful. The air is so clear every twig on every tree stands out and the sky is a bright bright cloudless blue. Not tomorrow though. Tomorrow snow is forecast, up to three inches.

Chapter Twenty

More Letters From America.

20th January 1985

Sunday Night Brrrrrrr!
Just got back from Pam and Mike Johnson's. They had a "Super Bowl" party–San Francisco 49'ers beat the Miami Dolphins (football) 32–16. The half-time show had to be seen to be believed it was so awful. Very big and very tacky. The JMU marching band was going to play in Washington tomorrow for the Presidential Inauguration but the parade has been cancelled. Ronald Carrier *[President of JMU]* must be grinding his teeth. And that's the reason for this letter heading–it's 15º below, which means it's 47º below freezing (F) and the wind-chill factor (only the Americans would go in for a wind-chill factor) is -60º and THAT is COLD! In this dry cold weather I've been building up static like Frankenstein's monster, so much so that yesterday I even got a shock when I touched the handle of the car door. So Carrie has given me her humidifier to put in my room. Allen suggested I had to walk about with a wire hanging down my trouser leg but I told him I already had that. It's not funny though, switching on a light and jumping at the same time, you can even see the blue spark from switch to finger, and when I take off my clothes at night they all jump right back on me, making sizzling noises.

Ekharts (a drugstore) are doing a special deal on 8 × 10's at $2 a print so I took a whole load of negs out there yesterday. It will still cost a small fortune but at $2 each who could turn it down? I didn't. Don't know why I'm writing this. It's way past bedtime and I've got an early class tomorrow.

16th February 1985

Saturday morning.

Allen has this MARVELLOUS typewriter. A Smith-Corona, the best ever–so here's a letter on it. I'm off to rehearsal in a minute. Rehearsal? I haven't yet had a full cast for a single rehearsal. There's so much going on: *J.C. Superstar, Five & Dime Jimmy Dean, Death of a Salesman,* DANCE CONCERTS, ILLNESS, GOING HOME FOR THE WEEK-END, A CAR SMASH (No one badly hurt fortunately) I think someone behind my back has been quoting the Scottish play. If I were the RSC the production would be postponed for a month but for me it's going to go on come hell or high water. We go up on Thursday. Yesterday I finally got a stage manager and board operator. Still haven't got FOH[24] manager. Haven't got any of my recorded sound effects–music, cannon, gunshots, etc. Tom Arthur can't learn his lines so I am learning them in case I have to take over his part at the last minute ... want any more?

Jessica, Pam Johnson's little girl and my very favourite child, has speech problems. At the moment she's having problems with her S's and T's. Her dad (Mike) has just bought a new truck so she told everyone at school "My daddy's got a big new blue fuck." So Mike spent half a night teaching her to say "van". Jessica went to school and told everyone, "My daddy's got a big new blue fuck van." Thought that would amuse you.

It's still very cold here but there is a smell of spring in the air. Should be much warmer by the time you arrive. Andy called last night and got very excited to hear you were coming. Did I tell you he's in a production of *Baby* at a dinner theatre in Maryland? He's not doing very much, chorus and covering, but he's really happy to be working and the legs seem to be holding up. He immediately said (when he

---
24 Front of house.

heard the news) that he would get someone to let him play one night so we could go and see him do something worthwhile.

There's no problem about meeting you. When I told Al the time of your arrival he immediately said, "Oh, good, we can go up for the day and play." Al likes playing. They got their tape recorder. I gave them five months rent in one lump sum, oh, wow! So they could afford it. Now its. "Just going up the mall to get a video."

And I must go to my rehearsal. Time's caught up with me. Hope your telly's going well. Love to Dave and the girls. Stay well–Oh, fuck! I still haven't written to Hyst Mum! Will do it tomorrow.

17th February 1985

Sunday Eve.

Just been watching *"Jewel in the Crown,"* the episode where old Mrs Leighton (Fabia Drake) dies. I'd forgotten they used *"Champagne Charlie"* in it so imagine my surprise when Barbie suddenly came out with "I've seen a deal of gaiety throughout my noisy life." When Allen got back from London all he sang was *Champagne Charlie*. and, if he started another number, it usually ended up as *Champagne Charlie*. Unfortunately he missed this week's episode of "Jewel" as he only got back from yet another theatre conference in Florida late this afternoon and went to bed early, so Anne and I watched it. Had a terrific snowfall the other night, about 4 inches. Made a snowman in the back yard and Jens gave him a carrot nose and cookie eyes but they kept falling out.

Rehearsals for *"Narrow Road"* are under way but I need another 3 or 4 boy bodies. I lost 5 in my class to *"J.C. Superstar"* and more to *"Five & Dime Jimmy Dean,"* mostly girls so that didn't matter but I miss the boys and have to look for them elsewhere. Have just finished going through the first assignments of the new writing class. I think there are some quite talented kids there, more so than last year, and they're much keener. I get to class at 5 to 10 and they're all sitting there, pens at the ready. It's a bit unnerving. It's great having my office in Lincoln House (the costume shop) more fun than Wampler. Have ordered a tape of "Seven Samurai" for both my classes to look at, especially the actors for "*Narrow Road*." They're handling the mime quite well but have no sense of style–yet.

As soon as I get my next pay cheque I'll send you a bank draft and you'll come over March/April. Fuck the problems; I'm bored with problems, I've spent my life worrying and trying to sort out problems. At the moment Allen and Anne are having the same sort of thing. They borrowed to go on their trip. Had a lovely lunch yesterday at a place called The Edinburgh Mill. Ed Steele took us and it looks like I'll be doing Wayside this summer, all things being equal. Sorry, Tom![25] Wayside will be much harder work but much more interesting.

Okay, so cheer up now and look forward to your holiday. You will disappoint a lot of people here if you don't come.

Chris came over, arriving at Dulles Airport on March 13th so once again, in between classes and rehearsals and invitations to luncheons and dinners, I became a tourist, showing him places I had written about: Tuttle & Spice, The Edinburgh Mill, Shenandoah Caverns, the Monterey Maple Fair. I took him to see The Wayside Theatre and we went down to Richmond with Allen to visit a high school, during which we came across a cast of kids rehearsing an Agatha Christie. I stuck my nose in (at their invitation) and gave direction for ten or fifteen minutes which left them shrieking "Don't go! Don't go!" when our host tapped his watch and said it was time to leave. We saw a student production in Wampler of *Death of a Salesman* and we visited George and Margaret Black in Charlottesville. At the university, George gave Chris a lesson in prosthetics, the making of a false nose for George Leybourne. Of course we had to have lunch at Ma Thomas's and spent the last day in Washington before I drove him back to Dulles for his flight home. Four days later I was back there, this time to meet Dave.

---

25 Tom Arthur was directing JMU Dinner Theatre for which I obviously was not going to be available, as he had hoped.

Chapter Twenty

18th April 1985

Oh, boy! The temperature is 89 and the sky is high, wide, and handsome, so they have all come out–everywhere! I've got twenty minutes before I have to leave for rehearsal so thought I would drop you a line. I suggested a game of tennis this morning and, after three strokes, my arm just seized up. Think I wrenched a muscle. It's very painful. Very. So I went to visit Gray who is sick with a strep throat, but didn't stay long. He missed rehearsal last night and it doesn't look as if he'll be there tonight *[He was playing Jesus in J.C.Superstar]* I told him if he didn't feel like doing his tutorial tomorrow to just forget it. The Lyndrups and Dave have gone out to dinner at another faculty member's house so there's just me and Ophelia (who has really got absurd) and Maisie. *[Two cats]*

Dave's been getting on well with everyone though some of the acting class were disappointed because, when he first walked in, they thought for a second or two you had come back, or so they told me. He is totally unimpressed with the beautiful Linda. Anne is getting Page (remember her? Babysitter?) to take Dave in hand–or something–so I will probably have time to start on Act 2 of *"Champagne Charlie."*

Friday–Boy, did I sweat in that theatre last night! As Allen would say, "we're talkin' heat here, boy." And today it is 91. They're on the rooftops and leaping all over the lawns, playing in the sprinklers. Gray called to say he was too tired and sick to do his tutorial which was fine by me because I was too hot and really didn't feel like it anyway. So I sent off some more Champagne Charlies and called it a day.

[I mailed over 300 brochures to colleges and universities across the states and received three replies: two saying thank you but no, and one from a Catholic college in Washington DC saying they would love to have the show but regretfully couldn't afford it.]

I'm sorry you're on your own to try sorting out the mess and I really wish I could do something about it but I've tried to sort out the mess for so long I'm a weary of it. Closed–I am tired too.

Jessica came to a bit of the rehearsal last night *[At that time she was the most adorable wide-eyed child with a smile that would make the angels weep, particularly in view of the pain that poor kid suffered. I believe because of a missing chromosome, or something like that, Jess was forever in and out of hospital and it broke my heart one day to hear her say, 'Please, no more needles.' She called me Ben, later it became Blin and she believed I lived in the middle of the world]* but got very upset at Dodge's coughing. "Ben's sick! Ben's sick!" Pam reassured her but she went home and told Brooke *[her sister]* "Ben's a mean, sick man." Unfortunately Jessica is sick herself today with her chest. I was wondering if it wasn't psychological but Pam thinks not. Can't believe you were here a whole month and didn't get to meet my very favourite baby.

Oh, the other day I got upstairs in Lincoln House and this number was waiting for me in the corridor. "Are you Glyn Jones? I was told you're the person I should see. I've written this script … my name is Bobby White." 'Oh. Yes,' I said, 'you were waiting on our table the other night.' I haven't had time to read it yet, what with all the others, and *Champagne Charlie* and "*Buried Child.*"

Allen has finally sold his truck, to a real redneck or, as he put it, "We're talkin' grit here." He only got $400 for it which was way below what he wanted but I think he was just so glad to get shot of it. Sunday we're having brunch at Tom and Kay's and then I think they're planning on taking Dave down to Charlottesville to see George and Margaret and *Good* which George has just directed. I'd like to go see it but I've got a dress rehearsal. Then Monday evening they are at Don and Martha Ann's.

Remember me to everyone. Love to special people. Ophelia sends pussy love to the girls; the Lyndrups send special humming bean love to you, and from me.

26th April, 1985

Just a quickie to put with all the stuff for Dave to bring back. Here is the new *Champagne Charlie*. You will find a lot of changes some minute, some quite large. A lot of stuff has been cut. If you feel it's necessary to put any of it back, well that's up to you.

Dave borrowed fifty dollars from me and I told him to return the equivalent to you in pounds. I have just had my final cheque from JMU but haven't had time to deal with all the financial matters. Will do that next week. Oh, shit! Pam got a whole lot of top hats from *A Chorus Line* and *42nd Street* and she is giving you one as a pressie and I was supposed to ask your hat size and I keep on forgetting so tell me next time we talk. Oh, by the way, your photo is up on the wall in Hotel Cantrell *[Not really a hotel, a student house]* Must have been taken the night you went to the party there. There is a party there tonight and, tomorrow night, one at Gray and Rob Yokum's to celebrate my birthday!!! Shee-it! Who's the most popular geriatric in town?

Only one more week of classes, than exam week, and I part company with JMU. It really has been a wonderful year–for me. I thought I was going to have all my evenings free next week but I read in today's JMU News that I am adjudicating The Directors' Workshop entries. I didn't know anything about it but Mike Doyle swears blind he asked me and I said yes. Bang goes my evenings but, as I am on top of the ladder at the moment and no one is taking pot shots at me, I better not rock it. There you are, the culminating achievement of my artistic life–I have attained stardom in Harrisonburg, Virginia. Well I couldn't have done it in a more beautiful place. Allen and Anne have given me a pink (!) windcheater with lettering on the front that reads, "London, Paris, Rome, Harrisonburg."

Jens came to me the other day and said he'd heard from his mom that he'd been offered a part in *The Innocents* and was considering it though he really felt he ought to see the script first. I ask you–eight years old! So I told him he would really like the part as he got to be terribly evil. "Oh, cool!" he said. 'Like do I get to throw spit balls at the teacher?'

The only problem I can see with Jens is that he'll be giving the rest of the cast notes. Evidently when he did Tiny Tim at Christmas he would come off stage and say to his dad who was playing Bob

Cratchett, "You blew your lines, dad." To which Allen would reply, "I know I blew my lines, Jens. Actors don't like to be told that."

"Yeah, I know, dad, but you blew your lines."

"Don't push it Jens."

"I'm only telling you you blew your…"

"JENS!"

They have both been studying though Jens has his ups and downs and crises of confidence. "Glyn, I've really been thinking about the play and I don't want to do it. It's too much to learn." Next day, "I learnt two pages today, Glyn." Next day, "Glyn I've really made up my mind about the play and I DON'T want to do it." And so forth and so forth.

Tom Arthur is also, by the way, hell at learning lines. I don't think he did one perf right in *Narrow Road to the Deep North*. He only had a small part, but every line got fucked up. I told the kids just to use it and get on with it no matter what he did or did not do. If he didn't come in, just to ride on regardless so they went on happily with Tom coming in when he could and when he remembered, and it worked. He had so much fun doing it it would have been really shitty of me to replace him, which I was thinking of doing at one despairing stage.

1st May 1985

Just given Anne a lovely foot massage. She was lying on the couch looking so tired so thought I'd give her a treat. Before I forget, Dave HAS to write to Liz. He has left a torch burning here and she will be very upset if she doesn't hear from him so please make sure he does.

[Dave made a great hit with the girls in Harrisonburg. He was a good-looking boy and charming with it and I think his sarf London accent had something to do with it but he found love in the house right next door and, once that happened, we didn't see much of Dave, at least not at night.]

I thought I would have all my evenings free after *Buried Child* but Monday and Tuesday evenings I had to go see *Hamlet* so Mary Kerr could pick my brains, and the rest of the week sitting in on "The

Director's Workshop" adjudicating. So far it hasn't been great shakes.

Today gave my last writing class and tomorrow will be the last acting one. I have told the writers I want their last assignment by Monday. This will give me two days to mark them and send in their grades. Then I can go to the E. Gray Lee farm on Wednesday. Did I tell you about my birthday? That Allen and Anne gave me a beautiful pewter cup with the JMU coat of arms? Anne baked a cake. Did Dave tell you about Jens and the freezer? Poor little bugger–he really was in the shit but put up a pretty good front considering the havoc (and loss) he had caused all through wanting a frankfurter in the middle of the night. That must have been the most expensive frank in the history of processed meats. So I had to make a huge chicken curry, a chicken in burgundy, and a chicken teriyaki to get rid of all that. In fact spent most of a day cooking chicken.

Okay, the main reason for writing this letter. Firstly I think you're missing Page 15 in your carbon copy. I have two fifteens anyway, so here it is. Secondly, on Page 10 after "near Newcastle" insert the following, "That's where I was born on March the 17th 1842."

Now I'm off to bed. It's gone twelve and it's been a long long day. I gave little Bobby White (the waiter) his script back and was vair kind. Told him to carry on writing as he obviously had a flair for it but that this particular effort was too derivative and to look on it simply as an exercise.

11th May 1985

I'll start this letter today although I probably won't send it off until after Wednesday when the pikkies come back. Needless to say I had a marvellous time at the E. Gray Lee farm in Covesville, Va. Actually it isn't really a farm anymore as they have sold all the animals and don't really do anything with it. Gray's mother, Shirley, who is delightful and full of fun, works as a physiotherapist in Charlottesville. She has a boy friend, George, who Gray refers to in his old-fashioned way as "my mother's fiancé." The situation is absolutely beautiful, the house being on the side of a mountain *[a hill really]* overlooking a valley and more mountains in the distance. Walton country. Gray and I sat on the front stoep watching the day disappear and getting pissed on the Bourbon he gave me for my birthday. We'd left Shirley and George in town getting pissed with friends "What music would be appropriate for this moment?" asks Gray. "I don't know," I reply, 'you choose.' So guess what he puts on–Siegfried's Funeral March. Oh, shee-it! Of all things to choose! With those mountains? And that sunset? And me getting sloshed? I couldn't bear it. Anyway, I reached for his hand across the table. Or, rather, I held out my open hand and he took it … and then …the dogs started to bark. And then … a fucking train came by (the line passes along the bottom of the hill) and blew its fucking whistle and then … the telephone rang and now we were both in hysterics and that, as they say, was that.

So he goes to answer the phone and I hear him suddenly get all deferential with "Yes, ma'am … yes, ma'am … thank you, ma'am… etc." and he comes back out onto the veranda quivering like a hunting dog with his little heart pattering away and, for a while, he can't even talk and then it all comes out in a rush. "That was Sissy Spacek and she would have loved to have lunch with me tomorrow and my friend from London but she's so sorry she and her daughter are going away in the morning for a month and she wouldn't make it and thank you so much for asking and she was so sorry." I said to him, "Gray, what did you do?" Well, he had found out her address (she lives not too far away) and written to her to say I was going to be at his home for a couple of days, I was a great admirer and would like to meet her and would she like to have lunch with us? So it was my turn to be slightly dumbfounded. I couldn't believe he had actually done that for me and not said a word about it. So I gave him a big hug and we yelled to the dogs to belt up and went back to our Bourbon, changing the music. Don't ask me to what, I don't remember. Then we went inside and watched *Cat Ballou* on the VCR and Shirley came home sloshed. I'm not sure he has recovered yet from talking to Miss Spacek. She evidently threw him a real blinder by starting off with "Gray?" and he answered "yes" and then she said, "This is Sissy Spacek" which

Chapter Twenty

sent him reeling and he never recovered enough to have a coherent conversation. He is so soft sometimes he is like a puppy. You should see him trying to pluck up enough courage to dive into the pool. It takes minutes of toe-dipping, walking around, going for a piss, pretend diving, more toe-dipping, walk around to the other side, have another look at the thermometer, look at the sky, blow hard a few times, dip the toe again. I said I wished I had a movie camera, it was pure Jacques Tati. Once he's in it's okay. Then he went to look for something in a chest on an upstairs veranda outside his room and a bee flew out of the chest. He practically fell down the stairs in his effort to get away, flapping his hands around his head all the while and all the while the bee was fifty yards away in the opposite direction. And yet, one night, driving through the centre of Harrisonburg, he suddenly slammed on the brakes and dashed out of the car and onto the sidewalk to stop a couple of guys beating up a helpless drunk. They fled under his attack and it was certainly something I don't think I would have the courage to do so I was rather glad they didn't hang around and so force me to go to his assistance. Talking of the pool, that was where most of our time was spent, in or around it and, needless to say, I have developed eight billion new freckles and, needless to say, been bitten umpteen times by summertime noonoos.[26] We went to Charlottesville on Wednesday to have lunch and took one lot of piks in. Then, as we had to wait an hour to get them back, we lay on the grass of the university campus. That is, I lay on the grass. Gray sat next to me admiring all the girls walking by.

Anyway, yesterday it was back to the pool. I gave him a massage–he liked that–then he made a sandwich for lunch and eventually we packed up and headed out. On the way I wanted to call in on a nursery to get some plants for Anne and Allen and, would you believe it, we got stopped by a cop who gave him a ticket for not showing his decals, and that's not dirty, it merely means his licence tags. He was in such a state as the cop walked over to the car. You have never seen such trembling. I think he expected the electric chair at the very

---
26 South African for insects.

least. Anyway, we went on to the nursery and I bought a clematis, two fuchsias, and a buddlea for 324 Franklin. Couldn't get a Black Night and was amazed I could get a buddlea at all, hardly anyone seems to have heard of them. It's such a scraggly little thing too.

Got back to Harrisonburg and, as it was suppertime, stopped at the Chinese. He was over the moon when the Chinese waiter assumed I was his dad come to take him back home after graduation. So I played along with it until the waiter nearly got me stumped by asking me which one I thought was the best Chinese restaurant in Charlottesville. Gray managed to get me out of that one. Harrisonburg, at the moment, is of course packed with mums and dads all come to fetch their babies or see them graduate. Today being graduation day I should think last night master Gray got pissed rotten and fucked rotten as well. The girls swarm around him like bees to the honey pot but it seems to be, to quote Dodge in "Buried Child", 'Had some of them in my day, never lasted more'n a week.' Anyway, I hope you don't mind but, as a farewell present, I have given him "The Lost Cause" my book on the civil war. It really is more fitted to his bookcase than mine. After all, he is one of the Lees of Virginia and great nephew to General Robert E. and the book is part of his heritage, not mine, although he now insists I am a Virginian by adoption. They are very proud of being the Lees of Virginia and the house is full of portraits of the family. In the guest room where I was there is also an antique map of Shropshire where the family originally came from. The fourth member of the household is Gray's younger brother, Henry Bedinger. But he wasn't there. He is in Pittsburgh studying photography. But I will probably meet him this summer as George and Shirley insist they are going to come up to Wayside. Must stop for a while, it's "Prairie Home Companion" time. *[Radio show I never missed.]*

To continue–The last morning we were lying by the pool he brought out the radio and plugged it in and guess what was playing? The end of "Valkure". You would have died, looking up at that mountain with that music playing. I couldn't do anything but close my eyes and let the music wash over me, echo and all. It was almost as if Wotan

Chapter Twenty

was actually there and maybe, somewhere on top of that mountain the fire is still burning and Brunnhilde still sleeps waiting for her Siegfried to appear.

I've just realised I spelt buddleia wrong up there–left out the i. Did you know it was named after a botanist named Buddle? Not the most romantic name in the world, is it? Now I'm going to read "The Innocents". Anne is busy studying and keeps asking me questions. What kind of a director is this who can't answer the questions yet? I'll put this aside till Wednesday.

Wednesday.

Right–here I am. Just got back from the Bluestone Inn. Took Robin and John there for dinner. Cost a fucking fortune but, after all the meals I (and you) have had at their house, can't really begrudge it. They ordered the "steak for two" and you should have seen the thing! Half of it or more was taken home in the doggy bag. There was enough there for six. That, plus baked stuffed potato and a salad and John had French chocolate cake and hot rolls and where the hell did he put it all? I had the Captain's Platter consisting of prawn, lobster tail, crab, scallops and flounder and couldn't finish it.

Have been playing tennis every day either with Anne or Allen and feel great. Unfortunately I'm too good for Anne and not good enough for Allen so I either win 6-0 or lose 0-6. We're taking the rackets to Middletown so, hopefully, will keep it up, especially as my game is improving all the time. By the way, I should have said when I was describing Gray plucking up courage to dive into the pool that the temperature of the water was 81–hardly chilly. Even you would have found it plenty warm enough. Haven't seen him all week except briefly at Lincoln House when he turned up for a fitting. He's rehearsing "*The Boy Friend*" for Dinner Theatre. Dave should really write to the Lyndrups as well to thank them for his holiday. In fact it's not a case of SHOULD, it's a case of MUST. Everyone here was very good to him and he can't just go away and forget it–so get him to pull his finger out–fast!

Just heard–Charlie Tucker *[a student]* in that car smash–drunk–lucky to be alive–flown to Richmond–face smashed in, punctured aorta–blood in the lungs–terrible. Face will need reconstructive surgery. Shit!

20th May 1985

Enclosed cheque for £100. Hope it helps. I'm well into Act III so hope to have the play finished by Thursday when I go up to Wayside. Tuesday we're going to see a new play about the cop who shot the gay mayor of Los Angeles. It's had great reviews [*Execution of Justice*] John Boy is also in Washington, in "Monte Cristo". Wonder what that's like. Allen calls it "Monte Crisco"–naughty. Back to the typewriter–about to reveal all! Wonder how my very first all-American play will be received. Anne reads it as it comes off the typewriter, can't wait for the next instalment. Sorry you're having such a tough time. Love you. Meece.

23rd May 1985

Well, here I am. Arrived last night and settled into the "Cottage". Start rehearsals this afternoon for *"Barefoot in the Park"*. Listening to a tape of Pavarotti at the moment. Can't find a classical programme on the radio. The cottage is very comfortable, like a beach or holiday home though the bedrooms are a bit like monk's cells. I've got it to myself until Anne and the kids come up. They went to Massanuttin today *[the time share]* and I am going to spend the day with them there on Monday as we have a free day. Don't ask me why we have a free day as we've only just started but Ed works in strange ways his wonders to perform. I had hoped to get the play finished before I came up here but ran out of time–with the final scene to go. So I want to go back to Harrisonburg tomorrow to finish it. I think we (Anne and I) were very clever at SETC[27] and have given Ed a very good company. David, who I hadn't met before is real cute. This is the one who also wants to be a writer. Gray is busy rehearsing dinner

---

27 South East Theatre Conference.

theatre so I haven't seen much of him. But we haven't said goodbye, just adieu. If I write anymore I won't have anything to talk about when I call so adieu to you too.

28th May 1985

Boy, did it rain last night! The heavens opened well and truly. The roof of the little red cottage didn't leak but the floor did!! Puddles just appeared. Thought I was going to float away like Noah's Ark but without the enemas. Massanuttin was fun. George and Margaret were there and asking after you. Spent most of the time (a) learning lines (b) working on the design for "*The Innocents*" with Allen and (c) playing tennis. I even forked out $20 to have a private lesson with Paul, the tennis pro, and then watch it on videotape. Paul's patter when I made good shots was, "Boom! There you go!"

I don't quite understand the time-share mentality. The unit (No 32) is very nice with everything except food provided and the village is right in the mountains with golf course, pool and, of course, tennis courts, and things like riding, climbing etc., but somehow going on holiday just ten miles from home doesn't seem to me like going on holiday, especially when you're popping back every now and again for something, or to do something.

Haven't had the new play copied yet but you'll get it just as soon as I do. It is called "Generations" and is set in Virginia on Route 33. It has a cast of four women, three white, one black. There is also a grandmother who sits on the veranda but is never actually seen or heard. I am going to send it to some theatres here (Louisville, Kentucky for example) and also to an agent in NY but not Laurence's one so don't say anything to him.

Went with Ed and George (technical director) today to lunch at the Strasburg Hotel. Wish I'd known about it when you were here– it's all Victorian. You would love it, especially the love seat in the lobby all in red and gilt. Evidently it was put up as a hospital for the railroad before it became a hotel. I don't know whether the railroad still goes through Strasburg but at least the hotel is still there. Like

The Wayside Inn all the bedrooms are period as well, and the public rooms. Unfortunately there are some anachronisms like modern America pile carpeting but it doesn't really spoil the effect if you choose to ignore it.

At the moment we're having it pretty easy, rehearsing afternoon and evening but that will end soon when two plays will be worked at one and the same time.

Sorry there's been no response to George *[the Leybourne brochures]* and I haven't heard from Auburn University about "Peter Pan" [?] so, should nothing happen soon, expect me back beginning of September and we will make another foray another time. C'est la vie. I miss you all anyway. Love the melody for "Ting Ting"–so sadly sweet. One day I will use it in something. Stay well. I'll send £'s soon. All the kids here are flat broke. Isn't that the way of the theatre?

The Wayside is a tiny theatre in a tiny town on Route 81, northern Virginia; so tiny you could walk from one end of town to the other in a matter of minutes. It has the theatre, a post office, a store, a wonderful 18th century coaching inn with six dining rooms and twenty one guest rooms all crammed to the rafters with antiques: a fire station, which boasted a notice warning, "No trespassing without permission"; a bank, an art gallery and framers, and a number of tennis courts. The theatre has a small gallery reached from the street by a circular iron staircase. This is because it was originally a cinema and segregated coloured folk sat in the gallery. I believe they sometimes made their feelings clear by spitting on the white folk below. There was also a roomy bar and on the first floor (second floor to the Americans) offices, a large rehearsal room and a costume and props shop in the basement. Members of the theatre company became honorary members of the Wayside Inn's 1797 Club, which entitled you to a daily luncheon special at a reduced rate and half price on any domestic beer served anytime the inn was open.

The town is Middletown and it is indeed in the middle of nowhere although with fairly large towns close by, Strasburg, Winchester, Front Royal, and not too far from Washington DC it has a large area from

Chapter Twenty

which to draw its audience. Allen Lyndrup was associated with the theatre and he had previously introduced me to C. Edward Steele, "Producing/Director." When we all had lunch at the Edinburgh Mill it was agreed I would play Victor Velasco in *Barefoot in the Park*, Pseudolus in *A Funny Thing Happened on the Way to the Forum*, and Elyot in *Private Lives*. The plays I would direct would be *The Innocents* and *Tribute* by Bernard Slade. My play out was *Crimes of the Heart*, a very popular play at that time.

As one of the directors I was expected to help cast the season so Anne and I had flown, courtesy of Eastern Airlines (one of the most uncomfortable trips I've ever made, it's no wonder they went belly-up shortly afterwards) down to Tampa, Florida for the South East Theatre Conference. Ed didn't make the trip. The conference was quite an experience. Theatre representatives from Alabama, Florida, Georgia, Kentucky, Mississippi, The Carolinas, Tennessee, Virginia, West Virginia, were there to audition hundreds of young hopefuls, 611 in all, who had already been sifted out from auditions in their home states. The auditions took place in a vast room in the Radisson Hotel, the drill being that if someone impressed your group you made a note of their name and, at the end of the day, pinned your list up on a board. The young hopefuls would than be interviewed in your hotel room and you would make your offer and final selection. Naturally the more talented would be invited to more than one callback and your theatre then wouldn't necessarily be their first choice so it was a matter of juggling as well. One kid was so brilliant we didn't even bother to take down his name as we all felt he would have at least a dozen calls, if not more. I remember feeling terribly sorry for the girl who followed him because he was certainly a hard act to follow. That evening he knocked on our door and waltzed into the room bright as a button (more cliché) one big beaming smile. 'You're not on our list,' I said.

'I know. I wasn't on anybody's list.' Obviously everyone had felt the same as us, this boy was going to get so many offers it would be a waste of time to interview him, but he certainly wasn't going to leave it at that and was doing the rounds off his own bat. We jumped at the opportunity of using him but naturally he got a better offer. Other than that we got our first choices.

I don't remember much about Tampa, most of my time being spent in the Radisson Hotel, but I was fascinated by the almost Moorish architecture of the university and Allen took us for a meal in a Spanish restaurant, The Columbia, situated on the longest urban street in the world, dead straight for miles and beautifully lit by streetlamps each with three hanging globes. The restaurant featured Luis Ortiz and his Mariachi of Mexico, Jose Greco and his Dance Company and Henry Tudela and his Continental Orchestra for dancing. Pam Johnson, who was also down there, took me to another restaurant beneath a giant ancient kapok tree.

I was glad not to have experienced Eastern Airlines a second time as we returned to Virginia in the student's van. Driving passed all the fruit sellers stalls at the side of the road, we went by one in front of which was a sign: "Closed. I am tard." Write it as you speak it.

The Lyndrups were closely associated with the Wayside Theatre, Allen mostly as a designer and Anne as actress under her maiden name of Marley, and what a talented actress she is. It was an absolute delight both to direct her in *The Innocents* and *Tribute* and to play opposite her in *Private Lives*.

At the rear of the theatre there was (is?) a small yard ending in the scene shop and, separately, the tiny cottage that Anne and I shared. It had a veranda with a wooden floor and the traditional swing seat, a main room with kitchen area (Anne had brought the microwave from Franklin Street), two bedrooms and a bathroom at the back. I would spend one of the happiest and most fulfilling summer's of my life in this little red cottage a hop, step, and a jump from the stage door. It soured slightly towards the end when, for some reason we never could fathom, Ed started to behave in a most peculiar and

Chapter Twenty

unfriendly fashion but, despite that, to partly quote Mr Dickens, it was the best of times, and never to be forgotten.

A theatre as small as The Wayside couldn't possibly survive on ticket sales and most of its income came from tax-deductible donations from a long list of individuals and commercial interests, the biggest benefactors were credited first as Angels, followed by Superstars, Stars, Backers, Donors, Friends, and finally, Supporters. The list was fairly extensive, especially where Friends were concerned but, even so, money was always in short supply and Ed was a genius at juggling. As she had been a member of the company the previous year, one of the first things Anne said to me, was, as soon as you get your cheque it's lickety-spit over to the bank to cash it just in case, and over to the bank the two of us would go, a rerun of the Naranj episode. The company were asked to be electricity conscious, a must where American kids are concerned, even to turning off lights others had obviously forgotten. The whole company were expected to be involved in a strike. As soon as a show went down everybody reported to the Technical Director for a job to work on. In the scene shop, which was always immaculately kept, after a strike and if sets were being dismantled, every screw that could be reused was saved and every piece of reusable wood, in fact anything that could be salvaged for future use.

The season opened with Neil Simon's *Barefoot in the Park* that got mixed reviews. The Harrisonburg paper headline read, "Wayside Stumbles In The Park" and someone named John Horton Jnr. writing in a paper the name of which I haven't kept, wrote "Wayside Opens With Sparkling Production." Lynn Price in *The Winchester Star* said, "although the play was more than twenty years old, 'Barefoot' Wears Well At Wayside." Of my own contribution in the sparkling production, "The two older characters are played with aplomb by Martha Hege and Glyn Jones. Their roles are designed to evoke the greatest mirth of the evening, and they both succeed to the hilt." In the wearing well production–"Glyn Jones adds just the right continental flavor as the eccentric upstairs neighbour, Victor Velasco," and in the stumbling production–"Glyn Jones as Victor Velasco the eccentric who lives in the attic is the only true actor on the stage. Jones is at ease with himself and the role, but unfortunately can do only so much on his own when surrounded by such weak performances." The weak performances did get their own measure of praise one way or another from the other two reviewers.

The Innocents followed and this was truly a family affair as Allan designed the set, Anne played Miss Giddens, the governess, and the children, Miles and Flora, were played by the Lyndrup children, Jens and Carrie. For Flora's piano playing I used one of Leybourne's lesser known songs, *The Broken Hearted Shepherd*, a very pretty and truly haunting melody most apt for a ghost play. All three reviewers gave the production the thumbs up but it is so strange that one wrote, "The only flaw technically are some of the sound effects, which instead of being chilling are merely distracting." While another wrote, "Eeriness is also achieved with good lighting and recorded sounds of heartbeats and whispers." You really cannot please everybody. Carrie was criticised, quite rightly, by all three as being a little inaudible at times but both children were otherwise highly praised and, as for Anne, Dean Kinley's revue in the Harrisonburg paper sums it up–"Anne Marley is the consummate actress ... and is providing a gripping flawless performance in "The Innocents," an eerie mystery based on Henry James' classic story..."

The Innocents was followed by Ed's one-man show based on the writings of Mark Twain. This gave us an extra week to rehearse *A Funny Thing Happened on the Way to the Forum*. Again with this one the critics were at odds with each other, Dean Kinley being odd man out with his headline "Unfunny 'Thing' At Wayside" and his revue, "The funny thing that supposedly happened on the way to the forum just isn't happening at Wayside Theatre. This overdone bit of musical sexism is being beaten to death by a cast that has no right to be attempting anything with music. Wayside patrons, paying $10,50 per person, deserve much more than gawking, squawking, and flat notes. There are thankfully some bright spots that just cannot be stifled. Harrisonburg area residents will recognise Glynn (sic) Jones in the lead role of Pseudolus, a Roman slave who never hesitates to make up the wildest tale. Jones is the genuine humor of this production. His instinct for comedy is remarkable, and his love of entertaining is evident always. His singing voice albeit is not magnificent, but compared to the rest of the cast, it is stellar. Why director Ed Steele chose to present a musical comedy this summer with such less-than-mediocre musical talent is a real puzzle."

John Horton Jnr. "Wayside's 'Funny Thing': The Frivolity Never Stops. Lunacy runs rampant during Wayside Theatre's production of the Steven Sondheim, musical which opened Wednesday for a two-week run. The show about some slight goings-on in ancient Rome, displays the Wayside company at its most exuberant–singing, dancing and clowning with abandon. The frivolity is virtually non-stop. The production staged and directed by Ed Steele treats the show as though it is being presented by some seedy road show company. The set and costumes are a garish melange of pinks, purples, and yellows and the attire ranges from togas to spats and boaters. Steele has been urging Wayside patrons for years to donate their unwanted knickknacks to the theater and it appears that a goodly quantity of them have been put to use in this production. The tackiness is so blatant that it attains a certain charm. Everyone is having such a good time that no one seems to care that nothing matches or fits a certain era. Nor does it matter that subtlety is a scarce commodity among the actors. It is meant to be played broadly and Steele's approach merely makes the cast's task, such as it is, easier. There are limits of course to how much foolishness an audience can absorb in one evening and at times the shenanigans make one feel surfeited. The cast of 15, led by Glyn Jones as the slave Pseudolus, is uniformly fine. Steele is the consummate dirty old man and David Harwell and Vicky Ellis are charming as the young lovers." He then goes on to say equally complimentary things about the rest of the cast.

Linda Gorton. 'A Funny Thing Is Funny, Thoroughly Entertaining.' ... "Wayside Theatre has creatively turned its inability to produce musical comedy in the grand manner into an asset. The result is as entertaining a bit of silliness as one is likely to see this summer. Instead of full orchestra, Wayside uses piano and drums for accompaniment and instead of authentic Roman costumes, the cast wears a hodgepodge of garments from the company wardrobe trunk: pseudo-Elizabethan tunics share the stage with yellow spats and bowler hats. Together these made-do measures give the performance an air of spontaneity that makes the audience fellow-conspirators in creating the make-believe world. The women in the play are primarily to be seen and not heard: this is a play in which the men are front and center. And the Wayside cast has no trouble in pulling it off. Glyn Jones's timing is superb. As Pseudolus, the street-smart slave who seeks to win his freedom by getting his gawky adolescent master, Hero (David Hartwell) (*sic*), married to the girl of his dreams (Vicki Ellis), Jones is onstage nearly every minute, keeping the action going. Hartwell's Hero is the personification of a love-struck teenager. He looks as if his brain is as bare as his knee caps and he uses what promises to be a good singing voice in a hopelessly cracked adolescent manner."

It was during the run of *Forum* that *Thriller of the Year* and *Doctor Who and The Space Museum* were brought to my attention when a letter was forwarded to me by Laurence Fitch saying a group of actresses in Hollywood wanted the rights to put on the play. Then a letter from an editor with the publishers, W.H.Allen, forwarded by Chris, enquired as to whether I was interested in the novelisation of the *Doctor Who*.

It was also during the run of *Forum* that Ed's ill humour started to surface. He had begun to use David as his whipping boy and I think the reason for his sudden animosity towards me was because of my siding with young Mr Harwell. There seemed to be no apparent reason

Chapter Twenty

for Ed's dislike but his attitude became more and more surly, as did that of Martha, his sidekick in the theatre. To get a smile or a greeting out of her was like pulling teeth without an anaesthetic. I still had to direct Ed in *Tribute* and hoped his attitude wouldn't affect what he was doing. Fortunately his professionalism got the upper hand at least for that and there was no problem. Due to a motorbike accident, Ed was an amputee and during the course of the play his character drops his trousers. I wondered if he would do it, displaying his artificial leg for all the world to see but even that caused no problem. The actor playing the son had already made it clear that he was unhappy at Wayside and wanted to leave, I believe because he wasn't getting the parts he felt were his due. When rehearsals started he was even more surly and unforthcoming than Ed but as that suited his character anyway I let him work out his sulks in his own time. The reviews for the play were good, the entire cast receiving well earned praise, and I learned something about casting I should have taken into account earlier in my career, typecasting to immediate thoughts doesn't always lead to the right choice.

The play is about a man dying from leukaemia and during the course of the action various friends appear to tell the audience what they think of him and to pay tribute. Included in those returning, ostensibly to say farewell, are the man's alienated son and his ex-wife, who he takes into the bedroom and makes love to for the last time. I had no say in the casting of this show and the actress playing the wife, Marilyn Mattys was, I have to say it, enormous, so large that part of the set had to be taken down and rebuilt as she was unable to get through an opening to go into the bedroom. This was hardly my idea of one half of a romantic liaison, not that Ed was an oil painting, but I had hoped for a more glamorous ex-wife. In the end I wouldn't have changed the one I had for the world. Lynn Price's headline was 'Tribute Touches Your Heart' and Marilyn's performance was one of the most moving I have seen in any theatre anywhere. I wasn't the only member of the audience in tears and I had lived with the show all through rehearsals.

No Official Umbrella

I was reminded of the time Chris and I went to Sadler's Wells to a special concert and the programme included a name I knew well, Joyce Barker, who was to sing the Liebestod from *Tristan and Isolde*. Joyce and her younger sister were both members of the choir at St. James' in Durban and Joyce had gone on to make a very successful career in opera. The curtains parted and shamefully the audience laughed. Joyce was so enormously fat, not by any stretch of the imagination could she possibly be an Isolde, but by the time she had finished singing she had the entire audience on its feet roaring their appreciation, call after call after call. So much for appearances. We went around to the stage door after the concert and she shrieked in a most unoperatic way when she saw me. 'Glun! Glun!' There was still more than a trace of that South African accent when she spoke. There were hugs and kisses and promises to keep in touch but that was the last time I saw her. A letter from my sister and a long newspaper obituary informed me of her death at the age of 60.

Dean Kinley's headline read: "Wayside's 'Tribute' lets Talent Shine Through. Wayside Theatre's 'Tribute' is a provocative comedy-drama that is certain to tug at the heartstrings and bring a tear to the eye. Bernard Slade's beautiful script is directed superbly and with great sensitivity by Glyn Jones. The story of an estranged husband and wife and their son growing to know one another after the father is stricken with leukaemia is brought to life by a talented cast that plays expertly off one another. Perhaps the most exciting performance is that offered by Tom Weber as Jud Templeton, son of leukaemia victim Scottie Templeton. *[So at least our disaffected young man went out in a blaze of glory]* The young Weber, a Lynchburg College graduate is a fine actor who builds gradually to an emotional outpouring that has been welling within Jud for years. His performance is particularly moving when the character reverts to a stutter, a problem from Jud's stormy youth.

In contrast, Ed Steel's portrayal of Jud's father Scottie is a steady stream of witticisms and jokes, most of them targeted at trying to get Jud to laugh. Steele too strikes an emotional nerve. He lures his audience into really liking Scottie, then practically breaks their hearts as his character faces death with great strength.

This play also has two other gems–Marilyn Mattys as Scottie's ex-wife and Jud's mother and Joe Mattys as Scottie's best friend, Lou Daniels. And of course Anne Marley turns in another A performance as Scottie's doctor. She is particularly memorable in this production for her concern about her dying patient and her character's convincing argument that Scottie should undergo treatment if not for himself, then for his son. The only drawback to this show is some real problems that a few of the major actors have with their lines. *[Meaning Ed of course without actually saying as much]* Misplaced and misspoken words tend to break the concentration and the piece is too beautiful for this to happen."

More Letters From America.

Monday. 3rd June 1985

Just started the first tech so you know what that means. Boy, it's warm! I'm glad the theatre is air-conditioned. I finished blocking "*The Innocents*" this morning, on paper that is. Allen has designed a beautiful set. What is the name of the lady who designs at Covent Garden who we like so much? I just can't think of it. Didn't she do "Enigma Variations?" You know who I mean–all the leaves. Well it's very much like that with the garden encroaching right into the house, which is what I wanted. Tell me her name or I'll go mad! *[Julia Trevelyan Oman.]*

I'm using "*The Broken Hearted Shepherd*" for Flora's song and am also thinking of using another Leybourne tune somewhere as a sort of music box theme–possibly "Mousetrap Man" or "Ting Ting"–not sure yet.

Oh, boy! It's going to be a long night. We've stopped already and started from the top again. The company are lovely, a really nice bunch of kids, I'm having trouble casting "Tribute" though. Tom and Bob both desperately want the part of the son, the part Andy wanted to come down for and, funnily enough, Tom is very like Andy. At the moment I've got three shows to worry about. Have already started to work on Pseudolus. Dying for a cup of coffee now. End of Act II and it's only ten-thirty. Not as bad as I thought.

Wednesday Morning.

Allen arrived with a rendering of the design *[For The Innocents]* so I plucked up courage to ask if I could have it. *[Now beautifully framed it hangs in the flat in Athens]* Last night wasn't too bad. Finished at 11.45. I really thought we were going to be there till the early hours. I am at last beginning to enjoy playing Victor. Been having problems with an accent, trying to do a Mittle European overlaid with American. Last night it worked for the first time in the second act. Act I I didn't have it, Act III I lost it. Was going to work on it this morning, if I get a chance.

Goom-bye, stay well and happy. Has Dave written to Allen and Anne yet? They no longer ask after him. I think there is a little hurt, a little disappointment there. They haven't said as much of course.

7th June 1985

David Harwell wants to be a writer and has already had a musical produced at his university which, he informed me, came second. Later it came out there were only two anyway! But he is bright so I am giving him all the encouragement he wants, writing wise. He's playing Hero in "Forum" so that should be fun. *"The Boy Friend"* in Harrisonburg got a good notice but they are still worried about *"Children Of A Lesser God"* which does seem a bizarre choice for dinner theatre. Tom being ambitious. It's been raining like crazy the last couple of days. Doesn't matter as they've been working days but now the racquets have arrived I'll want to play tennis again.

P.S. Allen and Anne did not like *"The Boy Friend."*

Chapter Twenty

12th June 1985

I'll probably only get this started tonight because I've already written to Pickle and Alex and Caroline and the show is nearly over. They're really enjoying it tonight. It's one laugh after another. This afternoon was great too. We had a whole busload of Black ladies from Washington and you should have heard them shriek! Only three perfs of "Barefoot" left, two of them sold out. Monday night I took off, decided to relax. (We don't perform Mondays and Tuesdays) It was actually a company day off but I rehearsed "Innocents" morning and afternoon and then in the evening five of us went into Winchester–3 guys and 2 polones. We were going to go to a "British pub" called "*Coalie Harry's*" but Coalie Harry's was closed so we went to "The Ground Round" where we ate peanuts and popcorn and chicken wings and drank pitchers of beer and danced the night away. What a little stir did I create. "Hey! You can really dance!!" I said I wasn't exactly in my wheelchair. "No, I mean you dance like a young man." (Thursday) Told you I wouldn't get very far last night. Well, surprise, surprise, after the show last night Gray turned up–with newest polone, Molly by name and playing Maisie in *The Boy Friend*. Pretty, cute, nice, dumpy. They had been to a movie in Harrisonburg and Gray decided he wanted to see me so up they came. We sat on the porch with Anne there too and we had chats and a great laugh as a slug appeared, quite the most enormous slug I have ever seen–six inches long at least and spotted like a leopard. Anyway, I fed it Honey Grahams and Gray fed it beer and we christened it Graham. Molly and Gray left about twelve-thirty and I went down to the boys' house to give David a hand with his new play–at his request. It was fun. He gets so excited over what he has written but doesn't take it badly when you come up with the criticisms, and the other guys send him up gently the whole time.

I had to yell at Jens for fooling around in rehearsal today and you know how I can yell. We had to scrape him off the ceiling and put him back into his skin but after he had behaved himself for a while, I gave him a big hug and a kiss and he was his old self again.

20th June 1985

My first free evening just to sit for a while although I will do some work on "Forum". We started rehearsals for it today. Have you ever blocked an entire musical (book) in one day? "Innocents" opened last night and went very well. Surprising considering we lost almost a day and had to change stage manager. Dramas! The girl Ed designated to do it just couldn't. She freaked out. There are 28 sound cues and 60 light cues. After we spent a couple of hours trying to get through the first three or four I took an executive decision and switched her with Miss Jessel. She broke into immediate sobs of relief. David did me a beautiful sound tape and worked on it for hours to get it dead right. He recorded "Broken Hearted Shepherd" for me and then at the top of the second act we've transposed it into the minor key and it is even more haunting and beautiful. The kids were great except that Carrie finds it difficult to keep up the projection and tends to gabble sometimes. Anne is a super Miss Giddons. We'll see what the notices say tomorrow. We haven't shown the cast the Harrisonburg notice for "Barefoot" as we thought (knew) it would upset them. Herb asked me about it one night and I had to lie through my teeth, especially as it was the night his parents were coming, having spent two days driving up from Georgia.

P.S. Went for a Chinese meal in Winchester and my fortune cookie read, "You will be drawn to the glamour of the stage."–Hysterics in restaurant. Now they tell me.

30th June 1985

(Jens is nine today)

Hey! I'm listening to Carrie's favourite tape – *Annie*. Remember when we went to see it? *"Innocents"* closed last night so we were working on strike till 1.30, except poor Dave and Geoff who were hanging lamps till four. Have just finished a music call. Am really enjoying the rehearsals for "Forum". Got another one at 6.30 so here I am, in between, to say got your letter yesterday, just as we were all

Chapter Twenty

beginning to worry about you. Oh, dear, how sad about Pip. I was (am) so sorry to hear about that but, as time goes by, we must inevitably lose more friends to the reaper. That is life–and death. I can't believe I am here, so full of excitement, and fun and energy and bubbling and beating twenty year olds at tennis and really feeling so good! What has happened? One last fling before the wheelchair? Yesterday I was dancing all over the Red Cottage to the strains of the can-can. Tom, Kay, June and Cindy all came to see the play last night and Kay said–"What's happened to you, you look marvellous!" Thanks. Great. They didn't say a single word about the play so presumably they didn't like it. And do you want to know something? Who fucking cares? I drove Anne and the kids to Berryville yesterday and we had lunch at "The Meeting Place"–menu enclosed for you. Very pretty town–pronounced "Burrville". Today they have all gone off to West Virginia. Our projected trip to N.Y. is off as the time has been cut so pooh fah! Instead I'll either go to Washington, or Gaithersburg to see Andy in "Oklahoma". Maybe we'll still make it to N.Y. later in the season. Thanks for sending the Allen *[W.H.]* stuff. Don't send them anything. I'll write. If there's not that much of a hurry it can wait a while–something to come home to, workwise I mean. I've got another two weeks before I write to various people in England to set (or try to set) wheels in motion.

6th July 1985

What a fucked up ole day! Apart, that is, from the pleasure of talking to you. Firstly, Gray was supposed to meet me for lunch at 12.15. I gave him an hour and, as he still didn't show, I pissed off. Got back to find Bar (M.D.) couldn't rehearse so shee-it! I meant to tell you on the phone I had an enlargement done of you, Tom, *[Arthur]* and Ma Thomas, but it was shitty when blown up, so I'll have to choose another. So how else has the day been fucked up? Yes, well, I thought, after rehearsal I'd have a game of tennis. Guess what? Pissing with rain. Well at least you are getting a letter out of it, which is something. If the beanpole were back from Philadelphia we could do some work. Shame, he is Ed's whipping boy at the moment and my admiration for him has gone up a thousand percent the way he is putting up with it. He really needs Ed's chiselling like a hole in the head. He is so gorgeous, all 6'2", 135 lbs of him, and you would love him, like a gangling pup. Anne fusses over him like a mother hen. Goes all mushy, which isn't hard to do with that baby face and those china blue eyes. I'm listening to Satie at the moment. I used "Trois Gymnopedes" at the end of "The Innocents" and Anne loved it so much I bought her a tape as a 1st night pressie, except she got it on the last night. Well, better late than never. I'm sorry you've had such a bad time. I don't know. We try and we try, don't we? Wish I could do something about it for you. Listening to the Satie has suddenly made me think of Sicily. I wonder why. So I am going to see Ed's one man "Mark Twain" show tonight. Hope it's a heap better than "The Boy Friend". *[JMU Dinner Theatre]* Yuk!" Ooh! Ouch! Oh, dear! Even Pam's costumes were awful and I never thought I'd ever say that. So was the set. In fact was there a redeeming feature? No, there wasn't. Gray was awful! But I love him so much I don't really care. High school dramatics and, in real life, he would never be asked to play Sir Percy anyway.

Chris Simmons has sent a Photostat copy of "Rock The Cradle, John" *[a Leybourne song]*, which is all he managed to come up with from The University of Indiana. The original Concanen[28] must be quite something. It is now early Wednesday morning, very early. The birds are singing the dawn chorus accompanied by distant thunder. "Forum" opens today and Friday I start rehearsing "Tribute". Haven't had a chance to look at it for ages but tomorrow I have all day so I can sit with the ground plan and do my homework. The set for "Forum" is wonderful. All pink, purple and reds–kitsch kitsch kitsch! It's quite amazing what you can do on so small a stage. Here come de rain, patter, patter, patter. I've been wiping the paper because I thought I had been drooling on it but it is rain coming through the window. It did it to me the other night and I was too lazy to get up and close

---

28 Illustrator of many Victorian music covers.

Chapter Twenty

the window so just lay there and got rained on. It was wonderful. The other night we had a fantastic electrical storm with lashings of rain and lightning all over the place and I went out naked into the yard at two in the morning and enjoyed every pagan minute of it. Stay well and try to be happy. I love you.

PS: "Mark Twain" was very good.

Thursday.
Five days since I started this letter! Will I never finish it? I've been trying to get to the bank to get you a money order. Anne has gone into Winchester today to do it for me while I sit here and block "Tribute" (this is a break). "Forum" seemed to go pretty well last night. Boy! Talk about sweating buckets! All that mad dashing about–overacting. W.O.T.T. *[way over the top]* Anyway, it's fun. Ed has directed it as a vaudeville troupe playing the piece so everyone has a ball being really hammy. No reviews yet but I will send them to you; good, bad, or indifferent. Okay, when Anne gets back I'll slip in the M.O. and this can finally be mailed.

Sunday.
Honey Chile!
Look, it's Sunday. Anne (would you believe this?) went to FIVE banks in Winchester and couldn't get an Int. M. Order. So, anyway, David and I are going to Washington tomorrow for our day off and I will do it then and eventually this will be mailed. Gray's mother and George (they are getting married August 31st) and two friends from Charlottesville came to see the show yesterday and enjoyed it. Wish they'd come second house. Your Glyn got the kind of American reception we only dream about. Wow! Yells! Whistles! You would have been so proud. I must admit it was the first time I felt really relaxed and had a ball. What an audience. They were with it right from the start so it was just love love love love all the way. Makes you feel real good.

I've finished blocking the play. Allen came to the show tonight and John Lee and Robin *[nee Haigh, ex-English ballerina]* The Lees enjoyed it. Allen didn't. I'm not surprised. After last night the gremlins decided to take over. It was okay though but okay not good enough. *[One strange thing about Forum was my song "Pretty Little Picture." I just could not keep those lyrics in my head and virtually every performance at some point or other I would have to tra-la-la it until I got back on track.]*

Thursday(No Date)

Listening to Zubin Mehta conducting the N.Y. Phil. playing orchestral extracts from *Götterdamarung* so thought I would stop learning "Private Lives" and write to you. Ah, those horns! Must go and take a shower. Found a new tennis opponent in Herb and Herb hits the ball like he's trying to kill it so I'm all of a mucky sweat anyway. I was only doing lines while drinking my coffee. Saw "Crimes Of The Heart" last night. It was really excellent, everyone very good. In fact, and I have to say it, I think it's probably the best show of the season. "Tribute" might have been if Ed had learned his lines but nobody has ever been able to get Ed to learn his lines. Going to stop now because it's Siegfried's funeral, poor Siggy. Ah, that was beautiful! What a treat. So, where were we? Valhalla's just biting the dust, hang on a mo. Aaaaaahhh! Cream knickers! Cream knickers! Right. Tuesday night, big dramas, mah deah. Half an hour before dress rehearsal David is suddenly taken with a dose of the extreme nasties. He's sitting on this couch as white as this paper, vomiting, eyes glazed, incoherent and almost unable to move with Anne applying ice packs and everyone standing around looking gormless. So I walked in, took one look at him, and the next thing he was in the car and we were haring up Route 11 for Winchester. I put my headlights on, put my foot on the gas and drove like a bat out of hell. 85 and not a cop car in sight. I was dying for one to stop me so I could say, "Give me an escort to the hospital" just like in the movies. But there's never a cop around when you want one. Anyway, it turned out to be acute gastroenteritis or a viral infection or something and three hours later we brought him

Chapter Twenty

back, weak but better and yesterday he did two shows. And very good he was too. I'll tell you more about it when I see you. Allen tells me the girl at JMU has changed her mind about directing "Generations" which actually is okay by me. I was wondering about her doing it with me not around and *[I was]* having second thoughts, especially after she said she found no humour in it. Wot! Have you known any Glyn Jones play without laughs? You have to be kidding. Right. Shower time. Bye! Bye ya'll. Love love love love love.

[Having refused an IV because it would add $20 or something to his dad's insurance, David sipped water even though there was a chance of his vomiting it up. That fortunately didn't happen and he gradually improved. I went off for a break and when I came back he was lying, completely covered under his sheet, with the two girls who had accompanied us standing by his bed pretending to be weeping and shocking the people passing by the open door. I gave them a slight ticking off for a not very funny practical joke as someone passing by might have just experienced their own loss for real. They were most subdued on the way back.]

22nd July 1985

Have a typed letter courtesy of Dave's machine. I've more or less got the morning off as they're setting up for *TRIBUTE* and the cast aren't called for rehearsal till three. Boo-hoo-hoo! *FORUM* is over. Oh, boy, did I have a ball? Can't remember when I enjoyed something on stage so much. And who's the tiny starlet of Middletown then? Gray came up on Wednesday and, after the show, he, Anne and I went to the Inn for a drink. Representatives of the World Bank had attended the performance that evening, a night out from Washington, and there they all were. As we walked in they broke into a round. Hey, I felt so good! Hardly like walking into Sardis after a first night but still good. Nothing like that had ever happened to me before. The first time I have walked into any place and twenty or more total strangers have stood up and applauded and wanted to shake hands and drinks that night were on the World Bank. Then David joined us and, after our drink, we drove to Stevens City to have a pancake breakfast. How did you like Dean's cutting crit? He obviously didn't get the point, that the squeaks and squawks were deliberate. Like that stupid bugger who read "Brood Of The Witch Queen" and said my dialogue was terrible. The DIALOGUE WAS MEANT TO BE EXACTLY WHAT IT WAS, YOU PRICK! HAVE YOU NEVER HEARD OF HIGH CAMP? Never mind, hey? The world is full of know it all idiots.

Have I written since Dave and I went to Washington? Had a great day. Hot as hell and humid with it and I walked the poor kid off his feet. Took him to Herb's, the sort of theatre restaurant you remember (?) for lunch then let him loose in the theatre shop, then let him loose in the record shop. The "Air And Space" *[museum]* didn't really grab him as his dad works for NASA and he was a bit blasé about it all. To use his expression, "Oh, pooh-fah!" The other one is, "Fan the merkin!" Then we had dinner at Front Royal on the way back. I thought we'd go to "My Father's Moustache" but it's closed on Mondays. Should have checked shouldn't I? Oh, what I meant to say was, instead of doing "The Air And Space" we went to The Archives instead to see the famous documents, Bill of Rights, etc. Also went to The Old Post Office and up the tower. You can see the whole city from up there.

24th July, 1985

What happened to the *DOCTOR WHO* script you were going to send? *TRIBUTE* opens tonight. This afternoon it was awful!! Leave early tomorrow for Harrisonburg then I think I'm going to stay in Covesville for a couple of days. Gray won't be there. He's gone to New York with his Molly. Hey! Today Anne and I went into J.C.Pennys and I bought a pair of tennis shorts on sale for $5 from $17. A bit good huh? And guess what??? I had to get a medium!!!! Hey? Wot? MEDIUM???? What happened to LARGE?

 C. Beeching £150
 Midland Bank £300
 Anglia Building Society £155

Chapter Twenty

I was going to send you 3 separate orders but they are now $10 each so can you do the separate bits please?

2nd August 1985

Here we are–August already! In six days time I will have been one whole year in the states. Anyway, let's bring you up to date. Sunday was spent mainly around the pool. Gray phoned between his shows and was surprised to find I was still there. So I hopped in the car and drove up to Harrisonburg and he came round to Franklin after the show and we talked till all hours. Then we had lunch on Monday and in the evening I went to a rehearsal of *"Under Milk Wood"* and Tuesday night went to the dinner Theatre to see *"Children Of A Lesser God"* which was wonderful. Kate Trammell was superb. A spark of genius by Tom to cast a dancer in that role but then everyone in the cast was good. I howled! Thank god I could, at last, say wonderful praising things to Tom, especially after the truly terrible *"Boy Friend"*. Gray was doing his understudy bit and he was good too. Afterwards I hugged and howled over everybody. What a mess! Then we went to Spankey's for dinner. At least Gray had food. I'd already eaten in the interval of course so just had a beer. There was a couple from Kentucky seated at my dinner theatre table. The wife who was the size of an army tent piled an absolute mountain of food on her plate, polished it off and went back for seconds just as large. Not only that but she had bread rolls, a generous side bowl of salad and TWO enormous desserts, worth at least 2000 calories a piece. They eat like tomorrow is famine time, and there is so much waste as well. It really is a disposable society when you see what the students put on their plates and then leave.

Then on Wednesday morning I met with Jacqui Donaldson who wanted to direct "Generations" at JMU. This is the girl who did such an incredible job on *"Five & Dime, Jimmy Dean." [But obviously she wasn't going to be sweet-talked into changing her mind]* Then I drove back to Middletown and David screamed, "Well, hi, Gleeee-yun! I missed ya!" And threw his arms around me for a big hug. Absence obviously makes the heart grow fonder. He's got himself a kitten that he has named Cleopatra. There were (are) two and Bob took the other one, which he has named "Space Traveller Merkin". I suppose a black kitten could look like a cunt wig at a push.

Back to Harrisonburg because Tom wanted to do an interview with WMRA/BBC. Afterwards had lunch with Al. Saw Pam and others. Everyone asking after you. Didn't see Gray. Presumably he was still with Molly. She evidently asked Eddie if our relationship is gay and Eddie told her, "No, it's more like father and son" which is more or less true.

5th August 1985

Went to the Kennedy Center last night to see "The Grand Kabuki". God, it was marvellous. I bought a souvenir programme for you. Also wanted to get you a T-shirt, black with a Japanese mask and "Grand Kabuki–Kennedy Center". The guy said to get it in the intermission, there were plenty. And so what? Sold-out weren't they? And they were the one thing cheap by Kennedy Center standards, only $8. The ticket cost $30 and the programme $7. Two dollars for a beer and $1.25 for a chocolate bar that normally sells for 45 cents. As George (our T.D.) says, when you cross into D.C. someone turns on a vacuum pump and all your dollars disappear. Well, it was worth it, but sorry about the T-shirt. The two plays were "*The Earth Spider*" and "*The Scarlet Princess of Edo*" which was wonderful Victorian melodrama. Read the synopsis. Didn't get back to M'town until about 1.30.

David's not talking to me. Basically he wanted me to work on a musical with him but when it came down to actually working on it he chickened out. Made every excuse he could think of not to write. There is something else bothering him as well but I know not what it is.

Okay, I'm going to practice my tennis now. No one to play with. Tom has left, Anne is rehearsing, George is working the shop so I'll just have to beat the board.

Chapter Twenty

18th August 1985

What a dreary old day–real London rain–non-stop. Just about to do our first on stage rehearsal of "P.Lives" I think it is going to be slightly hysterical or, as Andy would say, "holarious". Unfortunately the director's father died the day before yesterday so she had to fly to Cleveland today which meant, instead of rehearsing this afternoon, we had to be up for a nine o'clock, and that after a strike! It turned out to be almost useless anyway as they couldn't get a babysitter (her husband is playing Victor–a very good actor by the way) so we had a 6 and a 3 yr old to contend with, plus a "Sibyl" with allergies made grossly worse by having taken someone else's medicine. Boring! She said her first line and burst into tears–almost end of rehearsal. I think the end of summer is beginning to be felt. Some of the company have already left. More leave on Thursday after opening night. In fact we will be down to just under half a company. (19th) As I thought, last night's rehearsal was pigshit. It wasn't holarious at all–it just stank. Ed was doing his "cock-of-the-walk, I am the boss" bit and being highly objectionable. I think he is having girl-friend trouble and having got rid of half his teckies is (or has) screwed himself into the ground. The Leybourne nose looks very good (your letter arrived this morning) but WOT are you holding in your hand? We couldn't work it out. I said to Anne, "Do you think it could be Robert?" And she nearly choked over her coffee. I won't send the Leybourne pix back yet. George and Margaret will most probably come up for *"Private Lives"* and I'll show them. They should come up as one of the UVA faculty is in it and one of the UVA faculty directed it and then there is Anne *[a close friend]* and mois *[also a friend, not so close]* and I haven't said goodbye to them yet. This afternoon's rehearsal was a bit better. At least there weren't any moods or atmosphere to contend with. After Wednesday I'll start on the rewrites for *"Thriller of the Year."* *[For the Americans]* Must also talk to…*[Illegible]* at JMU about staying on in the US. Don't want to write to the immigration first and make a fuck-up. If I go down to Harrisonburg I'll call you. Haven't heard anything from Seattle yet. *[One of my unsuccessful job applications]*

Love to all. Stay well. That Bella is really too much. Saw Gus yesterday. He was barking after her.

Gus had written a letter to Bella back in June. It read -
Well hi-ya, Bella,
My name is Gus. I am two years old and I live in Richmond, Virginia and I am up here in M'town on a visit with my mistress whose name is Judith and she is the girl-friend of a guy named George–sounds like a musical doesn't it? "George And Judith." And this great guy Glen Glyn (slapped paws) showed me your picture and like WOW, man! Barf! Barf! You're cute. So I figured like, you know, I would kinda write you and see how things stand. Ouch! (slapped paws) I wasn't being gross. That's just the way it slipped out. Ouch! (slapped paws). Hey! I wish this guy would stop reading over my shoulder or I'm like gonna take a chunk outa his leg. No, I wouldn't do that. He did give me a piece of Jens' birthday cake. Mind you, Al was a bit pissed at him (Glen Glyn) making jokes about his (Al's) icing. Like it said "Hoppy Birthday" and Gleyn said why didn't he (Al) do a picture of a kangaroo? I didn't get the joke. What's a kangaroo? So send me a couple of sniffs, Bella.
Gus.
P.S. I'm a retriever, what are you?

Wednesday.
Well, here we are–the last five perfs at The Wayside. Just got back to find a letter from Bruce Gray *[Hollywood]* saying the production has been put off until the New year!! However they would still love to see me out there. In fact had a call from one of the producers day before yesterday saying they are putting me up and how much they are looking forward to it. She didn't say anything on the phone about postponement. Got Bruce's letter just after I had mailed off the rewrites and spent a lot of time at the travel agents. Got a lovely round trip of the states on Amtrak–thirty days unlimited travel for $325. Going via New Orleans (stopover) then Los Angeles (stopover)

Chapter Twenty

Seattle: return Los Angeles, Chicago, N.York–if I return, or want to.[?] At first I thought of cancelling it because of the postponement but then thought, why not go ahead anyway? I haven't heard anything from Seattle yet so will probably call them from H'burg next week and tell them what my plans are. I tried calling you the last couple of days but there was no reply.

Yesterday I went down to Covesville to see the sick puppy [*Gray, who had just had his tonsils out and was back home*] feeling very sorry for himself. But he'll be okay. Probably my last visit there so I had a skinny dip in the pool, dinner with them all, then headed back for H'burg. Driving back reminded me of a story I heard about a woman stopped for speeding. She wound down her window and smiled up at the cop about to write out a ticket. 'I know why you've stopped me, officer,' she said, 'you want me to buy tickets for the police ball.' He looked at her and said, 'Madam, State Troopers don't have balls.' She didn't get her ticket.

I've just heard that an amateur company in Winchester are thinking of doing "*Thriller of the Year*" this fall and they hadn't put 2 & 2 together–that it is mine I mean. They just chose it and it came up in conversation in the girl's dressing room. We've got one of them in "P.Lives" playing the maid and Anne said, 'Why don't you talk to the author? He's sitting right there in the next dressing room.' How about that for coincidence? Wonder if they'd like to try out the rewrites.

We've really had marvellous houses for "*Private Lives*". This afternoon was virtually full. One woman had the most extraordinary laugh. She nearly corpsed me in the last scene. Did Errol tell you I was offered two plays in Harrogate starting in September? He sounded a bit gloomy in his letter about the scene. Is it still that gloomy? Wish you were going to Hollywood with me. But you don't like long train rides do you? Not like me. And it takes 4 days from Charlottesville to L.A. Love to all and talk to you soon.

29th August 1985

Hi! Me again,

Sitting in the dressing room waiting for "Beginners" or, as they say in America, "Places". Started work today on "Doctor Who" *[sample of prose–yet another audition really]* and will send it off next week when I've typed it out on Al's machine. Now that David's left I don't have access to a typewriter here. Great excitement in Winchester today when the penny dropped and the lady who is directing *Thriller of the Year* is coming over to see me on Saturday. I wrote to Paul and Lionel just to warn them they may see me in N.Y. sometime. Anne has friends in New Orleans who we're hoping I might stay with. They're also friends with George and Margaret. I've decided, as we don't know what is happening, to leave a lot of stuff at 324 Franklin Street and get it at some future date.

Allen finally picked up the Wagner books a present from the good doctor. They are a Time-Life boxed set, very handsome 3 volumes. They will look very good sitting next to your "Ring" recording even if you never get around to reading them. Though how I get them to you is another matter. They weigh a ton. At the moment they are up in the attic with the rest of my stuff and they won't run away.

Show's over–another packed house–we're really going out with a bang. What a wonderful summer it's been. Wish you could have been here to share it. Maybe next year we'll visit and see a show.

Dean Kinley didn't write the review for *Private Lives*. This time *The Harrisonburg Daily News-Record* critic was one, Phyllis Quillen who wrote, ".... a delightfully funny evening's entertainment. Although the play shocked the staid 1931 first night audience in London with its kicking and fighting couples, modern audiences see domestic violence (and other sorts) graphically presented on stage, TV and films and are sadly more hardened. Coward's trademark is wit, and wit illuminates this not-so-simple tale of love."

She then continues with a résumé of the play before, "Coward's script creates delightful characters, and shows us the unique nature of the love between Elyot and Amanda with a keen ear and a shrewd eye. Both Amanda and Elyot are intelligent, sophisticated, mature people. Each is also unconventional (something that Coward himself reveled (*sic*) in) and while they are abrasive to each other, they are well matched.

The abandoned spouses, Sibyl and Victor show the opposite characteristics. Each is supremely conventional in different ways, he as the blustering but usually ineffectual male and she as the essentially manipulative young female of the species.

Glyn Jones' Elyot is a creature of contradiction. He looks and sounds like a perfectly conventional husband when we first meet him on the balcony with Sibyl. But as the play unfolds, his gift for saying exactly the most shocking thing at exactly the right moment appears. It is a gift in coping with the importunities of Sibyl, and a curse in leading to renewed warfare with Amanda, but thoroughly enjoyable for the audience.

His is a low-key performance that grows in force throughout the play. What is missing is a sense of the character's nervous force, his restless mental energy that prompts his outrageous lines. But as the play develops he seems to grow with it."

John Horton Jnr.–"The Wayside cast, ably directed by Marilyn Mattys, is fine. As the reunited lovers, Glyn Jones and Anne Marley are superb, displaying a wide range of emotions and a deft comedic touch, as well as a rather aggressive style of fighting. Both are exceedingly gifted actors and it is a delight to watch them at work.

Joe Mattys and Amanda Maxwell personify their roles as the new spouses: He (*sic*) is priggish and stuffy; she is empty-headed and prone to histrionics.

Susan Orlich completes the cast in the inexplicable role of the French maid."

Lynn Price–"Jones, a British actor, is perfectly cast as Elyot, a role originally played by Coward. Elyot is suave, debonair, and sarcastic and Jones has the looks and mannerisms that make him appealing. Miss Maxwell does well as Sibyl, his young bride. She is shrill and cutesy. When she whines "Ellllyyyyyot," you feel like someone has scratched chalk on the blackboard.

After two seasons with Wayside it is easy to recognise Miss Marley and her characters. She's got a great deadpan stare letting the audience in on the absurdity of it all. She's funny and likeable, especially in this role. Joe Mattys is appropriately rigid in his role as Victor. His exaggerated inhibitions are classic.

Four of the summer's best actors are cast in this play and it's been fun to watch them in their different roles. The play itself is rather uneven, sometimes insightful, [!] sometimes dumb, often funny, sometimes flat. It plays through to August 31st."

The end of a fabulous summer, slightly marred by a nightmarish scene with Ed. I had mentioned to Allen that I couldn't understand why Ed's behaviour had changed so much and he discussed it with a colleague at JMU, adding his opinion that he thought Ed was jealous. Why Ed should be jealous I do not know but this prick at JMU repeated Allen's words to him and he had Anne and me out on the street in front of the theatre where, literally puce with rage, he berated us loudly for Allen's remarks. I listened to this for a while and then I said, 'Ed, stop right there. Whatever Allen may or may not have said, it was Allen who said it so there is simply no point in having a go at Anne and myself, especially out here on the street in full view of passers by. If you think I am going to stand here being yelled at as though I were a naughty schoolboy you can think again. I apologise if you feel we have been disloyal to you in any way though I don't believe that is the case. You have a bee in your bonnet about something else entirely. I don't know what it is and I don't want to know what it is and that is the end of it. Anne and I are now going back into the theatre.' And that is what we did. I have a feeling Ed belatedly realised where my predilections lie and he hated what he called "faggot's theatre".

22nd August 1985

How strange it is suddenly. Hard to believe, in just one week, the summer is over. Somehow it seems all wrong that there isn't a hive of activity outside. Everything is so quiet, so still and deserted. David

Chapter Twenty

and Bob said their tearful farewells yesterday and now there are only the diehards of "*Private Lives*" left. It seems like only yesterday we were starting the first day of the season and SETC seems like a whole lifetime away. It's been a wonderful experience though and I'm not sad. It's been the kind of thing you could never repeat so I will always remember the summer of '85 in Middleton, lush and green and basking in the sun Have we really done six shows? Now all you hear are the crickets and the cicadas and the birds.

With the last strike, the season was over. We packed our things, said our goodbyes and headed back to Harrisonburg. Some time later the Wayside Board of Directors advertised for a new artistic director and I applied for the post. I presumed they had after all, seen my work both as actor and director. Naturally I didn't get it. It became an Equity theatre and, when I went back to JMU in 1988 I saw a production there of one of my favourite plays, Eugene O'Neil's *Desire Under the Elms*. It was so bad I wonder I managed to sit through to the end and that is not sour grapes. Neither the director nor any member of the cast came within a mile of that play. It was dull, it was boring, and it was tedious, one big yawn, and false from beginning to end.

My time in Virginia had very sadly come to an end and I knew I would miss it. The Lyndrups drove me to Charlottesville and said goodbye on the station platform as I boarded the train for an eight day journey that would take me on a round trip of America and through twenty one states.

Chapter Twenty One

The train pulled out of Charlottesville at 8.42 and a short while after it rattled over the road that ran up the hill to the Lee farm at Covesville and I wanted to see the house for what I thought would be the last time, but it was just out of view above the hill. I settled down in my seat to watch the passing countryside but that didn't last too long. The most revolting smell suddenly permeated the coach. The train had run over a skunk. I retired to the rest room at the end of the car to have a smoke and, fortunately, the smell of the skunk didn't last too long. I had my Walkman and half a dozen favourite cassettes for company and back in my seat I settled down with my music and my memories before I fell asleep. My ticket didn't allow me the luxury of a bed but in the reclining seat it wasn't too uncomfortable and, anyway, I was going to have seven nights of it so there was no point in complaining if I ended up with stiff joints.

I didn't know where we were when I woke up. We must have passed the Carolinas and were either in Georgia or Alabama. What I remember most about this stage of the journey was the kudzu. This vigorous broad leaf vine had been imported, so I was told, from Japan to line the railway embankments in an effort to stop erosion, and now had such a hold it could not be got rid of as a thick carpet of it spread everywhere, even climbing and killing the tallest trees, stark white skeletons now in their dark green winding sheets.

Alabama was not at all as I had imagined. The countryside we

Chapter Twenty One

passed through was more like a gently rolling, green English county. The food on the train was good though the menu limited and, as it would be virtually the same on every train I rode, I was getting a little weary of it towards the end. Mississippi and Louisiana to go before we pulled into New Orleans in the early evening where Ed Real and David Faust were waiting to take me to their dimity flat at 711 Barracks Street. Dimity because it was once slave quarters and slaves obviously didn't need room to swing any old cat. Was any room more than six by six? It didn't seem like it. It lay, one of a number, at the end of a fairly spacious courtyard entered from the street through a high-gated wall, and the courtyard I called Sebastian's garden with its tropical flora and the sweet scent of the ginger plant's white flowers.

Norleens, as it is pronounced down there, was another part of America I fell in love with and not surprisingly it is such a fascinating city, but my time there was too short. It wasn't a voluntary stopover. My connection to head out west was 2.30 the following day so we had to cram in as much as we could in twenty hours starting naturally with the French Quarter. I sent Gray a postcard of his famous great uncle standing in his leafy square and saw the last streetcar named Desire, now a museum piece. I drank beers in the bars and delicious milky French coffees beneath the shadow of the cathedral.

From New Orleans it was into Texas, stopping at Austin, which is nothing to talk about, and continuing on until suddenly we stopped in the middle of nowhere. One thing about train travel in America, you're kept well informed as to what is around you, like desert critters you might catch a glimpse of (I didn't) and the one hundred and one uses of yucca and right at this moment the fact that the hotbox, whatever that was, had broken down, one of the consequences of which was that there would no longer be air-conditioning so we were going to have to sit in the middle of nowhere and wait for a replacement. Never mind, we'll trot off to the diner for some lunch. It was while I was sitting in the diner that I witnessed the most amazing phenomenon, especially as we were in the middle of the desert. When I looked out of the windows to my right all I could see was a sheet of

No Official Umbrella

water as the rain pelted down and, when I looked out of the window on my left, all I could see was blue sky and bright sunshine. The train was literally bisecting the weather. It didn't last long. The ground had probably dried out before the replacement hotbox arrived which, eventually it did and we were on our way again: New Mexico, Arizona and, finally, California–Los Angeles where Eileen T-Kaye was waiting to meet me.

12th August 1985

Hollywood

Well, here I am in Tinseltown. Have met and dined with most everyone connected with *Thriller of the Year* that is Bruce, Irene, Sandra and Eileen. Hollywood is weird, not what I expected but it would take twenty pages to talk about it even after only two days. The journey was fantastic. Enjoyed every minute of it. When a Texan tells you Texas is big you'd better believe it. Norleens is amazing.

Hollywood at last! - But only as a visitor.

Chapter Twenty One

Yes–*"If Ever I Cease To Love"* is still the song and everybody knows it though not the words. *[If Ever I Cease to Love, a George Leybourne song that is used for the entrance of Comus at the grand ball during carnival]* and I amazed them by telling them all about George. They are now trying to find out more as their interest (Ed and David's) is thoroughly aroused.

Jerry Johnson Productions have delivered a huge electric typewriter for me to work on; maybe I ought to do something with it. Haven't met Jerry yet but Eileen took me to a specialist crime/thriller bookshop the proprietor of which being delighted to meet one of his authors!

Saturday night Sandra is taking me to a theatre party and I think tomorrow night Eileen is taking me to The Hollywood Bowl if she can get tickets. *[She didn't]* It's the last night of the season–Handel with fireworks.

Had lunch at The Soup Kitchen with a very charming actress, Joanna Miles whose husband is BIG. They are coming to England together next month even though they are parting company as a couple. Her husband is the man who started HBO and is a big theatre, film, and TV producer. He is at the moment president of Playboy and has (I think) three pictures to produce.

13th August 1985

I've just finished the last of the rewrites. Everyone here is so excited about it. Don't know how long the enthusiasm will last but they're saying it's a better play than *Deathtrap* and *Sleuth* would you believe? *[The play was never produced in Hollywood, not that year or the next]* Thrillers are the big thing here at the moment. People go off for weekends and train trips to work out "Whodunit?" Anyway I'll tell you all when I get home. Expect me around the beginning of the month. Anne called this morning to say there was a letter from Seattle to say I am no longer in the running so I have called Amtrak and rescheduled to go straight from here to New York next Thursday. In New York I'll arrange the flight home or, if no one can put me up, go straight

No Official Umbrella

to the airport and try for a stand-by. Funnily enough I wasn't that disappointed when I heard the news about Seattle. I've really grown so philosophical about it all. I made the attempt, did the right things, more than that I can't do.

I was not enthusiastic about Los Angeles/Hollywood, not what I saw of it anyway. Part of the problem might have been that I was without transport and without a car you're really stumped. In between doing my rewrites I had lunches and dinners with different people at various restaurants, called three of my ex-students now trying to make it there and visited them in their shacks on the wrong side of the tracks; and Tim Schroder, a friend from London who was now curator of silver at the museum. Being a Schroder, silver was certainly his metier. We met at the farmers' market where he did some shopping and then drove along one of those long palm-lined avenues and up a windy road to his house on a hill overlooking the city; the house not all that large, not exactly a mansion, but pretty impressive anyway.

To change my schedule I called Amtrak. The receiver at the other end was lifted almost as it rang. 'Amtrak. How may I help you?'
'Oh! (Expecting to hold on and taken by surprise at the alacrity of the response) 'I have a ticket to New York via Seattle and I want to change it and travel direct.'
'Your name, sir?'
'Jones, Glyn.'
'Thank you, sir. Your new ticket is waiting for you at Los Angeles. Have a pleasant trip.'
That was all it took. I doubt the call lasted a minute and I reckoned British Rail, as it then was, could have learnt a lesson or two from Amtrak.

Come time to leave, Eileen and I went for lunch at an Italian restaurant called *Fellini's*. The waiter approached our table and we ordered, adding a request for service to be fairly quick as I had a train to catch. The young man, no doubt a would-be actor, raised both eyebrows and, pulling himself up to his full height, said in tones dramatic, 'You're travelling Amtrak?'

'I am.'

'And what is wrong with flying, may I ask?'

'Firstly, flying bores me, you can't see much from forty thousand feet, secondly I love trains and, thirdly, can you get that order through fairly fast please?' Almost as fast as changing my ticket, two plates were slapped down on the table. 'Enjoy your meal,' he said as he sashayed away.

I don't know why but I had thought my train's departure time was two-thirty and, as we entered the very large parking lot at the station, over the tannoy I heard, 'This is the last call for The Desert Wind. The last call for The Desert Wind.'

'Jesus!,' I said to Eileen, 'That's my train!' I'd misread the time.

That day, I don't know why because I'd never seen it before and I don't know where it came from, Eileen was driving an open truck. I leapt out of the cab, grabbed my baggage from the bed at the back and yelled, 'I'll call you if I miss it!' And I was haring for the station. I got to the concourse which, as with everything else there, was vast and I thought as I surveyed eight miles of booking counter, 'Fuck the new ticket, there's no time,' and headed straight for the tunnel to be faced by another eight miles of that with branches off to left and right. Where was my train? It was extremely hot, I was carrying heavy luggage, I was a man in my fifties and it was probably just as well that I had been playing a lot of tennis because I ran. Passing half a dozen very long inclined side exits I decided I ought to surface and see where I was, so up one of the inclines I lumbered. Reaching the platform I saw my train was still two exits away but at least it was still there. Shit! What if I got there just as it was pulling out? By the time I reached the right exit I had slowed almost to a snail's pace, I was dripping with sweat, my chest was heaving, my legs were jelly. I was greeted by a smiling young woman: pretty, petite, blonde and cool; complete with clipboard and dressed in a uniform similar to that of an air hostess. 'Mr Jones?'

I nodded. I couldn't speak.

'Oh, good. You're our last one. We were waiting for you.'

Oh, dear, British Rail, beat that if you can. A whole trainload of people who should have left twenty minutes or so earlier had patiently waited for the last booked passenger to appear. With no hint of anything but consideration she showed me to my coach. The black attendant took my luggage; climbed up behind me carrying his little set of steps, and slammed the door behind him. Then he turned to me and said, 'You jes' stan' there a while, honey, an' have your heart attack, an' then I'll show you to your seat.'

I had no sooner sat down than the train was pulling out. Five minutes later there was an announcement. 'Mr and Mrs So and So are looking for a couple to make up a foursome at bridge. If anybody's interested they are in the observation car.' Later when I strolled up to the observation car the game was in full progress. I made friends with an eighty-year something lady from Florida who was a charming companion and who soon issued an invitation for me to visit when I was next in the states. A widow with a grown up family and grandchildren behind her, she was travelling simply for the sake of travelling, something she did quite often evidently. At dinner a couple were ushered into the seats opposite me and they had no sooner sat down than I heard, 'Hi. My name is Eric and this is my wife, Coreen.' At least that's what it sounded like. I sometimes had difficulty in understanding various American accents. For example on a train from Philadelphia to New York I went into the buffet car and ordered a coffee and a doughnut and heard, 'Plenawpdd.' She had to repeat it three or four times before, exasperated at talking to someone obviously brain-dead, she said extremely slowly, 'Plain … or … powdered,' meaning I presumed did I want my doughnut dusted with sugar. 'Oh!' I said. 'Powdered if you don't mind?' She gave me a very wry look. Eric went on to say he was a realtor which,

Chapter Twenty One

looking at the diamond ring, the diamond encrusted wristwatch, the gold bracelets and the gold necklaces didn't really surprise me, remembering what Eileen told me she had paid for her little mock Mexican hacienda and what Tim had paid for his more opulent dwelling. Needless to say Eric monopolised the conversation, a lot of it being about golf, a game I have little time for. Coreen said only a few words such as, 'Yes, dear,' and 'No, I don't think so, dear.' I also noticed she wore no jewellery.

So, from Los Angeles, it was back through Utah and a stop at Salt Lake City, a city that looked rather flat and dreary to me although the railway station was an impressive piece of architecture and I saw at a siding a goods truck with ACHESON TOPEKA & SANTE FE printed in large letters along its side: youthful memories of The Beverly Sisters. I don't remember whether it was in the wide flat country of Utah or whether it was Montana but the railway line ran for miles parallel to a dead straight road alongside of which there were occasional small rows of houses, maybe a dozen or so in all, maybe a few more, and in front of each house was parked, not an automobile, but a small plane, the road being used as the landing strip. 'Won't be long, honey, just flying down to the supermarket, vroom vroom.'

On into Colorado, a state of such breath-taking majestic scenery it seemed to me all the houses were plain and simple as though the people thought, how can we compete with nature when she's this grand? The train climbed into the mountains to the longest tunnel on the track and of course we were getting a running commentary, which was now all about how the tunnel was built. At this stage, our commentator informed us, because of the altitude, (we wouldn't be going any higher) Amtrak was prepared to give us a free health check. If we would be so good as to place our right hand against the nearest window? Of course, everybody did so, 'Now, if you can feel the pane,' the voice said, 'you're perfectly healthy.' There was a second or two before you heard the loudest concerted groan in the world at having been taken in by such an awful pun. Then of course the laughter followed and everybody felt good and neighbourly at being such a klutz. Descending on the far side the lights of Denver came into view spread out way below us, a wonderful sight as we descended, almost as though we were coming down from the sky. And so on through Nebraska, Iowa and Illinois to Chicago where we changed trains for New York.

It was back to Marcus Lutsky's apartment in Thompson Street, lugging my suitcase up those familiar six flights of stairs. The train had pulled in to Grand Central mid-afternoon and that evening we went into China Town to eat and then enjoyed the Mulberry Street Fair, it being the Feast of St. Gennaro. The next day I did a hot and sweaty round of the bucket shops and booked a cheap flight to London with Air India. A single by British Air was unbelievably expensive and we're talking cattle-car class. I said to the girl at the desk all I wanted was a single ticket to London, I didn't want to buy the aircraft. She was not amused. After that it was lunches and dinners and I attended a Director's Workshop at The Lincoln Center before having dinner at the Supreme Macaroni Company, the name making me think of The Automatic Meat Pie Restaurant in Liberia. Hairdressers and restaurants can come up with some lovely unusual names. After the Supreme Macaroni Company, I can't remember who with, I went on to see the play *Orphans* which I loved and saw again in London starring Albert Finney. That was at a special pro's matinee that brought the house down, and a play I would later get a chance to direct. It seems I also went one evening to a play reading at 39 Grove Street, *Shadow of an Outcast*, and a play of which I have no memory so it couldn't have impressed me at all. Also, all that week in New York, according to my diary, someone called Mary figures on a number of occasions and I'm afraid I have no memory of her either. Strange to say there's no mention of a visit to The Strand Bookshop. Could I have been a whole week in the Big Apple and not visited my favourite shop? On my last morning I had breakfast with Marcus and Jeff Dunn at Le Figaro, and from Thompson Street lugged my suitcase down those six flights of stairs, headed out to JFK and so to London.

Chapter Twenty One

Saying goodbye to New York was as big a wrench as saying goodbye to Virginia and when I stepped off the plane at Heathrow the sky was grey, all the world was grey. It was drizzling. After New York it was decidedly chilly and I was shivering. In the underground the people looked downcast, depressed dejected, dreary, they looked grey. They looked shabby. They looked the way I felt. I knew, once I was through our front door, I would be glad to see home again, but sitting in that train my heart was most definitely back in Virginia. Ah, well, I thought, it's back to the Labour Exchange.

Chapter Twenty Two

Too late for the two plays in Harrogate, after a meeting with Nigel Robinson the W.H.Allen editor, and my prose style being acceptable, I settled down to write the novelisation of *Doctor Who and The Space Museum*. I put Gray into it as leader of the rebels, changing his name to Gyar, and Lieutenant David C. Harwell, US Airforce as an exhibit in the museum. I should think Chris and possibly others are in it somewhere but I haven't read it for such a long time I don't remember where or how. I finished writing it at the turn of the year.

We rehearsed *Champagne Charlie* again and Chris performed it at The King's Head in Islington with Paul Knight now at the piano instead of Jeff Clarke. Jeremy was a drunken, noisy, and rather embarrassing member of the audience making what he thought were encouraging, but unnecessary, noises.

In November I auditioned for the part of the girl's father in *La Cages aux Folles* to go on at The London Palladium but sadly didn't get it. I would have enjoyed being in that glitzy, razzmatazz, gender-bender show even playing such a straight part. That same day I lunched with Jerry Johnson but there was no further news on the proposed Hollywood production of *Thriller of the Year* and I had already given up on that one. I thought I might make a few pennies selling photographs. After all I had, amongst others, some really beautiful pictures of Virginia, a riot of colour in the fall, but I was informed that agencies preferred transparencies and all my pictures were negative.

Chapter Twenty Two

So it seemed like pretty much everything was negative and, apart from my *Doctor Who*, the last three months of 1985 dwindled away in unmemorable fashion, except for one piece of excitement in the house. Impressed by the usefulness of the microwave oven at Wayside I, who being a Luddite had always been against it, went out and bought one. Dave wrote out a series of quite large signs with arrows which he taped up on the walls leading all the way from the front door and saying things like THIS WAY TO THE NEW MICRO and KEEP GOING and STRAIGHT AHEAD and YOU'RE ALMOST THERE and finally above the actual oven and with an arrow point down, the atomic symbol and TA RA! HERE IT IS! And here is a commercial break, a puff for SHARP; twenty years later that machine is still going strong.

Having finished and delivered *Doctor Who*, I went on to rewrite *Early One Morning* for Paul. Called *Pick Up* at first, the title was changed to *Fugue in Two Flats* and much much later I added a song brought about by an incident in Copenhagen. I was travelling in a trolley car and, at a stop, a beautiful young man got out and, before he walked away, he turned and gave me a look that set the pulse racing. Except that he was that much older than the boy in *Death in Venice* it was almost Death In Copenhagen time. The doors closed while I was still slightly in a state of shock and the song was right there in my head. Paul put a beautiful melody to my lyric, "Then a glance from a stranger, and my world could fall apart." I don't even remember where I was going that day.

Chris performed *Champagne Charlie* at The British Music Hall Association and various other venues around London and there were visits to the theatre: *Parsifal* at The Coliseum with the American Tenor, Warren Ellsworth; slender, lithe, a beautiful animal in movement and gesture and with such a voice. How does one describe a voice and avoid all the hackneyed expressions; honeyed, golden, thrilling, magnificent? The opera world suffered a grievous loss with his early death at forty-three. I can remember only five occasions in my life when I have written to someone to tell him or her how much I admired his or her work. Warren Ellsworth was one. Hildagard Hartwig, who I heard singing Octavian in *Der Rosenkavalier* in Hamburg and who was but the most perfect, most truly believable Octavian ever, again with a voice to raise the hair on the back of your neck was another. Then there was Peter Firth for *Equus* and both writer and director for the BBC's original and brilliant *The Lost Boys*, teleplay on Barrie and the Llewelyn boys. I call it the BBC's original because many years later I was in a programme of the same name but definitely not the same subject. I wrote to Jamie O'Neill in praise of his beautiful novel *Two Boys at Swim*. Oh, how I would dearly love to write a film script for that. Then of course there was my backstage visit to the cast of *March of the Falsettos* in Toronto so really I suppose that makes six in all.

We saw *The Critic* and *The Real Inspector Hound* at the National which we thought rather a rep production but with a lot more money thrown at it, *La Cages aux Folles* which I still wished I'd been in, *The Three Sisters, Barnum, Torch Song Trilogy* and *Café Puccini*, presented by Cameron Mackintosh and Andrew Lloyd Webber and written by Robin Ray which we thoroughly enjoyed despite it being hammered by the critics who were terribly snooty and highbrow in their reviews. So what was wrong with *Café Puccini*? Couldn't they lower their highbrows for one light-hearted enjoyable evening in the theatre? I mean! Did Puccini have the gift of melody or did he not? Obviously his gift of melody was not enough for that lot. I can't remember what radio programme I was listening to one day but it was one of those gather around and lets talk about something type programmes and this one was on modern music to which someone who sounded rather like a fruity old Colonel or Brigadier or some such obviously objected as he said, and I can't help but sympathise with him, "Tunes, my boy, tunes! That's what it's all about! Tunes!"

Towards the end of May, Gray paid a visit. We took him to The Players Theatre for a taste of Music Hall and in Golden Square at a

Chapter Twenty Two

"World Run" he was accosted by a grossly made-up queen in full drag, which didn't seem to faze him a bit so I took their photograph together. It was tourist time again as we took him down to Greenwich, to the Victoria and Albert Museum, London's east end, Brick Lane market and Jack the Ripper territory, Gordon's Wine Cellars at Charing Cross which he particularly liked. Covent Garden. He wanted to be left alone at Covent Garden so, making sure he knew how to get back to Stoke Newington, we left him to it. I was still up and about gone one in the morning when in he came with a girl he had picked up which obviously had been the object of the exercise. As he was sleeping in the spare bed in my study on the ground floor he obviously felt it was too easy to sneak in without disturbing anyone except that, though the fuck might have been a good one, I doubt they slept very well in that narrow single bed.

There was a positive orgy of theatre going of course, *Orpheus in the Underworld* at the ENO, *A Midsummer Night's Dream* at The Donmar, the awful *Mutiny* at The Piccadilly, *Lend me a Tenor* at The Globe, *Run for Your Wife* at The Criterion, a ballet triple bill at The Royal Opera House, a concert at St. Martin's In the Fields, *Chorus of Disapproval* at The Lyric, *Orphans* at The Apollo, *Noises Off* at The Savoy. He came with us down to the Cadbury Country Club near Bristol where Chris was doing yet another *Champagne Charlie* and, half way through his stay, the pair of them went up to Newcastle for a few days, while back in London I had an interview for The English Theatre of Hamburg followed by a reading with prospective cast and was contracted to play George in *Who's Afraid of Virginia Woolf?* towards the end of the year. The day before Gray left we had tea at The Savoy. This was one of our rare expensive treats. I took him to Gatwick Airport, we said good-by and I watched him go through the gate, disappointed that at the last minute he did not turn around for one final look.

The English Theatre of Hamburg is in a converted public baths on the first floor of a building mainly occupied by doctors' offices. It has a storeroom in the basement and that is where we gathered to rehearse

No Official Umbrella

With Suzanne Jefferies - Who's Afraid of Virginia Woolf - Hamburg

Virginia Woolf. Because the performances act as English lessons for German school kids the theatre works well audience wise. It was (is) run by an American couple, Clifford Dean and Robert Rumpf and Cliff was directing *Virginia Woolf.* Totally unwilling to take any suggestions from his actors we let him get on with it.

There was a flat for the men and another for the ladies and, although the young actor playing Nick was fine in the part, as a person I found him rather boring so we didn't see all that much of each other and where it would have been welcome to have had a companion on outings to concerts, museums etc., I either went on my own or to musical events with Michael Medlinger, the lighting designer, another American who fortunately was a music lover. There was also the fun Gudrun Kossak, our stage manager who made life a joy and who we're still in touch with.

Martha was played by a lady who put my back up from the moment I met her, a rep actress who gave her best performance at the curtain call, which was the only time she really looked at me in a way that told the audience how very much in love we really were. Other than that she more or less shut her cubicle door in my face and left me to do my own thing while she did hers.

There was very little wing space stage left, it was a really tight squeeze, and that was where the front door to the apartment was placed. At our first entrance, Cliff had it blocked that I went straight across to my chair downstage right, sat down, switched on the occasional lamp and lifted my newspaper to read while Martha stayed upstage behind the sofa doing her 'What a dump!' bit. The lights were not practical so my lamp had to be switched on from the lighting box, which was at the back of the auditorium. One night I duly reached out to switch it on and nothing happened. I glanced up at the box where I could see two figures that weren't looking at the stage at all but having an animated conversation. I tried the lamp two or three times and then, logically thinking the audience were going to have a great laugh if I started reading my paper in the dark, I got up and walked across to the chair downstage left. This unexpected movement alerted the lighting box so that, when I switched on that twin lamp it actually worked. But it completely threw our Martha who lost her lines and stood there gaping like a stranded fish until I put her back on track.

No matter my private thoughts on her acting, Martha received good reviews for her performance and so, I am glad to say, did I for George, though it is one of those parts you are never entirely satisfied with. I kept on finding new things, different reasons for what I was doing. For example, well into the run I suddenly thought even as I was doing it, "This is not the place to break down. George's breakdown should come later and he isn't crying for himself. He's crying for Martha." So I changed it. She was so wrapped up in herself she probably didn't even notice.

"In Glyn Jones the perfect George has been found, a master of cynical attitude"–Hamburger Abendblatt.

"More important however is Martha's husband, the weakling George who is suddenly prepared to do everything. Glyn Jones gives a masterful performance of hurtful revenge and intellectual self-pity"– Die Welt.

We gave ten o'clock in the morning performances for schools. Yuk! They tended to be a little on the noisy side but one rode it until one day the noise got to be too much. I presume it was kids not understanding something and asking each other questions but, at the top of act two George has a fairly long speech that does require a great deal of concentration so I stopped and turned to the audience and waited until you could hear a pin drop. Then I went into a spiel about you can hear us, we can hear you, we are live flesh and blood and not a television show so would you please keep the noise down just a little and I'll start all over again. Nick sat there with his jaw hitting the carpet. She, who wasn't even on stage, was terribly upset by my behaviour, how unprofessional it was. We continued in dead silence until, in the fight with Nick, as he clobbered me and I hit the floor, there was a rousing cheer that I couldn't help but smile at which got a round of applause. After the show one of the schoolmasters came backstage to apologise for his rowdy pupils.

Unfortunately I was to stop another ten o'clock show but this time certainly not deliberately, unless you call too many cigarettes and early morning coffees deliberate. Getting towards the end of the first act my heart suddenly started to thump rather wildly which of course made me tense up as I wondered whether I was going to get through to the end of the act, which made my heart thump even more violently. I came off stage and said to Gudrun, 'We have a problem.'
'Oh. Yes? And what is that?'
'Feel,' and I put her hand to my chest.
'Oh, my God!' She shrieked, and that was the end of the performance with that old cliché, 'Is there a doctor in the house?' There was, and if there hadn't have been, there were plenty in the building. I was all prepared to go back on stage if the heart calmed down in the interval but the doctor made me lie down on the dressing room

Chapter Twenty Two

floor, an ambulance was called and I was stretchered out to it, totally embarrassed and feeling an absolute prick. The Krankenhaus was within spitting distance of the theatre so that ambulance ride was the most expensive journey I have ever made, coming out as I remember it at the equivalent of about three hundred quid. At the hospital I was wheeled into A&E, asked a lot of questions in German hardly any of which I could answer, given a whiff of oxygen, put to bed and stayed there overnight. In the morning I walked out and back to the theatre a free man.

Unfortunately the theatre was not insured for loss of the performance which was a blow but I was insured for medical expenses so the insurance company paid that ridiculous ambulance bill.

I caught up with Peter Oeser after more than thirty years and he and his Elise wined and dined me most generously, took me to their holiday home on the island of Sylt–my God, was I nearly frozen to death? – To Lübeck where the marzipan comes from also to Travemunde where we sat in a tenth floor (or was it twelfth?) elegant restaurant and looked down on the bright lights of the town, the coming and going of traffic and the docks with cargo ships lined up alongside the wharfs. Then, if you lifted your gaze and stared across the water to the far side, all was pitch black broken by the occasional sweep of a searchlight. It was spine chilling. It was East Germany.

The Reeperbahn was not at all what I expected, not a narrow dirty little alley with its brothels, clubs, and sex-shops which of course it has but a wide avenue. Chris came for a visit and we went to the St Pauli Theatre there to see a play called *The Cuckoo's Egg* starring a seventy year old actress who could still high kick her leg over her head (and what a pair of legs she had) and just happened during the course of the play to have brought her music along so she could give us a couple of numbers. We had wondered what the piano was doing on the stage.

I also heard, from the gallery in the beautiful Baroque church of

No Official Umbrella

St. Michaeli, a glorious performance of *Verdi's Requiem* and, when I briefly thought of what was happening down there in and around the Reeperbahn, I realised I was more than happy to be up, as it were, with the angels in the gallery. I also went with Michael Medlinger to the Musikhalle to a performance of *Faure's Requiem* and to the same venue for a performance of *Buckner's Seventh Symphony*, my first experience of Bruckner live! I do honestly believe words are inadequate to describe that experience.

Music and opera going were well within one's pocket. A perfectly good seat in the opera house for a performance of *Turandot* cost me roughly eight pounds, a seat which in London at that time would have cost four or even five times as much. A big disappointment was a production of *West Side Story* that was touring Europe at the time and which Gudrun and I went to. God alone knows where it came from and who were supposed to be the "stars" that were mentioned in the blurb. It was being performed in a great barn of a place and in the interval I had to complain to the management about the constant use of flash as a particular member of the audience kept snapping away so, after an announcement, that at least stopped. Actually the production was so awful I wasn't particularly concerned. In a letter home I wrote, "*WEST SIDE STORY*" was a turkey. Maria had a voice like a tomcat having his balls squeezed in a vice. Anita, according to her bio, won third prize in the MISS DANCE COMPETITION OF GREAT BRITAIN 1983! As for the rest of the perfs let's not even talk about them. The sets were appalling; the lighting atrocious, the sound came through thick layers of cotton wool, and the German audience cheered itself hoarse. But the highlight of this raggle-taggle-gypsy-o piece of third rate tat was Anita's tits falling out of her bra so she had to finish singing '*I like to be in America*' holding her straps and dancing with one arm in a half nelson. There was a couple sitting right in front of us and I turned to Gudrun and said, 'That lady was a cat in a previous existence.' She had that kittenish quality about her and these enormous perfectly round eyes, just like a cat. She turned round and smiled at me and I thought, 'Oh, God! She heard what I said and she speaks English!' Anyway, she whispered something to her husband and turned around again, still smiling, and pretended to survey the audience. After doing this a couple more times she obviously couldn't contain herself any longer and almost jumped out of her cat skin to say, 'Excuse me, excuse me … you were wonderful … wonderful in *Virginia Woolf*.' 'Thank you,' I said, so I don't think she knew I had likened her to a cat, a nice cat. Mind you, with the audience screaming its tits off at *West Side Story*, should I take her praise with a pinch of salt?

The wonderful thing about Hamburg, apart from the music and the museums and the art galleries, apart from the Jungstil architecture that escaped allied bombing during World War II is that, without enormous skyscrapers and architectural monstrosities that simply wouldn't fit in, (I'm thinking here of what they've been doing to London) its scale in human terms makes it a beautiful and most liveable in city. Like Munich it has its reminder of a darker side of history nearby, in this case the site of the concentration camp that was Belsen. Apart from mounds covering mass graves, all signs of the horror are long since gone and it is a quiet park-like place in the midst of a vast expanse of heath, though standing there in the silence and chilled to the bone, it could still cause the deepest disquiet. Chris and I visited it because his father was one of the first British soldiers into the camp and Hyst Mum wanted us to go.

Four days before Christmas *Virginia Woolf* finished its run and I flew home to London. I had twelve days; most of it spent sorting out my income tax, before flying off again, this time to Denmark. It was during this brief hectic period that we got news of our friend Rosemary Matthews being taken to hospital. Rosemary's was a sad unfulfilled life both emotionally and as a would-be actress. She was well on in life when someone from her church actually courted and proposed to her, a proposal she accepted only to lose him to the grim reaper within a matter of days. Stanley Miller, he who invented names for people, also had a sometimes-unkind turn of phrase, and said of her, if she visited a battleship the ship would sink. I know what he meant because I took her to the Royal Opera House one evening where she embarrassed me not a little by falling upstairs! I telephoned the hospital and spoke to the matron asking for a prognosis and she said it was believed Rosemary could last a year. With this in mind and with so much to do I decided to leave visiting until I returned from Denmark. Alas, I hadn't been there more than a week when Chris telephoned to say Rosemary had died. I had ambivalent feelings towards Rosemary. On the one hand I felt great pity for her and on the other hand she irritated the shit out of me like grown women who say "mummy" and play at still being little girls. I had wanted for some time to write a play about sad unfulfilled Rosemary (and all the other Rosemarys of this world, male as well as female) but it just would not be born. After Chris's phone call, I sat down at the typewriter and, with no gestation period, or perhaps it had been gestating all these years without my realising it, I knocked off the play in less than a week. And this was alongside the amount of work I had to do at the school.

Mickey Fredie Pedersen was (is) an ex-ballroom dancing champion; the kind of man who wears a tan, a gold necklace, a shirt unbuttoned to the navel and who gets confidential and tearfully sentimental when in his cups. Already in possession of a dance studio, two large rooms, a sort of café/greenroom, changing rooms and showers, and an office outside of which was a largish lobby in which smaller classes could be held, I suppose it was a natural progression for him to think, with such premises, it was a good idea to start a theatre school, adding to his income already derived from dance classes for the toddlers who, to the annoyance of the "theatre" students, swarmed around the school like gnats whenever they had a class.

Mickey interviewed me in London and took me on. He wanted it to be for two semesters but I suggested we make it just one and see how it went. I also wanted to know how I could teach in Denmark when I had no knowledge of Danish. That was evidently no problem as all the kids were fluent in English, which proved to be almost true. This was to be the third season at DANMARKS SHOW OG TEATERSKOLE for which Mickey hired in England two teacher/directors; myself and Andy Smith, a dance teacher (modern and tap) and choreographer, Amie Sharpless, and a Musical Director, Roger Davidson. There was also a black American dance teacher of jazz by the name of Philip who lived in Malmo and crossed the water for his classes, a Danish singing teacher named Henning who had his students singing while doing push-ups which struck me as being just a teeny-weeny bit bizarre, but then what do I know about singing teachers and their methods? There was also an ancient retired chain-smoking ('Who cares as long as I've got the pills?') Danish actress who taught voice!

Letters From Denmark.

8th January 1987

Torsdag.

The Danes say 'Hi!" for 'Hello' and 'Hi' for goodbye so this is a hello Hi. I haven't learnt anything else in Danish because they all speak English, some of them so beautifully it fair makes you sick. But all about my skole (oh, another Danish word!). I can't believe almost a week has gone, but having been thrown in the deep end with four groups a day to teach (the third years are divided into two groups) I have been (a) pretty whacked and (b) getting my homework done. So far classes have gone well, touch wood. I haven't yet heard them sing or seen them dance but, as far as the acting is concerned, you could say I have started with raw material. Last year they had some American and the more they talk about him the more I wish they hadn't had him. For example today, Tom and Timm (sounds like a double act) and a girl whose name I can't remember, I can't remember the girls because like Tom and Timm, they are Unge, Inge, and Enge and I can't remember which is which. I remember Monica because she is SO cute and never stops smiling. And I remember

Heger because she always wants to do everything, and I remember Henrietta because, when I pointed to her to get up and do something she said, as she got to her feet, 'You don't know my name, do you?' To which I, in all honesty, replied, 'No, I've forgotten it.' 'Humph!' she sniffed. 'You don't know it because you didn't ask for it.' So I couldn't forget Henrietta now, could I? Anyway, Tom, Timm, and the girl did a scene from *My Fair Lady* in Danish and, after they'd done it and I made them do it again, I started to point out what I thought about it. In truth it was appalling. Tom said, 'But we did this time and time for the American, David, and he never told us these things. But you are right so why didn't David tell us?' There was of course no answer to that except that David just didn't know his arse from his elbow or was into "the method." I suspect the latter because he left the first years suspended from a limb not knowing their arses from their elbows, a totally confused bunch of kids.

The beautiful thing about them, and they are beautiful, is their eagerness. I finish something and there are cries of 'More! More!' or 'Can I do it again? I want to do it again.' *[This certainly didn't apply to all, as I was to find out]* Today I was a real shit. I made the boys do an *Equus* exercise, one student playing the horse and another, the boy, Alan Strang, who had to creep into the stable, take the horse into a field, make love to it, ride it, and cum. Flemyng did the Alan Strang and Jan did the horse. Timm, objected, saying he didn't believe Flemyng was emotionally involved with the horse so I had Timm do it and he was quite upset that everyone thought Flemyng was better. Timm and Jan (pronounced Jen) are very close friends so maybe Timm didn't realise this was making him somewhat inhibited. They are both nineteen and both beautiful. Timm is rather like Gray Lee. Jan is a big doll: tall, well-built; walks like John Wayne, has bushy eyebrows that meet in the middle and spiky blonde hair like a horse's mane. In fact he made a lovely horse. Flemyng was wonderful as the boy. He lives with one of the girls in the school. He is smallish, very quiet, but, boy, do still waters run deep. At first I tried to get the German, Christoff, to do Alan but he shied away totally. I asked him

Chapter Twenty Two

if he was afraid of it and he said, yes he was, he wasn't going to have anything to do with it, no way. So I turned to Flemyng sitting quietly in the corner and said, 'Flemyng?' and, without a word, he got up, led Jan to where he wanted him, and got on with it. There was no way that improvisation was going to be stopped until Flemyng had ridden his horse, had his orgasm, and recovered. Then he went back to his corner without a word and silently waited to hear what everyone had to say which wasn't all that much as they were all (except Timm) rocked back on their heels anyway. Jan, who had baulked at being asked to play a horse, was totally in Flemyng's control and was being a horse for all he was worth, like a puppet ceasing to be a puppet he became a horse in front of our very eyes. It was magical.

Then, for the girls, I gave them Jocasta impaling herself on the sword. Jan objected to this. He didn't see why she couldn't just stab herself, and all the girls yelled that it was sexually symbolic, didn't he see? And Jan went a beetroot colour and said, yes, okay, he did see. Anyway, there was only time for one girl to do it and who jumped up? Heger of course. One of the others said to me afterwards, 'What have you done to Heger last term she wouldn't get up and do anything and now she wants to do everything.' I don't recall doing anything in particular to Heger.

Yesterday afternoon I made my first timid foray into Copenhagen. Amager is an island and not considered, especially by the Amagerians or whatever they're called, to be part of the city proper, a bit like the Gozotans not being Maltese. I didn't get too far though. It was a lovely day without a cloud in the sky but it was -10c so I slipped into the National Museum and discovered another treasure house and a vending machine that makes the most delicious hot chocolate.

The only problem about the job so far is the living arrangements and I really don't know quite what to do about it. Space in Copenhagen is scarce and expensive. Most of the students live miles from the school, Roger and Amie are billeted with Mickey's in-laws and I am ensconced in Mickey's house. His wife, Suss, is very sweet and they've tried to make me comfortable. The room is almost a separate part of the house and is divided into two with an arch in the dividing wall so that it is like a bedroom and a living room, but both small. The bathroom is right next door and the only other person who uses it is the au pair so that's no problem. They said if I want to watch TV or just feel like sitting to go into their drawing room but I really don't want to do that. Most important, I can't cook. There's an electric plate on which I can make tea and coffee, and a fridge, but that's it. I can't even make toast. In fact there's not even a bread knife, not even a tin opener. There is one small saucepan and a little coffee maker, one of those glass ones with a plunger to hold down the grains, which does for tea as well. Suss did say if I wanted to cook to use their kitchen but I don't want to do that either. It's just not comfortable. It was different at Al and Anne's, there I lived en famille but this is really picnicking. Also Gigi has taken a great shine to me and wants to visit and it is boring. In the first place she is five years old, chatters incessantly in Danish, and won't leave when firmly pointed in the direction of the door. She's not supposed to visit of course and has been told as much a number of times but what do you do with a child of five, lock her up? She brings me all her treasures to look at. Yesterday I had to go through a whole box of ear rings and pretend I was really set back on my heels by them and this morning I found her in the bathroom brushing her teeth with my toothbrush! As I sit here and look around, most of my stuff seems to be scattered around the floor and, when I go out, I have to make sure things like toiletries, Walkman, etc., are all put up on top of the cupboard out of reach of little wandering fingers. Anyway, my room is cleaned for me, my laundry is done for me, my teas, coffees and snacks in the greenroom are free and Mickey even paid my bus pass which is all just as well, a very uninteresting takeaway pizza is £3.50. The meal we had at the local Amager hostelry the first night was wonderful but we only had one course (I had a dessert because the others had Irish coffee) and wine and the bill came to K1350, which in pounds is about 135.

When I'd finished class this afternoon Mickey said did I have time to talk scripts? So we went into his office and first he asked me how

Chapter Twenty Two

I felt about directing *Guys & Dolls*. I'd love to direct *Guys & Dolls* but definitely not with the students as they were so I said no to that one. Then he asked me how I felt about Brecht. Forget it, I said, I'm no Brechtian. There's only one thing of Brecht's I want to direct and that's *The Threepenny Opera*. 'I'm glad you said that,' he replied as he pushed the script across the desk. I had tried to persuade him to let me do *Candide* but he wouldn't buy it, firstly because it is not translated into Danish and secondly because he doesn't know it although the script is lying there in his office.

So, apart from classes, over the next nine weeks my projects are:

3rd Years: THREEPENNY OPERA (4 weeks) followed by a compilation WEST SIDE STORY / ROMEO & JULIET (5 weeks).
2nd Years: An evening made up of scenes from various musicals and plays.
1st Years: ANIMAL FARM which as a class they will translate into Danish.

I don't have a class tomorrow until 6 but I am going in for 9 in the morning to share Roger's, as I want to hear the third years sing. *[During Roger's class, with the students standing in a group around the piano, I moved from one to the other listening to voices as he put them through their exercises and, suddenly, there was this rich bass. Whoa! A budding Chaliapin. Who is that then? A boy named Lars who hadn't up to now been exactly in the forefront of things.]*

I will be going to Norway on the 18th. Will be in Oslo just for a weekend and the reason is there has been a whole heap of applications from Norwegians for places at the school, about 25, and Mickey is going over to audition them together with Roger and myself. Who am I to say no to a weekend in Oslo, even if I am working most of the time? Copenhagen (what I have seen of it) looks fascinating but,

No Official Umbrella

unfortunately, the graffiti freaks are rampant here and buildings look like New York subway trains. *[Before the big clean-up.]* Sad. The studio space is limited so, if he is going to take on more students, he will have to do something about it. I haven't yet been able to take the first years in a big space and I need to at least once. They don't even know the basic positions on the stage. I need a stage size space to show 'em. I believe Mickey is trying to get his hands on an actual theatre, possibly even negotiating for it at the moment. If the Norwegian invasion takes place he'll need it.

16th January 1987

This is the evening I've put together for the 2nd Years:
- COME TO THE CABARET (In Danish)
- COMEDY TONIGHT (in English)
- LITTLE GIRLS (in English)
- ADELAIDE'S LAMENT (Danish)
- GOOD TO MOMMA (English)
- A scene from THE LYSISTRATA (Danish)
- VITE VITE VITE (Cole Porter–English)
- A scene from BOYS IN THE BAND (English)
- A scene from ORPHANS (Danish)
- DENTIST (Little Shop of Horrors–English)
- NO TWO PEOPLE (Hans Christian Anderson–English)
- GET ME TO THE CHURCH ON TIME (Danish)
- BRUSH UP YOUR SHAKESPEARE (1st verse. Danish)
- Scene from TAMING OF THE SHREW (Danish)
- BRUSH UP YOUR SHAKESPEARE (2nd verse. Danish)
- Scene from TWELFTH NIGHT (Danish)
- BRUSH UP YOUR SHAKESPEARE (Last verse. Danish)
- THE FALLEN STAR–Music Hall song (English)
- THE BEST OF TIMES (English)
- IT'S NOT WHERE YOU START IT'S WHERE YOU FINISH. (English)

Chapter Twenty Two

I've given the list to Micky to sort out any copyright problems.

I told the kids if they had any favourites they wanted included to let me know but they didn't, so now they have to accept what I worked on which includes some of MY favourites.

Yesterday there was no heating in the building, maintenance or something. Fortunately the thermometer had shot up from arctic to only -2° so it wasn't, in fact, too bad.

Talking about walking living breathing dolls, another one has appeared on the scene. I saw it sitting against the wall in the green-room with its arms curled around its knees and, if Jan is a magnificent animal doll, this one is a piece of porcelain. In fact I really couldn't decide whether it was a boy or a girl until it stood up and then I saw it was most definitely a boy. Its name is Morten.

Oslo tomorrow and the number of auditionees, if that's the right word, has gone up to 31 so we're really going to have our work cut out. Some of them are travelling greater distances to get there than we are. I also took a class of juniors last week as Suss was ill. Out of a class of nine, three had difficulty with English but the others were quick to translate so there was no problem. They were great and one little girl sang from *Annie* ("Far Away?") with a belter that would have knocked Streisand off the stage. Then there was Tony who is ten: a mass of curly red hair, freckles, big brown eyes, a gap between his teeth, a smile that would melt Lucifer's heart and as bright as twenty brass buttons. I put my hand over his eyes and asked him the colour of everyone else's eyes and he got the lot. Okay, I thought, eyes are blue or brown, no big deal, so what is Penny wearing in her hair? 'A pink clip with blue flowers.'

'And what does so-and-so have on her T-shirt?'

'A laughing elephant.'

No flies on our Tony. Then, a couple of days later, I got Sasa to sing her song for Roger and his eyes were out on stalks. I got him yesterday to play "Dentist" which he didn't know and he could hardly play he was laughing so much. Ammy was her usual laughing self last night so I think her breakdown [!] did her good.

21st January 1987

Where is the time going? Half way through the third week already. Monday I start on *Animal Farm* (Really shitty, wanky, National Theatre type songs) and *Threepenny Opera*. So far we have got the German and Danish texts for that but no English, which is a fat lot of good to me. Hopefully the guy who is coming over Sunday *[Andy Smith]* is bringing it with him together with *Boys in the Band*. Would you believe they all want to do DRAG in their mixed-bag evening? Jan, Timm, Christoff and Tom are practically down on their knees begging me to include and let them do a version of "*I Am What I Am*". It's not been done here. Well, maybe not but I don't see why I should be the one to do it first, at least not with those four. Tom (who looks like Anthony Dowell with a big mouth) would be beautiful; tall and slender, moves like a dream and would be terrific in a frock. Timm possibly, Christoff possibly, but Jan? Never. He is the most beautiful of them all but he is beautiful as a man and would simply look ridiculous as a woman. And drag requires expertise and style to pull it off and these kids just ain't got that yet. The only thing Jan could do in drag is a burlesque of Mae West at which he would more'n likely bring the house down.

So let me tell you about Lars. I don't think I've mentioned Lars before. When I sat in on Roger's class I heard his voice for the first time (bass/baritone) and after the class I said to him. 'You have a very nice voice, what are you going to do with it?' He really didn't know what I was talking about so I took in the tape of the Faure Requiem and made him listen to the baritone. 'Now,' I said, 'do you think you can sing like that?' 'But that's classical!' He said. Precisely. Anyway, I'm casting him as Macheath so we'll see what he does with it.

Poor babes, they really don't have much place to go. You think we have it bad in England? This is what I have been told. There are no theatrical agents in Denmark. There is no theatre paper like *THE STAGE*, no casting directory like *SPOTLIGHT*. The National Theatre takes its new intake from state schools. There is a core of actors who are used over and over and new faces stay just that–worse–unknown faces. At least this is the picture that has been painted for me. So I have had to say things to them like 'Watch every programme on Danish TV and note the names of directors/producers. Then write to them with photo and CV. If you don't hear from them write again requesting an interview and/or audition, then follow it up with yet another letter. Same for going to the theatre. Mind you, if any of them, with one or two exceptions, auditioned for anything at the moment they wouldn't get too far. Third year students in England are miles ahead of this lot. Not that it's all their fault. The school is fairly new and Mickey himself is feeling his way. There is no doubt he is ambitious but in some things he really doesn't know his arse form his whatsit.

How did you like Carsten's painting? [*Picture sent with letter. Carsten was 13*] He does them all over his schoolbooks, his phantasy paintings he calls them. It's up to you to decide what they are. I decided mine is a Chinese fish. I took the juniors for two classes because of emergencies, so this is Carsten–'Are we having you again on Monday?'

'No.'

'Monday after?'

'No.'

'Not again at all?'

'No.

'When are you leaving?'

'April.'

(Squeal) 'Oh, no! Don't go. Don't go! Are you coming back?'

'Don't know.'

(Squeal) 'Yes, yes, please come back.'

'I haven't left yet.'

'I know. But after you've left you WILL come back. Won't you?'

The evening before yesterday I threw the first years in at the deep end. Played them the third movement of Shoshtokovitch's "Eighth," very dramatic, and told them to move as the music took them. I ended up with two more breakdowns. Christina I wasn't at all surprised at. She's at that age when everything's religion, horses, (she's 15) and melodrama, so I'm afraid I didn't take much notice of the tears but left her to some of the girls to hug and comfort and supply the needful shoulder to cry on or, in this case, substitute mother's breast. But, at the beginning I noticed Morten took an awful long time to get into it but, by the time I switched off, he was rolled into a little ball on the floor. It wasn't the end of the movement but I chickened out because I thought any moment now we were going to get a primal scream. So I got them all to talk about it, leaving Morten till last and, when I got to him, he just shook his head and said, 'Later, I'll talk later.' And later he did come up to me to tell me he was raped at age fourteen. He doesn't remember the actual rape because the guy laid him out cold with a length of wood but it was hospital time to repair the damage and he was under a psychiatrist for a year and a half afterwards. This was the first time he had thought about it since despite the fact that the guy, who also raped a young girl, was given only three years and could still be seen strutting about their home town. But yesterday Morten was a regular bouncing Bobby so I think the session possibly did him a lot of good. I certainly hope so. Christina too was running about the place and singing away. I said to Nathalie, (Rene Collo's daughter) after the class I thought I had better give up when I did. 'No, no!' She said, 'It was wonderful. It's just that you hit us really hard.' They all thought the music was fantastic and wanted to know what it was so, if nothing else, I've got them interested in something other than boom boom boom boom.

Timm in the greenroom yesterday was being totally outrageous though I'm not sure he was aware of it. He would be talking to someone and showing off and, every now and again, would glance my way to see if I was watching. It nearly got to the point where I said, 'If our eyes keep meeting like this people are going to talk.' But, before I could say anything, he was suddenly standing on his head. Anne-Marie was sitting next to me and I said to her, 'Watch Timm when he comes down, he's going to look straight in this direction to see if I've been watching him.' And, sure enough, that's exactly what happened. We both burst into laughter, which brought a right royal frown to Timm's

Chapter Twenty Two

brow, so I said to him, 'You really think you can wrap me round your little finger, don't you?'

'No I don't,' he said …. 'not yet.'

He'd finished school for the day and left a few minutes later. Five hours later he was back and I was back in the greenroom after a class. He came across to my table, sat down and said, 'What did you mean about ….?' and mimed wrapping around his little finger. He had been worrying about it all afternoon like a dog with a bone, so I said, 'Just because you're handsome, and sweet and nice and charming to me, don't think you're going to wrap me around your little finger.'

'Oh!' He said, blushing, I believe with pleasure, 'that's nice,' and went off happy as a sand boy.

31st January 1987

I didn't think I would come to Denmark to have one of the best evenings in the Opera House ever! First of all, the theatre, The Royal– it is so beautiful. There are actually two Royal Theatres, old and new, and we were in the old (Gamle Scene) dating from 1784. Magic. It was the perfect theatre in which to see an opera like *Don Pasquale*. It was one of the most imaginative, wonderful productions I have ever seen. So funny (even in Danish), beautifully staged in wonderful sets and, for the most part, the acting even knocked spots off the ENO. I say for the most part because there was an exception. Isn't it often the way? But even that could not spoil an enchanting evening. The orchestra were the pick of the bunch their playing was so good though a little bit too loud at times. The pit is large and totally open and it would make for a better balance if some of the musos were under the stage. The conductor had a Polish name and is a little mouse with glasses and a droopy moustache and musical fire in his belly. (I left my programme in the restaurant–fuck it!)

Norina was beautiful, marvellous coloratura, a little troubled now and again against the orchestra but, my god, can she act, and so totally believable. Also she was having herself a ball and her sheer effervescence came over those footlights …. Yes yes! Footlights!

.... Malatesta and Pasquale, equally high praise AND let us not forget Pasquale's manservant. A mute part, but what a part and what an actor playing it. His timing was perfection: neat and clean and nothing overdone. I would like every one of my kids to see this performance and learn what acting is all about. I'm afraid he did do a bit of upstaging (a bit?) wholly unintentionally I'm sure because sometimes you just could not take your eyes off him. You were listening to Pasquale and Malatesta, both in splendid voice, but watching the manservant whose reactions had you practically falling off your seat with laughter. He was doing no more than what was set down for him as Hamlet says, but doing it with such perfection how could you not help but watch it? It might have been better if the director hadn't placed him upstage centre but put him rather to one side. The high standard of the acting even went through the chorus. No one there stood out like a sore thumb, which brings me to the exception–the tenor–a blond lump who would probably be maladroit at playing Tony Lumpkin. Not only could he not move and not act and not sing but he was fat fat fat. In the Harlequin costume in Act III he looked like a potato sack. No woman, let alone the Norina we had, would look at him twice. He made a complete botch-up of the serenade and the ensuing duet in the garden. I could hear he was having chest problems, or maybe throat problems, or maybe both, but even so, forget it, a lurching disaster. That said, even he could not spoil the evening it had so much going for it.

    Roger, who had previously only seen two operas, both Verdi, and who said he hated opera but was prepared to give it one more try, came out of the theatre with stars in his eyes and didn't stop talking about it the rest of the evening. Lars enjoyed it too and the whole reason for going was to fire Lars with ambition. So, in the interval, I asked him whether he fancied playing the role of Malatesta? The look he gave me implied I had suddenly sprouted two heads and gone completely off both of them. 'Lars,' I said, 'has no one ever told you you really do have a very good voice?' The answer was no. Afterwards we went for a meal at a Thai restaurant and I pushed him further. I

Chapter Twenty Two

expounded on my idea that he should come to England at the end of term and stay with us for a week or two and I'd take him to Helen [*Helen Hillier, ex-Sadler's Wells Opera and Chris's teacher*] and, if she agreed with me that he did have potential, he could then decide for himself what he wanted to do. I told him she would say either go for it or forget it and, if it were the latter, well, he could return to Denmark and nothing was really lost. He listened to it all and then said just one word, "Yes." So in May we will be having a Danish visitor. Not the magnificent Jan, not the handsome Timm, not the cute Troels, not the beautiful Morten, but skinny, spotty, rather plain Lars who does have a certain charm and is very intelligent and whose voice seems to make the hairs prickle on the back of my neck.

Lars came to England and, although he was terribly nervous, he auditioned for Helen who agreed with me, the boy really did have a future. He returned to Denmark and we never heard another word from him, not so much as a thank you, but no thank you. A second Danish visitor though was Jan who arrived complete with his roller skates which was fortuitous because he auditioned for *Starlight Express* and was accepted. We did get a thank you letter from him, mailed from Japan. I never saw the show in London so don't know exactly what he did in it but, according to his letter, he was having a really great time, especially when the company got to Sydney. Another card told us this was "his city!"

4th February 1987

The snow has melted leaving the streets littered with dogshit. This sure ain't Hamburg and the pavements are infinitely worse even than London. I've never SEEN so much dogshit! Presumably, because of the snow, the street cleaners haven't been able to work and the Danes allow their dogs to shit everywhere, certainly in Amager.

I haven't started on the second year's revue yet and, when I do, it will be running side by side with the third years. *Animal Farm* is coming along and I think *Threepenny Opera* is going to be very good, two and

No Official Umbrella

a half weeks off and I lost one of my cast today, pregnant and flown off to Iceland, presumably to try and work things out with her boy friend. It's always such a waste of time having to go back and do it all over again with a replacement. The other thing about these projects, as Mickey calls them, is that though I have an MD and a choreographer, the animal known as a stage manager simply doesn't exist so like I am now going to have to sit down with scripts and go through prop lists. I solved the *Animal Farm* by telling them there simply aren't going to be any. *[A repeat of Narrow Road but a lot easier.]*

It would seem Mickey has got his theatre, a 625 seater called The Mercury–new.

Sunday.

Just going around to dinner at Roger and Ammy's. We're going to watch a video of *All that Jazz*. Thursday, Ammy, Troels and I went to see *Dames at Sea* but I left at the interval–nuff said. What a mess! Full house and been playing for months, god knows why. Haven't received *Fallen Star* yet. Have you sent it? Start rehearsals tomorrow.

Couldn't just say "no" to Mickey about the extra four weeks because he started off by asking me when I was going to America and I said I wasn't sure, and he said I told him I couldn't stay after March because I was going to America–trapped! He has a way of springing surprises like that.

Rehearsals for *Threepenny Opera* (TREEPENNY as they call it because they have difficulty pronouncing "th". Brown keeps calling MacHeath MacHeat) are going well and I am enjoying it, who would have thought? Yesterday when I was mooching around some junk shops looking for bits and pieces for the set, I found an old scarlet Danish postman's jacket so bought it. It was only K40 (about £4) and it can go in your wardrobe if ever you decide to perform something like MAFEKING NIGHT. The collar is wrong of course but it has a circle of gold braid around each cuff and two very nice silver badges on the collar. It fits Leif who is quite hefty so should be big enough for you.

Moggy Dooral [a Leybourne number] really is a very silly song,

Chapter Twenty Two

isn't it?

Saw part of a very beautiful Danish film on television last night called *My Grandmother's House* (Victorian story) and wish I'd seen it all. I was working on the play when Mickey popped his head in and suggested I join them for a glass of wine. Actually it was because he wanted me to watch the film with the most marvellous boy child in it, about ten I suppose. (See? Danish kids have talent was the message.) It was also beautifully photographed and beautifully acted all round from what I could judge. I'm sorry I missed the beginning.

22nd February 1987

Well, here it is! *Rosemary*. Hope you like it. Please do not–repeat–do not be tempted to look at the ending first. You'll spoil it for yourself.

Threepenny Opera went very well first house but they were WOTT in the second and I will have their guts for garters. No not really, but tomorrow will be post mort and I will lay it on the line, the difference between being professional and playing games in the village hall. Henning criticised it for not being sanggespracht [?] and Brechtian but Mickey was very pleased with it even though I wasn't. Needless to say he is delighted I'm staying the extra four weeks. Shit!

Last night was Troels' birthday party but we were all so knackered we left about 1.30. The food was good; his parents evidently run a posh restaurant. They were all upset because they knew I wasn't pleased with them though I tried to make light of it because of the party. To begin with everyone was given a glass of punch but thereafter if you wanted a drink you bought it at bar prices!

Today was the most beautiful day and I really should have got out and about and seen a bit of Copenhagen but I wanted to get the play finished and I did. There's discipline for you. The next three Sundays are all taken up with rehearsing the second years in their review. The trouble is they're divided into two groups, morning and afternoon, and Sunday is about the only time I can get them together to rehearse musical numbers. I was pleased with my settings for *Threepenny Opera*. First time I've tried my hand at it and even went in for a bit of real primitive choreog. Ammy of course did the more ambitious stuff for me.

Thank you for *The Fallen Star*. Eric will be delighted to get it. Nathalie Collo is still waiting for the Barbara Cook tape I promised her.

1st March 1987

Shit! March already? Got in from today's rehearsal and thought I'd have an hour's kip but, when I woke, I found it had stretched into three, that's how tired I was. Anyway, today is the halfway mark, if I stay the course. I've given Mickey a get-out by saying the other night that, if he had to change his mind for any reason about my staying the extra four weeks, I wouldn't hold him to it, silently hoping he would find a reason. He thought that was most generous of me. He really is a strange man, one minute talking sense, the next minute talking nonsense. He knows nothing about theatre and at the moment is driving me up the fucking wall. He takes great pride in maintaining he never interferes artistically but with ROMEO & JULIET/WEST SIDE STORY he has been a total pain in the arse. First of all he manipulated the casting and I acquiesced in everything except one. I told him that if Alex was cast as Romeo he would be minus a director and that was that. When he saw how serious I was he backed down. When I presented (his) cast list to the class I had tears and tantrums so I told them to go and talk to Mickey and he immediately turned around and said, oh no, he didn't do the casting, we did it together by discussion, and the decisions were finally mine. I am not popular but I couldn't very well contradict him without his losing a lot of face so we'll leave it at that. Then I was told no big production numbers in WSS. Then I was asked to present a schedule of rehearsals, which would enable him to take five of the company out at one time so they could work on some other little pet project. Then I was told he didn't care how bad the show was, it was the "work process" that mattered. I created merry hell at the prospect of losing five of my cast in the middle of rehearsals and told him it couldn't be done so he dropped

Chapter Twenty Two

that one. As it is I lose one every twenty minutes or so to the singing teacher for their "one-to-one" and you can bet your bottom dollar as soon as I turn around and say, 'Where is so-and-so?' the answer will be 'She/he has gone to Henning.' They slip in and out like cats. I wanted to include *Cool* in the WSS section but that was vetoed. 'No, they mustn't do that. They've done that.' There were more outraged howls from the class when it turned out it was the second years that had done it so I told him I was using it–one verse. The first act by the way is working beautifully and I am delighted with it. Last night came the real cracker in the caff.

MICKEY: I hear from the students that you are using more *Romeo and Juliet* than *West Side Story*. Is that right?
ME: I don't know, Mickey.
MICKEY: What do you mean, you don't know? You're the director, you should know.
ME: Well, I don't. I was going to run the first act today but I ran out of time.
MICKEY: Well I would rather you used more *West Side Story*.
ME: Oh, yes? And how do I do that?
MICKEY: You can use the songs.
ME: But I am using songs, Mickey, only you ordered me not to use big production numbers and, if you know your *West Side Story*, it is full of big production numbers.
MICKEY: Oh. (Silence) But you can use some other songs.
ME: Yes, but they're sung by the same principals, what would you like me to do with the rest of the cast?
MICKEY: Oh. (Silence) Well I don't want any more Shakespeare. They've done enough Shakespeare. They did *Midsummer Night's Dream* last term in Danish and this term in English.
ME: If they can do Shakespeare they can do anything.
MICKEY: Well they've done enough Shakespeare.

ME: And they still can't do Shakespeare.
MICKEY: Oh. (Silence)
ME: Anyway, you said you don't care how the show turns out. You keep saying it's the "work process" that matters so what's the difference if it is more Shakespeare than *West Side Story?* Which, by the way I don't believe it is, and Shakespeare in Danish is no longer Shakespeare anyway, at least not in the poetic sense.
MICKEY: Oh. (Silence) When you get to the last week tell me if you think it's going to be good and I'd like to invite some people to see it.
ME: I can't tell you if it's going to be good.
MICKEY: Why not? You're the director. You should know if it's going to be good or not.
ME: I don't speak Danish, Mickey. You would have to get the voice teacher or Henning in to tell you if it is good or not.
MICKEY: Oh. (Silence) Well you let me know and I'll invite some people in to see it. Fancy a beer?

End of conversation. Shit! Mickey's idea of the "work process" is to overload them with so much work they don't know whether they're coming or going. *The Elephant Man* on Friday night was appalling. I was not surprised. The second years have been working on that, plus *Grease*, plus the REVUE, plus *Equus*, plus classes. When I told Mickey he was out of his mind his reply was that they had four weeks and that was quite long enough. I said, 'No, Mickey, they do not have four weeks. I get them for one and a half hours three times a week, that, in total, is less than four days rehearsal.' He pointed out I had three extra rehearsals. 'Yes. Mickey, to do the big routines. It takes them two hours to pick up one number and, when you come back to it a week later, because that's the soonest you can get back to it, they've forgotten it and you have to start all over again.' But he just closes his ears and refuses to listen so I have got to the stage now when I am taking him at his word, that it is the fucking "work process" that matters and I just

Chapter Twenty Two

go ahead. The show will not be ready in time there is no doubt about that. Nothing they do is polished and they can't do two performances in a row without falling to pieces. There is no way I would dream of coming back here, not to put up with this sort of crap. Unless the whole running of the school changes dramatically disaster is on the way. I need this like a hole in the head. How attitudes can change in eight short weeks. Friday night I had to comfort poor Andy who was almost in tears over the debacle that was *The Elephant Man*. He said to me, 'I'm just fucking grateful if they remember to come on and go off at the right time. Second performance they didn't. Shambles.'

The thing is Mickey doesn't know how lucky he is with his Brit contingent. Four people who get on like a row of houses on fire, [!] we work our butts off, put in extra hours, and help out with each other's problems. Ammy's song and dance evening last night was great. At least they got that right and when it's right it's so exciting. She's an amazing girl, Ammy, only nineteen and very with it.

Roger works like no other muso I've ever met. He goes from my rehearsal to Ammy's class to ballet, to Andy's rehearsal and then, having put in more than a full day, some kid will come up to him and ask for help with a number for the café evening [*Students doing their own thing on top of everything else*] and he'll spend another hour on that. It would have just needed one of us to be a selfish shit to throw Mickey's entire programme totally out of balance. Whether he knows it or not he's not saying but I would work with this team any time and anywhere. The good things that have come out of all this are meeting with the other Brits, writing a new play, and growing in self-confidence as far as working on the floor is concerned. I haven't preplanned a thing [*with the revue*]. Everything's been off the top of my head right then and there. This afternoon I set LITTLE GIRLS, ADELAIDE'S LAMENT and GOOD TO MOMMA all in the space of half an hour. Roger sat at the piano and fed me the lines, I walked it for the girls, and they did it. Whether they will remember it or not is another matter. You would have thought I'd been directing musicals all my life!

The letter stopped there for three hours. Mickey knocked on the door and I had to join them for a sociable evening, which means listening to all his favourite records. Managed to slip in a few words of much-needed advice as he was in one of his receptive moods and it was 'dear Glyn' time. He says he's bringing thirteen musos from England for the end of term show. Oh, my God! They won't all be Roger Davidsons, that's for sure.

Going back to the SONG AND DANCE evening, one of the students, Ida, gave me a haircut so, in the evening I decided to wear a jacket and tie for the first time. My god, the reaction! Clothes maketh the man. You would have thought every sex symbol who ever existed had walked in. Ridiculous.

I don't know, in a funny kind of way I suppose I ought to be quite proud to have been chosen for this job despite all the drawbacks. Andy was telling me that in all the people who did apply (how many were there I wonder?) there were some quite high-powered names. But Mickey is the kind of person who goes on gut reaction rather than reputation. Oh well, let's see what tomorrow brings.

My prophesy of disaster was unfortunately spot on target. After I had left, Mickey contracted another Englishman to direct a production of *Chicago* in the theatre. I don't know whether or not he also brought his thirteen musos over from England but the result of this evident fiasco, as I heard it, was bankruptcy and he lost everything for which, despite all his faults, I couldn't help but feel exceedingly sorry.

The revue Ammy and I had worked so hard on was also a fiasco. I might have gone easier on the kids, knowing the amount of work they were asked to do, if it hadn't been for the fact that they dragged themselves in to the dress rehearsal looking and feeling like death after partying all night. The result was a total shambles. 'Right,' I said, when it was all over, 'you're going to do this show and you're going to do it for me, for Mickey, and any member of staff who perversely would want to suffer the torture of sitting through it. What you will not be

Chapter Twenty Two

doing is performing in front of an audience.' There was an immediate anguished howl. 'No parents,' I went on, 'no friends, not even other students. If, and as I see it it's a mighty big if, if you improve by tonight you may have an audience tomorrow. If not you will perform a second time to me and an empty room. That is it.' And I waved a hand in dismissal. I didn't even want to look at them.

Then a lone voice piped up. 'What if we don't do it at all?'

'Then you don't do it. It's no skin off my nose. My reputation and Ammy's is at stake here as much as yours thank you very much and I'm not going to let you make a fool of us which, according to what I have just seen and heard, is exactly what you're about to do.'

They slunk off without another word. I still had to have a go at Mickey, which I wasn't looking forward to, and that was because he had purchased a miniscule dimmer board and half a dozen lamps that wouldn't cast a beam as strong as a medium-size flashlight. I arranged them as best I could to cover as much of both halves of the show as possible, because I certainly wasn't interested in mounting a ladder and resetting during the interval. This was hardly imaginative lighting but wasn't it all part of Mickey's work process? I knew there was going to be a row when, during the first half I saw Mickey lean across to Andy and whisper something as he pointed up at the lights, though in this instance it wasn't actually the lamps' at fault. The kids just weren't up to finding their light.

The show, as expected, was appalling. They were all over the place. They forgot lines, they forgot moves, they stood looking at each other wondering what they were supposed to do next as though it had never been rehearsed, and I was going to have to sit through this a second time hoping they would at least have learned a lesson, which would have been some compensation. But now it was time to face an irate Mickey who wasn't angry because of the failure of the kids but because, as he saw it, I hadn't lit them properly with his new lights. Did I know how much he had paid for them? No, I didn't know how much he had paid for them and however much it was it was obviously too much.

'They were very expensive.'

'Then you were had, Mickey.'

'Had?'

'Taken for a ride. Did you get them out of a catalogue? They're useless, Mickey, no better than toys.'

'TOYS?'

I think it was the word 'toys' that really hurt and for which he found it hard to forgive me, if he forgave at all.

MORTEN.

In one of my final letters home I wrote, "Oh yes, there is the nineteen year old who looks like a Victorian porcelain doll (the one who was raped) but what a mess. Poor baby. I think… well… he asked me to go out with him to talk and he talked! Too long to tell you about it now. But I told him about you and, since then, he won't even look at me if he can avoid it. Well, that is up to him. I told him I would like it very much if he would consider me a friend but he has to come to me. I can't go to him. 'Thank you,' he said, looking straight ahead. He really is screaming inside but there's not much I can do unless he can let go and somehow I doubt he can."

Who hasn't heard of the Emperor Hadrian and his Antinous? Reading this letter now, how was it that at the time I didn't realise this was a young man in love? Was it because I couldn't believe that youth and beauty, not that youth and beauty is the be all and end all, could fall in love with someone so much older, especially when that someone older was I? We used a local pub called *Eric The Red* and one evening as I was eating in there, Morten walked in, saw me, and slipped onto the bench opposite. After a greeting and the offer of something to eat or a drink from me, an offer he declined, he looked down at the table and pretended to write my name a number of times, repeating it softly as he did so. This was when I said to myself, as though I still couldn't believe it, 'This boy is in love.' Aloud I said, 'Take me home,

Chapter Twenty Two

Morten.' Without another word we got up and left.

It was the easiest; I suppose the most natural thing in the world, to fall in love with Morten. In fact I became totally besotted with him and that was the way it was during the rest of my time in Denmark. To write about it now, after so many years, is to plunge into Mills and Boonish melodrama. Maybe it was that at the time but, even so, Morten will always be a part of my life. We corresponded for a number of years, he with some difficulty not being fluent in English, for example:

"Hello Glyn! You haven't had the Ragnall House address for three years. I have been looking in all of your's letter and I can't find the address to Hollings Farm. And I am nearly 100% certain that I have all your letters and card, but you can't bee to sure can you? Ha, I find it. The trip was a nice experience to take with you [?] I won't travel for 8 months again yo can't take it ah, [?] so many things so see and different's culture. So if I travel again only for a few months and only to two country at the time. I hope everything is fine with you and that you are writing the most beautiful manuscript in this century,
  You can do it Glyn
  Love Morten.

Finally I had a letter from him to say he was off to Tonga to see in the millennium and that was our last contact.

I also received a couple of affectionate letters from Timm Lausten but, unfortunately, I was tardy in replying and, by the time I did, he had moved and my letter was returned, "Not known at this address."

It was with one deep feeling of angst but otherwise with a sense of relief that I took train from Copenhagen to Hamburg for a short break. I shared my compartment with a very svelte Swedish gentleman who, like most Scandinavians, spoke perfect English. We got to talking about language and I said how strange I found Danish pronunciation to which he replied, 'The Danes don't have a language, they have a throat disease.' I wonder what the Danes think of Swedish. Chris joined me in Hamburg and we stayed with our friend Michael Medlinger. Lunches and dinners and evenings with friends, more visits to museums and galleries (and the street of rope makers of course) and, naturally, visits to the opera: *The Bartered Bride*, *Parsifal*, and at the English Theatre a performance of *Corpse* which was chosen over *Thriller of the Year* but which we enjoyed nevertheless, no hard feelings. At the end of our stay it was first class, travelling in style on the MS Hamburg to Harwich and back to London for a short while before our lives were due for yet another change.

Chapter Twenty Three

Dave left us to return to his south London roots, buying a property in conjunction with a couple of his mates, but his bedroom at 36 Farleigh Road didn't remain free for long. Another homeless puppy appeared. Out of the blue I received a reverse charge phone call, a rather desperate plea for help, from a penniless young man named Peter Jackson. It appeared he was at Victoria station and had absolutely no idea of what he was going to do with himself, so I told him to wait there and I would drive down and pick him up. Why, of all people, he cottoned onto us I really don't know and I wonder if I would have been quite so generous, or whether I would have been a little more cautious, had I known then that this was to be our third alcoholic. However, ignorance being bliss (another cliché) I duly picked up this rather shabby, sad looking character with a small, shabby, sadly battered suitcase, who wasn't even a friend of ours but an ex-friend of someone Chris knew through Sadler's Wells, and drove him back to Farleigh Road where he took over Dave's vacated room.

Jeremy had previously been exiled by Dave while we were away and had gone to live with another friend. It seemed one night he came home pie-eyed in the early hours and had gone to bed leaving the front door wide open; which meant not only could anyone walk in from the street in a high-crime area but, there being no gate, the dogs could walk out and they were not street smart dogs having always been taken out on a lead. Dave was naturally upset and furious and warned Jeremy if he did it again he would be out on his ear. He did it again.

It wasn't too long before, after a series of minor mishaps, like the hoarded Christmas cake that was tipped crashing to the floor ('The cat tripped me up') before we realised that one alcoholic had gone but another had arrived. When I questioned Peter as to where he was getting his booze, he promised me faithfully that he bought it at the local off-licence. Like the trusting and gullible idiot I am I believed him until, one Sunday morning, I realised he was positively legless and there was nowhere at that early hour of a Sunday he could have got alcohol from outside the house. For some years I had been making homemade wines and I immediately went down to the cellar to check on them. Practically every bottle, including a strawberry wine we hadn't even tasted, had gone. I went into the dining room where we kept our commercial stuff, mainly duty free spirits and liqueurs kept for dinners and the entertainment of guests. Every bottle had been emptied but for about a quarter of an inch or so in the bottom. That was it. I faced Peter with what he had done and told him he was no longer welcome but was to pack his shabby battered suitcase and leave with no further ado. There were tears and sobbing apologies and cries of 'What am I going to do?' But we had had all that before and I was no longer interested in what he was going to do apart from advising him to join AA or to see a doctor smartish and possibly get himself booked into a clinic. For weeks, while I thought he was trying to get himself sorted out, he had lived rent free with everything provided and now, as he stepped outside, the door was slammed behind him. We never saw or heard of him again.

In the bedroom we found empty bottles in and on top of the wardrobe, in every drawer, under the bed, under the pillows, under the mattress. Included were six bottles labelled *Strawberry, Extra Special*. It doesn't seem much now to have sent someone out into the street for but at the time I was too angry to stop and reflect on my reaction. As far as I was concerned he could find a soft touch elsewhere which I am sure he did.

Chapter Twenty Three

As I had been invited to return to JMU for another year, and with Dave gone, we had to seriously consider what to do with 36 Farleigh Road. It was much too big a house for Chris to live in on his own. We'd known Dave since he was fifteen. He was a close friend and one of a kind. To find someone as conscientious and amenable to take his place would seem like looking for that proverbial needle in a haystack (another cliché! I don't think I'll mention them anymore.) It was a shame in a way about Peter; there was no harm in him, he was quiet, unassuming, always smiling, tried to be helpful around the place when he wasn't falling over his feet, and someone who wouldn't hurt a fly. He might have taken Dave's place if it hadn't been for the addiction. He was obviously a lonely and unhappy human being and Farleigh Road could have been a home for him, but we decided now to put the house on the market, and the first idea we came up with was to buy a commercial property so that the ground floor could be let, providing Chris with an income while he lived in a flat above. But everything we saw was either in the wrong location or in such a terrible state and all so unbelievably expensive that the idea went out the window.

Chris's cousin, Jenny Gore, came to visit. She lived in a little West Yorkshire village called Heptonstall close to Hebden Bridge, one time hippy paradise and known even then as the Hampstead of the north, and she suggested we might like to look up there. 'Lots of artists are living there now,' she said, 'actors, directors, musicians.'

When Hyst Mum heard we were thinking of taking up Jenny's suggestion she freaked out. 'What do you want to go to Yorkshire for? There's nothing there. No trees. No trees. It's all electricity pylons!' Unfortunately many southerners have this image of Yorkshire that, apart from its wuthering (Yorkshire dialect. When the wind blows through the grass making waves the grass is said to be "wuthering") heights, it's all gloomy Wesleyan chapels, windswept moors, flat caps and ee bai goom whereas in fact, although it has all of that, it is also extraordinarily beautiful and, despite Hyst Mum's dire warnings, there are trees a plenty. In fact, backing the house we bought, we had our very own extensive bluebell wood. The approach to the house is down a long very steep drive, hellish in winter when slippery with fallen leaves, with a parking circle at the bottom and a builder's lad, butch and as straight as they come, once discovered behind his van masturbating over a girlie magazine, stood there one day looking around and said in awe and all seriousness, 'It's like fairyland!'

When Chris departed London to take a look around Hebden Bridge his last despairing cry was 'Don't banish me to Yorkshire!' But it wasn't too long before I received a phone call saying, 'I think you'd better come up.' So Dave was called into service once more to house sit while I took the bus to Halifax where I was met by Chris and Jenny and driven to Heptonstall. I thought this was my first visit to the area but, on the road from Halifax to Hebden Bridge, I recognised a number of landmarks, in particular a large chapel on a hill, remembered from a sightseeing expedition during the tour of *Grab Me a Gondola* all those years before and that I had up till then mistakenly associated in memory with Scotland.

The two of them then drove me around in Jenny's car, doing what the estate agents had previously done with Chris, showing me properties he knew I would reject before taking me to the one he had set his heart on–Hollings Farm.

Situated in a tiny hamlet named The Hollings halfway between Heptonstall, high on a hill, and Hebden Bridge down at the bottom, nestling beneath the bluebell wood and commanding a panoramic view across and down the valley, the Grade II listed farmhouse, which had been divided into two small cottages when we bought the place, was built, so the owner, Stanley Hitchen, informed us, in September 1600. He said the date was carved on a timber pillar in the kitchen called "the witching post", so called because every beam in the house was somehow attached to it via another beam and any loitering evil would run along the beams to the witching post and, like electricity, be safely earthed. But we never found it and, though it is possible the

Chapter Twenty Three

Hollings Farm - West Yorkshire

house was built at that time, I think Stanley was either kidding us about the carving or imagining it. There are other carvings though, especially in what became the winter parlour; the rose is prominent of course, as are the names of various members of the Hitchen family with dates, and a Latin inscription, "Veritas et Virtus Vincunt" which we translated not in truth but very rudely.

The house is a typical Yorkshire farmhouse, built of millstone grit under a slate roof and with flagged floors at ground level. A number of stone blocks low down in the walls are simply enormous and it must have been quite an achievement just to get them into place. Some of the windows were diamond pane; some replacements were sash of various sizes. The cottages were numbered 14 and 15 The Hollings. Number 14 consisted of one medium size room and one small on the ground floor and two small rooms above reached by a beautiful Japanese oak staircase that was evidently a present to his Mavis from Stanley on the occasion of their wedding. Part of the wall is panelled and there is a carving of Studley Pyke, a stone obelisk erected at the time of the Napoleonic wars that can be seen on the road from Hebden Bridge to Todmorden. On the carving, a cupid either side the pyke looks as though they are holding the edifice erect and the monument's name is carved in a scroll beneath. In other parts of the panelling are two roundels each holding a posy of flowers. In the floor of the bedroom, that is the ceiling of the parlour beneath, there is a coffin drop between the beams, the staircase being too narrow for bringing down coffins, and I thought it would be my coffin lowered through that hatch as I honestly believed Hollings Farm would be the house in which I would die, but fate has a way of contradicting our imaginings. I hadn't been prepared for dark damp Northern winters that seemed to last forever. In fact, as age crept up on me, if we had stayed longer at Hollings Farm it *would* have been my coffin lowered from above, and yet that beautiful house is the only part of England I still miss. The smaller of the two upstairs rooms at number 14 was converted into quite a spacious bathroom.

Number 15 consisted of one large room on the ground floor, part of which was partitioned off by a stud and pink-laminated hardboard wall into a narrow kitchenette. As there was no ventilation and it hadn't been cleaned in many a long day everything was inches thick in grease. The main section of the room itself was very dark with the only light coming in through two small dirt encrusted windows on the valley side. When Chris and Jenny were first invited into this room (and as I saw it on my first visit), there was a dull fire burning in the grate of an otherwise useless Victorian range, clothes were hanging en mass from beams, there was a bed covered in clothes beneath the dirty windows and, against the wall opposite the fireplace, a grimy sofa on which a bundle of clothes suddenly moved and a tremulous voice enquired, 'Who's there, Stanley? Who's there?' As Chris described it to me it was like old Sally in Dickens' *Oliver Twist*. In fact the whole place was Dickensian, a sketch by Boz. The voice belonged to Stanley's mother who must have been well into her eighties. On later visits she put on her best bonnet especially for our benefit. The third member of the household was Stanley's nineteen-year-old son John who wrote poetry in Yorkshire dialect. Stanley's spoken Yorkshire was so strong he sometimes had to say, 'What's that in English, John?'

Chapter Twenty Three

Beneath number 15 there is a barrel-vaulted cellar built in 1740, running the full length of the house from front to back with wide, built-in stone benches on either side and narrower stone shelves above. At the front end where the stone steps lead down, there is a well through which crystal clear spring water runs. Unfortunately this well was not all that deep and, when built, was not intended for use by washing machines and baths so, if the flow of water in summer was running low, you had to be extremely careful not to empty it or the pump would become air locked and have to be reprimed. You would be lying in the bath upstairs in 14 with the water running and suddenly hear the pump making dreadful noises as it suffered the mechanical equivalent of an embolism. In winter it was exactly the opposite when the spring could become a positive flood, overflowing the well and draining away down the outside before the water covered a wide step, or flowing over the step and draining away at the far end, or with really heavy flooding, disappearing down a drain in the centre of the floor itself.

Upstairs was a fairly large bedroom where father and his son John slept. This room boasted a long row of "weaver's windows", in front of which the women once sat to do their work. It also boasted a wall safe and a safe hidden in the windowsill, possible because the walls were more than two feet thick.

Outside number 14 was a flush toilet but no electric light and referred to by Stanley as "the shitoyl". Mid nineteenth century a large stone barn was added on the other end of the house and known as The Hollings Hatchery. On a rickety, wormy mezzanine floor we found and had to get rid of incubators for five thousand turkey chicks before pulling the whole rotten thing down. I should say Chris and Douglas had to get rid of them because by this time I was in America.

It was the end of July when Chris went up to Yorkshire and I followed in the first week of August. On my first viewing of Hollings Farm I agreed it was a stunningly beautiful place but I also thought to myself, 'We've worked on two houses, neither of them actually finished (as though a house is ever finished) but even in the state in which we found them they were child's play in comparison to what has to be done here.' Out loud I said, 'Do you realise just how much work it's going to take to make this house habitable?'

'Oh! Don't you want it then?' His disappointment was so palpable it didn't take much arm-twisting for me to agree that this was the house we were going to buy. Even when we had lived there some years he would still stand half way up the approach and, looking down at the house say, 'Aren't we lucky?' So Stanley and John marched us down to the estate agent in town who looked up with some surprise as we trooped into the office and raised his eyebrows even higher when Stanley slapped a hand on the counter and said, jerking a thumb in our direction, 'I want them to 'ave it.'

The agent, for some reason or other, seemed taken by surprise. With what appeared great consternation, he excused himself and went to talk to the girl sitting in the back office. She glanced out at us and whispered something to him. Very strange goings on. When he came back and started to hum and ha, possibly to say he had someone lined up who would offer more, Stanley was brooking no argument. 'I want them to 'ave it,' he repeated. So the process of buying Hollings Farm was put in motion. We later learned that the agent allegedly was trying to keep it for a client or friend of his who was still trying to raise the finance, hence his reaction.

We returned to London and put Farleigh Road in the hands of an Islington estate agent. This was on a Thursday and that evening he came around to view. Having decided on the price we wanted, enough to pay cash for the farm and for the work that was needed, he placed an advertisement in the property section of *The Observer* for that Sunday but, by Saturday night, the house was sold at above the asking price. What sold it so fast? It was an ordinary quite large Victorian terraced house in a fairly grotty street that over the years held fewer and fewer one family homes as house after house was bought by developers and converted into flats. This caused one enormous problem because a house divided into three or four flats meant that instead of one car requiring parking space in the road there were now three or four. It got to the point where we were parking our ancient Austin A60 station wagon three streets away, though on the last occasion of using it I did manage to find parking in front of the house, only to discover on going out in the morning to bring in the milk that that car had gone. It's a strange reaction you have, not to see something that you should be seeing. I brought in the milk, taking it all the way to the kitchen, thinking 'Where did I park last night? I'm sure I left the car outside the house.' I went back outside and stared at the empty space. I still couldn't really believe the car had gone. Chris was still in bed. I went upstairs and looked out the bedroom window. No doubt about it, there was definitely an empty space where I had parked the night before. 'The car's been nicked.' I said.

I reported it at Stoke Newington police station and, as it seemed I wasn't going to get the car back, eventually collected the insurance, which didn't amount to much. I also decided at this point that it was to be the last car we would have in London. It was simply no longer worth it. I never used the car to go into town anyway, it was too much hassle, and one could take a lot of buses and taxis for the cost of fuel and insurance, parking charges and road tax. One morning, some time later, there was an imperious knock on the door and I opened it to find an imperious gent complete with clipboard who flashed some identity at me, mumbled something about "Department of Transport" and barked, 'Mr Jones?'

'Yes?'

'Are you the owner of a green Austin A60, licence number blah blah blah blah?'

'I am'

'Would you kindly explain to me, sir, why said vehicle is not displaying the requisite road tax disc?'

I was intrigued. 'Where did you see the car?'

'I haven't seen it. The vehicle was reported by a police constable, as being parked in Amhurst Road,' which was two streets away at one end and joined Farleigh Road at the other. The car was most probably parked in front of the thief's house.

'Really? So why didn't this bright and alert young copper also report that I informed his station months ago that the car had been stolen?'

'Oh.' There was a long pause. 'Good day, sir. Sorry to have troubled you.'

Hackney has always been a high crime area. At Richmond Road in the early hours of one morning I heard Natalie somewhere downstairs barking and, although that was unusual for her, I didn't pay much attention to it. But in the morning when I went into the area, again to bring in the milk, I saw grubby putty or plasticine marks surrounded by a scratched circle in a kitchen window pane where someone was obviously going to try breaking in until Natalie put him off. Ours was about the only house in that area that never got done and I put it down simply to having two large dogs around. The fact that the dogs would probably have licked their hands had they managed to get in was not for the would-be burglars to know.

We think what sold Ragnall House in two days was not the aroma of freshly brewed coffee and baked bread but two very decorative stained glass windows with bird motifs we had bought while still in Richmond Road where we had no place for them but, in Farleigh Road, they went nicely in the extension and looked very pretty lit from behind.

Despite the monumental task that lay ahead of us in Yorkshire I would be relieved to get out of the city which was getting just too big, too loud, too dirty, too expensive and too dangerous. I was nearly rundown in Stoke Newington High Street by a speeding getaway car that mounted the pavement, and too often there was a tangible air of menace around. It could only get worse and judging from English newspapers it has (in many ways). It wouldn't be until the middle of November though that we would complete the sale of Ragnall House and be able to move into Hollings Farm. After two London houses, both bought in my name, I decided it was time Chris took a share of what we had. He became joint owner of a house, known in the hamlet

Chapter Twenty Three

as "the big house", and just under five acres of wuthering fields sloping steeply down to the village cricket pitch, with the river called Hebden Water on the far side. Actually the fields weren't all that wuthering. The one closest to the wood was so filled with saplings it was growing a wood of its own and we never did get around to clearing it. The second field was fairly clear except for patches of bramble and nettles I could never totally get rid of either. At the top of this field there was quite a wide flat length of land were we installed an old-fashioned cast iron hand pump to draw water up from an underground spring and I grew soft fruits and vegetables. There was also a totally useless chicken house whose floor had rotted and collapsed and was never used for anything except storing some firewood. In front of the house itself, in an area I started to cultivate as a garden and somewhere to plant a few fruit trees, was a quite substantial pigeon loft that Stanley thought a good selling point, Yorkshire being well known for its pigeon fanciers. I walked into it once to see what the interior looked like, locked it up and never went into it again.

We had some fruit trees at Farleigh Road, though not ones I put in, and as old as the house I guess. There was a giant pear tree and a plum, both of which gave an abundance of fruit, and a wonderful apple I discovered was a Blenheim Orange; the taste and texture of which knocked spots off your commercial green, yellow, and reds. Unfortunately the lady who bought the house asked Daphne and Gladstone next door if the pear bore fruit and when they said no she had it chopped down. At Hollings Farm I planted apple, pear, peach, and cherry but, apart from the apple, none had born fruit before we left. In Crete the one and only apple I planted was a total failure and the horticulturist at the agricultural co-op in Kalyves told us it was due to the fact that apples need hundreds of hours of really cold weather and that we normally just don't get. However, even if apples are a no go in our garden, other fruits we have in abundance: oranges, tangerines, lemons, grapes, plums, apricots, guavas, pears, loquats, figs, prickly pear, nectarine, passion fruit, walnuts and almonds, and what the Sicilians call a nut-peach, much smaller than a peach, with the constituency of a nectarine and twice the flavour. We discovered it in Sicily where the waiter at the restaurant assured us Sicily was the only place on earth where it would grow, like mastic on Xios, so when I saw one in a nursery near Xania, I snapped it up and it has produced masses of fruit. Unfortunately it has a very short season, unlike the goldenberries and strawberries that seem to fruit from February to October.

A stone walled path borders the second field at Hollings Farm. Part of the Pennine Way and much used by joggers and weekend ramblers it runs from a little humpbacked bridge over the river, steeply up the hill until it forks, one path continuing up to meet the Heptonstall Road, the other turning right to carry on along the top of the field, passed the shitoyl and between the house and two small semi-detached stone outhouses. These were probably even older than the house and once upon a time had a low roofed upper story where people slept while their animals were housed down below. The upper floors are long gone but to one side a flight of stone steps outside leads up to a small doorway that once led into them. The steps over the centuries have come to look almost basin shaped on both faces as, when the original top side got too worn down, the stones were taken up and turned over. In the first room there is a beehive oven that could heat both rooms. Someone told me this building is mentioned in the Domesday Book but I couldn't find it. We were also told that bread for the village was baked in the beehive oven but there was no confirmation of that either. We could close the path for one day a year for maintenance purposes but never did.

Further along, moving towards the wood and just below the parking circle is a jerry built corrugated iron garage and wood shed, its roof level with the edge of the circle. Douglas, having proudly taken and passed his driving test, once parked the car in neutral and forgot to put on the handbrake and the car ended up virtually on the garage roof. One of the neighbours alerted us to the fact. "Did you know your car is on the garage roof?" The rescue service and the insurance

Chapter Twenty Three

people couldn't believe it either. They really thought we were having them on. Fortunately photographs proved the situation to be for real. The damage to the car didn't look all that much but the bill for repairs came to over six hundred pounds and naturally the insurance premiums went up. Having heatedly argued with me that his driving instructor taught him never to park the car in gear, Douglas eventually came round and has never parked in neutral since. A neighbouring family higher up The Hollings whose roof was level with the road had to claim insurance for damage when a horse decided to stand on it. This really did require photographic evidence before the insurance company took it seriously.

Attached to the far wall of the barn via a short run that we turned into a small conservatory, (never finished: when we left, where there should be glass there was still plastic sheeting) was a pigsty that Douglas and I built up to become my study, far enough away from everybody for me to type away, pre-computer this was, without disturbing anyone. Chris made two large diamond pane windows for it. Stone lintels and mullion had been discovered when clearing out the barn where Douglas also discovered the remains of a very old table, three wormy legs and a stretcher possibly, judging by the carving, Elizabethan.

No longer owning a car in London, I hired a van for the move, packed it with essentials for camping in number 14, and with a large dog, Bella, and a cat in a basket, Bridget, who extended a paw through the mesh front and scratched the hell out of my back when I was in no position to stop and move her to a safer place I set off for Yorkshire. By the time I reached Halifax it was dark. I didn't know my way and started off on the road to Keighley until I realised, even in the dark, there was nothing I recognised so turned back and eventually found the right road. By the time I reached Hebden Bridge my patience with the poor animals was in short supply. By the time we reached Hollings Farm I think all three of us were pretty desperate for a pee and food and somewhere to lay our heads. Chris was staying in London to

No Official Umbrella

oversee the packing of our goods and shackles after which he would follow by train.

Having seen everything packed into pantechnicons and driven away, he locked up and made his way to King's Cross Station. As he was about to board his train who should he see walking down the platform but Jeremy Nightingale come to say goodbye. That sort of gesture was typical of Jer though maybe he was aware at the time or had a premonition that he would never see Hollings Farm or see us again, because two days later while at Jenny's house we had a phone call from the friend with whom he was staying to tell us he was dead. We passed the news on to Andy Moore and, as Jeremy died literally penniless, Andrew took it upon himself to see to Jeremy's affairs including his funeral. Jeremy was another who died too young but considering the trashing he gave his body with the alcohol it was not really surprising. One birthday we gave him a mug inscribed with "Lawyers do it with appeal." He never took it away with him so it is one of the few mementoes we still have of him: many many memories though. With all his faults, Jeremy was a good friend.

I clerked for him a few times when he was in a bit of a fix and I in a fallow period and, fascinating as it might have been, I soon gave it up when I came to the conclusion that the law and justice are two entirely different things. 'Why,' I enquired of Jeremy, describing a particular instance 'wasn't the defence lawyer asking the most obvious question?'

'It wouldn't have been politic,' was his reply.

'Why?'

'It would have annoyed the magistrate because it implied the police were lying.'

'But the police were lying. It was obvious they were lying.'

'It wouldn't have done any good to say so.'

The van had to be delivered up in Manchester and then I moved on to Ashley to buy the Toyota Tercel I was getting on Dave's advice. We certainly needed a four-wheel drive and it was a great little car I discovered very popular at that time, especially in America.

Chapter Twenty Three

It seemed every third car in Harrisonburg was a Tercel. It's true, Toyota engines never die but eventually the bodywork was in such a state the car wouldn't pass its MOT without a lot of expensive work and reluctantly we had to give it up. It was almost like parting with a dear friend. We went mad and, as with the Rover in London, bought a second-hand but splendid Subaru Legacy Estate that we could ill afford. But I run ahead of myself. I hadn't that much time in the Hollings before I was due back at James Madison, just enough time to meet Freda Kelsall and Chris Irvin who were on the point of starting a theatre company locally, called *Bridge Theatre* naturally, to talk to an architect in Todmorden about house renovations, to see an electrician, a chimney sweep and a plumber, and to sign on at the Labour Exchange. At the beginning of December I returned to London to attend Jeremy's funeral, collect my visa from the US Embassy, settled with the London estate agents and arranged travel to the US. Time was really moving so fast now. Douglas came down from Newcastle to spend Christmas with us. Dave and Poo came up to have a look-see. I made them a bed on the ground floor of number 15 and was horrified in the morning to find it had been so damp during the night, the bed was practically afloat. We all wished each other a happy new year and on the 4th of January I was in London, having dinner at Joe Allen's with Su Burrell. The following day I was on Air India Flight 103 bound for J.F.K.

Chapter Twenty Four

Taped to my office door one morning I found a notice printed in a large hand on a sheet of yellow legal pad. It read:

Du (*sic*) YOU WANT (Hand)SMOKED VENISON????!
IF SO FLIP PAGE.
JANICE O'ROURKE & PATRICK DOOLEY WILL SLAUGHTER A DEER AND SMOKE IT OVER HOT COALS FOR THE ONCE IN A LIFETIME OPPORTUNITY OF A BEAUTIFUL EXPLORATION INTO ACTING. 2 FINE ASPIRING ACTORS WILL BE TRAMPLED BY THE VISCIOUS (*sic*) BOARS OF ACTING INCOMPETENCE – UNLESS WE CAN GET OVERRIDES INTO YOUR CLASS!
PLEASE SAVE US!!!! We love you very much.

They got their overrides and proved to be two most talented young actors, Janice played the lead in *Generations* and Patrick was a wonderful Philip in *Orphans*.

This first semester at James Madison I had no writing class to take. I had a performance to give, this time to play Argon in Moliere's *The Imaginary Invalid*, which I thoroughly enjoyed once I got used to the idea that Tom King as the director was fond of saying, "Well, I really don't know about that."

Together with students who at least had some knowledge and a lot

Chapter Twenty Four

With Jane Learned in The Imaginary Invalid - J.M. University

of enthusiasm in my acting classes, I now had to try and instil some interest in a very large group of totally uninterested students in *Introduction to Theatre*. They were only taking the class because their degree required at least one course in the humanities and theatre it seemed to them could prove an easy trip, just as I, when a callow youth, thought acting would be an easy trip. They could attend lectures, so they thought, sit back, make a few notes, and do the minimum amount of work, enough to get a pass. There were forty of them.

'So just how much do any of you know about theatre?' I asked. I was met with forty blank stares. The answer obviously was nothing at all. 'Do any of you go to the theatre?' More blank stares. Football and baseball yes, pop concerts, rock concerts yes. Theatre? No.

Well attending lectures was not going to be enough. I wanted them to have hands-on experience so there were marks for volunteering to work in the costume shop or backstage, in the workshop, even ushering. I then gave them a shock by saying, 'I need to know just how much you do know about theatre.' I held up a sheaf of papers. 'I have here a list of questions that I put down off the top of my head. This is not, I repeat … this is not a test. It has nothing to do with grades so don't panic.' I could see by their reaction that they were already panicking. 'I promise you; it is simply to tell me what you do or do not know. Pass them out please and you have the rest of this period to write your answers.'

Silence ensued. At the end they put their papers on my desk and shuffled out without a word, which was not surprising when I looked at the results. Hardly a question had been answered.

INTRO TO THEATRE

1. Which American playwright wrote a play based on true incidents that took place in New England late in the seventeenth century? What was the subject of the play and what was its title? (6)
2. In ROMEO & JULIET, Romeo has two close friends and one fierce antagonist, name them. (6)
3. What composer took Teutonic myth as the basis for a cycle of four operas and what is the name of the cycle? (8)
4. What composer wrote the scores for the ballets ROMEO & JULIET and CINDERELLA? (4)
5. Andrew Lloyd Webber used another writer's work as the basis for his musical CATS. Who was the writer and what was the work? (4)
6. Who was it said, "There's a sucker born every minute"? (2)
7. What famous Russian playwright said, "I don't understand ballet at all. All I know is that in the intermissions the ballerinas stink like horses"? (Have a guess) (10)
8. Can you name two plays dealing in some way with the physically handicapped? (4)
9. What was the name of the first great American tragedian (2)
10. What is melodrama? (4)
11. What is a star trap? (2)
12. When performers refer to their "diaphragm" to what are they referring? (2)
13. What is a "Whiteface"? (2)
14. What is an "Auguste"? (2)
15. What is a "Lion Comique"? (20)

16. What is the meaning of "Deus ex machina"? (4)
17. What is "Pepper's Ghost"? (4)
18. Can you describe how it works? (6)
19. What do the following mean? To dim / To drop / To strike / To kill / To fade / To block. (12)

Out of a possible 104 marks no one reach ten. One girl with a splendid 0 merely wrote down each question as though it were also the answer. Another to question number 3 answered Andrew Lloyd Webber. I think, at this moment they must have hated me so, at the following class, looking at row after row of glum faces, I tried to reassure them. 'When I was your age,' I said, 'a hundred years ago, (the faintest glimmer of a smile) the first thing our teacher said to us was, "Imagine the theatre is like the most elaborately woven silk cushion with fringes and beautiful tassels. What you will learn about the theatre in a lifetime would be the equivalent of one silken thread of one silken tassel." Now that was many years ago: think how much more has happened from that time to this; think how many more plays have been written, how many more operas, how many ballets have been created, how many sets designed and built, how many more productions have been staged all over the world, how staging has developed, how sound and lighting have advanced. There is usually a practical reason for everything you know. Why do you suppose in earlier times, and indeed until quite recently, the footlights were referred to as floats? Any ideas?' No ideas. 'It was because the wick giving off the light was floated in oil. Later it was a candle and then it was gas. Gas however was extremely dangerous and many an actor's life was hazarded on the stage, even more so a dancer who happened to get too close to a flame wearing a non-fireproof tutu. Any number of theatres also went up in flames.' I certainly had their attention now with mention of death and destruction. 'Why do you think whistling in the theatre was forbidden and became a superstition some actors still believe in to this day? Any ideas?' No ideas. 'It was because stagehands didn't have the means of communication they have today, no cueing with red lights for stand-by and green for go, no cans or snug little earpiece to hear your cue; so they worked through a series of coded whistles and a whistle in the wrong place could be disaster. It could mean a drop, that is a stage cloth, a piece of scenery could come down from the flies, the area above the stage, at quite the wrong moment, possibly in front of the actors, hiding them from the audience and getting a great big laugh at the wrong moment, or worse, knocking someone's head off, possibly getting an even bigger laugh, human beings being what they are. And there you are, you've already started to separate your first silken thread from its tassel so let us go right back to the Greeks.'

Of all the classes I taught at James Madison I think I had a right to be proud of the final results of *Intro to Theatre*. From a body of total ignoramuses as far as theatre is concerned I ended up receiving highly knowledgeable and well thought out final essays with titles such as:

- *Puppets And Puppetry.*
- *Who Is Shakespeare?*
- *Theatre of the Absurd and the Existentialist Writers of the 50's.*
- *The Theatre As Liberation.*
- *20th Century Theatre. Stage Production in the U.S.*
- *Themes in "The Majestic Kid".*
- *The Theatre and Society.*
- *The Castle of Perseverance and Medieval Theatre in the Round.*
- *Edwin Forrest–Biography of an actor.*
- *Exit The King–by Eugene Ionesco*
- *Major Barbara–A Dialectical Approach.*
- *A Comparative Analysis of the Main Characters in Becket by Jean Anouilh & A Man For All Seasons by Robert Bolt.*
- *The Clash of Puck and Ariel*
- *Truthful Becoming–An essay on Acting.*
- *The Historical Authenticity of King Henry IV Part 1.*

And that was less than half of them.

Chapter Twenty Four

I was hardly back in Harrisonburg a week before David Harwell drove all the way over from Decatur, Illinois to visit. We had kept up a correspondence ever since the Wayside season and Anne was as delighted to see him as I was. It seemed to me to be an inordinately long way to drive but Americans don't appear to be phased by distances, which is probably just as well considering the size of their country. If you ask an Englishman the distance to a destination he will tell you in miles, an American will tell you in how many hours driving, and an Irishman will say, "Sure, it's just down the road," meaning it could be a matter of yards or a hundred miles or more, what's the difference? You're going to get there anyhow. David came to a rehearsal of *The Imaginary Invalid* and didn't say too much about it but there was no "Oh Poo fah!" or "fan the merkin!" so I presumed it wasn't too bad. He did ask who I was going to flirt with to which the answer was nobody though it was the beginning of our friendship with Tee Morris who, sometime during rehearsals, was looking particularly down in the mouth. When I asked him what the problem was it evidently all boiled down to the lack of twenty-five dollars. Tee's other great passion, apart from acting that is, was the marching band and he desperately wanted to go on a camp for which he needed twenty-five dollars. I gave it to him. I had it. He needed it. His need was greater than mine. I certainly wasn't interested in buying his body. How altruistic can you get? 'Pay it back if and when you've got it,' I said. He did.

The Imaginary Invalid was no sooner over when I had some casting of my own to do. Tom Arthur was determined I direct Athol Fugard's *Master Harold and the Boys* and the audition notices duly went up. My students warned me I would be hard put to it to find two good black actors and they were right. I did find one, but as I wanted to cast him in one role and he saw himself in the other and wouldn't be shifted, Master Harold was abandoned. I described it in a letter home.

"*MASTER HAROLD AND THE BOYS* is off thanks to a very stupid young man with a plank size chip on his shoulder. A plank?

A fucking tree! He walks into my office, he's perfect for the part of Willy, he's cast then and there. He walks out of my office and tells someone else he's not going to do it because he wants the part of Sam. Only three blacks applied to audition. One was much too young and totally inexperienced and could never have sustained either part. The other was dead right for Sam, so Troy got Willy. But Troy does not want Willy. He wants Sam. He doesn't even have the courtesy to tell me. I hear it second-hand. So Tom Arthur spoke to him in his class this morning and do you know what the man said? "He didn't even read me. He just gave me the part." So Tom said, 'Look, Glyn is a professional. He's been doing this for thirty years. He knows what he wants and he knows what he sees. If he casts you it's because he wants you. There are more ways of casting than reading.' So the boy says, "Well I'm too busy," and then sulks right through Tom's class. So thanks to him a production falls and the others are disappointed. I was over-blessed with Harolds–ten possibles–and, to be quite frank, I'm not sorry it's all over. Troy unwittingly did me a favour. I'm going to direct *ORPHANS*! Hurrah hurrah hurrah! If *MASTER HAROLD* had gone ahead I could sense nothing but troubles for six weeks and I am relieved not to be doing it. Preserve me!"

My play *Red in the Morning*, written all those years ago, in fact when I was in *Are You Now or Have You Ever Been?* in Birmingham had recently been bought for publication by Samuel French, New York. When the faculty offered to do a play of mine on the main stage I suggested *Red in the Morning* as it would give me a chance to see it and do any necessary rewrites, of which there were some, particularly one draggy scene in Act I which ended up cut virtually in half.

But Tom Arthur was being a bit iffy about doing the play main stage in case it offended some members of the Harrisonburg audience, which in fact it obviously did. (I had no sooner finished writing the play when an old lady in Oxford turned out to be almost a model of my leading character as far as her background was concerned and as late as August 2005, *The Sunday Times* ran an article about a Nazi war criminal working for British Intelligence after the war whose wife is still alive at 92 so it was quite legitimate for me to set the play in the 1980's). Tom was suggesting it be done in Wampler instead and Allen Lyndrup, who loved the play and wanted to design and direct it, certainly didn't want to direct it in the experimental theatre. He eventually won the argument. Meanwhile, slated for the experimental theatre was my play *Generations* to be directed by Chris Holloway. Someone was also looking for something with which to open the new country club and I gave him *Fugue in Two Flats* to read, at that time still titled *Pick Up*. He said he enjoyed the read but what would the blue-rinse ladies of Virginia think of a lyric that had the word 'ejaculation' in it?

Spring Break arrived; Allen and Anne went off with friends to Mexico. They wanted me to go with them but I felt it was a bit out of my range expenses wise so I flew to Decatur to visit David. Chris Holloway drove me to Charlottesville to take the plane, flying from there to Charlotte, North Carolina; to Dayton, Ohio; and finally Champagne, Illinois; still about forty-five miles from Decatur, so David drove over to pick me up. On the way to Charlottesville we took Route 33 and I showed Christian the house that inspired *Generations*. It looked exactly the same as it had four years previously with the same laundry hanging out on the veranda. It blew his mind as he had been quietly beavering away on the production without saying a word. He had his designer and crew and the play practically cast and I knew nothing about it until that moment. Later he drove down 33 on his own to take photographs and, back in Harrisonburg, was talking to some lady who said she remembered that house from when she was a child twenty years before and what looked like the exact same washing was hanging out even then. Now, she told him, whenever she drove past, her own kids would duck down on the car seat "in case someone in the house saw them!" Though who knew who would see them? It seemed no one had ever seen anyone in or around the place and no one knew who might live there which is strange in a rural community where everyone knows everyone even if they don't get along. It was no wonder I said, 'I'm going to write a play set in that house.'

The house on Route 33 that inspired the play Generations

Back in England Chris and Douglas were also beavering away with the improvements to Hollings Farm as well as Chris directing *Thriller of the Year* at the local Little Theatre and setting up dates for *Champagne Charlie* with Douglas as stage manager. The one man show (two if you count the accompanist) which originally travelled in a mini would now grow to such an extant it would need both a car and a hired van, and the accompaniment was augmented by trombone and cornet. Chris kept on working at it, improving the show with each performance.

In Decatur I found David hopping mad. Five English actors who were the absolute pits had just visited his university. Evidently, and here I nearly hit the roof when he told me, the British Arts Council paid them $18,000 for the week. I had the feeling the five were bullshitters from the left-wing fringe. David said he got the impression they couldn't get work in England so hauled their butts over to the states. Evidently they didn't even perform studied work, but read from scripts and were upset because the house lights were left on

Chapter Twenty Four

during the performance and they could see the students getting up and walking out. The students told David if the house lights hadn't been left on they'd have all gone to sleep anyway. The trouble is this kind of crap spoils it for others who really do have something to offer.

Decatur I found a totally uninspiring town in the middle of uninspiring countryside. I took my camera with me but somehow felt it probably wouldn't even come out of its case. It didn't. I met the head of theatre who asked me to give a talk to his students and I sat in on a class, "Music Theatre Literature" which was academically as cute as its title. I can't honestly say this was the greatest week of my life. In fact I know I would have had a lot more fun in Mexico but out of it did come my idea for *Third Drawer from the Top*.

The weekend in Charlottesville with Gray before returning to Harrisonburg was not only relaxing but also more rewarding. Took a long drive into the hills; wooden shack and "poh-white" country, very beautiful, and then had lunch at Sissy's Spaceck's favourite restaurant, or so Gray informed me, "The Book Gallery," a combined bookshop-restaurant with a bar and a pianist playing Bach and Debussy. We just had some beers at the bar and shared a bowl of caviar, very cheap, $4.95 and served with hardboiled egg, lettuce, onion, crackers and bread so quite filling. Eating out in America is not expensive which is why they do it all the time. Well it was cheap then, I don't know about now. Then, in a side street, we discovered another second-hand bookshop Gray didn't even know existed and my prize find was another book on *La Belle Otero* with lots of photographs. For more years than I can remember I had wanted to write a musical based on the life and career of this incredible woman and every bit of new information was a real find. More years were to pass though, and it wasn't until living in Crete, that I finally did get down to writing it.

The audition notices went up for *Orphans* and the classroom where they were being held was packed.

Tee Morris desperately wanted the part of Philip and I had more or less intimated it could be his, which was a stupid thing to do because for one thing I hadn't counted on Patrick Dooley. I don't remember the other boys auditioning for the part but I do remember Tee and I do remember Patrick. I wanted someone with a natural gift of movement and my instructions were simply, 'I want you to dash around this room like a blue-arsed fly. Go.'

Tee stood looking at me as if I were mad. 'Go on, Tee, do it,' I said. He walked sedately around the room on two very stiff legs. I had noticed during rehearsals for *The Imaginary Invalid* that if Tee was ever embarrassed, the walk would automatically follow and I got to calling it Tee's walk. It looked as though he had a giant carrot up his arse or was dying for a dump and desperately holding his buttocks together. Needless to say this wasn't going to get him the part.

Patrick took five seconds to practically trash the room as desks went flying and onlookers scurried out of his way. 'Enough! Enough!' I yelled. Patrick got the part.

It didn't take too long to cast Ron Copeland as Treat and Jim Anzide became the third member of the company as Harold. This was the difficult part to cast; to get a twenty year old to play a forty year old drunk and play it convincingly. Jim had some trouble getting there but he got it in the end quite magnificently. Ron too had trouble loosening up and letting it all hang out but he too eventually got there.

I wanted to get to know more about Patrick, particularly as to whether he could sustain a long part. He sat down opposite me and said, 'I don't know you. Are you that infamous man who gives those awesome classes on Tuesdays and Thursdays at twelve that everybody goes to?' This was before the offer of smoked venison and before he joined the class in the following semester. I discovered he had recently played Romeo so obviously he could sustain a long part. After a rehearsal he bounced into a Ralph Cohen rehearsal for Henry V to inform the entire company that "this man is a total genius!" I had this information from Ralph Cohen and Ron Copeland evidently raised a few eyebrows by announcing in front of various faculty members, 'At last, a director!' Shades of RADA.

Chapter Twenty Four

For once I couldn't say I hate actors who arrive late for rehearsals. They were there before me every time, set up and waiting. Ron, who was brought up in the Pentecostal closet was doing his best to shed its influence but unfortunately Pat had fallen recently under the spell of a rather charismatic adviser and had become a born-again Christian. I had a feeling it was a phase he was going through and he would get over it but I had to delete any reference to God or Jesus Christ in the script. He had no objections to anything else but did not want to take the name of his God in vain, that is outside church or his prayers. He asked if he could have Friday nights off to go to his church youth group but accepted it gracefully when I said no. 'It was worth a try,' he said, grinning. True I wanted someone for Philip who could really move but I didn't want someone who was capable of wrecking everything in his path including a plate glass window he went right through without sustaining so much as a scratch. 'I didn't touch it! I didn't touch it!' A piece of glass like a scimitar, about three feet long or more, eighteen inches wide at the top, narrowing to a needle sharp point at the bottom, hung there trembling like the sword of Damocles and, every now and again, someone would yell, 'Pat, stay away from there!' until security came along and removed the broken glass. The window was replaced and we heard no more about it. Unless we could get a more controlled performance from him I could see Pat either totally trashing the set or ending up in the Rockingham Memorial Hospital, possibly both. Before the window incident he had already knocked over a table and sent two chairs flying -'I planned that! I planned it!-and performed a somersault over the back of a couch with such force he missed the seat and landed on the floor in front of it flat on his back. I thought he must have cracked every vertebrae but he just looked up, grinning, and said, 'I meant that! I meant it!

Meanwhile, a very disappointed Tee Morris was mooching around campus trying to pluck up the courage to say yes he would like to play Alan Strang in *Equus*. I had decided to direct this in Wampler and had offered him the part but he was baulking at the idea of stripping off in front of his peers. I decided, if he didn't want to do it, I

No Official Umbrella

would direct *Streamers* instead. I could cast it without even having to audition but Tee eventually came through and said he would like to play Alan. The big problem now was how to convince his parents, who were vigorously against his doing it, that he wasn't merely engaging in a piece of porn. More Christians to win over. They came over to Harrisonburg and I took Tee and his mother to lunch to discuss it. It was clinched when I said, 'It's not as though he's going to perform with an erection, is it?' I don't think Mrs Morris had ever had a perfect stranger talk to her in so bald a fashion so she capitulated then and there and Tee was over the moon. 'I knew you could do it, Glyn.'

Carla, the girl I cast opposite him had absolutely no hesitation when told I wanted her nude. She didn't inform her family though and, as a punishment after the event, lost the use of her car for quite a lengthy period. Bad news. Without telephones and cars, life for most JMU students wasn't worth living. She didn't hold it against me though. A very pretty girl with a beautiful body, her big failing was her voice, high and squeaky, like the actress in the movie *Singing in the Rain*. 'I can't stand him!' I would have to work extremely hard on that voice but I had my two principals so put in my bid for a slot in Wampler. *Red in the Morning* was definitely down for the main stage in the fall and Chris Holloway now made his proposal for *Generations*. There was also Dinner Theatre in the summer and I felt sure there would be a lot more going on. The rest of the year was going to be very busy.

Orphans opened on the 19th April. The first performance was a little slow to start with and a couple of things went wrong technically but on the whole I was over the moon with it and so was the audience. Backstage after the show Ron and Pat revelled in a sea of female adulation. Whether this was because of their performances or because of who they were I don't really know. Pam Johnson's description of Patrick Dooley was, 'We're talking baby Jesus beautiful here,' and when considerably younger, Ron had sent his sister a photograph of himself with, written on the back, "To Edie from your fantastikly hansom brother, Ron" In both cases this was true. I like to think it was also because they were both fantastikly good actors. Jim wasn't the type to have girls fawning over him but congratulations on his performance were coming in from all directions.

I wasn't too sure about the review. Everyone was telling me what a good review it was whereas I was going around cursing under my breath because I honestly felt the reviewer had been privileged to see three of the best student performances she was likely to see in a lifetime and she didn't even know it. Though her headline screamed "*Orphans* Goes For The Emotional Jugular," I felt she did carp a bit too much although, "Lyle Kessler's *Orphans* makes a determined grab for the audience's emotional throat and Glyn Jones' production at James Madison University's Latimer-Schaeffer Theater Tuesday night came within an inch of getting that choke hold on the audience." Hopefully, after the first night's gremlins were ironed-out, we covered that last inch. The audiences certainly seemed to think so because it took the campus by storm and packed them in every performance. Even kids who never thought of going to the theatre were turning up. The same thing happened later with *Equus* but that was because word got around about the nudity so that every night an hour before the doors opened the line was around the block and many a disappointed young voyeur had to be turned away.

The revue for *Orphans* ended with, "This is no play for children of any ages; (*sic*) the language while perfectly appropriate for the characters, is raw and the violence is both implicit and explicit. Some scenes, although undeniably funny, will probably offend those of mature years and delicate sensibilities. But *Orphans* is a fascinating extended study of three very diverse characters and deserves to be seen."

She was dead right about the language. Harrisonburg Southern Baptists had never heard the word "cocksucker" on stage before but surprisingly there didn't seem to be an adverse reaction from those of "mature years and delicate sensibilities."

Tom Arthur was holding auditions for Dinner Theatre and, although he had already cast me in both plays, I decided to roll along and show willing with the other auditionees. Having greeted me in passing he moved on and into the room in the music department where the auditions were being held and we waited our turn outside in a corridor. There was nowhere to sit except on the cold concrete floor and, after Tom had gone through any number of hopefuls, leaving me sitting there like a spare prick at a wedding, I decided to call it a night and left, rather angry with him and sorry I had been wasting my time. For a while I even thought of telling him to stuff dinner theatre, I was flying back to England, but that impulse passed.

On my birthday there was an overflow of students in Wampler to hear the faculty's critiques of *Orphans*. It was going to be an event of high drama on its own account thanks to Tom King. For all his terminal degrees and obviously high intelligence, Tom King had the strangest approach to theatre of any man I have ever met and to this day I still wonder why he wasn't immersed in some other discipline, philosophy maybe. Either that or roaming the woods with his gun shooting bears, a pastime he seemed to be particularly fond of, or emigrating to Turkey, a country he visited whenever he could. Dealing with him was like walking on eggshells as he would sometimes erupt without warning and his rage was frightening to behold. What could have been nibbling away at this man I wonder? I remember one day when students who had been using Wampler left it totally trashed with rubbish strewn everywhere and, when I remarked on it, Tom blew. If that's the way the students wanted to leave the place so be it, who were we to criticise? Just leave them to do their thing, which in this case meant others wasting valuable time having to clean up after them. One of the rules for using Wampler was that you left it the way you found it and that included class use but in this instance, according to Tom, that obviously didn't apply. Despite having been directed by him twice I was never on Tom King's wavelength and yet there were students to whom he was a minor deity who could do no wrong.

This particular day he was in attack mode, starting off by making the stupidest and most insulting remarks about professionals in the

Chapter Twenty Four

theatre. In other words the only good theatre was amateur where plays are produced purely for the love of it. He then went on to say that in *Orphans* he had just seen three of the worst performances he was ever likely to witness. There was a collective gasp as numerous jaws hit the floor. My jaw didn't hit the floor. I couldn't believe what I had just heard. If Tom King wanted to attack me, that was fine, but I wasn't going to let him do it through the kids or get away with a remark like that. Was this the Ed Steele syndrome all over again? For the first time I really had a chance to tell him exactly how I felt and I pulled no punches. By now every jaw in the room was scraping the floor. Ron was sitting next to Pam Johnson who told me afterwards that he had his hand on her leg and it felt like his thumb and fingers were practically meeting at the bone. I said that, if Tom King wanted to criticise the production as a whole or my direction in particular that was fine by me. I was sure there were things wrong with it which deserved criticism, but I wouldn't have him crucify my cast for some obscure motivation of his own that nobody could fathom or even want to fathom. God alone knows what got into the man but I wanted to hear no more absurd crap from him and, shaking with anger, I stormed out of the room leaving a deafening silence behind me.

Having told him, exactly what I thought of him in front of faculty and virtually every communications student I wondered if Tom King would ever speak to me again, especially as I had arranged to stay in his house the following semester while he shuffled off to Turkey on sabbatical, but the next time I saw him it was as though nothing had happened.

The day had started off so well. In the morning, at Pam's request, I had gone to Jessica's school to read *Winnie the Pooh* to forty beautiful kids who sang. "Happy birthday, dear Glee-yun," and, in the evening, Anne made cheesecake and, with half a dozen favourite people, we indulged in champagne, not my favourite tipple but what the hell, it had certainly been a birthday to remember.

Chapter Twenty Five

Andy Leech arrived to move into "Westward Ho", the flat at the bottom of Franklin that Ron had named (it was decorated in an ancient wallpaper with a design of sailing ships) and was vacating for the summer. Andy, a seasoned tourer, trailed his goods and chattels with U-Haul and was soon settled in and ready to start rehearsals for *The Fantasticks*.

As was my wont, I wasn't prepared to study until after rehearsals started so was trying to get going on *Third Drawer from the Top*. A strange thing happens with me when writing plays. Up to page fourteen, and for some unknown reason it is always page fourteen, the progress is a slow struggle but after page fourteen momentum gathers apace. I wasn't yet on page fourteen so, when not wrestling with my own words, I was immersed in the Noel Coward diaries, hugging comfort to my bosom reading of all the shit the Master, as he eventually became known, had to put up with from critics and cretins, from cretinous critics. I was also into my newly found biography of *La Belle Otero* and told Andy how one New York critic revued her performance when she was appearing at Koster & Bial's with, "We have heard Otero dance and we have seen her sing." To which Andy's reply was, 'Mrs Lloyd Webber would be perfect casting.' New York was still being very unkind to Sarah Brightman at the time.

But life soon started to revolve around study, and rehearsals that certainly had their ups and downs as rehearsals are wont to do, though usually not quite to the extent that these were going to

Chapter Twenty Five

have. Tom directed like he was giving a class and intellectualized anything and everything at the slightest opportunity or came out with incomprehensible quotes such as 'Most of my decisions are unconscious and I take full responsibility for the unconscious.' We had barely started when he set down to run Act One before we had even blocked half of it and, as Tom didn't believe in blocking and changed so often, it seemed a pretty pointless exercise anyway.

It was fun working with my stage son, Andy, and watching him work, he so obviously enjoyed everything he did, that is until somebody, like the musical director, said something stupid and then the grin disappeared and the eyes narrowed to slits. But the moment never lasted and soon he was once more rolling merrily along.

I honestly believed that, good as he might be elsewhere, Tom just was not the right director for a musical. He would have been so much happier with *Hedda Gabler* or a Brecht (without Weil) and, listening to his sometimes interminable and unintelligible notes I found myself wishing Stanislavski had never been born.

The plays were to be performed in the round in a building called The Phillips Center; in a cavernous hall where the acoustics were evidently diabolical and technical staff were busy trying to solve the problem with flying panels.

Outside of rehearsals there was still signs of life about despite most students having left for home or summer jobs. Some who were still around kept coming up to me to say they'd registered for one or other of my classes for the following semester or for the summer session. I had a four week acting course to take once both Dinner Theatre plays were on their way. At the end of the semester students had submitted evaluations of their teachers. I don't remember this happening on my earlier visit not on paper anyway so was quite interested to read what my students thought of me. Putting all the valuations together I came out with straight A's I'm glad to say except for that one girl who objected to me for shouting at one of my students and James Madison really ought to be careful who they employed. But she was,

I am glad to say, the one dissenting voice and as she was a tedious and obnoxious little princess anyway I don't think anyone was too impressed with her criticism. I was a little worried by one though, comparisons sometimes being odious, which read, "It was marvellous to have someone who could actually teach acting. Tom King is a philosopher *[she obviously thought the same as I]*, Phil Grayson is a technician, Tom Arthur is a theorist, Roger Hall is a historian." I wondered what the aforementioned members of faculty thought of that and it rather goes against my earlier statement that you cannot teach someone to be an actor. Tom Arthur however was making very enthusiastic noises about my ability as a teacher, though of course not as good as the professionals.

I got home from rehearsal one night to find Anne had finished reading *Rosemary* and there was a note waiting for me on the kitchen table. "Must talk to you about ROSEMARY. It is wonderful. Absolutely wonderful! I smiled, I laughed, I cried. I cried so much I had to go out and clean the front porch to try and stop."

Normally the Lyndrups were in bed when I got in from rehearsal but the following night she was waiting for me and she just couldn't stop talking about the play. 'We must have a reading,' she said, so it looked like a third Glyn Jones play was going to be seen the following semester. But I couldn't help thinking, despite Anne's enthusiasm, about something I had read in one of my many book purchases in the states, *The Curtain Falls* by Joseph Verner Reed, published in 1935, "I looked at the play", he wrote. "It was a battered, dishevelled manuscript entitled *Blues* by Lynn Riggs. I went home and read it. In the light of the countless unproduced plays that I have since read, I can say that *Blues* is one of the most astounding plays I have ever come across. Why it has never been produced is one of these unaccountable irrelevancies of the theatre." This was in 1929. How many plays has this applied to since? *Rosemary*, so far, joins *Blues* as one of those unaccountable irrelevancies of the theatre. The $64,000 question though is, considering the number of large cast, multi-set flops and economic disasters Verner Reed did produce, why did he never think of doing *Blues*? What happens to all the hundreds of manuscripts that are sent out together with stamped addressed envelopes for their return if not wanted only for them seemingly to disappear into the great blue yonder? On my return to England in 1989 I sent *Rosemary* to Charlie Vance. Sixteen years later despite letters of love and assurance as to how he is such a big fan of my writing and he will read the play as soon as he gets a chance–I am still waiting for his reaction. These days of computers it costs next to nothing and takes minutes to print out a script, if and when needed, but in the old days it was a huge dent in the budget when scripts had to be printed by specialist companies and then, when submitted, including return postage, were never seen or heard of again.

We arrived at our first complete run-thru of *The Fantasticks* and it was terrible. At notes everyone flew at poor Tom and gave him hell. I love the man dearly and felt terribly sorry for him but even I couldn't resist throwing a temperament. He complained that people were stumbling over their words in the dialogue scenes which was hardly surprising as dialogue scenes had hardly been touched and you can learn words off the page till they're coming out of your ears instead of your mouth but unless you actually say them, hear your cues, are given responses, what's the point? But the biggest moan from the cast was the fact that, as Tom didn't believe in blocking (a case of "kicking it around" a little?) The opening and closing of acts had changed so often, none of us knew exactly which version we were supposed to be using. Technically it was a mess.

Little Jessica came to that rehearsal and sat open-mouthed through the entire evening so at least one person enjoyed it. And the entire season is a sell-out so we'd better get our act together fast, especially as we were now also about to start rehearsing *Fools*.

Keeping Jess company, a few students came and sat in, among whom was a girl with the prosaic name of Betsy Rook who looked like the young Sissy Spacek and was perfect for the younger daughter in

Generations. I fell in love on the spot and made her swear she would go to the auditions but when it came to it, much to my genuine disappointment, she didn't appear.

The musical opened and was playing to mixed receptions. The world had changed a great deal since 1960 and the fact that there had quite recently been two horrific rapes in the neighbourhood, one leading to the death of the victim, made me suggest to Tom that the rape song should be cut but he wouldn't hear of it. The result was, as soon as the word was mentioned, the audience reacted as if hit with a jet of icy water and we played to stony silence well into the second act. Tom was also verbally attacked in and outside the theatre by a number of offended ladies. It reminded me of the time Chris discovered a music hall number called *Why Don't We Nationalise the Ladies?* and decided to try it out at Chat's Palace in Hackney. It was received with boos and catcalls and, after the show he was virtually physically attacked by a bevy of furious, rather butch, East End girls waiting for him in the foyer, short haircuts, skin-tight jeans, Doc Martin's, and leather jackets. I came to his rescue only to have them turn on me as well and, in vain, did we plead the song was nothing more than a piece of light-hearted music hall history and should be taken as such, but no, it offended their sense of women's lib and women's rights and nothing would alter that. Chris immediately dropped the number, which was what should have happened in Harrisonburg with the rape song.

Fools is not Neil Simon at his best. It's a rather silly one-joke play and the audiences loved it. I don't know how many minutes their laughter added to performance times and it would have been even longer if the youngsters in the show had learned to ride their laughs instead of cutting them off but it certainly made a change and was great fun to do.

Now I had to take my four week acting class and sort myself out for the following semester with four classes scheduled. I was also looking forward to getting back to Hollings Farm for a short break once Dinner Theatre was over and before the semester began.

America was suffering the worst drought in fifty years and after days of temperatures in the upper nineties the heatwave suddenly broke one afternoon with the most almighty thunderstorm. I couldn't repeat my naked Wayside performance on Franklin but in a flash I was out on the front lawn in my little white shorts and giving myself up to the torrential rain. Anne stood on the porch and had hysterics. When he saw what a good time I was having Jens plucked up courage and dashed out in Bermudas and one of his dad's outsize old rugby shirts. He looked like a skeletal cast-off from a charity shop. What I, a fifty seven year old in my tiny white shorts looked like I have no idea, and quite frankly I didn't care. Sometimes in the searing heat of a Cretan midsummer's day when even the water in the garden hose is too hot to touch, I find myself wishing for one of those cold tropical downpours.

Then, suddenly, it was orientation time again and the campus was swarming with freshmen and their parents all being initiated into the workings of JMU. The university was fast becoming the most popular in the state, first choice with more applicants than The University of Virginia, Virginia Tech or William and Mary and with many more enquiries coming from outside Virginia. There was talk of raising the number of students from ten to sixteen thousand and I couldn't help but wonder what they would do about the parking problem. As it was, every car park was already jammed solid, and the university had a nice little earner in tickets. During *Imaginary Invalid* I received one while parked outside the theatre and despite all my protests with the campus police: there was no indication I couldn't park in that particular spot I said and, anyway, surely they wouldn't want to hand out a fine to an innocent visiting British professor. I even filled in the appeal form but all to no avail and it cost me a magnificent ten dollars.

Before semester started Tom sweet-talked me into taking an extra course. Would I share a course with him he asked? It was to be

'Theatre In The Fifties.' I would do Britain, he would do America, and the course would end with some high-powered guy from Yale and someone from the RSC guesting for America and Britain respectively. I liked the idea of meeting the high-powered geyser from Yale, as he was evidently quite influential, according to Tom, so I said yes. There was no mention of extra money for taking this course but in my mailbox I found a notice Tom had drawn up announcing "The New Course Being Offered dealing with (1) Theatre from the fifties to the eighties." [!] What happened to just the fifties? I suddenly thought of the research I would be required to undertake to cover four decades of theatre and, as for the eighties, I was totally out of touch. "(2) It is an evening block course, two lectures a week each of two hours twenty minutes duration." Now I was mad. Tom was fully aware that during that period I was committed to Brian Bolt to play Eddie in his production of *A View from the Bridge* and this would really put the mockers on it. I had a feeling I was being taken distinct advantage of and the time had come for a big fat NO! Unfortunately Tom was on the West Coast but I would tackle him the moment he got back. I don't think he realised what he was doing but he would make these vague suggestions and then elaborate on them behind one's back.

In the meantime other things were still preoccupying me. I had booked a room, M209, arranged a reading of *Rosemary* and cast it, so that needed to go into rehearsal. I was nearing the magic page 14 with *Third Drawer from the Top* (was actually on page 12) and, having finished reading the Otero biography, ways and means of writing the musical were going round and around in my head. The two big problems as I saw them were firstly how to make her sympathetic to an audience and secondly how to encapsulate in two and a half hours 96 years of someone's extraordinary life. I never imagined at that time that it would be another fourteen years before I would actually get down to writing it.

The reading of *Rosemary* went well; small audience which was a little disappointing though I was pleased to see unknown faces

Chapter Twenty Five

and the reaction was lovely and positive. If, in a more or less static reading, one gets only a fraction of a play's potential. I couldn't have been more encouraged by it. There was of course the usual dissenting voice; there has to be. A lady came up to me afterwards. Highly critical of the play because she "had been in geriatrics for many years" she didn't feel that the character of Walter was "fragmented" enough! Having based Walter on my personal experience of the real life model at Greenwoods I felt he was quite fragmented enough thank you. I let her ramble on with various other criticisms, just waiting for the punch line which I knew was coming and, sure enough, there it was, "Of course I write plays myself." She omitted to say, "plays better than this" but that certainly was what was implied. 'Ask her how many she's had done,' Anne whispered to me but I also knew the answer to that one. The same thing happened some time later when I took a directing class at The Little Theatre in Hebden Bridge using *Third Drawer from the Top* to work on and sure enough there just had to be another lady playwright in the group very sniffy about the play itself, never mind the workshop was supposed to be about directing not playwriting.

Of course, hearing it read, I found things wrong with *Rosemary*. There were a number of places where it needed tightening up. The Kenneth Williams story had to be cut in half at least but the story Walter tells of coming home Christmas eve to find his wife and kids gone had the audience by the short and curlies and the end, as with *The 88*, left them totally gob smacked, like Anne going out onto the porch to try and stop crying. God, I thought, how I would really like to direct this play but will I ever get the chance?

It had been a great day. Gray came up from Charlottesville as he wanted to attend the reading so, in the morning, Allen, Anne, Carrie, Gray and I went canoeing on the river, the Lyndrups in one canoe, Gray and I in another and it was beautiful. Not being an expert I managed to overturn the canoe and ditch us, fortunately where it was fairly shallow and not too close to rocks where we could have damaged both ourselves and the canoe so all we did was stand soaking wet, crotch deep in water and laugh, and it was still beautiful, one of those memories that stays with you for a lifetime.

Later, dried out, I took the cast of *Rosemary,* and Gray, for lunch at The Little Grill. I felt a bit like Alistair Sim in Edinburgh, choosing the cheapest place in town, although one could eat well at The Little Grill, and the whole shebang for seven people including beers and tips came to $35.

At Anne's suggestion I wrote to Hume Cronin and Jessica Tandy asking if I could send them the play. The reply was affirmative but the end result was not. Having read the play and praised its qualities–whether sincere or not but I like to think the former–the reaction was in Mr Cronin's own words, "at our age a little too close to home I'm afraid." Seventeen years later and *Rosemary* still lies neglected in the script cupboard.

Summer classes came to an end. My final one was a joy as my seven previously formless lumps suddenly came to life and gave me performances that didn't result in any A's but, at least, a complete string of B's rather than D's which, up till then, was what they had been heading for.

On the last night of *Fantasticks* we lost our "orchestra" right at the top of the first act when the electric piano simply died on us. Trooper Andy, with no hesitation and totally unphased, simply sang "*Love, What Is Love*" a capella with perfect pitch and eventually we got our orchestra back. He was also the hero of the softball game between waiters and actors at the company picnic. Evidently he looked around and said, "I think I'm the only homo here," proceeded to play like a Titan to put the macho breeders to shame, won the game for the actors and cracked a thigh bone in the process. Fortunately *Fools*, of which there were still seven performances to go didn't require him to put any strain on his legs.

There was a dinner dance for all those involved in the summer theatre and then I was off to Charlottesville to fly to Washington to fly to Manchester and so to Hollings Farm. From the moment of landing at Manchester it was two weeks non-stop activity starting with watching a performance of *Arms and the Man*, produced by Bridge Theatre, playing The Little Theatre and in which Chris was engaged as Sergius and performing it magnificently though I say it myself. With a smile on my face rather than a frown I didn't have to be kept away from the dressing room. There were new people to meet, among whom was Chris Cawkwell who had been giving a much needed and welcome helping hand with the refurbishment of the house. Hyst mum was on a visit, staying with cousin Jenny. There was the builder to see and central heating engineers, visits to Leeds and Halifax, to sale rooms and Thornton's Antiques, a treasure house of architectural salvage where I bought the magnificent fireplace. Dave and Poo arrived from London. There were lunches and dinners, and another shot at play going, this time to *Hedda Gabler*, not quite up to standard with some rather strange directorial choices I thought. *Champagne Charlie* was rehearsed a number of times, now with the two added musicians, Garry Pulleyn on trombone and Jules Wightman, trumpet doubling cornet for that nostalgic period sound. Paul Knight had come up from London to rehearse his orchestrations and play piano for the last time. The brass added a whole new dimension to the show and suddenly it was time to fly back to the states. I was due to take my first acting class the day following my flight.

Chapter Twenty Six

Shortly after Christian started rehearsing *Generations*, we started rehearsals for *A View from the Bridge* and then auditions were held for *Red in the Morning* with lots of new faces never seen before. Apart from my four classes, (don't remember what happened to Tom's blockbuster course. Guess I must have talked him out of it, or at least talked myself out of it) I was giving without charge private voice classes to individuals, but it wasn't all work. Sue Burrell came up from Richmond to see *Generations*, as did Gray from Charlottesville, and Scott Harrison came down from DC. The faculty might not have liked the play but they certainly seemed to be knocked out by it and I don't think, I hope anyway, it wasn't just because they were friends. We went to Dayton to have lunch at Ma Thomas's. It was the Autumn Festival so there was a street market and a Blue Grass band playing outside the fire station. The sad news was that Ma Thomas had died three weeks earlier. I think she was eighty-six, that wonderful old lady who had given me so much for *Generations*. I only wished she could have seen the play.

Two weekends of the Book Fair and more theatre books at two dollars a piece, performances of *Bridge* then it was *Red in the Morning* and the semester would be almost over. Chris scraped his pennies together to come over for the week of *Red in the Morning* as, *Champagne Charlie* aside; it is his favourite play of mine. Having seen it in production it was still his favourite.

Chapter Twenty Six

A View from the Bridge with Chris Ockler & Brian Kurlander - James Madison University

A View from the Bridge played to full houses and standing ovations which was gratifying and once again the Copeland family came up to see their son in a play, this time as Rodolpho. Su Burrell and Gray were also in town and everyone stayed with me in the King house so it was quite a party. Kim Russell, my fantastic stage manager from *Orphans* now had her acting cap on and made a really great job of Beatrice, despite her youth.

For once a play in the Experimental Theatre got a revue in the Harrisonburg paper. I don't know why but Phyllis Quillen came, saw, and reviewed. Headlined "Experience Gap Collapses JMU's Bridge" the revue ran, "From Redhook, the gullet of New York, to the Wampler Experimental Theatre at James Madison University can be a big leap, but without a detour to England for one of the actors, the production of '*A View from the Bridge*' might have wound up with a few broken spans. Not that there is anything wrong with director Brian Bolt's handling of Arthur Miller's uneven morality play-cum-psychological drama. *[It's fascinating the way people contradict themselves.]* And the audience Tuesday found itself so caught up in the conclusion that some people seemed inspired to leap onto the stage and rewrite Miller's ending with a little free improvisation. But without that stopover to cast Glyn Jones as Eddie Carbone, the Italian-American longshoreman whose view of the bridge of love is decidedly foreshortened, it is unlikely that Bolt's work or Miller's play would have raised more than tepid polite applause." She then goes on to give a résumé of the plot before continuing with, "For this play to work every character needs to be in balance and it takes considerable skill to imbue these characters with more than a surface comic-book life. Jones does it superbly. His Eddie is a tormented and tortured man, at odds with those whom he loves and with himself. His concept of who he is is so bound up with masculine stereotypes that he becomes incapable of seeing what he is doing and, more importantly, why he is doing it. In his mind everything is in black and white. But in his actions and in the perceptions that others have of him there are only infinite shades of gray." [*Phew!*]

I thought *A View from the Bridge* would be the last acting I would do but then I suddenly thought I would like to play Sir in *The Dresser* if I could talk someone into doing it the following semester. But then that darn old fate had other plans for me and I ended up playing Dysart in *Equus* instead.

Of *Red in the Morning* one student wrote, "In the combined tradition of Alfred Hitchcock's suspense and Stephen King's brutal force, RED IN THE MORNING takes the audience on a roller coaster ride filled with suspense, chills, and ultimately horror with a woman from hell. Both the characters and setting provide a tasty addition to Glyn Jones's gut wrenching play."

The general consensus among the younger generation was that the play was simply awesome. Not so among some of the older generation as a letter to Allen Lyndrup seemed to indicate.

Chapter Twenty Six

19th November 1988.

Re: *RED IN THE MORNING.*

Dear Sir,

We have been patrons of the drama department for several years and until now have thoroughly enjoyed your theatrical productions. We realise that as a teaching institution you must produce a wide spectrum of plays to give your students as broad a dramatic base as possible. The current production *RED IN THE MORNING* was not good theatre (*sic*–English spelling) The plot was nonexistent [?] and even after the final curtain we have yet to determine what the author was trying to portray other than a demented woman *[a woman from hell maybe but definitely not demented]* and physical violence beyond reason. *[The reason obviously being Edie's self-preservation.]* The kidnapping was the beginning of a good plot but even that fell flat in the end for it served no purpose and its motive was never revealed. *[A heavy ransom demand was no motive?]* All in all nothing strung together in a coherent plot leaving us the audience totally bewildered and thoroughly disgusted with the violence which left us with a very bad feeling.

To close on a higher note, our very sincere congratulations to Messrs Roggenkamp and Totten for a superb set. It is one of the best we have seen. Your department has an excellent reputation for scenic design and this was certainly one of your best. We are sorry to say that the set was the only redeeming feature of the current play.

Hoping for a better future,
Mr and Mrs Richard A. Thomas
Waynesboto [*sic*].

You bring to a play only what you can and you take from it what you can. In the case of this couple the bringing and the taking were obviously at ground zero. As for the play being plotless their brains must have been too wrapped up in their prejudices ("thoroughly disgusted") to be aware of what was going on. The play that receives

No Official Umbrella

universal acclimation has yet to be written but then that also applies to any of the arts. A painting entitled Red and Yellow Lines on a White Background and consisting of one red vertical line and one horizontal yellow lie on a white background, or even a single colour; Klein's red, orange, yellow, mean absolutely nothing to me except that the emperor's new clothes are around somewhere, some idiot critic has raved over it and some gallery has paid a fortune for it. Tretchikoff as he went laughing all the way to the bank could afford to ignore his critics, ditto Andrew Lloyd Webber. I once asked a composer in New York what he thought of Lloyd Webber's music and that was his exact response. When I went back to South Africa in '73 I took my mother a present, the Elizabeth Schwartzkopf recording of Richard Strauss's *Four last Songs*, to my mind an exquisite performance of some of the most beautiful music ever written and, despite being a singer herself and to my deep disappointment, she had no empathy with the music whatsoever. "I just don't understand it," she said. Her musical appreciation had stopped with Handel and popular arias from nineteenth century Italian opera.

In a similar frame of mind to Mr and Mrs Thomas of Waynesboro, Tom Arthur was thoroughly bemused by the play despite the fact that he had read and digested it in order finally to give it the go-ahead, and his evaluation was as follows–Firstly with a quotation from

"THE READER'S ENCYCLOPEDIA OF WORLD DRAMA", P.371

"Grand Guignol. A brief horror play about rape. Ghosts, murder, and the like, designed to shock and titillate the audience. *[The punctuation is as.]* Performed at the Parisian cabaret called Theatre du Grand Guignol the plays were very popular in Paris during the 1890's and 1900's and appeared in England in a somewhat modified form at the turn of the century."

Guignol was originally the name of a marionette in a kind of

Chapter Twenty Six

Punch and Judy show, dating from the end of the eighteenth century. The general cruel-heartedness of the puppet show and Guignol in particular provided the namesake for the Grand Guignol theatre.

I didn't want to do this play originally because I don't like the idea of "Grand Guignol". Cruelty and murder for the sake of titillation seems an unpleasant, cynical business. A friend who I respect called it "fun". I don't find it fun at all and thought it would disturb our audience too, and to no particularly good end that I could think of. After watching our audience watching RED IN THE MORNING onstage, I realise now that such worries were absurd; they were absolutely blasé about the play *[Mr and Mrs Thomas were anything but blasé]* for "titillation" of the sort offered by RED IN THE MORNING is available on television any night of the week. And of course that reaction worries me far more than my original objection. I have learned something I would rather not have known.

What has always been very good about Allen's work is that he has an acute sense of visual detail and style, as well as a good "eye" for character. *[Can one have an "eye" for character? And anyway, this is contradicted in the next paragraph.]* His musicals often sparkle. His comedies are genuinely funny a remarkably high percentage of the time. Furthermore, the products of Allen's directorial work have attained a gut intensity recently. HOLY GHOSTS came close to being a primal shriek, notwithstanding, even using the limits of its inexperienced cast. SIX CHARACTERS succeeded by harnessing an intensity of address which suggested a self-doubt which seemed to be shared by every character in the play. *[I'm not too sure what all that means but good on Al and his six characters and what about RED IN THE MORNING? Ah, here it comes.]*

RED IN THE MORNING had all the virtues mentioned above *[An inexperienced cast? An intensity of address? A self-doubt? What virtues?]* It too had an unusual immediacy, aided in no small measure by what was surely a director/lead actress decision to eschew overt signs of character cruelty. *["Surely a director/actress decision?" No, dear Tom, it was the author's decision, it's all there in the writing.]* The most frightening evil is terrifying precisely because it arises out of opacity rather than melodramatic foreshadowing. *[Exactly, which is why Evie is described as "lavender and lace" and the only foreshadowing that takes place at the top of the play is between Helena, the companion, and John, the manservant.]*

But the production was severely marred by its ending. Why did Allen, and presumably Glyn, back off from the killing of the invisible child, which was suggested by the script when the faculty first read it? Why were we let off the hook (pardon the pun) and allowed to believe that Evie ran off with the boy to live happily ever after? [!] Glyn and Allen may respond that what they did was make it possible to see the fate of the child in as happy or unhappy a light as one wishes. It won't do. The production lost much of its impact because of this failure of conviction, which in turn reduced the piece from "grand" to what might properly be called "mini" quignol.

[This is absolute nonsense. At no time, either in dialogue or action, is there the slightest suggestion that Evie goes off with the boy to live happily ever after. How Tom got this idea into his head I simply cannot fathom as earlier in the play Evie states categorically how much she detests the child, so it would hardly be likely she would go off with him and, at the play's end, it is obvious that Evie is the sole survivor. I go back to the film of The Servant, and the fight on the stairs. Was there a niche half way up the stairs and was there a figurine in that niche? What did Tom think he heard or saw that gave him this weird idea?]

I had heard from friends and read in the [news] paper before I went to the play that the first act was too long *[true–most of the cutting came in the first act]* and the second just about right, but found the opposite to be true. Glyn seems to me to have a good ear for low key, everyday dialogue which fairly oozes suppressed tension. But once the blood began to spurt in the second act, it was hard to keep up with the intricacies of the plot, at least for me. *[Guess he was in the same boat as the Thomas's at this point though looking in opposite directions because for them the plot they say was nonexistent, though I have to confess I don't know why Tom found it one thing and the Thomases another because I was asked to give a talk at a local old folks home and none of them seemed to have had any trouble with the plot other than the grand Guignol sequences churned them up a bit.]*

The script and/or production had a number of inconsistencies. If the play takes place in the present as indicated in the program, simple math dictates that, what with the last of the Nazi concentration camps being liberated in 1945, Evie is either getting on into her mid-eighties *[True, that's where I put her. The lady discovered in Oxford was of that age and, only recently, August 2005, the Sunday Times ran an article about a Nazi war criminal employed by British intelligence after the war whose wife at this time is 92 and who in her photograph looks pretty sprightly and well preserved with it. The point Tom is making I suppose is that someone in their eighties is capable of moving only with the help of a Zimmer frame, if at all, and probably has to be spoon fed. Of course there are people much younger who are well past it but certainly not everybody.]* Her actions in the script are unlikely for someone this old–though not impossible I suppose. *[What actions is he talking about? The physical action goes on all around her by the other characters while she remains serenely composed. She is required towards the end of the play to (a) fire a pistol and at the very end (b) fire a shotgun. Other than that it is mainly tea pouring time while she dictates the course of events and it doesn't require geriatric acrobatics to do that.]* She (Mary Szmagaj) didn't seem to be playing that age. *[Now it's a strange thing but any number of fledgling actors asked to play anyone over the age of sixty immediately assume the characteristics of someone of a hundred and five. Mary, as far as I was concerned played Evie beautifully, and you took into account her own youthful age. What happened to Tom's "using the limits of an inexperienced cast," though*

No Official Umbrella

in this case not inexperienced, merely young? And the same applied to John Harrell playing the part of the manservant John, and Shannon Wilson playing Helena who Tom criticised for the same reason. If he insisted upon authenticity of age students would never do plays with characters over the age of twenty-five or thereabouts.]

And how did Helena get into the cupboard with the two stiffs, one of which had to be hung up literally as a dead weight? *[On a meat hook hence the "no pun" remark above.]* Did Helena help her octogenarian employer rearrange the bodies in at least one unusual posture, *[Presumably the meat hook]* and then obligingly step into the closet before freaking out? *[No, Tom. Naturally we don't see the business of the actual hanging. It is revealed after the event but it is pretty obvious that a beefy manservant by the name of John was quite capable of lifting a dead body without the aid of Helena or the octogenarian and also of locking Helena in the cupboard with the stiffs.]*

What was the "business arrangement" between Evie and her husband? Her money for his help in (her) escaping from the Allies? Why wouldn't he simply have taken her money and turned her in rather than marrying a person he had every reason to think might kill him at the first opportunity?"

Now this is where one really begins to wonder what the point is of writing plays when they can be so misheard, misunderstood, misinterpreted. I have refuted Tom's critical points above but now I shake my head in despair that, having read the play (more than once maybe?) and sat through a performance, how could he get something so completely arse about face? From where did he get the impression that Evie had money of her own? It is stated quite clearly that the money, which makes Evie a rich woman is not hers but was bequeathed her by her husband whose ancestors made their fortune in the early days of rail travel, and the only reason her husband helped her escape the allies and married her was because he fell in love. There was no such thing as "a business arrangement." And why would she for one moment dream of killing her rescuer when her whole existence after the war relied on her remaining incognito, to all intents and purposes an aging, very charming English widow. To commit a murder would have been the height of stupidity. It could not have been clearer.

As with Harry Booth I don't mean to bite the hand that fed me but Tom must have had a lot on his mind or left his very clever brain at home the night he visited the playhouse. It's not unknown and unfortunately must happen more than one supposes.

But what did Phyllis Quillen have to say about the play? "Jones' Thriller Provides Chills." She obviously had no difficulty in following the plot and "the several hefty shocks" and on the whole it was a good review except for, "Much of the first act dawdles along in lackadaisical fashion and pointless exposition." Absolutely true, hence the cuts and rewrites. But it is what she says about the acting, in direct contradiction to Tom, which is most interesting. "Mary Szmagaj as Evie is pivotal to what happens and above all how it happens. This young actress literally takes center stage throughout most of the play, and most effectively manages it as Evie manages her house. She is Miss Marple outside, and Miss Malice inside, with a sweet, cold smile to mask her hidden past and true nature. Shanon Wilson as the flighty Helena, John Chidester Harrell as the lurking and lethal John, and Brian Kurlander and Ron Copeland as the duplicitous telephone engineers are equally outstanding."

This was the semester I moved into the King farmhouse at Mount Crawford about six miles out of Harrisonburg. I had the use of Tom King's car and, in bad weather, his truck. The livestock, mainly sheep, had been boarded out and I noticed the gun cabinet had been emptied. The only animals I saw around the house and for which I put out food were any number of feral cats and kittens. They fled in all directions the moment they saw me, except for one that didn't seem to know I was even there and, in fact that was the case. I picked it up and saw it was blind, its eyelids sealed with mucus and fly eggs.

No Official Umbrella

I got some baking soda and cotton wool from the supermarket the next time I went shopping and with a mixture of that and warm milk I bathed the kitten's eyes until gradually they opened and it could see again. I called her Sophie and she was a real cartoon cat; a silky pale grey and white. I would have loved to have taken her back to England with me but her airfare was three times mine so it was out of the question. Sophie took over as my social secretary.

Well hi there, ole buddy, or buddies, buddyroos. How ya'all doin? Chris, you know what that dirty sonofabitch did for Thanksgivin? Didn't say a word, jest upped an skedaddled an we never did see him for three hole days. Jest as well the last time he fed us he forgot to take the bag back inside so, when he made it back to the ole homestead, we found it mighty hard to walk up the path to give him a rousin hoe down howdy because it ain't easy tryin to walk with yer belly draggin along the groun. Now we don't see him hardly because he tells me he's practicin real hard for something called Ekweeyus an he's goin every night to somthin called the Directors Workshop, though if'n you wuz ter ask me I do declare he's visitin a cathouse, if'n you'all pardon the expression. I heerd about them places.

It's gotten mighty cold here now, Chris, so reckon as to how you jest mist it. We still got them clear blue Virginny skies but I am as froze as a turkey's nose in a icebox. Spencer, that stupid cat, an his new friend have cut loose an ain't bin seen around a while so there's jest me an Mathilda an Onyx hangin aroun the ole homestead. Caint figure out none where they got to. Jest took off for the hills I reckon. An that's about my news for now so I best get on to the messages I'm supposed to give yer.

What did he say now? Let me see ... Oh yeh ...he says to tell yer he done the rewritin on the play an Julie is now finishin it off so it can go to Mr Samuel French next week. He says he will also send it to you so you can see he cut off Mr Dell's nickname, whatever that means.

Well, I'm sure glad to have met you, Chris, an I look forward to meeting up with Dooglas sometime. Guess that's all for now so so long, fella. Talk at'cha some other time.

Chapter Twenty Six

*Yours Sincerely
Sophie*

*P.S
You forgot to take your Tammy Faye T-shirt.
Mathilda says to say mieow-hi an Onyx would cept he's so shy.
What does "giving head" mean anyways? Is it something to do with fish? I'm interested.*

18th December 1988

*Hi there, Buddy Boys,
You are NOT goin ter believe this! Ole shitface told me I gotta write you. I told him write? My paw is too small to hold a pin never you mind a pen. An anyway I got snow up to me asshole an it's given me frostbite. You ever had your asshole bitten by frost? Not somethin you want second time round let me inform you of that! An he says, "Earn your keep, slut." Slut! Slut!! Me? The original virginal Virginian pussy. Well ifn I'm to get any dinner tonite I best do like I'm told I suppoge. So here I am. He keeps on sayin how he would like to take me back to England with him cause I'm growing into SUCH a cute cat. A fat cute cat. But I don't reckon on it happenin cos it would cost dollars beaucoup, know what I mean? That is a French word, my ancestors havin come from the bayous of Louisiana. Spencer still hasn't come back but his stripey pretty frend has bin seen around. Trouble is, that ole bitch Mathilda don't reckon him none an belts the shit outa him every now an agin so he tends ter keep his distance. He says to tell you the Oxbridge Inn has bin sold at last* [After leaving college Gray went into partnership with a Greek in a bed and breakfast venture in Charlottesville and hated every minute of it] *and Gray will be out by end of February. He is quite a happy puppy about that. Gray I mean. Spencer's friend is a cat. Righty–I've earned my dinner. Goodbye.
Yours truly,
Sophie.*

No Official Umbrella

Presented by Washington & Lee University I took Ron Copeland over to Lexington to see *Sleeping Beauty* a "British Pantomime!" It was great fun even though, as I put it in a letter home, 'the kids were monstrously naff.' The Brokers' Men, two heralds named Shout and Bawl, were cute, looking like Tweedledum and Tweedledee, American version, and the one with the punch lines real deadpan like Buster Keaton, only pretty. I don't know what Al Gordon (the director) meant when he told me the Henry Street Playhouse was a Victorian Theatre. It might have been built in about 1898 but certainly never as a theatre. The interior is like Madison's Wampler only with a high ceiling and would seat about the same, two fifty at a pinch. So that was a bit of a disappointment though Lexington, home of the great General Lee is a pleasant little town and we automatically nosed out the second hand bookshops. Only ten books purchased this time but seven of them were plays for working on next semester so they didn't count. Gray had heard of a second hand bookstore in Culpepper that boasted having 16,000 volumes and wanted to visit it after Christmas. I promised Douglas faithfully by letter I would not buy 15,999 books.

Five days to Christmas and already I was thoroughly fed-up with the "festive season". On the radio Christmas music was played from morn to night. Guitarists played Christmas songs, flautists played Christmas songs, pianists and organists, jazz bands and orchestras; madrigal groups and choirs sang Christmas songs, as did José Carrerras, rather badly. To add to this constant barrage of halleluiahing faithful and warbling wonders, every local school band and singing group had to give a Christmas concert, and as their musicality was not exactly of a very high standard the result could be excruciating. I escaped from it for a few hours by locking myself in the sound booth at Latimer-Schaeffer with Joel Moritz, working on a sound tape for *Equus*.

Apart from computerised tills in the shops all jingling merry bells, the other sign of Christmas was the lighting up of house exteriors. The house on the crest of the hill above the King farm at night was completely outlined in red, white, and blue lights. There was a gigantic

Chapter Twenty Six

lit-up star on the front lawn and a couple of trees were doo-dahed up as well. Pam Johnston told me that in West Virginia it's like a feudin' an' a fightin' to see who can outdo who with the amount of lights they can stick up: all the way up the drive, all around the house, all around the garage and the barn, up the roof and the chimney stack and even on the weather vane.

Christmas I spent at Covesville and then Richmond and as we approached the New Year we were seriously thinking about Douglas paying a visit to the states during my last semester. In Richmond I went with Su to see *Camelot* at Theatre Virginia. It used to be The Museum Theatre but they upgraded it. Richmondites are such snobs. What a boring musical it is. Boring, boring, boring. King Pellinore and Mordred both excellent, the rest of the cast merely so-so. Direction was also so-so, the May Dance a toe-curling embarrassment and the fights simply awful. Was invited to a party afterwards and beat all the American actors at their own game,–Pool. Won five straight games in a row and then gave up before my luck ran out.

Chapter Twenty Seven

Sophie was unable to write the first letter of the New Year, she had got too fat. I can't remember but maybe I asked a neighbour to feed the cats while I was away because, after Richmond, Su and I went to the little town of Manteo on Roanoke Island, North Carolina, staying in the beautiful "Booth" house with its own private beach. The house was crammed with Victoriana, enough to fill half a dozen antique shops. The guest kitchen was liberally provided with crockery, cooking utensils, cutlery, vases, jugs, decanters, glasses, in fact anything that was needed and more, mostly antique. There were the most beautiful oil lamps everywhere but something was missing and that was quite simply any sign of an architectural feature. The whole place was lined with chip paper painted white and there was a definite need for figured wallpapers and mouldings to compliment all that Victoriana.

Also in the town was the most amazing shop called, naturally enough, "The Christmas Shop", open all year and selling nothing but Christmas goods; room after room, each one a glittering Aladdin's cave with red and gold the predominant colours of course. Owned by an ex-actor, he had done so well out of it he extended it with annexes and also now owned a brewery and Munich style beer hall and restaurant next door. The place was heaving as they were having an après-Christmas sale. Three large parking lots were jam packed with cars and they kept on coming.

It was weird to see the street in Manteo with English names: Sir

Chapter Twenty Seven

Walter Raleigh Street, Bedford Street, Essex, etcetera. Nag's head, The Outer Banks, just before you drive onto Roanoke Island, you pass miles and miles of hotels and big wooden beach houses, unpainted and the wood all weathered a uniform grey. As it was out of season and hardly anyone about, most of the cafés were closed and I couldn't help thinking it looked like a ghost town. I also couldn't help thinking it must be hell in summer with a million holiday makers and a million cars. There was one big plus for the area though, magnificent seafood. On the way back we stopped in Virginia Beach, very tacky, but with a great delicatessen.

El Rancho Sheepo
Virginia
1st November 1989

Dear Chris and Douglas,

I have a problem. I hope you don't mind me aksin fur advice. There is this guy I live with heer on the farm. He's a nice guy. He gives me what I want like food an lots of lovin. But I am real worried. You see, how can I put this? Sometimes he goes bananas an I cain't unnerstan why an I thought as to you bein two cool english cats you mebbe can tell me the answer to my problem. I go into the house (Mathilda comes too now) an I akses him politely an ladylike as I can–well I tell him really, hey shitface I'se hungry, you know, so he's all lovin an kind an he cuts me (an Mathilda an Onyx too sometimes) a piece o meat or sumthin like that an to save him the trouble of having to throw it down or bend over I run up his trouser leg to his hand. I mean, it's easy fur me. I jest have to use my claws, an then he goes apeshit (I learn these words from his students) an I cain't unnerstan why. What am I doin wrong? I mean he ought ter be pleased I save him the trouble, ain't that a fact now? Your advice would be gratefully received. Please send it in a plain envelope so he don't know I've wrote you. Thank you an looking forward to heerin from you. You all have a nice day now.

Concernedly yours,
Sophie.

No Official Umbrella

PS *You have ter admit it's one helluva problem. Bein nice doesn't allus get you what you want.*
Yours truly,
S.
PPS I am truly fearful for my fur. S.
PPPS Wouldn't you be?

The technical rehearsal for *Equus* went without a hitch except for one disappointment. I had intended that at the end of the play all my beautiful horses should, like the two principals, be starkers and they were all quite happy to go for it. But it just didn't work and I cut it. I knew Tee was going to be very good but I still hadn't got performances out of Hesther and Dalton which was worrying but I thought maybe they would come up to scratch at the dress. I was more than pleased with my lighting so was a little surprised when at the evaluations it was derisively criticised by Phil Grayson, but then Phil was the theatre technician and lighting specialist. I was also pleased with the hours Joel and I had spent working on the music and, at one point in the evening everything stopped dead. 'What's the matter?' I asked, or yelled rather.

'My hair's standing on end!'

'I've gone all goose pimples!'

Yells and whoops and stomping, American fashion.

'Okay, okay, get over it and we'll get on with the rehearsal and let's hope we have the same effect on the audience.'

There was no revue in the town paper but there was one in *The Breeze* the campus paper.

"A single spotlight illuminates center stage where a boy and a horse stand side by side. Five more horses approach from the sides of the stage and turn to face the audience. A man dressed in black stands among the horses. An eerie image of a giant horse skull hangs on the wall behind him. *[Not quite correct; it was a horse's head and a human skull within it]* The boy, Alan Strang, played by Tee Morris, has blinded six horses for reasons unknown. The horses are convincingly and gracefully played by ... The man in black, Dr, Martin Dysart played by Lance Johnson, is the analysing psychiatrist. ...The story is told in a series of memories and flashbacks, finally in an eerie flashback using only motion and lighting to reveal the reasoning behind the crime.

The play relies heavily on the viewer's imagination. The set, purposely plain, is set up like a stable with benches and horse blankets along the edges of the low stage and a stone wall across the back. A desk with a chair on either side of it sits in a corner. Locations other than Dysart's office are only vaguely implied with the placement of benches.

Throughout the play, audience tension grows steadily as more and more bizarre twists are added to the reasons behind Alan's crime. By the end of the final act, many people literally are on the edges of their seats, bodies leaning forward and eyes fixed intently on the action.

The performances by Tee Morris and Lance Johnson are exceptional. Morris conveys all the rage and confusion Alan feels with an almost frightening power. He flawlessly makes the transitions between frightened boy and an angry young man. Johnson portrays Dysart as a man torn between the choice of curing Alan at the risk of taking away a part of the boy's humanity and of letting him remain as he is–a boy in pain.

The horses are on stage during the entire performance but are not mere casual observers of the action. When something makes them nervous or angry they react. When Dysart asks Alan to tell him about Jill, played by Carla Yates, the girl he was with the night he committed the crime, the horses hiss and begin to grow restless, stomping their feet and tossing their heads.

The horses wear only brown loincloths; the scantily clad actors have bared themselves to the scrutiny of the audience, which enhances their portrayal of the animals. Alan mentions that horses are the most naked animals of all and that is a part of what makes them beautiful.

Equus is a thought provoking and sometimes shocking production. There is some nudity but it is done tastefully and necessary to the plot. The story of Alan Strang's horrible crime is a frightening one,

No Official Umbrella

full of sexual and family frustration, but it is also a touching story of a confused and lonely boy who finds a strange kind of companionship among the horses."

I'm sure Kim Thomas will forgive me for not giving her full text here but this was the gist of her revue. Tee really did come into his own with the part of Alan Strang. His parents came to the show and couldn't have been more complimentary. They thought it and he were both wonderful and the play certainly took the campus by storm. After the opening night I came out of class at four in the afternoon to find there was already a line two hours before the box office opened.

Meantime I had applied for a Judith E. Wilson Visiting Fellowship 1989-90 with the Faculty of English, Cambridge University but was given the thumbs down. "The Fund Committee have (*sic, and this from the English Department!*) agreed not to proceed further with your application."

Paid a second visit to Lexington, this time to see *Arden of Faversham* presented by Washington & Lee. This is a small university, about 2,500 students but rich, or so I am told. Lexington is also the home of the Virginia Military Academy and quite a few cadets were in the audience with their crew cuts and their skin-tight uniforms. If you're a roly-poly this is not the uniform for you. Saw Al Gordon who had a small part in the play and who visited England over Christmas and saw six pantos in six days–from Oxford to The Hackney Empire. He really is into panto in a big way. The play wasn't too bad and, as it is well known but unknown to me, I found it very interesting. The girl who played Arden's wife, Alice, wasn't up to it unfortunately. She seemed to believe passion is indicated by shouting. In fact there was altogether too much shouting. I'm a firm believer that if an actor resorts to shouting that actor doesn't know what he or she is doing. Sophie was doing a bit of shouting of her own.

Look you guys, you gotta have words with this big jerk. Yesterday was SO cold I aksed ifn I could come into the house an do you know what

Chapter Twenty Seven

he did? He tried to drag me into BED! Of course I weren't havin none of that, no siree. What kind of a girl does he take me for? Well I'm heer to tell you I am NOT THAT kind. But what is a girl to do? Do I freeze to death or do I pay the ultimate price? (Aint that a juicy saying for a poor pussy?) I am SO furious. I was considerin writing to President Bush an requestin for FBI protection. What do you think? I mean! The man's a pervert!! Your advice is eagerly awaited. In the meanwhile I will hide in the barn until the mailman delivers your letter. I can see the mailbox from the barn. I can peek through a crack in the door so he won't know I'm there.

Yours in secrecy,

Sophie.

P.S. My passport ain't come yet. I'll keep a lookout fur that at the same moment in time.

PPS. On the other paw, it was pretty warm an snugly under that theer blanket an, so long as he keeps his filthy hands to hisself, a girl could get used to it.

PPPS On the other paw, his hands ain't THAT filthy & it's a mite comfortin to be made a fuss of. I am seriously considerin I could jest give the ole barn a miss. Cancel your letter.

Yours purringly, Sophie

2nd December 1989

Just got back from my fencing. You will probably be asleep by now. It's 1.30 your time. I won. I never cease to surprise these kids. Good. Keeps them on their toes. My opponent, who is virtually one-third my age, did not expect to be beaten three in a row. Considering I haven't held a foil in my hand for a thousand years I rather surprised myself. All the tennis must have made me fit. Ten minutes of fencing usually (or used to) knock me sideways so how come I lasted half an hour and a whole match with hardly a sweat? Anyway, I forgot to tell you, Friday evening I went to the Music Department's production of The Mikado. Remembering the horror that was "Fiddler" I wasn't looking forward to it and surprise surprise! It was great. Beautifully sung, nicely staged (set in a Toyota factory) and Katisha played by a man, a genius stroke of casting. He was wonderful; great mezzo and played it absolutely straight–and SO ugly. The boy who played Ko-Ko so pretty and a gorgeous voice and camping himself silly in a butch kind of way. Pity he's a baritone. Give him another few years and he'd make a great heldentenor like Warren Ellsworth.

Also saw *Sexual Perversity In Chicago* in Wampler, a dreadful play. I was really offended by it. I mean I found it totally offensive. I wasn't shocked. Who am I to be shocked? But what a load of trash. As that American said the night we went to see *Satyricon*, it's the kinda trash that gives trash a bad name.

Goom-bye,
Willie & Sophie.

Dear People,
How dare that big klutz sign my name? I didn't aks him to and he never never never aksed my permission. The liberties some folks take! I can write my own letters thank you AND sign em. So! Heer is my signature–Sophie.

PS And HE talks about offence? Huh!
PPS Passport STILL hasn't come. Do you think Uncle Sam got my letter?

Two weeks to Spring Break and I was still working on *Third Drawer from the Top*. Maybe there were just too many distractions. I sent two plays to a New York agent, never heard a word from him, and Laurence Fitch wrote and gave me the names of two more but I think I was too disheartened for the moment to bother with them. There were two productions that week, one on main stage, one in Wampler. The first was Tom Arthur's production of a play called *On the Verge* something that came out of Yale I believe and which I didn't find either interesting or particularly good. Now I have no memory of it whatsoever. The play in Wampler was Allen Lyndrup reaching for

Chapter Twenty Seven

his Scandinavian roots by finally getting around to playing a Danish-American in that little domestic drama, *Vikings*. Now I had to sit down and write three critiques, none of which would be all that flattering, most especially "*Sexual Perversity.*"

Sophie didn't appear for breakfast one morning. I called and called and eventually she came around the corner of the house dragging a corpse twice as long as herself. God knows what it was. It was so mangled I couldn't tell whether it was flesh or fowl, feather or fur, and I wasn't going to take a close look. Disgusting!

Dear Boys,
What's he talkin about, disgustin? It is the unalienable right of every natural born American to be a hunter. It's written in the Bill of Rights. It's enshrined in the Constitution. So I'll go out and hunt a bar if'n I want to. I'll go out an hunt a hole sleuth of bars cept I don't think I know what a bar looks like so I guess I'll stick to squirls. If you think my writing is better I've been studying and reading the dictionary. Also "Hunters News". (No pictures of bars.)
Yours sincerely
Sophie.
PS He says do you know what a bar looks like?
PPS He says do you know what a squirl looks like?
PPPS He says I has to aks you do you know what a dildo looks like?
PPPPS What kind of a animal's that? Eek! It cain't be American.
Write soon.
Sophie.

25th February 1989

Sophie informs me she sent you the stills from "Oliverina". What she didn't tell you is that it is only a commercial for the local TV station for Purina Meow Mix. However, as they're paying her quite well, and as it doesn't look as though she's going to get her passport (she says), she's thinking of sending you over a few complimentary boxes of cat biscuits. (Depends upon the cost of postage she says.)

641

No Official Umbrella

She showed me part of the terrible script. 'Purr-lease, Miss, I want some more.' Just spent the whole day organising the Mid-term exam for Intro to Theatre and writing critiques for Monday's post-mortem so think I'll relax in a minute and watch some telly (Selina Scott–a programme from NY called "West 57th"– human interest stories, usually very good), and a lovely comedy programme called "*Golden Girls*"–three aging ladies living together and very funny, one of my favourites. These last few days have been bitterly cold again and the coast has been having blizzards with up to 12" of snow. Weird. The kids did a beautiful job of "*Greater Tuna*". I haven't laughed so much in a long time (not even at "Golden Girls"). I don't know though whether the play would transfer to England. It's not so much a play as an elongated revue sketch with four boys playing about twenty parts, including drag, and doing it wonderfully well. But "*Greater Tuna*" is a small town in Texas and the humour is SO Deep South, which is why I don't think the English would go for it.

Haven't got my act together yet for the Panto Symposium at SETC. Will work on it tomorrow. *[I had been invited to take part in this discussion on English Pantomime through my meeting Al Gordon.]*

Two more boxes of books on the way, Douglas. You better get those bookshelves up fast. Sophie says she'll come and lend you a paw (if she gets her passport) because she's very pawy with tools. If you ask me she's looking for an alternative in case her TV career fails. She tells me that limp-pawed Onyx got fired. He tried to do dirties behind a flat with the cameraman's cat (male). That's the way with a ginger cat; know what I mean, Vern?[29]

3rd February 1989

This 70° weather is causing confusion in dear old Mother Nature. Crocuses are up, bushes are budding, and birds have appeared other than hawks and rooks. As I sit here, the bare tree outside the kitchen window is a playground for cardinals and bluejays and a host of cheeky sparrers. Mathilda is sitting underneath eyeing what could

---
29 Tag from an American TV commercial at the time.

Chapter Twenty Seven

become breakfast if one of them gets too careless. I've invented a new word–"turdious". It means tedious shit, which is what the first half of the dance concert was last night, a modern work by someone called Sally Nash and titled *"Seven Dreams and an Awakening."* What? *"Seven Snores and Oblivion"* would have been more apt. The second half was much better and Robin's *[Haigh]* version of *"Les Biches"* wasn't at all bad. Unfortunately there are no boy dancers here. They're all like spastic sparrows at a Tupperware party.

Auditions for *"Uncle Vanya"* tonight and tomorrow. Fuck giving chances to lesser mortals. This time I'm going for the best and making it easier on myself, for a change.

The Mormons have just been but as they weren't pretty (unusual) they got short shrift and were sent away. But maybe there is a god. I was trying to think of something to cover a blank spot in a scene in *"Third Drawer"* and a visit by the Mormons, remembering the ones who came around to the house in London, would fill the gap beautifully. As they wouldn't be seen and only one talks, a cast member could double.

Boy! I can't wait to visit the *"Seven Days Ablaze"* Festival. Obviously we are going about theatre all the wrong way. Can you imagine Herb Titus? Is anybody named Herb Titus? Really! This was only part of a huge package of puff I got in my mail from colleges, publishers, etc. I must be on every computer around. "Third Drawer" is turning into a farcical-comedy (for want of a better description) I hadn't intended that but you know how plays eventually take over and start to write themselves and that's what it's doing. I'm half way through the first act. Josh has just got Bengay Rub all over his cock. I told you it was a farce.

I have read what he has written and it is TOTAL CRAP. Whoever heerd of someone rubbing Bengay on his you know what? Ridiculous. Then he's got a scene where this stupid guy treads on a cat! I'm going to report him to the S.P.C.A. I'm right glad the cat scratched him. If I was to be cast as the cat (hint hint) I'll do more than scratch I can tell you and I've got the claws for it. I'm thinking of auditioning for "Evita". What's Meryl Streep got that I ain't got.

Sophie.
PS Ho hum and fiddle-dee-dee, I could write a better play.

Come the beginning of March I flew to Louisville, Kentucky to be put up in a five star hotel, it was only for one night so I guess the university, or the department anyway, felt they could afford it as I was a sort of minor ambassador for JMU with taking part in the Panto Symposium. In the Chair was Philip Hill of Furman University who asked me if I would consider playing Dysart in his production of *Equus*. It would mean paying a visit to Greenville, South Carolina during Spring Break, first to suss out the university and also for Phil to audition me, which turned out to be a bit of a farce but, nevertheless, clinched the deal. The long drive down, 825 miles of it, was made easier by listening to a broadcast from the met; *Salome* with Helga Dernisch. I listened to it first by tuning in to the University of Tennessee Public Radio and, when I drove out of range, a slight adjustment and I was tuned into Virginia Tech so I could hear the complete opera. Coming in through The Appalachians I found east Tennessee to be real Hillbilly country but very pretty despite the signs of desperate poverty.

Furman's *Equus* was to be performed in The Playhouse, a small theatre of 150 seats and a thrust stage, very intimate. Furman is a small conservative protestant university, about the same size as Washington & Lee with a most beautiful campus spread around a lake. I realised just how conservative it was when I was told the drama students once complained to the Dean that they had been asked (told) to read "filthy" plays, the main play in question being *Streamers*.

The only problem I could foresee was timing; Phil's production clashing with the last weeks of the semester at JMU, so that had to be sorted out. It meant getting permission to leave JMU early, immediately after exams and marking of finals, and at the same time someone would stand in for me at Furman during the first couple of weeks of rehearsal.

Chapter Twenty Seven

But, back from Greenville, rehearsals went ahead for *Uncle Vanya*. Someone in Louisville had given me a cassette of Balalaika music so I decided to use some of it as incidental music in the play, or preshow music if nothing else. There were some real problems with the set but I think I overcame them and a problem with Astrov but, that apart, I was getting more and more excited with what my youthful cast were doing. Looking at the programme now I see I took little risk with my casting: James Anzide as Vanya, Brian Francoise as Serebryakov, John Harrell as Telegin, Mary Szmagaj as Sonya, the beautiful Lauren Kerr a much improved actress as Elenya. There were newcomers (to me) in the cast so I wasn't entirely selfish in my selection.

The script I used was Laurence Senelick's translation with permission to make changes and I see I made a number of cuts and some small changes in the dialogue, but the biggest change I made was in action, that is, having the attempted shooting of Serebryakov in full view of the audience rather than off stage.

Wade Lough, who designed the poster and programme, either had a delicious sense of humour or wasn't aware of what he was doing because his illustration featuring Vanya was the spitting image of Tom Arthur.

1st April 1989

Hi,

Just listening to *"Das Rheingold"* from the Met. Oops! Some very dodgy moments. The audience are applauding like crazy. I think you would be booing, like you did at "Parsifal". *[This production at The Royal Opera House was simply appalling and, in the interval, Chris stood up in the stalls and yelled 'Shoot Terry Hands!' much to the consternation of the corporate snobs surrounding us.]* Despite the presence of Jerusalem and Ludwig there are some cracking voices, dreadful vibrato and some of the messiest orchestral playing you have ever heard. (James Levine conducting).

The cherry blossom is out and it is beautiful. This week is "Cherry Blossom Festival" in DC. I meant to tell you I finally saw the Mary

No Official Umbrella

Martin "*Peter Pan*" on telly the other night and was very disappointed with it. Tacky!

It has just been reported on the news that a 77 year old man from Milwaukee, Wisconsin is being deported. He was evidently a Nazi and a guard at Buchenwald. Neighbours describe him as a kindly old man who shares his homegrown vegetables with them.

With temperatures up in the high sixties to low eighties all week we thought spring really was here but these last couple of days have been plummet time and out have come the warm clothes again. Brrr!

Rehearsals for "Uncle Vanya" are coming on.

JMU'S 'Uncle Vanya': Chekhov's Comic Sense.
So wrote Phyllis Quillen in the Daily News-Record.

"Anton Chekhov always insisted that most of his plays were comedies and not the dreary depictions of Russian ennui and stifled spirits that his contemporary stagers insisted on presenting. At least in the case of "Uncle Vanya" Chekhov was right. As performed at James Madison University's Latimer-Schaeffer Theater Tuesday night, it's Chekhov the comic genius who rouses the audience to giggles and guffaws–and proves that he really was a genius in the process. Chekhov the expositor however is a far duller fellow. Fortunately for us all, director Glyn Jones seems to have figured that out on his own and while there is little even he can do to speed up Chekhov's excruciatingly long first act, the other two fairly zip by.

After all, very little happens in Act 1 of a play written–sort of 90 some years ago. "*Uncle Vanya*" is really a condensed, trimmed down and eminently playable version of "*The Bear*" or "*The Bore*" (both titles have been used by translators). Even reading the original version is painful which may account for the latter title.

But somewhere around 1896, Chekhov's unwieldy work turned into "*Uncle Vanya*" and generations of audiences have been grateful."

She then gives a résumé of the play, a succinct summing up indeed, and goes on …

"Around these main characters is the rest of Chekhov's cast: the old

Chapter Twenty Seven

nurse, Marina; Vanya's mother, Mariya; and Telegin, a kind of hanger-on and friend of Vanya's with a fondness for playing the guitar."

The mention of "hanger-on" reminds me of a story I once heard and I wonder if it's true, that Gilbert and Sullivan wrote a pornographic opera for the edification of their close circle of friends. Titled *The Sod's Opera*, included in the cast are such characters as The Brothers Bollocks, a pair of hangers-on, and Scrotum, a wrinkled old retainer. But back to Phyllis. She tells of Serebryakov's decision to sell the estate and of Vanya's attempt to shoot him, and then …

"The Serebryakovs decide to leave, and life on the estate returns to its former placidity.
But life there cannot quite regain its former calm, for the characters, over the space of three acts, have grown and developed, learning to know themselves and each other much better than before. Chekhov manages to evoke an amazing amount of good-humoured fun out of this seemingly unlikely matter. But he seemed to realise for most people life is not a succession of high drama and world-shaking accomplishments. Whether living on an obscure country estate in turn-of-the-century Russia or a small town in Virginia, life for most people is family and friends and the small, apparently boring everyday events. This is part of what gives his plays such enduring appeal and charm, and in no small measure has contributed to the fact that they are still performed with gusto.
Director Jones has cast well. His young actors may lack the technique in some cases to completely embody all the complexities of these seemingly simple creations, but then with some adroit direction, a superb set by Allen Lyndrup and serviceable costumes by Pamela Johnson, they let their youth carry them." She then goes on to praise each actor personally, before, "Jones' vision of the play is measured and observant, production details are firmly in place, and his cast shows the effects of some relentless rehearsing. *[I sometimes wonder how critics know these things!]* In general his interpretation of "*Uncle*

Vanya" is as honest as can be. And as direct: people, not events, are persistently intriguing and downright hilarious at times no matter how bored, how limited, or how educated."

Douglas was due in 10.45 at Charlottesville and Chris Holloway drove over to pick him up. They arrived in Harrisonburg in time to join the first night party that was a standing feature of theatre production in Latimer-Schaeffer. Chris Holloway sent everyone into hysterics during the opening night party of *The Imaginary Invalid* when he said in all seriousness, 'Gosh, if they treat you like this after dress rehearsal, what's the first night party going to be like?'

'Chris, you've just had your first night.'

His jaw hit the floor. What did he think all those people were doing, sitting in the auditorium?

Dear Chris,

That big jerk! He sent me down to the bank to get this for you and I got attacked by this gross Doberman Pinscher an you owe me!! I nearly lost the first of my nine lives. I mean it was THAT close. I got so scared I peed all over this redneck guy walking close by. He ran to his truck for his hunting rifle and that was nearly life #2. I skedaddled for it across the road and was just about mowed down by a BIG MAC TRUCK and that was almost life #3. An it has gone back to winter an I scud on the ice an hit the kerb with my nose–#4. But I climbed up a tree an the branch gave way (even though I ain't as fat as I used ter be) an that was life #5. An I fell outta the tree right on top of a grizzly ole snake. I think it was a rattler, deadly poisonous anyway–#6. Then, on the way home, I was mugged (#7) an neerly raped. An as that is a fate WORSE than death that makes #8, which leaves me only one more life so from now on I gotta be real careful, don't you agree?

With love from
Sophie.

PS Banks are mighty dangerous places ifn you was to aks me. Supposin there'd been a robbery a goin on? Jes supposing it had been Bonny an Clyde. I could a gotten myself all shot up in the crossfire.

Chapter Twenty Seven

Sophie was turning into another Eudora Welty but that was her last, her very last letter. She was a truly amazing cat.

Chapter Twenty Eight

Lumbered down with luggage and having booked a sleeper, we took the train from Greenville to New York where we would stay in Mark Lutsky's apartment in Thompson Street. Mark had a lodger in the second bedroom at the time and moved out to a friend's flat so we could have his room. The lodger was South American I believe though I wouldn't know, as we never actually saw him. Paul and Lionel's flat, always our home from home while in New York, was suddenly not available to us. Before I could explain that Douglas was a family member and not some casual pickup, Lionel got all uppity and pursed lips when I asked if he could put the two of us up, so that was that. The Thompson Street apartment in floor area was about the same size as the kitchen at Hollings Farm. It was on the sixth floor and, without a lift, a long climb with heavy suitcases. Believe it or not though, the apartment before we arrived had been broken into by an intrepid burglar playing Spiderman, climbing up pipes in the area and entering through the tiny bathroom window.

We weren't to know it then but this was the last time I would be staying in Thompson Street. For my next and last visit to New York I stayed with Gray and Robert Yokum in their apartment close by Central park. They had moved to New York like so many aspiring young hopefuls in search of that crock of gold that would remain obstinately hidden. When I called Marcus's number the phone was answered by a petulant queenie voice informing me quite curtly that Marcus was dead, that he, queenie, was now in occupation and

Chapter Twenty Eight

Anyone for tennis? - Douglas at Furman University

not to bother him again, with which the phone was slammed down. Obviously an extremely bad hair day so I never did find out why, how or when Marcus had died.

We were catered for in Greenville with true southern hospitality, living in Phil and Marge Hill's beautiful house, situated a short distance from the spacious campus; very beautiful, green, with long drives lined with trees. Garden and mature trees also surround the Hill house, forest seeming to be a dominant feature of this part of the world. From bedroom to swimming pool was only a step but unfortunately the bees seemed to have taken up residence first and, as Douglas is paranoid about bees and wasps, that weren't so good. In what spare time we had I tried to get him to play table tennis and tennis but with no success. To Douglas, balls are supposed to come to him, he doesn't move to them so he would stand stock-still on court and watch the ball go flying by some distance away with no attempt to move whatsoever. I gave up. He was good at helping me learn lines though, mainly because he learned them faster than I did and could prompt without even looking at the book. I was having a tough time working on the play as an actor. Mr Shaffer's dialogue is a little like Agony Christie's: "What?" "Why?" "What then?" "Go on." "What happened next?" etcetera and I found it difficult getting the right question in the right place. Also I found I was constantly repeating other character's words. In fact, when it comes down to it, his dialogue is not the easiest to take in and that's putting it mildly.

The kids in the cast were, without exception, a delight to be with even if they did have their reservations about Douglas's uninhibited nudity. One night after rehearsal they invited us to go bowling but all the lanes were busy so we retired to a Pancake House to gorge ourselves silly. All that maple syrup and whipped cream! It was a fun evening with Elizabeth Chambless who played Hesther in fine form regaling us with stories such as when she was in a school production of *Once Upon a Mattress* and one of the teachers, playing the queen, offered her a lift home one night after a performance. The teacher was still in her costume, wimple and all. On the way they ran over a possum and the teacher, who was an animal lover, looking in her rear view mirror, saw the animal was still alive, or at least moving, so reversed over it. But now in the headlights she could see it was evidently still moving so she got out of the car, opened the boot (trunk), took out a travelling rug and a jack and, covering the animal with the rug, started to beat it to death, screaming hysterically "It's alive! It's alive!" Her action was cut short by a very loud masculine voice barking, 'Hold it right there, lady!' and there were two cops with guns pointing straight at her as she still shrieked. 'It's alive!" Another story was of a visit to a hospital where she sat waiting next to a woman holding a shoebox on her lap. Eventually consumed with curiosity she couldn't help but ask what was in it. 'My son's foot,' the woman replied.

Phil was a very sweet man but alas, in my opinion no great shakes as a director, another half-baked academic disciple of Stan the man. He didn't direct the kids other than to try and get them to find "the inner depth of the character", something which, in the limited experience

Chapter Twenty Eight

of their youth, they were quite unable to do, and the choreography for the horses consisted of finding the "truth" of being a horse which, having never had anything to do with horses, was also asking the impossible. As Douglas remarked, it was a bit difficult trying to find the "truth" of a horse's psyche having arms, legs, and headdresses that kept falling off; the headdresses, not the arms and legs. Phil's blocking consisted of getting up from one bench and crossing over to an opposite one so that you were not kept too long in one place with your back to that side of the house. The boy playing Alan was exquisitely beautiful, and I use the superlative without hesitation, but so up-tight he couldn't even fake an orgasm at the end of Act I which made nonsense of the whole thing. I have to admit I did enjoy wrapping him in my arms at the play's end though. The boy playing Dad sounded Australian, Dalton sounded stage Cockney cum Irish cum Scots, and the Nurse said everything ve–ry slow-ly-like–ev–er-y-thing-is-co-ming-out-with-great-diff-i-cul-ty and, as Dysart, I sometimes found it hard to keep a straight face. Douglas and I went around saying, 'Ek! He-goes-Doc-tor-Ek!-Ek!' To get the full effect, shoulders had to be lifted up to ears with each "Ek" and dropped again. So, altogether, neither of us thought much of the production, in direct contrast to the critics.

"Furman's *'Equus'* is superb production of difficult psycho-drama."

The Greenville News
"Talk about night and day: Following on the heels of Neil Simon at Furman comes one of the heavier and meatier–not to mention better plays–in contemporary theatre. A picnic in the park it's not, but Peter Shaffer's *"Equus"* is an intensely imaginative and provocative piece of theater that offers substantive food for thought for both actors and audience.

Furman is aided here by the presence of professional British actor Glyn Johns, *[Johns? Here we go again!]* who as psychiatrist Martin Dysart gives the show such a solid center that the pressure to carry off this most difficult of plays is taken off the students' shoulders, allowing them to more freely explore the possibilities given them by Shaffer. Add to that the imaginative and thoughtful direction by Phil Hill," etcetera etcetera.

Other headlines were "Exquisite Equus is a Success" and "Furman's *'Equus'* is spell-binding." So there you are, maybe Douglas and I were wrong, maybe from out front it was superb, exquisite and spell-binding. (*sic*)

Now in New York it would be play-play time for a few days before returning to England, but first it was necessary to secure me a flight home. There was no possibility of a seat on Douglas's return flight and BA's pricing policy was pricey to say the least so once again it was a dreary round of the bucket shops where eventually we came up with a moderately priced flight and, yes, once again via Air India. Unfortunately I would leave a couple of days before Douglas's but it was his first visit to New York and, as it was only a short one, I left him to make the most of it. I maintain that, after I left, he went to see *Into the Woods* a second time. He maintains he only went to *Cats*. One or other of our memories is faulty. Possibly he went to both.

During our peregrinations we were waiting at the kerb for the "Walk" sign on the corner of 42nd and Broadway when Douglas, much to the amusement of others standing by, started to do a tap dance.

'What on earth are you doing that for?'

'I can go home and say I danced on Broadway.'

The flight being found, booked, and paid for, like good tourists we toured Radio City Music Hall and, 'Oh, and who do we have here?' Said our guide. The superannuated Rockette in her dressing room doing her ironing. Surprise, Surprise! We gawped disbelievingly at the awful vulgarity of Trump Tower, rode the Staten Island Ferry and, at the Half Price Kiosk in Times Square, that same Times Square I found so uninspiring when Lionel first proudly showed it to me, we managed to get pretty good circle seats for *Into the Woods*. Unfortunately Douglas would not see the original cast, they had moved on but

Chapter Twenty Eight

both of us being Sondheim freaks I knew he would enjoy the show all the same. We settled into our seats, the houselights dimmed and the curtains were parted slightly which meant an announcement, probably a substitution, maybe not such a good start, even though we have seen understudies as good as, sometimes even better, than the named artiste. A bearded figure stepped out and, to Douglas's bewilderment, the full house erupted in instantaneous applause.

'Who's that? Who's that? What are they applauding for?' He growled. Douglas doesn't believe in applauding until he's been given something to applaud for.

'That, my dear, is Mr Sondheim himself.'

'Oh!' He immediately applauded as enthusiastically as everyone else. Eventually Mr Sondheim raised his hand to silence the applause and announced that, as the show that night was being filmed, the original cast were back for this one performance. How lucky could you get?

The Air India flight was comfortable and the service a delight. Whereas, after my first time in the states, I had to be dragged in chains, figuratively speaking, onto the plane for London, this time I had only expectations because Yorkshire and Hollings Farm, our new home I hardly had time to experience before leaving for America, was waiting for me. I knew it would be back to the Labour Exchange, but the Labour Exchange in Hebden Bridge, and later when it moved to Todmorden, was a genteel country tea party midst friendly faces in comparison to the atmosphere of resentment and the aggression that at times flared up in Hackney.

In 1984/5 while I was at JMU I wrote to so many colleges and universities in the states, with the backing of enthusiastic letters of reference from Tom, Allen, and Dean McConkey, in an effort to stay over there, perhaps even for good, but nothing came of my efforts. This time I hadn't bothered. This time the letters would go off to UK companies, theatres, managements and institutions and I have a big fat file headed APPLICATIONS, SUBMISSIONS & REJECTIONS.

HOLLINGS FARM 1991 – Presumably there must be, filed away somewhere else or still in files marked "Miscellaneous for sorting", applications, submissions & rejections for 89 -91.

The Queen and the Rebels was my first play for Bridge Theatre after which the diary's pages are mostly virginal except for noting Chris playing *Champagne Charlie* at various venues. After Paul Knight we now had a new pianist, a local musician, Dave Nelson, and Douglas was stage-managing so *Champagne Charlie* went back into rehearsal. It wasn't until well into August that I was back on stage again, still at the Hebden Bridge Little Theatre, this time as the headmaster in *Quartermaine's Terms*, after which the rest of 1989 is a blank except for the labour exchange and applications, submissions & rejections. Presumably my time was taken up with Hollings Farm, house and garden, and God knows there was enough to do and I was still more than happy with our move from London. One of my disappointing rejections that year was from Stuart Doughty at Yorkshire Television. As I now lived within commuting distance I thought it would be a grand idea to write for *Emmerdale* but, after an interview and submitting five scripts for him to get some idea of my work, Mr Doughty's letter giving me the brush-off gave as his reason that he didn't feel I would fit in with the team, as it appeared to him I wasn't "a company man." This just could have been his polite way of saying, "Get lost. I think your writing is shit." Jimmy Chinn, who I had encouraged all those years back, had been writing for *Emmerdale* for six years and, when I told him I was thinking of making an approach he wrote, "Sadly, I think your chances of getting on *Emmerdale* are very slim." He was close. They weren't just slim. They were nonexistent.

Errol McKinnon, my acting agent, died and, if I were to carry on acting, I would need to be on someone else's books. It seemed to have become quite fashionable, or a matter of necessity, for actors to form co-operatives and there was one in Hebden Bridge called "North of Watford" but, even if they would have accepted me and even though I worked with some of the members on stage, somehow I didn't really fancy being part of a co-operative. (Was Mr Doughty right?) My

Chapter Twenty Eight

behaviour throughout the rehearsals of *The Queen and the Rebels* was enough to put anybody off anyway so I doubt "North of Watford" would have been at all happy if I had applied to join them. Finding a new agent though was easier said than done and, as none of the agents I approached seemed particularly enthusiastic over my CV or my supposed talents and, as I was no longer particularly interested in the rat race anyway, I didn't push it too hard. The one interview I did have was so off-putting in front of a couple of self-opinionated, self-important, know-it-all-bigheads, one of whom could not have been more than a nineteen year old princess, (at least he gave the impression of being a nineteen year old princess) fair put me off. It never got further than the interview, which was hardly surprising. To be quite honest my body language alone, let alone the arrogant guff I was spouting, was enough to put anybody off.

Moving from London didn't mean we were lacking in culture, music, or theatre going. We had Northern Ballet Theatre in Halifax under the artistic directorship of Christopher Gable, City Varieties in Leeds where we enjoyed evenings of music hall, particularly if any friends were on the bill, Peter John, (*Nobody Loves A Fairy When She's Forty*) the lovely Annabelle Lee (*I'm always in the saddle on a Sunday*) Chris also performed at City Varieties, presenting a Leybourne number, *Oh The Fairies*! and of course there was the inimitable Roy Hudd. Kath George (*The Boy I Love Is Up In The Gallery*). Kath played Lydia in a production of *All My Sons* I directed for Bridge Theatre, which was presented at Venn Street in Huddersfield. The critic said Bridge Theatre needed to find a director Oh, my! We had Opera North in Leeds at the Grand, the theatre whose boards I had trod so many years before doing my Herring the bos'n bit.

Manchester with the Free Trades Hall and the Hallé, and its theatres, both permanent and touring, was a quick barrel down the M62: quick that was, if the stream of vehicles wasn't nose to tail usually due to what seemed like continuous road works and miles of coned-off single lane traffic. There was The Octagon, Bolton and the Coliseum in Oldham. Sheffield was within striking distance and the first play we saw there at the Crucible was *Brittanicas* with Michael Jenn in the company. We ventured even further afield driving as far as Leicester to see the musical *Mack & Mabel* at The Haymarket. There were good nonprofessional companies; two productions that stand out in my memory being *The Rink* in Oldham and, although I held no brief for the actual show, the production was one that could have shamed many a professional company. The other memory is of a hilarious production of *Nunsense* in a delightful little theatre in Ilkley. Halifax unfortunately was devoid of theatre except for the amateurs and seasonal pantomime. Our friend, Chris Cawkwell, decided he wanted to be more involved with theatre rather than just being an amateur player in Hebden Bridge and took a course at the College of Higher Education in Halifax. I went to see him in a part production of *Hamlet,* an exercise so appalling I wondered how the hell the instructor/director had ever gained employment in the first place let alone held on to it.

In Bradford there is the Alhambra and The Museum of Film and Photography with the Imax cinema and the original Cinerama, restored from bits and pieces garnered from all over the world.

Third Drawer from the Top was finished and I started to put out scripts. The first naturally went to Film Rights, but I then sent one to the Duke's Playhouse, Lancaster and never heard a word, and another to Rob Yokum in New York, and never heard a word. One also went to Laurence Senelick at Tufts but, according to him, it wasn't really the sort of play Tufts drama students would want to do. Tough titty.

By now Hollings Farm "The Big House", though far from finished, was more than comfortable with the barn divided into living area, dining area, mezzanine floor bedroom at one end, and, on the other side, a second mezzanine floor taking the place of the music room that was in Farleigh Road. Beneath that, the stalls in the byre had been converted into different parts of a workshop. Above the music room floor Douglas would eventually build a library and the two mezzanine sections were joined by a walkway, also lined with bookshelves. The

Chapter Twenty Eight

intended shower was still nothing more than a storage space but there was at least a fair-sized bathroom so the house now virtually invited guests. In March Tee and Mary Szmagaj came and they were followed by Stephen Mostad who arrived via Germany bringing us a piece of the Berlin Wall as a souvenir. My old drama teacher, Pearle Celine, and her husband, Alan arrived and, though we had kept in touch Christmas card wise, very much to our surprise after so long a time, Courtney Burr visited with new friend, Michael who, fortunately, Chris did not have to bake a pie for.

We did have some unexpected visitors that were not welcome. Douglas kept complaining there were too many dead or dying wasps in his bedroom and there must be a nest somewhere. I maintained they were flying in from outside but, at the head of his bed there were small holes in the ceiling from which dangled electric wires where light fittings were supposed to be fixed, so I took a torch and, from the top of a ladder, looked all around the roof space but could see no sign of any nest. Fortunately the trap in the ceiling was too small for me to squeeze through otherwise the exercise could have ended disastrously. However, satisfied with my inspection we left it at that until, one morning while Chris and I were at breakfast, there was a scream from the bedroom above and, dashing upstairs we found Douglas well and truly stung. There was only one thing for it and that was to call in the pest controller who duly arrived, looked around the loft as I had done, saw nothing, walked a short way up the track and looked from the outside and there, sure enough, wasps were flying in and out under the eaves. He soon put a stop to them.

Out in the garden, I was merrily digging away when I unearthed something that looked like the perished bladder from an old-fashioned football. I dug in my spade and fled for my life as the angry inhabitants swarmed out. I later went back when they had calmed down, and burnt them out. Ignorant townie, I didn't know wasps built nests underground and was to unearth a couple more, but with much greater care, before summer was out.

Now one of my many applications and submissions did not receive a rejection. I actually had a call from the Library Theatre in Manchester asking if I would go over and see one of their directors, Roger Haines, which I duly did, and he duly asked me to play Doctor Seward in *Dracula* to be performed at the Forum Theatre in Wythamshawe, just outside Manchester, one of those designed model towns like Welwyn Garden City. The theatre itself was a bit like an aircraft hanger but I enjoyed working for Roger even though Doctor Seward is one of those characters in which any actor, unless he's a genius, is "competent in the part". We even had a bomb scare one night which, instead of evacuating the theatre, we should simply have ignored. Who on earth would want to blow up the Forum Theatre, Wythamshawe, the centre of which has to be one of the dreariest litter strewn and grubbiest places in the UK? I suppose though you never can tell what cranky minds can dream up. The only other theatrical event that year was a trip to a Leeds studio to make a recording of *Champagne Charlie*.

Douglas now did two things totally out of character. Firstly he agreed to play squash with me at the municipal courts in Halifax. Douglas was actually going to race after a ball? Yes, indeed, Douglas was. Unfortunately we hadn't been playing more than a short time when the courts were closed for refurbishment and we never went back. Instead we signed on for night classes in Italian and German held in Sowerby Bridge. We didn't get very far with those either.

His second positive decision, in answer to a telephone call and a plea for help, was to agree to dance in an amateur production in Halifax of *Kismet*. This had us totally gob smacked, as Douglas hates being on stage probably more than anything else in life, a shame because he could have been quite a performer. *Equus* didn't freak him out because he was behind a mask, which was rather like a kid performing his party piece from behind the sofa. But he said he agreed to *Kismet* in order to get acquainted with some of the local amateurs so that Chris could be introduced as a possible director for musicals. Amateur companies paid professional directors quite well. Cawkwell and I went to see *Kismet* and had to stifle our laughter. We

Chapter Twenty Eight

left at the interval because Douglas had done his bit and he knew he was pretty terrible, the show wasn't too hot and there really was little point in staying.

His noble sacrifice was in vain anyway because he was no sooner into rehearsals for *Kismet* when Gary Pulleyn, who was playing in the pit for *Hello Dolly* at Rawden in Leeds and whose father was musical director there, called to ask Chris if he could step in and take over the direction of *Hello Dolly* as their director had suffered a heart attack. Poor man, I'm not surprised. The Rawden amateurs were the first lot I had a flaming row with and walked out on never to return. This was when Chris asked me to help out by directing his third production there the dialogue scenes in *Charlie Girl*. *Hello Dolly* was the beginning of our productions with amateur companies. His second in 1991 was *Guys & Dolls* and he was having terrible trouble finding a Lieutenant Brannigan. Like an idiot I said, if he really couldn't find one, I'd do it for him. Naturally he immediately stopped looking and, for the first time in over fifty years, I stepped out on stage, discounting college theatre, with a full amateur company and played Lieutenant Brannigan.

Apart from *Guys & Dolls*, 1991 saw a little more theatrical action than in the previous virtually barren year. In February *Champagne Charlie* was booked in for a performance at the Black-friars Arts Centre in Boston, Lincolnshire. The day before we woke up to find ourselves knee deep in snow and still snowing. The ice had formed stalactites so long their tips reached from the roof to the kitchen windows on the ground floor. The animals went out for a pee and disappeared. The car, with snow chains on, might just be able to make it up the track and out onto the road but whenever snow was forecast, everyone living in The Hollings left their cars parked on the main road at the top of the track. There was no way Douglas's old Lada (a present from his dad) with trailer was going to make it down the track and up again fully laden with costumes, sets, and props so we had to carry everything up the snowbound track. After a while it got dangerously slippery as the snow was impacted into ice. It was a long hard haul but eventually everything was loaded and the following morning we set off for Lincolnshire, Douglas driving the Lada and with an extra hand, a young lad named Gareth Thomas who was on lights. The pianist, Dave Nelson (who in the show also has reactions with Leybourne so is more than just a musician) drove himself and made it, but we lost our two brass players, as Garry couldn't even get out of snowbound Huddersfield. It was slow going and when we got beyond Sleaford we turned a corner to see ahead of us this long one and only hill in Lincolnshire jammed nose to tail with vehicles, mostly lorries, any number of which had slid off the road and landed up in ditches on either side. We could see Douglas, who had gone ahead of Chris and myself, was stuck in the middle of this massive unmoving jam but we also saw a turn-off to the right at the end of the tail and managed to sneak into it. It didn't matter where it led to initially as long as eventually it took us into Boston so, doing a complete detour; we finally approached that town from the south and by now it was dark. It had been a ten-hour journey. Douglas and Gareth eventually turned up, we did the get-in and thank goodness an audience braved the weather to see the show. We were put up in a beautiful old red brick house, the home of Paul and Harriet Bisson and their two lovely children. It was Paul who was responsible for booking the show and, when the family later left Boston, they moved to Yorkshire when Paul joined the staff of Fountains Abbey. At first they rented another beautiful old farmhouse close by, high on a hill and surrounded by sheep, before moving into their own house in Ripon. We still keep in touch even if it's only at Christmas.

I was invited to direct a play, *Female Transport* at a London theatre academy, ALRA[30] and went down on the Friday before my birthday to do a reading. But I was immediately home again and we celebrated my sixtieth with a memorable Sunday afternoon party: plenty to drink (one of the neighbours totally disgraced himself), wonderful food,

---

30 Academy of Live and Recorded Arts.

Chapter Twenty Eight

and so many many people: Hyst Mum, Douglas's whole family, mum, dad, brothers and sisters-in-law, all our new friends and acquaintances from up North, Roger Haines and his friend, Anthony, Dave and his new girl friend, Andy and Marianne Moore. Naturally, sixty being a landmark occasion, my sister and her husband were invited but sent regrets from South Africa saying that, much as they would love to be with us, they wouldn't be able to make it, but my nephew, Evan and his wife, Fiona were in England and would be there. I was called to the front door to greet them coming down the track and with them was this strange woman. 'Who's this?' I barked before the penny dropped and I recognised my sister. It had been a long time and what a reunion it was. I could hardly believe she was there. Of course Chris and Douglas were in on the secret and standing by with camcorder to film the moment. Unfortunately we made one huge faux pas; much to our shame we forgot to send an invitation to Chris's brother Roger and his wife, Jean and none of us can figure how this lapse from all three of us came about.

The following day I was back in London to start rehearsals for *Female Transport* and given much too much time in which to do it, five weeks as I remember it, not opening until the seventeenth of June. Three weeks would have been more than ample. They were good kids but I could never stop wondering what would happen to them when they went out into the great wide world and came up against that perpetual problem of a vastly overcrowded profession. While in London I stayed with Sheila Bernette but I hopped back and forth to Yorkshire (train fares weren't up in the stratosphere then, though a first class from Leeds to London was about the same as an economy flight to New York). By the end of production I was more than happy to be back in Yorkshire but not for long. Laurence informed me of Carnegie-Mellon's choosing to produce *Generations* in their showcase of new plays so it was Manchester to Pittsburgh. Although the play was a hit with audiences one lady told me she was going to write to

Frank Rich[31] about how wonderful it was! Fat lot of good that would do I thought but nice of her to think of it. On the return I stopped off in New York to stay with Gray. We went to a performance of *La Boheme* in the park: that is Gray, his current girl friend, and I went; after fifteen minutes I left, they stayed. I could not believe the New York Philistines who sat on the grass, eating, drinking and talking at the top of their voices, many with their backs to the stage so it was obviously not a musical occasion at all but a social one. The poor singers might as well have been miming to playback for all the impact they were making.

Back in Yorkshire it was home and gardens time again until rehearsals started for *Guys & Dolls* and the year ended with Chris and Douglas starting a whole new enterprise with the founding of PROSCENEIUM, an unexpected development that was to profoundly change the whole course of our lives.

---

31 New York Theatre critic.

Chapter Twenty Nine

Prosceneium is a company that builds and hires out theatre sets to amateur societies producing musicals and the spelling of the name is not a mistake. When a new name for the company was being discussed I thought it a good idea to add the extra E to proscenium so that the name could be printed PRO*SCENE*IUM.

The company originated as "Bradford Scenic", conducting business from a deconsecrated church in that city before it was sold to become "North West Scenery" that in 1991 was owned by a builder and amateur theatre enthusiast, Graham Kershaw. The company had been trading for some time but, by now, was really on its last legs with the word going around the societies, "Don't use North West Scenery". This was because there was also a total incompetent in charge who knew nothing about the shows he was asked to supply sets for, "I've got a backdrop of a Spanish galleon, will that do for *Anything Goes*?" Once the new company was formed Graham had to pay him off.

Also, unfortunately, a great deal of theatrical history had gone up in smoke or been ruined by the firemen's hoses when a fire broke out on the premises, (Graham was uninsured), and the remaining stock of scenery was so old-fashioned as to be unusable. We went with Graham to take a look at North West Scenery. At that time it was situated in Burnley in half a semi-derelict mill, the other half being a huge storage depot for coal and there being no complete dividing wall between the two halves, the coal dust didn't do much for painted scenery. Neither did the rain, which could be blown in through the wide gap between the top of the back wall and the roof to continue the rot where the firemen's hoses had left off. But it was a fascinating treasure house of now useless cloths, rostra, treads and theatrical memorabilia, a place for any theatre historian to ecstatically browse in. The cloths, those that weren't consumed or partly damaged by the fire, were reproductions of hit shows from the turn of, and the first years of the century when plays and operetta had numerous sets and managements could afford to employ gigantic casts: the Gilbert & Sullivan's, *Chu Chin Chows, Rosemaries*, The Princes, Princesses, Grand Duchesses, charming vagabonds, beer swilling students and all those other imagined creations from mythical lands somewhere in the romantic Balkans. The scene painting was so beautifully executed it almost took your breath away; the cloths were literally giant works of art in their own right and should have been museum pieces, like the beautiful Victorian forest set erected in the Georgian Theatre in Richmond, Yorkshire, a museum in itself and one now so fragile it can only be used for a limited number of performances a year. On one occasion there I asked the manager if it would be possible for me to take off my shoes and walk on that set. He agreed with some trepidation and it was sheer magic, even with him keeping a beady eye on me.

   Unfortunately these old cloths at North West were useless for another reason, and that was they were made for major theatres and were forty foot in width on pitch pine battens top and bottom that weighed a ton and some of the old paint had cracked, was stained, or flaking away. On some of the battens there were small oval ivory discs bearing the number of the cloth, and on the frame of one flat of unusual construction was stamped "Property of Jack Buchanan". Unfortunately there was no indication of what show it was from. Where black and white photographs from the original productions accompanied the cloths you did know which shows they were from. The photographs luckily were not destroyed in the fire and many of them show not just the sets, but are stills from actual productions showing the enormous casts.

Chapter Twenty Nine

If it can be said that the reason for my originally going to America was because of a pair of yellow socks, then the cause of my coming to live in Greece was a theatrical prop; a flesh-eating plant. Graham Kershaw's own amateur society was at Whitworth who were scheduled to do *Little Shop of Horrors* and North West Scenery did not have any Audrey 2's, so the incompetent manager called a local scenic designer by the name of John Thomas who we were also friends with, asking him if he could provide the said props. John's answer was negative but he got in touch with Chris and Douglas who agreed to make them and duly did so. They delivered the plants, sent in their bill and awaited payment from North West Scenery, which was not forthcoming. After a couple of reminders, they discovered the proprietor of North West Scenery was Graham so they sent him a letter threatening legal action if the account wasn't settled. It was, with no further delay, Graham laying the reason for non-payment fairly and squarely at the feet of the incompetent manager for not having passed the bill on to him.

Graham then paid a visit to Hollings Farm. We think he took a look at the big house, the original paintings, the antiques (most of which were bargains bought for peanuts, for example a genuine Biedemeier sofa found in a junk shop in the Queens Road, Dalston and got for £5.), and thought, 'Ah, there's money here.' In fact that's where all the money was, in and on the walls. The actual bank account if not in the red was pretty well close to it. So weren't there any rich relatives around? No, no rich relatives. Still, money or no money, something had to be done if North West Scenery was to be saved and he invited Chris and Douglas to go in with him in the scenery hire business; Chris as designer, Douglas as super-efficient production manager, and himself as managing director and Mr Moneyman. And that was how Prosceneium was born, from the need for an Audrey 2.

Although I was not officially part of the company I did consider myself to be "a company man" (unpaid) from the very start. The first set to be designed and built was for Sandy Wilson's *The Boy Friend* and its first outing would be for Whitworth. A space was cleared and cleaned in the Burnley premises and work started on cloths but it was soon apparent that somewhere would have to be found where they could be hung. A couple of doors down from Graham's offices in Rochdale was a welder's workshop with sufficient height and a bar from which a cloth could hang and we moved in there. I say we because this was the start of my helping hand and I think we all nearly froze to death it was so cold in there. It was obvious that permanent premises had to be found so I accompanied the others on their rounds inspecting various possibilities and eventually we saw Sladen Wood Mill near Littleborough and North West Scenery with its new name had found its new home. As work progressed, first of all shifting stuff from Burnley to Littleborough into this vast empty building while carrying on building sets, we still nearly froze to death. Quite often I could be found at the mill, canvassing and priming flats, painting, decorating cloths, shopping, preparing meals, anything that I could do that needed doing to ease the pressure because Prosceneium took off very fast and very successfully. In five years, twenty-four new sets were constructed for musicals and pantomimes, all to Chris's designs. Two years down the line when it came to *Peter Pan*, everything was so far behind, even with permanent personel working flat out, Douglas's brother, William came down from Newcastle to provide an extra hand.

Life was getting extremely busy in other directions as well. Just before Christmas Chris was asked to take over a couple of parts in *Pinocchio* at City Varieties in Leeds when someone fell out and, as we moved into 1992, two evenings a week meant a drive to Ripon when we started rehearsals for *Carousel*, myself directing, Chris choreographing, having also designed the set which Prosceneium delivered. In March we had another surprise visitor from the states, Ron Copeland on his way to join his current girl friend (very rich evidently) in Paris, his first and possibly only trip abroad. *Carousel* having opened in Harrogate and played its week, life quietened down for a while. In June there were Pat Dooley more visiting ex-students, Brian Françoise and Jen Suhenic, and in August we welcomed Chris

Chapter Twenty Nine

Holloway who came down for a visit when he had a break from a production he was with at the Edinburgh Festival. He made another remark almost as good as his first night party faux pas when he saw an electric kettle, obviously for the first time, 'Oh, my! A teapot with an element!' I do so regret we've lost touch.

In September we had to go down to London as Hyst Mum had suffered a stroke and we visited her in Harold Wood Hospital. She had been out picking blackberries and was found lying in the road next to her cycle so that at first it was assumed she was the possible victim of a hit and run but it turned out not to be so. While in London we saw *Grand Hotel*, a production Chris and Douglas loved. I didn't.

Back in Yorkshire, rehearsals started for *Charlie Girl*. Over the next few years I was to direct and fall out with a number of amateur operatic societies. For Ripon I directed *Orpheus in the Underworld*, again with Chris doing the choreography and *My Fair Lady* choreographed by Ian Stead who had played Bacchus in *Orpheus*. I got on extremely well with the Ripon Company, the only society I truly enjoyed working with. They at least showed some discipline though there was sometimes the usual political flak flying about that seems to be par for the course with amateurs. The only reason we came to a parting of the ways was because they then wanted me to direct *Showboat*. This is not an all time favourite of mine and I didn't want to direct something in which people had to black up because there was no way we going to find artistes of the right colour in Ripon, so I declined the offer. Unfortunately the musical director stated that if I wasn't going to do it, neither was he, and as he had been with the company for a good many productions they weren't too pleased with me over losing him.

Graham asked me to direct *Underneath the Arches* at Whitworth. After three or four rehearsal calls where I hardly saw the same faces twice I gave up. Then, for another society, came *Whitehorse Inn* one of those archaic bits of nonsensical fluff that should have been buried years ago. I arrived at rehearsal one evening to find the committee had invited a photographer to take shots of the cast for the programme. Naturally they hadn't thought to inform me of this fact so I sat around most of the evening twiddling my thumbs because no one was willing to leave the vicinity of the photographer in case they missed out on a mug shot. I asked if anyone was prepared to do extra rehearsals because I felt they badly needed it. Only Ian Stead, dancing again, and his partner volunteered. From the rest there was a deep depressing silence. Then one of the leads couldn't attend rehearsals as he was a butcher and needed time to dress his turkeys for Christmas. They didn't like me. I didn't like them. We parted company. Finally came *42nd Street*, and what should have been a really exciting engagement that turned out to be another battle. This one I didn't walk out on, though I was tempted to a few times. Long before auditions I asked the committee one of the most important questions as far as *42nd Street* is concerned, 'Can you guarantee enough dancers, particularly boys.'

'Oh, absolutely,' was the response, 'no problem at all. We'll get them from other societies.'

I ended up with about a dozen girls of all shapes, sizes, ages and abilities and a twelve-year-old boy who, admittedly, was very good, but girls had to pretend to be boys and just looked like girls pretending to be boys. It's quite amazing how amateur societies select shows with very little forethought. *42nd Street* was all in vogue at that time. Everyone was doing it so everyone else had to do it. I had a phone call from St Ives; I seem to remember it was St Ives, somewhere in Cornwall, asking if I would direct it down there. Wonderful getaway it would have been, I thought, I could stay down there and write. I note from an entry in my appointments diary I had actually started these memoirs. But there were questions. Were they aware of how much dancing was involved? Could they supply the dancers, dancers who were good at tap? Was their stage bigger than a postage stamp? The answer to all was a big fat no so they dropped the idea in favour of something less ambitious which I wasn't invited to direct

Back to my own *42nd Street*; the committee wanted to drive up to Glasgow to see another society's production at the King's Theatre

Chapter Twenty Nine

(another house whose boards I once trod) and it was quite a memorable trip because, like *The Rink*, the production was fabulous: imaginatively directed, beautifully performed, the band was first class, the chorus work and the tap routines so exciting. I loved it. My committee however didn't seem at all impressed, if not damning with faint praise they were rather dismissive in fact. 'Ours will be better,' they all said. Pardon me for having doubts about that but apart from, 'We're only amateurs you know' whenever they're taken to task, the other cry is, 'We are better than anyone else, even the professionals.'

Auditions had been interesting and fairly successful. There was one cute little girl, young woman rather, with a sparkling personality and so adorably cookie, a natural madcap, and I immediately wanted to cast her in a part but, oh no, she didn't do parts, only chorus. Nothing I could say, no amount of encouragement, no amount of pleading would change her mind; it was chorus or nothing. In other words she was another Douglas and terrified of having to go solo. We cast one actor, of course I never had final say in this process, who came up to me afterwards and said what I expected him to say, 'I really don't understand this character, I'm going to need all the help I can get.' In other words, if I turn in a lousy performance, which I'm sure I will, it will be all your fault. There's always one and, if he thought I was going to spend more time with him than anyone else he had another think coming.

Before rehearsals start I always check everyone's availability and then spend a great deal of time working on a schedule so that cast members are not called unnecessarily or kept hanging about. Everyone gets a copy, including committee and stage management and, on receiving it, is asked to approve. If there are any objections there is still time to make changes. So what happened? My young leading lady is called for a Wednesday but at the end of a previous rehearsal informs me she won't be able to make it because she wants to go to a pop concert. Obviously when I made out the schedule she hadn't realised the boy band that had her all of a quiver was only in town for that one night. The fact that the entire rehearsal was scheduled around all her scenes was of no importance. I was furious.

I could never start rehearsals on time. Scheduled to start at seven, people were still rolling in at half past or even later. The usual excuse was late leaving work. It drove me mad. I offered to start rehearsals half an hour later but they wouldn't have that. One rehearsal took place on a bank holiday. 'Right,' I said, Monday's a holiday. None of you are at work. I expect you to be here at ten to seven ready to go at seven. All right?' It was a promise and, believe it or not, they kept it. All who were called were there by ten to seven. And what happened? The committee en bloc didn't arrive with the key until half an hour later leaving all of us hanging about the street waiting, and they couldn't understand why I blew my top.

When it came to moving into the theatre for the dress rehearsal, the set that had been booked even before I was on the scene, proved too big to get on the stage. By one in the morning I told the cast to go home and left stage management to sort out the problem of their own making. I had had enough. I attended the first night more out of duty than anything else and it wasn't as bad as I thought it was going to be, but that was mainly due to my wonderful choreographer on whose strong shoulders I laid most of the burden and who literally almost made a silk purse out of a sow's ear, if I can mix my metaphors. That was the end of me and directing for amateurs.

The previous year, 1993, Chris and Douglas, now with a certain security behind them in the shape of the company, felt they badly needed a holiday and they decided on Greece. They had a choice of two cut-price packages, one on Cephalonia, and the other on Crete. The Cretan holiday was at Plakias on the south side of the island and they chose this, firstly because it was a fair distance from Heraklion airport and secondly because they were advised to take a torch and this indicated they were less likely to be surrounded by lager louts or families with kids.

Chapter Twenty Nine

This was the year I would make my last appearance as an actor. I received a phone call from a BBC producer/director in London by the name of Bridget Sneyd asking me to go down for an interview if I was interested in playing a part in a *Crimewatch File*. I went down to London to a now totally nonsmoking BBC, which was boring as I was still a smoker. I lit a cigarette before going in, met Bridget, chatted, and read for her. The programme would be in two parts titled *The Lost Boys*, about a gang of murderous paedophiles and Bridget was interested in me for the lead, a revolting character by the name of Sydney Cooke. I thanked her for seeing me and asked as a matter of interest how she found me. 'From Spotlight'[32] she said. 'Must have been a very old Spotlight,' I said, 'I haven't been in it for years.' She looked at the cover and smiled ruefully. Yes, it was, but lucky for me because, although I didn't think for one moment I had got the part, I was no sooner back in Yorkshire when the phone rang and it was Bridget again, offering it to me. I enjoyed working for Bridget and I actually enjoyed playing the part. As I have no paedophile tendencies … No, that's a silly thing to say. If I do have any paedophile tendencies I would never act on them and I am certainly no murderer so I had no guilt feelings about playing Sydney Cooke. I found it an interesting experience to be actually locked up in one of Her Majesty's prisons. After the programme was broadcast over two weeks in October 1994 I was quite prepared to be attacked by umbrella wielding old ladies in Hebden Bridge but nothing of the sort happened. All everybody kept saying was, 'How could you play a part like that?' Then one morning I walked into the local bakery and the lady who served me said, 'Oh, the last time you came in, you nearly gave me a heart attack. I thought, "Oh, my God, he's out!" And then I said to myself, "don't be silly, he's only an actor." That will be £1.25 please.'

Towards the end of wrestling with *42nd Street* and while the show was playing Chris and Douglas took a second fortnight's break. Douglas suggested they try somewhere different but Chris said why

---
[32] Actor's directory.

not go back to Plakias where they knew people and could start the holiday immediately without needing time to settle in and suss things out. So back to Plakias they went where they were remembered and greeted like old friends. And I now had a second call out of the blue from a total stranger by the name of Garth Harrison. Someone had told him I played dame in pantomime. I told him he was misinformed. Chris played dame in a number of pantos at Rochdale; as for me I was a writer. That interested him. Could I write a version of *Peter Pan* for him to present in Weston this coming Christmas? I most certainly could. My God! Was I actually going to get a paid commission after all this time when the only money coming in from writing were the small amounts in royalties from *Thriller of the Year?* Not only was I going to write *Peter Pan,* he also, after we had met and talked, asked me if I would like to direct it and that was a generous gesture I had no hesitation in taking up.

Garibaldi, the musical, and *When the Devil Rides,* the screenplay, were put to one side as I concentrated on *Peter Pan* and I am glad Garth's faith in me was justified when it broke all records at the theatre that Christmas. It was almost a disaster before it even opened. Douglas delivered the set just before Christmas. The pirate ship and the flats for the nursery were on castors for smooth, easy scene change. Fred, Garth's trusted stage manager, an ancient with many a theatrical anecdote to regale everyone with, informed Prosceneium he wanted light casters with rubber tyres so that the scene shifting would be absolutely noiseless. The scene shifting far from being noiseless went with a clunk clunk clunk until it ground to a standstill as the light plastic and metal castors bent beneath the weight of the set and stopped turning. Consternation reigned. Garth, completely overlooking the fact that the castors were the choice of his own stage manager, was screaming about broken contracts and threatening all sorts of legal action. Fred was beside himself as phone calls were made to Yorkshire for replacements. How did one find replacements when everything was closing down for Christmas? Douglas was stage managing the panto in Rochdale where Chris was

Chapter Twenty Nine

playing dame but after their show they went down to the Mill were they removed every solid castor they could find on existing sets and packed them up, so that the following morning they could be sent to Weston. Les Jones, the transport manager for Prosceneium sent them by courier. When we heard that our hearts sunk, but miraculously the castors did arrive in time and Garth's blood pressure went back to what could be called as near normal as dammit. What Fred was on about to begin with, when the scene changes were covered with music anyway, I really don't know.

The following year Chris and Douglas insisted I join them in what had become their annual visit to Plakias. 'You've got to see Crete. You'll love it.'

Once again the Footes, Bill and Beryl, came down from North Shields to look after Hollings Farm were vandalism and crime were already beginning to encroach, even in such an out of the way location. Youths drove over from Burnley to get up to theft and mischief before hightailing it back over the border into Lancashire and Bill's car was broken into both times they came to look after the place. The security light we had placed high in a tree beside the parking circle was smashed with a well-aimed stone. Others in the hamlet had their cars vandalised and it actually got bad enough for all of us in The Hollings to form a vigilante group, taking it in turns to stay up at night in the hopes of catching the villains at it. As is always the way, as soon as we did that they stopped coming for a while and we gave up.

The guys were right, I loved Crete and, sitting at our favourite taverna, Glaros, (Seagull) run by our friend Nikos Makrimanolakis, on the last night of our holiday, watching the sun set over the mountains across the bay, a beautiful sight I loved watching every evening, I said, 'Why do we have to go back tomorrow?'

'We don't have to,' Douglas said.

Well, this time we did have to, but we decided the following year we would extend the holiday by a week in order to house hunt. We were already taking night classes in Greek at that College of Higher Education where I had sat through that abysmal *Hamlet* and we had a brochure from an Englishman with Cretan connections. I would sit at the kitchen table looking through it again and again with the photographs of stone Cretan houses while, at the same time, trying to learn more Greek from a book. When I went to direct *Peter Pan* on the Isle of Man my Greek phrase book went with me. It was a very old one; one that Chris had bought in Athens many years previously when he danced in the theatre Herodes Atticus at a Bach Festival. We decided to take the holiday in July to test the heat of the day because the second reason for my wanting to leave Yorkshire was the winter. As I grew older the winter seemed to get longer, darker, colder, and wetter every year until, eventually, I thought, 'If I spend one more winter here I will be dead.' I never thought it would happen and even now I still find myself missing Hollings Farm. Apart from certain friends that's all I do miss of England.

So, in the middle of July in the middle of the days' heat, we went house hunting on Crete. There was only one criterion, whichever house it was going to be, presuming we found one, all three had to say yes, two out of three as happened with a few properties, was not good enough.

But we did find the house. The three of us sat in the courtyard and said, mentally, if not aloud, 'This is it.'

On the 12th December 1996 contracts were exchanged. Janis Kulakis, through whom we had been dealing, telephoned to pass on the news and to add. 'May you be very happy in your new home on Crete.' But that is a whole other story.

CODA

I had originally thought of sub-titling these memoirs *The Diary of a Failure* but was dissuaded by my friends from doing so. After all, my reasoning went, as a playwright I am not a Tom Stoppard or an Alan Aykbourn, a Bennett, Frayn, Shepard, or Arthur Miller. As a lyricist I am not Sondheim. As an actor I am not up there with Ian McKellen, with Derek Jaccobi, David Jason, Michael Gambon or multi-million dollar film stars and, as a director, I am not in the same league as Daldry, Hands, Nunn, Hall or Hytner. And yet, and yet …. It's been a good life, I can say in all honesty and without boasting I have been well loved, and there are many things other than that for which I must be truly grateful, so maybe my friends were right, not such a failure after all even though as the good lady said, "he's only an actor."

November 1984

Dear Glyn,

We all want to express our deep appreciation for giving us the opportunity to work with you. You are the best director most (if not all) of us have worked with and someone who is truly a gentleman. Rehearsals were something to look forward to because working with you and learning from you was such a delight for all of us. Throughout the whole process of putting on the show we in the cast would talk among ourselves of how easy it was to work with you "professionally" and how much we liked you personally for everything from your tremendous patience to your wonderful British humor.

When we heard you were staying next semester we were (and still are) thrilled because of the professionalism and "class" you bring to the department and just because we like having you around and want you to continue as part of our family. We feel so relaxed and comfortable around you that we'd like you to stay on indefinitely.

For all of us "*The Country Wife*" was one of, if not THE most educational and enjoyable theatre experiences we've ever had and you've made an impression on us such that we'll never forget you.

No matter how long you stay or where you go afterward, always remember there are 15 American kids who love you.

Love,
Missy Mayers and the cast of
THE COUNTRY WIFE. JMU

28th April 1985

Glyn,

Sometime during semester someone asked me who the best director was I ever worked with and I said Glyn Jones. I explained that I liked him because he has definite ideas that he communicates well, he is knowledgeable about a variety of technical aspects and they aren't shrouded [*sic*] in some ego. I learned so much working with you, not necessarily big things, but lots of little things which are perhaps more useful. You are probably the most patient and in command, though not in a manipulative sense, director I've known. Now, working with you as an actor, I am fairly overwhelmed at the magnitude of your abilities. Much of what you possess is what I wish to aspire to. Thanks for coming to JMU because you have truly inspired me.

Sincere thanks and best wishes
Gregg O'Donnell
"BURIED CHILD."

CODA

HILDEGARDE H DREAMED (WITH A SIGH)
WOULDN'T IT BE NICE IF SHE COULD FLY?
BUT SHE'S FAR TOO ROUND,
AND CLOSE TO THE GROUND,
FOR SUCH RIDICULOUS PIE IN THE SKY.
AH, WELL ....

Many years ago Laurence Fitch of blessed memory said to me, 'Glyn, dear boy, you're such a good writer and you've waited so long. But with you it's always bread today and jam tomorrow.'

Who knows? Maybe there's still time for a spoonful of jam.

There have been so many many people influencing my life, whose love and friendship I have appreciated and who I would like to have mentioned, and to them all I can only apologise, hand on heart, that in this writing they have been neglected. Perhaps if I had spent my life in the shade of an official umbrella there would have been fewer, but my life would have been so much the poorer for it. To all, I can only say a heartfelt thank you. G.I.J.

PS: Yes, *A King's Story* WAS nominated for an Oscar in 1967.

Index

A

Actors Equity Association 10, 12, 35, 44, 141, 206, 239, 364, 533
Actors' Studio 40
ACTT 362-363
Adams, Douglas 312
Africa 3, 8, 28, 42, 45-46, 48-49, 57, 68-69, 72-73, 76-77, 79-80, 83, 99, 115, 119, 153, 162, 165, 167, 170, 178, 185, 188, 200, 202, 259, 278, 280, 292, 294, 336, 338, 345, 353, 360, 374, 382-383, 391, 411, 424, 461, 624, 663
African National Congress Party 79
Akenglen - Production Company 444
Aldridge, Michael 376
Alge, Robert 379, 488
Allyson, June 264, 269
Amsterdam 80-81, 351
Anderson, Lindsay 38-39, 401
Animals:
  Natalie 368-371, 382, 385, 422, 455, 588
  Sophie 630-631, 634-635, 638-639 - 642, 644, 648-649
Anzide, Jim 385, 604
Arctic Circle 135
Arden, John 315
Arnott (Lady) Turner 227
Arrambide, Mario 439
Arthur, Kay 160, 327
Arthur's Seat, Edinburgh 70
Arthur, Tom 160, 327-328, 440, 441, 466-467, 474, 477, 480-481, 486, 490, 492, 494, 496, 498, 519, 525-526, 599-601, 607-608, 611-616, 620, 624, 626-629, 640, 645, 655
Ashton, Ellis 457
Askey, Arthur 224
Associated British Productions Limited 401
Associated-Rediffusion 206, 242-243
Athens, Greece 1, 133, 188, 282, 372, 456, 516, 676. *See* Greece
Audin, W.H. 206
Audreson, Michael 363
Austin, Ray 301
Austin, Tom 189, 208, 212
Australia 44, 49, 51, 53, 136, 184-

185, 244, 293, 294, 342,
   383-384, 443
Aykbourn, Alan 203, 677
Aznavour, Charles 386, 391

B

Babycham 21
Bailey, Gillian 363
Ballet Rambert 245
Banbury, Frith 376
Bannister, Trevor 31, 33, 294, 313.
   See also Plays, Pantomimes
   & Musicals:: Early One
   Morning
Barker, Felix 404
Barker, Joyce 514
Barkworth, Peter 359
Barnes, Larry 457
Barrie, J.M. 140, 144, 219-220, 546
Barrow, Janet 201
Bart, Lionel 145
Barton, John 313
Bass, Alfie 301
Bayldon, Oliver 137
Beaulieu-Sur-Mer 30
Beeching, Christopher 1, 81-82,
   195, 229-231, 236, 245-247,
   256-257, 259-260, 282, 292,
   302, 305, 309, 312, 329-330,
   342, 348, 350, 353, 356, 362,
   365, 367, 369, 373-374, 378,
   382, 387-388, 390, 393, 408,
   414, 420-423, 425, 432, 437,
   440-441, 444, 447, 449, 451-
   452, 454-455, 457-459, 461-
   462, 467-468, 475, 483, 485,
   494, 512, 514, 544-545, 547,
   551, 553-554, 567, 578-579,
   581-582, 584-585, 587-588,
   591, 602, 614, 630, 635, 645,
   656, 657, 659-664, 667-669,
   672-676
Beeching, Jean 422
Beeching, Roger 231, 422, 452

Beethoven 267
Behean, Katy 219, 435
Bell, Melissa 140
Belsen 115, 553
Bernette, Sheila 152, 197, 663
Biko, Steve 79, 80
Bioscope - Cinema 114, 297
Birken, Andrew 220
Bishop of Zululand 102
Bisson, Paul & Harriet 662
Blakely, Colin 455
Bloemfontein 53
Blue Hills Farm 59, 73-74, 120,
   123-125, 153, 269
Bluett, Ray 293, 333
Blythe, Eric 217, 224
Bob Jones University 331-334
Boer War 200
Bogarde, Dirk 30
Bogart, Humphrey 110
Bogdanov, Michael 354
Boksburg 153
Bolt, Brian 261, 616, 621
Bolt, Robert. See also Plays,
   Pantomimes & Musicals::
   Tiger and the Horse, The
Bond, Edward 436, 472, 486
Books:
   A Christmas Carol 109, 471
   A History of the Liverpool Play-
      house 426
   Angel - Glyn Jones 2, 252, 350
   A Pictorial History of South
      Africa 27-28
   Baron in the Trees 215-216
   Black Beauty 72
   Brood Of The Witch Queen 524
   David Copperfield 109
   Dead on Time - Glyn Jones
      319. See also Television:: A
      Model's Lot is Not a Happy
      One
   Fear, Anxiety, Neurosis and the
      Wolfenden Report 251
   Great Expectations 109
   Hildegarde H and Her Friends -

Glyn Jones 305
Lost on the Prairie 109
Oliver Twist 109, 584
Prancing Nigger 139
Priceless 190
Seven Centuries of English Cooking 369
The City and the Pillar 176
The Lost Cause 502
The Man from Moscow 372
The Naked Civil Servant 191
The Pictorial Book of Philosophy 231
The Space Museum - Glyn Jones 2, 6, 294, 296, 512, 544. *See also* Television:: Doctor Who
The Virginian 464
The Wrong People 374
Two Boys at Swim 546
Who's Who In The Theatre 235
Booth, Harry 23, 260, 296, 303, 312, 365, 629
Booth, Michael 74
Boothroyd, Basil 36, 145
Borrodaile, Mary Tucker 254-255
Box, Muriel 8, 30
Box, Sydney 8, 24, 28, 30, 216, 281, 285, 351
Bracco, Roberto 225
Braemar Castle 178-179. *See also* Union Castle Line
Brahms 12, 14, 267, 432
Branagh, Kenneth 17, 130, 151-152, 207, 314, 408, 434-435, 440, 617
Brandt, Wieland 371
Brecht 220, 237, 559, 611
Brian Brooke Company 114
Bridge, Alexander 6
Bridge Theatre Company 593, 619, 656, 657
Brightman, Sarah 610
British Arts Council 227-228, 246, 602
British Broadcasting Corporation 2, 6, 38, 137, 201, 206, 215, 218, 224-235, 247, 269, 293, 296, 309, 319, 355, 364, 383, 390, 393, 526, 546, 673
Brooke, Peter 359
Buckner 552
Buffery, Mark 405, 407
Bullen Street - Durban South Africa 46, 50, 53-54, 58, 144
Burrell, Susan 160, 362, 471, 477, 593, 621
Burr III, Courtney 374, 378, 452, 659
Bush Davies Dance School 245, 246
Butters, Paul 203, 244
Byng, Douglas 227

C

Cadby Hall, Joe Lyons 213
Cagney, James 110
Cairney, John 232
Caltanissetta 45, 446
Calvino, Italo 215
Cambodia 3
Candia 65. *See also* Crete
Cape Town 49, 53, 114, 164, 181
Cardinal Paino 52
Cargill, Patrick 135
Carnegie Mellon University 205, 239, 467, 663
Carpenter, Richard 457
Carr, Jane 455
Cassily, Richard 387
Cawkwell, Chris 619, 658
Celine, Pearle 113-115, 194, 293, 659
Cellier, Peter 381
Century Films Productions 296
Chadwick Street Labour Exchange 30
Chambless, Elizabeth 652
Champagne Charlie. *See also* Plays, Pantomimes & Musicals::

Champagne Charlie
Chaplin, Sidney 373
Charlottesville 12, 362, 464-465, 494, 496, 499, 501-502, 521, 529, 533-534, 601, 603, 617, 619-620, 631, 648
Chasen, Heather 316
Chenoweth, Ian 294
Chetwyn, Robert 249, 250-251
Chevalier, Albert 460
Children's Film Foundation 2, 296, 298
Chinn, Jimmy 223, 656
Chopin 8, 265
Christie, Agatha 235, 494
Cinerama 208, 658
Clark, Bruce 363
Clarke, Jeff 468, 544
Clark, Petula 245
Clayton, Alex 136, 245
Clayton, Kenny 136-137, 186, 245, 489
Clayton, Vicky 132, 245, 512
Clinton, Hilary Rodham 148
Clive, Philip 13
Clouston, Erlend 396
Comrie, Billy 103, 110
Conan Doyle, Arthur 30
Congreve, William 433
Connaught Rangers, The 308, 315, 320, 322, 410-411
Cook, Barbara 570
Cooke, Sydney 673
Copeland, Ron 198, 262, 330, 385, 604, 629, 632, 668
Copp, Donald 184
Corner Tea Rooms 213
Costumiers:
  Alkits 23
  Bermans 265
  Moss Bros 23
Coward, Noel 132, 180, 280, 378, 610
Crawford, Michael 218, 225
Creighton, Anthony 314
Cretan 78, 615, 672, 676

Crete 1-2, 28, 31, 48, 65, 132, 148, 160, 180-181, 283, 326, 349, 372, 374, 387, 429, 449, 589, 603, 672, 675-676. *See also* Greece
Crewe Junction 222
Crisp, Quentin 191
Cronin, Hume 618
Cruttwell, Hugh 419, 430, 439
Cugat, Xavier 289, 303
Cutts, John 187, 251

D

Dachau 82, 115
Dalby, John 390
Daldry, Stephen 205
Daly, James 308, 322, 405-407, 410
Dame Edith Evans 438
Dankworth, Johnny 139
Dar-es-Salaam 165, 167
Darrell, Teddy 159
Davidson, Andy 140
Davidson, Roger 357, 555, 557, 559, 561-562, 566, 568, 573-574
Dean, Clifford 548
Dean, Peter 140, 143
Dearsley, A.P. 130
Delon, Alain 246
Denbigh, Wales 42
Dench, Judy 387
Denison, Michael 194, 358
Dexter, John 38
Dillman, Bradford 386, 391
Dixon, Jack 329
Domesday Book 590
Donaldson, Jacqui 525
Donovan, Terence 354
Dooley, Patrick 385, 594, 604, 606, 668
Dors, Diana 4
Doughty, Stuart 656
Dowager Lady Hardinge of Penshurst 24
Dowdeswell, Caroline 194

Drake, Charlie 224
Drake, Fabia 493
Drummond, Vivienne 162
Duke of Windsor 23-24, 27, 29
Dunn, Jeffrey 357, 542
Durban, South Africa 27, 42, 53-54, 60-61, 64-66, 69, 71, 74, 77-78, 83, 92, 95, 101, 110-111, 113, 115, 119, 121, 123-124, 153, 180, 185, 196, 263, 268-269, 272, 276, 278, 286, 379, 475, 514
Durwell Productions Limited 286, 288, 291, 293
Dyer, Charles 455

E

Eddington, Paul 455
Edinburgh Festival 232, 669
Edward VIII 28, 29. *See also* Duke of Windsor
Egbuna, Obi 293
El Cordobes 304
El Greco 190
Ellison, Carey 151
Ellsworth, Warren 545-546, 640
Emmerson, Michael 319
Empress Of Canada 244
England 1, 4, 10, 14, 22, 25, 51, 53, 55, 62, 74, 77-78, 115, 120, 125, 128, 133, 144, 160, 162, 164, 174, 176, 178, 181, 184-185, 197, 199, 205, 208, 239, 244, 260, 279, 293-294, 301, 305, 307-308, 317, 324-326, 393, 411, 426, 431, 435, 443, 453, 456, 474, 519, 537, 555, 562-563, 567, 574, 584, 596, 602, 608, 613, 621, 624, 630-631, 638, 642, 654, 663, 676. *See also* Great Britain
Entabeni 63, 92, 242
Eshowe 27
Europe 3, 165, 170, 181, 339, 411, 454, 467, 552
Evans, Margo 288
Eyre, Ronald 383

F

Family:
  Blodwen - Aunt 42-43, 56-57
  Brockman, James 44, 46
  Brockman, Maria Charlotte 44-46, 51, 57
  Brockman, Rosie 44
  Ceridwen - Aunt 42, 57, 68
  Ceridwen Gwyneth (Ceri) - Sister 62-64, 69, 76, 126, 212, 244
  da Costa, Sarah - Aunt 49
  da Costa, Tony - Cousin 49, 50-51
  Hendry, Robin 380
  Jillorma 49
  Jones, Llewellyn Idris - Father 43, 57
  Josepina 49
  Marie 46, 48, 51-52, 55
  Paino, Antonino - Uncle 46
  Paino, Bartolo 44-45, 49
  Paino, Francesco - Uncle 45-46, 48
  Paino, Grazzia Conzella - Aunt 46
  Paino, Janet 201, 294, 411
  Paino, Maria - Aunt 44, 46
  Paino, Rosa Angela - Mother 46, 58
  Paino, Rosina - Aunt 48
  Paino, Umberto 49
  Paino, Vincenzo - Uncle 45-49, 53, 259, 442
  Reverend Alfred Ebden Padday 55
Fanning, Rio 354
Farhi, Moris 354
Farrow, Eileen 6
Farrow, Mia 386
Fauré's Requiem 552

684

Faust, David 535
Fazan, Eleanor 387
Ferriman, Arthur 301
Feydeau 390
Fielding, Fenella 318
Fields, Gracie 67
Film:
- A King's Story - Columbia Pictures 2, 23, 28, 30, 260, 296, 300-301, 679
- All That Jazz 568
- A Midsummer Night's Dream 373
- Captain Hornblower 153
- Carry on Films 59
- Finishing School 300, 308
- Go for a Take 443
- Henry V 435
- Maurice 374
- Monsieur Hulot's Holiday 443
- My Grandmother's House 569
- Plein Soliel 246
- Privates on Parade 431
- Quills 374
- River Rivals - Childrens Film Foundation 312
- Satyricon 640
- Snows of Kilimanjaro 166
- Speed 377, 379, 382, 386, 390-391, 414
- Stop 313
- Suddenly Last Summer 81
- The Color Purple 274
- The Lone Ranger 155
- The Madness of King George 79
- The Master Craftsman 308
- The Servant 438, 626
- This Sporting Life 38
- West of Zanzibar 170

Film Rights 52, 658. *See also* Fitch, Laurence
Finch, Peter 31, 33, 386, 391
Finney, Albert 41, 483-484, 542
Firbank, Ronald 139
Firth, Peter 356, 363, 391, 546
Fitch, Laurence 35, 242, 249, 387, 512, 640, 679
Flanagan Jnr, Bud 164
Flynn, Daniel 417
Foote, Douglas 1, 319, 329-333, 336, 348, 355, 585, 590-591, 593, 602, 632-633, 635, 642, 648-664, 667-669, 671-675
Forbes, Bryan 402
Forde, Brindsley 363
Fosse, Bob 373
Fowlds, Derek 379
France 30-31, 57, 245, 302, 308, 364, 411, 442, 456
Fraser, Bill 383
Fraser, Donald 394
French's acting editions 233
Fugard, Athol 79, 599
Furman University 330, 331, 434, 644, 651-654

G

Gable, Christopher 657
Garibaldi 51, 144, 147, 674
Garonzik, Elan 238
Gaskill, Bill 40, 361
Gassman, Michael 317-318
Gay, Chris 374
Geddes, Henry 298
General Smuts 72
Genoa 180-182
George, Kath 657
George V docks 14, 183
George VI 185
German East Africa Line 69
German, Edward (Jones) 43
German measles 94, 246, 247
Gibson, Chloe 38, 217, 224, 319
Gibson, William 288
Gielgud, John 129, 198, 253, 332, 362, 438
Gilbert and Sullivan 311, 318, 647
Gilmar, Brian 286, 288
Gingold, Hermoine 388
Gister, Earle 463

Glenwood High, Durban 71, 112, 150, 207, 269, 271, 278, 324
Glover, Paul 147, 373
Gordon, Al 632, 638, 642
Gordon, John 9, 12
Gore, Jenny 581
Goring, Marius 224
Gorton, Linda 512
Gothenburg 133
Granada Television 200, 224
Grand Guignol 201, 624, 625
Grant, Julian 293
Grant, Steve 322
Grant, Tilly 176
Gray, Bruce 528
Gray, Dulcie 358
Great Britain 3, 181
Greece 4, 59-60, 327, 424, 430, 667, 672. *See also* Athens, Greece; *See also* Crete
Green, Guy 386, 391
Greenville - South Carolina 330, 332, 334, 644-645, 650-651, 653
Grieves, Donald 266
Gubbay, Raymond 451, 457
Guinness, Alec 129
Guinness Lecture 319
Guthrie, Tyrone 402

H

Haines, Roger 224, 660, 663
Hale, Georgina 455
Hales, John 313-315
Hall, Adelaide 139
Hallé Orchestra 657
Hall, Willis 348
Halpin Film Productions 377, 390
Hamilton, Gabrielle 316
Hamilton, Lionel 233, 237
Hancock, Tony 224
Handel 61, 266, 537, 624
Hardy, Laurence 318
Harker, Diana 397
Harrisonburg 160, 282, 312, 329, 380, 426, 440, 452, 462, 466, 471, 472, 474, 482, 497-498, 501-502, 504, 509-511, 516-518, 524-527, 530, 533, 593, 599-601, 603, 606-607, 614, 621, 629, 648
Harrison, Debbie Lee 143
Harrison, Garth 141, 674
Harrison, Scott 238, 620
Harte, Judith 316
Hartnell, William 295
Hartwig, Hildagard 546
Harwell, David 159, 358, 441, 465, 511-516, 599
Hatfield, Mark 435
Hawker, Karl 258
Hawkins, Jack 31
Hawthorne, Ben 246, 281, 285, 288, 291, 316, 412
Hawthorne, Nigel 79-80
Hayes, Melvyn 388
Hebden Bridge 427, 428, 581-583, 591, 617, 655-656, 658, 673
Hege, Martha 509
Hempel, Anoushka 194
Henderson's Procedure 428
Hillier, Helen 567
Hill, Philip 644
Hinton, Pip 132
Hitler 3
HMV 24
Hollings Farm 577, 582-586, 588-592, 602, 614, 619, 650, 655-656, 658, 661, 667, 675-676
Holloway, Christian 467, 601, 606, 648
Homosexuality 211, 335
Horton Jnr, John 509, 511
Hotspur. *See* Plays, Pantomimes & Musicals:: Henry IV Part One
Howard, Frankie 224
Howard, Trevor 198
Huby, Roberta 4. *See also* Plays, Pantomimes & Musicals:: Grab Me a Gondola

Hudd, Roy 451, 657
Hudson, Rock 211
Humby, Caroline 305
Hurt, John 191
Huxley, Elspeth 176

I

Ibsen, Henrik 17, 430
Idi Amin 3
Imax 658
IRA 410
Isle of Wight 22, 129-130, 152
Italy 45-46, 52, 144, 308, 365

J

Jackley, Nat 115
Jackson, Peter 579
James, Henry 318, 510
James Madison University 6, 78, 198, 203, 330, 440-442, 462-465, 470-471, 473, 481, 487, 491, 494, 497, 499, 520, 523, 525, 527, 532-533, 581, 606-607, 615, 621, 644, 646, 655, 678
James, Sid 59
J. Arthur Rank 30
Jenkins, Florence Foster 373
Jenkins, Herbert 301
Jenn, Michael 374, 456, 462, 474, 658
Jerry Johnson Productions 537
Joe Coral, Bookmakers 13
Johannesburg 56, 77, 114, 118, 153, 159, 164
John, Elton 398
John Horton Jnr 509, 511, 531
John, Peter 657
Johnson, Jerry 537, 544
Johnson, Pam 465, 491-492, 508, 606, 609, 647
Johnston, Lloyd 393

Jones, Clifton 250, 252
Jones, Elwyn 216
Jones, Gareth 393
Jonson, Ben 109

K

Kaye, Danny 211
Kaye, Gordon 360
Keel, Howard 110
Keith, Penelope 441
Kemsley Newspapers 186, 187, 200, 207, 213. *See also* Newspapers & Periodicals:: The Sunday Mail
Kern, Wolf 282
Kerridge, Mary 438
Kershaw, Graham 665, 667
Kessler, Lyle 607
Kimberley 53
King Arthur 307, 379
King, Beryl 388
King, Tom 470, 472, 594, 608-609, 612, 629
Knight, Joan 387
Knight, Paul 40, 544, 619, 656
Konstam, Nigel 188
Kossak, Gudrun 548
Kossof, David 38-40
Kramer, Josef 115
Kurlander, Brian 621, 629

L

La Belle Époque 148
La Belle Otero 148, 603, 610
La Colombe D'or 31
La Donna è Mobile 20-21. *See also* Opera:: Rigoletto
Laine, Cleo 139
Langford, Bonnie 378
Lars 559, 562, 566, 567
Larsson, Ulf 133, 386
Latrobe, Peter 212

Lawton, Leslie 395, 396, 397
Lawton, Mark 243
Layton, Joe 378
Lee, Annabelle 457, 657
Leech, Andy 440, 462, 471, 610
Leech, Richard 349
Lee III, Gray 12, 362, 495, 497, 499-504, 517, 519-521, 523-526, 529, 535, 544, 546-547, 556, 603, 617-618, 620-621, 631-632, 650, 664
Lehmann, Beatrix 376
Lehr, Milton 303-304
Leighton, Margaret 376-377
Leine, Morten 257
Lennox, Vera 234, 235
Leonard, Michael 188
Leverson, Sarah Rachel 254
Le Vien, Jack 23, 26, 28, 146. *See* A King's Story
Levin, Bernard 408
Lewis, John 102, 207, 212, 438
Leybourne, George 457-458, 461, 462, 468, 482, 487-488, 494, 506, 510, 515, 520, 527, 537, 568, 657, 662. *See also* Plays, Pantomimes & Musicals:: Champagne Charlie
Lilley, Valerie 79
Linklater, Dick 227
Littlewood, Christopher 148
Llangibby Castle 207. *See also* Union Castle Line
Lloyd, Arthur 255
Lloyd, Sue 300-301
Lloyd Webber, Andrew 546, 596-597, 624
Loach, Ken 235, 237
London 3, 10, 12-14, 20, 32, 35-37, 40-41, 53, 74, 132, 136, 145, 152, 164-165, 183-184, 188, 190-191, 193, 197, 203, 207-209, 213, 217, 219, 222, 228, 235, 243, 246, 265, 280, 286, 301, 304, 307-308, 318-319, 322-323, 330, 335, 340, 345-347, 349, 354-355, 359, 365-366, 370-371, 374, 376, 388, 391, 393-397, 409, 412-413, 421, 433, 440-441, 444-446, 454, 458, 467, 471, 481, 483, 487, 493, 497-498, 500, 527, 530, 538, 542, 544-545, 547, 552-554, 567, 578-579, 582, 586-588, 591, 593, 619, 643, 655-657, 662-663, 669, 673
Lord Camrose 186
Lord Chamberlain 289-291
Lord Kemsley 186
Lord Kitchener 77, 211
Lord Leighton 192
Lunts 359
Lusby, Rick 431
Lutsky, Marcus 452, 542
Lyn, David 237
Lyndrups, Allen & Anne 282, 312, 427, 463, 467, 471, 479, 483, 487, 489, 491-497, 499, 501, 503-505, 507-508, 510, 515-516, 521-523, 530, 532-533, 601, 612, 617, 622, 625-626, 641, 647, 655

M

MacCarthy, Fiona 34, 37
Mackie, Peter 131, 194, 208, 215, 367, 382, 453, 455
Mackintosh, Cameron 137, 148-149, 546
Mack, Warren 92
Macmiadechain, Padraig 192, 259-260, 302
Macnab, David Scott 65, 280
MacQueen Pope 229-230
Makrimanolakis, Nikos 675
Malikyan, Kevork 354
Mandela, Nelson 79
Marlborough, Frank 152, 197
Marowitz, Charles 387-388, 390
Marquis of Bath 304
Marshall, Cindy 327, 472, 474

Martin, Mary 646
Mason, James 8-9, 109, 129. See also Plays, Pantomimes & Musicals:: Seventh Veil, The
Masque School of Theatre and Ballet 113
Mastoids 92
Matcham, Frank 143
Matthews, Rosemary 202, 553. See also Plays, Pantomimes & Musicals:: Rosemary
Mattys, Marilyn 513, 515, 531
Maugham, Robin 374
Maugham, Somerset 43, 240
Mau Mau 171-172, 175, 177
Mayes, Richard 40, 387-388
McCambridge, Mercedes 471
McClure, James 454
McConkey, Don 474
McCulloch, Jane 403
McEnery, Peter 30
McGann, Paul 430
McKellen, Ian 360, 381, 677
McKendry, Maxime 369
Mckillop, Don 395
McKinnon, Errol 352-353, 656
McLure, James 239
Medlinger, Michael 548, 552, 578
Method Acting 236-237, 262, 556
M.G.M 166
Michel, Keith 136
Miles, Bernard 163, 383
Miles, Joanna 537
Miles, Roy 190, 305, 308, 365
Millar, Ronald 359
Mill, Callum 232
Miller, Sandy 417
Miller, Stanley 38, 208, 213, 553
Milligan, Spike 385
Mills and Boon 130
Mills, Hayley 176
Mineo, Sal 23, 74, 374, 378
Moét & Chandon 8
Moffatt, Kathleen 316
Moliere 594
Mombassa 166-168, 170-171, 174, 178-179
Monica, Fay Henwood 268
Moody, Ron 455
Moore, Andy 301, 352, 379, 424, 592
Morley-Priestman, Anne 402
Morrison, Bill 79
Morris, Tee 599, 603-606, 636-638, 659
Morten 257, 561, 564, 567, 576-577
Morvan, Michel 260
Mostad, Stephen 453, 659
Moth to the Flame 454
Mozambique 73, 117-118
Mr Mears 427, 428-429
Mugabe, Robert 3. See herein Zimbabwe
Munich 81-82, 282, 371, 468, 553, 634
Murray, Alistair 268
Music Hall Society 457
Mynhardt, Siegfried 162

N

Nakuru Players 173
Napoli 45
Naranj, Manu 336
Natal 56, 58-60, 64, 74, 104, 268, 279, 338
National Service 196
National Union of Seamen 10
Ndola 116
Nel, Betty 124-125, 127-128
Nelson, Dave 656, 662
Ness, Agnes 426
Newspapers & Periodicals:
  Beano 118
  Daily Mail 36, 202
  Evening News 404
  Evening Standard 36
  Gambit 225
  Harrisonburg Daily News-Record 530

Kemsley Newspapers 186
Punch 36
Radio Times 80
The Breeze 472, 636
The Daily Telegraph 397
The Financial Times 402
The Greenville News 653
The Guardian 34
The Liverpool Post 396
The Observer 186, 322, 404, 586
The Stage 10, 356, 562
The Sun 36, 365
The Sunday Express 300
The Sunday Mail 186
The Sunday Sun 186
The Sunday Times 186, 600, 627
The Times 408
The Winchester Star 509
Variety 390
Zeta 317-318, 353
Ngakane, Lionel 336
Niagara Falls 452. *See also* The Maid of the Mist
Nichols, Beverly 191
Nightingale, Sir Geoffrey 310
Noakes, Cecil 267, 276-277
Noble, Adrian 431
Noel, Magali 373
Norman, Andy 378
Norman, Barry 36
Northern Ballet Theatre 657
Northern Rhodesia 115. *See also* Zambia
Norway 257, 357, 559

O

Obey, Andre 199
Ockler, Chris 621
O'Connell, Patrick 250, 252
O'Connor, Donald 110
O'Donnell, Gregg 478, 678
Oeser, Peter 190, 551
Offenbach 353
O'Gormon, George 287

Olivier, Laurence 4, 211, 332, 360, 362, 435
Oman, Julia Trevelyan 515
O'Neil, Eugene 239, 533
O'Neill, Jamie 546
Opera:
  Carmen 20
  Caro Mio Ben 61
  Das Rheingold 645
  Der Rosenkavalier 546
  Don Pasquale 565
  Four last Songs 624
  Götterdamarung 522
  Il Seraglio 468
  La Boheme 164, 330, 664
  Largo, Handel 61, 266
  L'enfant et les Sortileges 309
  Mazeppa 489
  Orpheus in the Underworld 353, 547, 669
  Parsifal 545, 578, 645
  Rigoletto 20
  Salome 644
  Samson and Delilah 61, 353
    Softly Awakes My Heart 61, 266
  The Bartered Bride 578
  The Pearl Fishers 330
  The Sod's Opera 647
  Tristan and Isolde 382, 514
  Turandot 552
Opera North 657
Oracle Productions 313
O'Rourke, Janice 594
Orton, Joe 414
Osborne, Charles 227
Oscar 8, 23, 52, 212, 280, 679
Oslo 357, 559, 561
Our Gang 297-298

P

Palmer, William 52
Pan African Films 251
Parkyn, Derek 132

Paton, Alan 59
Patrick, Nigel 31, 376, 418
Paulsen, Carl 129
Payne, Bruce 430
Peck, Gregory 153
Pedersen, Mickey Fredie 357, 554-555, 557-560, 563, 568-576
Pemberton, Antonia 229
Pennell, Nicky 453
Pennine Way 590
Penrose, John 10-11, 22, 129
Penry Jones, Peter 247
Pepys, Samuel 3, 217
Perry, John 305
Perth 49, 294, 342, 387
Pertwee, Michael 130
Peterson, Mark 313
Peters, Ray 347, 421
Petherbridge, Edward 219
Philips, Bob 379
Philips, Graham 184
Pietermaritzburg 58, 66, 83, 111, 268, 272, 278
Pillars of Society 430, 433
Pink, Pearl 426
Pinner, Charles 376, 391-392, 398
Pinter, Harold 233, 350
Plakias-Crete 672, 674-675
Plays, Pantomimes & Musicals:
  42nd Street 373, 497, 670, 673
  A Chorus Line 335, 497
  A Coat of Varnish 359, 441
  A Doll's House 292, 430
  A Flea in Her Ear 435
  A Funny Thing Happened on the Way to the Forum 507, 510
  A Lesson from Aloes 79
  A Little Night Music 149, 374, 387-388
  All My Sons 657
  Amadeus 402
  A Man About the House 114
  A Man for all Seasons 44, 246, 248, 260
  Anastasia 287, 292, 359, 373
  An Inspector Calls 414-415

Annie 518, 561
Another Country 207, 374, 474
A Private Matter 379, 381
Are You Now or Have You Ever Been? 4, 359, 600
Are You Sitting Comfortably? 18, 316
Arms and the Man 619
Ashes of Thebes, The 354
Au Pair 386
A View from the Bridge 6, 261, 354, 616, 620-622
Babes in the Wood 330
Barefoot in the Park 504, 507, 509
Barnum 546
Bay Rum 228, 289-292
Beautiful For Ever 2, 252-255, 258, 487
Beauty and the Beast 414
Best Little Whorehouse In Texas 474
Between Two Sighs 206, 228, 488
Billy Liar 313-314, 483
Black Maria 137-138
Blithe Spirit 419
Blues 383, 612-613
Bourbon and Laundry 454
Boy Friend, The 236, 503, 516-517, 520, 525, 667
Boys in the Band 562
Breaking Point 260
Brief Encounter 37
Brighton Beach Memoirs 474
Brittanicas 658
Buried Child 6, 472-473, 486, 496, 498, 502
Café Puccini 546
Camelot 633
Candide 559
Captain Brassbound's Conversion 441
Caretaker, The 233-234, 361
Carousel 668
Cats 388, 425, 440-441, 654
Champagne Charlie 420, 487.

See Leybourne, George
Charlie Girl 661, 669
Cherry Orchard, The 198
Chicago 453, 529, 542, 574, 640
Children of a Lesser God 516, 525
Chorus of Disapproval 547
Cinderella 2, 237, 309
Circus Boy 37, 40, 229
Cole 388, 560
Come Laughing Home 348
Corn is Green, The 6
Country Wife, The 6, 464-465, 468, 477-480, 483, 485, 487, 489, 678
Coventry Nativity Play of the Company of Shearmen and Tailors 109
Crimes of the Heart 479, 481, 507
Crisis at the Crow's Nest 9
Critic, The 546
Crucible, The 139, 456
Cry the Beloved Country 59
Cuckoo's Egg, The 551
Cupid & Psyche 136
Daggers Drawn 203, 244
Dames at Sea 568
Dark Victory 150-151
Day the Welsh Rose, The 393
Death and Brown Windsor 130
Death of a Salesman 492, 494
Deathtrap 537
Desire Under the Elms 533
Dial M for Murder 203
Dick Whittington 362
Doctor in the House 151-152
Don't Walk About With Nothing On 390
Dracula 224, 414, 416-418, 660
Dresser, The 197, 483-484, 622
Each Evening at Five Past Eight, A Holiday Entertainment 259
Early One Morning 30-33, 35-37, 40-41, 252, 261, 291, 402, 545
Earth Spider, The 526
Educating Rita 471
Edward II 198
Elephant Man, The 425, 572-573
Enter Anthony 130, 248, 292
Epitaph for George Dillon 314
Equus 330, 434, 546, 556, 572, 605, 607, 622, 632, 636-637, 644, 653-654, 660
Fantasticks, The 610, 613, 618
Female Transport 662-663
Fifty Mark, The 199
Five & Dime, Jimmy Dean 492-493, 525
Fly Away Peter 130
Fools 613-614, 618
Fugue in Two Flats 40-41, 545, 601. *See also* Plays, Pantomimes & Musicals:: Early One Morning
Generations 2, 205, 239, 467, 505, 523, 525, 594, 601-602, 606, 614, 620, 663
Ghost Train, The 150
Gin Game, The 483
Gone with the Wind 378, 483
Gorky Brigade, The 40, 388
Grab Me a Gondola 3, 212, 221, 223, 582
Grand Hotel 669
Grease 572
Great Society, The 384
Guys & Dolls 559, 661, 664
Haircut, The 239
Hamlet 107, 232-233, 293, 390, 438, 440, 498, 566, 658, 676
Hassan 115
Hear the Hyena Laugh 454, 487
Hedda Gabler 611, 619
Hello Dolly 661
Henry IV Part One 109
High Bid, The 318
HMS Pinafore 451
Hobson's Choice 196, 360, 441
How Do You Like Your Wagner

387
Imaginary Invalid, The 6, 594-595, 599, 604, 615, 648
Inadmissible Evidence 314-315
Innocents, The 185, 497, 503, 505, 507-508, 510, 515-516, 520
Into the Woods 149, 654
Irma la Douce 6, 132, 316
Jane Eyre 235
J.C. Superstar 492-493
Joe Egg 206
Journey's End 114
Julius Caesar 150, 223-224
Kill Two Birds 260
Kismet 660-661
La Cages aux Folles 544-546
Lear 197, 307, 484
Lend me a Tenor 547
Little Footsteps on the Petals 152, 197
Little Hut, The 292
Little Mary Sunshine 442
Little Saint, The 225
Little Shop of Horrors 560, 667
Live Like Pigs 315
Lodger, The 288
Lone Star 454
Look Back in Anger 314-315, 408
Loot 414, 418
Lovely to Look At 9
Lovers Dancing 455, 486
Lysistrata 150
Mack & Mabel 658
March of the Falsettos 453, 546
Marriage Go Round 288
Master Harold and the Boys 599
Measure For Measure 387-388, 390
Merchant of Venice, The 229
Merlin 308, 454
Moby Dick 225
Monkey's Paw, The 109
Mousetrap, The 32, 235, 482, 515
Mutiny 547

My Fair Lady 556, 669
My Lovely Trumpeter 228
My Three Angels 292
Narrow Lane, The 228
Narrow Road to the Deep North 472, 486, 493-494, 498, 568
Night Mother 471
Noah 199, 200, 505
Noble Spaniard, The 240
Noises Off 547
Nothing Doing Tonight 150
Nunsense 658
Oedipus 198
Off the Record 173
Oh Brother! 2, 38, 139, 228, 249-252, 319
Old Batchelor, The 322, 433, 435, 440
Old Time Music Hall 132, 292, 457
Oliver 109, 137, 219, 329, 371, 451, 453, 455, 584
Once Upon a Mattress 467, 652
One Touch of Pity 38-39
On the Verge 640
Onward Victoria 147
Opus One 148
Orphans 198, 385, 542, 547, 594, 603, 606-609, 621
Pacific Overtures 149, 330
Paint Your Wagon 185
Paradise is Closing Down 436
Paradise Road 228
Penny for a Song 315
Peter Pan 2, 140-141, 143-145, 219-220, 326, 506, 646, 668, 674, 676
Pickwick 139, 144, 251
Pickwick Papers, The 139
Pillars of Society 430
Pinocchio 468, 668
Porgy and Bess 185
Power and the Glory, The 199
Prancing Nigger 228
Private Lives 37, 287, 507-508, 522, 527, 529-530, 533

Quartermaine's Terms 656
Queen and the Rebels, The 428, 656-657
Questioning of Nick, The 436
Rattle of a Simple Man 36, 286, 288
Real Inspector Hound, The 546
Red in the Morning 6, 200, 274, 371, 476, 600, 606, 620, 622
Red Shoes, The 8
Relapse, The 465
Reluctant Debutante, The 10
Reluctant Heroes 7
Reunion in Vienna 376-377, 391, 418
Richard II 114
Ring for Catty 135
Rink, The 658, 671
Rivals, The 417, 436, 437
River of Sand, The 200-203, 206, 228
River Rats 474
Romulus the Great 232
Rosemary 2, 202-205, 310, 353, 553-554, 569, 612-613, 616-618
Run for Your Wife 547
Salad Days 148, 236, 292
Saved 436
Scarlet Princess of Edo, The 526
Scenes and Revelations 238
See Naples and Die 113
Seven Brides for Seven Brothers 477, 479
Seventh Veil, The 8-9, 109, 129
Sexual Perversity in Chicago 640-641
Shadow of an Outcast 542
She Stoops to Conquer 199
Shop at Sly Corner 6
Showboat 669
Sleeping Beauty 632
Sleuth 537
Something's Burning 383
Starlight Express 567
STATEMENTS after an arrest under the Immorality Act 79, 393
Strauss Galas 457
Streamers 395-398, 606, 644
Sunday in the Park with George 149
Sweeny Todd 149
Sweet Charity 350, 373
Taming of the Shrew, The 435
Tell Me You Love Me 387. *See also* Plays, Pantomimes & Musicals:: How Do You Like Your Wagner
Tempest, The 114
The 88 2, 317, 319, 323, 349, 354, 395, 401-403, 406-408, 411-414, 437, 617
Third Drawer from the Top 2, 335, 442, 603, 610, 616-617, 640, 643, 658
Threepenny Opera, The 559, 562, 567-569
Three Sisters 437, 546
Thriller of the Year 2, 308, 316, 353, 512, 527, 529-530, 536, 544, 578, 602, 674
Tiger and the Horse, The 1, 234
Tis Pity She's a Whore 431
Torch Song Trilogy 454, 477, 546
Trap for a lonely Man 292
Treasure Island 163, 384-386, 444
Trial by Jury 451
Tribute 507-508, 513-514, 516, 520-524
Tsafendas 80
Twelfth Night 164
Twilight of Aunt Edna 203, 326, 335, 381
Two Bouquets, The 185
Two for the See-Saw 288-289
Uncle Vanya 643, 645-646, 648
Under Milk Wood 386, 525
Underneath the Arches 669
Unexpected Guest, The 260
Valmouth 139

Venice Preserved 198
Vincent in Brixton 40
Virginia Woolf 37, 438, 547-548, 553
Visit, The 359
Volpone 107, 109, 158, 162
Waiting or Crimes of the Heart 479
War Music 394
West Side Story 243, 329-330, 552-553, 571-572
When the Devil Rides 52, 674
When the Lights go on Again 132
Whitehorse Inn 669
Who Goes Bare 197, 241, 307, 379
Who's Afraid of Virginia Woolf 438, 547-548
Wild Duck, The 17
Wind in the Willows, The 195
Wind Versus Polygamy 293
Women Around 2, 193, 349
You Can't Take it With You 229
Pocock, Tom 36
Poland 4, 259
Pol Pot 3. *See also* Cambodia
Pooley, Barbara 375
Postlethwaite, Pete 384
Praxiteles 81
Prescod, Pearl 139
Prestatyn 42-43, 70, 74, 126-127
Price, Lynn 509, 513, 531
Prince of Wales 25, 28, 147, 359, 360
Princess Margaret 185
Prosceneium 664-665, 667-668, 674-675
Prospect Theatre Company 395, 402
Publishers:
  Abydos Publishing 306
  Pan Books 365
  Weidenfeld and Nicolson 369
  W.H.Allen 296, 512, 544
Pulleyn, Garry 619

Q

Quayle, Anthony 358-360
Queen Elizabeth 185, 451
Quillen, Phyllis 530, 621, 629, 646

R

Rabe, David 395-398
Rachmaninov 113
Radio Play:
  People Are Living There 390
  Prairie Home Companion 502
  Robben Island 390
Ragnall House 451, 577, 588
Railway Companies:
  Acheson Topeka & Santa Fe 541
  Amtrak 316, 452, 528, 537-539, 541
Rainer, Rex 136, 289, 366
Randall, Leslie 217
Ratlidge, Mike 394
Ravel 268, 309
Ray, Andrew 247
Rayner, David 286-288
Ray, Robin 546
Real, Ed 535
Reddy, Peter 259
Redfarn, Roger 360
Redgrave, Michael 37, 191, 229
Redgrave, Vanessa 389
Reed, Oliver 219
Reeperbahn 551-552
Reggio Calabria, Italy 44, 52
Reid, Beryl 200, 201
Reinhardt, Max 239
Reynolds, Joan 217
Rhodes, Cecil 211
Rice, Tim 149
Richardson, Dick 463
Rich, David 164
Richins, Trevor 130
Richmond, Natal 74, 94-98, 100, 101, 110, 120, 122-123, 284
Ridgeway, Philip 351

Ridley, Arnold 150
Rietti, Papa 225
Riggs, Lynn 612
Robert Hale & Co 214
Robertson, Toby 395, 402
Robinson, Osborne 234
Robson, Flora 185, 200, 202
Rockwell, Norman 12
Roderick, William 248
Rooney, Mickey 373
Roose-Evans, James 37-38
Rowlandson 372
Royal Academy of Dramatic Arts 11, 195, 196, 219, 239, 322, 354, 417, 419, 425, 430-431, 435-436, 439, 453, 475, 604
Royal Shakespeare Company 162, 219, 313, 374, 431, 437, 492, 616
Rumpf, Robert 548
Rushton, William 385
Russ, Debbie 363
Russell, Kim 385, 621

S

Salter, Ivor 295
Samuel French Ltd 252, 316, 387, 487, 600, 630
Saunders, Peter 32, 34, 387
Scase, David 224
Schofield, Paul 199
Schroder, Tim 538
Schulman, Milton 40
Schwab, Steven 469
Schwartzkopf, Elizabeth 624
Screenplay:
  Brigadier Gerrard 30, 281
Sea Scouts 264, 265
Secombe, Harry 97, 139, 144
Selbie, Christopher 405
Senelick, Laurence 426, 645, 658
Senter, Susan 327, 474
Seyler, Athene 362
Shaftesbury Avenue 41, 129

Shakespeare 109-110, 219, 223, 331-332, 431, 571, 598
Sharpeville 79, 83
Sharpless, Amie 555
Shaw, Richard 295
Sheekey's Fish Restaurant 20
Shenandoah Phi Beta Kappa Association 470
Sheridan, Dinah 391
Sherwood, Robert E. 376
Shulman, Milton 402
Sicily 44-45, 52, 147, 446, 520, 590
Sim, Alistair 136, 379, 442, 618
Simmonds, Douglas 363-364
Simmons, Chris 487, 520
Simmons, Jean 388
Simon, Neil 442, 509, 614, 653
Simpson, Roy 296, 356, 364-365, 377, 387, 391, 443
Simpson, Wallace Mrs. 25
Sim, Sheila 170
Sindon, Jeremy 40, 185, 310-311, 315, 318, 352, 366-367, 371, 386, 392, 421, 425, 443-445, 448, 544, 579, 592-593
Singh, Ronnie 308
Sircom, Malcolm 139, 251
Slade, Bernard 507, 514
Sladen Wood Mill 668
Smith, Andy 555, 562
Smith, Maggie 41
Soft Machine 394
Sondheim, Stephen 149, 388, 511, 655, 677
Songs:
  Bless 'em All 135
  Cliquot Cliquot 468
  Cool 571
  Fallen Star 568, 570
  Gilbert the Filbert 457
  I Am What I Am 562
  If Ever I Cease To Love 537. *See also* Leybourne, George
  If You Were the Only Boy in the World 16
  I like to be in America 552

I'm sitting on top of the world, just rolling along, just singing a song 285
I Wonder Who's Kissing Her Now. 16
Jesus is Walking on the Water 125
Just a Song at Twilight 61
Keep the Home Fires Burning 67
Knees Up Mother Brown 16
London Pride 132
Love's Old Sweet Song 61
Moggy Dooral 568. *See also* Leybourne, George
My Old Man said Follow the Van 16
Nobody Loves A Fairy When She's Forty 657
Oh The Fairies! 657. *See also* Leybourne, George
On Mother Kelly's Doorstep 16
Red Sails in the Sunset 62
Rocking at the Cannon Ball! 4
Rock The Cradle, John 520. *See also* Leybourne, George
Roll Out the Barrel 135
Somewhere a Voice is Calling 61
The Boy I Love Is Up In The Gallery 657
The Broken Hearted Shepherd 510, 515. *See also* Leybourne, George
The Lambeth Walk 68
The Tailor and The Crow 487
The Twi-Twi-Twilight, 1
Why Don't We Nationalise the Ladies? 614
Wish Me Luck As You Wave Me Goodbye 67
You Made Me Love You 16
Sonneveld, Wim 442
South Africa 3, 8, 27-28, 42-49, 53-57, 68, 72-79, 83, 99, 115, 119, 153, 162, 165-166, 170, 185, 188, 200, 202, 259, 278, 280, 292, 353, 374, 382-383, 391, 424, 461, 624, 663
South African National Theatre 107, 115
South African Railways & Harbours 55
Southcott, Ron 294
Southern Rhodesia 56, 116-118, 165. *See* Zimbabwe
Southworth, John 250
Soweto 79, 80
Spacek, Sissy 500, 613
Spencer, Jeremy 185
Spiers, Derek 74, 123
Spooner, Dennis 295
Spooner, John 143
Spring, Dorothy 164
S.S. Canberra 244
SS Watussi. *See also* German East Africa Line
Stanislavski 237, 611
Stanyon, Brian 229, 235
Steele, Anthony 170
Steele, C. Edward 507
Steele, Ed 358, 494, 511, 609
Steele, Tina 241
Stevens, Alfred Peck. *See also* The Great Vance
Stevens, Dudley 132, 149, 292
Stevens, Laura 221, 353
Stevens, Leslie 288
Stevenson, Geraldine 457
Stevens, Ronnie 404-405
Stockholm 132, 133
Stoke Newington Cemetery 458
St Paul du Vence 31
Strand Electric 152, 283
Strauss, Richard 624
Stuart, Malcolm 36
Studley Pyke 583
Suez Canal 180
Sun City 73
Sutton, Michael 187
Swanage, Dorset 259
Swaziland 102
Sweden 132-133, 135, 386
Szmagaj, Mary 627, 629, 645, 659

T

Tabert, John 480
Tandy, Jessica 618
Taormina 446-447
Taraborrelli, Arnaldo 305-306
Tate and Lyle Golden Syrup 123
Tati, Jacques 443, 501
Taurian 13, 18, 91-92, 160, 184, 359, 416
Taylor, Elizabeth 362, 456
Taylor, Jonathan Scott 385
Taylor. Kenneth Alan 130, 151-152
Teck, Alex 305, 306, 382, 413, 517, 570
Television:
  Act of Terror 224
  A Hard Look at Software 352
  Alice in Winterland 398
  Amelia 233
  A Model's Lot is Not a Happy One 318
  Bathtime 304, 349, 350
  Bindle 2, 301
  Books, Plays, & Poems 383
  Boyd QC, 218
  Breakaway Girls 355, 393
  Charlie Chester 218
  Child of Hope 80
  Colditz 215
  Crimewatch File 673
  Cugat in Madrid 305
  Dad's Army 150
  Diary of Samuel Pepys 217
  Doctor Who 2, 104, 294-296, 512, 524, 530, 544-545
    The Crusaders 296
    The Sontaran Experiment 104
    The Space Museum 2, 6, 294, 296, 512, 544
  Eastenders 140
  Emmerdale 656
  Golden Girls 642
  Hancock's Half Hour 224
  Hill Street Blues 383
  Homicide 383
  Hotel Imperial 218
  Jewel in the Crown 493
  Joan and Leslie 217
  Lady of the Camellias 217
  Marcia 393
  Murder Bag 217
  Neighbours 140, 646
  No Friendly Star 38, 224
  One Candle for Jenny 242
  Play For Today 80. *See also* Child of Hope
  Queen's Champion 218
  Softly Softly 224, 309, 353
  The Army Game 224, 265
  The Arthur Askey Show 224
  The Avengers 318
  The Charlie Drake Show 224
  The Eggspert 387
  The English Captain 225
  The Expert 224, 356
  The Flame Trees of Thika 176
  The Forsythe Saga 453
  The Frankie Howard Show 224
  The Golden Spur 218
  The Gold Robbers 2, 349
  The Hump of the Camel 351
  The Infamous John Friend 224
  The Jack Hylton Show 218
  The Liver Birds 393, 471
  The Lost Boys 220, 546, 673
  The Magnificent 6½ 298, 356
    Peewee's Pianola 298, 300
  The Mercury Theatre 354
  The Secret Kingdom 224
  The Trojan Women 206
  The Windscale Affair 393
  Three Golden Nobles 218
  Xavier Cugat show 289
  You Are There 218
Terblanche, Terry 98
Terence 72
The Alliance of Resident Theatres/New York 488
The Almost Free Theatre Company 80

Theatres:
  Actor's Studio, New York 239
  African Consolidated Theatres 153
  Aldwych Theatre 455
  Alhambra - Bradford 115, 658
  Arts Theatre 30
  Belgrade Theatre, Coventry 37, 206
  Birmingham Rep 4-5
  Buxton 132, 236, 285, 288, 290, 292-293, 309, 430
  Chelmsford 30-31, 35, 261, 354
  Citizen's Theatre, Glasgow 232-233
  City Varieties 657, 668
  Connaught Theatre Worthing 193
  Crucible Theatre 435
  Danmarks Show Og Teaterskole 555
  Derby Playhouse 415
  Forum Theatre - Wythamshawe 660
  Free Trades Hall 657
  Gaité Lyrique 373
  Georgian Theatre - Richmond 666
  Golders Green Hippodrome 316
  Hackney Empire 638
  Henry Street Playhouse 632
  Herodes Atticus - Athens 676
  Institute of Contemporary Art. 225
  Ipswich 139, 249, 251, 252
  King's Theatre, Hammersmith 4, 197, 670
  King's Theatre, Southsea 4
  Krannert Center for the Performing Arts 442
  Latimer-Schaeffer Theater - James Madison University 465, 470, 607, 646
  Library Theatre, Manchester 223, 660
  Liverpool Playhouse 78-79, 395-397, 426
  Lyric Theatre, Hammersmith 198
  Mayfair Theatre 459, 461
  Mermaid Theatre 163, 384
  Mowlem Theatre 259
  National Theatre 40, 107, 115, 139, 200, 205, 360, 562
  New End, Hampstead 80
  New Tyne Theatre 329
  Nottingham Playhouse 39
  Phoenix Theatre, Leicester 199, 313
  Piccadilly 184, 186, 208, 260, 373, 376, 547
  Playhouse Theatre, London 40
  Prince Edward 208
  Queen Elizabeth Hall 451
  Queen's Theatre, Hornchurch 219, 245
  Radio City Music Hall 454, 654
  Riksteatern 133
  Roundhouse London 395
  Royal at Northampton 233
  Royal Court 40, 205, 314, 361, 401, 441
  Sadler's Wells 193, 309, 312, 365, 489, 514, 567, 579
  St Pauli Theatre 551
  The Apollo 547
  Theatre Royal Covent Garden 20, 23, 260, 330, 386, 482, 515, 547, 645
  Theatre Royal Drury Lane 335, 378, 413
  Theatre Royal, Haymarket 441
  The Barbican 220
  The Belgrade 37, 206, 233
  The Bristol Hippodrome 144
  The Chichester Festival theatre 376
  The Colliseum - English National Opera 164, 365
  The Commonwealth Institute Theatre 139
  The Criterion 547

The Forum, Wythemshawe 224
The Gaiety Theatre, Douglas, Isle of Man 143
The Gaiety Theatre - Dublin 411
The Globe 547
The Hampstead Theatre Club 37
The Haymarket 187, 200, 360, 379, 658
The Haymarket - Leicester 658
The Intimate Theatre, Palmers Green 462
The Lincoln Centre 454
The Little Theatre - Hebden Bridge 617, 619
The Lyric 547
The Mercury - Denmark 354, 568
The Mermaid 163, 318, 385, 389, 444
The National Theatre 40, 200, 360, 562
The New London 440
The Octagon, Bolton 657
The Oldham Coliseum 152, 164, 545, 657
The Old Vic 198, 317, 394-395, 402-403, 406, 408-409, 438
The Open Space 387-388
The Opera House, Pretoria. 158
The Phillips Center 611
The Phoenix Theatre 199
The Players Theatre 132, 546
The Playhouse - Furman University 644
The Playhouse, Weston-Super-Mare 140
The Royal Alexandra, Toronto 452
The Royal - Denmark 40, 192, 205, 293, 314, 330, 361, 386, 440-441, 452, 547, 565, 645
The Savoy 547
The Source Theatre, Washington 474
The Vanburgh 196
The Wayside 471, 483, 494, 506, 509, 528, 531
The Winter Garden - Ventnor 136
The Wyvern, Swindon 241
Tivoli, Fordsberg (cinema) 6-7, 11, 131, 153-154, 156, 158
Tivoli Theatre, New Brighton 6-13, 129, 131, 153-154, 156, 158
Toronto Free Theatre 453
Venn Street 657
Victoria Palace 164
Wampler, the Experimental Theatre 261
Wayside Theatre 159, 358, 465, 494, 508, 510-512, 514
Westcliffe 6. *See also* Plays, Pantomimes & Musicals:: Irma la Douce
West Yorkshire Playhouse 203-204
The Belfast Festival 319
The British Music Hall Association 545
The Crazy Gang 165
The Double Deckers 2, 44, 298, 303, 305, 356, 360, 362-363, 365, 376, 388
The English Theatre Of Hamburg 547
The Festival Hall 23
The Galloping Snail. 121
The Great Vance 30, 33, 37, 44, 246-247, 319, 468, 613
The Hackney Festival 457
The Haymarket 187, 200, 360, 379, 658
The Maid of the Mist 452
The Museum of Film and Photography 658
The Rose and Crown, Ilford 15
The Royal Academy 192, 440
The Royal Ballet Touring Company 293
The Strand - Book Store 426
The Taverners 199

The Twi-Twi-Twilight,. *See also* Songs:
The Watch Tower 49
The Welsh Theatre Company 246
Thomas, Dylan 386
Thomas, Gareth 662
Thomas, John 667
Thurber 184
Timson, Bruce 212
Tippet, Sir Michael 258
Tolbert, A.B. 336
Tom and Jerry cartoon 240
Toothill, Paul 407
Trafalgar Square 70
Trident Television 402, 404, 409-410
Trigger, John 313, 354
Trinder, Tommy 458
Tufts University 426
Tummon, Susan 143
Turner, Yolande 31, 33. *See also* Plays, Pantomimes & Musicals:: Early One Morning
Twentieth Century Fox 363-365
Twilight Zone, The 1
Tyler, Watt 384
Tynan, Kenneth 17, 314, 408

U

Uganda 3
Umbilo, Durban 64-65, 92, 325
Union Castle Line 1
University of Indiana 520
University of Natal 64
Unwin, Stanley 352

V

Valentine, Dickie 206, 218
Vance, Charles 30, 33, 37, 44, 246-247, 319
van Gyseghem, Andre 39

Vardi, Yair 329, 330
Vardy, Michael 9
Vaughan, Peter 349
Venice Film Festival 4
Ventnor 22, 129-132, 135-136, 150, 152, 292
Verdi 20, 552, 566
Verner Reed, Joseph 612
Verwoerd, Hendrik 80
Vibert, Trevor 315
Vicky Lind. *See* Clayton, Vicky
Victoria and Albert Museum 355, 547
Victorian illusion 454. *See also* Moth to the Flame
Victorio Emanuel III 46
Vidal, Gore 176, 191-192, 211
Vilane, Priscilla Jane 73, 74, 75, 76, 123, 128
Virginia, USA 12, 78, 159-160, 237, 282, 312, 322, 330, 334, 358, 397, 441, 456, 462, 464-465, 471, 474, 483, 487, 497, 502, 505-508, 519, 528, 533, 543-544, 601, 615, 633, 635, 638, 644, 647
Vlaminck 191
Vocal Aids:
  Negroids 7
  Sanderson's Specific 7
Vu, Michel 31

W

Wales 14, 25, 28, 42-43, 46, 56, 68, 69, 126, 127, 147, 184, 246, 247, 252-253, 258, 359, 360, 393, 407, 451
Walker, Patrick 188
Waterhouse, Keith 348
Watkins, Darton 259
Watson, Paul 243
Watty, Bessie 6. *See also* Plays, Pantomimes & Musicals:: Shop at Sly

Corner
Weaver, Elizabeth 316
Webster, Nina 293
Welch, Joan Kemp 206
Welles, Orson 225
Wessels, Gerrit 161
Weston, Ernest 136
Whitehouse, Mary 289
Whittaker, David 295
Wightman, Jules 619
Wiles, Tony 32
Wilkinson, Tom 4-5.
See also Plays, Pantomimes & Musicals:: Are You Now or Have You Ever Been?
Williamsburg 160, 488
Williams, Emlyn 6
Williams, Nona 132, 288, 291
Wilson, Lionel 147, 373, 421
Wilson, Sandy 139, 236, 667
Wise, Frank 162
Wolfitt, Donald 197
Woodward, Edward 318
Woolworths 9, 12, 14
World War I 2, 11, 67
World War II 12, 133, 256, 553
Wrede, Casper 206
Wren, Geoffrey 130-131
Wright, Nicholas 40
Wynne, Greville 372

X

Xhosa 194

Y

Y.M.C.A 187, 189, 194
Yokum, Robert 650
Yorkshire 51-52, 144, 176, 203-204, 247, 260, 330, 336, 351, 356, 375, 427-428, 444-445, 451, 454, 581-585, 588-589, 591, 655-656, 662-664, 666, 669, 673-674, 676
Yorkshire Television 52, 656

Z

Zambia 115
Zimbabwe 3, 56
Zulu 27, 77, 86, 104, 194
Zweig, Stefan 107, 109

www.ingramcontent.com/pod-product-compliance
Lightning Source LLC
Chambersburg PA
CBHW031609160426
43196CB00006B/69